T0342568

DISTRESS IN THE FIELDS

Indian Agriculture after Liberalization

DISTRESS IN THE FIELDS

INDIAN AGRICULTURE AFTER LIBERALIZATION

EDITED BY

R. RAMAKUMAR

 Tulika Books

Published by
Tulika Books
44 (first floor), Shahpur Jat, New Delhi 110 049, India
www.tulikabooks.in

First edition (hardback) 2022

ISBN: 978-81-950559-0-6

For

Vineet

Vineet Kohli (1979–2018)

Contents

Tables and Figures

5 Public Spending Priorities for Agriculture and Allied Sectors in Recent Years: Insights from the Union and Select States

6 WTO and Agricultural Support in India: Promise Unkept

9 Price Support and Access to MSPs in Indian Agriculture

10 Costs of Cultivation and Profitability in Indian Agriculture: A Plot-level Analysis

13 Agricultural Insurance in India: History, Issues and Recent Performance

15 Reform of Agricultural Markets in India: A Critical Analysis

16 Food Security Policy and Reforms in the Public Distribution System

Preface

'The Punjab peasant is born in debt, lives in debt and dies in debt', so wrote Sir Malcolm Darling in his famous book of 1925 titled *The Punjab Peasant in Prosperity and Debt*. The peasant's life, he wrote, was 'dominated by *kismet* (luck)'; he has a 'mind that is often as empty as the horizon that surrounds him'; and '[h]ardly a week passes without some reference in debate or the Press to the economic disabilities of the cultivator and to his "poverty and misery"'. If we return to read Darling close to a century after his book was published, we realize how true that description would be of the Indian farmer in 2022 despite the great transformations that have overtaken the country and its economy.

The experience of Indian agriculture in the first forty years after independence was marred with contradictions. On the one hand, India failed to base its developmental journey on an egalitarian rural society, as countries like China or South Korea did. India's First Five-Year Plan in 1950 had drawn up a progressive vision for Indian agriculture. The Plan reflected the critical nature of the land question – a major concern for the peasantry, which had participated in the freedom movement with extraordinary fervour. The First Plan document argued that 'the future of land ownership and cultivation constitutes perhaps the most fundamental issue in national development. To a large extent, the pattern of economic and social organization [in independent India] will depend upon the manner in which the land problem is resolved' (Government of India 1951).

Here was a vision that linked the land question to the idea of national development. The land problem was also central to Daniel Thorner's use of the term 'built-in depressor', to capture the 'complex of legal, economic and social relations' under colonialism (see Thorner 1962). The built-in depressor created strong disincentives for private investment and the overall development of productive forces, and thus was 'a formidable block against the modernization of Indian agriculture'. Land was also the material basis for multiple forms of social discrimination in the rural society, founded on caste, gender and religion.

The Indian state's failure to implement land reforms after independence did not just stymie the possibilities of structural change in the economy. It also allowed inequalities in land ownership and possession, and *ipso facto* the material basis for social discrimination, to persist. In the ultimate analysis, the high frequency with which caste- and gender-based atrocities are reported from rural India even today, as well as the relatively less reported everyday forms of exploitation, have its roots in the control of a few over land.

On the other hand, India attained foodgrain self-sufficiency between the 1960s and the 1990s. The technology-led package of the green revolution, aided ably by a series of public institutional support measures in the realm of prices, subsidies, credit, marketing, research and extension, raised the productivity of crops like paddy and wheat and allowed India to be free from dependence on external food aid. To achieve this goal, public policy consciously targeted and utilized the richer sections of the peasantry and regions well-endowed with irrigation to lead the green revolution. The technology eventually spilled over to other sections of the peasantry and other regions too. Yet, given the inequalities in land distribution, the green revolution was also associated with an entrenchment of rural power structures.

Liberalization of the economy after 1991 disturbed the precarious equilibrium that marked the rural economy and society after the 1960s. The Indian state weakened, if not dismantled, many of the public institutional support structures erected in the rural areas during the green revolution. Procurement, support prices, input subsidies, rural banks, regulated markets, and public research and extension came under attack. These spheres were adversely affected by regimes of fiscal austerity, and the *social* purpose of their institution was sought to be undermined by prioritizing a set of *commercial* goals. In this period, the fortunes of India's agricultural economy were also increasingly integrated with free trade and imperfect global markets.

Thus, a new phase of distress was inaugurated in the countryside. This book is essentially about this phase of agrarian distress after 1991 until the advent of the Covid-19 crisis in 2020. Much has been written about this phase, but this book tries to depart from other studies in a few important respects.

First, it does not treat the post-1991 phase in Indian agriculture as independent of the phase that preceded it. It places the developments after 1991 in a *historical context*; identifies elements of *continuity* and *change*, and ensures that the treatment of policy is not delinked from its *differentiated impact* on the rural social structure.

Secondly, the book is based strongly on quantitative data – both from secondary sources and from intensive village surveys. While secondary data are used to provide the critical macro-narratives on theory and policy, village survey data open up opportunities to undertake a richer and nuanced analysis of how the outcomes of policy are experienced by different sections of the rural society. To the best of my knowledge, most recent studies on Indian agriculture tend to compartmentalize these realms of analysis.

Thirdly, the book covers and discusses a wider range of policies and issues than usual accounts undertake. The introduction to the volume and the sixteen chapters analyse how policies and issues related to land ownership, tenancy, prices, trade, crop incomes, subsidies, fertilizers, credit, insurance, research and extension, marketing and food distribution have changed after 1991, and their impact on the agrarian economy.

Finally, the book also performs the function of policy documentation, as well as tries to position itself as classroom reading/reference material on Indian agriculture. My introductory essay is a product of about fifteen years of classroom engagement at the Tata Institute of Social Sciences (TISS), Mumbai, which have forced me to expand the canvas of my analysis and finetune my understanding of the subject. Much of this learning finds expression in the introductory essay as well as in the choice of the contents of chapters and their authors.

Admittedly, there are gaps in what the book tries to cover. Extended papers on research, extension and the allied sectors of agriculture – livestock and fisheries – could not be included due to constraints of space. Similarly, concerns relating to climate change and sustainable development had to be excluded. These are issues I hope to cover in another forthcoming volume. The challenges thrown up by the Covid-19 pandemic are also not covered in this book; several of us have written about it elsewhere (see Ramakumar 2022).

I must thank several friends and colleagues for helping me with the preparation of this volume. Almost all the papers included here were first presented at a national seminar on 'Indian Agriculture: Policy Shifts and Emerging Challenges', held on 20–21 June 2019 at TISS, Mumbai. The seminar was organized when I was the National Bank for Agriculture and Rural Development (NABARD) Chair Professor in the School of Development Studies, and NABARD financed the organization of the seminar. Without implicating the institution in the arguments made in this book, I must thank NABARD at the outset. I also thank Aardra Surendran,

Ranjini Basu, Ashish Kamra and colleagues at the School of Development Studies at TISS who helped me in the organization of the seminar.

A special mention must be made of scholars who read the manuscript version of the book and provided encouraging words of endorsement: Barbara Harriss-White, J. Mohan Rao, Jens Lerche and P. Sainath. I am also grateful to all the scholars who agreed to contribute to this volume.

Tulika Books, New Delhi did an excellent job of copy-editing, designing and publishing the book in such a fine form. I thank Indira Chandrasekhar and H. Basantarani for their perseverance and patience over the many months of production of this book. The delightful cover of the book was designed by Alpana Khare, who uses a line drawing of Chittaprosad, dated 3 January 1945, most probably drawn in Nagar during his tour of Maharashtra; I thank her too.

My family has been a pillar of support over the years, and it would be inappropriate if I do not acknowledge their role in my life as an academic.

I hope you like the book.

15 July 2022   R. Ramakumar
Mumbai

References

Government of India (1951), *First Five Year Plan*, New Delhi: Planning Commission, Government of India.

Thorner, Daniel (1962), *Land and Labour in India*, New Delhi: Asia Publishing House.

Ramakumar, R. (2022), 'India's Agricultural Economy During the Covid-19 Lockdown: An Empirical Assessment', *Indian Journal of Agricultural Economics*, vol. 77, no. 1.

INTRODUCTION
Economic Reforms and Agricultural Policy in India

R. Ramakumar

This chapter is an introduction to the volume. At the same time, it is an extended discussion on the nature of agricultural growth in India after independence, with specific reference to the last three decades of liberalization of the agricultural sector.

The long story of post-independence Indian agriculture has passed through multiple phases of short growth spurts and long periods of stagnation. From a position of growth stagnation and acute food deficiency till the mid-1960s, India's agriculture grew to become self-sufficient in foodgrain production by the 1980s. At the same time the agrarian constraint to economic growth persisted, as the Indian state failed to undertake radical land reform or invest in agricultural infrastructure. Consequently, agricultural growth in the 1970s and 1980s stood differentiated across crops, classes and regions. By the 1990s, the Indian state adopted the agenda of liberalization. Gradually, over about three decades, external exposure of agriculture increased, and many policy measures and institutional interventions in agriculture were reversed or diluted. Overall, even as capitalist development in agriculture proceeded, the liberalization agenda did not increase growth in agriculture; rather, it led to what scholars call 'agrarian distress'. The agrarian distress opened doors to a new set of contradictions in the rural economy. Even as the absence of land reform and public investment retained economic inequalities, the new policies stymied the potential for a rise in income for a large section of the rural workforce.

This volume is about this long story of Indian agriculture, but with special reference to the period of economic liberalization after 1991. It documents and examines various aspects of agricultural policy and their impact on farmers at a disaggregated level and at the level of various sub-sectors within agriculture. It covers various themes including macroeconomic changes in agriculture, land ownership, tenancy, prices, trade, crop incomes, subsidies, seeds, fertilizers, pesticides, credit, insurance, research, extension, marketing and food distribution. In sum, it aims to arrive at a composite and critical account of changes in India's agricultural policy in the 1990s, 2000s and 2010s.

There are sixteen chapters in this volume besides this introductory chapter. When the volume was conceptualized in 2019, we wanted it to broadly meet four objectives. First, we wanted it to be an extensive review of the policies of liberalization in Indian agriculture. Second, we wanted the discussion on liberalization policies to be placed in the historical context of the evolution of agricultural policies in India. Third, we wanted the volume to be essential reading material for students of Indian agriculture in universities. Fourth, we wanted it to be a ready reference for researchers with regard to empirical information, including quantitative data, used in analyses.

This introductory chapter is arranged as follows. The first section delineates the different phases of agricultural growth in India after independence. The second section discusses the major policies, factors and processes associated with the performance of agriculture in these phases. The official agricultural policy after 1991 and attempts to relate the outcomes of policy shifts to patterns of growth across time are critically analysed. The last section is the concluding section. We depart from the usual practice of including a section that summarizes each chapter. Instead, these summaries are absorbed into the discussion in this introductory chapter; appropriate references are provided where necessary.

Phases of Agricultural Growth in India

This section is an overview of the different phases of growth and slowdown in Indian agriculture. We rely on aggregate macro-indicators for this purpose. In India, data on agricultural production are available from two major sources. First, the Ministry of Agriculture (MoA) releases the index numbers of area under cultivation, production and yield of a set of forty-six crops, called forecast crops. A major limitation of these index numbers, however, is the exclusion of non-forecast crops.

Second, the Central Statistics Office (CSO) provides the gross value of output (GVO) for a set of crops that includes non-forecast crops. However, the base year for the calculation of GVO has changed at frequent intervals, and alongside, the weights attached to crops in the estimation have also changed. For instance, when the base year changed from 1980–81 to 1993–94, the weights attached to fruits and vegetables (non-forecast crops) were revised upwards. Such changes in weights were continued when more recent series with base years 2004–05 and 2011–12 were released.

Rates of Growth Across Phases

Data from the MoA and the CSO show that four broad phases of growth can be delineated in the evolution of India's agricultural economy after 1947.[1] The first is the period of fifteen years after national planning began, from 1950–51 to 1964–65. The second phase, called the 'early green revolution phase', roughly spans the period between the mid-1960s till the beginning of the 1980s. The third phase, the 'late green revolution phase', extends from the early 1980s to early 1990s. The fourth phase covers the period after 1991–92, when there were major changes in agricultural policies towards domestic liberalization and integration with the global economy.

In the first phase, i.e. between 1949–50 and 1964–65, the index of agricultural production (IAP) grew by 3.2 per cent per annum, driven by not a rise in yields but a rise in area cultivated (Table 1). Yields began to rise from the mid-1960s; nevertheless, the annual growth rate of IAP fell to 2.8 per cent in the early green revolution phase. The real recovery of growth rate of IAP happened in the late green revolution phase, when the IAP grew at 3.4 per cent per annum and yields grew at 2.6 per cent per annum. In the liberalization phase, i.e. between 1992–93 and 2019–20, the annual growth rate of IAP fell to 2.2 per cent, the lowest for any period after 1949–50. The above periodization remains valid when we consider the data on GVO for all crops from the CSO also, except in that growth rates remained largely stagnant between the late green revolution phase and the liberalization phase (Table 2).

If we consider the allied sectors of agriculture – livestock and fisheries – the trend is that growth rate of GVO rose in the second and third phases, only to fall in the fourth phase. Within the livestock sector, the sub-sectors of milk, meat and eggs also show such a pattern of growth (see Table 2). In other words, there is overwhelming evidence that growth rates of production and GVO in agriculture and allied sectors were lower in the fourth phase as compared to the third phase.

Our analysis of yields in agriculture gives us results similar to that of production in agriculture, except in the case of maize and coarse cereals. While the growth rate of index of area remained at less than 1 per cent per annum after the mid-1960s, the index of yields rose through the second and third phases before slowing down after 1992–93 (see Table 1).

Rates of Growth Across Sub-Phases after 1992–93

Data in Tables 2 and 3 also show that agricultural growth rates after 1992–93 were not uniform throughout. There were three distinct sub-phases in agricultural growth after 1992–93: (a) between 1992–93 and 2002–03; (b) between 2003–04 and 2010–11; and (c) between 2011–12 and 2019–20.

Between 1992–93 and 2002–03, IAP grew at just 0.6 per cent per

Table 1 *Compound growth rates of index numbers of area, production and yield per hectare of major crops in India, estimates of Ministry of Agriculture and Farmers Welfare, 1949–50 to 2019–20, base year 1981–82=100, in per cent per annum*

Crop group	Area				Production				Yield			
	1949–50 to 1964–65	1965–66 to 1980–81	1981–82 to 1991–92	1992–93 to 2019–20	1949–50 to 1964–65	1965–66 to 1980–81	1981–82 to 1991–92	1992–93 to 2019–20	1949–50 to 1964–65	1965–66 to 1980–81	1981–82 to 1991–92	1992–93 to 2019–20
Foodgrains	1.3	0.4	-0.3	0.3	2.8	3.0	2.9	1.9	1.4	2.0	2.6	2.0
Cereals	1.2	0.6	-0.4	0.1	3.2	3.5	3.2	1.8	1.8	2.3	3.0	2.1
Rice	1.2	0.9	0.6	0.1	3.5	3.0	4.1	1.6	2.2	2.1	3.4	1.5
Wheat	2.7	3.7	0.2	0.9	4.0	7.5	3.4	2.1	1.3	3.6	3.2	1.2
Maize	2.7	5.2	0.1	2.0	3.9	0.8	2.2	3.7	1.2	0.2	2.1	1.7
Coarse cereals	0.9	-0.8	-1.8	-0.9	2.3	1.3	-0.1	1.6	1.2	2.0	1.6	2.7
Pulses	1.7	0.3	-0.1	1.0	1.4	0.5	1.0	2.2	-0.2	0.3	1.2	1.3
Oilseeds	2.7	0.2	2.4	0.2	3.2	1.6	5.8	1.4	0.3	1.4	2.2-	1.7
Non-foodgrains	2.2	0.8	1.9	1.4	3.7	2.5	4.3	2.8	0.9	1.6	2.2	1.6
All crops	1.6	0.6	0.2	0.7	3.2	2.8	3.4	2.2	1.2	1.8	2.6	2.1

Source: Computed from data collected from Department of Food and Agriculture, Government of India.

Table 2 *Compound growth rates of value of production of major items of agri-culture in India, estimates from National Accounts Statistics, 1965–66 to 2018–19, base year 2011–12 = 100,* in per cent per annum

Crop group	Compound growth rates of value of production (per cent per annum)					
	1965–66 to 1980–81	1981–82 to 1991–92	1992–93 to 2018–19	1992–93 to 2002–03	2003–04 to 2010–11	2011–12 to 2018–19
Cereals	3.5	3.0	1.5	0.8	2.0	1.1
Paddy	3.0	4.0	1.4	0.8	1.4	1.2
Wheat	7.4	3.3	1.9	1.9	3.1	1.2
Jowar	1.9	−1.1	−3.5	−4.7	−0.1	−5.6
Bajra	0.5	0.4	−1.1	−1.1	−2.3	−1.1
Maize	1.4	2.2	4.5	2.6	5.5	3.5
Ragi	4.3	−0.5	−1.7	−3.0	−0.9	−3.9
Pulses	0.7	1.1	2.1	−0.5	1.8	5.2
Oilseeds	1.7	5.7	1.7	−1.7	1.9	−0.03
Spices and condiments	3.3	4.2	4.3	4.5	2.7	4.9
Fruits and vegetables	4.7	2.1	4.5	5.4	5.2	3.9
Crops, total	2.8	2.4	2.5	2.3	2.7	1.6
Milk	3.8	5.1	4.3	4.1	4.3	5.7
Meat	1.4	5.1	5.0	2.6	5.5	7.9
Eggs	4.4	7.2	5.0	3.9	6.3	4.9
Livestock, total	3.1	4.5	4.3	3.6	4.4	6.0
Fisheries, total	3.3	5.9	4.7	4.1	4.1	9.7

Source: Computed from National Accounts Statistics, Central Statistics Office.

annum, and the GVO for all crops grew at 2.3 per cent per annum. However, between 2003–04 and 2010–11, the IAP recorded an annual growth rate of 3.1 per cent; this appears to have been driven largely by a sharp growth of yield indices. Similarly, between 2003–04 and 2010–11, the GVO for all crops grew at 2.7 per cent. However, in the third sub-phase, the growth rate of IAP fell to 1.8 per cent per annum (between 2011–12 and 2019–20) and that of GVO fell to 1.6 per cent per annum (between 2011–12 and 2018–19). In other words, the revival of growth rates between 2003–04 and 2010–11 did not raise the growth rates of agricultural production of the combined period between 1992–93 and 2019–20 to a level above the growth rates of the 1980s.

Table 3 *Compound growth rates of index numbers of area, production and yield per hectare of major crops in India, estimates of Ministry of Agriculture and Farmers Welfare, 1992–93 to 2019–20, base year 1981–82=100,* in per cent per annum

Crop group	Area				Production				Yield			
	1992–93 to 2019–20	1992–93 to 2002–03	2003–04 to 2010–11	2011–12 to 2019–20	1992–93 to 2019–20	1992–93 to 2002–03	2003–04 to 2010–11	2011–12 to 2019–20	1992–93 to 2019–20	1992–93 to 2002–03	2003–04 to 2010–11	2011–12 to 2019–20
Foodgrains	0.3	-0.4	0.5	0.6	1.9	0.6	2.5	2.2	2.0	0.6	3.0	1.6
Cereals	0.1	-0.4	0.3	-0.01	1.8	0.9	2.4	1.6	2.1	0.8	3.3	1.6
Rice	0.1	0.3	0.2	0.1	1.6	0.8	1.4	1.6	1.5	0.5	1.2	1.5
Wheat	0.9	0.3	1.4	0.1	2.1	1.7	3.1	1.7	1.2	1.3	1.8	1.6
Maize	2.0	1.4	2.1	1.1	3.7	2.8	2.0	3.7	1.7	1.5	0.0	2.6
Coarse cereals	-0.9	-2.1	-0.9	-0.7	1.6	-1.5	2.0	1.4	2.7	0.1	4.9	2.1
Pulses	1.0	-0.8	1.4	3.0	2.2	-1.0	2.4	4.6	1.3	-0.4	1.2	1.6
Oilseeds	0.2	-0.7	0.0	-0.4	1.4	-1.8	1.2	1.1	1.7	-0.6	1.2	1.6
Non-foodgrains	1.4	-0.2	2.7	0.5	2.8	0.5	4.3	1.4	1.6	-0.2	2.1	1.0
All crops	0.7	-0.3	1.3	0.5	2.2	0.6	3.1	1.8	2.1	0.3	3.3	1.3

Source: Computed from data collected from Department of Food and Agriculture, Government of India.

Crop-Specific Growth Rates

There were also important crop-specific differences in the growth of production after 1992–93 compared to the 1980s (see Tables 1, 2 and 3). For foodgrains, cereals, rice and wheat, the growth rate of IAP and GVO declined significantly in the liberalization phase; for all the four crops/crop groups, there was a marked reduction in the growth of yields too. Within the liberalization phase, the growth rates of production and yield of foodgrains and cereals were higher between 2003–04 and 2010–11 than between 1992–93 and 2002–03 or between 2011–12 and 2019–20. The index of production as well as GVO for oilseeds recorded a decline of growth rates of production and yield between the late green revolution phase and the liberalization phase. In the sub-period after 2011–12, the value of production of oilseeds fell in absolute terms too.

Two contrary features of growth after 1992–93 also need to be noted. First, while the area under coarse cereals fell in absolute terms in the liberalization phase, the growth rates of IAP and GVO improved due to a rapid rise in yields after 2002–03. Disaggregated data further show that the growth of production and yield in coarse cereals was largely led by a growth of production and yield in maize. Secondly, the area under pulses rose in the liberalization phase, which led to a higher growth rate of pulses production. Within the liberalization phase, this was a phenomenon noted specifically between 2011–12 and 2019–20, when the area cultivated with pulses grew by 3 per cent per annum. There was also a moderate rise in the yield of pulses after 2002–03. In combination, this led to a rise in the production of pulses after 2002–03, but more specifically after 2010–11.

The only crop group that showed a consistently high growth rate of production between 1992–93 and 2018–19 was 'fruits and vegetables'. The production and GVO of fruits and vegetables grew after 1992–93 at a rate almost double that in the 1980s; the growth rate of GVO was above 5 per cent per annum between 1992–93 and 2010–11, though it did slow down to a more moderate level of 3.9 per cent per annum between 2011–12 and 2018–19 (see Table 2).

Shifts in Public Policy Across Phases

At the time of independence, India had an increasingly lopsided agricultural economy marked by low, and at times declining, yield of crops, low share of irrigated area, large extent of cultivable land left fallow, deterioration of soil quality and the use of poor quality seeds and poorly yielding livestock (Nanavati and Anjaria 1947). Between 1896 and 1947, foodgrain production in India grew at a meagre 0.1 per cent per annum; foodgrain availability per head, which was about 200 kg in the triennium ending in 1918, fell to about 150 kg in the triennium ending 1947 (Blyn 1966).

The reasons for the deteriorating state of agriculture under colonialism are many and complex. Nevertheless, *the* one overarching reason is backward and oppressive relations of production in agriculture. Big landlordism was a dominant feature of agrarian relations. All the land systems of British India, though diverse in their features, were united in their outcomes: namely, sub-division and extreme fragmentation of operated land, sub-infeudation of holdings, insecurity of tenures, rack-renting, illegal cesses and usury (see Habib 2008).

Post-Independence Agricultural Policy

After independence, the Indian state embarked on a system of national planning for the economy. The necessary condition for a rapid increase in the growth of the agrarian economy was a radical transformation of land relations. However, notwithstanding the emphasis on the land question in the plan documents, agricultural policy after independence never really considered the reform of property rights in land as a means of eliminating structural inequalities in the economy and expanding the home market (see Rao 1994).

First, land reforms in India were a major failure. The number of households that received land in the first 60 years after independence was just 5.4 million. Between 1947 and 2007, only 4.89 million acres of land were redistributed (Mishra 2007). The total extent of land redistributed accounted for less than 2 per cent of total operated area. The total extent of land over which tenants were conferred ownership rights accounted for less than 4 per cent of total area operated. Except in three states – Kerala, West Bengal and Tripura – the area redistributed in each state was less than 1 per cent of the area operated (Ramachandran and Ramakumar 2000).

Secondly, agriculture was viewed as a 'bargain sector', i.e. a sector where output can be increased with very little additional investment (Chakravarty 1973). If about 20 per cent of the plan outlay was kept aside for irrigation in the first plan, the share fell from the second plan onwards to roughly 8 to 10 per cent of the plan outlay. As a result, the share of irrigated area in the total area increased very slowly, which in turn contributed to a slow growth of crop yields.

Poor levels of agricultural growth also affected the prospects of industrialization and overall economic growth. An important precondition for the success of planning for industrialization was effective government control over the supply of wage goods. By the mid-60s, the possibilities of agricultural growth through expansion of area were exhausted; as data in Table 1 show, the growth rate of area was high for almost all crops between 1949–50 and 1964–65. Agricultural production was slowly headed towards a plateau. There were also frequent food shortages and spikes in food prices in the late 1950s and early 1960s. The wage goods constraint intensified, and the food crisis threatened to derail the planning process itself. The shift of agricultural strategy in the mid-60s must be seen in this context.

The New Agricultural Strategy of the 1960s

In response to fears of inadequacy of food production, a number of programmes for 'intensive agricultural development' were introduced from the early 1960s. These programmes were aimed at encouraging the adoption of a 'package' of high-yielding seeds combined with other improved technologies, credit and assured irrigation (Dantwala 1986). It was this new agricultural strategy (NAS) that came to be called the 'green revolution'. After the mid-1960s, there was also a rise in public investment in agricultural research and extension; the technologies of the green revolution were a product of the National Agricultural Research System (NARS).

While the NAS was mainly a technology-led programme, it was also supported by four forms of institutional support – *price* support, *credit* support, *input subsidy* support and *marketing* support.

Price support. The adoption of new technologies required price incentives at two levels: higher output prices for the producers, and lower and affordable prices for the consumers. The national food policy after 1965 was an effort to reconcile these contradictory objectives. In 1959, a report submitted by the Ford Foundation had already flagged the importance of 'a guaranteed minimum price' for producers (GoI 1959). Taking this recommendation forward, the Agricultural Prices Commission (later renamed as the Commission for Agricultural Costs and Prices, or CACP) was established in 1965, which estimated and announced support prices and procurement prices. The Food Corporation of India (FCI), established in 1965, undertook the task of procuring foodgrains from farmers in the surplus areas at procurement/support prices, storing and transporting them to deficit areas for distribution through the network of ration shops under the public distribution system (PDS).

Credit support. The policy of nationalization of commercial banks in 1969 helped to significantly raise the availability of credit for peasants. First, according to the new branch licensing policy, commercial banks were required to open four branches in unbanked rural areas for every branch opened in metropolitan or port areas. Secondly, 40 per cent of the net bank credit was to be provided to the priority sectors, of which agriculture and allied activities were to receive 18 per cent. Thirdly, the differential interest rate scheme was introduced in 1974, where loans were provided at concessional interest rates on advances to agriculture. These steps helped to mop up the new liquidity in the rural areas, improve the geographical spread and functional reach of public banks, and weaken the hold of usurious moneylenders in rural areas (Shetty 1997; Ramachandran and Swaminathan, eds 2005; Chavan 2002).

Input subsidy support. The subsidy policy of the 1970s covered the pricing of important inputs like fertilizers, pesticides and electricity for irrigation. The prices of major inputs in agriculture were 'controlled' to promote their adoption.

Marketing support. Agricultural Produce and Marketing Committee (APMC) Acts were passed in the states to regulate the marketing of farm produce by minimizing distortions in exchange. Under the APMC Acts, a number of regulated markets (*mandis*) were set up across the country (Acharya and Agarwal 2004). These *mandis* ensured a stable and standardized market for farmers adopting the new technology package.

The NAS made a signal contribution towards reducing India's dependence on food imports. It was instrumental in transforming the 'ship-to-mouth' predicament of India in the 1960s and, as M.S. Swaminathan pointed out, 'established the linkage between [national] sovereignty and food self-sufficiency'. Yet, for all its technological advantages, the outcomes of the NAS were unequal and far below potential.

As Rao (1994) argued, the limitations of NAS have to be understood in terms of the 'failure of planners . . . to see agriculture as a strategic, system transforming sector'. According to Rao, such a shift in policy would have required a 'focus away from the supply side to the centrality of property relations and mass demand as a propellant for the whole economy' (ibid., p. 133). The implementation of land reforms was a crucial factor in determining the extent of technological diffusion; the limits of NAS lay in its circumvention of this strategic choice. Consequently, the benefits of the green revolution were distributed unevenly with a '*region*-wise, *crop*-wise and *class*-wise concentration of production' (P. Patnaik 1975, p. 28). The NAS focused on regions well-endowed with irrigation, on just two crops (rice and wheat), and on sections of the peasantry that could mobilize the investment necessary for adopting the new technology.

A contrary view in this period came from M.L. Dantwala (1970). Following the argument of Theodore Schultz, Dantwala noted that 'the transformation of traditional agriculture is a qualitative technical phenomenon'. He further argued that land reforms were no more important in the Indian context, as technical change ushered in by the green revolution had resolved the problem of agricultural surplus rendering 'institutional changes practically sterile and ineffective'.

But as opposed to Dantwala's 'technocratic' view – to borrow the phrase used by Patel (1980) – stood the 'institutional' view, which was widely held by scholars of Marxist and structuralist persuasions (see U. Patnaik 1986; Raj 1969; Chakravarty 1977). Drawing from a comparative analysis of Taiwan, Mexico and India, Raj (1969) argued that in the absence of institutional reforms, the transformation of traditional agriculture would get reduced to just a promotion of dualism. According to Chakravarty (1977), the diffusion of agricultural innovations would be ineffective if the system of property rights 'inhibits risk-taking or channelization of scarce resources'.

> The crux of the agricultural problem would lie in devising effective organizational forms under which inputs, such as fertilizers, new seeds, electricity and water can be made available to as large a group of cultivators as possible. If we were unable to devise such organizational forms, technological innovations are bound to create tensions in the agrarian society through accentuating inequalities even if there were no inherent biases in the new technology in favour of large producers. (Ibid., p. 228)

It was in this context of close linkages between effective organizational forms and the structure of property rights that land reform emerged as a crucial factor that determined the extent of technological diffusion. In its absence, the potential of green revolution remained unexploited, and its benefits were spread unequally across crops, classes and regions in the early phases of the green revolution.

The Agricultural Recovery of the 1980s

By the late green revolution phase, the 1980s, agricultural growth spread to new regions and more crops (Bhalla and Singh 2010). Two important factors contributed to the turnaround of agricultural growth in the 1980s.

First, there was a major jump in production in the eastern region of the country, particularly in the state of West Bengal. Studies have traced the production achievements of West Bengal in the 1980s to the tenancy reforms – Operation Barga – undertaken by the Left Front government after 1977–78 (Mishra 1991; Rao 1995; Ramachandran 1997; Rawal 1999; Mishra and Rawal 2002). Two major achievements of these reforms were the provision of security of tenure to tenants and the fixation of fair rents. Sharecroppers across the state were registered in the land records through massive political mobilization. According to Mishra (1991), about 1.4 million sharecroppers were registered till 1990. The state government acquired about 1.4 million acres of ceiling-surplus land; out of this, about 1.1 million acres were distributed to approximately 2.5 million households.

These measures, combined with an increase in the supply of bank credit and input support to small farmers, were instrumental in West Bengal registering the highest growth rate of agricultural production among all states in the 1980s (Ramachandran, Swaminathan and Rawal 2003). As

Abhijit Sen put it, 'West Bengal, with a growth rate of over 7 per cent per annum in agricultural value added – more than two-and-a-half times the national average – can be described as the agricultural success story of the eighties' (Sen 1992, p. 10).

Secondly, there was an improvement in the production of oilseeds in the central Indian region. The quantum jump in the production of oilseeds in the 1980s was achieved mainly due to technological breakthroughs accompanied by public support on various fronts. The Technology Mission on Oilseeds was launched in 1986 to reduce dependence on imports and achieve self-reliance. The Mission's first achievement came in 1987–88, when, in spite of a drought, oilseeds production was significantly higher than in the earlier years (MoA 1988). As the figures in Table 1 show, oilseeds production grew at a rate of 5.8 per cent per year in the late green revolution phase, as compared to 1.6 per cent per year in the early green revolution phase (see also the CSO figures in Table 2).

The Advocacy for Liberalization in the 1990s

As distinct from earlier periods, agricultural policy in the 1990s took a different turn. If rejection of the need for institutional changes to transform the traditional institutional framework of agriculture was *implicit* in the technocratic view of the green revolution periods, India's neoliberal economic 'reform' after 1991 *explicitly* rejected it. The basic premise of the reform programme was that with increased openness of the economy, the barriers to expansion of agricultural surplus could be overcome by using external trade as an instrument. Thus land reform did not just take a backseat; the effort was to reverse the implementation of land reform.[2]

The critique of agricultural policy till the 1980s was first put forward by international financial institutions such as the World Bank, and then willingly embraced by India's ruling class (World Bank 1986, 1991; Parikh 1993, 1997; Pursell and Gulati 1993). In the new discourse, the importance of terms of trade dominated discussion on agricultural policy, and embedded in it was the exalted role bestowed on prices to allocate resources efficiently. It was argued that the earlier policy deliberately skewed the terms of trade against agriculture through protectionist industrial and trade policies, and an overvalued exchange rate. According to Gulati, Hanson and Purcell (1989), this policy-induced shift of terms of trade against agriculture was equivalent to 'net taxation' of agriculture. The argument went, once we 'get the prices right', the incentive structure in agriculture would improve and farmers would respond to higher prices by producing more. The National Agriculture Policy (NAP) of 2000 noted that 'the government will endeavour to create a favourable economic environment for increasing capital formation and farmers' own investments by removal of distortions in the incentive regime for agriculture, improving the terms of trade with manufacturing sectors and bringing about external and domestic market reforms' (GoI 2000, p. 8).[3]

How do you shift the terms of trade in favour of agriculture? Apart from reforms in the industrial sector and exchange rate policies, the suggested pathways were the embrace of free trade on the external front and the liberalization of agriculture on the domestic front. On the external front, a reversal of India's 'autarkic approach' would bring gains from trade, additional foreign exchange earnings, and, consequently, end the net taxation of agriculture (Gulati, Hanson and Pursell 1989). India had major comparative advantages in diversifying its cropping pattern in favour of high-value, export-oriented crops like fruits, vegetables and flowers. A free trade policy would not just 'promote farmers' own investments', but also 'investments by industries producing inputs for agriculture and agro-based industries' in these crops (GoI 2000, p. 8). It was based on a series of such expectations that India signed the World Trade Organization (WTO) agreement in 1994.

On the domestic front, the liberalization of agriculture included, first, changes in the policies of input subsidies. According to one author, subsidies in agriculture were 'fiscally unsustainable . . . inefficient and costly to farmers' (Parikh 1997, p. 11). Subsidies also resulted in an irrational use of inputs by farmers. If India cut down its input subsidy bill, it could save resources to raise public investment in agriculture (Gulati and Sharma 1995). Thus, the NAP of 2000 stated that:

> A time-bound strategy for rationalization and transparent pricing of inputs will be formulated to encourage judicious input use and to generate resources for agriculture. Input subsidy reforms will be pursued as a combination of price and institutional reforms to cut down costs of these inputs for agriculture. Resource allocation regime will be reviewed with a view to rechannelizing the available resources from support measures towards asset formation in rural sector. (GoI 2000, p. 9)

A second component of domestic liberalization was related to output price support. The argument went as follows. The minimum support price (MSP) tied farmers to *lower* price realization and denied them *higher* open market prices (and, by extending the same logic, higher export prices). The MSP and foodgrain procurement systems were fiscal burdens on the budget. The government was an 'inefficient' player in the foodgrain market. So the government should gradually retreat from the functions of procurement and distribution of food (Parikh 1997, p. 12). At one end, the large buffer stocks of food should be gradually brought down to a basic minimum. At the other end, the PDS need not be universally accessible, and should be converted into a targeted system that uses means-testing to identify 'needy' beneficiaries. In the place of public procurement and PDS, private trade could be relied upon to 'import or export . . . build or shed inventories, as and when they expect tightness or slack in the domestic market' (ibid.). The optimal private holding of stocks would be greatly assisted by the 'creation of futures markets' for agricultural products (ibid.).[4]

The agenda for domestic liberalization included several additional components. First, in line with financial liberalization, the M. Narasimham Committee argued that banks should function on a commercial basis with profitability as their prime concern (RBI 1991). As part of this approach, the earlier 4:1 ratio for opening bank branches was discarded and banks were permitted to rationalize their rural branch network. The norms related to coverage of priority sector lending, and agricultural credit itself, were considerably diluted.[5]

Secondly, it was argued that the existing laws on agricultural marketing discriminated against farmers by not allowing them to interact directly with the big buyers. As a result, India was unable to diversify its cropping pattern away from rice and wheat. Contract farming was suggested as a way out. To promote contract farming, state-level APMC Acts would need amendment whereby any private market or rural collection centre can freely emerge anywhere without approval of the APMC or payment of a *mandi* tax to them. The three Farm Laws of 2020 (later repealed in 2021) gave legislative approval to these changes in agricultural marketing. Corporate farming was also suggested as a solution. To promote corporate farming, it was argued that land ceiling provisions in the land reform laws have to be diluted so that larger landowners and agribusiness firms can freely lease in or purchase land. The belief was that if permitted, such consolidation of landholdings could impart economies of scale by attracting potential investors, including corporate players, into agriculture.[6]

Thirdly, though the official policy often reaffirmed its commitment to encourage public agricultural research, promotion of private sector research was seen as a definitive solution.[7] According to Manmohan Singh, 'the first green revolution came due to innovations developed in the public sector. The second green revolution may well come from technologies developed in the private sector' (M. Singh 2009). To encourage the private sector and meet the commitments of the WTO agreement, an Intellectual Property Rights (IPR) regime was endorsed in agricultural research.[8]

Fourthly, the agricultural extension system was to be reorganized by encouraging more public–private ventures as well as NGO-based extension networks. Cost recovery was seen as an important feature of the reformed extension system; as the NAP of 2000 stated, 'the government will endeavour to move towards a regime of financial sustainability of extension services through affecting in a phased manner, a more realistic cost recovery of extension services and inputs' (GoI 2000, p. 7).

More than a quarter century has passed since the implementation of free trade policies and domestic liberalization of agriculture. Data in Tables 1 and 3 show that the long phase of liberalization between 1992–93 and 2019–20 was marked by a slowdown in agricultural growth rates. There was a definite pick-up of growth rates in production between 2003–04 and 2010–11. However, this short stretch of growth was inadequate to raise the growth rates of the period 1992–93 to 2019–20 above the growth rates of the 1980s. While there was growth in some crops for some periods, the overall record of liberalization in raising agricultural growth was poor.

The next section examines, in greater detail, each argument raised in favour of liberalization and its specific impact on Indian agriculture.

The Era of Agricultural Liberalization
The Reversal of Land Reform Laws
Economic policies after 1991 were premised on a rejection of the need for basic institutional transformation in the rural economy. It was no surprise, then, that one of their most important features was a rejection, and reversal, of state-led land reform. In fact, post-1991 policies aimed at removing ceiling limits by diluting land reform laws and allowing private firms to cultivate unlimited areas of land (see Ramachandran and Ramakumar 2000; Athreya 2003). Such a policy stance is expected to widen agrarian inequalities, especially in access to and distribution of land as a productive resource.

Two chapters included in this volume deal directly with the question of land distribution. **Vikas Rawal and Vaishali Bansal** review multiple sources of secondary data on land distribution including the NSSO Surveys of Land and Livestock Holdings (NSSO-SLLH) and the National Family Health Survey (NFHS). According to NSSO-SLLH, 40.8 per cent of rural households in India were landless in 2018–19, up from 34.5 per cent in 2012–13. According to NFHS, 47.4 per cent of rural households were landless in 2015–16. High levels of landlessness coexist with extreme concentration of land ownership and possession. Thus, the top 20 per cent of rural households owned 76 per cent of all land in 2018–19 (as per NSSO-SLLH) and 83.1 per cent of all land in 2015–16 (as per NFHS). All data sources also show a rise in the extent of landlessness in rural India between 1991–92 and 2018–19. Advocacy for land reforms in India is usually responded to with the refrain that there is already a predominance of small and marginal holdings. Rawal and Bansal argue that this refrain may be misplaced; a significant proportion of holdings are more than 2 hectares in size. The share of holdings above 2 hectares in size was 41.7 per cent as per the NSSO-SLLH of 2018–19 and 71.2 per cent as per the NFHS of 2015–16.

Madhura Swaminathan, in her chapter, presents interesting village-level primary data on the distribution of land. In eleven of the nineteen villages that she studied as part of the Project on Agrarian Relations in India (PARI), the top 5 per cent of households owned more than 40 per cent of all agricultural land in the village. In a Bihar village, the corresponding share was 68 per cent. On the other hand, the bottom 50 per cent of households in these eleven villages owned either no land at all or less than 5 per cent of all agricultural land. Clearly, the case for land reform in India is alive.

Geetanjoy Sahu, in his chapter, deals with the land question among Adivasis in India, which is fundamentally different from that among Dalits and other landless sections. For Adivasis, the problem is related to reversing land alienation resulting from encroachment and takeover of land by real estate interests and settlers. After many decades of struggle, the union government passed the Forest Rights Act (FRA) in 2006, which aimed at recognizing and vesting rights over forest land on Adivasis and other forest-dwelling communities. Sahu assesses the progress of vesting individual forest rights under the FRA in India, and finds that its implementation was uneven across the country. From his fieldwork in Maharashtra, he notes that successful implementation of FRA is critically dependent on the extent to which the Adivasis' land problem was politicized and institutional support ensured for the potential beneficiaries.

These chapters underline the continuing relevance of land reform in India. In this context, the liberalization agenda of undermining land-ceiling laws is widely expected to encourage absentee farming by large farmers and corporations (Ramachandran and Ramakumar 2000). It is also expected to reduce the extent of ceiling-surplus land, while a substantial proportion of rural households are still landless.[9]

The land question, as Swaminathan, Rawal and Bansal, and Sahu elaborate, continues to be an important challenge for rural transformation in India. Even in the period of economic reforms, the process of development of capitalist relations in agriculture has been shown to be uneven and differentiated (Ramachandran 2011). These features of unevenness and differentiation are manifested in the outcomes of almost every socio-economic process in rural India. Profitability from farming, distribution of benefits from government schemes, the spread of markets and the provision of bank credit, among others, are all intermediated by the nature of rural social formation. In this volume, such differentiations are a recurring theme even as we focus on changes in public policy.

The Stagnation of Public Capital Formation in Agriculture

Public expenditure on agriculture has a significant impact on agricultural growth. It is crucial to the expansion of the productive base of agriculture. Public investment *crowds in* private investment in several spheres, including infrastructure, human capital and research. In most of these cases public investment is necessary because the pervasiveness of market failures disincentivizes private investment. Public investment also contributes to reducing the risks and uncertainties in agricultural production. According to Fan, Hazell and Thorat (2000), who examined Indian data between 1970 and 1993, government spending on productivity-enhancing investments, such as rural infrastructure, irrigation and agricultural research, significantly aided the growth in agricultural productivity and reduction of rural poverty (see also Sen 1997).

Trends in investment

The most immediate source of information on agricultural investment in India is the data on gross fixed capital formation (GFCF) from the Central Statistics Office (CSO). Here, we are looking at that part of the nation's total expenditure on agriculture that is not consumed but added to the nation's fixed tangible assets. In India, GFCF in agriculture primarily includes investment in major and medium irrigation projects.

First, the declining trend in total GFCF in agriculture (public + private) began in the second half of the 1980s and continued into the 1990s (Table 4). From the early 2000s, the share of agricultural GFCF in agricultural GDP began to rise, reaching 14.1 per cent in 2005–06 and 16.2 per cent in 2010–11. For the years after 2011–12, we considered GFCF as a share of GVA from agriculture under the new base year of 2011–12. Here, the share of GFCF in GVA fell from 18.2 per cent in 2011–12 to 17 per cent in 2019–20. In other words, the short period of rise in public investment in the mid-2000s was not carried over into the 2010s.

Secondly, within the GFCF in agriculture, the share of public investment was declining. As a share of agricultural GDP, public investment began to decline from the early 1980s and continued to decline in the 1990s, 2000s and 2010s (except for a moderate improvement between 2004–05 and 2007–08). The data series under the new base year after 2011–12 also does not show any discernible rise in public investment in agriculture.

Thirdly, the share of private investment was rising within GFCF in agriculture. The growth of private investment stagnated in the 1980s, increased moderately in the 1990s and increased rapidly in the 2000s, but slowed down in the 2010s. In the 1980s and 1990s, the rise in private investment was insufficient to compensate for the fall in public investment. However, in the 2000s, the rise in total GFCF was aided significantly by the growth in private investment. The pattern changed again in the 2010s, when private investment fell alongside public investment, which led to an overall compression of GFCF as a share of GVA from agriculture.

In his chapter in this volume, **S.L. Shetty** argues that public investment was crucial for the success of green revolution in India. In the phase

Table 4 *Gross fixed capital formation (GFCF) in agriculture as a share of GDP/ GVA from agriculture, India, in constant prices, 1950–51 to 2019–20,* in per cent

Period/Year	GFCF in agriculture as a share of agricultural GDP/GVA		
	Public sector	Private sector	Total GFCF
As share of GDP from agriculture (%)			
1950–51 to 1954–55	–	–	4.2
1955–56 to 1959–60	–	–	5.3
1960–61 to 1964–65	2.0	2.9	5.0
1965–66 to 1969–70	1.8	3.5	5.4
1970–71 to 1974–75	2.2	4.0	6.2
1975–76 to 1979–80	3.6	6.1	9.7
1980–81 to 1984–85	3.7	4.6	8.5
1985–86 to 1989–90	3.1	5.0	8.2
1990–91 to 1994–95	2.2	5.4	7.6
1995–96 to 1999–00	1.9	6.1	8.1
2000–01	1.8	9.0	10.8
2001–02	2.1	11.1	13.1
2002–03	2.0	11.7	13.6
2003–04	2.3	9.7	12.0
2004–05	2.9	10.6	13.5
2005–06	3.3	10.9	14.1
2006–07	3.5	10.4	14.0
2007–08	3.3	11.4	14.7
2008–09	2.9	14.5	17.4
2009–10	3.1	13.7	16.8
2010–11	2.6	13.5	16.2
As share of GVA from agriculture (%)			
2011–12	2.4	15.9	18.2
2012–13	2.4	14.1	16.5
2013–14	2.1	15.6	17.7
2014–15	2.3	14.7	17.0
2015–16	2.6	12.1	14.7
2016–17	2.8	12.8	15.6
2017–18	2.5	12.3	14.8
2018–19	2.9	13.1	16.0
2019–20	2.7	14.3	17.0

Source: Publications of the Central Statistics Office, New Delhi.

of liberalization, private investment assumed the dominant role in GFCF. According to him, this rise in private investment was aided by four factors after the late 2000s: a global commodity boom; a rise in terms of trade in agriculture; a faster flow of institutional credit to agriculture; and a faster growth of farm wages that led farmers to invest in labour-saving machines.

The breakdown of complementarity

Till the 1980s, a characteristic feature of GFCF in Indian agriculture was the complementarity between public and private investments (Shetty 1990; Storm 1993; Dhawan 1988; Rao 1998). In a growing economy, public investment induces or crowds in private investment by farmers. Thus, typically, public investment in irrigation leads to complementary private investment in constructing field channels and bunds, drainage and levelling of fields (Mishra and Chand 1995). Similarly, public investment in rural infrastructure, such as in electrification, can help mobilize significant private finance in irrigation investment (Rawal 1999).

But data from the 2000s show that there was a shift in this relationship of complementarity. Private investment grew even in the absence of preceding or associated public investment. It may be argued that the autonomous nature that private investment attained in the 1990s and after may well be a response to a sustained stagnation in public investment, particularly in surface irrigation. Such a conclusion can be discerned from the results of the All-India Debt and Investment Surveys (AIDIS) in 1992, 2003, 2013 and 2019. Two sets of patterns emerge from the AIDIS.

First, the proportion of rural households that reported any fixed capital expenditure fell between 1992 and 2003 (from 15.4 per cent to 13.2 per cent), and rose between 2003 and 2013 (to 31.1 per cent) and 2013 and 2019 (to 34.9 per cent). Also, the share of fixed capital expenditure in farm business in the total fixed capital expenditure fell from 32.8 per cent in 1992 to 21.8 per cent in 2003, but then rose to 23.3 per cent in 2013 and 26 per cent in 2019.

Secondly, most of the rise in the private fixed capital formation went into the construction of wells and farmhouses and purchase of tractors and tillers, the sales of which rapidly increased in the 1990s and after (see Sarkar 2013). In 2013 and 2019, respectively, about 28 per cent and 23 per cent of fixed capital formation by rural households was on transport equipment; about 23 per cent and 15.2 per cent was on wells and other irrigation sources; and 11 per cent and 18.7 per cent was on agricultural machinery and implements. These – constituting 62 per cent in 2013 and 57 per cent in 2019 of the overall fixed capital formation – represented investment in the purchase of tractors/tillers as well as in the digging of tube wells and bore wells. The extent of investment on tube/bore wells shows that in the absence of public investment in surface irrigation, there was an autonomous rise in investment by rural households in the exploitation of groundwater. These figures also show a fall in private investment in groundwater between 2013 and 2019, which is in line with the figures in Table 4.

However, sustained exploitation of groundwater in the absence of investment in surface irrigation has its limits. According to an assessment of groundwater resources in 6,881 'assessment units' (blocks or *talukas* or watersheds) of India by the Ministry of Jal Shakti in 2017, about 17 per cent were classified as 'over-exploited', 5 per cent as 'critical' and 14 per cent as 'semi-critical'. The corresponding shares in 2011 were 15 per cent, 4 per cent and 10 per cent (see GoI 2011). Unregulated expansion of groundwater irrigation without allowing for sustainable recharge of wells from surface sources and water conservation structures could have adverse implications such as: stagnation of yields, loss of soil fertility, salinity, increase in pumping depths, rise in pumping costs, reduction of well yields and scarcity of groundwater in summer months (Planning Commission 2007).

Tapas Singh Modak addresses the question of poor public investment in irrigation and its implications for farmers in his chapter. Modak uses data from the Central Water Commission, Ministry of Agriculture and Farmers' Welfare and the Minor Irrigation Census to show that the period of declining public investment in irrigation was associated with a shift from surface irrigation to groundwater irrigation. If the share of area irrigated by surface irrigation and groundwater irrigation was 57 per cent and 29 per cent respectively in 1950–51, these shares were 25 per cent and 64 per cent respectively in 2015–16. Public policy aided this shift to groundwater irrigation by increasing the supply of bank credit, supply of free electricity and public tube well programmes. As public investment in surface irrigation continued to be low in the 1990s and after, farmers intensified their investment in groundwater irrigation with the attendant ecological externalities.

In sum, agricultural policy after 1991 failed to decisively raise levels of public fixed capital investment in agriculture. Almost all the increase in total fixed capital investment in the 2000s and 2010s came from private sources.

Public Investment in Agricultural Research and Extension
Agricultural research

Conceptually, spending on research and extension are considered 'investments' as opposed to non-investment 'expenditures'. Zhang and Fan (2004) refer to public investment as those public expenditures 'providing various public goods, such as research and development (R&D), infrastructure, and education' (ibid., p. 89). Studies show that public investment in R&D has 'the single largest effect on sectoral growth' in agriculture, particularly in the long run (Mogues *et al.* 2012).

Historically, the government was the leading investor in agricultural research, which was considered a public good. In the developed world, public investment on agricultural research as a share of agricultural GDP ranged between 2 and 3 per cent (Byerlee, Alex and Echeverría 2003). For all the developing countries put together, the corresponding share was 0.6 per cent (see Ramasamy 2013; Nin-Pratt 2021). In India, public investment on agricultural research and education was 0.38 per cent of the agricultural GVA in 1996–97, which rose marginally to 0.6 per cent by 2018–19 (Figure 1). In other words, India's share was not above the average for the developing world (see also Pal 2017). A target of 1 per cent of agricultural GDP was fixed for public investment in agricultural research in the Ninth Five-Year Plan (1997–2002), but this was not achieved even in 2019–20. In fact, there was a fall in public investment as a share of agricultural GVA after 2011–12.

In the 1990s and after, private firms increasingly substituted for public institutions in agricultural research.[10] However, globally, private sector research has never been considered a substitute for public sector research. Pardey and Beintema (2001) noted that private research across the world

Figure 1 *Public spending on agricultural research and extension as a share of GVA from agriculture, India, combined for centre and state, 1987–88 to 2018–19,* in per cent

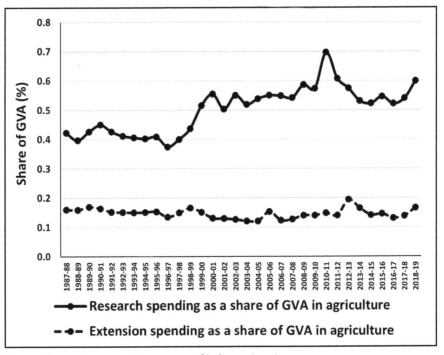

Source: Finance Accounts, Government of India, various issues.

covered only a 'small sub-set of the needs of the poor.' Technologies developed by the private sector were mainly suited to 'capital-intensive forms of commercial agriculture with high value-added aspects off the farm'. Private sector research focused mainly on the development of herbicides, insecticides and technologies related to food storage, transport and processing technologies (see also Alston *et al.* 2000). In India too, private sector agricultural research is confined to a few crops, such as maize, sunflower, cotton, pearl millet, oil seeds and sorghum, where expected profit levels are high. A detailed discussion of private investment in the seed sector – attempted in the following sub-section – will help amplify these concerns.

Illustration: seed research

Post-independence efforts in India to improve the quality of seeds began with the establishment of the National Seed Corporation Limited (NSCL) in the public sector in 1963. The Seeds Act was passed in 1966, by which quality control of seeds was envisaged to be attained through voluntary certification and compulsory labelling of notified seeds. The State Farms Corporation of India (SFCI) was established in 1969 for the production of certified seeds. State Seed Corporations (SSCs) were set up in the states under the three phases of implementation of the National Seeds Project (NSP) – NSP I in 1976, NSP II in 1978 and NSP III in 1987. SSCs were to acquire breeder seeds from national institutes or State Agricultural Universities, and then produce and distribute certified seeds to farmers.

After 1991, there were major shifts in the official policy on agricultural research and extension. While NSP I and NSP II focused only on the public sector, NSP III aimed at encouraging seed production in the private sector as well. As per the new industrial policy of 1986, seed and biotechnology firms were re-classified as core industries, with the result that the entry of large firms became easier. As per the new Seed Policy in 1988, the domestic seed industry was further liberalized with considerable incentives offered to private players to enter into seed production. Earlier, foreign equity in a seed company was limited to 40 per cent under the Foreign Exchange Regulation Act (FERA), 1973. After 1991, 100 per cent foreign equity was allowed in the seed industry and seed imports were allowed for research purposes under open general licence (OGL). The introduction of IPRs in plant breeding was an important component of the WTO agreement in 1995.

Today, as a general rule, private seed companies produce low-volume, high-value seeds with the focus on hybrids of oilseeds, maize, cotton and vegetable crops. The public sector, on the other hand, produces high-volume, low-value seeds. Nevertheless, a majority of seeds that are planted continue to be farmer-saved seeds and not certified seeds. It is the official position of the Indian Council of Agricultural Research (ICAR) that certified seeds yield more than farm-saved seeds, and the productivity levels of many crops could be raised by 20 per cent if certified seeds are used in place of farm-saved seeds. Seed replacement rates, i.e. the share of total area sown with certified seeds, were very low in the 1980s. In 1987, among field crops, the share of commercial/bought seeds in total quantity of seeds planted was less than 10 per cent; the rest was farm-saved (Pray 1990).

Official estimates for 2011 suggest an improvement in seed replacement rates. In rice and wheat, the seed replacement rates were 40 per cent and 33 per cent respectively; in certain crops with strong private sector interest in the development of hybrid seeds, such as hybrid maize, the seed replacement rate was higher, at about 57 per cent. In cotton, where there is a substantial private sector presence, the seed replacement rate was close to 100 per cent. In all such crops where seed replacement rates improved significantly, it was the private sector that gained market dominance through higher sales of hybrid seeds.

Of the total quantity of seeds sold in India in 2014–15, about 59 per cent was sold by the private sector. The shares of private sector seeds in total quantity of seeds sold in paddy and wheat were 42.5 per cent and 53.4 per cent respectively. But in specific crops like cotton, maize and sunflower, the share of private sector seeds in total quantity of seeds sold was above 95 per cent. If we consider the total quantity of hybrid seeds sold in India in 2008, the share of private sector hybrids was 100 per cent for cotton, sunflower and vegetables, 98 per cent for maize, 90 per cent for paddy, and 82 per cent for millets (see Schenkelaars, Vriend and Kalaitzandonakes 2011). For crops like bajra and jowar too, the share of the private sector in seed production was between 80 and 90 per cent.

In effect, encouragement to the private seed industry has implied encouragement to seed oligopolies. In anticipation of favourable changes in investment policies, a number of mergers and acquisitions took place in the Indian seed industry after the 1990s (Spielman *et al.* 2011). Public or non-profit research institutions have found access to critical technologies denied or restricted through unduly expensive royalties; the outcome has been the stifling of open-access research. Research priorities have gradually drifted away from socially desirable objectives. The rise in share of private sector seeds has been accompanied by a rise in seed prices, which has raised the cost of cultivation of specific crops, such as cotton (see Ashish Kamra's chapter in this volume for estimates of rise in seed costs).

Agricultural extension

In agricultural extension, the official argument was that agricultural information had acquired the characteristics of a 'private good' (see Reddy 2008 for a brief review). According to the NAP of 2000, 'the government will endeavour to move towards a regime of financial sustainability of extension services through effecting . . . a more realistic cost recovery of extension services and inputs' (GoI 2000). The new policy argued that the supply emphasis of the earlier training and visit (T&V) system was misplaced, and should be replaced with a demand-driven and competitive extension network. In this view, the government was to withdraw subsidies on extension services so that it could compete with the private sector on a level playing field.

Evidence shows that there was considerable weakening of the public agricultural extension system in rural India after 1991 (see Figure 1). Balakrishnan, Golait and Kumar (2008) noted that there was a slowing down of the growth of public spending in agricultural extension in India in the 1990s and 2000s. According to a Planning Commission review, the sluggish growth in Indian agriculture in the 1990s was mainly due to 'weakened support systems', and in particular, 'unresponsive agricultural research, nearly broken down extension [and] inadequate seed production, distribution and regulation' (GoI 2005, p. 197).

The evidence from Andhra Pradesh from the 1990s and early 2000s was rather striking in this respect. A government commission noted that 'the collapse of public agricultural extension services in the State has been one of the most important contributory factors to the generalized agrarian crisis' (see GoA 2004). The decline in the quality of extension system and the weakening of the SSC led to a sharp rise in the quantity of spurious seeds sold. Traders who sold the spurious seeds to farmers were also doubling up as moneylenders; the cost of seeds was considered as loans at high rates of interest.

Data from two rounds of Situation Assessment Surveys (SAS) of agricultural households, conducted in 2012–13 and 2018–19, starkly bring out the increasing weakening of the public extension system in the last decade (see Table 5). While a higher share of agricultural households accessed technical advice between 2012–13 and 2018–19, the share of households who accessed public sources fell from 18.1 per cent to 16.5 per cent in the July–December season and from 13.9 per cent to 12.1 per cent in the January–June season. The sharpest rise was in the share of agricultural households who accessed private sources, including input dealers and commercial agents, from 7.4 per cent to 21.1 per cent in July–December and from 6.6 per cent to 20 per cent in January–June.

One important reason for the poor show of public extension was the poor density of extension personnel. In India, there were only 0.12 million extension personnel to serve 158 million operational holdings covering 141 million hectares of net cropped area (Sajesh and Suresh 2016). There were also wide variations in the net cropped area covered by extension per-

Table 5 *Share of agricultural households accessing technical advice, by sources and season, 2012–13 and 2018–19, India,* in per cent

Source of technical advice	July–December season		January–June season	
	2013	2019	2013	2019
Government extension agent/ATMA	6.2	3.1	3.8	1.5
Krishi Vigyan Kendra	2.7	1.3	2.4	0.5
Agricultural universities/colleges	1.2	0.3	0.9	0.2
Veterinary department	8.0	6.6	6.8	6.8
Cooperatives/Farmer producer organizations	–	3.2	–	2.1
Agri-clinics and agribusiness centres	–	0.5	–	0.3
Kisan Call Centres	–	1.5	–	0.7
Sub-total: sum of all public sources	*18.1*	*16.5*	*13.9*	*12.1*
Progressive farmers	20.0	22.8	18.4	20.3
Private input dealers and commercial agents	7.4	21.1	6.6	20.0
Private processors	–	2.1	–	2.3
NGOs	1.2	0.6	0.9	0.7
Radio/TV/print media/smart phone apps	19.6	19.7	17.0	13.1
Sub-total: sum of all non-public sources	*48.2*	*66.3*	*42.9*	*56.4*
Any source	40.6	48.7	35.0	42.2

Source: Situation Assessment of Agricultural Households, NSSO, various issues.

sonnel; the figures ranged from 531 hectares, 553 hectares and 606 hectares in Kerala, Bihar and Tamil Nadu, respectively, to 2,608 hectares, 2,799 hectares, 2,982 hectares, 3,194 hectares and 3,154 hectares in Andhra Pradesh, Gujarat, Punjab, Rajasthan and Karnataka, respectively.

Alongside a reversal of the decline in public investment in agricultural infrastructure, a reversal of the slowdowns in public investment in research and extension was equally a critical factor associated with a revival of agricultural growth in India.

Trends in Public Expenditure

Apart from public investments, the union and state governments in India intervened in the agricultural sector through considerable revenue expenditures. These expenditures, which covered direct payments to farmers, input subsidies and administrative costs, were extremely important in the day-to-day functioning of the governments and their interface with farmers.

Gurpreet Singh and Sridhar Kundu, in their chapter, examine the trends in public expenditure by the union and state governments. According to them, there was a long-term decline in the expenditures of the centre and the states in agriculture between the 1990s and the 2010s. While there was rise in the centre's expenditure on agriculture in the late 2010s, this was largely owing to one new scheme – called PM-KISAN – of direct cash transfer to the farmers. In fact, in the 2010s, Singh and Kundu argue, there was a certain shift in the priorities of public expenditure away from creating infrastructure and undertaking 'core' activities. Increasingly, the governments were favouring individual-centric cash transfers and loan waivers as solutions to the crisis in agriculture. As a result, the spending of the government on allied sectors of agriculture (like dairying and fisheries) and on key inputs (like seed, soil and water) were falling. Such a fiscal stance of the governments did not augur well for the long-term health of the agricultural sector.

The Promise of Free Trade

Trade liberalization in Indian agriculture involved a series of policy measures, beginning with the rupee devaluation of 1991.[11] First, subsidies on the exports of a set of commercial crops, such as tea and coffee, were withdrawn. Secondly, consequent to India's signing of the WTO agreement in 1994, export controls on almost all crops were gradually phased out. Thirdly, quantitative restrictions on the imports of commodities like wheat and wheat products, rice, pulses and oilseeds were removed from 2000 onwards. In fact, the use of quotas as an instrument of trade policy itself was discontinued. Fourthly, trade policy began to use tariffs as the primary instrument of regulation. After the late 1990s, applied tariffs on the imports of most crops declined and were kept much below the bound levels of tariffs set by the WTO agreement.

All these changes were expected to improve the prospects of export-led growth in agriculture. However, this promise remained unfulfilled. In Figure 2, we have plotted the real values of agricultural exports and imports in India. In Figure 3, we have plotted the ratios of the rupee values of agricultural exports and imports in India. Some broad patterns emerge from these figures.

First, India has always had a trade surplus in agriculture. In the early 1990s, the value of agricultural exports was about four to five times the value of agricultural imports. Secondly, from the mid-1990s till 2009–10, there was no sign of any break in the trends of agricultural exports. But agricultural imports rose after the mid-1990s, leading to a sharp fall in

Figure 2 *Value of agricultural exports and imports, India, deflated at 2011–12 = 100, 1990–91 to 2019–20,* in Rs crore

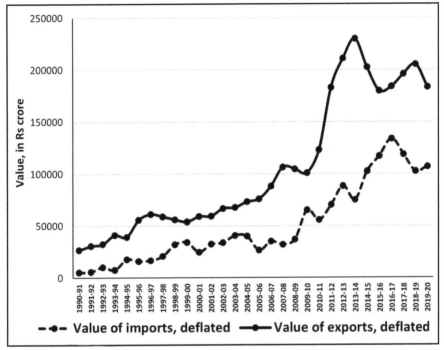

Source: 'Agricultural Statistics at a Glance', various issues.

the ratio of exports to imports to levels less than two by 2004–05. Thirdly, there was a short period of rise of agricultural exports between 2009–10 and 2013–14, which increased the export–import ratio from 1.6 to 3.1. But the increase in exports over this short period was limited to just three commodities: rice, bovine meat and cotton (GoI 2020). Fourthly, after 2013–14, agricultural exports fell even as agricultural imports continued to rise, leading to a fall in the export–import ratio from 3.1 in 2013–14 to 1.7 in 2019–20. In 2019, the value of exports was above US$ 1 billion in only four commodities: rice, frozen shrimps, bovine meat and cotton. On the other hand, most of India's agricultural imports after the mid-1990s were in vegetable oils, spices, pulses, cereals (mainly wheat) and horticultural products.

Overall, between 1990–91 and 2019–20, if agricultural exports grew by 13.8 per cent, agricultural imports grew by 18 per cent. If we disaggregate these growth rates across the three sub-phases after 1990–91, we see that between 1990–91 and 2002–03, agricultural exports grew at 15.7 per cent while agricultural imports grew at 25 per cent. Between 2003–04 and 2010–11, agricultural exports grew at 18 per cent while agricultural imports grew at 13 per cent. But between 2011–12 and 2019–20, agricul-

Figure 3 *Ratio of rupee value of agricultural exports to rupee value of agricultural imports, India, 1990–91 to 2019–20*

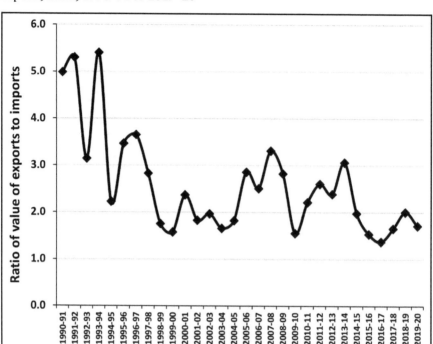

Source: 'Agricultural Statistics at a Glance', various issues.

tural exports grew at just 4 per cent, while agricultural imports grew at 10 per cent. Thus, in two out of the three sub-phases after 1990–91, agricultural imports grew at a much faster rate than agricultural exports.

Sachin Kumar Sharma, Teesta Lahiri and Suvayan Neogi, in their chapter, analyse India's engagement with the WTO in great detail. They identify two important reasons why developing countries like India were unable to take advantage and raise exports after the WTO agreement was signed. First, the Agreement on Agriculture (AoA), 1994 was systemically biased against the interests of the developing world. The AoA did not create a level playing field across developed and developing countries. Countries that were already heavily subsidizing their agricultures in 1986–88 (i.e. developed countries) received much more policy space to retain or reduce these subsidies than other countries (i.e. developing countries). Secondly, the methodology to compute the extent of support to agriculture was flawed and outdated. The reference price used to compute the Aggregate Measurement of Support (AMS) is still indexed to 1986–88 prices. Unless the methodology was changed and indexed to a more recent year, the developed countries would be able to continue to provide trade-distorting support.

India did not transform itself into a fully free trade area even after signing the WTO agreement. It retained its freedom to ban exports,[12] raise import tariffs[13] and keep its applied tariffs lower than bound tariffs for a range of agricultural commodities.[14] Given this cushion, India was able to insulate its domestic market from the extraordinary volatilities of the world market, such as the global food price spike of 2007–08.

Yet, two features of the period after 1995 are notable. First, while there was no discernible deviation of agricultural exports from its long-term trend; and indeed, there was a discernible deviation of agricultural imports from its long-term trend. The importance of imports can also be judged from another indicator: the number of 'import surges'. By one year of import surge, we refer to a year in which the value of imports was higher by 10 per cent than the average value of imports over the previous three years. If we take a count of such surge years in the twenty-seven-year period between 1993–94 and 2019–20, there were fifteen surge years for agricultural imports into India.

Secondly, international prices and domestic prices in agriculture were more integrated after the mid-1990s than before (see Table 6). For instance, the correlation between international and domestic prices of maize, rice, wheat and sugar rose phenomenally from 0.1 to 0.2 between 1981 and 1995, to 0.7 to 0.8 between 1996 and 2009. In Table 6, I have also included the correlation coefficient for the period between 2000 and 2019, and the relationship stands unaffected.[15] This increased alignment of domestic and world prices effectively imported the volatility of international prices – formed in highly imperfect and monopolized market environments – into Indian agriculture. Trade policy did intervene occasionally by either banning exports or raising applied tariffs, or using the MSP/procurement system to maintain domestic prices. However, given volatilities in global prices, there was strong transmission of the global volatilities into domestic markets.

Given the import surges and increased integration between domestic and international prices, there was a constant downward pull for the

Table 6 *Correlation between domestic and world prices of selected commodities, India, 1981 to 2009*

Period	Correlation co-efficient			
	Maize	Rice	Wheat	Sugar
1981–95	0.122	0.165	0.198	0.286
1996–2009	0.753	0.808	0.835	0.877
2000–19	–	0.791	0.696	0.739

Source: Chand and Bajar (2012) for 1981–1995 and 1996–2009; computed by the author for 2000–19.

domestic prices of many commodities – cotton, tea, coffee, spices, and many fruits and vegetables – after the mid-1990s. Despite trade controls that were often invoked, the import surges in various crops contributed in different degrees to the declines in their domestic prices (Bhalla 2004; Ghosh 2005). Further, even the minor gains from trade that resulted were unevenly distributed within India; according to Chand and Bajar (2012), the post-liberalization pattern of trade was 'favourable for States with higher per capita income and adverse for States with lower per capita income' (ibid., p. 41).

Is Indian Agriculture Net-Taxed?

It is in the context of the poor promise of trade and highly volatile international markets that the argument of 'net taxation' of Indian agriculture should be examined. As we discussed earlier, a major rationale offered in favour of liberalizing Indian agriculture was that farmers were 'net-taxed'. In other words, the incomes of farmers were kept artificially lower than what they should have been. It was argued that this 'net taxation' existed because protectionist policies deprived farmers of higher international prices, and the administered price system deprived farmers of higher domestic market prices. If there were more liberal domestic markets and freer global trade, the prices received by farmers would rise.

For this purpose, scholars use estimates of effective protection coefficient (EPC) or producer support estimates (PSE). EPC is the ratio between value added measured at domestic prices and value added measured at international prices.[16] PSE is estimated using a methodology advocated by the Organization for Economic Co-operation and Development (OECD). It has two components. The first is market price support (MPS). MPS is that part of the gross transfers to producers arising from 'a gap between domestic market prices and border prices of a specific agricultural commodity'. The second is budgetary transfers (BOT). BOT include all budgetary expenditures on policies that support agricultural production. PSE is the sum of MPS and BOT, expressed also as a percentage of the value of agricultural production (see Sharma, Mathur and Akhter 2021). Both EPC and PSE are based, thus, on the differential deemed to exist between international and domestic agricultural prices.

Right from the 1980s and 1990s, EPC and PSE were used to argue that Indian agriculture was net-taxed (see Gulati, Hanson and Pursell 1989 for the use of EPC; and OECD 2018 for the use of PSE). For instance, OECD (2018) found that PSE in Indian agriculture was –6 per cent between 2014–15 and 2016–17. In contrast, PSE in the OECD countries was +18.2 per cent, +19.6 per cent in the EU countries, and +9.5 per cent in the United States. The negative figure for PSE emerged largely because of a negative MPS despite a positive BOT. In 2019, India's MPS was Rs –4,61,804 crore, or −15.5 per cent of the value of production, and India's BOT was Rs +2,99,064 crore, or +10.1 per cent of the value of agricultural production. The argument was that if India adopted free trade and liberalized its domestic markets, it can 'get the prices right', net taxation can be eliminated and farmers' prices can be raised.

The major problem with such a methodology (EPC or PSE) that bases itself on the differential between domestic price and international price is that the international price is assumed to be a benchmark with no reference to the actual possibilities of domestic producers obtaining that price (Ramakumar 2021a). Let us assume a commodity 'A' whose international price is higher than its domestic price. First, 'A' may be produced in large quantities but may also be essential for the country's domestic food security. Hence, it may not be regularly exported. Yet its MPS will be estimated as negative. Examples of such commodities in India are rice and wheat.

Secondly, most short-term changes in MPS may be illusory if they result from short-term fluctuations of international prices, or relative exchange rates, or shocks to global demand or supply. Such fluctuations are more pronounced in agriculture because international agricultural markets are imperfect, narrow and dominated by monopolistic multinational companies.

Thirdly, if a country starts exporting 'A' to benefit from higher international prices, will the differential between international and domestic prices remain? In the mainstream trade literature, a 'small country assumption' is used where all countries are assumed to be price-takers and no single country is considered capable of triggering a major rise or fall in prices. But this is an unrealistic assumption. The international market for most agricultural commodities is small, while countries like India are large producers. Even if India exported a small additional share of the production of 'A', its impact on international prices will be disproportionately inverse. Consequently, the differential between domestic and international prices would considerably narrow, if not simply disappear.

Due to such fluctuations in MPS, the PSE also fluctuates widely. The PSE for Indian agriculture was +1.9 per cent in 2000. It fell to −14 per cent in 2004, −20.4 per cent in 2008 and −27.8 per cent in 2013. Later, it rose to −3.8 per cent in 2015 and −5.5 per cent in 2019. These fluctuating PSEs mean nothing in terms of taxation or subsidization of producers. They only mean that international prices were volatile.

In summary, over the period of liberalization, indicators like EPC and MPS or PSE were freely used to argue for further opening up Indian agriculture to the global market and reducing domestic price support measures. The fact is that such indicators are poor measures of taxation in agriculture because the international prices are no 'true prices' to be accepted as benchmarks of what producers can obtain. At best, they indicate short-term export possibilities in a commodity. Further, a negative MPS or PSE by itself implies neither a government that squeezes revenues out of farmers nor the absence of absolute profitability in agriculture.

Trends in the Terms of Trade

Most arguments to liberalize Indian agriculture on the external and domestic fronts have linked such policy changes to their ability to tilt the terms of trade in favour of agriculture. Once the terms of trade improve, the resulting price incentives would generate a significant supply response. Supply response is defined as a rise in area or production that results from a percentage change in prices. Accordingly, most policy discussions on agriculture give an exalted status to 'prices'; if prices are set 'right', resources would be efficiently allocated and area or production would rise.

What is the relationship between terms of trade and supply response in agriculture? Is it desirable to see prices as being singularly capable of raising area or production? I argue in this section that the conceptual and empirical basis for arguing so is weak, for many reasons.

First, the vast literature on the supply-responsiveness of farmers shows that the relationship between prices and output is weak (Rao 1988, 1989; Sen 1992; Ghosh 1992; Nayyar and Sen 1994; Hazell, Misra and Hojjati 1999; Vaidyanathan 2000). To begin with, there are major difficulties related to the accuracy of economic models used to estimate supply response, including in the measurement and control of different effects. Nevertheless, in a careful and extensive survey of the literature, Rao (1989) found that the range of long-run supply elasticity of aggregate agricultural output was historically between 0.1 and 0.5 in the developing countries. Rao's conclusion was that the resulting 'efficiency loss is quite small' (ibid., p. 41).[17] The responsiveness of yield-raising inputs to output prices was also not statistically significant. In fact, it was non-price factors – i.e. inputs, technology, institutions and infrastructure – that significantly determined growth in farm output.

Secondly, many studies have questioned the basic premise of the argument in favour of 'price incentives' and the alignment of domestic prices to world prices. Nayyar and Sen (1994) argued that the analytical construct of the terms of trade argument is very narrow, given their excessive concern with static allocative efficiency and ignorance of inter-temporal considerations. Also, it assumes that resources have perfect substitutability across uses and perfect mobility across sectors, both of which underestimate structural rigidities in the economy.

Thirdly, as Desai and D'Souza (1999) pointed out, the impact of an improvement in the terms of trade on marketed surplus will be intermediated by both the wealth effect and the substitution effect. Assuming no use of hired labour, it can be argued that a rise in family incomes due to improved terms of trade could either reduce family labour supply (wealth effect) or increase family labour supply (substitution effect). While output would fall in the former case, it would rise in the latter case; the aggregate effect is complex and unknown.

Fourthly, if the price of one crop rises, will all farmers shift to the cultivation of that crop? It would be difficult to argue so because the shift in allocations of area between crops is significantly constrained by the specificities of soil, climate and irrigation, which are diverse across regions (Vaidyanathan 2000).

Fifthly, as already discussed, current world prices (based on which most simulations are run) may be poor predictors of future world prices, particularly given that world prices are subject to significant volatility (Rao 1989; see also Gill and Brar 1996).

Finally, seen from a structuralist point of view, even if terms of trade were depressed by import-substituting policies in industry, the resulting growth in non-agricultural employment can lead to a faster growth in per capita agricultural incomes than in a protected scenario (Sen 1992).

In sum, while a rise in output prices is always welcome for a farmer's profitability, to assume that relative price changes can be enforced and used by policy to significantly raise output or shift cropping patterns will be an overstatement. A singular focus on prices, sidelining the relevance of non-price factors, would be poor policy.

In India, the idea of terms of trade is used in two senses. The first is the 'net barter terms of trade for farmers', which is the ratio between the index of prices received and index of prices paid for final consumption, intermediate consumption and capital formation. The second is the 'terms of trade between agricultural and the non-agricultural sectors'. The difference between the two is that hired labour is not included in the estimation of intermediate consumption in the latter (see Mahendra Dev and Rao 2015).

In India, the net barter terms of trade for farmers showed a moderate rise in the 1980s, a stagnation till the late 1990s and a slight fall till 2003–04 (Figure 4A). Between 2004–05 and 2010–11, the barter terms of trade showed a rising trend (Figure 4B). The rise of terms of trade after 2004–05 was achieved largely due to a rise in the international agricultural prices and a rise in the domestic MSP for rice and wheat. After 2011–12, the net barter terms of trade fell and remained depressed till 2019–20. These trends in the barter terms of trade for farmers were broadly in line with agricultural growth rates during each of these phases. However, it would be erroneous to see terms of trade as the predominant explanation for agricul-

Figure 4A *Net barter terms of trade for farmers and terms of trade between agriculture and non-agriculture, India, 1982–83 to 2003–04,* base year 1990–91 = 100

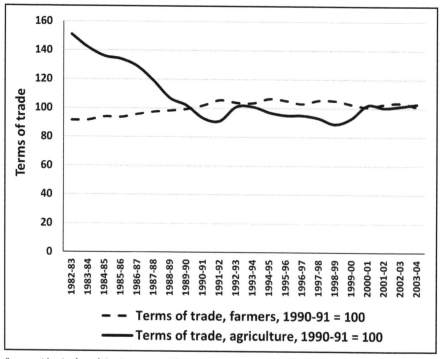

Source: 'Agricultural Statistics at a Glance', various issues.

tural growth between 2004–05 and 2011–12, as several non-price factors like public expenditure, availability of credit and improved technology also shifted favourably in this period.

At the same time, the terms of trade between the agricultural and non-agricultural sectors showed no clear relationship with agricultural growth. In the 1980s, the terms of trade for agriculture fell, but agriculture was growing rapidly. Terms of trade for agriculture did rise after 2004–05 till 2010–11, but unlike the barter terms of trade, it continued to grow between 2011–12 and 2019–20. What this shows is that hired labour was an important constraint on the profitability of agriculture for farmers between 2011–12 and 2019–20.

The trends in net barter terms of trade for farmers, however, does broadly suggest that profitability of cultivation might be an important explanatory factor for poor agricultural growth. It is to this topic that we now turn.

Figure 4B *Net barter terms of trade for farmers and terms of trade between agriculture and non-agriculture, India, 2004–05 to 2019–20*, base year 2004–05 = 100

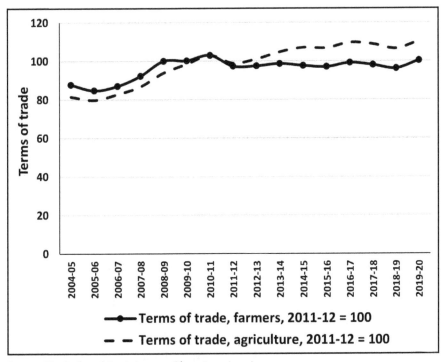

Source: 'Agricultural Statistics at a Glance', various issues.

Profitability Per Unit Area

Profitability in cultivation is dependent on various factors. These include the ratio between input price and output price, the type of crops grown, the yields of crops, the number of crops grown in a year, the ability to raise affordable credit for investment, the size of farms, and, finally, the ratio between trends in farm income and the cost-of-living index. Any rise in profitability in cultivation, then, requires addressing concerns related to a wide array of factors that determine returns from farming.

Let us first review studies on profitability across crops and regions in the 1990s and early 2000s (Sen 2004; Sen and Bhatia 2004; Surjit 2008). Using data from the 'Comprehensive Scheme for Studying Cost of Cultivation/Production of Principal Crops' (CCPC), Sen (2004) underlined three changes that affected profitability in the 1990s. One, there was a general slowdown in the diffusion of yield-increasing technologies and inputs in the 1990s as compared to the 1980s. Two, mechanization in agriculture grew faster in the 1990s than in the 1980s, though at varying rates across regions. Three, there were important technological changes and shifts in output prices. Sen's careful conclusion was that profitability in agriculture fell in the 1990s as compared to the 1980s.

> During the 1980s, when yield growth was higher and prices of most crops tended to rise faster than the cost of living, the real per hectare margin of GVO [gross value of output] over cost . . . increased for all crops except maize. . . . During the 1990s, with yield growth slowing down for most crops, and prices of crops other than cereals and sugarcane rising slower than the cost of living, the real GVO–cost margin fell for most crops other than wheat, sugarcane, barley and tur. . . . Across States also, increases in GVO–cost margins were less evident during the 1990s than during the 1980s. (Sen 2004, p. 38)

In this section, I use data from CCPC and the results of Ashish Kamra's chapter in this volume to extend the analysis to the 2000s and 2010s. I use the ratio between the GVO and C2 and A2 costs of cultivation to analyse changes in profitability in more recent years. Illustrative national-level data for rice, wheat, maize and cotton are provided in Figure 5.

First, in rice and wheat, there was a fall in profitability in the 1990s and early 2000s, a rise in profitability between 2004–05 and 2007–08, and a fall in profitability between 2007–08 and 2018–19. In the case of maize and cotton, there was fall in profitability till 2001–02, a steady rise in prof-itability between 2001–02 and 2010–11, and then a fall in profitability between 2011–12 and 2018–19. Secondly, in all four crops, the fall in GVO to C2 ratio was steeper than GVO to A2 ratio in the 2010s. Thirdly, if we consider GVO to C2 ratios, the profitability ratio was below 1 for many years between 1996–97 and 2018–19 in all four crops; in other words, cultivation was loss-making if opportunity costs of land and labour were added to the costs.

Ashish Kamra's chapter expands on this theme in greater detail. He analyses plot-level CCPC data for thirteen crops over seventeen years, between 2000–01 and 2016–17. After a critical examination of the reliabil-ity of CCPC data, he focuses on the cost of cultivation, GVO and profitabil-ity for each crop in the major cultivating states. Across crops, he reaches the unequivocal conclusion that profitability ratios, after showing some prom-ise in the 2000s, either fell or stagnated in most states in the 2010s. For many crops, profitability levels in 2016–17 fell back to the profitability lev-els recorded in the early 2000s. In Kamra's analysis, the fall in profitability was lower and more pronounced in smaller-sized farms than in larger-sized farms. According to him, the crunch in profitability was mainly due to a 'double whammy' of decline or stagnation in output prices and an increase in input prices.

The outcome of such a sharp fall in profitability was an absolute

Figure 5 *Profitability ratios (ratio of GVO to cost A2 and cost C2), paddy, wheat, maize and cotton, 1996–97 to 2018–19, India*

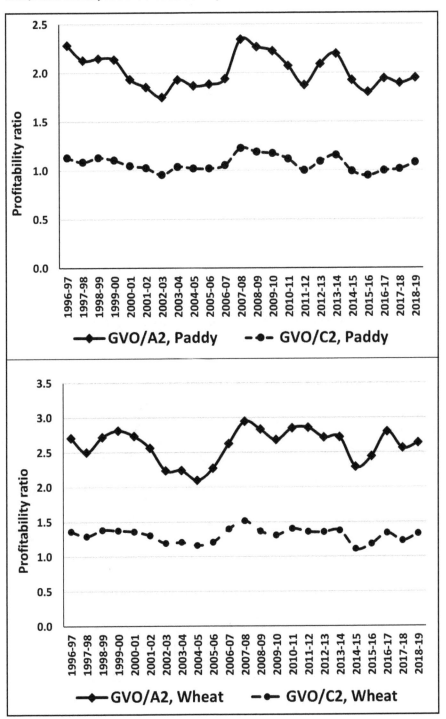

Figure 5 *(continued)*

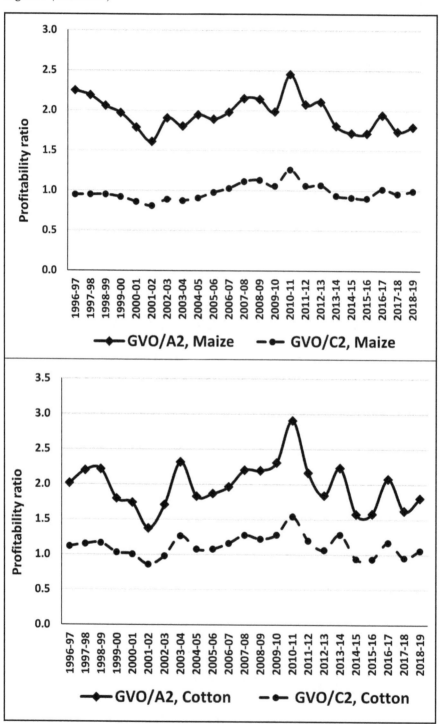

Source: CMIE Economic Outlook.

Table 7 *Incomes of agricultural households, India, 2012–13 and 2018–19, by sources, nominal and real*, in Rs per month

Source of income	Nominal incomes		Real incomes	
	2012–13	2018–19	2012–13	2018–19
Cultivation	3081	3798 (23.3)	2855	2816 (–1.4)
Animal farming	763	1582 (107.3)	707	1173 (65.9)
Wages	2071	4063 (96.2)	1919	3012 (57.0)
Non-farm business	512	641 (25.2)	474	475 (0.2)
Total	6426	10218 (59.0)	5954	7477 (25.6)

Note: Figures in parentheses are percentage changes from the previous survey.
Source: NSSO, 'Situation Assessment of Agricultural Households', various issues.

shrinkage of real incomes from cultivation for agricultural households. Data from the SAS of 2012–13 and 2018–19 attest to this (see Table 7). Over this six-year period, the total monthly income of agricultural households rose by 59 per cent in nominal terms, but only by 26 per cent in real terms. Further, and more importantly, the monthly income from 'cultivation' fell in real terms from Rs 2,855 to Rs 2,816 (a –1.4 per cent fall). Total incomes rose because of a rise in incomes from animal farming and wages. The enormity of the contemporary distress in India's agrarian society is fully borne out by the absolute fall in real incomes from cultivation.

Aparajita Bakshi, in her chapter, builds on this theme with a detailed, unit-level analysis of agricultural incomes from the SAS, 2012–13. She argues that low and declining levels of profitability translated into low levels of incomes from agriculture. The incomes were so low that average total income was lower than average consumption expenditure for 60 per cent of agricultural households. When only incomes from crop production and animal husbandry were considered, this share rose to 80 per cent. Bakshi further argues that the total incomes of 43 per cent of agricultural households were below the poverty line. When only income was considered, the share rose to 67 per cent from crop husbandry and animal husbandry. She fortifies her arguments with detailed income data from a set of village surveys across India. But she cautions against the view that all classes of agricultural households have low incomes; the 'income problem in agriculture' was a differentiated phenomenon. Landlords and capitalist farmers did obtain much higher levels of incomes from agriculture and non-agricultural activities than smaller farmers.

In her chapter in this volume, Madhura Swaminathan too addresses the problem of low incomes and unequal distribution of incomes across socio-economic classes. In ten of her seventeen surveyed villages, the Gini coefficient of income distribution was more than 0.5. In every surveyed village, the net income per unit of land was lower for smaller farmers than for larger farmers.

We now return to the discussion on profitability. Ashish Kamra's conclusion about a 'double whammy' invites our attention to two distinct issues: output prices and input costs. I discuss the two separately below.

Output Prices and the Role of MSPs

An important determinant of output prices in India is the administered prices announced by the union government. MSPs are announced for twenty-three crops in India, though only a few crops – like paddy, wheat, pulses, cotton and groundnut – are actually procured from the farmers. Some state governments procure a small quantity of coarse grains also. For sugarcane, a fair and remunerative price (FRP) is announced at which the sugar mills purchase cane from farmers. Two features are worth mentioning on the spread and reach of MSPs in India.

First, notwithstanding the general view that MSPs are inaccessible to farmers and irrelevant to farmers' welfare, there was a major improvement in the procurement system for major crops in India over the past two decades (Gupta, Khera and Narayanan 2021). In this period, many states began to undertake their own Decentralized Procurement Schemes (DCP). Further, procurement moved out of the traditional centres of Punjab, Haryana and western Uttar Pradesh into other states. Still further, governments began to procure pulses in significant quantities in the second half of the 2010s. Between 2014–15 and 2018–19, the National Agricultural Cooperative Marketing Federation of India Ltd. (NAFED) made a record procurement of 91.1 lakh tons of oilseeds and pulses (61.3 lakh tons of pulses and 30.3 lakh tons of oilseeds) under the Price Support Scheme, up by 1205 per cent from the 7 lakh tons procured between 2009–10 and 2013–14. In other words, the MSP became available for a larger proportion of farmers by the late 2010s than in the early 2000s.

Experience also shows that whenever market prices fell below the MSPs, farmers increasingly preferred to sell to the government at the MSPs. It would also be erroneous to assume that MSPs do not affect the prices received by farmers who did not sell at the MSP. In fact, MSPs served as an upward pull on farm gate prices even when the farm gate prices ruled lower than the MSPs.

Secondly, while access to the MSP system and procurement may have expanded over the years, it remains limited in their direct reach.

According to SAS data, a majority of farmers in India were not even aware of MSPs in the *kharif* and *rabi* seasons of 2018–19; only 40.7 per cent of paddy farmers, 37.1 per cent of wheat farmers, 28.3 per cent of soybean farmers and 30.7 per cent of cotton farmers were aware of MSPs. Further, only 14.5 per cent of paddy farmers, 9.7 per cent of wheat farmers, 8.6 per cent of soybean farmers and 8 per cent of cotton farmers sold to a procurement agency. In terms of quantities sold, only 23.7 per cent of paddy, 20.8 per cent of wheat, 13.1 per cent of soybean and 7.6 per cent of cotton were sold at their respective MSPs.

There is more. Even in 2019–20, in many states, there was no public procurement of crops for which MSPs were announced. Even when market prices fell below the MSP, procurement was not initiated in many states and crops. When procurement was indeed initiated, a large proportion of farmers were left out due to the poor spread of procurement agencies. In addition, there were regular complaints from farmers that the MSPs were fixed too low and did not adequately cover the cost of production.[18] Even in periods when MSPs rose, the rise covered just the rise in input costs and nothing more. For example, addressing the theme of the rapid rise of MSPs in the second half of the 2000s, Mahendra Dev and Rao (2010) noted that:

> . . . the farming community is not necessarily better off as a result of higher support prices, as these prices are meant to compensate for the rising CoP [cost of production]. . . . [R]ising costs necessitated higher support prices to sustain the long-run margin of 20 per cent over total costs. . . . [I]f the MSPs were not hiked sufficiently as in case of rice in the late-1990s and early years of the new millennium, margins would have gone down and distress would have spread. (Ibid., p. 180)

The case against expansion of MSPs, as made by a section of economists, has rested on the claim that higher procurement would lead farmers to raise their mark-up over the marginal costs of production. As our discussion shows, the empirical basis for such a claim is weak. The problem in the output market, it would appear, is not hegemony of the MSP but its limited reach among farmers. At the current levels, MSPs hardly cover the costs of production. In fact, in the context of the deteriorating economics of farming, MSPs perform the salutary function of a protective cover for farmers.

Biplab Sarkar's chapter addresses this important question of adequacy of, and access to, MSPs. Using CCPC data, he shows that MSPs do not compensate for the actual cost of production of rice, wheat, cotton, sugarcane, jute and arhar in most states. At the national level, MSPs accounted for only 68 per cent of C2 costs in paddy, 71 per cent of C2 costs in wheat, 63 per cent of C2 costs in cotton and 78 per cent of C2 costs in sugarcane. Using a dataset from intensive village surveys across states, Sarkar also shows that farm harvest prices for paddy were considerably lower than MSPs in seven out of twelve villages. At the same time, farm harvest prices were higher than the MSP in the case of wheat in all the villages, which shows the potential of MSP to function as a floor price for other crops.

Rise in Input Costs

Profitability was not stymied by low MSPs alone. The steady rise in input costs absorbed most of the increases in MSPs. Consequently, profitability rates were either stagnant or declining. A good proportion of the rise in input costs was consciously induced by shifts in public policy that aimed at restricting subsidy provisions, particularly for fertilizers, diesel and power (Gulati and Sharma 1995).

The argument in favour of reducing subsidies is based on four reasons: first, the prices of subsidized inputs do not reflect their relative scarcity value, which encourages their irrational application; secondly, most subsidies are pocketed by the larger farmers; thirdly, subsidies constitute a substantial burden on the finances of the government; finally, subsidies crowd out public investment by diverting resources (see also Mahendra Dev 1997; Vaidyanathan 2000; Gulati and Narayanan 2003; Gulati and Mullen 2003).

All these reasons are questionable. First, whether inputs are used rationally or irrationally is not a derivative of their prices alone; it depends more on the level of awareness of farmers and the strength of the extension system. In India, the rationale for input subsidies has always been to provide inputs to farmers at affordable and stable prices so as to incentivize them to adopt new technologies. Subsidies also help to compensate for imperfections in the capital market and the risks associated with the adoption of new and high-cost technologies. There is, by now, agreement that input subsidies significantly aided the process of adoption of new technologies during and after the green revolution. For example, Sen (1992) showed that the agricultural growth of the 1980s was primarily due to more intensive use of fertilizers and pesticides, and that there was a perfect negative correlation between yield of foodgrains and prices of fertilizers relative to foodgrains. Any withdrawal of subsidies will raise input prices, adversely affect input use and, in turn, reduce yields.

Secondly, there is enough evidence to show that marginal and small farmers benefit significantly from input subsidies. Estimates in Acharya and Jogi (2004) show that 36.4 per cent of the total input subsidies were availed by marginal and small farmers, while their corresponding share in the ownership of operated area was 36 per cent.

Thirdly, higher yields owing to faster diffusion of technologies could restrain the growth of food prices and enable the government and industry to keep price-indexed wage bills low (Acharya 2000). In this sense, input subsidies lead to lower wage bills for the government and industry. If we net these gains out, input subsidies may not constitute any real fiscal burden on the government.

Finally, as **S.L. Shetty** argues in his chapter, subsidies and investment are not perfect substitutes. In many cases, subsidies are necessitated by the overall distorted pattern of the development process, where a number of other more market-distorting and inefficiency-inducing uses of public expenditures exist. There are also better ways of mobilizing revenues for the government to afford subsidies, such as higher taxes on the urban rich and corporates. In reality, as he underlines, the subsidy–investment dichotomy is nothing but a disingenuous way to cut subsidies without any clear commitment to raise public investment.

Broadly, the union government's policy in the 2000s was to compress input subsidies, to allow input prices to rise, and to try and compensate farmers through a rise in MSP. This was one reason why input costs and MSPs rose concurrently for a period after 2004–05. However, such a strategy could be argued to be undesirable for two reasons. First, a large number of farmers in India do not generate a marketable surplus; most of the production of marginal and small farmers enter into self-consumption, and these groups would be adversely affected by higher input prices. Secondly, most small and marginal farmers in India are net buyers of food, and a rise in MSPs will raise their food bills without any compensatory allowance. Finally, procurement operations take place only in a few states and regions. As such, the geographical reach of the benefits of a rise in MSP is limited. For these reasons, among others flagged by Shetty, input subsidies and public investment cannot be treated as 'substitutes'.

In the following three sub-sections, I try to look more specifically at three types of input costs: fertilizers, pesticides and labour.

Fertilizer prices

Fertilizer prices rose sharply in the 1990s and after. In India, an average of 15 to 20 per cent of the total paid-out costs per acre of land are incurred on fertilizers. A feature of fertilizer use was that the consumption of nitrogenous (N), phosphatic (P) and potassic (K) fertilizers rose from 86.7 kg/hectare in 2001 to 146.3 kg/hectare in 2011, but fell to 133.1 kg/hectare by 2019. In other words, there was a rise in NPK consumption per hectare when agriculture was growing and a fall in NPK consumption per hectare when agricultural growth slowed down.

There are four stylized facts about fertilizers in India. First, while India produces about 75 per cent of its requirement of N fertilizers, it is dependent on imports for about 50 per cent of the final production of, and about 90 per cent of the raw materials for, P fertilizers. There is 100 per cent dependence on imports for K fertilizers due to the absence of domestic potash sources.

Secondly, there was very little addition to the domestic production capacity of fertilizers in the 2000s and 2010s. While no new public sector fertilizer company was established to increase capacity, five units of Fertilizer Corporation of India Ltd. (FCIL) and three units of Hindustan Fertilizer Corporation Ltd. (HFCL) were closed down in 2002. There has been a plan to revive five of the closed fertilizer plants – four of FCIL in Talcher, Ramagundam, Gorakhpur and Sindri, and one of HFCL in Barauni – but these were unlikely to be completed before 2022. As a result, one, there was increasing dependence on imports of fertilizers; and two, about half of the total production of N fertilizers and about three-fourths of the production of P fertilizers were with the private sector.

Thirdly, the prices of fertilizers in India were controlled by the government till 1992. The control regime was based on the Retention Price Scheme (RPS) for urea in 1977 and complex fertilizers in 1979. Under this regime, the subsidy to farmers represented the difference between the normative cost of production/distribution for each company and the fixed retail price. In 1992, partial decontrol of fertilizer prices was undertaken as part of the economic reforms programme. The prices of P and K fertilizers were decontrolled, while the prices of urea (N) continued to be controlled. After 1997, there was an effort to restore the parity in prices through a concession scheme, and in 2003, the RPS on urea was replaced with a Group Pricing Scheme (GPS) that was functional till 2009. Nevertheless, the relative price differences persisted.

Such an irrational policy on fertilizer prices seriously upset the nutrient balance in Indian soils. The consumption of N fertilizers increased rapidly, while that of P and K fertilizers fell in relative terms. The imbalance in use led to a declining fertilizer response in fertile irrigated regions and a depletion of micro-nutrients from the soil, leading to a deterioration of soil fertility in different degrees.

In 2009, the government introduced the Nutrient Based Subsidy (NBS) scheme. Here, a fixed amount of subsidy, decided on an annual basis, was provided for each fertilizer depending on its nutrient content. In other words, the subsidy on nitrogen, phosphorus, potash and sulphur contained in each fertilizer were fixed by the government. The actual retail prices of the fertilizers were left to the discretion of the fertilizer companies depending on the costs of production.

After the introduction of the NBS, the government reduced the subsidy per kg of nutrient. In 2010–11, the subsidy per kg was Rs 23.2 for nitrogen, Rs 26.3 for phosphorus and Rs 24.5 for potash. In 2011–12, this was reduced to Rs 20 for nitrogen, Rs 20 for phosphorus and Rs 21 for potash. In 2019–20, the subsidy per kg stood at Rs 18.9 for nitrogen, Rs 15.2 for phosphorous and Rs 11.1 for potash. On a per ton basis, between 2010 and 2019, the NBS for di-ammonium phosphate (DAP) fell from Rs 16,268 to Rs 10,402; for single super phosphate (SSP) from Rs 4,400 to Rs 2,826; and for muriate of potash (MOP) from Rs 14,692 to Rs 6,674.

Due to these shifts in policy, the prices of fertilizers skyrocketed after 2010–11. While the prices of fertilizers like ammonium sulphate and SSP had begun to rise in the 1990s itself, there was a very sharp rise in the prices of all fertilizers (except urea) after the introduction of the NBS scheme in 2009. Figure 6 provides data on the wholesale price indices (WPI) and Figure 7 provides data on the maximum retail prices (MRP) of major fertilizers in India.

In sum, the major features of fertilizer policy after 1991 were: (1) the absence of new capacity generation; (2) the growing importance of the private sector in fertilizer production; (3) increasing loss of self-reliance and dependence on imports; and (4) a shift in the pricing policy that aimed at reduction of subsidy and full deregulation of MRPs of P and K fertilizers.

Figure 6 *Wholesale price indices (WPI) of fertilizers, India, 2005 to 2018*, base year 2004–05 = 100

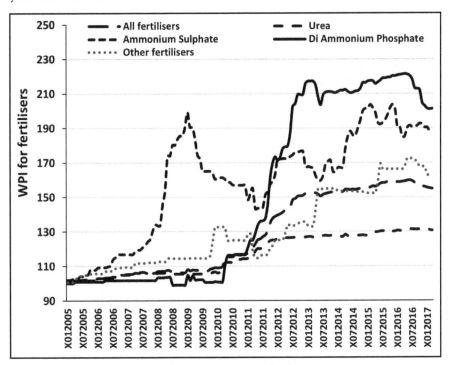

Source: Office of the Economic Advisor, Government of India.

Figure 7 *Maximum retail prices (MRP) of urea, ammonium sulphate, di-ammonium phosphate (DAP), single super phosphate (SSP) and muriate of potash (MOP), in terms of nutrients, India, 1981 to 2019*, in Rs per kg of nutrients

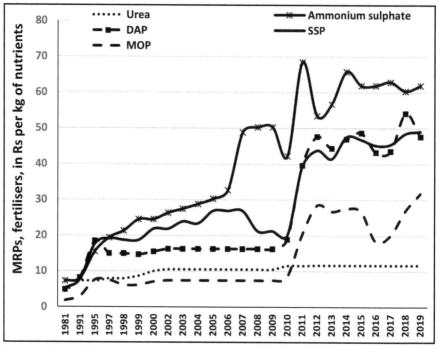

Source: Office of the Economic Advisor, Government of India.

Fertilizer prices, and costs of production in agriculture, rose sharply as a result. Particularly after the introduction of the NBS scheme in 2009, the prices of P and K fertilizers have either tripled or quadrupled.

The chapter by **Prachi Bansal and Vikas Rawal** is a detailed review and analysis of the political economy of fertilizer sector reforms in India. It meticulously documents changes in fertilizer policies after 1992 and shows that there were irrational changes in fertilizer consumption across different phases of the reforms. The chapter demonstrates how reforms led to differential changes in fertilizer prices alongside a sharp rise in the prices of P and K fertilizers. The introduction of the goods and services tax (GST) also contributed to the rise in fertilizer prices. In one section of the chapter, Bansal and Rawal focus specifically on urea policies. They argue that neem-coating of urea, introduced to improve nitrogen absorption, had no scientific backing in terms of its ability to raise yields. Other initiatives like reducing the size of one bag of urea from 50 kg to 45 kg were also based on poor evidence. Finally, they critically assess the desirability of scrapping fertilizer subsidies and replacing them with a direct cash transfer. They demonstrate that the move will have serious adverse consequences for the peasantry.

Large numbers of farmers, tenants in particular, are likely to be excluded from the scheme due to the poor state of land records management and the failure of the Soil Health Card scheme. The use of Aadhaar and biometrics to distribute cash transfers would further add to the problems of exclusion of farmers from the scheme.

Pesticide prices

The consumption of chemical pesticides in India declined over the two decades after 1991. Between 1990–91 and 2011–12, the consumption of chemical pesticides declined from 75,033 MT to 50,583 MT, and then rose to 60,599 MT in 2019–20.[19] There are many reasons for such an over-all fall in the consumption of chemical pesticides. Across these three decades, pesticide science advanced. The conventional pesticides were mostly highly toxic organophosphorus and carbamate compounds. New pesticides were products of advanced molecular research. These new generation pesticide molecules came with comparatively less toxicity, more effectiveness, specificity (narrow range) and low dosages. As a result, the total quantity of chemical pesticides used in the contemporary period is lower than the quantity used in the 1980s and 1990s.

India is a net exporter of pesticides. Even though self-sufficient in terms of total requirements, private pesticide firms also import patented pesticides for re-sale in India. There were about 60 pesticide companies based in India. However, about 90 per cent of the total production of pesticides was in the private sector. The government was largely a facilitator and regulator of private investment. The major public sector producer – Hindustan Insecticides Ltd. – produced less than 8 per cent of the total production of pesticides. But two private producers – United Phosphorus Ltd. and Sabero Organics Ltd. – accounted for more than 50 per cent of the total production of pesticides. In other words, the pesticide industry in India closely resembled a situation of oligopoly (Acharya and Agarwal 2004).

Till the 1990s, the government provided subsidy on pesticides under different crop-based schemes, such as for oilseeds. However, pesticide subsidy effectively ended by the early 1990s (Birthal 2003). In the 1990s and 2000s, pesticide prices were completely deregulated. At present, no price control measures exist under the Insecticides Act of 1968, which is the most important regulating legislation for pesticides. The government's claim has been that the 1968 Act ensures competition between producers, which keeps pesticide prices affordable. In fact, in line with this thinking, the Department of Chemicals and Petrochemicals officially stated in 2013 that:

> There is no problem with regard to availability and the cost at which [pesticides] are being sold. The companies are in competition with each other

Figure 8 *Wholesale price indices (WPI) of pesticides, India, 2005 to 2018,* base year 2004–05 = 100

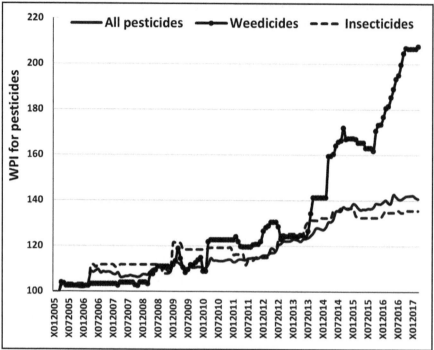

Source: Office of the Economic Advisor, Government of India.

to reduce the cost. . . . All types of pesticides which are used in India are actually available at fairly reasonable price. There is intense competition in the market. . . . That brings down the cost and that helps the farmers also. (Lok Sabha Secretariat 2013, pp. 18–19)

However, data on pesticide prices show the government's claim was only partly true. Non-availability of officially validated data constrains a long-run analysis of the price trends. Nevertheless, results from Figure 8 provide some indication of the rise in pesticide prices. There was a clear uptick in the wholesale prices of pesticides from about 2012. In particular, weedicide/herbicide prices show a very sharp rise. I also tried to collect data on the MRPs of specific pesticide brands across years. Between 2005–06 and 2019–20, the price of Quinalphos 5% GR rose from Rs 25 per L to Rs 340 per L; the price of Monocrotophos 36% SL rose from Rs 286 per L to Rs 550 per L; and the price of Acephate 75% WP rose from Rs 329 per L to Rs 760 per L.

Labour costs

The third component of input costs that rose sharply was wages for labourers. Labour costs are not controlled by policy, but they were the largest component of costs of cultivation. The trends were as follows. Real wages in all agricultural operations fell between 1997–98 and 2004–05 (Figure 9). Wages then rose marginally till 2008–09, and then rose sharply till 2016–17. Das and Usami (2017) note that the growth rate of agricultural wages between 2007–08 and 2016–17 was 'above 5.5 per cent per annum for most large States, and across all occupations, agricultural and non-agricultural, and for males and females'. Between 2009–10 and 2019–20, real wage rates rose by 250 per cent.

The reasons for the rise in wage rates after 2009–10 were varied. There was a reasonable growth in the non-agricultural sector – particularly the construction sector – that drew workers out of agriculture. There was also the Mahatma Gandhi National Rural Employment Guarantee Scheme (MGNREGS), India's flagship rural public works programme, which provided millions of person-days of work every year in the rural areas (see

Figure 9 *Average real wage rates for rural labourers engaged in agricultural occupations, India, annual, by sex, 1997–98 to 2019–20*, in Rs per day

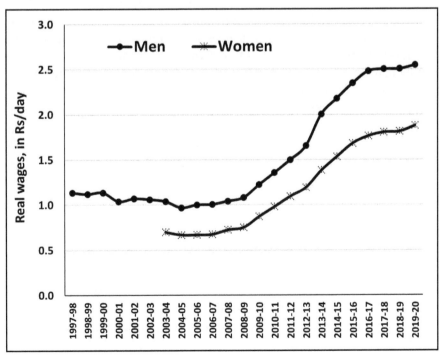

Source: CMIE Economic Outlook.

Acharya 2018). Both these phenomena might have led to a tightening of the rural labour market after 2009–10, leading to a rise in wages.

Figure 9 also shows that real wages stagnated after 2016–17, which is largely credited to the disastrous demonetization experiment in November 2016 (see Ramakumar, ed. 2018). MGNREGS did not expand in this period to compensate for the loss of jobs. A report by India Ratings argued that though MGNREGS 'may have helped shield the nominal wages from fall-ing' after 2016–17, the scheme 'did not provide the necessary impetus to strengthen real wage growth and reduce rural distress in a significant way' (Bharadwaj 2018).

Availability of Credit to Agriculture

There were three phases of change and continuity in the sphere of agricultural credit in India after 1991–92. The first phase was the period between 1991–92 and 2003–04. This phase of financial liberalization wit-nessed a reversal of several achievements of bank nationalization. There were: (1) large-scale closures of commercial bank branches in rural areas; (2) a sharp fall in the growth of credit flow to agriculture; (3) a widen-ing of inter-state inequalities in credit provision; (4) increased sidelining of small and marginal farmers in the supply of agricultural credit; and (5) increased exclusion of Dalits and Adivasis from the formal financial sys-tem (for details, see Ramachandran and Swaminathan, eds 2005; Chavan 2005, 2007). A consequence of this squeeze of formal credit in the 1990s was the resurgence, in different degrees across India, of the informal sector of credit, particularly moneylenders. Expansion of the informal sector of credit sharply raised the costs of credit in agriculture in the 1990s.

The second phase began from 2003–04 and continued till 2011–12. In this phase the downward trend of agricultural was reversed, and there was a revival. However, agricultural credit assumed a totally dif-ferent role – of increasingly financing new forms of commercial, export-oriented and capital-intensive agriculture, including by corporate houses (see Ramakumar and Chavan 2007, 2013). In their chapter in this volume, **Pallavi Chavan and R. Ramakumar** describe four features of agricultural credit in this phase. One, a part of the revival in agricultural credit was on account of a dramatic increase in *indirect* finance as opposed to *direct* finance to farmers. The definition of agricultural credit itself was diluted to allow banks to provide more indirect finance and include them under the priority sector. Two, even within direct finance and surely so within indirect finance, there was a rapid growth of large-sized loans that were unlikely to be borrowed by marginal, small- and medium-sized farmers. Most of the large-sized loans were given to large agribusiness enterprises including corporates, partnership firms and joint-stock companies. Three, about one-fourth of the direct finance and more than half the indirect finance were provided by urban and metropolitan branches of banks. Four, about half of the agricultural credit in a year was disbursed by banks in the January–March quarter, when all operations in farming were completed.

The third phase was between 2011–12 and 2018–19. While some of the essential features of the second phase continued into the third phase, Chavan and Ramakumar show that there were strong elements of discontinuity also. The growth of agricultural credit slowed down after 2011–12, but the slowdown was more pronounced in the case of indirect finance than direct finance. From the second half of the 2000s, the Reserve Bank of India (RBI) also introduced regulatory changes that led to a rise in the number of rural bank branches, limited the role of credit to corporate agribusinesses, introduced a new sub-target for small and marginal farmers, monitored bank targets on a quarterly basis, and allowed inter-bank trading of priority sector portfolios. As a result, while the diversion of agricultural credit continued in the third phase also, corrective measures by the RBI helped to contain it to an extent.

Results from the AIDIS reports of 1992, 2003, 2013 and 2019 reaffirm many of the above conclusions (see Table 8). The AIDIS provides household-level data on indebtedness for two groups: all 'rural households' and 'cultivator households'. All rural households operating at least 0.002 hectare of land were treated as 'cultivator households'.

First, public policy after nationalization of banks in 1969 had aimed to increase the share of institutional sources in the debt outstanding of households. The share of institutional sources in the total debt outstanding of rural and cultivator households fell sharply between 1992 and 2013, but rose back to the levels of 1992 between 2013 and 2019. Clearly, close to three decades were lost in expanding the access of rural households to institutional credit.

Secondly, the share of debt outstanding of rural and cultivator households from non-institutional sources, as well as from moneylenders specifically, rose sharply between 1992 and 2013 and fell between 2013 and 2019. Yet, their share in 2019 remained higher than in 1992. About one-third of the debt outstanding of rural and cultivator households came from non-institutional sources even in 2019.

Thirdly, there was a rise in the incidence of indebtedness alongside a rise in the debt–asset ratios (which shows the extent to which debt is a drain on the value of owned assets) of rural and cultivator households. The debt–asset ratio for cultivator households rose phenomenally from 1.6 in 1992 to 3.4 in 2019. The intensification of the debt burdens of rural and cultivator households, then, is a clear feature of the period of financial liberalization after 1992.

Table 8 *Selected basic indicators of household debt in rural India, rural and cultivator households, AIDIS, 1992 to 2019,* in number and per cent

Type of household/Item	1992	2002	2013	2019
(a) Incidence of indebtedness (%)				
Cultivator households	25.9	29.7	35.0	40.3
All rural households	23.4	26.5	31.4	35.0
(b) Debt–Asset ratio				
Cultivator households	1.6	2.5	2.8	3.4
All rural households	1.8	2.8	3.2	3.8
(c) Share of institutional sources in total debt (%)				
Cultivator households	66.3	61.1	58.0	67.0
All rural households	64.0	57.1	56.0	66.1
(d) Share of commercial banks in total debt (%)				
Cultivator households	35.2	26.3	27.7	42.6
All rural households	33.7	24.5	25.1	41.9
(e) Share of non-institutional sources in total debt (%)				
Cultivator households	30.6	38.9	41.6	32.9
All rural households	32.7	42.9	44.0	33.8
(f) Share of moneylenders in total debt (%)				
Cultivator households	17.5	26.8	31.5	22.6
All rural households	17.5	29.6	33.2	22.8

Source: AIDIS reports, various years.

What also emerges is a sharp contrast between aggregate banking data from the RBI and household data on indebtedness from sources like the AIDIS. A disaggregated analysis shows that aggregate banking data from the RBI hide several disquieting features in the distribution of credit. Across two decades of financial liberalization, the status of cultivator households appears to be worse off than before.

Crop Insurance

Crop insurance is one of the most important mechanisms against such risks as are associated with monsoons; it protects farmers against the uncertainty of crop production and helps minimize income instability. Over the years, India has never had a comprehensive crop insurance programme. Different crop insurance schemes were marred by low coverage, inadequacy of cover, high premium, low awareness, complexity of claim assessments and delay in settling claims. In 2016, the union government introduced, with much fanfare, the Pradhan Mantri Fasal Bima Yojana (PMFBY). The

PMFBY was an extension of the earlier schemes with certain modifications, such as lower premiums, wider coverage and faster settlement of claims. The objective was to increase the share of gross cropped area insured from 22 per cent to 40 per cent.

Awanish Kumar, in his chapter, shows that the functioning of the PMFBY was starkly different from the tall claims of the government. According to data from the SAS of 2018–19, only 8.3 per cent of paddy farmers and 6.8 per cent of wheat farmers in India reported their crops as insured. He argues, first, that PMFBY only attempted managing yield risks and the income variability that resulted from such risks. It did not cover price volatility and resultant income variability. In other words, PMFBY was not a *comprehensive* crop and income insurance scheme. Secondly, PMFBY continued to be marred by the problem of low coverage. It mandatorily covered loanee farmers while only theoretically covering non-loanee farmers. A large number of small and marginal farmers were excluded from the scheme since they could not afford the premium. Kumar shows that the number of farmers insured and the area insured under PMFBY were on a decline between 2016 and 2020.

Thirdly, the unit of measurement for loss calculation in PMFBY has remained contentious. The homogenous or area-based approach followed in PMFBY ignored agro-ecological variations and the specificities of individual farms. The crop-cutting experiments continued to be based on the block or *tehsil* level. There was little investment made to institute structures and capacities to collect data at the village and farm levels. As a result, the number of pending claims under PMFBY rose between 2016 and 2020. Fourthly, PMFBY proposed to calculate threshold yield for a given area by looking at weighted averages of yield over the previous seven years excluding up to two calamity years. This was against the interests of the majority of farmers in semi-arid and dry regions. Finally, PMFBY opened up the crop insurance sector to corporate profiteering by private insurance companies.

Surely, the need of the hour, as Kumar argues, is a universal and comprehensive crop insurance scheme with a special focus on small and marginal farmers.

Deregulation of Agricultural Marketing and Contract Farming

Sudha Narayanan, in her chapter in this volume, lays down the important challenges in agricultural marketing in India. First, there are problems related to uneven market access to farmers in different parts of India. While some regions are better served by *mandi*s, there are other regions prone to the monopsony power of traders. Even when APMC *mandi*s are functional, trader collusion remains a persistent complaint. As a result, the producer's share of the consumer's rupee is low. Secondly, continued barri-

ers to movement of goods, varying market charges and poor price dissemination leads to a situation of fragmentation of agricultural markets. Thirdly,
initiatives that could help improve quality of the produce, such as assaying,
are poorly developed in agricultural markets. Fourthly, aggregation of the
farmer's produce at the farm level remains a major challenge, which gives
rise to high levels of transaction costs. Fifthly, modern storage facilities like
cold storages and refrigerated transport are poorly developed, which results
in substantial post-harvest losses. Historically, these problems have limited
the ability of farmers to obtain better prices and access stable markets.

In this context, agricultural marketing reforms suggested by the
government after the 1990s have had four major objectives: (1) legalization of contract farming; (2) legalization of direct purchase of agricultural
produce from farmers by retail chains, bypassing regulated APMC *mandi*s; (3) permission for private players to open and control new agricultural
markets; and (4) removal of stock limits on traders to attract more private
investment into storage and warehousing.

Constitutionally, agricultural marketing was always recognized as
under the jurisdiction of state governments. In 2003, the union government
prepared a model Act on agricultural marketing and circulated it to the
states for passage in state legislative assemblies. This model Act contained
clauses on reforms in APMC *mandi*s as well as approving regulations on
contract farming. In 2017 and 2018, the 2003 model Act was split into
two model Acts, where reforms in APMC *mandi*s were separated from the
regulation of contract farming.

Reception of these model Acts was neither dismissive nor welcom-
ing. Many states selected a few clauses that they found suitable to their contexts, and accordingly amended their APMC Acts between 2003 and 2020.
Only one state – Bihar – used the occasion to completely annul its APMC
Act in 2006 (see Narayanan's chapter for a list of these legislative changes
in states). These included the freedom to establish private market yards/pri-
vate markets, to allow direct purchase of agricultural produce from farmers, establish farmer's/consumer's markets, to allow for contract farming, to
facilitate single-point levy of market fees, and to allow single registration/
license for trade/transaction in more than one market in the state. In other
words, substantial progress was achieved in addressing the different state-
specific challenges in agricultural marketing between 2003 and 2019; these
changes were also customized for each state given the state-level specificities
of agriculture.

It was in this context that the union government decided to break
the constitutional consensus that held till then, bypass the state governments, and issue three ordinances on agricultural marketing reforms in
May 2020. These three ordinances were later passed as three 'Farm Acts' of

the Parliament in September 2020. These Acts were to be national legislations, of a one-size-fits-all variety, applicable to all states in the country. The passage of the Farm Acts triggered a historic farmers' agitation all over the country in 2020 and 2021, till they were finally withdrawn in November 2021 (Ramakumar 2021b).

The Three Farm Acts

Prior to the now repealed Farm Acts, each APMC *mandi* had a 'notified area', which was its broad area of jurisdiction. Within this notified area, market activities were regulated. Establishing a private market or a rural collection centre within this notified area required a licence from the concerned APMC. The sponsor also had to pay a *mandi* tax to the APMC, just as other traders transacting in the *mandi* did. The Farmers' Produce Trade and Commerce (Promotion and Facilitation) Act, 2020 removed this jurisdictional power of the APMCs, and limited it to the principal market yards, sub-market yards and market sub-yards of the APMC. All areas outside these spaces were called the 'trade area', where traders and farmers may engage in the trade of agricultural commodities without approval from the APMCs, and without paying any cess, tax or levy. Thus, according to the government, this Act provided free choice of sale for farmers. The government also claimed that middlemen would be eliminated, and that farmers would receive higher prices than before.

The second legislation – The Farmers (Empowerment and Protection) Agreement on Price Assurance and Farm Services Act, 2020 – according to the government, provided an ideal *regulatory* framework for contract farming on a level playing field and without fear of exploitation. It would transfer the risk of market unpredictability from the farmer to the sponsor, and enable the farmer to access modern technology and better inputs.

The third legislation – The Essential Commodities (Amendment) Act, 2020 – removed basic food items including cereals, pulses, oilseeds, edible oils, onions and potatoes from the list of 'essential commodities'. All stock limits were removed for traders, processors and exporters. The government's claim was that this would help address private investors' concerns of excessive regulatory interference, and would attract more private investment into storage and warehousing.

The question of constitutionality

The first and foremost criticism against the Farm Acts was regarding their legal validity. Agriculture is a state subject in the Indian Constitution, listed as Entry 14 in the State List (List II). This apart, Entry 26 in List II refers to 'trade and commerce within the State'; Entry 27 refers to 'production, supply and distribution of goods'; and Entry 28 refers to 'markets and fairs'. For these reasons, intra-state marketing in agriculture was always considered a legislative prerogative of the states.

Seen in this perspective, the Parliament's passage of the Farm Bills was an extraordinary step (see Ramakumar 2020). For this extraordinary intervention, the union government invoked Entry 33 in the Concurrent List (List III). Entry 26 and 27 in List II are listed as 'subject to the provisions of Entry 33 of List III'.[20] Entry 33 in List III mentions 'trade and commerce in, and the production, supply and distribution of' a certain set of agricultural items. The question here is if the union government could use Entry 33 to intervene in the legislative domain of the states.

The first issue was whether 'marketing' of crops by farmers at the farm gate can be held equivalent to 'trade' as listed in Entry 33. To begin with, if marketing is concerned with *commodities*, trading is concerned with *products*. A commodity is a raw material used to produce another good. In contrast, a product refers to the finished goods so produced and sold to buyers. In other words, commodities and products are distinct entities that appear at different stages of the value chain. In our context, while Entry 33 might apply to the trading of products, it might not be applicable to farmers marketing at the farm gate. A related point is also that Entry 28 in List II – 'markets and fairs' – is *not* subject to Entry 33 in List III. As APMC *mandi*s fall under Entry 28, the union government would have no authority to define a 'trade area' overriding the concept of a 'notified area'.

In many of its judgements, the Supreme Court of India has also upheld the legislative powers of the states in intra-state agricultural marketing. Most notable is the ruling of the five-judge constitutional bench in *ITC Limited vs Agricultural Produce Market Committee (APMC) and Others* in 2002. The Tobacco Board Act, 1975 had brought the development of the tobacco industry under the union government. However, Bihar's APMC Act continued to list tobacco as an agricultural produce. In this case, the question was if the APMC in Monghyr could charge a levy on ITC for the purchase of unprocessed tobacco leaves from growers. An earlier judgement had held that the state APMC Act will be repugnant to the central Act and hence was *ultra vires*.

The constitutional bench in 2002 upheld the validity of the state APMC Act, and ruled that (1) market fees can be charged from ITC under the state APMC Act; (2) state laws become repugnant only if the state and centre enact laws on the same subject matter under an Entry in List III; and (3) in those cases outside List III, one has to first examine if the subject matter was an exclusive entry under List I or List II, and only after determining this can one decide on the dominant legislation that would prevail. In the case of the Farm Acts of 2020, the applicable points are (1) and (3). Regarding (1), states could continue to charge *mandi* taxes from private markets anywhere in the notified area regardless of the central Act. Regarding (3), the state legislation should prevail as agriculture was an exclusive subject matter, Entry 14, in List II.

In short, there was a strong case to reasonably argue that the Farm Acts had poor legal validity, if not outrightly unconstitutional.

Criticisms on the contents

In this sub-section, I shall attempt to critically examine each claim made by the government and its empirical validity. These claims and responses remain valid even after the repeal of the three Farm Laws, as the spirit of reforms in agricultural marketing retains its earlier conceptual perspective.

The claim of farmer's freedom to sell. A majority of the sale of farmers' produce in India already happens outside the *mandis*. Data from SAS, 2012–13 show that only 29 per cent of paddy and 44 per cent wheat were sold by farmers directly at a *mandi*, while the rest was sold to either a local private trader or others.

Farmers were forced to sell outside the *mandis* for two reasons. The first is that there were not enough *mandis*. In 1976, there were 4,145 large markets in India with the average area served at 775 km². The National Commission on Agriculture (NCA) in 1976 had recommended that every Indian farmer should be able to reach a *mandi* in one hour by a cart. The average area to be served by a *mandi* was thus estimated at 80 km². To meet this goal, the number of *mandis* required was at least 42,000. However, there were only 6,630 *mandis* in 2019 with an average area served of 463 km². Of course, roads and transport facilities have improved after 1976 and the 80 km² criterion need not be held as sacrosanct. Hence, using another set of criteria, the Doubling Farmers' Income Committee of the government found in 2016 that there should be at least 10,130 *mandis*. So, by all counts, India needed not less but more *mandis*.

The second reason was that most small and marginal farmers, given their limited marketable surplus, did not find it economical to bear the transport costs and take their harvests to the *mandis*. Thus, most of them ended up selling harvests to a village trader even if at a lower price. Even if private markets replaced *mandis*, in the absence of facilities of aggregation, it is only reasonable to expect that small and marginal farmers would continue to sell to traders in the village itself.

In sum, there is poor empirical basis for the claim that *mandis* were monopsonies that needed to be broken down. *Mandis* needed internal reform, but to weaken them to the status of irrelevance was equivalent to throwing the baby out with the bathwater.

The claim of elimination of middlemen. There is little evidence to argue that private markets would replace middlemen. First, private markets and private collection centres incurred significant transaction costs in purchasing small quantities of produce from many small and marginal farmers. These large transaction costs were a strong disincentive for private players to invest in rural markets. A possible solution is the aggregation of farmers' produce by farmers themselves. According to the government, Farmer Producer Organizations (FPO) can effectively play the role of aggregators at the farm level. However, the avenues for such aggregation remained limited. While several FPOs exist on paper, many of them were non-functional and a majority were under-capitalized (see Neti, Govil and Rao 2019).

Secondly, for the very reason of high transaction costs, the experience with states where APMC reforms were undertaken does not inspire confidence in the possibility of private investments. Bihar, which annulled its APMC Act in 2006, is a good example.[21] In Bihar, formal and regulated trade in the erstwhile *mandi*s were replaced by informal and unregulated trade, leading to poorer price realization for farmers.

The claim of higher prices for farmers. Will farmers earn better prices due to competition between *mandi*s and private markets? We have already referred to the poor potential of private markets to replace *mandi*s. But even if private markets were established, the possibility of higher prices for farmers would depend on whether the private transactions costs were likely to be lower than the existing *mandi* tax structure. If the transaction costs were higher than the *mandi* taxes, which was more likely because private players add margins to costs, these expenses were likely to be transferred either to farmers as lower prices or to consumers as higher prices or both.

The claim on the potential of contract farming. The overall criticism of The Farmers (Empowerment and Protection) Agreement on Price Assurance and Farm Services Act, 2020 was that it was more promotional than regulatory.

Sukhpal Singh, in his chapter in this volume, undertakes a detailed examination of the potential of contract farming and the role of the 2020 Act. He begins by reviewing the experience with contract farming across the world. First, contract farming companies tend to exclude small landholders and favour large landholders due to the high transaction costs of dealing with small farmers. Secondly, companies and farmers breach contracts when open market conditions are more favourable than specified in the contract. Thirdly, contract farming arrangements do not adequately take account of the considerations of ecological sustainability, such as monocultures and heavy use of chemicals. While there are exceptions, companies engage with environmental concerns only when the market demands so. Finally, contract farming is also associated with an increase in labour displacement, intensified casualization of labour, and increased use of low-paid women workers and child labour (see also S. Singh 2002).

For these reasons, Singh does not consider contract faming as useful per se. But contract farming can be a useful tool for price discovery and risk reduction for farmers if their interests are protected. State policy should ensure that there is collective action across farmers (i.e. group contracts in place of individual contracts), a fair and transparent negotiation process, equitable sharing of risk, competition for procurement instead of monopsony, an effective and trusted payment mechanism, and an effective grievance redressal mechanism. According to Singh, The Farmers (Empowerment and Protection) Agreement on Price Assurance and Farm Services Act, 2020 did not ensure adequate safeguards for the small farmers and would not have led to efficient and inclusive contract farming arrangements.

Private investment in storage and warehousing. Contrary to the government's claims, it was unclear if stock limits on traders were the reason for poor private investments in storage and warehousing. Surplus of agricultural produce in India is scattered and fragmented across space and crops. For private companies to be incentivized to invest, a certain homogeneity in the kind of surplus and facilities for aggregation across small producers and regions are necessary. Such a situation does not exist in large parts of India. As a result, it was unlikely that significant amounts of private investment would enter the sector.

At the same time, a few private corporate players were likely to create a foothold in certain crops and regions where favourable conditions prevail. Over a short period, private companies like the Adani Group had increased their investment in storage and warehousing. In the long run, if the procurement system was weakened and the *mandi*s withered away, it was expected that such investments would strike gold. In such circumstances, the bargaining power of small and marginal farmers would decline and the stranglehold of large agribusiness in agricultural marketing would expand.

India requires major public investments in storage and warehousing. Given the emphasis that public policy has placed on the National Food Security Act (NFSA) and the potential diversification of cropping patterns, such investments would be imperative. Unfortunately, public investment was falling, and policy has continued to favour private corporate investments in the sector.

Summary. The overall fear about the three Farm Acts was the growing clout of private corporates in Indian agriculture. Given that India's agrarian system was dominated by small and marginal farmers, their ability to effectively engage with a corporate-dominant market system is rightfully expected to be poor. This was one reason why the farmers' protest spread across states in 2020 and 2021 and attained a pan-Indian dimension. The withdrawal of the Acts in November 2021 showed that the union government was wary of such a spread of unrest across rural India.

PDS Reforms

Anmol Somanchi, in his chapter in this volume, discusses the functioning of PDS and assesses the reform undertaken within PDS in the decade of 2010s. The foodgrains procured by the union government using MSP and the procurement mechanism are distributed to the people using PDS. The neoliberal focus on restricting procurement in the long run had moved hand-in-hand with an effort to restrict the scope of the PDS from a universal system to a targeted system. Somanchi's chapter is an assessment of PDS in the neoliberal period. He argues that between the mid-1990s and the mid-2000s, the goal of targeting had failed as it led to a reduction of PDS coverage, exclusion of large numbers of the needy population, a fall in per capita purchases, a decline in the viability of PDS outlets and an increase in the diversion of foodgrains.

However, he also notes that there was an improvement in the functioning of the PDS after 2004–05 when it became a contentious political issue in India. In 2013, the National Food Security Act (NFSA) was passed, which enlarged the population eligible to access PDS and made food subsidy a legal entitlement. Yet, he notes, problems of exclusion persisted in the PDS. The continued focus on targeting the beneficiaries led the government to attempt technocratic solutions to further reform the PDS. But these technocratic solutions – often being solutions in search of problems – introduced new elements of exclusion in the PDS. These included the indiscriminate use of Aadhaar (India's biometric-linked unique identity scheme) in the delivery of PDS benefits. Somanchi also rejects the neoliberal solution of shutting down PDS and moving to a cash transfer programme by monetizing the food subsidy. In conclusion, his analysis underlines the need to transform PDS from a targeted system back to a universal system.

Concluding Comments

Agricultural development in post-independence India was marked by a failure of the state to resolve the agrarian question, i.e. ending the extreme concentration of land ownership and use, and weakening the factors that fostered disincentives in investment and technology adoption, tied workers to a social system with considerable pre-modern features and compressed purchasing power. While this failure shaped the pattern and nature of agricultural growth in India after 1947, the implementation of economic reforms after 1991 introduced new dimensions to the contradictions of the earlier regime. The Washington Consensus-inspired policies in agriculture have had acute adverse effects on the conditions of life and work in rural India.

The green revolution of the 1960s and 1970s helped Indian agriculture overcome a 'ship-to-mouth' existence and achieve self-sufficiency in production. This achievement was built on a platform of state support: in prices, subsidies, credit, marketing, research and extension. This interventionist role of the state in the 1970s and 1980s led to the creation of a network of institutional support structures in rural areas. Indeed, given the unreformed agrarian economy and stagnant public investment, the benefits of these support structures were distributed unequally – across crops, classes and regions.

Economic reforms after 1991 explicitly rejected the need for institutional transformation in agriculture. Instead it was argued that with increased openness, the barriers to raising agricultural surplus could be overcome through free trade. Diversification away from foodgrains, and towards export-oriented crops, was sought to be promoted. Land reform laws were amended in many states to raise land ceilings and encourage private corporate investment.

Over the long period of reform between 1992–93 and 2019–20, agricultural growth rates slowed down. In the 1990s and after, there was a steady weakening of public institutional support to agriculture. The growth of public capital formation in agriculture stagnated, as did the growth of public expenditure on research and extension. The protection offered to agriculture from predatory imports was removed, resulting in a downward pull on the commodity prices. As part of fiscal reforms, the input subsidy system was restructured, due to which input prices and costs of production increased sharply. Profitability in cultivation fell, leading to a fall in the incomes of agricultural households in real terms. The expansion of rural credit slowed down in the 1990s, reopening the doors to moneylenders. After the 2000s, public banks increasingly catered to the needs of large farmers and corporate agribusiness groups. Regulated markets came to be treated as obstacles to efficient marketing, and they were deregulated through new legislations.

The chapters in this volume elaborate on the impact of these new policies on the agricultural sector. They demonstrate that the impact was adverse in general, and acutely adverse in certain cases. At the same time, even as withdrawal of the state proceeded, there was growth of private investment; this was evident from the increase in the use of fertilizers and electricity, and the purchase of tractors and tillers. Not all crops witnessed a fall in the growth rates of production. Bank credit continued to be easily available to richer sections in the countryside. Due to these complex changes, even as there was little growth of large-scale agrarian capital from

below, peasant transformation continued to be characterized by land transfers and differentiation. This unevenness of agrarian change in rural India
is also amply illustrated by the chapters in this volume.

Notes

[1] This periodization of the economy builds on, and extends, an earlier exercise by Rao (1998).

[2] As the then Prime Minister Manmohan Singh noted in 2004, 'it has to be appre-ciated that the scope for a successful classical land reform involving large-scale redistribution of land is very limited' in India.

[3] The importance attached to terms of trade in determining agricultural policy was retained in the 'National Policy for Farmers' released in 2007.

[4] The NAP of 2000 stated: '[T]he Government will enlarge the coverage of futures markets to minimize the wide fluctuations in commodity prices as also for hedg-ing their risks. The endeavour will be to cover all important agricultural products under futures trading in course of time' (GoI 2000, p. 14).

[5] As the NAP of 2000 stated: '[P]articular attention will be paid to removal of distor-tions in the priority sector lending by commercial banks for agriculture and rural sectors' (GoI 2000, p. 12).

[6] As the NAP of 2000 stated: '[P]rivate sector participation will be promoted through contract farming and land leasing arrangements to allow accelerated technology transfer, capital inflow and assured markets for crop production, especially of oil-seeds, cotton and horticultural crops' (GoI 2000, p. 11).

[7] As the NAP of 2000 stated: '[P]rivate sector investments in agriculture will also be encouraged more particularly in areas like agricultural research' (GoI 2000, pp. 9–10). It also stated that 'development, production and distribution of improved varieties of seeds and planting materials . . . with private sector participation will receive a high priority' (ibid., p. 7).

[8] As the NAP of 2000 stated: '[P]rotection to plant varieties through a *sui generis* legislation, will be granted to encourage research and breeding of new varieties particularly in the private sector in line with India's obligations under TRIPS Agreement' (GoI 2000, p. 7).

[9] At present, direct farming by corporate houses – that could be called 'corporate farming' – is limited to a few pockets of India. There are two major reasons for the small extent of land under corporate farming. First, only a few states have amended their land reform laws to allow large-scale cultivation by corporate houses. Many states continue to have laws that allow only 'agriculturists' to purchase agricultural land. Secondly, as many farming households own small holdings, the transaction costs of working with these households are large and this renders the economics of direct farming fragile for corporates. Due to these reasons, a corporate presence in Indian agriculture is not yet visible in direct cultivation.

[10] Globally, too, there were sharp declines in the growth rates of public funding to agricultural research after the 1990s, compared to earlier decades. Studies show the increasing control of private research firms over agricultural research consequent to the shrinking of resources to public research. Globally, donors of the Consultative Group on International Agricultural Research (CGIAR) reduced their funding for research; as a result, CGIAR centres have had to focus more on own-revenue gen-eration by commercializing their research findings and entering into partnerships with the private sector in the development of new technologies.

[11] As we discussed earlier, an overvalued exchange rate was argued to be an impor-tant reason for the poor export orientation of Indian commodities, including in agriculture.

[12] For example, India banned the export of wheat between 1997–98 to 2000–01, and of rice and wheat between 2007–08 and 2011–12 (Saini and Gulati 2017).

[13] For example, India's average Most Favoured Nation (MFN) tariff rate rose from 10 per cent in 2010–11 to 13 percent in 2014–15 and this rise was mainly in cereals, oilseeds, and sugar (Saini and Gulati 2017).

[14] For example, while India's bound tariffs in agriculture are between 10 and 300 per cent, its applied tariffs are between 0 and 150 per cent (Saini and Gulati 2017).

[15] The correlation coefficient between 2010 and 2019 fell for rice and wheat; this was largely because international prices fell (for wheat) or remained stagnant (for rice), while domestic prices were maintained at a higher level in part by the MSP system/procurement and in part by raising applied tariffs. In the case of sugar, however, the correlation coefficient remained high even after 2010.

[16] Of course, the international price is adjusted for transport costs, marketing margins and other costs incurred.

[17] As Vaidyanathan (2000) argued, 'even a 15 per cent improvement in ToT with a price elasticity of aggregate supply of 0.3, will raise output by about 5 per cent, equal to less than the additional output in two years at present growth rates. Hardly the basis to project a *sustained* increase in the growth rate!'

[18] According to the National Commission for Farmers (NCF) in 2006, MSPs should be fixed at 150 per cent of the C2 cost of production. However, even in 2019–20, MSPs were not fixed above 150 per cent of the A2+FL cost of production.

[19] On the other hand, the consumption of bio-pesticides rose from 123 MT in 1990–91 to 8,110 MT in 2011–12 and 7,804 MT in 2019–20.

[20] The introduction of Entry 33 in List III was itself a matter of controversy in 1954 (see Ramakumar 2020 for a discussion).

[21] See Akhilesh Pandey, 'Bihar's failing PACS system shows what could happen after the farm laws', *Caravan*, 16 January 2021; and Sayantan Bera, 'What trade freedom gave to Bihar's farmers', *Livemint*, 8 March 2021.

Bibliography

Acharya, S.S. (2000), 'Subsidies in Indian Agriculture and Their Beneficiaries', *Agricultural Situation in India*, vol. 47, no. 5, pp. 251–60.

Acharya, S.S. and N.L. Agarwal (2004), *Agricultural Marketing in India*, New Delhi: Oxford and IBM Publishing Co.

Acharya, S.S. and R.L. Jogi (2004), 'Farm Input Subsidies in Indian Agriculture', Working Paper 140, Institute of Development Studies, Jaipur.

Alagh, V.K. (2011), 'The Future of Indian Agriculture', Dr B.P. Pal Memorial Lecture, Indian Agricultural Research Institute, New Delhi.

Alston, J.M., M.C. Marra, P.G. Pardey and T.J. Wyatt (2000), 'A Meta-Analysis of Rates of Return to Agricultural R&D: Ex Pede Herculem?', Research Report No. 113, International Food Policy Research Institute, Washington D.C.

Athreya, V. (2003), 'Redistributive Land Reforms in India: Some Reflections in the Current Context', Paper presented at the All-India Conference on Agriculture and Rural Society in Contemporary India, Barddhaman, 17–20 December.

Balakrishnan, P., R. Golait and P. Kumar (2008), 'Agricultural Growth in India since 1991', Study No. 27, Development Study Group, Reserve Bank of India, Mumbai.

Bharadwaj, S. (2018), 'Rural Wage Growth No Less Important than Doubling Farmers' Income', Press release, India Ratings, Mumbai.

Birthal, P.S. (2003), 'Economic Potential of Biological Substitutes for Agrochemicals', Policy Paper 18, National Centre for Agricultural Economics and Policy Research, New Delhi.

Bhalla, G.S. (2004), *Globalization and Indian Agriculture, State of the Indian Farmer: A Millennium Study*, vol. 19, New Delhi: Academic Foundation.

Bhalla, G.S. and G. Singh (2010), 'Growth of Indian Agriculture: A District Level Study', Final Report on Planning Commission Project, Planning Commission, New Delhi.

Blyn, G. (1966), *Agricultural Trends in India 1891–1949: Output, Area and Productivity*, Philadelphia: University of Pennsylvania Press.

Byerlee, D., G. Alex and R.G. Echeverría (2002), 'The Evolution of Public Research Systems in Developing Countries: Facing New Challenges', in D. Byerlee and R.G. Echeverría, eds, *Agricultural Research Policy in an Era of Privatization*, Oxon, United Kingdom: CABI, pp. 19–34.

Chakravarty, S. ([1973] 1997), *Writings on Development*, New Delhi: Oxford University Press.

Chakravarthy, S. (1977), 'Some Reflections on the Growth Process in Indian Economy', reprinted in C.D. Wadhwa, ed., *Some Problems of Economic Policy*, Bombay: Tata McGraw Hill.

Chand, R. and S. Bajar (2012), 'Agricultural Trade Liberalization Policies in India: Balancing Producer and Consumer Interests', in R. Banga and A. Das, eds, *Twenty Years of India's Liberalization*, New Delhi: Centre for WTO Studies and United Nations.

Chavan, P. (2002), 'Some Features of Rural Credit in India: A Study after the Period of Bank Nationalization', M.Phil thesis, Indira Gandhi Institute of Development Research, Mumbai.

———— (2005), 'Banking Sector Liberalization and the Growth and Regional Distribution of Rural Banking', in V.K. Ramachandran and M. Swaminathan, eds, *Financial Liberalization and Rural Credit in India*, New Delhi: Tulika Books.

———— (2007), 'Access to Bank Credit: Implications for Rural Dalit Households', *Economic and Political Weekly*, vol. 42, no. 31, 4–10 August, pp. 3219–23.

Dantwala, M.L. (1970), 'From Stagnation to Growth', Presidential Address delivered at the 53rd Annual Conference of the Indian Economic Association, December.

———— (1986), 'Strategy of Agricultural Development since Independence', in *Indian Agricul-tural Development since Independence: A Collection of Essays*, New Delhi: Oxford and IBH Publishing Co., pp. 1–15.

Das, A. and Y. Usami (2017), 'Wage Rates in Rural India, 1998–99 to 2016–17', *Review of Agrarian Studies*, vol. 7, no. 2.

Dhawan, B.D. (1988), *Irrigation in India's Agricultural Development: Productivity, Stability, Equity*, New Delhi: Institute of Economic Growth and Sage Publications.

Fan, S., P. Hazell and S. Thorat (2000), 'Government Spending, Growth and Poverty in Rural India', *American Journal of Agricultural Economics*, vol. 82, no. 4, November, pp. 1038–51.

Ghosh, J. (1992), 'Twelve Theses on Agricultural Prices', *Social Scientist*, vol. 20, no. 11, pp. 20–25.

———— (2005), 'Trade Liberalization in Agriculture: An Examination of Impact and Policy Strategies with Special Reference to India', Background paper for *Human Development Report 2005*, New Delhi.

Gill, S.S. and J.S. Brar (1996), 'Global Market and Competitiveness of Indian Agriculture: Some Issues', *Economic and Political Weekly*, vol. 31, no. 32, 10 August, pp. 2167–77.

Government of Andhra Pradesh (GoA) (2004), *Report of the Commission on Farmers' Welfare*, Hyderabad.

Government of India (GoI) (1959), *India's Food Crisis and Steps to Meet It*, Ministry of Food and Agriculture, New Delhi.

———— (2000), 'National Agriculture Policy', Ministry of Agriculture, New Delhi.

———— (2005), 'Agriculture and Food Security', Mid-term Review of the Tenth Five-Year Plan, Part II, Chapter 5, Planning Commission, New Delhi.

———— (2011) 'Annual Report 2009–10', Ministry of Water Resources, New Delhi.

———— (2020), 'HLEG REPORT on Agriculture Exports', Fifteenth Finance Commission (Chairperson: Sanjiv Puri), New Delhi.

Gulati, A., J. Hanson and G. Pursell (1989), 'Effective Incentives in India's Agriculture: Cotton, Groundnuts, Wheat and Rice', WPS 332, World Bank, New Delhi.

Gulati, A. and K. Mullen (2003), 'Responding to Policy Reform: Indian Agriculture in the 1990s and After', Working Paper No. 189, Stanford Center for International Development, Stanford.

Gulati, A. and S. Narayanan (2003), *Subsidy Syndrome in Indian Agriculture*, New Delhi: Oxford University Press.

Gulati, A. and A. Sharma (1995), 'Subsidy Syndrome in Indian Agriculture', *Economic and Political Weekly*, vol. 30, no. 39, 30 September, pp. A93–A102.

Gupta, P., R. Khera and S. Narayanan (2021), 'Minimum Support Prices in India: Distilling the Facts', *Review of Agrarian Studies*, vol. 10, no. 2, pp. 49–71.

Habib, I. (2008), *Indian Economy, 1858–1914*, A People's History of India 28, New Delhi: Tulika Books.

Hazell, P.B.R., V.N. Misra and B. Hojjati (1999), 'Role of Terms of Trade in Indian Agricultural Growth: A National and State Level Analysis', EPTD Discussion Paper 15, International Food Policy Research Institute, Washington D.C.

Lok Sabha Secretariat (2013), 'Production and Availability of Pesticides', 36th Report of the Standing Committee on Chemicals and Fertilizers, 15th Lok Sabha, presented on 6 August, New Delhi.

Mahendra Dev, S. (1997), 'Subsidies and Investments in Indian Agriculture: Issues and Perspectives', Rajiv Gandhi Institute for Contemporary Studies, New Delhi.

Mahendra Dev, S. and N.C. Rao (2010), 'Agricultural Price Policy, Farm Profitability and Food Security', *Economic and Political Weekly*, vol. 45, nos 26–27, pp. 174–82.

———— (2015), 'Improved Terms of Trade for Agriculture: Results from Revised Methodology', *Economic and Political Weekly*, vol. 50, no. 15, pp. 19–22.

Ministry of Agriculture (MoA) (1988), *Technology Mission on Oilseeds*, Indian Council of Agricultural Research, New Delhi.

———— (2013), *State of Indian Agriculture, 2012–13*, New Delhi.

Mishra, S.N. and R. Chand (1995), 'Public and Private Capital Formation in Indian Agriculture: Comments on the Complementarity Hypothesis and Others', *Economic and Political Weekly*, vol. 30, no. 25, 24 June.

Mishra, S.K. (1991), *An Alternative Approach to Rural Development: Land Reforms and Panchayats*, Government of West Bengal, Kolkata.

———— (2007), 'On Agrarian Transition in West Bengal', *The Marxist*, vol. 23, no. 2, pp. 1–22.

Mishra, S.K. and V. Rawal (2002), 'Agrarian Relations in Contemporary West Bengal and Tasks for the Left', in V.K. Ramachandran and M. Swaminathan, eds, *Agrarian Studies: Essays on Agrarian Relations in Less-Developed Countries*, New Delhi: Tulika Books, pp. 329–55.

Mogues, T., B. Yu, F. Fan and L. McBride (2012), 'The Impacts of Public Investment in and for Agriculture: Synthesis of the Existing Evidence', ESA Working Paper No. 12–07, Agricultural Development Economics Division, Food and Agriculture Organization (FAO), Rome.

Nanavati, M.B. and J.J. Anjaria (1947), *The Indian Rural Problem*, Bombay: Vora and Co.

National Commission of Farmers (NCF) (2005, 2006), *Reports*, New Delhi.

Nayyar, D. and A. Sen (1994), 'International Trade and the Agricultural Sector in India', *Economic and Political Weekly*, 14 May, pp. 1187–203.

Neti, A., R. Govil and M.R. Rao (2019), 'Farmer Producer Companies in India: Demystifying the Numbers,' *Review of Agrarian Studies*, vol. 9, no. 2, pp. 92–113.

Nin-Pratt, A. (2021), 'Agricultural R&D Investment Intensity: A Misleading Conventional

Measure and a New Intensity Index', *Agricultural Economics*, vol. 52, no. 2, March, pp. 317–28.

OECD (2018), 'Review of Agricultural Policies in India', Organization for Economic Co-operation and Development, Paris.

Pal, S. (2017), 'The Funding, Institutional Development and Policy Perspective of Agricultural Research in India', in S. Pal, ed., *Agricultural R&D Policy in India: The Funding, Institutions and Impact*, New Delhi: ICAR and National Institute of Agricultural Economics and Policy Research.

Pardey, P.G. and N.M. Beintema (2001), 'Slow Magic: Agricultural R&D after Mendel', International Food Policy Research Institute, Washington D.C.

Parikh, K.S. (1993), 'Economic Reforms and Food and Agriculture Policy', Indira Gandhi Institute of Development Research, Mumbai.

———— (1997), 'Overview: Prospects and Retrospect', in K.S. Parikh, ed., *India Development Report 1997*, Indira Gandhi Institute of Development Research, Mumbai: Oxford University Press.

Patel, S.J. (1980), 'Planned Development in India: Review of Major Changes,' *Mainstream*, vol. 5, pp. 1–10.

Patnaik, P. (1975), 'Current Inflation in India', *Social Scientist*, vol. 3, nos 6 and 7, Special Number on Inflationary Crisis, January–February, pp. 22–42.

Patnaik, U. (1986), 'The Agrarian Question and Development of Capitalism in India', *Economic and Political Weekly*, vol. 21, no. 18, 3 May.

———— (2002), 'Deflation and Deja vu: Indian Agriculture in the World Economy', in V.K. Ramachandran and M. Swaminathan, eds, *Agrarian Studies: Essays on Agrarian Relations in Less-Developed Countries*, New Delhi: Tulika Books, pp. 111–43.

Planning Commission (2007), 'Report of the Expert Group on Groundwater Management and Ownership' (Chairperson: K.S. Parikh), New Delhi.

Pray, C. (1990), 'The Potential Impact of Liberalizing India's Seed Laws', *Food Policy*, vol. 15, no. 3, pp. 193–98.

Pursell, G. and A. Gulati (1993), 'Liberalizing Indian Agriculture: An Agenda for Reform', World Bank, Report No. WPS 11721993, Washington.

Raj, K.N. (1969), 'Some Questions Concerning Growth, Transformation and Planning of Agriculture in the Light of Experience in Mexico, Taiwan and India', *Journal of Development Planning*, vol. 1, no. 1.

Ramachandran, V.K. (1997), 'Achievements in the Countryside', *Frontline*, 11 July.

———— (2011), 'The State of Agrarian Relations in India Today', *The Marxist*, vol. 27, nos 1 and 2, pp. 51–89.

Ramachandran, V.K. and R. Ramakumar (2000), 'Agrarian Reforms and Rural Development Policies in India: A Note', Paper presented at the International Conference on 'Agrarian Reform and Rural Development', Department of Agrarian Reform, Government of the Philippines and the Philippines Development Academy, Tagaytay City, 5–8 December.

Ramachandran, V.K. and M. Swaminathan (2002), 'Introduction', in V.K. Ramachandran and M. Swaminathan, eds, *Agrarian Studies: Essays on Agrarian Relations in Less-Developed Countries*, New Delhi: Tulika Books.

Ramachandran, V.K. and M. Swaminathan, eds (2005), *Financial Liberalization and Rural Credit in India*, New Delhi: Tulika Books.

Ramachandran, V.K., M. Swaminathan and V. Rawal (2003), 'Agricultural Growth in West Bengal', Paper presented at the All-India Conference on 'Agriculture and Rural Society in Contemporary India', Barddhaman, 17–20 December.

Ramakumar, R. (2020), 'Farm Acts: Unwanted Constitutional Adventurism', *The Hindu*, 6 October.

———— (2021a), 'Farm Laws and "Taxation" of Farmers', *The Hindu*, 16 February.

———— (2021b), 'The Death of Hubris, A Confrontation on Hold', *The Hindu*, 20 November.

Ramakumar, R., ed. (2018), *Note-Bandi: Demonetization and India's Elusive Chase for Black Money*, New Delhi: Oxford University Press.

Ramakumar, R. and P. Chavan (2007), 'Revival of Agricultural Credit in the 2000s: An Explanation', *Economic and Political Weekly*, vol. 42, no. 52, 29 December, pp. 57–63.

——— (2014), 'Bank Credit to Agriculture in India in the 2000s: Dissecting the Revival', *Review of Agrarian Studies*, vol. 4, no. 1.

Ramasamy, C. (2013), 'Indian Agricultural R&D: An Introspection and Way Forward', *Agricultural Economics Research Review*, vol. 26, no. 1, January–June, pp. 1–20.

Rao, J.M. (1988), 'Agricultural Supply Response: A Survey', *Agricultural Economics*, vol. 3, no. 1, pp. 1–22.

——— (1989), 'Getting Agricultural Prices Right', *Food Policy*, vol. 14, no. 1, February, pp. 28–42.

——— (1994), 'Agricultural Development under State Planning', in T.J. Byres, eds, *State, Planning and Liberalization in India*, New Delhi: Oxford University Press.

——— (1995), 'Agrarian Forces and Relations in West Bengal', *Economic and Political Weekly*, vol. 30, no. 30, July, pp. 1939–40.

——— (1998), 'Food, Agriculture and Reforms: Change and Continuity', *Economic and Political Weekly*, vol. 33, nos 29 and 30, 18 July, pp. 1955–60.

Rawal, V. (1999), 'Irrigation Development in West Bengal: 1977–78 to 1995–96', PhD thesis, Indira Gandhi Institute of Development Research, Mumbai.

Reddy, B. (2008), 'The Status of Public Agricultural Extension Services: A Case Study in Rural Maharashtra', MA Dissertation in Development Studies, Tata Institute of Social Sciences, Mumbai.

Reserve Bank of India (RBI) (1991), *Report of the Committee on Financial Systems* (Chairperson: M. Narasimham), Mumbai.

Saini, S. and A. Gulati (2017), 'Price Distortions in Indian Agriculture', The World Bank, Washington D.C.

Sajesh, V.K. and A. Suresh (2016), 'Public-Sector Agricultural Extension in India: A Note', *Review of Agrarian Studies*, vol. 6, no. 1, pp. 116–31.

Schenkelaars, P., H.D. Vriend and N. Kalaitzandonakes (2011), 'Drivers of Consolidation in the Seed Industry and its Consequences for Innovation', Commission on Genetic Modification (COGEM), Missouri.

Sen, A. (1992), 'Economic Liberalization and Agriculture in India', *Social Scientist*, vol. 20, no. 11, November, pp. 4–19.

——— (1997), 'Agricultural Growth and Rural Poverty', in G.K. Chaddha and A.N. Sharma, eds, *Growth, Employment, Poverty Change and Continuity in Rural India*, Indian Society of Labour Economics, New Delhi.

——— (2002), 'Agriculture, Employment and Poverty: Recent Trends in Rural India', in V.K. Ramachandran and M. Swaminathan, eds, *Agrarian Studies: Essays on Agrarian Relations in Less-Developed Countries*, New Delhi: Tulika Books, pp. 392–444.

——— (2004), 'Changes in Cost Structure and Farm Business Incomes, 1981–82 to 1999–2000', Paper presented at the All-India Conference on 'Agriculture and Rural Society in Contemporary India', Barddhaman, 17–20 December.

Sen, A. and M.L. Bhatia (2004), *Cost of Cultivation and Farm Incomes*, State of Indian Farmers: A Millennium Study, vol. 14, New Delhi: Academic Foundation.

Sharma, S.K., P. Mathur and R. Akhter (2021), 'Negative Support to Farmers: Myth or Reality', *Frontline*, 26 March.

Shetty, S.L. (1997), 'Financial Sector Reforms in India: An Evaluation', *Prajnan*, vol. 25, nos 3–4, pp. 253–87.

——— (1990), 'Investment in Agriculture: A Brief Review of Recent Trends', *Economic and Political Weekly*, 17 February.

Singh, M. (2009), Inaugural address to the 5th Asian Regional Conference of the International Commission on Irrigation and Drainage, New Delhi, available at http://pmindia. nic.in/content_print.php?nodeid=836&nodetype=2.

———— (2012), Speech at the Golden Jubilee of Indian Agricultural Research Institute, New Delhi, available at http://pmindia.nic.in/speech-details.php?nodeid=1141.

Singh, S. (2002), 'Contracting out Solutions: Political Economy of Contract Farming in the Indian Punjab', *World Development*, vol. 30, no. 9, pp. 1621–38.

Spielman, D.J., D. Kolady, A. Cavalieri and N.C. Rao (2011), 'The Seed and Agricultural Biotechnology Industries in India', IFPRI Discussion Paper 01103, International Food Policy Research Institute, Washington D.C.

Storm, S. (1993), *Macroeconomic Considerations in the Choice of an Agricultural Policy: A Study into Sectoral Interdependence with Reference to India*, Aldershot: Avebury Press.

Surjit, V. (2008), 'Farm Business Incomes in India: A Study of Two Rice Growing Villages of Thanjavur Region, Tamil Nadu', PhD Thesis submitted to the University of Calcutta, Indian Statistical Institute, Kolkata.

Swaminathan, M.S. (1999), 'For an "Evergreen Revolution"', Interview to Parvathi Menon, *Frontline*, vol. 16, no. 27.

Vaidyanathan, A. (2000), 'India's Agricultural Development Policy', *Economic and Political Weekly*, 13 May, pp. 1735–41.

World Bank (1986), *World Development Report 1986*, New York: Oxford University Press.

———— (1991), '1991 Country Memorandum for India', New York.

Zhang, X. and S. Fan (2004), 'Public Investment and Regional Inequality in Rural China', *Agricultural Economics*, vol. 30, pp. 89–100.

I
Land and Agrarian Relations

1

Agrarian Inequalities in India

Madhura Swaminathan[1]

Introduction

There is a substantial literature on the trajectory of growth of Indian agriculture after independence, but much less on the differential benefits of growth. Following a brief sketch of the trajectory of growth, this chapter argues that serious problems continue to beset agrarian India, arising out of growing inequalities across crops, regions, castes and classes.

The chapter draws on official statistics as well as evidence from village-level surveys across the country. The national surveys conducted by the National Sample Survey Office (NSSO or NSO) on consumer expenditure, on landholdings and on assets can be used to estimate levels and trends in inequality. Two special surveys of the NSSO of particular relevance to the rural economy are the Situation Assessment Surveys (SAS) of 2002–03 and 2012–13. These surveys, for the first time in India, collected data on household incomes including incomes from crop farming.

To understand inequality in incomes, especially inequality across classes and castes, this chapter also uses data collected from in-depth village surveys conducted by the Foundation for Agrarian Studies (FAS) as part of its Project on Agrarian Relations in India (PARI).[2] To date, PARI has a data archive on around twenty-eight villages located in different agro-ecological regions across twelve states of India. We have drawn on data from nineteen villages (in nine states), as described in Appendix Table 1. The advantages of the PARI data are: (1) reduction in non-sampling errors on account of better quality of data collection; (2) less exclusion of richer households on account of it being a census of all households; and (3) availability of information on household incomes as well as on caste, land ownership, and other parameters of relevance.

Various measures of dispersion, such as the coefficient of variation, are used to capture inequality. Simple indicators that describe a distribution are based on percentiles (such as the median or the top one per cent). One of the commonly used summary measures of inequality is the Gini coefficient. This coefficient measures the extent to which the distribution of incomes (defined using a Lorenz curve) deviates from a perfectly equal distribution, and ranges from 0 (perfect equality) to 1 (perfect inequality).[3]

Growth Performance

If we take a long-term perspective, the agricultural economy of India changed dramatically after independence. Using a 100-year time series on gross value of output or GVO at constant (1960) prices, Takashi Kurosaki showed that after a half-century of stagnation (1901–47), with total output growing at less than half a per cent a year, and with output per capita and output per acre both showing a negative growth, there was a remarkable change in the next 50 years (Kurosaki 2006).[4] From 1948 to 2002, GVO increased at almost 3 per cent per annum, and GVO per unit of area or productivity at over 6 per cent a year.

For the first 50-year period from 1960 onwards, a useful categorization of phases of growth of agricultural output (based on Chand and Shinoj 2012) is the following:

1. Phase 1: Pre-green revolution period, 1960–61 to 1968–69.
2. Phase 2: Early green revolution period, 1968–69 to 1975–76.
3. Phase 3: Period of wider technology dissemination, 1975–76 to 1988–89.
4. Phase 4: Period of diversification, 1988–89 to 1995–96.
5. Phase 5: Post-reform or liberalization period, 1995–96 to 2004–05.
6. Phase 6: Period of recovery, 2004–05 to 2010–11.

The first three phases correspond to the pre-green revolution period, the early years of the green revolution (GR), and the late green revolution years with the more extensive spread of modern technology.[5] In the pre-GR phase, the growth in foodgrain production, of nearly 3 per cent a year, was on account of both growth in area and in yield, with area growth dominating in several crops including wheat and maize. This was the period of extensive growth, i.e., growth in output through expansion of area cultivated. The pattern of growth was very different in the early green revolution and wider dissemination phases, with the growth in yield becoming the major contributor to growth of output. In the decade of the 1980s, for example, taking all foodgrains, there was a small decline in area cultivated while yield grew at over 3 per cent a year.

The decade of the late 1980s to mid-1990s was a period of growth in non-cereal crops and a period of crop diversification. Data on area under different crops from the triennium ending 1970–71 to that ending 2007–08 show that in the aggregate, the share of area under cultivation of non-food grain crops rose steadily, from around 20 per cent to 26 per cent (Kannan and Sundaram 2011). Notable components here are the expansion of area under oilseed crops, fruits and vegetables. Correspondingly, the share of foodgrain crops in area cultivated fell. The relative decline in area under foodgrain, however, was primarily on account of a big fall in share of area sown to coarse cereals (such as barley and sorghum). Rice was the single most important crop in India, accounting throughout the period for around 23 per cent of the gross cropped area. Similarly, the data on GVO show that the contribution of cereals to total value of agricultural output declined, while that of fruits and vegetables increased from 16 per cent in 1970–71 to 24 per cent in 2007–08 (ibid. 2011).

The late 1990s was when the effects of policies of liberalization, initiated a decade earlier and that accelerated in the early 1990s, began to be felt. There was a major slowdown of the agricultural economy. The agricultural sector was adversely affected by the policies of trade and financial liberalization and structural adjustment introduced after 1991 (Ramachandran and Swaminathan 2002). Immediate effects were seen in the form of reduction in public investment in agriculture, irrigation, research and development, and extension. There were structural changes as well, such as in the access to credit and terms of trade. The neglect of agriculture became visible in the slowing down of growth of yield and output of rice and wheat, as well as cereals and foodgrains in the aggregate. Indeed, the period from the late 1990s to mid-2000s (1998–2004 to be more precise) has been characterized as one of the worst periods for agricultural growth in the post-independence era (Ramachandran and Rawal 2010).[6] However, production of pulses and oilseeds, and cotton grew more rapidly in the 2000s than in the 1990s. The latter was not sustained and the growth of output of pulses and oilseeds declined afterwards.

After 2004, there was a phase of recovery associated with policy changes, notably an increase in public investment in agriculture, in provision of more institutional credit to agriculture, and higher minimum support prices (MSP), resulting in favourable terms of trade for agriculture (Himanshu 2019). Agricultural output grew at 1.8 per cent a year between 1998 and 2004, but at 3.8 per cent between 2004 and 2012 (ibid.).

The following quote summarizes the phases of agricultural growth from the 1960s to mid-2010s:

> In a nutshell, the growth series clearly establishes a steady increase in the growth rate for three decades after the advent of the green revolution, followed by a gradual tapering off and decline after the mid-1990s, which

lasted for a decade. This was succeeded by an unambiguous turnaround in the years coinciding with the Eleventh Five Year Plan (2007–12). (Chand and Shinoj 2012, p. 56)

The agricultural economy has seen a setback between 2011–12 and 2019–20 (see Ramakumar's introduction to this volume). Agricultural output grew at 1.6 per cent per annum from 2011–12 to 2019–20. The crop sector within agriculture showed a collapse of incomes following a reversal of many policies resulting in a decline in public investment and worsening terms of trade. Gross value of output in the crop sector grew at only half a per cent a year in real terms (Himanshu 2019).

Inequality Across Regions

Early studies on inter-state and inter-district variations in agricultural growth were led by G.S. Bhalla (Bhalla and Alagh 1979; Bhalla and Tyagi 1989; Bhalla and Singh 2012), which clearly showed major differences in growth performance across states and regions of India. In Table 1.1, we report state-level variations in the growth of GVO from Bhalla and Singh (2012), with the analysis extended to the most recent period.

In broad terms, the north-west region took the lead, followed by the southern and eastern regions; pockets of the central region remain laggards. In the early phase, Punjab and Haryana were the states with the highest rate of growth of output. In the 1980s, agricultural growth in eastern India, especially West Bengal, accelerated. In fact, West Bengal was one of the fastest growing states in terms of GVO in the 1980s. Growth in the southern and central regions also picked up in the 1980s.

But between 1990 and 2005, the growth of agricultural output in the northern and eastern regions lagged behind that in central and southern regions. Other studies find a similar pattern of regional differences, and argue that the increase in GVO in southern and western/central regions came from crop diversification and expansion in cultivation of high-value crops (see Birthal *et al.* 2013, cited in Tochkov, Goyari and Paltasingh 2017). Another important point to note from the Bhalla and Singh (2012) is the sharp rise in the coefficient of variation in the period of liberalization (1990 to 2005–08), an indicator of growing divergence in the performance of states.

Growth performance was disappointing in the most recent period also, i.e. 2011–12 to 2017–18, and it varied across states and regions. Growth was negative in four states including Haryana and less than 2 per cent in eight states as well as at the all-India level. Madhya Pradesh, Andhra Pradesh and Uttar Pradesh were the only three states with a growth rate of over 3 per cent.

Differences in cropping pattern are an important explanation for the

Table 1.1 *State- and region-wise growth of value of output, 1962–65 to 2017–18,* in per cent

Sl. no.	State and Region	Annual compound growth rate (%)				
		1962–65 to 1980–83	1980–83 to 1990–93	1990–93 to 2005–08	1962–65 to 2005–08	2011–12 to 2017–18
1	Haryana	3.74	5.04	2.35	3.55	–0.56
2	Himachal Pradesh	2.01	2.74	0.68	1.71	2.27
3	Jammu &Kashmir	4.31	0.17	0.61	2.04	0.87
4	Punjab	5.58	4.22	1.64	3.87	1.58
5	Uttar Pradesh	2.67	3.06	1.31	2.28	3.14
	North-west region	3.39	3.55	1.54	2.78	–
6	Assam	2.38	2.42	–1.73	0.93	2.66
7	Bihar	0.27	2.07	1.23	1.02	1.41
8	Orissa	1.91	2.86	–0.27	1.36	0.03
9	West Bengal	1.43	5.98	1.80	2.60	2.00
	Eastern region	1.30	3.61	0.78	1.65	–
10	Gujarat	2.52	0.90	4.70	2.89	1.19
11	Madhya Pradesh	1.59	4.52	2.03	2.42	7.12
12	Maharashtra	1.91	1.92	3.86	2.58	1.04
13	Rajasthan	2.59	6.06	2.61	3.40	–0.23
	Central region	2.06	3.27	3.23	2.75	–
14	Andhra Pradesh	2.41	3.40	2.54	2.69	5.75
15	Karnataka	2.46	3.66	2.13	2.62	1.83
16	Kerala	1.28	1.77	1.74	1.55	–2.95
17	Tamil Nadu	0.90	4.06	1.16	1.72	–1.45
	Southern region	1.82	3.41	1.98	2.25	1.34
	India	2.24	3.37	2.10	2.46	1.75
	Coefficient of variation (%)	54.19	51.08	87.86	37.09	–

Notes: In Bhalla and Singh (2012), the value output is measured as the sum of output value of 44 crops at 1990–93 constant prices. For 2011–12 to 2017–18, value of output is at 2011–12 base prices. Bhalla and Singh (2012) consider 1962–65 to 1980–83 as the initial period of green revolution, 1980–83 to 1990–93 as the maturing of green revolution, and 1990–93 to 2005–08 as the post-reform period. For the period 2011–17, we have used GoI (2020). We did not compute the regional averages and the coefficient of variation.

Source: Bhalla and Singh (2012) for first four columns; last column estimated from GoI, *State-Wise and Item-Wise Value of Output from Agriculture, Forestry and Fishing Year: 2011–12 to 2017–18*, National Statistical Office, Ministry of Statistics and Programme Implementation, 2020.

observed differences in growth rates across states. Even within foodgrains, for example, wheat yields and production accelerated in the early years of the green revolution, whereas yields and output of rice grew faster in the 1980s. These differences in growth performance of crops were reflected in regional differences: Punjab outperformed all states between 1962 and 1980–83 (Table 1.1). West Bengal and eastern India in general did not share in the growth story of the 1960s and 1970s. Indeed, the period of 1949–80 was one of stagnation in agricultural production in West Bengal, with growth of rice output (1.7 per cent a year) lagging behind that the population growth rate of 2.4 per cent a year (Boyce 1987). There was, however, a sea-change in the 1980s in all of eastern India, with foodgrain production in West Bengal (growing at 6.4 per cent per annum) surpassing that of all other major rice-growing states (Saha and Swaminathan 1994). The picture in respect of crop performance is more complicated in recent years, as diversification into high-value crops was associated with higher variability in GVO on account of both fluctuations in production and in prices and is a matter for separate study.[7]

Improvement in irrigation and water management were the base of growth in production for most crops. Not surprisingly, then, production and yield did not show the same pace of growth in regions with little or no irrigation and in crops grown on dryland areas. Indeed, it is widely recognized that the next push for agricultural growth will come from increased production of neglected crops and in less well-endowed regions.

Inequalities in Land Ownership

We now turn to interpersonal inequalities or inequalities across households in a given population. We begin with land, recognized as the most critical asset in an agrarian society both in terms of being a productive asset and also an indicator of social and economic status and basis for further wealth accumulation. Inequality in ownership of land is in many ways at the base of other interpersonal inequalities in rural areas.

Data on land ownership for households in all states of India are available from the decennial NSSO surveys. The Gini coefficient for ownership of land computed from these data show that inequality in respect of ownership of land has been very high through the last 50 years (with a Gini coefficient of over 0.7) and has risen even further in the last decade to a historical high (Table 1.2).[8] The current patterns of distribution of land ownership, of course, arise from historical inequalities, but the evidence shows that policies of the Indian government, notably land reform policies, have not dented these inequalities (with the exception of a few states). Inequality is a little lower when we look at operational distribution of landholding (that is, on the basis of who operates the land and not who owns the land),

Table 1.2 *Gini coefficients for the distribution of operational and ownership holdings of land, India, 1960–61 to 2003–04*

Type of holding	1960–61	1970–71	1980–81	1990–91	2003–04
Operational holdings	0.58	0.59	0.63	0.64	0.62
Ownership holdings	0.73	0.71	0.71	0.71	0.74

Note: Ownership holdings in these estimates refer to ownership of any type of land including homestead land.
Source: National Sample Survey (NSS) on land and livestock holdings as cited in Ramachandran and Rawal (2010).

suggesting that a section of households without ownership of land are able to lease in and operate land.

Even these high numbers (in Table 1.2) may be underestimates of the true inequality. It has been established that NSS Land and Holdings surveys underestimate the ownership holdings of large landowners on account of many factors, notably the method of the stratification chosen for sampling (Kumar 2016). For this reason, we present data from PARI surveys of 19 villages located in a variety of agro-ecological zones to depict ground-level inequalities.

Building on the material presented in Ramachandran and Rawal (2010), data in Table 1.3 show the extreme concentration of land ownership in the villages surveyed under PARI. Among all resident households, the top 5 per cent of households accounted 40 per cent or more of total agricultural land in eleven of the nineteen villages for which data are presented in Table 1.3. For example, the top 5 per cent of households owned 54 per cent of total agricultural land in the village of Ananthavaram in Guntur district of Andhra Pradesh, as well as in Tehang village of Jalandhar district of Punjab. Both these villages (from coastal Andhra Pradesh and the Doaba region) had access to canal and groundwater irrigation and were regions of cereal production with high agricultural productivity. While most of the villages with extremely high concentration of land were villages with access to irrigation, there were some like Zhapur village (Kalaburagi district, Karnataka) that belonged to a dry zone but where *zamindari* was prevalent before independence. At the same time, the bottom 50 per cent owned no land of their own or less than 5 per cent of total land in the same eleven villages.

There was a variety of reasons that could explain the pattern of ownership in villages with somewhat less unequal distribution of landholdings. We have, for example, two villages of West Bengal where the top 5 per cent controlled 20–24 per cent of total landholdings (Kalmandasguri and Amarsinghi). These two villages were characterized by the predominance of landowners with marginal or small holdings. We also have two villages

Table 1.3 *Share of agricultural land owned by the 5 per cent of households with the largest ownership holdings and the 50 per cent with the smallest ownership holdings, by village, 2006–2010*, in per cent

Village, Region	Share of agricultural land owned by	
	top 5 per cent	bottom 50 per cent
Ananthavaram, Guntur district, South Coastal region, Andhra Pradesh	54	0
Bukkacherla, Anantapur district, Rayalaseema region, South-West Andhra Pradesh	33	17
Kothapalle, Karimnagar district, North Telangana region, North Andhra Pradesh	41	1
Harevli, Bijnaur district, Western Uttar Pradesh	39	2
Mahatwar, Ballia district, Eastern Uttar Pradesh	40	6
Nimshirgaon, Kolhapur district, South Konkan Coastal region, Maharashtra	24	5
Warwat Khanderao, Buldhana district, Vidarbha region, Maharashtra	35	10
25F Gulabewala, Sri Ganganagar district, Gang Canal region, Rajasthan	43	0
Gharsondi, Gwalior district, Grid region, Madhya Pradesh	46	5
Alabujanahalli, Mandya district, Southern Dry Zone region, Karnataka	26	9
Siresandra, Kolar district, Eastern Dry Zone region, Karnataka	26	17
Zhapur, Kalaburagi district, North-East Dry Zone region, Karnataka	48	3
Rewasi, Sikar district, Rajasthan	23	18
Amarsinghi, Malda district, New Alluvial Zone region, West Bengal	24	9
Kalmandasguri, Koch Bihar district, Tarai Zone region, West Bengal	20	10
Panahar, Bankura district, Old Alluvial Zone region, West Bengal	46	2
Tehang, Jalandhar district, Doaba region, Punjab	54	0
Katkuian, West Champaran district, North-West Alluvial Gangetic region, Bihar	68	0
Nayanagar, Samastipur district, North-West Alluvial Gangetic region, Bihar	50	0

Note: Agricultural land includes net sown area and current fallows.
Source: Survey data, Foundation for Agrarian Studies, and Ramachandran and Rawal (2010).

of Karnataka in this category of relatively low inequality (Siresandra and Alabujanahalli), and these were villages comprising largely of peasants and with a very small section of landless households.

Inequalities in Incomes

As non-agricultural sectors and employment expand, the dependence on land for income generation and further capital accumulation may weaken. So, we turn now to inequalities in income. A serious problem arises here from the lack of secondary data on household incomes in India. The statistical system in India does not collect serial data on household incomes. Typically, the data from consumer expenditure surveys (CES) on monthly per capita expenditure is used as a proxy for income. This approximation is unsatisfactory as incomes exceed expenditure for the upper income groups and fall behind expenditure for the lower income groups. Inequality in expenditure is therefore likely to be much lower than inequality in incomes. To illustrate, inequality of consumption expenditure in rural areas, as measured by the Gini coefficient, is shown in Table 1.4. By this measure, rural India would be characterized as region of low 'income' inequality, since a Gini coefficient less than 0.5 can be termed as low.

In response to the agrarian crisis of the late 1990s and early 2000s, the first ever large-scale sample survey of income of rural households was conducted in 2002–03, as part of the SAS.[9] A second round was completed in 2012–13. There are serious questions about the methodology of SAS including the definition of farmers and the concept of income used. Nevertheless, the SAS surveys provide the first national-level estimates of incomes of cultivators.[10] Turning to data from the two rounds of SAS, first, inequality in income (as expected) is much higher than inequality in consumer expenditure. The Gini coefficient for income was 0.52 in 2002–3 with a small increase to 0.53 in the SAS of 2012–13 (Table 1.5).

Let me turn again to data from the PARI village surveys in which detailed information was collected to estimate household incomes. This

Table 1.4 *Trends in consumption expenditure inequality, rural India, 1993–94 to 2011–12*

Year	Gini coefficient
1993–94	0.286
2004–05	0.305
2011–12	0.311

Source: Mahendra Dev (2018).

Table 1.5 *Trends in income inequality, rural India, 2002–03 to 2012–13*

Year	Gini coefficient
2002–03	0.52
2012–13	0.53

Source: Mahendra Dev (2018).

Table 1.6 *Inequality in income as measured by Gini coefficient of per capita household income, study villages*

Village, Region	Gini coefficient
Ananthavaram, Guntur district, South Coastal region, Andhra Pradesh	0.602
Bukkacherla, Anantapur district, Rayalaseema region, South-West Andhra Pradesh	0.539
Kothapalle, Karimnagar district, North Telangana region, North Andhra Pradesh	0.565
Harevli, Bijnaur district, Western Uttar Pradesh	0.598
Mahatwar, Ballia district, Eastern Uttar Pradesh	0.516
Nimshirgaon, Kolhapur district, South Konkan Coastal region, Maharashtra	0.491
Warwat Khanderao, Buldhana district, Vidarbha region, Maharashtra	0.531
25F Gulabewala, Sri Ganganagar district, Gang Canal region, Rajasthan	0.686
Gharsondi, Gwalior district, Grid region, Madhya Pradesh	0.721
Alabujanahalli, Mandya district, Southern Dry Zone region, Karnataka	0.467
Siresandra, Kolar district, Eastern Dry Zone region, Karnataka	0.453
Zhapur, Kalaburagi district, North-East Dry Zone region, Karnataka	0.485
Rewasi, Sikar district, Rajasthan	0.465
Amarsinghi, Malda district, New Alluvial Zone region, West Bengal	0.370
Kalmandasguri, Koch Bihar district, Tarai Zone region, West Bengal	0.547
Panahar, Bankura district, Old Alluvial Zone region, West Bengal	0.334
Tehang, Jalandhar district, Doaba region, Punjab	0.608

Source: PARI Survey Data.

included income from crop production, other allied activities, agricultural and non-agricultural employment, salaries, business and remittances. In ten of the seventeen villages listed in Table 1.6, the Gini coefficient was greater than 0.5, i.e. the national average reported in Table 1.5. These villages spanned different agro-ecological regions. Extremely high inequality, with a Gini coefficient of over 0.6, was observed in four villages, three of which (Ananthavaram, Tehang and 25F Gulabewala) were characterized by the availability of good quality irrigation, high cropping intensity, high crop productivity and a significant section of landless manual worker households. The exception was Gharsondi (Gwalior district, Madhya Pradesh) where there was crop failure during the survey year, but where the village economy was dominated by one landlord household. In the rest of the villages, except two, the Gini coefficient was between 0.4 and 0.5. The two villages reporting the lowest income inequality were in West Bengal, and these villages were characterized by a smallholder economy.

There are many factors affecting income distribution including concentration of land ownership, level of incomes from crop production and access to non-agricultural sources of income, among others. Nevertheless, the overall picture is one of high levels of income inequality.

Incomes from Crop Production and Extent of Landholding

While there has been extensive debate about farm size or extent of landholding and productivity, there is less of debate on farm size and profitability.[11] Our concern in this section is with net incomes or profits from agriculture and whether incomes differ across farm sizes. We argue, based on village-level data, that in most cases, large farmers tend to get higher returns than small farmers.

Table 1.7 draws on Das and Swaminathan (2018) who computed net incomes (GVO net of costs) for small and large farmer households, with the former defined as all those with less than 5 acres of irrigated land or 15 acres of rainfed land, in sixteen villages. With a few exceptions, it is clear that in every village, the net income from crop cultivation per unit of land was lower for small farmers than large farmers (Table 1.7). In other words, even within the same agro-ecological context, small farmers tended to earn less per hectare than large farmers.

In some villages, the difference was substantial.[12] In Ananthavaram village (Guntur district, Andhra Pradesh), small farmers who were largely tenants made losses from paddy cultivation on account of the high rents paid whereas large farmers received more than a lakh of rupees per hectare (see Ramachandran and Rawal 2010). In Harveli (Bijnaur district, Uttar Pradesh), another village with a significant income difference, large farmers cultivated a different mix of crops including sugar cane, and made higher profits than paddy-growing small farmers. Of the three exceptions to the rule, in two villages, the number of observations of large farmers was small.[13] A further exploration of these data showed that differences in incomes as between small and large farmers was not primarily on account of differences in yield but on account of differences in costs of production and realized prices (Das and Swaminathan 2017).[14]

Table 1.7 *Average net incomes from crop production per hectare of operational holding by farmer category, study villages, 2010–11 prices*, rupees per hectare

Village, Region	Small farmer	Large farmer
Ananthavaram, Guntur district, South Coastal region, Andhra Pradesh	(–) 1,294	1,36,275
Bukkacherla, Anantapur district, Rayalaseema region, South-West Andhra Pradesh	3,666	295*
Kothapalle, Karimnagar district, North Telangana region, North Andhra Pradesh	11,244	7,678*
Harevli, Bijnaur district, Western Uttar Pradesh	14,317	33,420
Mahatwar, Ballia district, Eastern Uttar Pradesh	8,604	11,155
Nimshirgaon, Kolhapur district, South Konkan Coastal region, Maharashtra	43,208	32,722#
Warwat Khanderao, Buldhana district, Vidarbha region, Maharashtra	24,031	25,399
25F Gulabewala, Sri Ganganagar district, Gang Canal region, Rajasthan	9,671	25,916
Gharsondi, Gwalior district, Grid region, Madhya Pradesh	16,462	18,226
Alabujanahalli, Mandya district, Southern Dry Zone region, Karnataka	40,843	46,660
Siresandra, Kolar district, Eastern Dry Zone region, Karnataka	18,402	55,407
Zhapur, Kalaburagi district, North-East Dry Zone region, Karnataka	3,123	7,559
Rewasi, Sikar district, Rajasthan	4,254	13,967
Amarsinghi, Malda district, New Alluvial Zone region, West Bengal	49,064	N.A.
Kalmandasguri, Koch Bihar district, Tarai Zone region, West Bengal	39,527	N.A.
Panahar, Bankura district, Old Alluvial Zone region, West Bengal	25,323	29,954
Tehang, Jalandhar district, Doaba region, Punjab	49,332	65,775

Notes: N.A. refers to not applicable; * refers to less than ten observations; # refers to population estimate based on weighted data from sample.
Source: Das and Swaminathan (2017).

Inequalities in Income Across Caste

Caste is a pervasive feature of rural society, and discrimination or exclusion on the basis of caste results in differential access to productive resources and inequalities in observed economic status. Nationally, 31 per cent of rural households were reported as landless in 2003–4, but the proportion was 41 per cent among Dalit or Scheduled Caste households (Appendix Table 3).

The PARI village surveys permit us to study differences in household incomes across caste groups. In Table 1.8, we report the median value of per capita annual household income for Dalit (Scheduled Caste) and Adivasi (Scheduled Tribe) households in each village as compared to other households excluding Muslims (generally, other Hindu households) in the same village.[15] The striking result is that across this diversity of villages, differing in agro-ecological and socio-economic and demographic characteristics, the median Dalit or Adivasi household usually received a lower income than a household belonging to other non-Muslim households. This was so even in villages such as Mahatwar (eastern Uttar Pradesh) and 25F Gulabewala (Sikar district, Rajasthan) where Scheduled Castes constituted a majority of the village population.[16] There were three interesting exceptions. In Kalmandasguri village (Koch Bihar district, West Bengal), Scheduled Caste households were major beneficiaries of land reform and were thus among landowning peasant households. In Zhapur village of northern Karnataka, there were crop losses in the survey year, and several large caste Hindu landowning households made large incomes losses. In Rewasi village (Sikar district, Rajasthan), a good section of Scheduled Tribes was from the Meena tribe, a group that had gained access to land and sources of non-farm employment, and was relatively well-off.

Conclusions: Worsening Agrarian Inequalities

Agricultural growth in India took on a new trajectory from the mid-1960s, lasting for over thirty years, with the growth in output of several crops driven largely by improvements in yield. A disquieting feature of the same period, however, was the growth of inequalities in the agricultural economy. As Rao and Storm (1998, p. 199) put it in their analysis, 'the spread of growth has been uneven over time, across space and among agrarian classes'. In the last thirty years since the liberalization of the Indian economy, the unequalizing tendencies have been aggravated.

In this chapter, we tried to unpack aggregate performance of the agricultural economy by examining inequalities in different dimensions. Data for over 50 years showed that there have been and continue to be large variations in growth across states and regions, with north-western India having led growth in early years. While growth spread to other regions (such as eastern India), regional differences remain. Detailed crop-level, district-level and agroclimatic-level analyses are needed to identify ways of addressing these gaps.

The major part of the chapter focused on interpersonal inequali-

Table 1.8 *Median per capita annual household income, Dalit (SC) and Adivasi (ST) households and other households, PARI villages, 2010–11,* prices in rupees

Village, Region	SC/ST	Other
Ananthavaram, Guntur district, South Coastal region, Andhra Pradesh	10,162	18,676
Bukkacherla, Anantapur district, Rayalaseema region, South-West Andhra Pradesh	6,730	9,947
Kothapalle, Karimnagar district, North Telangana region, North Andhra Pradesh	7,087	11,001
Harevli, Bijnaur district, Western Uttar Pradesh	5,996	13,404
Mahatwar, Ballia district, Eastern Uttar Pradesh	4,864	5,306
Nimshirgaon, Kolhapur district, South Konkan Coastal region, Maharashtra	9,197	17,424
Warwat Khanderao, Buldhana district, Vidarbha region, Maharashtra	5,627	12,540
25F Gulabewala, Sri Ganganagar district, Gang Canal region, Rajasthan	7,053	49,770*
Gharsondi, Gwalior district, Grid region, Madhya Pradesh	5,955	9,560
Alabujanahalli, Mandya district, Southern Dry Zone region, Karnataka	12,095	17,352
Siresandra, Kolar district, Eastern Dry Zone region, Karnataka	14,537	23,940
Zhapur, Kalaburagi district, North-East Dry Zone region, Karnataka	11,714	10,698
Rewasi, Sikar district, Rajasthan	18,432	16,532
Amarsinghi, Malda district, New Alluvial Zone region, West Bengal	8,048	9,071
Kalmandasguri, Koch Bihar district, Tarai Zone region, West Bengal	12,691	12,368
Panahar, Bankura district, Old Alluvial Zone region, West Bengal	6,532	9,292
Tehang, Jalandhar district, Doaba region, Punjab	13,929	38,710
Katkuian, West Champaran district, North-West Alluvial Gangetic region, Bihar	7,219	9,995
Nayanagar, Samastipur district, North-West Alluvial Gangetic region, Bihar	7,007	10,997

Notes: *In 25F Gulabewala village, the SCs were Majhabi Sikhs and the other group comprised Jat Sikhs. Muslims are excluded from the other group of households.
Source: Survey data, Foundation for Agrarian Studies, and Ramachandran and Rawal (2010).

ties, and examined disparities across households in respect of ownership of land and income. We argued that large-scale national survey data are not very useful for studying inequalities across households, both on account of the lack of accurate data on certain parameters such as household income, and on account of serious underestimation of the rich (and hence of inequality). Nevertheless, the macro data indicate a worsening of inequality with respect to ownership of land and other assets, per capita consumption expenditure and household income in rural areas.

We drew upon the PARI village data archive to bring out the multiple inequalities experienced by rural households including inequalities across caste and class (as measured by differences between small and large farmers). The village data were rich in detail and provided a cross-sectional view of inequality in a range of diverse agro-ecological settings. These data cannot be used to generalize for India or to establish trends but they do provide a depiction of the grim ground-level realities of inequality. The overwhelming message is that inequalities in villages across the country are unconscionably high and linked to access to land and other productive resources as well as entrenched caste deprivation.

Notes

[1] I am grateful to Kaushik Bora and Arindam Das for help in the analysis of the PARI data.

[2] For further details, see https://fas.org.in/category/research/project-on-agrarian-relations-in-india-pari/

[3] For different ways of calculating and interpreting the Gini coefficient, see Anand (1983).

[4] Kurosaki has taken the sum of gross value of output of eighteen crops.

[5] These three phases are similar to the periodization in Rao and Storm (1998).

[6] Indeed, the agrarian crisis of this period has been noted as one reason for the defeat of the NDA government in the election of 2004. The 'India shining' campaign of the NDA was countered with data on rural India (see Mahendra Dev 2004).

[7] Diversification into high-value crops can bring high returns but also losses on account of fluctuations in market prices, such as in the case of rubber in Kerala.

[8] A similar trend of rising inequality is evident from data on total household assets or wealth (that is all assets including land) as shown in Appendix Table 2.

[9] There is a very regular data series on crop incomes, namely the data from the Cost of Cultivation Surveys (CCPC) conducted by the Ministry of Agriculture, but these refer to production of single crops on selected plots and do not tell us about the cultivator household (which may have multiple plots and grow a combination of crops). For a comprehensive discussion of CCPC data, see Surjit (2017).

[10] On features of methodology of SAS and problems in comparing the two survey rounds, see Sarkar (2017).

[11] Some scholars arguing that benefits of new technology such as the green revolution go to larger farmers and others argue that the technology is scale-neural and benefits cultivators irrespective of extent of landholding.

[12] The difference was statistically significant in four villages: Ananthavaram, Harevli, Rewasi and Tehang (Das and Swaminathan 2017, p. 115).

[13] There were very few observations on large farmers in Bukkacherla and Kothapalle

villages, and a significant section of the large farmers incurred losses due to crop failure in the survey year.

[14] There are, of course, many factors contributing to these income differences, as discussed in Swaminathan and Baksi, eds (2018).

[15] As the income distribution is skewed in all villages, the median was chosen to represent average incomes.

[16] In an earlier paper, with data on eight villages, it had been demonstrated that 'Dalit households were under-represented in the top income quintile in all villages but one, but over-represented in the lower quintiles' (Rawal and Swaminathan 2011).

References

Anand, S. (1983), *Poverty and Inequality in Malaysia: Measurement and Decomposition*, Oxford: Oxford University Press.

Bakshi, A. (2008), 'Social Inequality in Land Ownership in India: A Study with Particular Reference to West Bengal', *Social Scientist*, vol. 36, nos 9 and 10, pp. 95–116.

Bhalla, G.S. and Y.K. Alagh (1979), *Performance of Indian Agriculture: A District-Wise Study*, New Delhi: Sterling Publishers.

Bhalla, G.S. and D.S. Tyagi (1989), *Patterns in Indian Agricultural Development: A District-level Study*, New Delhi: Institute for Studies in Industrial Development.

Bhalla, G.S. and G. Singh (2012), *Economic Liberalization and Indian Agriculture: A District-level Study*, New Delhi: Sage Publications.

Birthal, P.S., P.K. Joshi, D.S. Negi and S. Agarwal (2013), 'Changing Sources of Growth in Indian Agriculture: Implications for Regional Priorities for Accelerating Agricultural Growth', Discussion Paper, International Food Policy and Research Institute, New Delhi.

Boyce, J.K. (1987), *Agrarian Impasse in Bengal*, Oxford: Oxford University Press.

Chand, R. and P. Shinoj (2012), 'Temporal and Spatial Variations in Agricultural Growth and Its Determinants', *Economic and Political Weekly*, vol. 47, nos 26 and 27, pp. 55–64.

Das, A. and M. Swaminathan (2018), 'Cropping Pattern, Productivity and Incomes from Crop Production', in M. Swaminathan and S. Baksi, eds, *How Do Small Farmers Fare: Evidence from Village Studies in India*, New Delhi: Tulika Books, pp. 95–125.

Himanshu (2019), 'India's Farm Crisis: Decades Old and with Deep Roots', *Ideas for India*, 12 April, available at https://www.ideasforindia.in/topics/agriculture/indias-farm-crisis-decades-old-and-with-deep-roots.html, accessed 19 March 2021.

Kannan, E. and S. Sundaram (2011), 'Analysis of Trends in India's Agricultural Growth', Working Paper no. 276, Institute for Social and Economic Change, Bengaluru.

Kumar, D. (2016), 'Discrepancies in Data on Landholdings in Rural India', *Review of Agrarian Studies*, vol. 6, no. 1, pp. 39–62, available at http://ras.org.in/discrepancies_in_data_on_landholdings_in_rural_india, accessed 19 March 2021.

Kurosaki, T. (2006), 'Long-Term Agricultural Growth and Crop Shifts in India and Pakistan', *Journal of International Economic Studies*, vol. 20, pp. 19–35.

Mahendra Dev, S. (2004), 'How to make Rural India Shine', *Economic and Political Weekly*, vol. 39, no. 40.

————— (2018), 'Transformation of Indian Agriculture: Growth, Inclusiveness and Sustainability', Presidential Address, 78th Annual Conference on Indian Society of Agricultural Economics, New Delhi.

Tochkov, K., P. Goyari and K.R. Paltasingh (2017), 'Indian Agriculture after the Green Revolution: An Overview', in B. Goswami, M.P. Bezbaruah and R. Mandal, eds, *Indian Agriculture after the Green Revolution: Changes and Challenges*, London and New York: Routledge.

Ramachandran, V.K. and M. Swaminathan (2002), 'Introduction', in V.K. Ramachandran and M. Swaminathan, eds, *Agrarian Studies: Essays on Agrarian Relations in Less*

Developed Countries, New Delhi: Tulika Books.

Ramachandran, V.K. and V. Rawal (2010), 'The Impact of Liberalization and Globalization on India's Agrarian Economy', *Global Labour Journal*, vol. 1, no. 1, pp. 56–91.

Ramachandran, V.K., V. Rawal and M. Swaminathan, eds (2010) *Socio-Economic Surveys of Three Villages of Andhra Pradesh*, New Delhi: Tulika Books.

J.M. Rao and S. Storm (1998), 'Distribution and Growth in Indian Agriculture', in T.J. Byres, ed., *The Indian Economy: Major Debates Since Independence*, Delhi: Oxford University Press, pp. 193–248.

Rawal, V. and M. Swaminathan (2011), 'Income Inequality in Rural India and the Role of Caste', *Review of Agrarian Studies*, vol. 1, no. 2, pp. 108–33, available at http://ras.org.in/index.php?Article=income_inequality_and_caste_in_village_india&q=rawal&keys=rawal, accessed 19 March 2021.

Saha, A. and M. Swaminathan (1994), 'Agricultural Growth in West Bengal in the 1980s', *Economic and Political Weekly*, vol. 29, no. 43, pp. 3858–60.

Sarkar, B. (2017), 'The Situation Assessment Surveys: An Evaluation', *Review of Agrarian Studies* vol. 7, no. 2, pp. 111–22, available at http://ras.org.in/index.php?citation=the_situation_assessment_surveys&citation_status=1, accessed 19 March 2021.

Surjit, V. (2017), 'The Evolution of Farm Income Statistics in India: A Review', *Review of Agrarian Studies* vol. 7, no. 2, pp. 39–61, available at http://ras.org.in/index.php?Article=the_evolution_of_farm_income_statistics_in_india&q=surjit&keys=surjit, accessed 19 March 2021.

Swaminathan, M. and S. Baksi, eds (2018), *How Do Small Farmers Fare? Evidence from Village Studies in India*, New Delhi: Tulika Books.

Appendix

Appendix Table 1 *List of study villages with district, state and year of survey*

Village	District	State	Survey year	Number of surveyed households
Ananthavaram	Guntur	Andhra Pradesh	2005–06	664
Bukkacherla	Anantapur	Andhra Pradesh	2005–06	292
Kothapalle	Karimnagar	Telangana	2005–06	370
Harevli	Bijnaur	Uttar Pradesh	2005–06	109
Mahatwar	Ballia	Uttar Pradesh	2005–06	156
Nimshirgaon	Kolhapur	Maharashtra	2006–07	137
Warwat Khanderao	Buldhana	Maharashtra	2006–07	250
25 F Gulabewala	Sri Ganganagar	Rajasthan	2006–07	204
Rewasi	Sikar	Rajasthan	2009–10	219
Gharsondi	Gwalior	Madhya Pradesh	2007–08	263
Alabujanahalli	Mandya	Karnataka	2008–09	243
Siresandra	Kolar	Karnataka	2008–09	79
Zhapur	Kalaburagi	Karnataka	2008–09	109
Amarsinghi	Maldah	West Bengal	2009–10	127
Panahar	Bankura	West Bengal	2009–10	248
Kalmandasguri	Koch Bihar	West Bengal	2009–10	147
Tehang	Jalandhar	Punjab	2010–11	681

Source: PARI Survey data.

Appendix Table 2 *Gini coefficient for ownership of all assets, rural India, 1992 to 2012*

Year	Gini coefficient
1991–92	0.62
2001–02	0.63
2011–12	0.67

Source: Mahendra Dev (2018).

Appendix Table 3 *Proportion of rural households that do not own any land other than homesteads (excluding cultivated part of homestead) as proportion of total households, by social group, all India, 2003–04,* in per cent

	Adivasi	Dalit	Non-Dalit/Adivasi	All
India	26.4	41.4	28.5	31.1

Source: Computed from NSS Land and Livestock Holdings Survey, 59th Round, as cited in Bakshi (2008).

2

The Land Question in Contemporary Rural India

Vikas Rawal and Vaishali Bansal

Introduction

Resolution of the land question in contemporary rural India remains an unfinished task and a critical issue. With neoliberalism as the dominant ideology guiding state policy, Indian state has abdicated the responsibility of implementing land reforms. This makes it even more important for people interested in progressive change to revisit the land question and the need for land reforms. What is the land question in rural India today? How unequally is land distributed in rural India and how has land distribution changed over time? What have been the trends in respect of landlessness in rural India? Are land reforms still relevant?

This paper deals with these concerns. It presents a detailed analysis of data on landholdings to answer some of these questions.

The paper is organized as follows. In the second section, we discuss the data and their limitations. The third section presents a discussion on the extent of landlessness in Indian states and in India. It also discusses disparities in land ownership among different social groups and gender. In the fourth section, we present data on inequality in ownership of land in India. In this section, we specifically examine whether there has been a proliferation of small holdings in India and if the large landholdings have disintegrated in recent times. The fifth section presents a discussion on variation in incidence and forms of tenancy in India. In the concluding section, we argue that the evidence presented in the paper points at continued relevance of land reforms in India.

Data on Landholdings of Rural Households

Official statistics on land are poor and severely understate inequality in the access of rural households to land. Agricultural Censuses and the NSSO Surveys of Land and Livestock Holdings (NSSO-SLLH) are the two most widely used sources of data on landholdings.

Agricultural Censuses are based on retabulation of land records in most states.[1] There are, however, no clear guidelines on how this retabulation is done. The task is done at the state-level, with little supervision to ensure uniformity. Land records are records of ownership of land by individuals. Since tenancy is seldom recorded in land records, only a small proportion of tenancy is captured in Agricultural Censuses. Land records also do not contain any information on households. Although operational holdings in agricultural censuses refer to land operated as a single technical unit, it is not clear how land operated by households but registered under the names of various members of households (and other family members) are identified and aggregated to obtain operational holdings. Such parcels of land may even be located in different villages. Land records are often outdated and do not reflect the correct status of ownership and possession. They are also, in most states, very poorly maintained (Mishra and Suhag 2017). In most states, computerization of land records is an ongoing task. For the 2015–16 Agricultural Census, an unsuccessful attempt was made to use computerized land records database in Gujarat and Maharashtra. However, the effort was abandoned because of inadequacy of information available in the database and other teething problems.[2]

Identification of *de facto* operational holdings from the records of individual ownership of land is an almost impossible exercise. In reality, no serious effort is undertaken to identify operational holdings for Agricultural Censuses. Since India had about 16.8 crore rural households as per the 2011 Census, and anything between 30–50 per cent of rural households are landless, the total number of operational holdings recorded in the Agricultural Census (13.8 crores in 2011–12) is clearly an overstatement. This is likely to be a result of poor enumeration based on land records.

Until the 70th round (for 2012–13), NSSO-SLLH are conducted once in ten years. A detailed assessment of these surveys and issues related to the comparability of estimates from different rounds of these surveys can be seen in Rawal (2008), and Bansal, Usami and Rawal (2018). It was recently decided that the surveys on agriculture and landholdings would be conducted once in five years rather than once in ten years. In addition, in the 77th round, the survey on land and livestock holdings was merged with the Situational Assessment Survey.[3] This was a major improvement, as canvassing Land and Livestock Survey and Situational Assessment Survey on two separate samples of households meant that information on related aspects of agrarian economy could not be analysed together. This problem has been resolved with the merging of the two surveys. There were, however, two important changes in the way questions on landholdings were administered. First, the new survey schedule did not collect plot-by-plot information on landholdings. As a result, the data cannot be used for analysing parcelization (or fragmentation) of holdings. Secondly, data on extent of holdings were recorded in acres rather than in hectares, with 0.01 acres (rather than 0.01 hectares) being the smallest unit of enumeration of land. This can have a bearing on estimates of landlessness (see Rawal 2013) and adjustments should be done when estimating landlessness for comparison with estimates from the previous surveys.

Until recently, NSSO also collected data on operational holdings of land in the quinquennial surveys of consumption expenditure and employment (see Rawal [2013] for a detailed assessment). However, after the 68th round, the employment surveys (NSSO-Employment and Unemployment Surveys [EUS]) were replaced with the Periodic Labour Force Surveys (PLFS) and questions related to land were excluded. Data from the last round of the consumption survey (for 2017–18) have also not been released. Consequently, data on operational holdings of land from these surveys are only available up to the 68th round (for 2011–12).

In this paper, we use two additional sources of data on landholdings.

In the Socio-Economic Caste Census (SECC) conducted in 2011, information on ownership of land was collected from all rural households. Although household-level data from the SECC are not available, and therefore it is not possible to examine inequality in ownership of land, the aggregated tables provide information on the proportion of landless households, and proportion of households that have irrigated and unirrigated land, at the national, state, district and taluk levels.

The National Family Health Surveys (NFHSs), which are large, nationally representative surveys, also collect limited but useful information on ownership of agricultural land. Since 1992–93, five rounds of NFHSs have been conducted. The data for the last round, for 2019–20, have not yet been released. While the first three rounds covered about 60,000 rural households in the sample, the sample size for the 2015–16 round was much bigger and included over 4,25,000 rural households (Table 2.1). There have been some changes in the way data were collected on agricultural land in different NFHS rounds.

(1) In all the surveys, sample households were first asked whether they owned any agricultural land. This can be used to obtain comparable estimates of proportion of households that do not own land from all the surveys.

(2) In the 1992–93 survey, if a sample household reported that they owned some agricultural land, it was asked how much irrigated and how much unirrigated land they owned. This was a slightly complicated way of asking for the information as the lack of information on irrigation status resulted in a significant number of blank values – neither a zero nor a positive number – being left in columns for irrigated and unirrigated land. In such cases, it was not possible to estimate total amount of land because of these blank entries.

Table 2.1 *Number of rural households in the sample, different rounds, National Family Health Surveys, India*

Year	Sample
1992–93	59,740
1998–99	61,800
2005–06	58,805
2015–16	4,25,563

Source: Based on different rounds of the National Family Health Surveys.

In subsequent surveys, the households were instead asked how much total land they owned, and then a third question was added about how much of their owned land was irrigated. In these rounds, information on total amount of land was recorded even if there is some ambiguity about the irrigation status. This difference makes the data on the extent of ownership holdings from the 1992–93 survey non-comparable with subsequent rounds of the National Family Health Surveys.

(3) In the 1992–93 survey, information on the extent of land was recorded only in acres and saved in the database as such. In the subsequent three surveys, information was recorded in acres and, at the stage of data entry, also converted into and recorded in hectares. In the first three surveys, the fields recorded three digits of information with largest allowed number being 995 (acres or hectares). Numbers from 996–999 were reserved as special codes. In the fourth round, only two digits were allowed with 95 being the largest number allowed. In this case, numbers 96–99 were reserved as special codes.

This means that, in the 1992–93 survey, the largest extent of land recorded was 995 acres (about 402 hectares). In the 1998–99 and 2005–06 surveys, the largest amount of land that could be recorded was 995 hectares. And in the 2015–16 survey, the largest amount of land that could be recorded was 95 hectares. These differences affect the accuracy with which land of large owners is provided in the data from the surveys. To make the data comparable, we have imposed a ceiling of 95 hectares on all surveys. That is, all households that had more than 95 hectares, were treated as having 95 hectares. This results in some underestimation of inequality and the share of area under large landholdings.

(4) In the 2005–06 and 2015–16 surveys, field investigators were also allowed to record information if the information could not be converted to acres. This was done for about 4.5 per cent rural households in 2005–06 and 18.6 per cent rural households in 2015–16. The survey schedule did not require field investigators to even mention what non-standard unit was being

used. This is a problem because, for such observations, the number cannot be converted to a standard unit (acres or hectares) and the proportion of such households is significant in the 2015–16 survey.

(5) In the latest two rounds, NFHS-4 and NFHS-5, an additional question on whether the land was owned solely by the male member of the family and/or by the female member of the family was also added. This additional question provides particularly useful data on the status of land ownership by women in India.

Unlike the NSSO-SLLH surveys, NSSO-EUS, SECC and NFHS ask only a few questions on land and these questions are part of a survey in which land is not the main focus. A distinguishing aspect of NFHSs is also that women are the primary respondents. It is possible that respondents are less likely to conceal the true extent of land that they own/operate when this information is obtained through just one or two questions as part of a survey that deals with many other things rather than in a survey that focuses on land and involves a detailed investigation about the extent, nature and use of landholdings.

Landlessness in Rural India

All nationally representative surveys with data on landholdings show that a large proportion of rural households in India do not own any agricultural land (Table 2.2). This proportion increased significantly over the last three decades.

As per the latest NSSO-SLLH, about 41 per cent of households in rural India did not own any agricultural land in 2018–19. Other national surveys suggest that the proportion of landless households in rural areas might be significantly higher than what is estimated in NSSO-SLLH. The Socio-Economic Caste Census (SECC) conducted in 2011 found that 56 per cent of rural households did not own any agricultural land. As per the last round of the National Family Health Surveys (NFHS-4) for which data are available, 47.4 per cent of rural households did not own any agricultural land in 2015–16. NSSO-EUS can be used to get estimates of proportion of households that do not cultivate any land. Since these surveys are unlikely to capture tenancy, it is not surprising that the estimates of proportion of households that do not cultivate any land (49 per cent in 2001–12) are close to the estimates of proportion of households that do not own any land from the NFHS (47.4 per cent in 2015–16).

Data from all the sources show that the extent of landlessness among rural households has increased since the early 1990s (Table 2.2). As per NSSO-SLLH, proportion of landless households increased by about 12 percentage points between 1991–92 and 2018–19. The NFHSs show a similar level of increase between 1992–93 and 2015–16.

Table 2.2 *Proportion of households that do not own any agricultural land, 1991–92 to 2018–19, rural India,* in per cent

Year	NSSO-SLLH	NFHS	SECC	NSSO-EUS*
1991–92	29.3	–	–	–
1992–93	–	35.4	–	–
1993–94	–	–	–	35.0
1998–99	–	38.7	–	–
1999–00	–	–	–	39.0
2002–03	32.1	–	–	–
2004–05	–	–	–	43.0
2005–06	–	41.5	–	–
2009–10	–	–	–	47.0
2011	–	–	56.4	–
2011–12	–	–	–	49.0
2012–13	34.5	–	–	–
2015–16	–	47.4	–	–
2018–19	40.8	–	–	–

Note: Estimates based on NSSO-EUS are for households without operational holdings of land. See Rawal (2013).
Source: Based on NSSO Surveys of Land and Livestock Holdings, National Family Health Surveys, Socio-Economic Caste Census and NSSO Employment-Unemployment Surveys.

As can be seen in Table 2.3, at the state-level, the estimates of proportion of landless households from NFHS in 2015–16 were close to the proportion of landless households computed from the SECC. Landlessness was high in Kerala, West Bengal and Tripura despite a significant amount of land redistribution in these states through land reforms. These states had an exceedingly high population density, which meant that despite redistribution and very small size of holdings, a large proportion of households continued to remain landless. The extent of landlessness in these states may be overstated because the data do not account for cultivation on homestead lands. Distribution of homestead lands was an important component of land reforms in these states and allowed beneficiaries to use it for marginal cultivation. Landlessness was also high in states like Punjab, Haryana, Andhra Pradesh and Tamil Nadu, where no land redistribution has been done through land reforms and agricultural transformation has increased rural inequalities.

The land question in India is inextricably linked to the caste question. Historically, as part of the caste system, Dalits were denied the right to own agricultural lands. While such practices were outlawed in the Constitution of independent India, the impact of historical injustice and continuation of

Table 2.3 *Proportion of households that do not own any agricultural land, by state*, in per cent

States	NSSO-SLLH (2012–13)	NSSO-SLLH (2018–19)	SECC (2011)	NFHS-4 (2015–16)
Himachal Pradesh	24.2	10.9	22	28.4
Punjab	46.3	64.5	64.5	65.0
Haryana	27.9	47.9	55.9	55.8
Bihar	49.3	49.9	65.6	54.1
West Bengal	43.4	55.0	69.6	62.1
Jharkhand	17.9	20.0	37.7	30.9
Odisha	28.3	43.4	54.3	41.9
Rajasthan	15.3	25.0	38.0	33.8
Gujarat	32.4	37.4	55.3	43.3
Maharashtra	38.9	40.9	53.7	44.8
Andhra Pradesh	54.4	63.7	73.4	60.9
Karnataka	34.5	34.5	46.6	44.3
Kerala	27.0	37.5	72.5	79.7
Tamil Nadu	52.4	65.3	73.4	69.1
Telangana	42.5	41.5	57.5	44.5
Uttarakhand	33.4	29.7	43.3	41.9
Uttar Pradesh	22.2	32.6	44.8	33.2
Chhattisgarh	24.1	34.6	46.7	33.8
Madhya Pradesh	29.3	31.9	54.7	39.0
Assam	25.6	39.4	56.7	51.9
Jammu and Kashmir	9.3	13.9	22.4	20.3
Sikkim	46.5	22.1	39.8	34.7
Arunachal Pradesh	17.6	14.4	44.1	39.4
Nagaland	31.9	8.8	42.6	38.5
Manipur	18.2	23.2	70.0	69.4
Goa	82.3	54.5	91.6	82.6
Mizoram	12.1	21.5	79.5	46.8
Tripura	60.8	54.4	68.3	72.7
Meghalaya	19.6	19.6	76.0	66.3
India (including UTs)	34.5	40.8	56.4	47.4

Source: Based on NSSO Surveys of Land and Livestock Holdings, 70th round, Socio-Economic Caste Census and National Family Health Survey, 4th round.

discriminatory social practices in various forms have meant that disparities in land ownership across Dalits and caste Hindus did not decline (Bakshi 2008; Rawal 2014; Thorat and Newman 2007; Thorat and Newman, eds 2012). Along with Dalits, Muslim households in rural India also face discrimination in access to land (Sachar Committee 2006). Thus, landlessness among Dalit and Muslim households in rural India continues to be disproportionately high. While the disparities were seen in all the data sources, the NFHS recorded a higher degree of landlessness among Dalits and Muslim households than the NSSO surveys. As per the NFHS data for 2015–16, 62 per cent of rural Dalit households and 61 per cent of rural Muslim households did not own any land. Adivasis faced exclusion from ownership of land in multi-caste villages. They have also been dispossessed from land because of land acquisition for mining, industrial and other projects. As per the NFHS, 41 per cent of Adivasi households were recorded as landless in 2015–16. Both NSSO and NFHS data show a sharp rise in landlessness among Dalits, Adivasis and Muslim households from 2012–13 to 2018–19 (Table 2.4).

An important aspect of land rights in India is that land is mostly registered in the name of men and is inherited only by male descendants. In the latest round of NFHS (for 2015–16), a question was asked about whether land was registered in name of men, women or both. These data show that, in the country as a whole, land titles for 89 per cent of the landowning households were only in the name of men (Table 2.5). The land titles were in the name of women in only 8.2 per cent of landowning households and were shared by both men and women in 2.1 per cent of landowning

Table 2.4 *Proportion of households with no owned land, by social group, 1991–92 to 2018–19, rural India,* in per cent

Social group	Dalit	Adivasi	Muslim	Others
NSSO Land and Livestock Surveys				
1991–92	42.4	22.9	–	–
2002–03	41.8	24.8	39.2	28.6
2012–13	46.2	26.7	41.9	30.6
2018–19	57.3	32.8	53.1	35.2
National Family Health Surveys				
1992–93	51.2	30.2	46.3	31.3
1998–99	54.7	32.4	51.8	31.8
2005–06	57.4	33	54.5	34.5
2015–16	61.7	40.8	61.3	40.3

Source: Based on different rounds of NSSO-SLLH and the NFHS.

Table 2.5 *Share of landowning households with land titles in the names of women (single or joint), 2015–16,* in per cent

State	Per cent	State	Per cent
Andhra Pradesh	17.0	Meghalaya	77.6
Assam	7.3	Mizoram	15.3
Bihar	7.7	Nagaland	18.6
Chhattisgarh	11.1	Odisha	7.2
Goa	19.8	Punjab	7.3
Gujarat	8.2	Rajasthan	7.2
Haryana	5.5	Sikkim	5.1
Himachal Pradesh	19.4	Tamil Nadu	10.6
Jammu and Kashmir	5.1	Telangana	17.9
Jharkhand	8.4	Tripura	13.3
Karnataka	14.8	Uttar Pradesh	10.9
Kerala	32.0	Uttarakhand	14.7
Madhya Pradesh	9.2	West Bengal	6.6
Maharashtra	9.9	Union Territories	12.8
Manipur	8.6	All-India	10.3

Source: Based on National Family Health Survey, 2015–16.

households. Two states, Meghalaya and Kerala, where some communities and castes have had a tradition of matrilineal inheritance of land, stood out in respect of proportion of households where land titles were in the name of women. In Meghalaya, 78 per cent of landowning households and in Kerala 32 per cent of landowning households had land registered in the name of women (alone or jointly).

Land Inequality

Not only are a large proportion of rural households in India landless, land is also highly unequally distributed among the rest. As per the latest NSSO-SLLH data, in 2018–19, the top 20 per cent households owned about 76 per cent of all the land (Table 2.6). The NFHS data show an even higher level of concentration. As per the NFHS data, the top 20 per cent households owned 83 per cent of all the land in 2015–16. This was 9 percentage points higher than the estimate for 1998–99.

Has There Been a Proliferation of Tiny Landholdings?

It is commonly argued by scholars of different persuasions as well as policymakers that landholdings in India have got highly disintegrated over

Table 2.6 *Distribution of owned land across quintiles of ownership holdings,*
1991–92 to 2018–19, in per cent

Quintiles	NSSO-SLLH			NFHS		
	1991–92	2012–13	2018–19	1998–99	2005–06	2015–16
Bottom 20 per cent households	0	0	0	0	0	0
20–40 per cent households	1.3	0.8	0	1.4	0.7	0.1
40–60 per cent households	9.3	8.5	4.8	6.8	5.8	3.7
60–80 per cent households	21.5	20.5	19.5	17.7	17.4	13.0
Top 20 per cent households	67.8	70.2	75.7	74.1	76.1	83.1
All households	100.0	100.0	100.0	100.0	100.0	100.0

Source: Based on NSSO Surveys of Land and Livestock Holdings, 48th, 70th rounds and National Family Health Surveys, 2nd, 3rd and 4th rounds.

the years because of population growth and subdivision, or partitioning between the inheritors of land. There has been, it is argued, a proliferation of uneconomic and unviable very small holdings.

Although such arguments are not new, they have been widely used in the recent years. For example, Thimmaiah (2001) wrote that

> the area as well as the number of small and marginal farms increased phenomenally during the last three decades. Though efforts were made to consolidate landholdings that were sub-divided and fragmented, operation of the provisions of land reforms and laws of inheritance prevented economically viable holdings from emerging as a normal feature of Indian agriculture. (Thimmaiah 2001, p. 191)

Hazell (2005) argued that 'continuing rural population growth on a fixed land base is creating a situation where the subdivision of small farms has or is approaching the point where many farms may now be too small to be efficient or to survive' (Hazell 2005, p. 95). S. Singh (2006) wrote that 'small farms are highly fragmented. Land transactions have led to further fragmentation making them non-viable in terms of resource use as well as family sustenance' (S. Singh 2006, p. 18). Padhee and Joshi (2019) claimed that 'about 1.5 million-2 million new marginal and small farmers are added every year due to the law of inheritance'. Satyasai and Mehrotra (2016) stated that 'the structure of Indian agriculture is skewed towards small producers operating tiny and uneconomical holdings' (Satyasai and Mehrotra 2016, p. 23).

These arguments were also reiterated in many recent official policy documents. For example, the Tenth Five-Year Plan document stated that 'with increasing population, landholdings are getting fragmented and becoming unviable' (Planning Commission 2003). Planning Commission (2008) argued that 'small land-owners who would otherwise have to operate small uneconomic holdings should have the opportunity to legally lease out land to other farmers with the assurance of being able to resume possession at the end of the stated period of tenancy'. Montek Ahluwalia, in an article about the approach of the Twelfth Five-Year Plan, wrote that 'as holdings are subdivided and become uneconomic, very small and marginal farmers may be better off leasing out their land to more viable farmers' (Ahluwalia 2011). Dalwai Committee (2018) argued that 'under the conditions of agricultural production system obtaining in India, farming is faced with inefficient scales of operation due to small and marginal size of farms'. NITI Aayog (2015) elaborated the argument and stated that

> over the generations, as families have grown, landholdings have come to be divided and fragmented into small economically unviable parcels and plots. Onerous leasing laws have prevented consolidation of these hold-ings. On the one hand, these smallholdings force owners to seek alternative means of livelihood and on the other their plots remain uncultivated with no prospect of being joined to other plots to produce more viable holdings.

These arguments were used as the rationale for the model Land Leasing Act designed to promote reverse leasing as a mechanism for increas-ing the scale of production. The Haque Committee, which drafted the model Land Leasing Act, argued that 'marginal and small farmers would be better off leasing out their land to more viable farmers for rent, while seeking paid employment within or outside agriculture' (Haque Committee 2016).

Most of these studies and official documents cite Agricultural Censuses to show the proliferation of very small holdings. As described in Section 2, Agricultural Censuses do not have a systematic way of iden-tifying household operational holdings. In states where they are based on land records, they are likely to separately record holdings of individuals as operational holdings. The Agricultural Censuses also do not have a speci-fied mechanism for aggregating land owned across different administrative units. Such problems are likely to result in false data showing high level of fragmentation of holdings.

What do other sources of data show? All large-scale household sur-veys except the last two rounds of NSSO-SLLH found that more than half of total area is in holdings that are larger than 2 hectares (Table 2.7). As per the NFHSs, over 70 per cent of the land was owned by households with two hectares of land or more. These are not tiny, uneconomic holdings. Although official surveys do not capture large holdings very well, and thus overstate

Table 2.7 *Proportion of land in holdings of two hectares or more, 1987–88 to 2018–19*, in per cent

Year	NSSO-SLLH	NFHS	NSSO-EUS*
1987–88	–	–	68.4
1991–92	64.4	–	–
1993–94	–	–	63.9
1998–99	–	70.9	–
1999–00	–	–	58.7
2002–03	59.6	–	–
2004–05	–	–	57.0
2005–06	–	62.6	–
2009–10	–	–	57.3
2011–12	–	–	54.0
2012–13	43.1	–	–
2015–16	–	71.2	–
2018–19	41.7	–	–

Note: Estimates based on NSSO-EUS data are for households without operational holdings. See Rawal (2013).
Source: Based on NSSO Surveys of Land and Livestock Holdings, National Family Health Surveys and NSSO Employment-Unemployment Surveys.

the prevalence of smaller holdings, even they do not show that most of the land is divided into uneconomic holdings.

The NFHSs, which are the only surveys that record large landholdings, show that the changes in land distribution were such that, on the one hand, there was a swelling in the ranks of the landless households and, on the other, a considerable accumulation of land by large landowners. The data do not show an increase in proportion of landowners owning very small amounts of land (Table 2.8).

Low level of incomes from agriculture is a problem exacerbated by neoliberal policies. These policies have also hastened the process of differentiation resulting in a sharp increase in landlessness and land inequality. While a discussion of causes of this crisis of incomes is beyond the scope of this paper, presenting the crisis of incomes in agriculture as a crisis caused because of proliferation of uneconomic holdings is an argument based on poor evidence. This has been a common position of mainstream economists and policymakers, and is nothing more than an attempt to conceal the real causes of the agrarian crisis.

Table 2.8 *Distribution of households and owned land across size-classes of ownership holdings, NFHS, 1998–99, 2005–06 and 2015–16,* in per cent

	Households			Area		
	1998–99	2005–06	2015–16	1998–99	2005–06	2015–16
Landless	38.7	41.5	47.4	0	0	0
Marginal (0–1 ha)	34.9	33.8	19.6	14.0	19.5	14.9
Small (1–2 ha)	11.7	9.9	6.9	15.0	17.9	13.9
Marginal & Small	46.6	43.7	26.5	29.0	37.4	28.8
Medium-I (2–4 ha)	8.2	6.2	4.6	20.0	21.3	17.4
Medium-II (4–10 ha)	4.7	3.4	2.1	25.4	24.9	17.8
Medium	12.9	9.6	6.7	45.4	46.2	35.2
Large-I (10–20 ha)	0.9	0.5	0.4	11.5	8.4	7.8
Large-II (20–30 ha)	0.3	0.1	0.1	5.8	3.4	3.5
Large-III (>30 ha)	0.2	0.1	0.2	8.2	4.6	24.7
Large	1.4	0.7	0.7	25.5	16.4	36.0
Land specified in non-standard units	0.6	4.5	18.6	0.0	0.0	0.0
Total	100.0	100.0	100.0	100.0	100.0	100.0

Note: In the last two rounds of NFHS, data on land for some households were recorded in non-standard, local units. These holdings are likely to be small. We have estimated that, depending on different assumptions about these non-standard local units, if these households are classified into different size-classes, it results in a small increase in share of land in the marginal and small holdings, and the share of the largest size-class falls slightly. In 2015–16, under different assumptions about the size of these non-standard units, the share of the top size-class varies between 20 and 24.7 per cent.
Source: Based on various rounds of National Family Health Surveys.

Existence of Large Landholdings

The flip side of the argument that there was a proliferation of uneconomic holdings is that large holdings were subdivided due to inheritance and population growth. This is used to argue that redistributive land reforms were not relevant anymore.

Of the various sources of data on landholdings, NFHSs are the only ones that capture large-scale holdings. The NFHS data show that a significant part of land is owned by those who have large amounts of land. A comparison of data from different rounds of NFHS also suggests that the share of holdings in the largest size-class (30 hectares or more) actually increased over the last two decades (Table 2.8). The state-level estimates show that, among large states, the share of land owned by households with more than

Table **2.9** *Share of land owned by households with more than 30 ha of land, by state, NFHS, 2015–16*, in per cent

States	2015–16	States	2015–16
Andhra Pradesh	1.4	Madhya Pradesh	17.2
Assam	6.4	Maharashtra	18.7
Bihar	28.8	Odisha	37.5
Chhattisgarh	4.6	Punjab	10.9
Gujarat	6.6	Rajasthan	11.1
Haryana	18.6	Tamil Nadu	65.1
Himachal Pradesh	18.4	Telangana	9.1
Jammu and Kashmir	23.8	Uttar Pradesh	7.1
Jharkhand	21.6	Uttarakhand	27.4
Karnataka	16.9	West Bengal	24.3
Kerala	10.8	*India*	20.4

Notes: Households owning more than 95 hectares of land were recorded as having 95 hectares of land in the data.
Source: Based on National Family Health Survey, 2015–16.

30 hectares of land was highest in Tamil Nadu, Odisha and Bihar (Table 2.9).

It is relevant here to note that many village studies have also shown continued presence of large landholdings in Indian villages (Arora 2021; Ramachandran, Rawal and Swaminathan 2010; Rawal and Ramachandran 2013; Swaminathan and Das, eds 2017). Primary data-based studies have also shown that, barring the context when land ceiling acts were actively implemented in a few states, land market transactions resulted in the consolidation of holdings as dominant classes accumulated more and the best lands (Rawal 2001).

The Question of Tenancy

Tenancy relations in India, barring exceptions like West Bengal, are almost entirely informal. Such informal, insecure and exploitative tenancy contracts, often interlocked with unfree relations of labour, are not only unjust but can also be growth-retarding. Mainstream positions on tenancy range from considering tenancy (and thus, tenancy reforms) as a marginal aspect of land relations to treating state-led tenancy reforms as a cause of prevalence of insecure tenancy. Along with an uneven and distorted penetration of capitalist relations in the Indian countryside, there were also significant changes in the extent of use of tenancy, in the class configuration of tenants and lessors, and in the form of tenancy contracts over the last few decades. With the state unwilling to effectively implement land reforms in most parts of India, tenancy relations have continued to be informal, exploitative and embedded in socio-economic power relations.

NSSO Surveys on Land and Livestock (NSSO-SLLH) are the only source of large-scale survey-based data on tenancy. The incidence of tenancy is likely to be under-reported in these surveys. It is therefore important to interpret results from these surveys carefully.

Increasing Incidence of Tenancy

The first main finding from our analysis of the NSSO-SLLH data is that, at the national level, there was a significant increase in the incidence of tenancy between 2002–03 and 2018–19.

In Table 2.10, we have compiled the estimates given in NSSO reports for the 26th and 37th rounds of NSSO-SLLH surveys. Our estimates based on unit-level data from the subsequent three surveys. These estimates show that the proportion of tenants among rural households and proportion of leased-in land in total operated area fell between 1971–72 and 2002–03. The decline in tenancy over this period was explained variously, including on account of problems of data (that is, inability of NSSO-SLLH to capture all tenancy contracts), reduction in supply of land for lease (eviction of tenants because of tenancy reform legislation, increasing dominance of marginal holdings, and resuming self-cultivation for better utilization of capital invested by landowners in machinery and irrigation), and reduction in demand for leasing land (declining unemployment and poverty, and rising wages, during the 1980s).

The trends between 2002–03 and 2018–19, presented in Table 2.10, are in sharp contrast to the trends over the previous decades. At the national

Table 2.10 *Tenants as a proportion of all rural and cultivator households, leased-in land as a proportion of total operated area, rural India, 1971–72, 1982, 1991–92, 2002–03, 2012–13 and 2018–19*, in per cent

Year	NSSO Round	Tenants/ Rural households	Tenants/ Cultivator households	Leased-in area/ Operated area
1971–72	26.0	25.3	–	10.6
1982	37.0	17.8	24.0	7.2
1991–92	48.0	9.3	12.8	8.7
2002–03	59.0	8.0	11.4	6.7
2012–13	70.0	10.3	15.0	11.1
2018–19	77.0	10.9	17.4	21.8

Source: Estimates for 1971–72 and 1982 taken from NSSO (1986, 1987); estimates for 1991–92, 2002–03, 2012–13 and 2018–19 computed using the corrected unit-level data for each round.

level, proportion of tenants among rural households increased from 8 per cent in 2002–03 to 10.9 per cent in 2018–19. The share of leased-in land in operated area increased from about 6.7 per cent in 2002–03 and 11.1 per cent in 2012–13 to 21.8 per cent in 2018–19. It is important to note that while the proportion of tenants rose only by 0.6 percentage points between 2012–13 and 2018–19, the share of leased-in land in the operated area almost doubled. This implies a significant rise in average area leased-in by a tenant, suggesting a shift towards leasing of land by large tenants.

It should be pointed out that the extent of tenancy reported by the lessors of land is considerably lower than the extent of tenancy reported by lessees or tenants. Sawant (1991) showed that there is a large concealment of tenancy in the data on leasing out in NSSO-SLLH, and that the extent of concealment is non-uniform across classes and states. Similarly, agricultural censuses also record very low levels of tenancy. In comparison with estimates presented in Table 2.10, only 0.94 per cent of the operated area was reported as being under tenancy contracts in the Agricultural Census for 2010–11. Given that most of the tenancy contracts in India are informal and short-term, and do not comply with tenancy reform laws, landowners do not register tenancy contracts in land records.[4]

Increase in Fixed-rent Tenancy

Another trend that stands out clearly in the data is the increase in fixed-rent tenancy, and within that, of rental payments paid in money. The share of land cultivated on fixed rent in total leased-in land increased from about 33 per cent in 1991–92 and 47 per cent in 2002–03 to 55 per cent in 2012–13 and 2018–19 (Table 2.11). Since 2012–13, fixed rental payments in money have become the singlemost important category of types of tenancy contracts, and accounted for about 43 per cent of leased-in land in 2018–19.

In 2018–19, fixed money rent was the dominant type of contract in Punjab, Haryana, Maharashtra, Tamil Nadu, Andhra Pradesh and Telangana. In Punjab, about 94 per cent of the leased-in land was under fixed money contracts. On the other hand, sharecropping was the dominant type of contract in Uttar Pradesh, Bihar, Tripura, Jharkhand, Chhattisgarh and Orissa with over 40 per cent leased-in land under sharecropping contracts.

The rise of fixed rent tenancy has been argued to be a result of, on the one hand, increasing access to irrigation, improved productivity and a reduction in uncertainty of production, and on the other, increased demand for leasing land because of increasing landlessness, lack of availability of decent non-agricultural employment and entry of large landowners in tenancy market. Fixed money rents are typically paid in advance and, therefore, are particularly favourable for richer tenants. However, if increasing landlessness, lack of mobility among workers, and entry of rich tenants into the tenancy

Table 2.11 *Distribution of total leased-in area under various terms of lease, rural India, 1961–62, 1971–72, 1982, 1991–92, 2002–03, 2012–13 and 2018–19*, in per cent

Year	Fixed rent			Produce Share	Others and unspecified
	Fixed money	Fixed produce	Total		
1961–62	25.6	12.9	38.5	39.2	22.3
1971–72	15.4	11.6	27.1	47.9	25.1
1982	10.9	6.3	17.1	44.7	38.2
1991–92	19.0	14.5	33.5	34.4	32.1
2002–03	28.9	18.6	47.5	40.7	11.8
2012–13	39.9	15.2	55.1	30.8	14.1
2018–19	42.6	12.2	54.8	27.7	7.4

Source: Estimates for 1961–62, 1971–72 and 1982 taken from NSSO (1986); for 1991–92 from NSSO (1992); and rest computed using unit-level data.

market increase the competition for leasing in land, credit-constrained poor landless households may also be forced to accept fixed rent and other kinds of highly exploitative contracts (Rawal and Osmani 2009).

Land-Class Position of Tenant Households

How are tenant households distributed across deciles and quintiles of ownership holdings? In which classes do we find an increase in incidence of leasing in? Table 2.12 shows the distribution of tenants and leased-in land across deciles of ownership holding. It shows that the bottom deciles, comprising landless households, had disproportionately low access to tenancy. Bulk of tenants are in the middle deciles. Although, the proportion of households that leased in land in the top decile of ownership holdings was smaller than the proportion in middle deciles, households in the top decile of ownership holding leased in large extents of land, and thus accounted for a disproportionately high share in the total area of land leased in.

Not only do middle and large landowners lease in a substantial proportion of land, there are also other resource-rich households that do not own any land but lease in substantial amounts of land. In fact, it is noteworthy that tenants who do not own any land are not all small peasants. A significant share of them are tenants with operational holdings in middle to top deciles. Table 2.13 shows that, over time, the proportion of landless tenants (tenants who did not own any land) whose operational holdings were in top two deciles of operational holding has increased. In 2018–19, about 24 per cent of landless tenants were in the top two deciles of operational holdings.

Table 2.12 *Distribution of tenant households and area leased in, across deciles of ownership holding, rural India,* in per cent

Deciles	Distribution of tenants		Distribution of leased-in land	
	2002–03	2018–19	2002–03	2018–19
D1	7.9	9.8	6.3	7.8
D2	7.9	9.8	6.3	7.8
D3	7.9	9.8	6.3	7.8
D4	13.1	9.8	9.5	7.8
D5	11.9	9.6	8.8	6.1
D6	12.7	10.7	10.3	8.2
D7	13.0	10.5	10.6	8.7
D8	10.9	11.5	11.6	11.4
D9	8.2	9.9	10.8	12.6
D10	6.6	8.4	19.7	22.0
Total	100.0	100.0	100.0	100.0

Note: Tenants not owning any land were proportionately divided among bottom deciles comprising landless households.
Source: Based on NSSO Surveys of Land and Livestock Holdings.

Table 2.13 *Distribution of landless tenant households and area leased in, across deciles of operational holding, rural India,* in per cent

Deciles	Distribution of landless tenants		Distribution of leased-in land by landless tenants	
	2002–03	2018–19	2002–03	2018–19
D1	0	0	0	0
D2	0	0	0	0
D3	0	0	0	0
D4	15.5	3.9	2.0	0.7
D5	16.2	17.3	6.8	6.4
D6	17.6	18.3	7.8	9.9
D7	18.6	18.7	12.7	11.7
D8	14.4	19.0	15.7	19.1
D9	11.1	13.0	21.0	20.1
D10	6.6	9.8	33.9	32.0
Total	100.0	100.0	100.0	100.0

Source: Based on NSSO Surveys of Land and Livestock Holdings.

These tenants, in the top two deciles of operational holding, accounted for 52 per cent of land leased-in by landless tenants. In contrast, bottom 40 per cent of landless tenants accounted for only 17 per cent of total land leased in by landless tenants.

These results are broadly consistent with findings of several other studies that have noted the entry of large, resource-rich tenants into the lease market (see, for example, Bharadwaj and Das 1975; Jodha 1981; Murty 2004; Nadkarni 1976; Ramachandran, Rawal and Swaminathan, eds 2010; Sidhu 2005; Srivastava 1989; Vyas 1970).

Reverse Tenancy

Reverse tenancy refers to tenancy transactions in which small, resource-poor landowners lease out land to large, resource-rich cultivators. Although the term reverse tenancy was not yet in vogue, in one of the earliest discussions of reverse tenancy, Nadkarni lucidly described the process as one in which,

> members of the dominant class in rural society are entering into formal and informal lease agreements with the poor landholders for cultivation by the former, particularly in regions having the prospects of agricultural prosperity. Thus, the small owners surrender their operational control over land – if not ownership itself – in favour of the dominant. (Nadkarni 1976)

The term reverse tenancy started to be used to describe such tenancy contracts from around 1980. In the Indian context, Vyas (1970) and Nadkarni (1976) were among the earliest commentators to argue that there is an increasing tendency of households from among dominant classes using tenancy to extend their operational control over land.

In several empirical studies of tenancy that followed, the increase in the proportion of large landowning households who leased in land was used to imply an increasing incidence of reverse tenancy in India. In one of the most widely cited study on reverse tenancy in India, I. Singh (1989) argued that reverse tenancy in central Punjab was on the rise even though most of the land in the primary data used in the paper was leased out by middle and large owners. Similarly, Deb *et al.* (2015) found that a substantial amount of land in The International Crops Research Institute for the Semi-Arid Tropics (ICRISAT) survey villages was leased in by large farmers, and interpreted it as an evidence of reverse tenancy. Sharma (2010) used another flawed measure – a greater increase in proportion of land leased out by marginal and small landowners than the increase in proportion of land leased in by the same category of landowners is seen as an indicator of increasing incidence of reverse tenancy.[5] In many other studies, increasing incidence of reverse tenancy in India has been more of an assertion than a finding (see, for example, Kumar 2006; Ramakumar 2000; and S. Singh 2002, 2012). Despite the weak evidence, several other scholars cited some of these studies, often further misinterpreting the evidence, and asserted that incidence of reverse tenancy was on the rise, particularly in the affluent states like Punjab and Haryana (see, for example, Parthasarthy 1991; Shah and Harriss-White 2011).

In contrast, most primary data-based studies that looked at the class-status of both lessors and tenants have come to different conclusions. Sheila Bhalla (1983), in her detailed study of tenancy relations in Haryana, found that 'small cultivators, in particular, have not chosen to lease out some or all of their land and to go to work as farm labourers'. She found that, apart from the large landowners, land was also leased out by small landowners who were engaged in non-agricultural occupations outside the village. On the relative class-position of lessors and tenants, she wrote that, 'in many cases, the tenant and the owners are social and economic equals, especially if the tenant is a man who owns some land in addition to the land he takes on rent' (Bhalla 1983). Birthal and Singh (1994) studied tenancy contracts in Mirzapur and Varanasi districts of Uttar Pradesh. The data presented by them showed that only 2.63 per cent of tenancy contracts in the sample from Mirzapur and 6.18 per cent of tenancy contracts in the sample from Varanasi involved a small landowner leasing out land to a middle or a large landowning tenant.

Sharma and Dréze (1996) noted that in Palanpur (UP), 'there seems to be some tendency for people to refrain from entering into tenancy contracts with individuals who own either a lot more or a lot less land than themselves'. While fixed rent tenancy was found to have become more prevalent in Palanpur in recent times, reverse tenancy was not found to be a significant phenomenon in more recent studies either (Tyagi and Himanshu 2011b, 2011a). In their study based on longitudinal surveys of thirty-six villages in Bihar, Sharma and Rodgers (2015) noted that while there had been a decline in the practice of landless households cultivating land on lease because of increased migration of workers from landless households, the incidence of reverse tenancy was small and had not increased. In PARI village studies, done in many different states of India since 2005–06, reverse tenancy was not found to be a dominant form of tenancy in any village (Ramachandran, Rawal and Swaminathan, eds 2010; Rawal and Osmani 2009; Swaminathan and Das, eds 2017; Swaminathan and Rawal, eds 2015).

Given this context, the pertinent question to ask is: what do the NSSO-SLLH data show about prevalence of reverse tenancy in India? Before we deal with this question, we must reiterate some important limitations of NSSO-SLLH data. In NSSO-SLLH, no information is collected from tenants in the sample that could be used to identify the class status of lessors from whom they lease in land. Similarly, lessors in the sample are not asked information that could be used to identify the class-status of their tenants. Given this, the information provided in NSSO-SLLH is inadequate to identify tenancy contracts in which a small landowner leases out land to a large cultivator. This is a major limitation in using NSSO data to estimate the extent of reverse tenancy.

Given this constraint, the only possible way of using NSSO data to examine whether reverse tenancy is prevalent in any substantial measure is through a comparison of the distribution of lessors and tenants. If the distribution of leased-in land shows a greater concentration of larger landowners than the distribution of leased-out land, one could argue that tenancy is resulting in a net transfer of land from the small landowners to large landowners. Such a comparison, however, must be preceded by the caution that the extent of leasing out reported by landowners suffers from much greater under-reporting than the reporting by tenants. In the 77th round survey, only 2,705 sample households, out of 58,022 sample households for which data on landholdings were collected, reported having leased out any land. In comparison, 8,366 households had leased in some land. The estimate of total leased-out land for 2012–13 was only 5.1 million hectares; in comparison, the estimate for total leased-in land was 21.7 million hectares. Since large landowners are more likely to under-report leasing out, the distribution of leased-out land may be distorted to show less concentration of large landowners, and thus may falsely indicate the existence of reverse tenancy.

With these caveats, we compare the distribution of leased-in land (Table 2.12) and of leased-out land (Table 2.14) across deciles of ownership holdings. The tables show that there was a greater concentration of leased-out land than leased-in land in the hands of large landowners. In 2018–19, top-two deciles accounted for about 35 per cent of all leased-in land and

Table 2.14 *Distribution of lessor households and area leased out, across deciles of ownership holding, rural India,* in per cent

Deciles	Distribution of lessor households		Distribution of area leased out	
	2002–03	2018–19	2002–03	2018–19
D1	0	0	0	0
D2	0	0	0	0
D3	1.8	0	2.0	0
D4	4.7	0	4.8	0
D5	7.6	10.1	4.5	2.3
D6	9.6	10.6	6.4	4.2
D7	16.0	14.2	8.0	7.7
D8	13.5	19.4	24.0	11.5
D9	20.8	19.1	22.6	18.4
D10	25.9	26.5	27.6	55.9
Total	100.0	100.0	100.0	100.0

Source: Based on NSSO Surveys of Land and Livestock Holdings.

74 per cent of all leased-out land. Between 2002–03 and 2018–19, there has been a significant increase in the dominance of large landowners in the distribution of leased-out land. While the proportion of lessors in the top two deciles of land ownership has remained almost the same at about 26 per cent, their share in total leased-out land has increased by 24 percentage points between 2002–03 and 2018–19. Small changes in the distribution of leased-out land seen in lower deciles of land ownership are primarily a result of increased landlessness. Small landowners account for a very small share in the total leased-out land. In 2018–19, the bottom 20 per cent households had leased out only 6.5 per cent of the total leased land.

In other words, these data do not support the possibility of a large-scale prevalence of reverse tenancy in India. In fact, NSSO-SLLH data are consistent with the conclusion that most tenancy contracts in India are either between large landowning lessors and poor tenants, or, lateral tenancy contracts, in which land is leased out by a household to another with a similar socio-economic status.[6] The clearest example of dominance of lateral tenancy is seen in Punjab, where land is primarily owned by medium to large landowners belonging to Jat Sikh community, while landless households, mostly Dalits, are excluded from tenancy markets as well. Data on tenancy in Punjab shows that the tenancy transactions take place only among the top few deciles of landowning, non-Dalit households.

Continued Relevance of Land Reforms

It is well known that over the first four decades after Independence, land reform laws were enacted but were turned into paper tigers in most states because of a lack of serious political commitment to implement land reforms (Appu 1996). After 1991, with the adoption of neoliberal policies, the state became even more hostile to the idea of implementation of land reforms. Not only did the implementation of land reforms cease to be on the policy agenda of the government, but provisions of land reform laws were also relaxed to varying degrees in most states. In West Bengal and Tripura, two states that had an impressive record of implementation of land reforms, electoral losses of the Left in the recent years have opened the floodgates to the demands for a reversal of land reforms.

From providing security of tenure and land to the tiller, state policy has moved to ensuring free and unrestricted functioning of land markets and assuring the rural rich that they need not fear losing land because of pro-poor interventions of the state. The model Land Leasing Act 2016, which the central government has been pushing all states to adopt, provides for 'complete security of land ownership right' and has a provision for automatic eviction of the tenant after the fixed duration of the lease 'without requiring any minimum area of land to be left with the tenant'. The model Act also sets the stage for the state to abdicate the right to enforce rent ceilings or to out-law exploitative provisions in rent agreements. The proposed act allows for

> the terms and conditions of lease to be determined mutually by the land-owner and the tenant without any fear on the part of the landowner of losing land right or undue expectation on the part of the tenant of acquir-ing occupancy right for continuous possession of leased land for any fixed period.

The evidence presented in the foregoing sections strongly points to the continued relevance of redistributive land reform in India. A large proportion of rural households in India are landless, inequality in ownership and opera-tional holdings of land is very high, and ownership of a significant amount of land continues to be concentrated in the hands of the large landowners. We have argued that the common narratives – that there has been a proliferation of small and uneconomic holdings; that large landholdings have disintegrated due to population growth and inheritance; and that tenancy has almost disap-peared – are based on weak evidence. A careful assessment of the data show that landlessness and inequality in access to land increased sharply over the last few decades. The share of land owned by the large landowners also rose sharply. Along with this, the prevalence of informal and insecure tenancy also increased. There was also an increasing tendency of resource-rich farmers expanding their scale of production through leasing of land. This resulted in a marginalization of poor households in the tenancy markets.

Given the vast rural inequalities, redistributive land reforms remain critical for progressive change in India. A push for capitalist development in agriculture and the state-facilitated corporate penetration in agriculture in recent times have meant that rural poverty has deepened, rural inequalities have exacerbated, and caste and gender-based exclusion has remained deeply entrenched in all aspects of life. In states where a serious effort for implemen-tation of land reforms was made, the path of development turned to a more progressive direction. In Kerala, land reforms were the critical foundation on which developments in the areas of education, health and democratic polity were built (Ramachandran 2000). In West Bengal, land reforms created the impetus for agricultural growth and formed the basis for democratization of institutions of local governments (Mishra and Rawal 2002). In Tripura, land reforms paved the way for impressive gains in the areas of education and health, and social and economic empowerment of Adivasis and women (Government of Tripura 2007). However, with the emergence of national gov-ernments and state-level political forces that are hostile to land reforms, these gains remained limited and are now under threat. Direct political intervention, discrimination in fiscal transfers and provision of credit, and creation of hurdles in the implementation of government schemes meant that even these states were not able to fully build upon the foundations provided by land reforms.

Political prospects of implementing land reforms have become bleak in recent decades. This needs to change. Important struggles for land titles of forest dwellers under the Forest Rights Act and for redistribution of public and ceiling-surplus lands to landless households have been taking place in many parts of India. It is important that these are strengthened and the implementation of redistributive land reforms brought back on to the national policy agenda. The Indian countryside is characterized by a vast mass of peasantry and rural workers who live in abject poverty, do not have access to decent education and health care and to basic amenities necessary for living a decent life. The implementation of land reforms is a precondition for this to change in a significant way.

We are grateful to Jesim Pais, Abhijit Sen, Surajit Mazumdar and R. Ramakumar for comments on this paper. The discussion on tenancy is based on work done jointly with Yoshifumi Usami.

Notes

[1] The system of plot-by-plot enumeration for land records exists only in areas that were under temporary settlements during the British period. In such areas, land records form the basis for Agricultural Censuses. In states that were under the Permanent Settlement as well as in the North-Eastern states, systems of plot-by-plot enumeration for land records do not exist. In these states, Agricultural Censuses are based on sample surveys.

[2] http://agcensus.nic.in/egov.html.

[3] The latest 77th round NSSO survey, 2018–19 is called the Survey of Land and Livestock Holding of Households and Situational Assessment of Agricultural Households. In this paper, we use the term NSSO-SLLH to refer to all rounds of the Surveys on Land and Livestock Holding.

[4] West Bengal, where registration of a substantial proportion of tenants in land records was achieved through Operation Barga in the late 1970s and early 1980s, is the only noteworthy exception on this account.

[5] The measure does not account for the fact that, as per the NSSO data, proportion of marginal and small landowner households and share of total land owned by these households also increased over the same period. Also, since the share of marginal and small landowner households in land leased in remained much greater than the share of these classes in land leased out, the indicator does not necessarily imply an increase in leasing of land by small landowners to large landowners.

[6] Having analysed earlier rounds of NSSO-SLLH surveys, Sharma (1995, 2009) also noted lack of conclusive evidence about an increase in incidence of reverse tenancy. He concluded that 'the lessors and lessees belonging to not very different farm size categories dominate the lease market in most of the states' (Sharma 2009, p. 107).

References

Ahluwalia, M.S. (2011), 'Prospects and Policy Challenges in the Twelfth Plan', *Economic and Political Weekly*, vol. 46, no. 21, pp. 88–105.

Appu, P.S. (1996), *Land Reforms in India: A Survey of Policy, Legislation and Implementation*, Delhi: Vikas Publishing House.

Arora, S. (2021), 'A Study of Land Distribution, Tenancy and the Land Market in a Central Indian Village', SSER Monograph 21/1, Society for Social and Economic Research (SSER), New Delhi, available at http://archive.indianstatistics.org/sserwp/sserwp2101.pdf, accessed 30 July 2022.

Bakshi, A. (2008), 'Social Inequality in Land Ownership in India: A Study with Particular Reference to West Bengal', *Social Scientist*, vol. 36, nos 9 and 10, pp. 95–116.

Bansal, V., Y. Usami and V. Rawal (2018), 'Agricultural Tenancy in Contemporary India: An Analytical Report and a Compendium of Statistical Tables Based on NSSO Surveys of Land and Livestock Holdings', SSER Monograph 18/1, Society for Social and Economic Research (SSER), New Delhi, available at http://archive.indianstatistics.org/sserwp/sserwp1801.pdf, accessed 30 July 2022.

Bhalla, S. (1983), 'Tenancy Today: New Factors in Determination of Mode and Level of Rent Payments for Agricultural Land', *Economic and Political Weekly*, vol. 18, nos 19–21, pp. 835–54.

Bharadwaj, K. and P.K. Das (1975), 'Tenurial Conditions and Mode of Exploitation: A Study of Some Villages in Orissa', *Economic and Political Weekly*, vol. 10, nos 5–7, pp. 221–40.

Birthal, P.S. and R.P. Singh (1994), 'Contractual Arrangements in Agriculture of a Developing Economy', *Indian Journal of Agricultural Economics*, vol. 49, no. 2, pp. 187.

Dalwai Committee (2018), 'Report of the Committee on Doubling Farmers' Income: Structural Reforms and Governance Framework', Committee on Doubling Farmers' Income, vol. 13, Department of Agriculture, Cooperation and Farmers' Welfare, Ministry of Agriculture and Farmers' Welfare, Government of India, New Delhi, available at https://agricoop.gov.in/sites/default/files/DFI%20Volume%2013.pdf, accessed 30 July 2022.

Deb, U., S. Pramanik, P.E. Khan and C. Bantilan (2015), 'Revisiting Tenancy and Agricultural Productivity in Southern India: Insights from Longitudinal Household Surveys', ICAE Conference on Agriculture in an Interconnected World, Milan, Italy, 8–14 August, available at http://oar.icrisat.org/9009/1/Revisiting%20Tenancy.pdf, accessed 30 July 2022.

Government of Tripura (2007), *Human Development Report 2007*, Agartala, Government of Tripura, available at http://tripura.nic.in/hdr/welcome.html, accessed 30 July 2022.

Haque Committee (2016), 'Report of the Expert Committee on Land Leasing', NITI Aayog, Government of India, New Delhi, available at http://niti.gov.in/writereaddata/files/writereaddata/files/document_publication/Final_Report_Expert_Group_on_Land_Leasing.pdf, accessed 30 July 2022.

Hazell, P.B.R. (2005), 'Is There a Future for Small Farms?', *Agricultural Economics*, vol. 32, no. 1.

Jodha, N.S. (1981), 'Agricultural Tenancy Fresh Evidence from Dryland Areas in India,' *Economic and Political Weekly*, vol. 16, no. 52, pp. A118–28.

Kumar, P. (2006), 'Contract Farming Through Agribusiness Firms and State Corporation: A Case Study in Punjab', *Economic and Political Weekly*, vol. 41, no. 52, pp. 5367–75.

Mishra, P. and R. Suhag (2017), 'Land Records and Titles in India', *PRS Legislative Research*, New Delhi, available at http://www.prsindia.org/uploads/media/Analytical%20Report/Land%20Records%20and%20Titles%20in%20India.pdf, accessed 30 July 2022.

Mishra, S.K. and V. Rawal (2002), 'Agrarian Relations in Contemporary West Bengal and Tasks for the Left', in *Agrarian Studies: Essays on Agrarian Relations in Less-Developed Countries*, pp. 329–55, Tulika Books, New Delhi.

Murty, C.S. (2004), 'Large Farmers in the Lease Market: How and Why Do They Enter the Market? Are Marginal Farmers Affected in the Process?', Working Paper No. 55, Centre for Economic and Social Studies, Hyderabad, available at http://www.cess.ac.in/cesshome/wp/wp-55.pdf, accessed 30 July 2022.

Nadkarni, M.V. (1976), 'Tenants from the Dominant Class: A Developing Contradiction in Land Reforms', *Economic and Political Weekly*, vol. 11, no. 52, pp. A137–50.

National Sample Survey Organisation (NSSO) (1986), 'Some Aspects of Operational Holdings', Report No. 331, NSSO 37th Round, January–December, 1982, NSSO, Department of Statistics, Government of India, New Delhi, available at http://mospi.nic.in/sites/default/files/publication_reports/nss_report_331.pdf.

———— (1987), 'Some Aspects of Household Ownership Holdings', Report No. 330, NSSO 37th Round, January–December, 1982, NSSO, Department of Statistics, Government of India, New Delhi, available at http://mospi.nic.in/sites/default/files/publication_reports/nss_report_330_0.pdf.

———— (1992), 'Operational Land Holdings in India, 1991–92: Salient Features', Report No. 407, Land and Livestock Holdings Survey, NSSO 48th Round, January-December, 1992. NSSO, Ministry of Statistics, Programme Implementation, Government of India, New Delhi. http://mospi.nic.in/sites/default/files/publication_reports/407_final.pdf.

NITI Aayog (2015), 'Raising Agricultural Productivity and Making Farming Remunerative for Farmers', Government of India, available at: http://niti.gov.in/sites/default/files/2019-07/RAP3.pdf.

Padhee, A.K. and P.K. Joshi (2019), 'Why India Needs a Land Leasing Framework', IFPRI Blog, available at https://www.ifpri.org/blog/why-india-needs-land-leasing-framework.

Parthasarthy, G. (1991), 'Lease Market, Poverty Alleviation and Policy Options', *Economic and Political Weekly*, vol. 26, no. 13, pp. A31–38.

Planning Commission (2003), 'Tenth Five Year Plan: Volume II, Sectoral Policies and Programmes', Planning Commission, Government of India, New Delhi.

———— (2008), 'Eleventh Five Year Plan, Volume III: Agriculture, Rural Development, Industry, Services, and Physical Infrastructure', Planning Commission, Government of India, New Delhi.

Ramachandran, V.K. (2000), 'Kerala's Development Achievements and Their Replicability', in G. Parayil, ed., *Kerala: The Development Experience, Reflections on Sustainability and Replicability*, pp. 88–115.

Ramachandran, V.K., V. Rawal and M. Swaminathan, eds (2010), *Socio-Economic Surveys of Three Villages in Andhra Pradesh: A Study of Agrarian Relations*, New Delhi: Tulika Books.

Ramakumar, R. (2000), 'Magnitude and Terms of Agricultural Tenancy in India: A State-Wise Analysis of Changes in 1980s', *Indian Journal of Agricultural Economics*, vol. 55, no. 3.

Rawal, V. (2001), 'Agrarian Reform and Land Markets: A Study of Land Transactions in Two Villages of West Bengal, 1977–1995', *Economic Development and Cultural Change*, vol. 49, no. 3, pp. 611–29.

———— (2008), 'Ownership Holdings of Land in Rural India: Putting the Record Straight', *Economic and Political Weekly*, vol. 43, no. 10, pp. 43–47.

———— (2013), 'Changes in Distribution of Operational Holdings of Land in Rural India'. *Review of Agrarian Studies*, vol. 3, no. 2, pp. 73–104, available at http://www.ras.org.in/changes_in_the_distribution_of_operational_landholdings_in_rural_india.

———— (2014), 'Variations in Land and Asset Inequality', in V.K. Ramachandran and M. Swaminathan, eds, *Dalit Households in Village Economies*, New Delhi: Tulika Books.

Rawal, V. and S. Osmani (2009), 'Economic Policies, Tenancy Relations and Household Incomes: Insights from Three Selected Villages in India', available at http://archive.indianstatistics.org/misc/vrosmani2009.pdf.

Rawal, V. and V.K. Ramachandran (2013), 'Socio-Economic Surveys of Selected Villages in Rajasthan', Report, University Grants Commission, New Delhi.

Sachar Committee (2006), 'Social, Economic and Educational Status of the Muslim Community of India: A Report', Prime Minister's High-Level Committee for Preparation of Report on Social, Economic and Educational Status of the Muslim Community of India, Government of India, New Delhi, available at, http://mhrd.gov.in/sites/upload_files/mhrd/files/sachar_comm.pdf.

Satyasai, K.J.S. and N. Mehrotra (2016), 'Enhancing Farmers' Income', available at http://agricoop.nic.in/sites/default/files/12%20July%202016%20Sat%20kjss%20NM. pdf, accessed 30 July 2022.

Sawant, S.D. (1991), 'Comparative Analysis of Tenancy Statistics: Implications of Concealed Tenancy', *Artha Vijnana*, vol. 33, no. 1, pp. 12–23.

Shah, A. and B. Harriss-White (2011), 'Resurrecting Scholarship on Agrarian Transformations', *Economic and Political Weekly*, vol. 46, no. 39, pp. 13–18.

Sharma, A.N. and G. Rodgers (2015), 'Structural Change in Bihar's Rural Economy', *Economic and Political Weekly*, vol. 50, no. 52, pp. 45–53.

Sharma, H.R. (1995), *Agrarian Relations in India*, New Delhi: Har-Anand Publications.

———— (2009), 'Changing Tenancy Relations in Rural India', in D.N. Reddy, eds, *Agrarian Reforms, Land Markets and Rural Poor*, Centre for Rural Studies, Lal Bahadur Shastri National Academy of Administration, Mussoorie, New Delhi: Concept Publishing Company.

———— (2010), 'Magnitude, Structure and Determinants of Tenancy in Rural India: A State-Level Analysis', *Indian Journal of Agricultural Economics*, vol. 65, no. 1, p. 80.

Sharma, N. and J. Dréze (1996), 'Sharecropping in a North Indian Village', *The Journal of Development Studies*, vol. 33, no. 1, pp. 1–39, available at https://doi.org/10.1080/00220389608422451, accessed 30 July 2022.

Sidhu, H.S. (2005), 'Production Conditions in Contemporary Punjab Agriculture', *Journal of Punjab Studies*, vol. 12, no. 2, pp. 197–217.

Singh, I. (1989), 'Reverse Tenancy in Punjab Agriculture: Impact of Technological Change', *Economic and Political Weekly*, vol. 24, no. 25.

Singh, S. (2002), 'Contracting Out Solutions: Political Economy of Contract Farming in the Indian Punjab', *World Development*, vol. 30, no. 9, pp. 1621–38, available at http://www.sciencedirect.com/science/article/pii/S0305750X02000591, accessed 30 July 2022.

———— (2006), 'Corporate Farming in India: Is It a Must for Agricultural Development?', Indian Institute of Management, Ahmedabad.

———— (2012), 'Institutional and Policy Aspects of Punjab Agriculture: A Smallholder Perspective', *Economic and Political Weekly*, vol. 47, no. 4, pp. 51–57.

Srivastava, R. (1989), 'Tenancy Contracts during Transition: A Study Based on Fieldwork in Uttar Pradesh (India)', *The Journal of Peasant Studies*, vol. 16, no. 3, pp. 339–95.

Swaminathan, M. and A. Das, eds (2017), *Socio-Economic Surveys of Three Villages in Karnataka: A Study of Agrarian Relations*, New Delhi: Tulika Books.

Swaminathan, M. and V. Rawal, eds (2015), *Socio-Economic Surveys of Two Villages in Rajasthan: A Study of Agrarian Relations*, New Delhi: Tulika Books.

Thimmaiah, G. (2001), 'New Perspectives on Land Reforms in India', *Journal of Social and Economic Development*, available at http://www.isec.ac.in/Journal%203(2). pdf#page=5, accessed 30 July 2022.

Thorat, S. and K.S. Newman (2007), 'Caste and Economic Discrimination: Causes, Consequences and Remedies', *Economic and Political Weekly*, vol. 42, no. 41.

Thorat, S. and K.S. Newman, eds (2012), *Blocked by Caste: Economic Discrimination in Modern India*, New Delhi: Oxford University Press.

Tyagi, A. and Himanshu (2011a), 'Change and Continuity: Agriculture in Palanpur', Working Paper 48, Asia Research Centre, London School of Economics and Political Science, London, Available at: http://eprints.lse.ac.uk/38375/1/ARCWP48-TyagiHimanshu. pdf, accessed 30 July 2022.

———— (2011b), 'Tenancy in Palanpur', *Asia Research Centre*, London School of Economics and Political Science, London, available at http://eprints.lse.ac.uk/38374/1/ARCWP47-TyagiHimanshu.pdf.

Vyas, V.S. (1970), 'Tenancy in a Dynamic Setting', *Economic and Political Weekly*, vol. 5, no. 26, pp. A73–80.

3

The Forest Land Rights of Tribals

India's Experience with Special Reference to Maharashtra

Geetanjoy Sahu

With the enactment of the Scheduled Tribe and Other Traditional Forest Dwellers (Recognition of Forest Rights) Act, 2006 (henceforth FRA), an important shift in forest tenure occurred in India. At least 13 million acres of forest land were recognized or legally transferred to local forest dwellers across the country as of 31 December 2020 (MoTA 2020). Of these 13 million acres, 42,31,270 acres and 89,49,533 acres were recognized or transferred as individual forest rights (IFR) and community forest rights (CFR), respectively. The national average for the recognized forest area for IFR was still low at 2.2 acres as of 31 December 2020. However, the changes they brought in were significant. A total number of 19,20,507 IFR claims were recognized across the country.

There have been many reports and studies on the recognition process and the impact of CFR on local livelihoods and well-beings. But there is less evidence on the IFR recognition process under FRA and its impact on the livelihoods of forest title holders. In this chapter, an attempt is made to critically assess the role of state and non-state actors in the recognition of IFR and its implications on the livelihoods of forest dwellers. While we present national figures too, special focus is maintained on the experiences in the Palghar district of Maharashtra.

This chapter is divided into eight sections. The first section gives an overview of the forest-rights claims and recognition between 2008 and 2020. The second section outlines the method employed to collect the primary and secondary information. An overview of the study area is provided in the third section. In the fourth section, the institutional framework to enforce the recognition of IFR is discussed. The role of state and non-state actors in the recognition of IFR in the study area is highlighted in the fifth section and the status of recognition of IFR claims in presented. The sixth section assesses the implication of recognized IFR claims on the livelihoods in the study area. Conclusions summarize the discussion.

Key Provisions and Status of Implementation

The preamble of the FRA begins with a progressive statement emphasizing that this legislation is '. . . an Act to recognize and vest the forest rights and occupation in forest land in forest-dwelling Scheduled Tribes and other traditional forest dwellers who have been residing in such forests for generations but whose rights could not be recorded'.

In other words, the FRA is not a land distribution act; rather, it recognizes the pre-existing rights that forest dwellers enjoyed before colonial rule. The preamble further emphasizes that the non-regularization and non-recognition of forest dwellers' rights over forest lands, both during the colonial period and in independent India, have resulted in historical injustice to forest-dwelling communities. The FRA was an attempt to address this historical injustice by recognizing and vesting in forest dwellers, rights over all types of forests, irrespective of their ownership and classification. A careful reading of Section 2(a) of the FRA suggests that forest dwellers are eligible to claim not only their rights over the forest land within the boundary of their respective revenue villages, but also are entitled to own, access, use and manage their forest land within the traditional and customary boundaries of the village, irrespective of the classification of the forest. In other words, forest dwellers who have lived in and depended on any type of forest land on or before 13 December 2005 are eligible to claim their rights over this forest land. Another important dimension of the FRA is that the recognized rights can be inherited by family members of the title holder, which means that the title deed will pass on to the next generation of the title holder and cannot be alienated after his/her demise.

Sections 3(1) and 3(2) of the FRA recognizes all the customary and traditional rights of forest-dwelling communities over forest lands. Section 3(1) recognizes a bundle of rights. The bundle of rights is broadly divided into two types of rights: individual forest rights (IFR) and community forest rights (CFR). The provisions for IFR include the rights of forest dwellers to hold and live on the forest land under individual or common occupation for habitation or self-cultivation purposes. The provisions of CFR seek to restore all customary and traditional usufruct rights of forest-dwelling communities within the traditional or customary boundaries of the village, irrespective of the ownership, classification and size of forests. These rights include grazing and fishing rights, nistar rights,[1] and ownership, access, use and disposal rights of minor forest products traditionally collected within or outside village boundaries.

Status of Implementation of FRA

This section gives an overview of forest rights-claims and trends in the recognition of both IFR and CFR claims between 2008 and 2020. It is followed by a discussion on the major issues and concerns in the implementation of the FRA.

The MoTA, being the nodal agency, maintains a state-wise data set on the implementation status of FRA and presents it under two broad categories: IFR and CFR. In the absence of any other authentic data set on the status of the FRA across the country, Tables 3.1 and 3.2 present an analysis of the MoTA's Monthly Progress Report (MPR) data set, which documents claims till 31 December 2020.

The data in Tables 3.1 and 3.2 reveals that 96 per cent of the claims filed and recognized were for IFR. A deeper analysis of the data set further reveals that 64 per cent of IFR claims were from Odisha, Madhya Pradesh,

Table 3.1 *Status of individual forest rights claims till 31 December 2020*

Total number of IFR claims filed at the gram sabha level	41,09,105.0
Total number of IFR claims recommended by the gram sabha to SDLC*	27,35,229.0
Total number of IFR claims recommended by SDLC to DLC*	22,09,198.0
Total number of recognized IFR claims	19,20,507.0
Total number of rejected IFR claims	17,06,914.0
Total number of pending IFR claims	4,81,684.0
Total recognized forest areas (acres)	42,31,270.0
Average IFR recognized area (acres)	2.2

Note: * SDLC: Sub-divisional level committee; DLC: District level committee.
Source: MoTA (2020).

Table 3.2 *Status of community forest rights claims till 31 December 2020*

Total number of CFR claims filed at the gram sabha level	1,50,280.0
Total number of CFR claims recommended by the gram sabha to SDLC	1,06,868.0
Total number of CFR claims recommended by SDLC to DLC	98,078.0
Total number of recognized CFR claims	77,271.0
Total number of rejected CFR claims	47,984.0
Total number of pending CFR claims	25,025.0
Total recognized forest areas (acres)	89,49,532.5
Average CFR recognized area (acres)	115.8

Source: MoTA (2020).

Chhattisgarh, Maharashtra and Tripura (see Table 3.3). These five states also accounted for 71 per cent of the total number of recognized IFR claims and 76 per cent of the total recognized IFR lands in the country. Similarly, around 72 per cent of CFR claims were from Odisha, Madhya Pradesh, Chhattisgarh, Maharashtra and Gujarat; these states also constituted 87 per cent of recognized CFR claims and 86 per cent of total recognized CFR lands in the country (see Table 3.4).

The above analysis of the data set on the status of FRA implementation in 2008–20 reveals that its enforcement has been very uneven across the country. Several studies have also pointed to the serious concerns at the level of implementation of the FRA. In most villages across states, forest dwellers were simply unaware of the provisions of FRA. But even when they applied for their rights, especially IFR, their claims in many cases were: (i) left pending for several years; (ii) wrongly rejected; (iii) only partially granted; (iv) granted with the imposition of unreasonable conditions; (v) granted much smaller areas than claimed by the forest dwellers; (vi) not processed in the

Table 3.3 *Top five states with recognized IFR claims*, in numbers and acres

Name of the State	Claims received	Claims recognized	Area recognized (in acres)
Chhattisgarh	8,58,682	4,01,251	8,52,977.5
Odisha	6,23,252	4,41,529	6,65,580.0
Madhya Pradesh	5,85,266	2,30,028	8,27,160.0
Maharashtra	3,62,679	1,66,082	3,97,532.5
Tripura	2,00,696	1,27,981	4,65,572.5
Total	26,30,575	13,66,871	32,08,822.5

Source: MoTA (2020).

Table 3.4 *Top five states with recognized CFR claims*, in numbers and acres

Name of the State	Claims received	Claims recognized	Area recognized (in acres)
Madhya Pradesh	42,187	27,976	14,82,277.5
Chhattisgarh	31,558	21,967	20,62,022.5
Odisha	15,073	6,649	2,44,967.5
Maharashtra	12,087	7,084	27,68,720.0
Gujarat	7,187	3,887	11,79,722.5
Total	1,08,092	67,563	77,37,710.0

Source: MoTA (2020).

protected areas; and/or (vi) granted and recognized but the titles were not converted into record of rights (RoR) (Sundar 2019; Broome *et al.* 2019; TISS 2017; CFR-LA 2016).

Methodology

The analysis in the remaining sections of this chapter is largely based on primary data collected through personal interviews with forest-rights holders in the Palghar district of Maharashtra. For the analysis, 108 forest-rights holders were interviewed from twenty-two hamlets located in seven revenue villages under three blocks in Palghar district. The block-wise

Table 3.5 *Distribution of respondents in the study area*

District	Block	Gram Panchayat (village assembly)	Name of the hamlet	Type of Scheduled Tribes		
				Malhar Koli	Warli	Katkari
Palghar (108)	Dahanu (37)	Ambesari (10)	Ambesari	0	10	0
		Jamshet (27)	Dongripada	0	13	0
			Vasantwadi	0	11	0
			Mangadpada	0	3	0
	Palghar (34)	Tandulwadi (9)	Tandulwadi	0	7	0
			Dongarpada	0	2	0
		Saphale-Umbarpada (14)	Saphala	1	0	0
			Rodkhadpada	4	1	0
			Dehupada	1	0	0
			Raipada (Sartodi)	2	0	0
			Saruchapada	2	0	0
			Sarupada	0	3	0
		Maikhope (11)	Patilpada	2	0	0
			Zanzroli	3	1	0
			Bandate	2	2	0
			Dhondhalpada	0	1	0
	Vasai (37)	Tilher (13)	Tilher	8	0	0
			Jadhavpada	3	1	0
			Dhumalpada	1	0	0
		Batane (24)	Batane	0	3	0
			Batanepada	0	16	1
			Thalyachapada	0	4	0

Source: Survey data, 2019.

distribution of respondents was: Dahanu (37), Palghar (34) and Vasai (37). All the interviewed forest-rights holders were Scheduled Tribes (ST), though they were from different tribal communities. Out of the 108 respondents, 78 respondents belonged to the Warli tribe, 29 to the Malhar Koli tribe and one to the Katkari tribe. The main criterion to select respondents was the recognition of titles of forest dwellers before December 2015 so as to capture the impact of recognized rights on their livelihoods. The data collection was completed over two phases: April–May and November–December 2019.

We also interviewed the intervening actors, including both state and non-state actors, to assess their role in the recognition of IFR process and the provision of post-recognition support to the forest-rights holders.

Background to the Study Area

Palghar is located in the Konkan division of Maharashtra. It consists of eight administrative blocks namely, Jawhar, Mokhada, Talasari, Vasai, Vikramgad, Palghar, Dahanu and Wada. The district had a total population of 29,90,116 covering over 4,69,699 hectares of the total geographical area of Maharashtra. The tribal population in the Palghar district is 11,18,000, which constituted around 37 per cent of the total population in the district. Palghar was earlier part of Thane district and became a separate district on 1 August 2014. The formation of Palghar district was the outcome of a long struggle of tribals and farmers in this region. Land rights of tribal people was and continues to be a contentious issue in this region (see Khan 2015). Despite constitutional provisions for the protection and promotion of land rights in the Fifth Scheduled Areas,[2] alienation and deprivation of land continued in Palghar. In addition to lack of administration, support towards regularization of rights of people over land, the forest dwellers and farmers in Palghar also faced competing pressures from a number of infrastructure projects and real-estate projects. Because of its proximity to the Mumbai Metropolitan Region, the demand for land in Palghar district was always high. Several reports indicated that illegal selling of land, diversion of land for industrial projects and encroachment of land by real-estate agents, industrial forces and non-tribals were perceived by the tribal communities as an attempt to undermine Adivasi autonomy and evict them from their ancestral land (NCST 2019; Nair 2018; The Free Press Journal 2017).

Due to the lack of political and administrative will to regularize the land rights, increasing diversion of land and illegal occupation of tribal lands by non-tribals, land struggles and movements were an integral part of the Palghar history. Mobilization and formation of grassroots organizations began from the inception years and continues till date to assert tribal rights over land and forest resources. Some historical movements over land in this region include the Warli land-reforms movement, Gramdan movement,

Bhoodan movement, movement against Reliance Power Plant in Dahanu and the recent movement against the proposed bullet train project between Ahmedabad and Mumbai via Palghar (Sahu and Chawla 2011; Poyam 2020). These movements were historic because they sustained over the years and, to a great extent, successfully managed to negotiate their demands and rights over both agricultural land and forest land. With the FRA of 2006, another chapter in this struggle was inaugurated.

Between 2008 and 2020, a total number of 19,20,570 IFR and 77,271 CFR claims were recognized across India. However, the recognition of forest-rights claims varied from state to state and also within the states. Maharashtra was one of the leading states in recognizing IFR and CFR rights. The recognized IFR claims in Maharashtra constituted around 11 per cent of the total recognized claims in India. A total number of 3,74,766 forest rights claims, out of which 3,62,679 were IFR claims, 12,087 were CFR claims, were filed across Maharashtra as on 31 December 2020. The total number of recognized claims was 1,73,166 out of which 1,66,082 were IFR claims and 7,084 were CFR claims. Rights were recognized over 31,66,253 acres of forest land.

Within Maharashtra, Palghar district stood apart from the rest of the districts especially in the recognition of IFR claims. The highest number of IFR claims and recognitions in Maharashtra were effected in Palghar, followed by Gadchiroli and Nashik. A total number of 29,505 IFR claims were recognized in Palghar, which constituted 41 per cent of the total recognized IFR claims in the state (Sahu 2020). In this context, it will be interesting to investigate the claim processes, the factors that contributed to the enforcement of IFR and the outcomes of FRA execution in Palghar. The remainder of this chapter discusses these issues.

Institutional Framework for the Recognition of IFR

Section 6, Chapter IV of FRA outlines a highly democratic and decentralized procedure and institutional arrangement to recognize and vest forest rights in the forest-dwelling communities. A three-tier institutional arrangement is prescribed. The process of recognition begins at the gram sabha (village assembly) level with the formation of a Forest Rights Committee (FRC) consisting of not less than ten but not more than fifteen members. The president of the FRC shall be from the ST community. Two-thirds of the members of the FRC should be from the ST community and one-third of the members of the FRC should be women. The FRC is the executive arm of the gram sabha to receive claims, consolidate them, verify them and place them before the gram sabha to pass a resolution to that effect. Afterwards, a copy of the decision is forwarded to the second-tier body i.e. sub-divisional level committee (SDLC) at the tehsil level.

The SDLC consists of six members representing one member each from the revenue, forest and tribal welfare departments, and three members of the block- or tehsil-level panchayats (rural local bodies). The primary responsibility of the SDLC is to orient the gram sabha about the FRA provisions and provide necessary documents to gram sabhas during the claim filing process. The received claims from the gram sabhas need to be verified at the SDLC and forward the received claims to the district level committee (DLC) for final decision.

The DLC is the final authority to decide upon the claims forwarded to it by the SDLC. The DLC also consists of six members that include District Collector, Divisional Forest Officer, Officer of the District Tribal Welfare Department and three members of the district panchayats (rural local bodies). The DLC members have to examine all claims received from the SDLC and take a final decision over the submitted claims. It is also the responsibility of the DLC to issue directions for incorporation of the recognized forest rights in the relevant government records including record of rights.

Any person aggrieved by a decision of the gram sabha over his/her claim may, within a period of 60 days from the date of the resolution, file a petition to the SDLC. A similar procedure is also laid down for forest dwellers to appeal to the DLC if they are aggrieved by the decision of SDLC. It is also important to note here that no such petition shall be disposed of against the aggrieved person, unless he has been given a reasonable opportunity to present his/her case. To avoid any arbitrariness, Section 12 (A) (3) of FRA specifies that no claim can be rejected without communicating in person to the claimant. In a recent notification, the Office of the Governor of Maharashtra introduced another institutional arrangement i.e. a divisional level committee which will hear appeals from the claimants against the decision of the DLC. With this background about the institutional arrangement for the process of recognition, we now move on to discuss the nature and process of forest-rights recognition in the study areas.

Drivers of Implementation of Individual Forest Rights in Palghar

Over the last two decades, India has witnessed a series of unprecedented rights-based policies enacted by both the union and state governments. Some of them include the Mahatma Gandhi National Rural Employment Guarantee Act 2005; Right to Information Act 2005; National Rural Health Mission 2005; Forest Rights Act 2006; Right of Children to Free and Compulsory Education Act 2009; National Food Security Act 2013; and Right to Fair Compensation and Transparency in Land Acquisition, Rehabilitation and Resettlement Act 2013. These policies were unprecedented not only due to their socialist outlook but also because of the wide support they received across the political and civil society spectrum. Political regimes changed, but the policies continued. However, the major challenge for these policies has been their implementation at the grassroots level.

Non-implementation and non-compliance of policy and law is a common phenomenon in India. Several reasons explain this state of affairs but the most important reason is the lack of administrative and political will. This has resulted in interventions by many non-governmental organizations (NGOs) and non-registered public-spirited organizations at the grassroots to facilitate and bridge the gap between implementing agencies and potential beneficiaries (Yadav 2010). Though the chances of success of policy implementation due to the intervention of NGOs vary from policy to policy and also state to state, their presence and role in the policy implementation process has increased over the last two decades.

The case of FRA implementation in India is testimony to this increasing role of NGOs in driving the process of implementation at the grassroots level. Existing research and *prima facie* evidence suggest that there are broadly four types of grassroot interventions to enforce the FRA. First, intervention by the nodal agency of the FRA i.e. tribal department and authorities at local sub-district and district administration to provide information to people about the Act and their rights and the process to be followed to claim their occupied land. Second, the *suo moto* initiatives, mobilization and collective action by the villagers to assert their rights under FRA. Third, a group of villagers forming a village federation and working unitedly to claim their rights over the forest land as recognized under FRA. Fourth, interventions and facilitation by the NGOs and grassroots organizations including political parties in providing information, training and enabling the forest dwellers to claim their rights under the Act. Among these four interventions, several studies show that the nodal agency and district and sub-district administration failed in discharging their statutory duties. *Suo moto* and village federation initiatives were very rare and limited to few pockets in the country with a long history of collective action and forest management practice. So, the most crucial role and intervention in facilitating the implementation of FRA was by the NGOs and grassroots organizations, including political parties.

As in other parts of India, in the case of Palghar too, the role of four important organizations namely, Kashtakari Sanghatana, Bhoomi Sena, Shramjeevi Sanghatana (Organization of Toiling People), and the Communist Party of India (Marxist) are worth discussing. Before we explain the role and significance of each one of them in the forest-rights claims and recognition process, a brief description of these organizations is important.

The Kashtakari Sanghatana is a non-registered mass organization of mainly landless and marginal Adivasi farmers and labourers, which has been working in Thane and Palghar districts since 1978. According to the Sanghatana, it has organized its members to struggle for their rights over land (including forest land, tenancy land, land diversion for projects, encroachment by real estate groups, etc.), forests, health, education, water, rights of migrant labour, women's rights, against corruption and the implementation of rights-based legislations. The Sanghatana does not contest elections but has occasionally, including in the recent elections, supported the left parties.

The Bhoomi Sena (Land Army) was initiated in the early 1970s by Kaluram Dhodade, one of the most powerful voices among Adivasi leaders in India. Ever since its inception, the Bhoomi Sena was struggling against exploitation and injustice, either in the field or in the factory. This non-registered organization's main goal was 'land to tiller'. The organization largely believed in constitutional methods to achieve its goals by focusing on protest, mobilization, legal advocacy and dialogue strategies in the study areas of Palghar.

The Shramjeevi Sanghatana (Organization of Toiling People), constituted in the late 1970s, has led struggles to release and rehabilitate bonded labourers in Maharashtra. They fought to release thousands of bonded tribal families and organized them against the bonded-labour system in Palghar. The movement later spread to other parts of India. The organization also mobilized various movements of tribals, labourers and marginal farmers to fight for their minimum wages, for the restoration of alienated land and for the right to education for migrant child labourers. In the recent past, the organization has expressed its support to the right-wing political party i.e., Bharatiya Janata Party (BJP).

The Community Party of India (Marxist), or the CPI (M), was very active in Palghar since the late 1940s itself. After the famous Warli revolt that it led in 1947 in the Thane district, the CPI (M), through its affiliated organizations like Maharashtra Rajya Kisan Sabha, mobilized people around issues of ownership of land by Adivasis, the low prices their products fetched, their lack of access to forests, the low wages paid to landless labourers, and the system of forced labour.[3] Over the last seven decades, the CPI (M) was steadfast in fighting for the land rights of forest dwellers and had broadened its support base beyond the peasant classes (Khan 2015). It is the only political party that has been very vocal and also in the forefront in Maharashtra demanding the effective implementation of FRA and PESA. It has also led massive protests across Maharashtra challenging the arbitrary rejection of forest rights claims by the authorities.

Though these organizations have different ideological positions and support bases, what was common was their consistent demand for recognition to land rights of people and ending the exploitation by landlords and state agencies. These organizations supported each other on certain issues but also fought bitter political battles against each other, including violence and killing of each other's workers and leaders in the past (Singh 2013). The conflict of interest and organized support base of each of these organizations resulted in each identifying their intervening areas and respecting others' areas of work by not interfering in each other's demarcated villages in advancing their goals. The field insights from three blocks clearly illustrated the demarcated areas of operation of these organizations in mobilizing forest dwellers for the claims under FRA. Nevertheless, the role of each one of them was significant in driving the process of forest-rights claims and recognition at the implementation level. The activities of these organizations included capacity building and awareness among forest dwellers about the forest rights act, mobilizing forest dwellers to assert their rights, facilitating the claim filing process, demarcation of claimed land, and gathering evidence on the claimed land. Legally, these initiatives were supposed to be undertaken by the SDLC, but data in Table 3.6 clearly show how non-state actors were crucial in informing the forest dwellers about the provisions of the Act. Only four IFR holders said that they came to know about FRA from the revenue officer.

Secondly, around 90 per cent of the claims submitted in the study areas were initiated by the non-state actors. More importantly, as Table 3.7 shows, majority of the claims were from the landless forest dwellers. This clearly reflects the goal of the grassroots organizations and the CPI (M) to ensure land titles to the most marginalized communities in the study areas.

Thirdly, while thousands of villagers across India were still struggling and were yet to file their forest-rights claims even after twelve years of FRA implementation, 90 per cent of the claims were filed in the study villages in the first year of FRA implementation itself (see Table 3.8). This was unique and was possible due to the presence and consistent struggle of the non-state actors demanding land rights to the forest dwellers.

Table 3.6 *Awareness about the Forest Rights Act, Palghar district, 2019*

From whom did you come to know about the Forest Rights Act?	Frequency	Percentage
Villagers	3	2.8
Gram sabha meeting	2	1.9
Gram sevak (rural local body secretary)	1	0.9
NGOs/grassroots organizations	79	73.1
Forest rights committee	1	0.9
Communist Party of India (Marxist)	17	15.7
Revenue officer	4	3.7
Others	1	0.9
Total	108	100.0

Source: Survey data, 2019.

Table 3.7 *Facilitating agencies and landholding status of claimants*

Name of facilitating agencies	Number of claims facilitated	Land holding status of the claimants	
		Was owner of revenue land before filing forest rights claim	Was landless but cultivating over forestland before filing of forest rights claim
Kashtakari Sanghatana	11	8	3
Shramjeevi Sanghatana	48	12	36
CPI (M)	16	6	10
Bhoomi Sena	23	3	20
Local Government Officers	10	6	4
Total	108	35	73

Source: Survey data, 2019.

Table 3.8 *Title recognition trend in the study areas*

Year	IFR claim filed (frequency)	Percentage	IFR claim recognized (frequency)	Percentage
2008	90	83.3	1	0.9
2009	5	4.6	1	0.9
2010	6	5.6	61	56.5
2011	2	1.9	0	0.0
2012	2	1.9	0	0.0
2013	2	1.9	31	28.7
2012	0	0.0	12	11.1
2015	1	0.9	2	1.9
Total	108	100.0	108	100.0

Source: Survey data, 2019.

Fourthly, under Section 4 (3) of the FRA, the claimant, irrespective of being a tribal or any other traditional forest dweller, had to prove that he/she was primarily residing in forest or forests land and dependent on the forest or forests land for bonafide livelihoods prior to 13 December 2005.[4] In the case of other traditional forest dwellers (OTFD), it was required to prove that they were primarily residing in and dependent on the forests or forest land for bonafide livelihood needs for at least three generations (each generation being twenty-five years).[5] Several studies have found that major-

Table 3.9 *Types of evidence attached by the forest rights claimants*

Sl. No	Types of evidence submitted	Number of claimants
1	Fine receipts issued by the forest department	57
2	Oral evidence of senior citizens	24
3	Name in the encroachment list of government	05
4	Grazing tax	10
5	Miscellaneous	12
	Total number of applicants	108

Source: Survey data, 2019.

ity of the claims that were rejected across India were due to the failure of claimants to submit two minimum evidential documents proving that the claimed land was under her/his occupation on or before 13 December 2005 (TISS 2017).

But in Palghar, producing minimum two evidential documents was not a difficult task for the claimants, due to the commendable role played by the facilitating organizations. These organizations, through their long association with the villagers, collected and consolidated all the government records, notifications, fine receipts of the forest department and all the past judgments of the Maharashtra High Court and the Supreme Court of India applicable to the villages (see Table 3.9). The government records, fine receipts and court orders recognized their presence, even though it recognized them as encroachers in many cases and not as the legal entitles. These government records were sufficient to prove that they were living or dependent on that forest land for their livelihood. The forest dwellers, whom the authorities earlier labelled as encroachers, were now recognized as the legal holders of that land under the FRA.

The above discussion helps us to understand how difficult it could be to process IFR claims in the absence of well-organized grassroots organizations and the political will of political parties. A recent report on the status of FRA implementation also suggests that in all the top five leading states in the recognition of IFR claims – Odisha, Maharashtra, Madhya Pradesh, Chhattisgarh and Tripura – the engagement of forest rights groups, NGOs, facilitating civil society groups and the CPI (M) made a huge difference in comparison to other states (TISS 2017). The analysis of the database of forest rights claims in Palghar reveals that not a single claim was rejected at the DLC level, and only 1,275 claims were pending at the DLC level against the 60,304 filed claims by the forest dwellers, which was just 2.1 per cent of the total filed IFR claims. The rejected and pending claims at the DLC level in Palghar were also very low compared to the national-level figures.

At the national level, the rejected claims constituted 41.5 per cent of the filed IFR claims, and the pending claims constituted 11.7 per cent of the filed IFR claims.

There were, however, a few challenges in getting the total claimed area approved and converting the recognized forest land into the RoR. A recent study showed that while the FRA promised to recognize up to a maximum 4 hectares for IFR claims, the average recognized area for IFR claims in India was only 2.18 acres (Sahoo and Sahu 2019). The average IFR recognized area in Maharashtra was 2.33 acres, but the average IFR recognized area in Palghar was only 1.03 acres. There was, thus, a huge gap between the claimed area and the recognized area in Palghar. In the study area, the average recognized area was 0.73 acre (see Table 3.10).

Table 3.11 presents a comparative picture of the role of facilitating organizations in their respective intervening areas. The highest number of claims were facilitated by Shramajeevi Sanghatana and lowest number of claims were facilitated by the local government office. The maximum area for IFR claim was made with the help of Shramajeevi Sanghatana and the local government office, whereas the claims facilitated by CPI (M) had lesser area. The average time taken to get the claimed area recognized was not less than three years. Out of 108 IFR claimants, only ten claimants received the claimed area and two facilitating organizations namely, Sarmajeevi Sanghatana and CPI (M), had appealed against the lesser recognized claims on behalf of thirty-five claimants. All the IFR claimants received their title's original document copy, except sixteen IFR claimants. However, irrespective of whether the original title was received or not, or whether the recognized area was lesser than the claimed area, the forest dwellers continued to occupy and carry on their agricultural activities on the claimed land. Not a single IFR claimant faced any obstacle to continue their activities because they had been told by the facilitating agencies that they were the legal owners of the forest land occupied before 13 December 2005.

Table 3.10 *Gap in the claimed and recognized area in the study areas*

Palghar		Dahanu		Vasai		Study sample IFR claims (108)	
Total claims: 34		Total claims: 37		Total claims: 37			
Average IFR claimed areas (in acres)	Average IFR recognized areas (in acres)	Average IFR claimed areas (in acres)	Average IFR recognized areas (in acres)	Average IFR claimed areas (in acres)	Average IFR recognized areas (in acres)	Average IFR claimed areas (in acres)	Average IFR recognized areas (in acres)
2.046	1.388	2.47	1.397	3.25	1.1	2.56	0.730

Source: Survey data, 2019.

Table 3.11 *Overall performance of facilitating organizations*

Name of facilitating agencies	Total number of claims facilitated	Average claimed area (in acres)	Average recognized area (in acres)	Number of appeals against the lesser recognized area	Average time taken to get the title (years)	Recognized area same as claimed area	Total number of record of rights prepared
Kashtakari Sanghatana	11	1.79	0.725	0	4.64	0	0
Shramajeevi Sanghatana	48	3.29	0.638	23	2.52	3	0
CPI (M)	16	1.56	0.714	11	4.25	5	0
Bhoomi Sena	23	1.71	0.922	0	3.56	2	0
Local government office	10	3.40	0.857	1	2.00	0	0
Total	108	2.56	0.731	35	3.40	10	0

Source: Survey data, 2019.

Implications of the Recognized IFR Claims

Legally protected individual forest tenure is widely recognized as an essential foundation for improving the socio-economic and material conditions of the households. The impacts of forest tenure security rights on local poverty and socio-economic benefits have been widely established. Although the security benefits of community forest tenure on local well-being are well recognized, the impacts of individual forest tenure security rights under the FRA have not been adequately assessed.

Section 16 of the FRA Amendment Rules of 2012 specifies that the state government shall ensure through its departments that all government schemes including those relating to land improvement, land productivity, basic amenities and other livelihood measures are provided to such claimants and communities whose rights have been recognized and vested under the Act.

Maharashtra was not only one of the leading states to recognize different types of rights, it also led the country in its interventions after the recognition of community forest rights. A recent analysis of post-FRA intervention in Maharashtra showed that a total number of 87 orders, guidelines and notifications were issued between 2008 and 2018 by different departments, including the Tribal Development Department, Governor Office, Rural Development, Revenue and Forest Department and Planning Department of Maharashtra to upscale the implementation of FRA, enhance the livelihoods of forest dwellers and prepare forest management plans (Sahu *et al.* 2019). For example, in its resolution issued on 22 March 2016, the Tribal Development

Department allocated Rs 18 crores for the installation of solar/bore pump sets on IFR-recognized areas from a special central assistance scheme.

However, there were several challenges too. The forest-rights claim recognized under the FRA is a legal title in the form of a signed document by the competent authority. The recognized title is non-transferable and inalienable, but heritable. Therefore, the final title document given to the forest-rights holder should have a clear description of the forest right conferred, the demarcation of boundaries and other relevant information. In reference to the RoR, Rule 12 A of the FR Rules (as amended on 6 September 2012) provides that on the completion of the process of recognition of rights and issue of titles, the Revenue and Forest Departments are required to prepare a final map of forest land so vested. The concerned authorities are also required to incorporate the forest rights so vested in the revenue and the forest records within a specified period of record updating. This position has been reiterated in the Ministry of Tribal Affairs circular dated 3 March 2014, which noted that the FRA process will be complete only when the RoR was created.

On 2 January 2012, the Revenue and Forest Department of Maharashtra issued an order stating that all titles issued under FRA should be recorded in the 7/12 (RoR) extract under the column 'Other Rights'. The titles under FRA will be heritable, but non-alienable. The names of the husband and the wife should be recorded as title holders. In case the title holder(s) is without a direct heir, the nearest family member should be appointed as the heir. The ownership of the land, however, will continue to be under the Forest Department, Government of Maharashtra. Similarly, on 28 December 2018, the Tribal Development Department issued an order directing to ensure that IFR title holders are issued independent 7/12 (RoR) extracts by actual measurement of the land.

However, despite these clarifications from the MoTA and state government, the district administration in Palghar did not initiate efforts towards recording in the RoR. There was no database available in the public domain on the status of RoR. It was found that out of 108 surveyed forest-rights-recognized claims, not a single forest-rights holder received 7/12 (RoR) with their name in the 'Other Rights' column. This resulted in multiple disabilities and denial of full enjoyment of rights recognized under the Act. The lack of proper RoR resulted, amongst others, in the denial of credit from financial institutions; forced mortgaging of land; lack of access to crop insurance and loan waiver; lack of crop loss compensation; and lack of access to various schemes for farmers, which required producing the RoR. The system of giving only titles in the form of a signed document was also totally incapable of handling the inheritance claims that came up. There was the lack of a well-structured land management framework as provided under the Maharashtra Land Record Code to address these issues.

Our survey showed that the facilitating organizations did not pay adequate attention to the RoR issue. The Revenue and Forest Department took notice of the fact that IFR titles in some districts of Maharashtra were not given 7/12 (RoR) copies and that such IFR titles were still classified as forest compartments. It therefore issued a circular on 2 November 2016 stating that such title holders should be given access to bank loans and other schemes based on their IFR titles. On 28 December 2018, the Tribal Development Department issue an order requesting the district collectors to inform the banks to remove the hurdles in accessing formal credit. The collector was also required to chalk out plans to allow the IFR title holders to access other government schemes. It also stated that the IFR title holders should be given priority in land improvement schemes and income-augmenting schemes. They should also be given preferential priority for the shortlisting of beneficiaries for schemes under the departments of agriculture, tribal development and rural development.

Nevertheless, these schemes continued to be out of access for forest dwellers and their applications were not processed on the ground that their title had not been recorded as RoR. Despite government orders, no respondent received any bank loan. Here, the role of the facilitating agencies was poor. Discussions with the IFR title holders showed that no interest was taken by the facilitating agencies to link their recognized title to government schemes. The only scheme that was integrated with the IFR land was the MGNREGS (Table 3.12).

There is increasing recognition in the literature that legally secured individual forest rights provide a critical foundation for household income generation and land productivity. Past experiences with land reforms in India also suggest that there were multiple challenges in the improvement of the productivity of the land after its distribution. The analysis of post-recognition

Table 3.12 *Status of post-forest rights recognition benefits and interventions*

Name of the taluka	Total number of claimants interviewed	Conversion of record of rights of recognized claims	Bank loan provided to the recognized claimants	Total number of beneficiaries of MGNREGS for land labelling
Palghar	34	0	0	29
Dahanu	37	0	0	14
Vasai	37	0	0	29
Total	*108*	*0*	*0*	*63*

Source: Survey data, 2019.

impacts in Palghar suggests that there was no learning from past experiences. Promising progress has been made in many countries that opted for secure tenure rights, particularly in Latin America and China, by providing technical and institutional support and targeted policies to improve land productivity (DFID 2002). In the study areas, however, these strategies remained absent, and their implementation and enforcement were far from materializing.

Conclusions

This study on the recognition process for IFR claims and its impact on the local livelihood and land productivity of the recognized forest areas aimed to contribute to efforts to improve the quality of implementation process of FRA and identify the challenges to integrate line department schemes with forest rights holders' recognized lands. It is hoped that the results will be useful for state administrators, practitioners and forest-rights groups who are engaged in this process. It is also expected that this study will generate interest among research scholars to focus on the impact of individual forest tenure security on the socio-economic and material conditions of forest dwellers in rural areas.

Notes

[1] *Nistar* rights refer to concession rights over forest land and resources as recognized by erstwhile rulers or zamindars before independence.

[2] Under Article 244 (1) of the Constitution of India, the 'Scheduled Areas' are defined as 'such areas as the President may by order declare to be Scheduled Areas' – as per paragraph 6(1) of the Fifth Schedule. The criteria for declaring any area as a 'Scheduled Area' under the Fifth Schedule are: preponderance of tribal population, compactness and reasonable size of the area, a viable administrative entity such as a district, block or taluk, and economic backwardness of the area as compared to the neighbouring areas. These criteria are not spelt out in the Constitution of India but have become well established. The Fifth Schedule provides protective legal provisions, such as increased Adivasi control over land rights as well as self-governance in predominantly Adivasi areas. It also provides for laws with specific applicability only to these areas. The Panchayats (Extension to Scheduled Areas) Act, 1996, further protects the Adivasi community's access to land and resources. These laws mandate prior consent of the community for land acquisition for any public or private project.

[3] The Warli revolt of 1947 was a wide struggle against exploitation and oppression that sought to change production relations in the Thane district, and it provided the Kisan Sabha with a base among the Adivasis of the region, enabling it to take up issues affecting the Adivasi people even after the revolt was over.

[4] There is no scientific or specific reason why the cut-off date is 13 December 2005. It was kept in accordance with the day the bill was tabled in the Parliament.

[5] Experts involved in the drafting of the Act were of the opinion that the clause of 75 years of occupation and dependent on forest land was introduced at the eleventh hour by the MoTA and there was no clarity and justification on why there was a separate provision for OTFDs.

References

Broome, N.P., S. Ajit and M. Tatpati (2019), 'The Indian Forest Act's Proposed Amendment is Dangerous and Fanciful', 3 May, *Down To Earth*, available at https://www.downtoearth.org.in/blog/forests/the-indian-forest-act-s-proposed-amendment-is-dangerous-and-fanciful-64319, accessed 10 January 2020.

Community Forest Rights-Learning Advocacy (CFR-LA) (2016), 'Promise and Performance: Ten Years of the Forest Rights Act in India', Citizens' Report of the Promise and Performance of The Scheduled Tribe and Other Traditional Forest Dwellers (Recognition of Forest Rights) Act 2006, after 10 years of its Enactment, December 2016, Produced as part of Community Forest Rights-Learning Advocacy Process (CFR-LA), India, 2006, www.fra.org.in.

Department for International Development (DFID) (2002), 'Better livelihoods for Poor People: The Role of Land Policy', available at https://www.iatp.org/sites/default/files/Better_Livelihoods_for_Poor_People_The_Role_of.htm, accessed on 10 January 2020.

Khan, S. (2015), 'The Kisan Sabha and Adivasi Struggles in Thane District after 1947', *Review of Agrarian Studies*, vol. 5, no. 1, January–June, pp. 112–36.

Ministry of Tribal Affairs (MoTA) (2020), 'Monthly Progress Report on Forest Rights Act', Government of India, New Delhi, available at https://tribal.nic.in/FRA.aspx.

Nair, S. (2018), 'Even as Vasai Man was Fighting for His Land, 4 Buildings on it got OC', *The Times of India*, 10 November, available at https://timesofindia.indiatimes.com/city/mumbai/even-as-vasai-man-was-fighting-for-his-land-4-buildings-on-it-got-oc/articleshow/66562774.cms, accessed 20 April 2020.

National Commission for Scheduled Tribes (NCST) (2019), 'On the Spot Inquiry Report in the Matter of Alienation of ST Land by Non-ST at Sativali Village, Palghar', available at https://ncst.nic.in/sites/default/files/hearings_proceedings/2371.pdf, accessed 20 April 2020.

Poyam, A. (2020), 'In Palghar a Site of Historic Resistance, Adivasis Once Evicted, Oppose a Bullet Train Project', *Caravan Magazine*, 25 March, available at https://caravanmagazine.in/communities/in-palghar-site-of-historic-resistance-adivasis-once-evicted-oppose-a-bullet-train-project, accessed 20 April 2020.

Sahoo, U. and G. Sahu (2019), 'Twelve Years Later: Implementation of the Scheduled Tribes and Other Traditional Forest Dwellers (Recognition of Forest Rights) Act 2006', *Indian Journal of Social Work*, vol. 80, no. 4, pp. 423–38.

Sahu, G., P.S. Fernandes, A.A. Date, J. Dongare and H. Patange (2019), 'Compendium of Orders, Circulars, Resolutions and Notifications of Maharashtra Government in the Post-Forest Rights Act Enactment Phase From 2008–2018', Tata Institute of Social Sciences, Mumbai.

Sahu, G. (2020), 'Community Forest Rights Implementation: Experiences in the Vidarbha Region of Maharashtra', *Economic and Political Weekly*, vol. 55, no. 18, 2 May, pp. 42–48.

Sahu, G. and M. Chawla (2011), 'Environmental Movements in Dahanu: Competing Pulls', *Economic and Political Weekly*, vol. 46, no. 49, 3 December, pp. 10–14.

Singh, C.U. (2013), 'CPI-M Supporters Renew Campaign of Terror Against Villages Dominated by Kashtakari Sanghatana', *India Today*, 17 July, available at https://www.indiatoday.in/magazine/indiascope/story/19831031-cpi-m-supporters-renew-campaign-of-terror-against-villages-dominated-by-kashtakari-sanghatana-771160-2013-07-17, accessed 20 April 2020.

Sundar, N. (2019), 'A Mahagatbandhan in the Forests is the Need of the Hour', The Hindu Centre for Politics and Public Policy, 23 April, available at https://www.thehinducentre.com/the-arena/current-issues/article26862187.ece, accessed 20 April 2020.

Tata Institute of Social Sciences (TISS) (2017), 'A Rapid Assessment Study on Rights Recognition Process Under Forest Rights Act: Reasons of Rejection and Impact of

Rights Recognized on Livelihood in Odisha, Jharkhand and Chhattisgarh', Project Report, Mumbai.

The Free Press Journal (2017), 'Maharashtra: Despite Protests, 460 Hectares of Tribal Land in Palghar to be Diverted for Development of Industries', 27 November, available https://www.freepressjournal.in/cmcm/maharashtra-despite-protests-460-hectares-of-tribal-land-in-palghar-to-be-diverted-for-development-of-industries, accessed on 20th April 2020.

Yadav, S. (2010), 'Public Policy and Governance in India: The Politics of Implementation', *The Indian Journal of Political Science*, vol. 71, no. 2, April–June, pp. 439–57.

II

Investment and Expenditure in Agriculture

4

Agricultural Investment in India

A Chequered History

S.L. Shetty

There is surely a case for taking a wholesome view of overall economic development to further the cause of agricultural development in India (see Shetty 1990). This chapter is devoted to the singular aspect of the vicissitudes in agricultural investment over different phases of the country's development and the relative shares of public and private investment in agriculture. Additionally, the chapter also deals with questions on whether agricultural subsidies have crowded out public investment in agriculture, the motivation for private investment in the context of changes in terms of trade, the adoption of labour-saving mechanization and the growth of institutional credit flow, which are all crucial issues that have surfaced in the debate on agricultural investment in India.

Introduction

Undoubtedly, Indian agriculture has been facing a crisis situation over the past quarter of a century. When the erstwhile Planning Commission introduced a radical departure in the plan objectives in the form of 'not just faster growth but also inclusive growth' in the then Eleventh Five-Year Plan (2007–08 to 2011–12) document, one of the important strategies proposed was to recognize the neglect of agriculture in the planning process and correct it. It aimed at nearly doubling the average agricultural growth from about 2.4 per cent per annum during the then Tenth Plan period (2002–03 to 2006–07) to 4 per cent per annum in the Eleventh Plan period and also to similarly accelerate the growth of public sector capital stock in agriculture from about 2.3 per cent per annum in the Tenth Plan to 4.0 per cent in the Eleventh Plan period.

In fact, amongst different phases that Indian agriculture passed through after the green revolution of the 1970s, the year 2004–05 in the middle of the Tenth Plan was a turning point in agricultural growth. With a view to correcting the development crisis faced by the agricultural sector, the Mid-Term Appraisal of the Tenth Five-Year Plan (2002–03 to 2006–07) proposed multipronged steps to address the malaise: large budgetary allocations for agriculture, a National Horticulture Mission, reforming of the agricultural extension system, improving the agricultural terms of trade, reforming the agricultural marketing arrangements through the model Agricultural Produce Market Committees (APMC) Act, Bharat Nirman Project to upgrade the rural infrastructure, and finally, doubling of bank credit for agriculture (See Deokar and Shetty 2014). However, as the then Twelfth Plan document (2012–13 to 2016–17) summed up, many of these pious goals remained unfulfilled.

> Public investment in agriculture, which was stepped up very substantially in the last three years of the Tenth Plan, stagnated in the Eleventh Plan. This was mainly because of a large shortfall in planned investment in irrigation. As a result, a key part of the Eleventh Plan strategy to achieve 4 per cent agricultural growth, which was to increase public investment in agriculture to 4 per cent of agricultural GDP and thereby achieve growth of public sector capital stock in agriculture at least equal to the required 4 per cent growth of total capital stock, had not fructified. (Planning Commission 2013)

As Bisaliah, Mahendra Dev and Saifullah (2013) wrote, a series of steps would be required to rejuvenate agricultural growth, of which public investment would be the most critical.

> All these growth promoting agents require investment in agriculture. But one of the most disquieting developments in the agricultural sector during the last decade has been the neglect of capital formation in agriculture, especially in public sector. Many of the problems of agricultural sectors, viz., low productivity, low employment opportunities, high intensity of poverty and inadequate infrastructure, are attributed to inadequate and progressive decline in public investment in physical capital [irrigation and electrification, roads, markets, etc.], human capital [health, education and training] and development of non-farm sector. (Bisaliah, Mahendra Dev and Saifullah 2013, p. 62)

Secondly, in a detailed study on the existing status of agriculture, Kumar, Chauhan and Maredia (2013) pointed out another facet of investment in agriculture. They noted that

> agriculture [was] facing complex challenges of declining factor productivity, degrading soil and water resources, rising food and energy prices, and increasing frequency of extreme climatic events. On the other hand,

resources for research are scarce; India spends only about 0.6 per cent of its agricultural gross domestic product in agricultural research, much less than the average of about 2–25 per cent in developed countries. (Kumar, Maredia and Chauhan 2013, p. 374)

Thirdly, structural change in the Indian economy has implied that there was a steady decline in the share of agricultural GDP (AGDP) in the aggregate GDP from about 55 per cent in 1950–51 to 17.8 per cent in 2019–20. However, about 53 per cent of the country's workforce continued to be dependent on agriculture. Obviating this dichotomy would require that India focusses on the condition of its small and marginal farmers.

Fourthly, following from the third point, one of the most complex issues of India's agrarian scene that hinders sizeable agricultural investment is the increasing marginalization of landholdings along with rising fragmentation. Data from the Agricultural Census show that the number of operational holdings more than doubled from 70.5 million in 1970–71 to 146 million in 2015–16. Due to high population pressure and the uneconomic nature of tiny holdings, the average size of operational holdings dwindled from 2.3 hectares in 1970–71 to 1.08 hectares in 2015–16. Due to these structural features including urban migration, the total area operated declined from 162 million hectares in 1970–71 to 157.8 million hectares in 2015–16. More significantly, 68.5 per cent of operational holdings are marginal holdings of below one hectare as against 50.6 per cent in 1970–71. If the small farmer category of 1 to 2 hectares is also included (which stood at 22.9 per cent of all holdings in 2015–16), as much as 86 per cent of operational holdings belonged to the small and marginal categories. Together, they accounted for about 46.9 per cent of the total operated area in 2015–16. They possessed such tiny operated areas with the averages for marginal and small holdings at 0.38 hectares and 1.4 hectares, respectively.

Fifthly, reform and developmental activities in the agricultural sector will have to be focussed on the marginal farmer category. The mass of farmer households belonging to marginal holding category – as much as 69 per cent of total operational holdings accounting for about 24 per cent of the land operated – become the obvious candidates for moving out of agriculture. Their economic situation may be characterized as unsustainable. Improving their skill levels for non-farm activities ought to be one of the most important priority areas for policy action. It should also be facilitated by amending tenancy regulations, which will in turn allow banks to provide credit facilities for tenant cultivators.

Finally, added to all the above and/or as a consequence of all the above, India has the spectacle of a highly unequal growth scenario in the agricultural sector. To quote Bisaliah, Mahendra Dev and Saifullah (2013):

Polarized growth instead of broad-based virtuous growth has given rise to growth enclaves, bypassing a large segmentation of agriculture. The outcome of this polarized growth is agricultural segmentation with the rural affluent elite, dynamic farmers with roots in agriculture, and home and footloose farmers waiting for the 'opportunity' to leave agriculture. (Bisaliah, Mahendra Dev and Saifullah 2013, p. 61)

It is in this broad background that we discuss the trends and patterns of public and private investments in agriculture in this chapter.

Phase-Wise Behaviour of Agricultural Investment
Periodization of the Trends in Agricultural GCF
To begin with, we have attempted a broad overview of the trends in agricultural gross capital formation (GCF) between 1950–51 and 2016–17. The time series data are based on the Central Statistics Office's National Accounts Statistics (NAS); they relate to (1) back series of 1993–94 base year data; (2) back series of 2004–05 base year data; and (3) the series based on the current 2011–12 series. Thus, we have the long time-series of GCF in agriculture for six decades and seven years (1950–51 to 2016–17). As the vast series are based on different base years, we have the data for some common years for various base year series for comparison purposes.

Based on the nature of public policies that have evolved over years for agriculture growth, the long period of 67 years since the economic planning process began in 1950–51 has been classified into the following five phases, with an attempt to caricature the broad trends in agriculture investment, as also investments by public and private sectors separately. This periodization was largely derived from the Twelfth Five-Year Plan document (Planning Commission 2013, pp. 4–10).

(1) The pre-green revolution period, 1951–52 to 1967–68
(2) The green revolution period, 1968–69 to 1980–81
(3) The mild liberalization period, 1981–82 to 1990–91
(4) Early liberalization period, 1990–91 to 1997–98
(5) The late liberalization period, 1998–99 to 2016–17

The summary of the major changes in policies and trends across these five phases are presented in Table 4.1.

Methods of Measuring Agricultural Investment
Amongst possible multiple measures of indicating the importance of agricultural investment, we have chosen two simple and commonly-used measures:

(a) Agricultural GCF as a percentage of the economy-wide GCF indicat-

Table 4.1 *A summary of the different phases of agricultural investment growth*

Phases	Nature of agricultural investment behaviour
Pre-green revolution period (1951–52 to 1967–68)	There was some flush of enthusiasm in the first decade of planning on large-scale irrigation projects and hence higher public sector investment in agriculture. Otherwise, after some initial push, overall agricultural investment rate stagnated.
Green revolution period (1968–69 to 1980–81)	This period saw a steady improvement in public sector investment in agriculture and some fractional improvement in private investment. Overall, this was the best period when the total agricultural GFC to agricultural GDP was the highest in post-independence India.
Wider coverage and mild liberalization period (1981–82 to 1990–91)	This was the period when focus shifted from intensification of green revolution in select areas to new areas. This was also the period when the nature and quality of state intervention in the economy began to be weakened, particularly in the fiscal, monetary and trade policies. This period also saw a distinct edging down of public sector investment, a moderate increase in private investment and a relative stagnation in total investment.
Early liberalization period (1990–91 to 1997–98)	This period saw a steady decline in public investment, reductions in private investment and a slump in total agricultural investment.
Period of private investment revival (1998–99 to 2016–17)	This period saw a slowdown in public investment, but accompanied by a rapid increase in private investment and also an increase in overall investment (as shown by GCF to agricultural GDP/GVA ratios). These could be traced to the commodity boom, rise in terms of trade, the faster flow of institutional credit to agriculture and faster growth of farm wages, which provided an inducement to labour-substituting investment.

ing the relative importance of investment in agriculture in aggregate investment of the economy;

(b) Agricultural GCF as percentage of GDP/GVA (gross value added) originating in the agricultural sector, the sector being defined in a broad way comprising crops, forestry, and logging and fishing.[1] This ratio is presented separately for public and private sectors.

Agricultural GCF to Total GCF Ratios

Figures 4.1, 4.2 and 4.3 present the crude year-wise ratios of agricultural GCF as percentages of nation-wide GCF as per the 1993–94, 2004–05 and 2011–12 series, respectively. The results presented for overlapping years

Figure 4.1 *Agricultural GCF as a percentage of aggregate GCF at current and constant prices (based on 1993–94 series): 1950–51 to 2002–03*

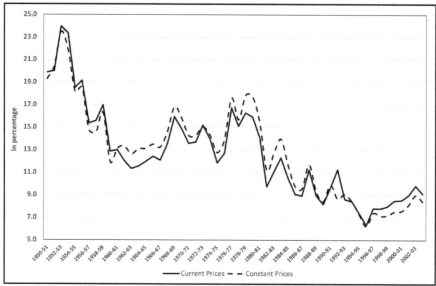

Source: The original data are from the Central Statistics Office's National Accounts Statistics, various issues.

Figure 4.2 *Agricultural GCF as a percentage of aggregate GCF at current and constant prices (based on 2004–05 series): 1980–81 to 2012–13*

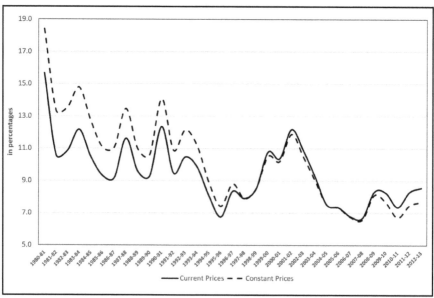

Source: The original data are from the Central Statistics Office's National Accounts Statistics, various issues.

Figure 4.3 *Agricultural GCF as a percentage of aggregate GCF at current and constant prices (based on 2011–12 series): 2011–12 to 2018–19*

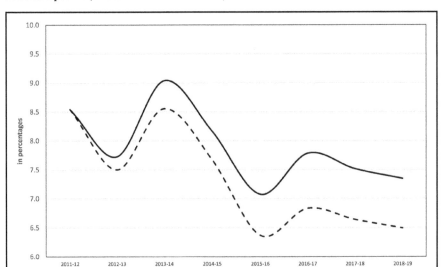

Source: The original data are from the Central Statistics Office's National Accounts Statistics, various issues.

differ but the overall trend appears comparable. For 1980–81, for instance, the 1993–94 series provides an agricultural GCF to total GCF ratio at current prices of 14.1 per cent, but the corresponding ratio at the 2004–05 series was 15.7 per cent. For the next year 1981–82, there was a sharp decline to 9.7 per cent as per the 1993–94 series and 10.6 per cent as per the 2004–05 series. In other words, the trends appear comparable.

The crude ratios presented in the figures provide interesting results. First, the share of agricultural GCF in total GCF declined over time, both at current and constant prices. Second, the share was hovering around 12 per cent to 20 per cent during the first three decades of the 1950s, 1960s and 1970s. Thereafter, it steeply dipped to lower levels, generally ranging from 7 per cent to 10 per cent and touching as low as less than 7 per cent in some years.

Some interesting revelations emerge from a comparison of these ratios of GCF at current and constant prices. Conceptually, if the current price ratio is higher than the constant price ratio, it implies that the farmers have to bear a relatively higher cost of capital goods prices than the average price other sectors pay for capital goods. This was the situation during the early 1950s of the pre-green revolution period. The situation was reversed in the post-green revolution period when current price ratios became lower than the constant price ratios and the farmers faced relatively lower prices for capital goods.

Interestingly, this trend continued till about the end of the early liberalization period (1997–98). There was thus a long period in the post-green revolution period when the farmers paid relatively lower prices for their investment goods than the average prices of capital goods borne by other sectors. Interestingly, after the start of the commodity boom and significant improvement in agricultural terms of trade, there was a queer behaviour of the agricultural GCF to total GCF ratios across current and constant price estimates. As shown in Table 4.2, agricultural terms of trade distinctly improved during the last period, but the GCF ratios at current prices were

Table 4.2 *Agricultural terms of trade index based on wholesale price indices (WPI)*

Year	Food and non-food articles index	Manufactured products index	Terms of trade index (2/3*100)
(1)	(2)	(3)	(4)
WPI – Base Year 2004–05 = 100			
2005–06	103.39	102.42	100.95
2006–07	112.49	108.22	103.95
2007–08	121.47	113.39	107.13
2008–09	133.51	120.38	110.90
2009–10	151.00	123.05	122.71
2010–11	176.65	130.07	135.81
2011–12	190.44	139.51	136.51
2012–13	209.55	147.06	142.50
2013–14	232.98	151.46	153.83
2014–15	243.92	155.12	157.25
2015–16	252.32	153.42	164.46
2016–17	265.04	157.38	168.41
WPI – Base Year 2011–12 = 100			
2012–13	111.41	105.30	105.80
2013–14	123.20	108.50	113.55
2014–15	128.01	111.20	115.12
2015–16	131.35	109.20	120.28
2016–17	136.45	110.70	123.26
2017–18	138.18	113.80	121.43
2018–19	139.32	117.90	118.17
2019–20	150.04	118.30	126.83

Note: Column 4 is derived by author.
Source: Office of the Economic Advisor, Ministry of Commerce and Industry, Government of India.

higher, though fractionally, than the constant price estimates (see Figures 4.1, 4.2 and 4.3). A possible explanation for this could be that during the commodity boom period, prices of capital goods too rose at a rapid rate and, hence, farmers did not receive any extra benefit insofar as their relative cost of investment goods were concerned.

Agricultural GCF to Agricultural GDP/GVA

We now attempt to study the trends in agricultural GCF in relation to agricultural GDP/GVA. An interesting revelation in the estimates of agricultural GCF to agricultural GDP ratios is the distinct contrast they show against the trends in the ratios of agricultural GCF to total GCF. The former showed some distinct improvement in the past decade or so, unlike in the ratios of agricultural GCF to total GCF. They had remained generally below the two-digit level for five decades i.e., until the end of the 1990s. Thereafter, it steadily increased from 8.4 per cent in 1998–99 to 13.5 per cent in 2004–05 and 18.2 per cent in 2011–12; finally, it settled down at around 15 per cent. But the ratio of agricultural GCF to total GCF showed a persistent decline over the decades. This probably reflects the persistent decline in the share of agriculture in the country's total GDP.

We also present these ratios separately for public and private sectors. Figures 4.4, 4.5 and 4.6 and Figures 4.7, 4.8 and 4.9 depict long-term trends in these series. As the figures show, the trends in agricultural investment rates fit into various phases of agricultural growth summarized in Table 4.1. In the pre-green revolution period, for instance, the GCF–GDP ratio hardly showed any uptrend. It showed an initial increase from 3.4 per cent in 1950–51 to 5.5 per cent of agricultural GDP in 1955–56 but thereafter, through the second and third plan periods, the ratio steadily fell to 4.4 per cent in 1967–68, i.e., on the eve of the green revolution period. As brought out earlier, the green revolution period was the best period for agriculture if we go by the agricultural investment ratios. Agricultural GCF to agricultural GDP ratio steadily firmed up during the period and attained the highest level of 10 per cent in 1978–79 or 10.7 per cent in 1979–80 (Figure 4.4). Throughout the subsequent phases of agricultural development, such a concentrated focus on agricultural sector was lost in the milieu of liberalization and the urban orientation of the development process.

Slowdown in Public Sector Investment

The concentrated focus on agricultural investment, referred to above, concerned higher tempo of investment by the public sector. As shown in Figure 4.7, during the green revolution period, public sector investment rate steadily rose from 1.4 per cent in 1967–68 to 4.2 per cent in 1979–80, the best in post-independence history. But this dynamism in public sector invest-

Figure 4.4 *Agricultural GCF as a percentage of agricultural GDP at current and constant prices (based on 1993–94 series): 1950–51 to 2001–02*

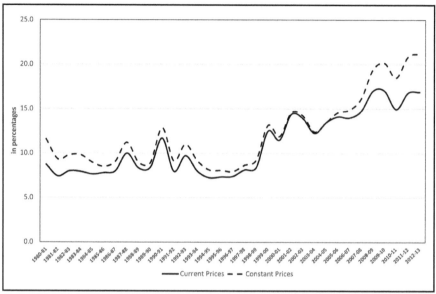

Source: Central Statistics Office's National Accounts Statistics 2005 (1993–94 series) and new series of National Accounts Statistics (base year 1993–94).

Figure 4.5 *Agricultural GCF as a percentage of agricultural GDP at current and constant prices (based on 2004–05 series): 1980–81 to 2012–13*

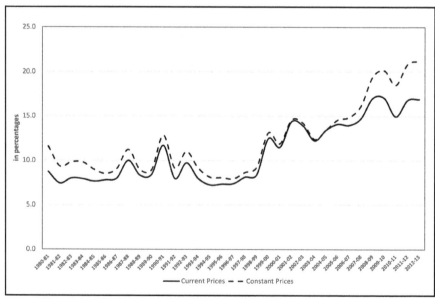

Source: The original data are from the Central Statistics Office's National Accounts Statistics, various issues.

Figure 4.6 *Agricultural GCF as a percentage of agricultural GVA at current and constant prices (based on 2011–12 series): 2011–12 to 2018–19*

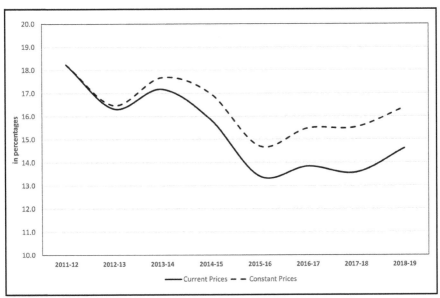

Source: The original data are from the Central Statistics Office's National Accounts Statistics, various issues.

Figure 4.7 *Agricultural GCF as a percentage of agricultural GDP – public and private sectors (based on 1993–94 series): 1960–61 to 2002–03*

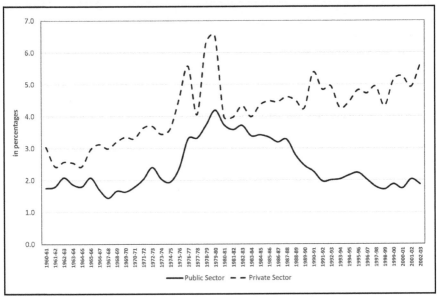

Source: Central Statistics Office's National Accounts Statistics 2005 (1993–94 series) and new series of National Accounts Statistics, (base year 1993–94).

Figure 4.8 *Agricultural GCF as a percentage of agricultural GDP: public and private sectors (based on 2004–05 series): 1980–81 to 2012–13*

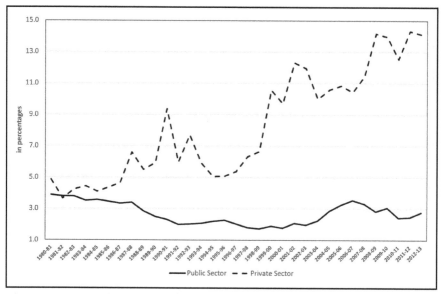

Source: Central Statistics Office's National Accounts Statistics 2005 (1993–94 series) and new series of National Accounts Statistics (base year 1993–94).

Figure 4.9 *Agricultural GCF as a percentage of agricultural GVA for public and private sector (based on 2011–12 series): 2011–12 to 2018–19*

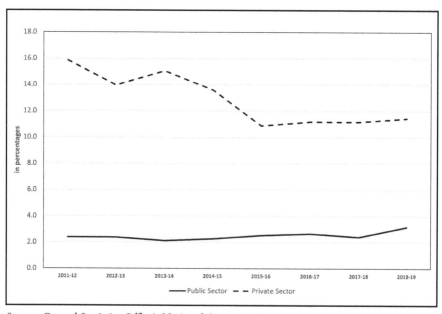

Source: Central Statistics Office's National Accounts Statistics, various issues.

ment did not last thereafter. Public sector investment rate slowed down in the 1980s but after liberalization in the 1990s, the fall was much steeper. The public sector GCF rate, which had attained the peak of 4.2 per cent in 1979–80, finally ruled at less than 2 per cent in the late 1990s, both as per the 1993–94 NAS series as well as the 2004–05 series.

The Twelfth Five-Year Plan document (Planning Commission 2013) had corroborated the above; it brought out how the average annual growth in public sector net fixed capital stock in agriculture had slipped from 3.9 per cent in the 1980s to 2 per cent in the early liberalization period and 1.4 per cent in the Ninth Five-Year Plan period (i.e. 1997–98 to 2001–02).

Departure from the Trend after the Commodity Boom, 2000–01 Onwards

As depicted in Figures 4.7 and 4.8, historically, the private sector investment rate behaved parallel to the public sector investment rate for four decades until the end of the 1980s. While we have not attempted any rigorous econometric exercise here, the broad behaviour of the rates of public and private investments does suggest that public sector investment crowded in private sector investment, and that increases in private sector investment largely followed the increases in public sector investment.[2]

Public sector investment rate rose from just 1.8 per cent of agricultural GDP in 1960–61 to 4.2 per cent in 1979–80 i.e., at the height of the green revolution period. Concurrently, the rate of private sector investment rose from 3.0 per cent in 1960–61 to the peak of 6.5 per cent in 1979–80. For the next decade or so, both public and private sector rates of capital formation were lower than those in the preceding period: a little over 3 per cent in the public sector and a little over 4 per cent in the private sector.

But after the economic reforms began in the early 1990s, there was a distinct divergence between private sector investment rate and public sector investment rate (Figures 4.8 and 4.9). As per the 2004–05 series of NAS, public sector investment rate in agriculture, which had ruled at 3.9 per cent in 1980–81 and 3.4 per cent in 1987–88, steadily fell thereafter and reached the low level of just 1.8 per cent in 2000–01. Contrariwise, the corresponding private investment rate in agriculture, which was at 4.9 per cent in 1980–81, increased to 6.6 per cent in 1987–88, and thereafter, though the rate fluctuated, overall, it has been on an uptrend, touching the high rates of 10.6 per cent in 1999–2000 and 9.7 per cent in 2000–01.

What was more noteworthy was the vastly rapid increases in the private sector investment rate after the beginning of the current century. The rate, which was at 9.7 per cent in 2000–01, steadily increased to 14.1 per cent in 2012–13 as per the 2004–05 series, or a value in the range of 13.6 per cent to 15.9 per cent between 2011–12 and 2014–15 as per the revised 2011–12 series.[3] The Planning Commission in the Twelfth Five-Year Plan document attributed it to two key factors (see Planning Commission 2013, pp. 7–10):

(1) The main driver of this was a large relative price shift in favour of agriculture, showing that farmers respond to price incentives; and
(2) While private investment in irrigation and water-saving devices did increase, the largest increase was in labour-saving mechanization. This was a natural response to growing labour scarcity which is reflected in rising wages (ibid., p. 8).

Making a critical assessment of the implications of these phenomena, the same plan document further cautioned thus:

> Labour saving mechanization, a significant contributor to the sharp increase of private investment in the Eleventh Plan period, was a natural response to tighter labour markets and rising wages. But while mechanization helped farmers to cope with labour scarcity, it exacerbated a decline in capital productivity. Private capital stock in agriculture has increased twice as fast as agricultural GDP since the Ninth Plan and, although mitigated by terms of trade gains and a debt write-off, continued investment with declining capital productivity may not be sustainable.
>
> While greater private investment in farming is desirable where it reflects both an ability to invest and a desire to increase farm productivity, the same phenomenon can become a source of distress if farmers keep investing to cope with shrinking natural resources, more frequent adverse weather and less assured labour supply, and do not get adequate returns for this investment. (Ibid., p. 9)

Alleged Trade-Offs Between Subsidies, Agricultural Investment and Other Productive Expenditures

There is enough empirical evidence that inadequate and rapidly declining rate of public investment was a constraint on agricultural growth. This – associated with inadequate attention to institutional changes in agriculture like tenancy reforms, strengthening of extension agencies, greater attention on agricultural education and research and building up of rural infrastructure – was the cause for the sector's poor growth performance.

A major allegation in this context was that the decline in agricultural investment and infrastructure was because of an unsustainable rise in the subsidy burden in the government's budget. These subsidies were extracted by the politically powerful rich farmers' lobby through huge amounts of input and other agricultural subsidies. A number of studies argued in favour of reducing agricultural subsidies and increasing public investment in agriculture (Chand 2009; Mahendra Dev 1997). Varied deleterious effects of agricultural subsidies on ground water utilization, climate change and increasing inequalities in the distribution of benefits were highlighted. Even the then Planning Commission in its Twelfth Five-Year Plan document argued thus: 'The imbalance between subsidy expenditure and expenditure on public investment raises the issue whether a shift away from subsidies and towards greater public investment would not be beneficial' (Planning Commission 2013, p. 13).

The Plan document also provided 'evidence' on this imbalance between subsidies and public investment. Table 4.3 reproduces these data. It shows that the size of subsidies grew more than three-fold from Rs 35,001 crore in 2002–03 to Rs 1,16,488 crore in 2010–11; as per a reply to a question in the Parliament, it rose further to Rs 1,53,743 crore in 2011–12. Also, this size of subsidies constituted three times the size of public investment in agriculture.

We, however, wish to take a more cautious view on this issue. While we agree that there are some broad inequalities in the distribution of agricultural subsidies, withdrawal of input subsidies in agriculture may cause serious disturbances in agricultural prices and result in unsustainable levels of inflation and other distortions in the economy. Subsidies are indeed a very inefficient way of resorting to public expenditures for development. But they are necessitated by a distorted pattern of overall development. By the same logic, there are many forms of inefficient and unequal uses of public expenditure, all of which need to be addressed in a wholesome manner and not in a partial and truncated manner. Above all, the question of growing inequality is relevant in the context of the greatly unequal way of mobilizing tax resources. The best example is the way marginal tax rate for the urban richer segments was reduced from 40 per cent to 30 per cent by the union government.

Overall, there is a case for reducing current expenditures as farm subsidies and expanding capital expenditures for agriculture. But, such a change in development strategy cannot be undertaken in isolation. It has to be a part of a wider strategy of inclusive development under which intensive focus should be conferred on both the sides of public finance: resource mobilization as well as more balanced distribution of expenditures. There is an acute need for public expenditures on social sectors or for physical infrastructures and manufacturing. This is a behavioral question of public policy planners. If they were serious about the acute need for public investment in agriculture, more tax mobilization should be made possible. But in reality, the planners showed no interest in raising public investment in agriculture after the easy flush of enthusiasm in the first two decades of planning on large-scale irrigation projects.

Indeed, the next stage of diversification in agriculture called for somewhat different sets of investments in a series of rural and agricultural infrastructures including networks of warehouses, go-downs, commercial refrigerators and extension infrastructure. The failure was, in retrospect,

Table 4.3 *Public sector capital formation and subsidies to agriculture (centre and states)*, in Rs crore and as per cent to GDP from agriculture and allied activities at current prices

1	Public GCF agriculture and allied		Budgetary subsidies (CSO)		Food subsidy		Total fertilizer subsidy		Subsidy on indigenous urea		All other agriculture subsidies		Total subsidies other than food subsidy (5+6+7)	
	2		3		4		5		6		7		8	
Tenth Plan														
2002–03	9,563	2.0	43,597	9.0	24,176	5.0	11,015	2.3	7,790	1.6	16,196	3.3	35,001	7.2
2003–04	12,218	2.2	43,765	8.0	25,181	4.6	11,847	2.2	8,521	1.6	15,258	2.8	35,626	6.6
2004–05	16,187	2.9	47,655	8.4	25,798	4.6	15,879	2.8	10,243	1.8	16,221	2.9	42,343	7.5
2005-06	20,739	3.3	51,065	8.0	23,077	3.6	18,460	2.9	10,653	1.7	20,181	3.2	49,294	7.8
2006-07	25,606	3.5	59,510	8.2	24,014	3.3	26,222	3.6	12,650	1.7	21,924	3.0	60,796	8.3
Eleventh Plan														
2007-08	27,638	3.3	85,698	10.2	31,328	3.7	32,490	3.9	12,950	1.5	34,830	4.2	80,270	9.6
2008-09	26,692	2.8	1,56,823	16.6	43,751	4.6	76,603	8.1	17,969	1.9	54,438	5.8	1,49,010	15.8
2009-10	33,237	3.1	1,39,248	12.9	58,443	5.4	61,264	5.7	17,580	1.6	37,121	3.4	1,15,965	10.7
2010-11	34,548	2.7	1,50,170	11.8	63,844	5	62,301	4.9	15,081	1.2	39,106	3.1	1,16,488	9.2
2011-12	36,887												Total Rs. 1,53,743 Crore	10.2

The following figures of agricultural subsidies were revealed in a Parliamentary Reply dated 8 February 2014 for 2011–12:

Note: As explained in the source, public sector agricultural GCF and agricultural GDP are from CSO, National Accounts Division; budgetary subsidies are also from CSO and are based on the economic and purpose classification of Government expenditure. Food and fertilizer subsidies are from budget documents of the Central Government. 'All other agriculture subsidies' in the table are defined as budgetary subsidies (CSO) plus subsidy on indigenous urea minus food subsidy. This is because CSO classifies food subsidy as subsidy to agriculture bur classifies subsidies on indigenous urea as subsidy to industry.
Source: Planning Commission (2013).

in the absence of inclusive planning and not necessarily in the diversion of resources in favour of subsidies away from agricultural investment. Therefore, in my view, it is wrong to argue that 'the main reason for decline in public sector investments is the diversion of resources from capital account to current account i.e., from capital formation to subsidies' as Chand (2009) argued.

Role of Institutional Credit in Private Investment in Agriculture

While explaining the key drivers of accelerated private investment in agriculture in the recent period, the Twelfth Five-Year Plan document restricted itself to two factors: relative price shift in favour of agriculture, and impetus to labour-saving mechanization. We, however, find that a major public policy shift in the form of doubling of farm credit under 'priority sector' bank credit dispensation also played a key role in facilitating private investment in agriculture.

The 'comprehensive credit policy' announced in 2004 envisaged doubling of agricultural credit every three years, or at a rate of 30 per cent every year, starting from 2004–05. The policy was carried forward for many blocks of successive three years. Data presented in Table 4.4 show how rapid increases took place in the flow of institutional credit after 2004–05. There was a 103 per cent increase between 2004–05 and 2007–08 and a 75 per cent increase between 2007–08 and 2010–11. The credit flow was sizeable even in relation to agricultural GDP/GVA estimates. Credit to GDP ratio in agriculture shot up from 16.0 per cent in 2003–04 to 22.2 per cent in 2004–05, to 35.5 per cent in 2009–10 and to 42.9 per cent in 2016–17.

It should be conceded that the bulk of the institutional credit was in the form of short-term production credit – generally more than two-thirds of the total credit flow. Even so, the extent of term loans granted was impressive in relation to the amount of private capital formation in agriculture. As shown in Table 4.5, term loans as percentage of private GCF in agriculture shot up from 36.0 per cent in 1999–2000 to 108.6 per cent in 2005–6 and 120.5 per cent in 2006–07. Though the proportion fell thereafter, it remained high ranging from 48 per cent to 135 per cent, implying that the availability of institutional funds played a key role in the acceleration of private investment in agriculture year after year.[4] As noted by the Planning Commission, this was the period when farm wages firmed up and farmers chose to adopt labour-saving mechanization. The confluence of the three factors – better terms of trade, inducement to use labour-saving mechanization and liberal availability of institutional loans – contributed to a noticeable improvement in private investment in agriculture without any push from public investment. To an extent, this situation cannot be sustained, and there is vast scope for the public sector to expand its investment in agricultural extension, education and research – a role which only the public agencies can play.

Table 4.4 *Flow of institutional credit to agricultural credit*, in Rs crore

Year	Production (short-term) credit	Medium-term/long-term credit	Grand total	Agricultural GDP/GVA	Production (ST) credit	MT/LT credit	Grand total
					As percentage of agricultural GDP/GVA		
(1)	(2)	(3)	4= (2)+(3)	(5)	(6)	(7)	(8)
1999–2000	28,965	17,903	46,868	4,55,302	6.4	3.9	10.3
2000–01	33,314	19,513	52,827	4,60,608	7.2	4.2	11.5
2001–02	40,509	21,536	62,045	4,98,620	8.1	4.3	12.4
2002–03	45,586	23,974	69,560	4,85,080	9.4	4.9	14.3
2003–04	54,977	32,004	86,981	5,44,667	10.1	5.9	16.0
2004–05	76,062	49,247	1,25,309	5,65,427	13.5	8.7	22.2
2005–06	1,05,350	75,136	1,80,486	6,37,772	16.5	11.8	28.3
2006–07	1,38,455	90,945	2,29,400	7,22,984	19.2	12.6	31.7
2007–08	1,81,393	73,265	2,54,658	8,36,518	21.7	8.8	30.4
2008–09	2,10,461	91,447	3,01,908	9,43,204	22.3	9.7	32.0
2009–10	2,76,656	1,07,858	3,84,514	10,83,514	25.5	10.0	35.5
2010–11	3,19,108	1,27,671	4,46,779	13,19,686	24.2	9.7	33.9
2011–12	3,96,158	1,14,871	5,11,029	15,01,947	26.4	7.6	34.0
2012–13	4,73,500	1,33,875	6,07,375	16,75,107	28.3	8.0	36.3
2013–14	5,48,435	1,81,687	7,30,122	19,26,372	28.5	9.4	37.9
2014–15	6,35,412	2,09,916	8,45,328	20,93,612	30.4	10.0	40.4
2015–16	6,65,312	2,50,197	9,15,509	22,25,368	29.9	11.2	41.1
2016–17	6,89,457	3,76,298	10,65,755	25,18,662	27.4	14.9	42.3
2017–18	7,54,972	4,13,531	11,68,503	27,96,908	27.0	14.8	41.8
2018–19	7,52,209	5,04,620	12,56,830	29,22,846	25.7	17.3	43.0

Source: Agricultural Statistics at a Glance 2014, 2017 and 2019, Ministry of Agriculture and Farmers' Welfare.

Concluding Observations

We shall make four concluding observations in summary.

(1) The absence of an inclusive planning strategy was reflected rather conspicuously in the persistent neglect of agricultural investment throughout the post-independence era except for a brief green revolution period.

(2) Restive farm households extracted concessions from the state, in the form of varied subsidies and increased credit flows from institutional agencies. Growing subsidies arose from a distorted pattern of development.

Table 4.5 *Agricultural GCF financed by term loans of financial institutions*

Year	Term loans (Rs crore)	GCF – agriculture, forestry and fishing (Rs crore) (private)	Term loans as % of private GCF (agriculture, forestry and fishing)
1999–00	17,303	48,126	36.0
2000–01	19,513	44,751	43.6
2001–02	21,536	61,341	35.1
2002–03	23,974	57,959	41.4
2003–04	32,004	54,472	58.8
2004–05	49,247	59,909	82.2
2005–06	75,136	69,204	108.6
2006–07	90,945	75,496	120.5
2007–08	73,265	95,679	76.6
2008–09	91,447	1,33,655	68.4
2009–10	1,07,858	1,51,325	71.3
2010–11	1,32,741	1,65,396	80.3
2011–12	1,14,871	2,38,174	48.2
2012–13	1,33,875	2,33,747	57.3
2013–14	1,81,687	2,90,009	62.6
2014–15	2,09,916	2,84,544	73.8
2015–16	2,50,197	2,42,388	103.2
2016–17	3,76,298	2,81,529	133.7
2017–18	4,13,531	3,12,487	132.3
2018–19	5,04,620	3,34,525	150.8

Source: Term loan figures are compiled from Agricultural Statistics at a Glance, 2019, 2017 and 2014; GCF figures have been culled out from various publications of National Account Statistics. Data for base year 2011–12 has been used for the years from 2011–12 to 2016–17 and data for base year 2004–05 has been used for the years from 2004–05 to 2010–11.

Unless an egalitarian pattern of development is adopted, mere withdrawal of subsidies will give rise to many distortions in the macroeconomy.

(3) Despite the absence of public sector investment support, the farm community responded to the market forces – reflected in high terms of trade for agriculture and higher farm wages – in the form of higher private investment through labour-saving mechanization. This process was substantially facilitated by the increased availability of institutional credit.

(4) All of these, together, contributed to an accentuation of overall inequalities in the farm sector.

The author wishes to place on record his sincere appreciation of the help rendered by Bipin Deokar, Vijayata Sawant, Harshada Parab, Pravin Jadhav and K. Srinivasan. He also sincerely thanks J. Dennis Rajakumar for his comments on an earlier version of this paper.

Notes

[1] We have compiled extensive data on the trends in GCF in all these sectors separately but not discussed here. For instance, private GCF in the 'fishing' sector during the past two decades has been quite impressive. We have also worked out gross fixed capital formation (GFCF) to GDP ratios; the broad results presented here do not contradict their trends and hence they are not discussed here.

[2] This is a profound theme requiring some rigorous econometric exercise on causal relationships, which we have not attempted here. Our observation is based on the visual view of the behaviour of data series and their graphs and some informed economic logic. A comprehensive historical study on this theme has been that of Gulati and Bathla (2001).

[3] The CSO has reported a higher revision of 9.4 per cent in the GCF of 'agricultural and allied activities' in the revised 2011–12 series as compared with the earlier estimates of GCF as per 2004–05 series (CSO 2015, p. 131).

[4] The proportions of credit to investment ruling at more than 100 per cent appear odd indeed. Even credit share coming closer to 100 appears odd as banks do keep margins against assets. These possibly are attributable to estimational issues in credit flow as well as capital formation. There is no way of reconciling them here. But overall trend appears realistic and reliable.

References

Bisaliah, S., S. Mahendra Dev and S. Saifullah (2013), *Investment in Indian Agriculture: Macro and Micro Evidences*, New Delhi: Academic Foundation, in association with Mumbai: Indira Gandhi Institute of Development Research (IGIDR).

Central Statistics Office (CSO) (2015), *Changes in Methodology and Data Sources in the New Series of National Accounts: Base Year 2011–12*, Ministry of Statistics and Programme Implementation, Government of India, New Delhi, June.

Chand, R. (2009): 'Capital Formation in Indian Agriculture: National and State Level Analysis', in D.N. Reddy and S. Mishra, eds, *Agrarian Crisis in India*, New Delhi: Oxford University Press, pp. 44–60.

Deokar, B.K and S.L. Shetty (2014), 'Growth in Indian Agriculture: Responding to Policy Initiatives since 2004–05', *Economic and Political Weekly*, Review of Rural Affairs, vol. 49, nos 26 and 27, 28 June, pp. 101–04.

Gulati, A. and B. Seema (2001), 'Capital Formation in Indian Agriculture: Revisiting the Debate', *Economic and Political Weekly*, Special Article, vol. 36, no. 20, 19 May, pp. 1697–708.

Kumar, S., S. Chauhan and M.K. Maredia (2013), 'Research Priorities for Faster, Sustainable and Inclusive Growth in Indian Agriculture', *Indian Journal of Agricultural Economics*, Conference Number, vol. 68, no. 3, July–September, pp. 373–88.

Mahendra Dev, S. (1997), 'Subsidies and Investments in Indian Agriculture: Issues and Perspectives', RGICS paper no. 39, Rajiv Gandhi Institute for Contemporary Studies (RGICS), New Delhi.

Planning Commission (2013), *Twelfth Five Year Plan (2012–2017): Economic Sectors*, vol. 2, New Delhi: Sage Publications.

Shetty, S.L. (1990), 'Investment in Agriculture: Brief Review of Recent Trends', *Economic and Political Weekly*, Special Article, vol. 25, no. 7–8, 17–24 February, pp. 389–98.

5

Public Spending Priorities for Agriculture and Allied Sectors in Recent Years

Insights from the Union and Select States

Gurpreet Singh and Sridhar Kundu

Introduction
Background

Following the adoption of neoliberal economic reforms in the early 1990s, India witnessed drastic changes in its fiscal policy. It led to reduced budgetary support towards a number of areas, which adversely impacted all those sectors (e.g., in education, health and agriculture) where public sector provisioning was crucial in the context of a low-income country with harsh economic, social and regional disparities. In the subsequent phases of economic reforms, especially after mid-1990s, public provisioning for agriculture and allied sector witnessed squeezing, with an overall shrinking (or stagnation) in public spending of the country through its annual budgets (Acharya and Das 2012; Jha and Acharya 2011). The decline in public spending in agriculture had severe implications on the livelihoods of millions of workers. Inadequate public spending in agriculture was associated with declining farm income and increasing cost of cultivation, which made farming, especially small farming, less viable (Misra and Hazell 1996; Gill and Singh 2006; Vaidyanathan 2006; Fan, Gulati and Thorat 2008; Reddy and Mishra 2010).

A number of policies and budgetary measures were introduced in the later part of 2000s to revive the agrarian economy. As a result, there was some improvement in the growth of the agricultural sector (Acharya and Das 2012). Despite these improvements, the level of farm income did not witness much increase. The growth of farm income in real terms increased by only 3.6 per cent between 2003–04 and 2013–14. In the recent years too, a number of schemes and programmes were implemented by the union as well as state governments, most notably an income support scheme to double the farmers' income by 2022 (Chand 2017). However, there were still no signs of recovery. The country witnessed unrest among the farming community manifested in various agitations and increasing number of farm suicides.

A robust and sustained revival of the agricultural sector necessarily requires a number of significant changes in the overall policy framework for the agrarian sector. Complementary provisioning of resources from the union and state budgets for the agriculture and allied sectors would be crucial in this regard. Given this backdrop, the present article makes an attempt to understand the recent trends and composition of public spending by the union and select states based on a spatial, temporal and sector-wise dataset of public expenditure in agriculture and allied sectors.

Scope and Questions

This chapter focuses primarily on the union government's expenditure towards agriculture and allied sectors. It also tries to unpack the analysis for four selected states: Bihar, Gujarat, Karnataka and Odisha. The selection of states was done on the basis of regional representation as well as diversity in agroclimatic conditions. These states are different in terms of soil, climate, water availability and thus, they differ in terms of diversity and pattern of agricultural production. The chapter broadly addresses four questions pertaining to the public spending in agriculture and allied sectors.

First, what are the important trends in public spending on agriculture and allied sectors?

Second, what is the composition of public spending in agriculture and allied sectors by the central government and the governments of the selected states?

Third, what is the direction provided to public spending in the sector by the union government? It has been argued that the capacity of the state governments to plan and design schemes had weakened considerably between 2000 and 2015 because of the following reasons: (1) the state governments faced a severe fiscal crunch during the early 2000s, which reduced the states' capacity to plan and design programmes to address the challenges at the grassroots level; (2) the public spending by the union government increased in the later part of 2000s due to various new schemes. Some of these programmes continued till 2014–15. However, due to changes in the terms of the Fourteenth Finance Commission (FFC), a major shift was witnessed towards direct benefit transfers to the farmers. Of late, some states also followed this strategy of the union government.

Fourth, what are the gaps in public spending in agriculture and allied sectors? There are a number of key components of public spending in agriculture that directly influence the capacity of the sector. Therefore, it is important to unpack some of those important areas of public spending in the sector.

Data and Methodology

To understand the long-term trend of public spending, a relatively longer time period i.e., from 1995–96 to 2019–20 is taken for the analysis of union government spending and a combined (union and state) spending. For the states' expenditures, the time period is 2015–16 to 2019–20, which is the period of the FFC. This period was so selected for the sake of consistency in analysis, as the centre–state fund-sharing formula was revised by the FFC. Therefore, this chapter largely limits the period of analysis to the period of FFC.

The analysis is based on union, states and combined budget documents. To understand the long-term trend of public spending, the data was taken from India Public Finance Statistics, Ministry of Finance, Government of India (union and combined budget analysis). For the analysis of important components and the schemes, budget expenditure data was taken from the Detailed Demand for Grants (DDG) of the respective states and the union governments. There are other sources of data, such as the RBI's study on state finances that does not disaggregate but consolidates the spending based on heads of accounts.

Agricultural sector has been defined broadly, going beyond the definition of 'agricultural and allied activities' as in the accounting classification conventionally and maintained in the budgets. This analysis takes into account the public spending made under crop husbandry, animal husbandry, food storage and warehousing, minor irrigation, flood control, village and small industries, rural development, and special area programmes. So, this broad definition includes the functional classification of expenditures as it provides a better way to understand the trends in public spending. 'Agriculture and allied sectors' and 'agricultural sector' are used interchangeably in this chapter.

Limitations

There are certain limitations of such an analysis: first, the state-level analysis is limited only to four states, which is not sufficient in providing the insights of public spending in other regions. Secondly, the analysis considers public spending only for the period 2014–15 to 2019–20 and does not provide a long-term analysis due to the consistency issues in centre–state funds sharing formula. Thirdly, as lot of variations can be found within the states in terms of production conditions, the chapter does not comment on public spending within the states. Likewise, the analysis is limited to examining the quantity of funds but misses out the quality aspects of public expenditure in agriculture.

The second section discusses the trends and patterns of public spending towards agriculture and allied sectors for union, union and states combined, and select states. The third section examines the composition of public spending across various departments concerning agriculture and allied activities by the union government and the select states. The fourth section maps the changing priorities of public spending in the sector by the union government. The analysis of public spending in the context of agrarian crisis has been presented in the fifth section. The last section concludes the discussion.

Trends in Public Spending
Union and States' Combined Spending

As a result of neoliberal policies, a drastic change in budgetary spending towards the agricultural sector was observed in the 1990s. Figure 5.1 provides the share of budgetary spending of the union and states combined, and the union government towards agricultural sector in India's GDP. A declining trend is observed for both the share of spending for union and states combined (from 1.0 per cent to 0.8 per cent) as well as union (0.3 per cent to 0.2 per cent) in the GDP during 1995–96 to 2005–06.

A robust and sustained revival of agriculture and the rural economy requires a number of structural changes in the overall policy framework. As a policy response to declining agricultural growth, a focus was given to a number of programmes, such as the Rashtriya Krishi Vikas Yojana (RKVY) during the Eleventh Five-Year Plan. There was a visible increase in the budgetary spending on agriculture during this period (Figure 5.1). As a result, the share of public spending of the change to union and states, and the union, increased from the lowest level of 0.8 per cent and 0.2 per cent in 2005–06 to 1.1 per cent and 0.3 per cent of GDP in 2016–17, respectively. This moderate rise in public expenditure, both at the levels of union and states, was associated with a period of growth in agriculture. However, given that the rise was only moderate, this growth momentum could not translate into a sustained growth of farm income.

Union Government's Spending

After the new government assumed power in 2014, one of the important goals was to double farmers' income. A series of interventions were attempted to revive the growth of this sector through a substantial increase in the budget allocation/expenditure. Interventions such as the Pradhan Mantri Kisan Samman Nidhi (PM-Kisan), the Pradhan Mantri Fasal Bima Yojana (PMFBY), among others, were the major initiatives towards fulfilling the objective of doubling farmers' income by 2022, taking 2015–16 as the base year (Chand 2017). In this direction, there was a significant increase in allocation to agriculture and allied sectors by Rs 75,000 crores under PM-Kisan in 2019–20. This apart, expenditure under the interest subvention scheme was earlier covered under the Ministry of Finance.[1] Since 2016–17, expenditure under this head was accounted under the Ministry of Agriculture and

Figure 5.1 *Share of the budgetary spending of the centre and states combined and central government towards agricultural sector in India's GDP, 1995–96 to 2016–17,* in per cent

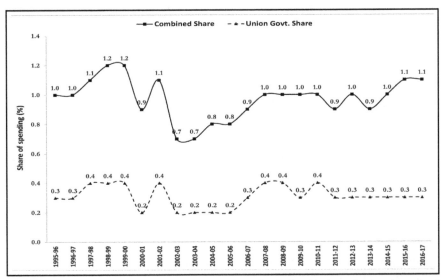

Note: Spending in agricultural sector includes only under the heads of crop husbandry, animal husbandry, food storage and warehousing, other allied programmes and minor irrigation
Source: India Public Finance Statistics, 1995–96 to 2016–17.

Figure 5.2 *The allocation for agriculture and allied sectors as proportion of total union budget and GDP, 2014–15 to 2019–20,* in per cent

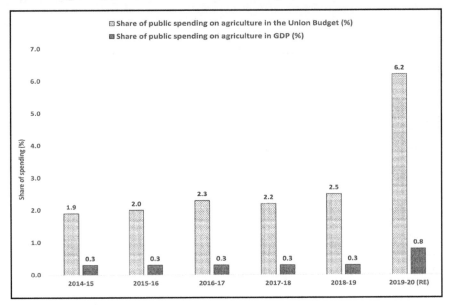

Note: RE-Revised Estimates
Source: Union budget documents, various years.

Farmers' Welfare. This introduction of one new scheme and a reclassification results in expenditures rising under specific heads. Due to the introduction of PM-Kisan scheme, the share of public expenditure in agriculture rose from 2.5 per cent in 2018–19 to 6.2 per cent in 2019–20 (see Figure 5.2).

State Governments' Spending

The state budgets too have not provided adequate attention to agricultural sector, despite it being a state subject. In Gujarat, the agriculture budget constitutes 3.4 per cent of the state budget in 2019–20. Between 2014–15 and 2019–20, the budget provision for agricultural sector never crossed 5 per cent; the share remained within the range of 3.2 to 4.8 per cent (Figure 5.3).[2] In Bihar, the share of spending towards agriculture in the total budget was 3.2 per cent in 2019–20; between 2014–15 and 2019–20, the share remained within the range of 2 per cent to 5 per cent (Figure 5.3).[3] However, the corresponding share rose from 5.8 per cent to 7.6 per cent in Odisha and from 6.4 per cent to 8.2 per cent in Karnataka between 2014–15 and 2019–20.[4]

Figure 5.3 *Share of public spending towards agricultural sector in total state budgets of select states,* in per cent

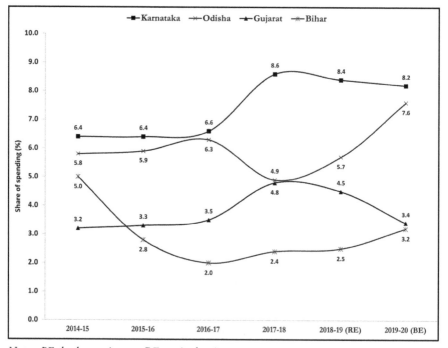

Notes: BE- budget estimates; RE- revised estimates.
For the states, agriculture spending includes Departments of Agriculture, Departments of Co-operation and Departments of Farmers' Welfare. These departments are not uniform across states and some departments are either named differently or merged with the other departments.
Source: Union and State Budget Documents for 2016–17 to 2019–20.

Composition of Public Spending on Agriculture

The role of allied sectors of agriculture is important in supplementing rural household incomes. Animal husbandry is one of the crucial allied sectors which contributes around 12 per cent of the total income of agricultural households in India (GoI 2016). Small and marginal farmers are also largely dependent on non-crop income sources (Vatta *et al.* 2018). An important feature of allied sectors is that they are relatively less vulnerable to weather conditions and thus provide complementary income to the households. This section analyses the composition of public spending in various departments related to agriculture and allied sectors by the central and state governments.

Composition of Public Spending by the Union Government

In the budget of the union government, the crop sector received the highest priority, whereas allied sectors like animal husbandry, fisheries, dairy development, and education and research were relatively neglected over the years. A new Ministry of Fisheries, Animal Husbandry and Dairying was cre-

Figure 5.4 *Share of departmental spending in total union budget allocation to the Ministry of Agriculture and Farmers' Welfare, and Ministry of Fisheries, Animal Husbandry and Dairying,* in per cent

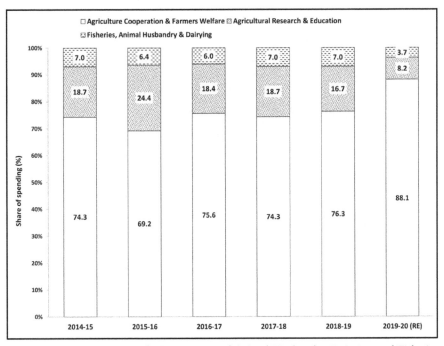

Note: From 2019–20 onwards, Department of Animal Husbandry, Dairying and Fisheries became a separate ministry (Ministry of Fisheries, Animal Husbandry and Dairying), which was initially part of the Ministry of Agriculture and Farmers' Welfare.
Source: Union budget documents from 2014–15 to 2020–21.

ated in 2019. Even then, the Department of Agriculture and Farmers' Welfare (DoAFW) received the largest share in the total allocation and it showed an increasing trend over the years. In 2014–15, the share of DoAFW was 74.3 per cent, which went up to 88.1 per cent in 2019–20 (Figure 5.4). The increase in budgetary allocation to DoAFW was on account of the introduction of the PM-Kisan scheme with additional fund allocation of Rs 75,000 crores in 2019–20. However, no such increment was provided to the other departments.

The Department of Animal Husbandry had the lowest share: 7 per cent in 2014–15, which came down to just 3.7 per cent in 2019–20 (Figure 5.4). There was an increment of a meagre Rs 1,300 crores in the five years for this department. The Department of Agricultural Research and Education was also not given adequate importance. The funds allocated for this department saw a minimal increase, from Rs 4,840 crores in 2014–15 to Rs 7,846 crores in 2019–20. The share of funds for this department came down from 19 per cent in 2014–15 to 8.2 per cent in 2019–20.

Composition of Public Spending by the State Governments
As far as the states are concerned, some provided high priority to the allied sectors. For instance, Karnataka and Gujarat gave relatively high priority to the allied sectors compared to Odisha and Bihar. In 2015–16, allied sectors'

Figure 5.5 *Share of public spending in allied sectors in the total state agriculture budget,* in per cent

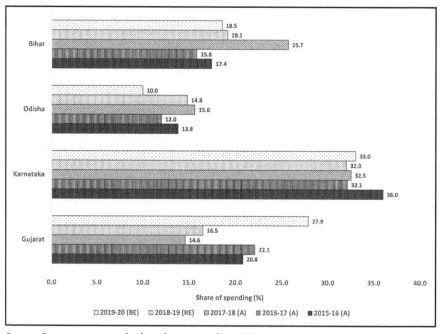

Source: State government budget documents from 2014–15 to 2019–20.

share in Odisha's agriculture budget was 13 per cent, which came down to 10 per cent in 2019–20. In Bihar, the share showed a marginal increase from 17 per cent to 18.5 per cent in the same period. On the other hand, in Karnataka's total agricultural budget, the share of allied sectors was 36 per cent in 2014–15 and 33 per cent in 2019–20. In Gujarat, the share fluctuated within a range of 20 to 27.9 per cent between 2014–15 and 2019–20 (Figure 5.5).

In sum, the crop sector remained at the core of public spending, both at the centre and state levels, whereas the share of other two departments declined significantly during the period of analysis. It indicated that the funding for important activities such as animal husbandry, fisheries, dairying and agricultural research were not prioritized both at the union and the state levels.

Shifting Priorities

As we discussed, while there was a revival of public spending in the agricultural sector, it was largely due to a shift in spending towards income support, interest subvention and crop insurance (CBGA 2020). The problem, however, is that this policy framework might fail to address some of the root causes of agrarian crisis in India. Of late, some states also followed this strategy of the union government and introduced schemes, such as Rythu Bandhu for Andhra Pradesh, Krushak Assistance for Livelihood and Income Augmentation (KALIA) for Odisha and loan waivers in various States (Acharya and Singh 2020). So, it is important to examine the change in the direction of public spending in agriculture for the union government.

Only four schemes – PM-Kisan, Pradhan Mantri Fasal Bima Yojana, the Interest Subvention Scheme and the Price Support Scheme – constituted a major proportion of the public spending of the union government. We call these schemes part of 'non-core' interventions as opposed to 'core' interventions that focus on direct spending and investment to raise production and productivity (CBGA 2020). The core component includes public spending on schemes, such as the Rashtriya Krishi Vikas Yojana (RKVY), the Paramparagat Krishi Vikas Yojana (PKVY), the Pradhan Mantri Krishi Sinchai Yojana (PMKSY), the Blue Revolution and White Revolution, which directly contribute in enhancing the production.

The shares of 'core' and 'non-core' interventions in agriculture were 72 per cent and 28 per cent respectively in 2014–15 (Figure 5.6). Even before the introduction of PM-Kisan, the share of allocations in non-core interventions had started to rise and accounted for more than half the total public spending in agriculture. But in 2019–20, the share of non-core interventions increased sharply to 82 per cent while that of core interventions fell to just 18 per cent (Figure 5.6).

A number of studies have argued that public expenditure on rural public goods such as rural connectivity and storage facilities provides impetus

Figure 5.6 *Share of union government expenditure on core vs. other interventions for agriculture and allied sectors,* in per cent

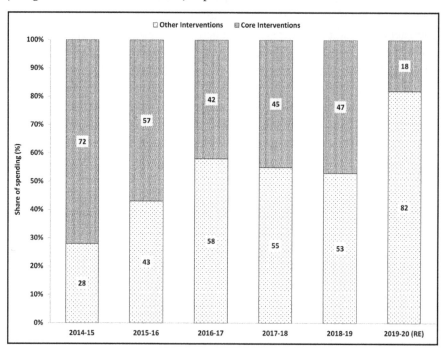

Notes: i) Core interventions include the schemes meant for crop and non-crop sectors and other systemic interventions in Agriculture and Allied Activities sectors; ii) Other non-core interventions include budget allocations/expenditure on PM-Kisan, Crop Insurance, Price Support and Interest Subvention.
Source: Union budget documents, various years.

to agricultural growth across regions, although with varying degrees; and within agriculture, expenditure on infrastructure and research and development (R&D) is the most desirable way of increasing farm profitability (Fan, Gulati and Thorat 1999; Singh 2011; Singh, Pal and Jha 2015; Bathla 2017; Mahendra Dev 2018). So, this major shift in the composition of public spending within the agricultural sector, from core to other interventions, raises questions on the strategy to achieve the stated objectives of higher growth in agriculture and farmers' income. Secondly, increased public spending by way of introducing such schemes indicates that the concerned departments are not carrying out their core mandate of enhancing capacity and infrastructure but are performing the role of facilitator in disbursing the cash flows to farmers either through banks or insurance companies.

Gaps in Public Spending on Agriculture and Allied Sectors

This section tries to highlight some of the gaps in public spending in agriculture and allied sectors. Although agriculture remains a state subject (in terms of the division of responsibilities as per the Constitution of India), the pervasive agrarian crisis in the country has pushed the union government to supplement public expenditure by states through a range of interventions (in the form of centrally sponsored schemes and additional resources for state schemes) for the development of agricultural sector. However, there are key components like seeds, irrigation, soil and marketing where state governments play a crucial role. Therefore, this section focuses on public spending on key components of the agricultural sector by the states.

During the last decade or so, agriculture managed to achieve a reasonable rate of growth. However, one cannot observe any relief from the prevailing distress. Between 2002–03 and 2012–13, agricultural income in real terms increased by only 3.6 per cent annually (Gulati and Roy 2019). The C2 cost that includes the paid-out costs by farmers plus imputed rental costs of owned land, imputed interest on owned capital and imputed value of family labour employed increased rapidly, which resulted in declining profitability of important crops in major producing states (Narayanamoorthy 2013; Chand 2017; Srivastava, Chand and Singh 2017).

Secondly, due to lower levels of income, a major proportion of income was spent on household consumption. As per the 70th round of Situational Assessment Survey of Agricultural Households, the average monthly income per agricultural household during the agricultural year July 2012–June 2013 was Rs 6,426 out of which approximately 97 per cent (Rs 6,223) was consumption expenditure (GoI 2016). As households needed funds to carry out production activities, such as expenditure on inputs and productive resources, they complemented the requirement for additional funds through loans. Around 52 per cent of agricultural households reported outstanding loans, out of which 40 per cent have taken loans from informal sources (GoI 2016). Any crop failure or income shock often leads to increase in indebtedness, which exacerbates distress. Thus, weak provisioning for supportive services such as R&D, extension and irrigation are the key reasons for increasing cost of cultivation and declining incomes.

Rashtriya Krishi Vikas Yojana (RKVY)

Under the RKVY, the union government urged state governments to spend on capital formation and infrastructure in the agricultural sector so that post-harvest operations in the production system can be strengthened. RKVY was launched in 2007–08 as a state plan scheme with additional central assistance from the union government for the development of agricultural sector.

After 2017–18, many state governments cut down their spending under RKVY (Figure 5.7). In 2014–15, Bihar allocated Rs 523 crore under this scheme, which came down to Rs 253 crores in 2019–20. Budget alloca-

Figure 5.7 *State governments' spending on Rashtriya Krishi Vikas Yojana,* in Rs crore

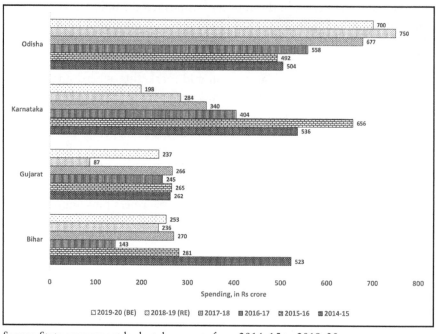

Source: State government budget documents from 2014–15 to 2019–20.

tion for the RKVY scheme for Karnataka and Gujarat followed the similar trend. In Gujarat, the budget allocation for the RKVY scheme came down from Rs 262 crores to Rs 237 crores. In Karnataka, there was a substantial reduction of allocation by Rs 338 crores between 2014–15 and 2019–20. The only exception was Odisha. In Odisha, there is no reduction in fund allocation; in fact, the fund allocation increased by Rs 200 crores over the same period. The reduction in spending on capital formation will have long-term impact on the growth on the sector especially in states like Bihar where agricultural growth between 2011–12 and 2019–20 was negative.

Seeds

A large number of small and marginal farmers in India do not get quality seeds. Majority of the farmers are dependent upon seeds available in the market. Also, a significant proportion of the farmers seek advice from the commission agents and seed traders about the selection of seeds variety and quality, even in the agriculturally advanced states of the country (Verma and Sidhu 2009). Many incidents of crop failure have been reported due to spurious seed quality. Also, the indigenous seed varieties are disappearing due to which seed diversity is vanishing.

A number of measures have been adopted by the union and the

Figure 5.8 *State governments' spending on seeds*, in Rs crore

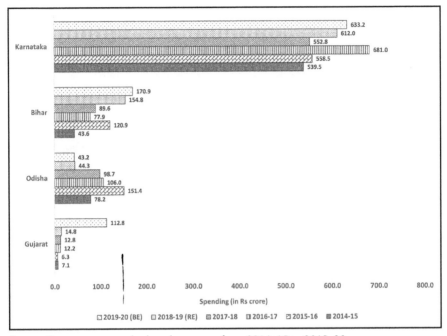

Source: State government budget documents from 2014–15 to 2019–20.

state governments to upgrade the quality of seeds. In 2010, the government launched a programme called National Mission on Agricultural Extension and Technology (NMAET) with the aim of facilitating infusion of modern technology in the agricultural sector. The scheme Submission of Seeds and Planting Material (SMSP) falls within the scope of the NMAET. The aim of the scheme was to grow good quality seeds through research and development. However, state government's spending on seeds, including in SMSP, remained small. In 2014–15, Gujarat was spending just Rs 7.1 crore on seeds followed by Bihar (Rs 43 crore) and Odisha (Rs 78 crore) (see Figure 5.8). However, Karnataka was spending relatively more than the other three States i.e., Rs 540 crores on seeds. By 2019–20, the spending on seeds increased in Gujarat (Rs 113 crore), Bihar (Rs 171 crore) and Karnataka (Rs 633 crore) whereas in Odisha it witnessed a fall to Rs 43 crores. It shows that a relatively small amount has been spent on seed research and extension and the funding has also remained unstable.

Soil and Water Conservation
The production conditions depend upon the agroclimatic conditions of a region, type of soil and availability of irrigation sources. A number of studies have highlighted that several factors (natural as well as current agri-

Figure 5.9 *State governments' spending on soil and water conservation*, Rs crore

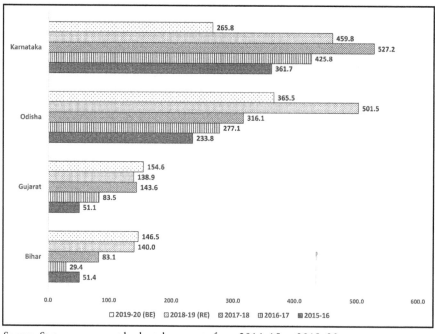

Source: State government budget documents from 2014–15 to 2019–20.

cultural practices) cause the degradation of soil and water resources, making the future of agriculture unsustainable. Therefore, conservation of soil and water is very important for sustainability of agriculture. States such as Bihar, where agricultural sector is badly affected due to natural reasons, demand more public provisioning towards improving soil and water management. However, the state government's support to soil and water conservation is very low. Both Bihar and Gujarat have the same level of budget provision, though both face different challenges related to soil and climate. In 2015–16, both the states had a budget provisioning of around Rs 50 crores approximately, which increased to about Rs 150 crores approximately in 2019–20. However, Karnataka and Odisha spent a little higher than both Bihar and Gujarat on soil and water conservation (Figure 5.9). The pace of degradation of soil and water, and frequency of crop loss due to natural factors, justify the need for higher budgetary allocations.

Food Security

A major part of agricultural household income is spent on consumption expenditure. Hence, ensuring food security is important not only in the context of poverty and hunger, but also from the perspective of safeguarding overall income. A sustained growth in production is needed to support the

Figure 5.10 *State budget allocation for National Food Security Mission*, in Rs crore

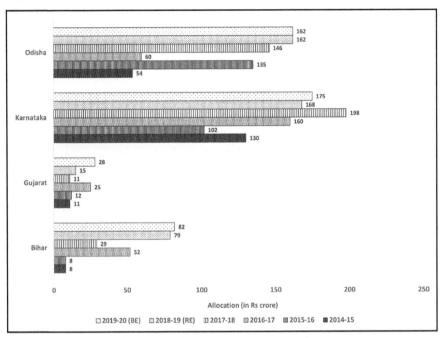

Source: State government budget documents from 2014–15 to 2019–20.

food requirement of billion plus population. National Food Security Mission (NFSM) launched in 2007 aimed at enhancing production of paddy, millets and pulses.[5]

There was a rise in budget allocation for NFSM by the state governments. In Gujarat, the government spending increased from Rs 11 crores in 2014–15 to Rs 28 crores in 2019–20, while in Karnataka, it increased from Rs 130 crores to Rs 175 crores during the same period. In Odisha, the budget allocation was Rs 54 crores in 2014–15 and it went up to Rs 162 crores in 2019–20. In Bihar, the budget allocation under NFSM was less than in many other states. In 2014–15, total budget allocation under this scheme was only Rs 8 crores, which went up to Rs 82 crores in 2019–20 BE (Figure 5.10).

Public spending under important constituents of agricultural growth such as seeds, water and soil witnessed a declining trend in the recent years. Like the centre, most of the states were also prioritizing cash-based programmes, which left less space for spending on enhancing productive capacity in the sector.

Concluding Remarks

The dismal performance of agricultural sector has been a subject of serious concern. Compression in public spending amongst various other factors is one of the important factors behind the agrarian crisis. This chapter examined the trends and composition of public spending in agriculture and allied sectors, and particularly for select states. It also examined the direction of change in the public spending by the union government. Finally, the chapter highlighted the gaps in public spending in a number of key components of agricultural sector across select states.

The long-term trends of public spending by the centre, and the centre and states combined in the agricultural sector were declining from the late 1990s to mid-2000s; it then increased till 2019–20. However, the share of spending (both for the centre, and centre and states combined) to GDP did not increase to the levels of 1990s. The states' expenditure in agriculture did not increase significantly, between 2014–15 and 2019–20.

The expenditure in agriculture remained skewed towards crop sector both for union and the states. The share of crop sector in union's spending in total agriculture budget was rising and reached as high as 88 per cent in 2019–20. Similarly, allied sectors in the selected states also did not receive importance as far as the budgetary allocations were concerned.

The union government's provisioning for the sector was moving towards direct cash transfer of benefits with less focus on creating infra-structure. The share of public spending on 'core activities' declined from 72 per cent in 2014–15 to just 18 per cent in 2019–20. State governments were also relying on the policy template set by the union government; a number of states introduced income support schemes and loan waiver schemes. Such individual-centric transfers undermine collective community approaches to solve the crisis in agriculture.

Finally, there were glaring gaps between the approach of public spending and the challenges faced by the sector. Public spending in key component areas like seeds, soil and water did not receive much priority. Such a neglect of public spending on agricultural infrastructure was a cause of concern for the long-term viability of the sector.

There is a need to redesign the policy framework and deliver adequate budgetary support in agriculture. An enabling macro policy framework and complementary provisioning of resources for the agriculture and allied sec-tors would be crucial in this regard. The budgetary framework must also address the challenges faced by the allied sectors in agriculture. Farmers require handholding support. Therefore, the approach of need-based plan-ning and budgeting is required for the sector. Last but not the least, public expenditure framework requires a strong co-operative federalism whereby provisioning of resources from the union government supplements the resource requirements of states.

Notes

[1] Under the Interest Subvention Scheme, with the government intervention, farmers access credit from the banks at relatively lower interest rate than the market rate of interest. The interest subsidy is borne by the union government from the budget. It does not include union government spending under the category of interest subvention and income support to farmers.

[2] Gujarat agriculture spending includes spending on Department of Agriculture, Farmers' Welfare and Co-operation.

[3] Bihar agriculture spending includes spending on Department of Animal and Fisheries Resource, and Department of Co-operatives.

[4] Karnataka agriculture spending includes spending on Department of Agriculture and Horticulture, Department of Animal Husbandry and Fisheries, and Department of Co-operation.

[5] It is a centrally sponsored scheme with 60 per cent allocation from the union government, and 40 per cent from state governments since 2015–16.

References

Acharya, N. and S. Das (2012), 'Revitalizing Agriculture in Eastern India: Investment and Policy Priorities', *IDS Bulletin*, vol. 43, no. s1, pp. 104–12.

Bathla, S. (2017), 'Public Investment in Agriculture and Growth: An Analysis of Relationship in the Indian Context', in S. Bathla and A. Dubey, eds, *Changing Contours of Indian Agriculture*, Singapore: Springer, pp. 13–28.

Centre for Budget and Governance Accountability (CBGA) (2020), 'Decoding the Priorities: An Analysis of Union Budget 2020–21', Centre for Budget and Governance Accountability (CGBA), New Delhi, February, available at https://www.cbgaindia.org/wpcontent/uploads/2020/02/Decoding-the-Priorities-An-Analysis-of-Union-Budget-2020-21-2.pdf, accessed 9 November 2020.

Chand, R. (2017), 'Doubling Farmers' Income: Rational, Strategy, Prospects and Action Plan', NITI Policy Paper no. 1, NITI Aayog, Government of India, New Delhi, March.

Fan, S., A. Gulati and S. Thorat (2008), 'Investment, Subsidies, and Pro-Poor Growth in Rural India', *Agricultural Economics*, vol. 39, no. 2, pp. 163–70.

Fan, S., P.B.R. Hazell and S. Thorat (1999), 'Linkages between Government Spending, Growth and Poverty in Rural India', Report no. 110, International Food Policy Research Institute, Washington D.C.

Gill, A. and L. Singh (2006), 'Farmers' Suicides and Response of Public Policy: Evidence, Diagnosis and Alternatives from Punjab', *Economic and Political Weekly*, vol. 41, no. 26, pp. 2762–68.

Government of India (GoI) (2016), 'Income, Expenditure, Productive Assets and Indebtedness of Agricultural Households in India', Situational Assessment Survey of Agricultural Households, 70th Round 2013, National Sample Survey Office, Report no. 576, April, Government of India.

Gulati, A. and R. Roy (2019), 'Wooing the Farmer', *Seminar*, available at http://www.india-seminar.com/2018/701/701_a_gulati_and_r_roy.htm, accessed 23 January 2021.

Jha, P. and N. Acharya (2011), 'Expenditure on the Rural Economy in India's Budgets since the 1950s: An Assessment', *Review of Agrarian Studies*, vol. 1, no. 2, pp. 134–56, available at http://ras.org.in/expenditure_on_the_rural_economy_in_indias_budgets_since_the_1950s, accessed 10 January 2021.

Mahendra Dev, S. (2018), 'Transformation of Indian Agriculture: Growth, Inclusiveness and Sustainability', Working Paper No. 2018–026, Indira Gandhi Institute of Development Research, Mumbai, December.

Misra, V.N. and P.B.R. Hazell (1996), 'Terms of Trade, Rural Poverty, Technology and Investment: The Indian Experience, 1952–53 to 1990–91', *Economic and Political Weekly*, vol. 31, no. 13, pp. A2–A13.

Narayanamoorthy, A. (2013), 'Profitability in Crops Cultivation in India: Some Evidence from Cost of Cultivation Survey Data', *Indian Journal of Agricultural Economics*, vol. 68, no. 1, pp. 104–21.

Reddy, D.N. and S. Mishra (2010), *Agrarian Crisis in India*, New Delhi: Oxford University Press.

Singh, A. (2011), 'The Changing Landscape of Public Expenditure and Investments in Agriculture: Implications for Growth Trajectory', *Indian Journal of Agricultural Economics*, vol. 66, no. 3, pp. 301–13.

Singh, A., S. Pal and G.K. Jha (2015), 'Transitioning India's Public Expenditure in Agriculture Towards Higher Growth and Equity', *Indian Journal of Agricultural Economics*, vol. 70, no. 3, pp. 246–58.

Singh, G. and N. Acharya (2020), 'Shifting Priorities of Union Government's Budgetary Support for Agriculture: An Analysis', Working Paper No. 1, Farm Sector Policy and Budget Analysis Series, September, Centre for Budget Governance and Accountability (CBGA), New Delhi.

Srivastava, S.K., R. Chand and J. Singh (2017), 'Changing Crop Production Cost in India: Input Prices, Substitution and Technological Effects', *Agricultural Economics Research Review*, vol. 30, Conference issue, pp. 171–82.

Vaidyanathan, A. (2006), 'Farmers' Suicides and the Agrarian Crisis', *Economic and Political Weekly*, vol. 41, no. 38, pp. 4009–13.

Vatta, K., G. Singh, N. Sharma and P.B. Bhoi (2018), 'Regional Dimensions and Determinants of Income Diversification in Rural India', *Agricultural Economics Research Review*, vol. 31, Conference issue, pp. 33–46.

Verma, S. and M.S. Sidhu (2009), 'Sources, Replacement and Management of Paddy Seed by Farmers in Punjab', *Agricultural Economics Research Review*, vol. 22, no. 2, pp. 323–28.

III
Agricultural Trade

6

WTO and Agricultural Support in India

Promise Unkept

Sachin Kumar Sharma, Teesta Lahiri and Suvayan Neogi

Introduction

The agricultural sector is crucial to India's economic development and transformation, especially considering its significant role in employment, GDP, safety net programmes, food security, international trade and economic development. In 2019–20, the share of agriculture in India's total employment and GDP was 43 per cent and around 17 per cent, respectively. About 86 per cent of Indian farmers were small and marginal farmers, and 99 per cent of Indian farmers had an average landholding of less than 10 hectares in the same period (GoI 2020; Sharma *et al.* 2020b). Most farmers face insurmountable challenges due to small and fragmented landholding, low farm income, high price volatility, burdensome farm debts, poor irrigation, and lack of marketing and mechanization facilities, among others (Sharma 2016; Taylor 2014). The severity of the volatilities and challenges faced by this sector are often the causes of the long-standing agrarian distress in India and farmers' suicides.

Given the importance and sensitivities of agriculture at the domestic front, trade liberalization under the World Trade Organization (WTO) was always contentious for Indian farmers and other stakeholders. The Agreement on Agriculture (AoA) of the WTO deals specifically with various aspects of agricultural trade, such as domestic support, export subsidies and market access. Of the several issues, disciplining domestic support to agriculture was the priority for the negotiating members in the WTO negotiations. All WTO members, irrespective of their status as developed, developing or least developed countries (LDCs), provide support to their agricultural sectors through different measures. Given the impact of these measures on price and output of agriculture products, these measures can be categorized as trade-distorting and non-trade distorting support.

The AoA categorizes various domestic support measures under different boxes based on the trade-distorting impact they can have, along with respective financial limits. Amber box, Green box, Blue box and Development box are the various components of domestic support to agriculture under the AoA.

Measures such as general services, pest management, rural development and direct payments under the Annex 2 of the AoA are deemed to be not or minimally trade-distorting support and are classified as Green box measures. All the members can provide support without any financial limits under the Green box. However, some other measures influence the prices and output of agricultural commodities by providing an incentive to farmers to produce more irrespective of market signals. Price support and price deficiency payments are examples of such measures, which are treated as trade-distorting support and are dealt under the provisions of the Amber box. Unlike the Green box, members have limited policy space to provide support under the Amber box. The AoA allows the members to provide the minimum level of Amber box support in the form of the *de-minimis* limit, which is 5 and 10 per cent of the value of production (VoP) of a concerned product for developed and developing members, respectively.

Further, the flexibilities to provide support under this box are not the same for all the members but are determined based on the historical support provided by a member during the Uruguay Round negotiations. Those members who provided higher trade-distorting support during the base-period (1986–88) got a larger policy space to reduce support under the Amber box compared to members like India who were not historically distorting agricultural trade (Birovljev and Ćetković 2013).

Such differential treatment led to an important and systemic skewness in the AoA across developing and developed countries. On the one hand, most developing members did not provide Amber box support beyond the *de-minimis* limit in 1986–88. Therefore, their future flexibilities to provide product-specific support were capped by the applicable *de-minimis* limit. On the other hand, most developed members were already providing Amber box support more than the *de-minimis* limit in 1986–88. Therefore, they obtained more flexibilities in the form of the aggregate measurement of support (AMS) entitlement to provide support beyond the *de-minimis* limit. The developing members were deeply affected by this structural asymmetry, which long permitted developed countries to provide huge agricultural subsidies without breaching their commitments (Sharma *et al.* 2020a). As a result of the larger policy space under the Amber box, developed members enjoyed artificial comparative advantages in agricultural trade at the expense of the low-income and resource-poor farmers of the developing countries (Josling 2015; Tania and Mapulanga-Hulston 2016). In fact, literature frequently suggests that high levels of trade-distorting support provided by developed members led to overproduction and the subsequent depression of international prices of agricultural commodities were detrimental to the farmers in developing countries (Schmitz, Schmitz and Rossi 2006; Hawkes and Plahe 2012; Sharma and Das 2018).

Rather than eliminating their Amber box entitlement, developed members attacked the support measures of the developing members, including price support and input subsidies (Sharma 2020). Like for most developing members, the policy space to provide Amber box support for India is also capped by the *de-minimis* limit. Within the Amber box, the Indian government provides product-specific support in the form of market price support (MPS) through the minimum support price (MSP) mechanism. Under this mechanism, farmers can sell their produce to the government agencies at the MSP, which is announced by the government at the recommendation of the Commission for Agricultural Costs and Prices (CACP). The price support-backed procurement plays a role in not only mitigating the adverse impact of price fluctuations on farm income but also in providing food security to more than 800 million people under the National Food Security Act (NFSA) of 2013 (Sharma and Das 2017). Being a developing member, the Indian government can provide input subsidies to low income or resource-poor farmers without any financial limit under the AoA.

Yet, due to the limited policy space under the Amber box, the MSP-based support to Indian agriculture has been frequently questioned and challenged at the WTO. Developed members are demanding to reduce India's flexibility in the agriculture negotiations. In response, India has been consistently asking for addressing the asymmetries in domestic support by eliminating the AMS entitlement of the developed members.

Against this background, this chapter critically analyses the trend in domestic support to Indian agriculture and highlights the relevant and contentious issues for India in agriculture negotiations. This chapter is organized into five sections. The following section, which is the second section, gives a brief description of the classification of domestic support measures under the AoA. The third section provides a snapshot of the overall trends in India's domestic support policies. The fourth section addresses India's main challenges in implementing domestic support policies, and the final section summarizes the main content of this study.

Classification of Domestic Support Measures under the AoA

The Green box covers all policies that have no or at most minimal trade-distorting effects on production. This support should be public-funded and shall not have the effect of providing price support to producers. General services, public stockholding for food security purposes, domestic food aid and direct payments are the main components of the Green box. All WTO members can provide unlimited Green box support to the agricultural sector provided all the conditions attached with Annex 2 of the AoA are satisfied.

Like the Green box, members can provide unlimited support under the Blue box in the form of direct payments to specific products subject to the production-limiting conditions given in Article 6.5. The direct payments can be based on (1) fixed area and yields; or (2) 85 per cent or less of the base level of production; or (3) a fixed number of livestock heads. Only a few members like EU, Norway, Japan, Iceland and China, among others, have used Blue box measures in recent years.

Unlike the Green and Blue boxes, only developing members are entitled to provide unlimited support under the Development box (Article 6.2) as a part of special and differential treatment (S&D) provisions to support its agriculture. Developing members can provide (1) investment subsidies generally available to agriculture; (2) agricultural input subsidies generally available to low-income or resource-poor producers; and (3) subsidies given to producers to encourage diversification from producing illicit narcotics under this box.

All domestic support measures that cannot be covered under the Green, Blue or Development boxes are categorized under the Amber box (Table 6.1). The support provided to farmers under this box includes product-specific support (PSS) for agricultural products such as rice, wheat, milk, etc. in the form of price support, deficiency payments, budgetary allocations, etc., as well as non-product specific support (NPS) in the form of input subsidies such as seed, fertilizer, irrigation and electricity subsidies to farmers. Support

Table 6.1 *A snapshot of the classification of domestic support measures under the AoA*

Category	Financial Limit	Coverage
Green box (no or at most minimal trade-distorting)	no limit	general services; public stockholding for food security; domestic food aid; direct payments to producers
Article 6.2 (Development box)	no limit for developing countries	investment and input subsidies to low income or resource-poor farmers
Blue box (production limiting)	no limit	direct payments based on fixed area and yields; or made on 85 per cent or less of base-level production; or made on a fixed number of livestock heads.
Amber box (trade-distorting)	strict financial limit	MPS, price deficiency payments and other budgetary support

Source: Authors' compilation based on the AoA text.

under the Amber box is considered trade-distorting and thus subject to strict financial limits and reduction commitments.

A certain percentage of Amber box support, or the *de-minimis* limit, is exempt from these limits and reductions. The *de-minimis* limit is based on the VoP of a specific product for PSS and the VoP of total agriculture for NPS. All developing members except China are entitled to a *de-minimis* limit of 10 per cent for both product and non-product specific support. The applicable *de-minimis* for developed members is set at 5 per cent, and for China at 8.5 per cent of the VoP.

During the Uruguay Rounds, when the General Agreement on Tariffs and Trade (GATT) contracting parties negotiated the domestic support disciplines on agriculture, the *de-minimis* percentage was set out as the minimum entitlement. Those members that were already providing trade-distorting support more than the set *de-minimis* level during the Uruguay Round were entitled to provide Amber box support beyond the *de-minimis* limit under the AoA. Many developed members such as the United States (US), the European Union (EU), Japan, Australia, Canada, among others, were already providing huge trade-distorting support during the base period of 1986–88. The Amber box support provided during the base period was called base AMS. On the other hand, most developing members, including India, had been providing negligible trade-distorting support in the base-period of 1986–88. Since these members were providing Amber box support within the *de-minimis* limit, their Amber box support entitlement got capped at the applicable *de-minimis* level only. For these developing members, *de minimis* limit also serves as a maximum limit for the Amber box.

In the AoA, developed countries committed to reduce their base AMS by 20 per cent over six years (1995–2000), while developing countries had to cut down their entitlements by 13.3 per cent over a ten-year period (1995–2004). Despite the reductions, most of the developed members still have huge trade-distorting support entitlements. For instance, the US had been providing more than US$ 24 billion as Amber box support in the base period. Even after the applicable 20 per cent reductions, the US has an AMS entitlement of US$ 19.1 billion as per its last domestic support notification in 2017. Besides the developed members, a few developing members were also entitled to the AMS, as they had also been provided Amber box support in excess of the *de-minimis* limit in the 1986–88 period. However, the share of these developing members in total AMS entitlement at the global level is barely 5 per cent, whereas the developed members account for more than 95 per cent of global entitlement (Sharma *et al.* 2020b). For instance, the US and the EU had AMS entitlements of US$ 19 billion and US$ 81 billion in 2019, while all the developing members enjoying the AMS entitlement together had a total of just US$ 6.7 billion.

Tables 6.2 and 6.3 provide a glimpse into India's Amber box support during the base years of 1986–88. During the base period, both product and non-product specific support provided by India was either negative or within the *de-minimis* level. As a result, India did not get any AMS entitlement but was only allowed to provide support up to the *de-minimis* level of 10 per cent of VoP for each product.

Currently, India along with many other developing members at the WTO face a severe crunch in policy space since they cannot provide price support scheme to their agricultural sector beyond the *de-minimis* limit, and as a result are often held back from enacting policies that are attuned with their national socio-economic needs of mitigating poverty, hunger, and issues

Table 6.2 *Product-specific support by India in 1986–88*, in Rs million

Description of basic products	Base product-specific AMS	Description of basic products	Base product-specific AMS
Rice	−77,235	Cotton	−14,543
Wheat	−89,880	Soybean (yellow) and	
Bajra	−6,822	Soybean (black)	−16
Jawar	−16,454	Urad	−1,394
Maize	−12,517	Moong	−1,752
Barley	−4,203	Tur	−4,550
Gram	−4,945	Tobacco	11
Groundnut	−20,494	Jute	−3,833
Rapeseed Toria	−8,694	Sugar cane	2,405
		Total product-specific AMS:	−2,44,422

Source: Based on India's Schedule of Commitments (WTO Doc: G/AG/AGST/IND).

Table 6.3 *Non-product-specific aggregate measurement of support, 1986–89*, in Rs million

Description of subsidy	Base AMS (1986–89)
Fertilizer subsidy	10,205
Electricity subsidy	15,814
Irrigation subsidy	17,927
Credit subsidy	998
Seed subsidy	820
Total non-product-specific AMS	45,814

Source: Based on India's Schedule of Commitments[1] (WTO Doc: G/AG/AGST/IND).

of livelihood security and rural development. On the other hand, due to their AMS entitlements, most developed nations continue to support their agricultural sectors beyond the applicable *de-minimis* limit. This clearly shows how the domestic support provisions in the AoA are inherently asymmetric.

Trends in Domestic Support to Indian Agriculture

All members provide support to their agricultural producers through various measures. India also supports its millions of farmers through a wide variety of measures, which may be categorized under the Green box, Development box and the Amber box of the AoA.

Green Box

Measures under the Green box of the AoA are perceived to be minimally trade-distorting in nature. For simplicity, India's Green box expenditure is divided into three sub-parts: (1) general services; (2) public stockholding (PSH) for food security purposes and domestic food aid; and (3) direct payments to producers.

Under the general services, India incurred US$ 3.5 billion in 2018–19 on various programs related to agricultural research, training, pest and disease control, inspection, extension and advisory services, marketing and promotion, and infrastructure services. However, expenditure under the PSH programmes for food security purposes accounted for the major share in the Green box for India. Under this head, the government agencies procure foodgrains like wheat, rice, coarse cereals and pulses from the farmers at the administered prices, or the market prices. It is noteworthy that the procurement of foodgrains at the administered prices for public stockholding programmes is subject to the provisions related to product-specific support under the Amber box also. The procured foodgrains are distributed through the public distribution system (PDS) as well as other welfare programmes to the eligible population at highly subsidized rates. Currently, the PSH programmes form the backbone of the National Food Security Act (NFSA) of 2013, which makes the right to food a legal entitlement by providing subsidized foodgrains to nearly two-thirds of the population. In implementing the NFSA, the Food Corporation of India (FCI) procures foodgrains and distributes them to the poor at subsidized prices through the public distribution system (PDS). The PSH component played an essential role in mitigating the adverse impact of the Covid-19 pandemic on poor people by providing foodgrains free of cost to the eligible population under the PM Garib Kalyan Anna Yojana.

Many other developing members are also providing foodgrains at a subsidized rate to their population. For instance, Indonesia implements the RASKIN (Beras untuk Rakyat Miskin) programme through which subsidized rice is provided to the eligible population by its government agency BULOG (Indonesian Bureau of Logistics) (Sharma 2018). As of 2018–19, India spent more than US$ 17 billion on its PSH programmes, which amounted to almost 76 per cent of its total Green box expenditure (Table 6.4). Given the fact that more than 195 million Indian people suffer from undernourishment, the importance of PSH programmes in achieving the zero-hunger goal of the United Nation's Sustainable Development Goals (SDGs) cannot be underestimated. Even a developed member like the US provided US$ 99 billion as domestic food aid to the American people in 2017.

The Indian government also supported the farmers through direct payments under the Green box. Direct payments under this box may include any form of decoupled income-support, government participation in income-insurance and income-safety nets, crop-insurance payments in times of natural disasters, and producer and resource retirement programs, among others. As a direct payment, the government provides support under a crop insurance programme called the PM Fasal Bima Yojana (PMFBY). Additionally, the government provides direct payments in the form of Pradhan Mantri Kisan Samman Nidhi (PM-KISAN), which aims to ensure the livelihood security of farming families by providing them with an income of Rs 6,000 per annum in the form of a direct benefit transfer. On an ad-hoc basis, the government has also occasionally supported Indian farmers in the past through debt waiver programmes. The Green box expenditure increased substantially in 2017–18 because of such support through debt-waivers in 2017–18 (Table 6.4).

The total Green box support in India for 2018–19 was US$ 22 billion,

Table 6.4 *India's domestic support trend under the Green box and Article 6.2, 1995–96 to 2018–19*, million USD

Year	General service	Public stockholding for food security purposes	Direct payment	Total Green box	Development box (Article 6.2)
1995–96	397.6	1,569.7	228.3	2,196.0	254.0
2000–01	86.3	2,629.2	135.8	2,851.0	8,478.0
2005–06	488.4	5,211.4	207.5	5,907.0	12,316.0
2010–11	1,124.4	13,812.5	4,542.2	19,479.0	31,610.0
2015–16	2,725.9	15,644.9	NA	18,371.0	23,553.0
2016–17	2,812.9	16,271.5	NA	19,693.0	22,831.0
2017–18	3,611.2	18,040.8	9,791.0	31,443.0	22,574.0
2018–19	3,537.3	17,212.0	1,732.0	22,482.0	24,184.0

Sources: India's domestic support notifications to WTO.

which was significantly lower than the US and the EU, which spent US$ 118 billion and US$ 74 billion respectively in 2017. Domestic food aid accounted for the major share of Green box support in the US, whereas the EU's Green box support was mainly in the form of direct payments to the farmers.

Development Box (Article 6.2)

Under this box, a developing member can provide three types of support comprising investment aid, input subsidies to low income or resource poor farmers and support for crop diversification from illicit narcotic crops. However, India mainly utilizes this box to provide input subsidies like irrigation, fertilizer and electricity subsidies to its low-income and resource-poor farmers. The AoA does not provide the definition for low-income resource-poor farmers. As a result, developing members use their objective criteria to identify low-income resource-poor farmers. India uses 'average landholding' as its criteria and categorizes all farmers with an average landholding up to 10 hectares as low-income or resource-poor. As per the Agriculture Census of 2015–16, 99.45 per cent of Indian farmers had landholding less than 10 hectares and thus, were classified as resource-poor farmers. Over the years, India's expenditure under this box has increased to US$ 24 billion and it is the largest user of this box among the developing members of the WTO (Table 6.4).

Blue Box

Like most WTO members, India has never notified any domestic support measure under the Blue box. As earlier mentioned, the Blue box categorizes direct payments made under production limiting programmes that comply with the given conditions under Article 6.5 of the AoA. Despite being trade-distorting, these payments are exempt from any financial limits due to their production-limiting nature. Until 2016, only five developed members, namely the EU, US, Japan, Norway and Iceland, had used the Blue box to support their producers. However, in 2016, China became the first among the developing members to provide support under this box.

Amber Box

The Amber Box is used to categorize all measures that do not fall under any of the aforementioned categories. Input subsidies not specific to any product are classified as non-product-specific support (NPS), whereas support given to a specific product is classified as product-specific support (PSS). As India did not provide Amber box support above the *de-minimis* limit, the maximum support under the NPS is 10 per cent of VoP of agriculture for a relevant year. However, India notifies input subsidies under the Development box rather than as NPS in the Amber box. Currently, India notifies a portion of insurance premium subsidies under the PMFBY, which does not satisfy the conditions of Green box, as NPS in the Amber box. Thus, India's NPS Amber box expenditure includes mainly a portion of insurance premium subsidies. Since crop insurance is an 'input' *per se*, this can also be categorized in the Development box.

India provides PSS through the MSP policy, which is treated as MPS under the AoA. In India, based on the CACP recommendations, the government announces the MSP for twenty-four major crops which include rice, wheat, coarse cereals, pulses, certain oilseeds and cotton. The government agencies like FCI are responsible for procuring the foodgrains at administered prices, stocking and distributing these foodgrains at subsidized prices to the targeted food-insecure population through the PDS. All expenditure incurred in the procurement of the foodgrains at the administered prices is categorized as part of the product-specific Amber box. India can provide product-specific support up to 10 per cent of the VoP of a specific product. In case, India exceeds the 10 per cent limit, then other members can challenge the MSP by initiating a dispute at the WTO.

Besides the limit of 10 per cent capping under the *de-minimis* limit, a related issue is pertaining to the methodology to compute the MPS. As per the AoA, the MPS is calculated by comparing the applied administered prices (AAP) and a fixed external reference price (FERP). The difference between these two variables is multiplied by the eligible production. The resultant support amount for a specific product in India should not be more than the 10 per cent of the VoP in a relevant year. For India, the MSP is treated as the AAP for purposes of calculation. The FERP for a specific product is the average FOB (free on board) unit price for the said agricultural product in net-exporting countries, and the average CIF (cost-insurance freight) unit price for the product in net importing countries during 1986–88.

In the base period of 1986–88, when India's entitlements were being calculated, the difference between the AAP and the FERP had been negative, which resulted in negative support to rice (Table 6.5). This was also true for almost all the products notified in India's schedule of commitments (Table 6.2). The low level of support during the base period led to the capping of policy space under the Amber box by the 10 per cent *de-minimis* limit.

India has submitted domestic support notifications to the WTO from 1995–96 to 2018–19. In these notifications, the portion of market surplus procured by the government agencies at the MSP is treated as the eligible production. This definition of eligible production has been questioned in various meetings of the committee on agriculture (CoA) by developed members who argue that total production should be treated as eligible production in the absence of procurement targets. Despite taking the actual procurement as eligible production, the PSS to rice has increased over the years due to increase

Table 6.5 *Product-specific support to rice during 1986–88*, in Rs million

Year	Applied administered prices	External reference price	Eligible production	Total market price support
	Rs/ton	Rs/ton	Million ton	Rs millions
1	2	3	4	5 = [(2–3)* 4]
1986–87	2,190	3,520	60.56	–80,545
1987–88	2,250	3,520	56.86	–72,212
1988–89	2,400	3,520	70.49	–78,949
1986–88, average	2,280	3,520	62.64	–77,235

Source: Based on India's Schedule of Commitments (WTO Doc. G/AG/AGST/IND).

Table 6.6 *Product-specific support calculation for rice, India, 2011–12 to 2018–19*

Year	Applied administered price (AAP)	FERP	Eligible production	Total market price support (MPS)	PSS as % of VoP
	US$/tonne	US$/tonne	Million ton	US$ million	(%)
2011–12	338.06	262.51	35.04	2,647.39	7.44
2012–13	344.67	262.51	34.04	2,796.70	7.67
2013–14	324.79	262.51	31.85	1,983.73	5.45
2014–15	333.66	262.51	32.04	2,279.66	6.15
2015–16	323.06	262.51	33.54	2,030.96	5.85
2016–17	328.75	262.51	38.10	2,524.19	6.67
2017–18	360.72	262.51	38.134	3,745.04	8.87
2018–19	375.41	262.51	44.331	5,004.97	11.46

Source: Authors' calculation.

in the MSP over the years, whereas the FERP had remained fixed, i.e. US$ 262.51/ton. As a result, India faces a severe constraint in policy space to implement its price-support schemes and continue to comply with its *de-minimis* limit commitments. In 2018–19, India exceeded the *de-minimis* limit of 10 per cent for rice (Table 6.6). To ensure the continuation of the MSP for rice, which also forms a part of India's food security programmes, India invoked the Peace Clause under the Bali Round. As per this decision, WTO members shall refrain from challenging the developing members' domestic support policies on staple crops in pursuance of PSH programmes for food security.

It is evident that there has been an overall increase in India's domestic support from 1995 to 2019–20, both in absolute and relative terms (Table

Table 6.7 *Trend of India's total domestic support notification, 1995–96 to 2018–19,* in million US$

Year	Amber box	Blue Box	Article 6.2 (Development box)	Article 6	Green Box	Total domestic support (TDS)	TDS as % of VoP
	1	2	3	4=1+2+3	5	6 = 4+5	7
1995–96	5,956	0	254	6,210	2,196	8,406	8.38
2000–01	0	0	8,478	8,478	2,851	11,329	10.09
2005–06	2	0	12,316	12,318	5,907	18,225	11.26
2010–11	2,282	0	31,610	33,892	19,479	53,364	16.73
2015–16	1,505	0	23,553	25,058	18,371	43,449	11.51
2016–17	4,757	0	22,831	26,271	19,693	45,964	11.17
2017–18	6,460	0	22,574	29,034	31,443	60,477	13.29
2018–19	9,790	0	24,184	33,974	22,482	56,456	12.52

Sources: India's submissions to WTO.

6.7). Due to limited policy space under the Amber box along with the constraining and outdated MPS methodology discussed above, India, like many other developing members, is facing a lack of policy space to provide product-specific support. Over the years, India's domestic support measures such as the MSP and input subsidy policies have been frequently questioned at the WTO.

Issues and Challenges Related to Domestic Support

India's biggest challenge regarding its economic policies is ensuring the food and livelihood security of the millions of poverty-stricken Indians. Given the high price volatility of agriculture and the general nature of subsistence-oriented agriculture for the millions of small and marginal Indian farmers, it becomes imperative for the government to enact agricultural policies that can help alleviate farm distress as well as address the broader issues of food and livelihood security of the farm population. There are some issues related to domestic support to agriculture, which have major implications for the welfare of Indian farmers.

Issues Related to Market Price Support-Backed Procurement

The price support-backed procurement system is one such tool that the Indian government uses to minimize the negative impact of price fluctuations to ensure remunerative prices to farmers. This policy is used not only by India; rather, it forms an essential component of food and income security programmes in many developing members such as China, Indonesia,

Kenya, Pakistan and Turkey, among several others. However, developing members, including India, are increasingly finding it challenging to provide price support due to two main reasons. First, unlike developed members, most developing members cannot provide PSS beyond the *de- minimis* limit.

Second, the outdated methodology comparing the AAP with the FERP, where AAP is for the current year and FERP is based on 1986–88 prices, results in an inflated figure for PSS (Panos and George 2014). Though Article 18.4 of the AoA mentions consideration of the impact of inflation on a member's commitments during the review process, it is not a unilateral right of the member. The uncertainty in the review process under the committee on agriculture (CoA) has been a major issue in the MPS methodology. It was because of this uncertainty that India has consistently demanded using an updated FERP based on a moving average of the last three or five years' export or import price (WTO 2012; South Centre 2014). Alternatively, members should be allowed to adjust the FERP for accumulative or excessive inflation since 1986–88 (Sharma 2018). Currently, many WTO members including India have been notifying domestic support notifications in US$. The advantage of notifying in a strong currency is that currency deprecation is considered in the MPS methodology. Despite this, the FERP of most agricultural products in India are lower than the MSP, resulting in positive market price support. In the case of rice, India used the Bali Peace Clause for the year 2018–19 as the product-specific support was more than 10 per cent. Without the Peace Clause, the MSP for rice would have been prone to legal challenge at the WTO.

Figure 6.1 *Fixed external reference price and MSP of selected agricultural products in India (US$/ton) for the marketing year 2018–19*

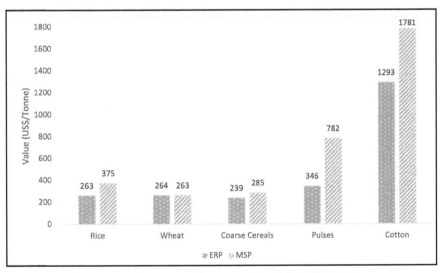

Source: India's latest DS:1 submission to WTO (Doc No. G/AG/N/IND/18).

Attack on De-minimis Limit

In the recent years, some members have also attacked the limited policy space available to developing members in the form of the *de-minimis* limit. As mentioned above, the Indian government can provide product-specific support up to 10 per cent of the VoP. Developing members find it challenging to implement product-specific measures, including price support, owing to the constraining limit of 10 per cent of the VoP. In agriculture negotiations, many developed members like Australia, New Zealand, Canada, EU and the US are demanding a reduction in the existing flexibility of the *de-minimis* limit for the developing members. Further, it is stated that the *de-minimis* limit for the developing members is 10 per cent in comparison to 5 per cent for the developed members. According to them, developing members need to undertake a proportional reduction in the Amber box for disciplining the trade-distorting support.

This argument by the developed countries is an attempt to dilute the special and differential treatment (S&D) provisions available to the developing members under the existing AoA. It ignores the huge flexibilities available to the developed members because of the historically high levels of AMS entitlement. India, along with other developing members, is demanding the elimination of the AMS entitlement as a pre-requisite for further strengthening the provisions for trade-distorting support.

The AMS Entitlement of Members

Most of the developing members cannot provide the Amber box support beyond the *de-minimis* limit as per their schedule of commitments. On the other hand, most developed members have the AMS entitlement to provide high levels of product-specific support beyond their applicable *de-minimis* limit. For instance, the US has subsidized coffee and bananas to the extent of 189 per cent and 64 per cent of the VoP, respectively, according to its 2017 notification. Similarly, the EU had given PSS to the extent of 60 per cent of the VoP in the past in 2008–09 (Figure 6.2). With these huge support levels, these members tend to gain artificial comparative advantages on select products, which in turn depresses the international prices of agriculture commodities and thus adversely affects the welfare of farmers in the developing nations.

Developing nations have often argued that the nature of the AMS entitlement is inherently distorting in nature. Members entitled to the AMS got their entitlements by virtue of having provided trade-distorting support in excess of their *de-minimis* limits in the base-period. Moreover, this entitlement is enjoyed by the members over and above their already applicable *de-minimis* limits. This, coupled with the fact that the AMS entitlement allows entitled members great flexibility in concentrating PSS to few select products, is the reason why developing nations believe, that any disciplines

Figure 6.2 *PSS support in excess of de-minimis limit by AMS entitled members,* in per cent

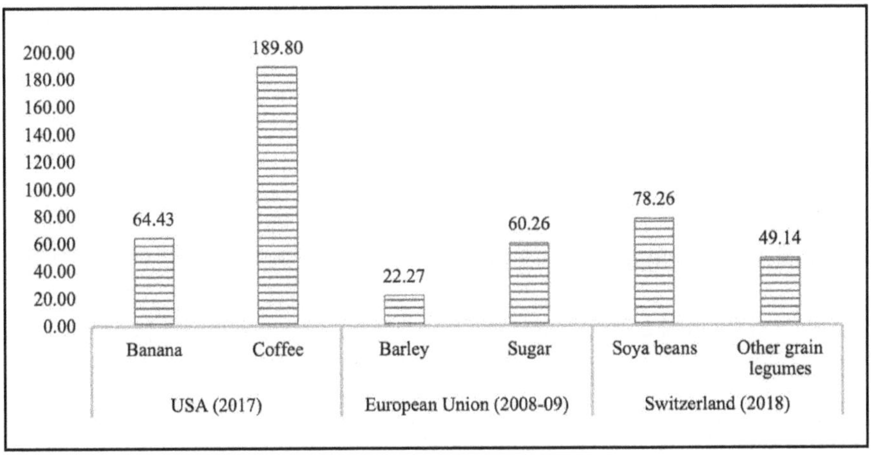

Source: Members' WTO notifications.

on domestic support should first and foremost seek to remove the asymmetrical AMS entitlement (WTO 2017b, 2018).

Capping Development Box Support and an Attack on S&D

The developed members not only attacked the existing *de-minimis* limit in the negotiations but have also attacked the developing members' entitlements under Article 6.2 of the AoA, by attempting to impose financial limits on Development box spending (WTO 2017a). This box has allowed the developing members to provide investment aid and input subsidies to low-income or resource-poor farmers without any financial limit under the AoA. Many developing and LDC members are using this box's provisions to support their vulnerable and poor farmers. Further, this is the foremost and significant S&D provision for the developing members under the AoA. Owing to its importance, many developing members strongly oppose any attempt to limit this flexibility in the agriculture negotiations.

The Bali Ministerial Decision and the Peace Clause

The importance of public stockholding and MSP procurement for food security purposes in developing economies has already been emphasized in previous subsections. In 2013, at the 9th Ministerial Conference of the WTO at Bali, the members agreed to a peace clause for the interim period till a permanent solution could be reached. This peace clause prevented any legal challenge to a developing members' existing PSH programmes for supporting traditional staple food crops in pursuance of food security. To use the peace clause, a developing member must notify that it is either breaching or about to breach its *de-minimis* limit on certain products to the committee on agriculture and must continue to provide regular domestic support notifications as well as additional information regarding all public stockholding programmes it maintains. On 31 March 2020, India became the first developing member to invoke the Bali peace clause, when it crossed the *de-minimis* limit on rice by providing PSS up to 11.46 per cent of the VoP.

While the peace clause provides a necessary shield from legal attacks on developing nations' PSH programmes, it has certain constraints of its own. Firstly, the peace clause covers only 'traditional staple food-crops' based on the predominant diet patterns in a certain developing member. This implies a very restrictive view of food security and ignores the larger concerns of the livelihood securities of cash crop farmers. Secondly, the Peace Clause's protection is only restricted to PSH programs that had been in existence at the time of the Bali Ministerial. Thus, it cannot be extended to protect future PSH programmes by developing members. Moreover, most developing nations find it onerous to comply with all the additional notification obligations imposed by the Bali decision on public stockholding. Due to this, along with other developing members, India has been demanding a permanent solution to the issues of PSH programmes for food security purposes, which is compatible with the socio-economic situations in the developing countries and will provide greater flexibility than the existing interim solution under the Bali peace clause.

Per-Farmer Support as a Negotiating Position

The basic principles and objectives of the multilateral trading system acknowledge that there exists a wide gap between the standards of living in the developing and the developed members. This is the main rationale behind all the S&D provisions under the various WTO agreements. This gap between economic realities of the two groups of members can be clearly seen from the fact that while farmers respectively hold at least 180 hectares or 315 hectares of land on an average in the US and Canada, farmers in India have an average landholding of 1.08 hectares only. Moreover, while more than 196 million people in India are dependent on agriculture and allied activities, the US farm sector comprises only 2.11 million farmers. Thus, it is essential to focus on actual per-farmer support received by agricultural producers in developed and developing nations. Most developed members provide support in the form of direct payments under the Green box along with the AMS entitlements for the Amber box. If only the Amber box per-farmer support is considered, an Indian farmer only gets US$ 49 per year, while his American and Canadian counterparts get US$ 7,253 and US$ 7,414, respectively. In case of per-farmer total support, it can be observed that farmers in the US received more than US$ 61,200 as per-farmer support in 2016, while in comparison Indian farmers received only US$ 282 in 2018–19.

This shows the manifest difference in the socio-economic realities of domestic support entitlements of developed members on the one hand and heavily populated farm-dependent developing members like India on the other. It is important to use the per-farmer-based domestic support criteria as an instrument in the agricultural negotiations at the WTO to create fairer rules of agricultural trade. It is necessary to eliminate the existing asymmetries in domestic support and create a level-playing field in agricultural trade, keeping in mind the interests of the millions of food-insecure and poverty-stricken farmers in developing members, such as India.

Conclusions

The Doha Declaration had promised substantial reductions in trade-distorting domestic support as well as mandated S&D for developing nations almost two decades ago. However, there was little progress in disciplining domestic support in the developed world. Instead, in the negotiating arena, there have been attacks on the developing members' policy space to provide domestic support to deflect attention from the disproportionate nature of entitlements enjoyed by some developed members of the WTO. As a result, members have highly polarized positions on domestic support at the WTO, making agricultural negotiations highly contentious.

Majority of Indian farmers are low-income or resource-poor farmers, and mostly engaged in rain-fed subsistence agriculture. They are additionally plagued by small landholding size, farm debt, poverty, livelihood insecurities and overwhelming farm distress. Most of India's farm support policies are targeted at the welfare of these distressed farmers. However, India faces several challenges about implementing domestic support policies that are in coherence with its socio-economic realities due to the inherent asymmetrical nature of domestic support provisions of the AoA. Domestic support measures of India have been consistently questioned by the developed members at the various meetings of the Committee on Agriculture. Attacks on India's price support policies on sugar is a glaring example of this fact. Price support measures of India for rice, wheat, pulses and other cash crops have also been cross-examined at the WTO through questioning or counter-notifications.[2] On the other hand, Indian farmers face an unfair playing field due to huge product-specific support and high per farmer support in the developed members.

In the agriculture negotiations, developing members need to be cautious about disciplining the trade-distorting support. Developing members should forcefully demand to change the outdated methodology for calculating the market price support. The external reference price should be based on recent years rather than based on 1986–88 prices. Limiting the flexibilities under the Development box as well as the reduction in the *de-minimis* limit will have substantial adverse implications for the policy space for the developing members. Instead, developing members need to continue to demand the elimination of the AMS entitlement as a primary requirement for reforming the rules pertaining to domestic support. In this regard, per-farmer support should be an integral part of agriculture negotiations to make future agricultural trade rules fairer for the poor farmers of the developing members.

Notes

[1] Schedule of Commitments here refers to a member's 'Supporting Tables for Commitments on Agricultural Subsidization' which includes detailed information on the provision of domestic support and export subsidies during the agreed base-period by the said member.

[2] A counter notification can be filed by a member at the COA opposing or questioning a Domestic Support notification filed by another member. In 2018–19, several of India's measures were challenged through this method by the US, Canada and Australia.

References

Birovljev, J. and B. Ćetković (2013), 'The Impact of the WTO Agreement on Agriculture on Food Security in Developing Countries', Paper presented in 135th Seminar of European Association of Agricultural Economists, Belgrade, Serbia, European Association of Agricultural Economists, 28–30 August 2013.

Government of India (GoI) (2020), 'Agriculture and Food Management', *Economic Survey 2019–20*, vol. 2, Ministry of Finance, Government of India, available at https://www.indiabudget.gov.in/economicsurvey/, accessed 22 March 2021.

Hawkes, S. and J.K. Plahe (2012), 'Worlds Apart: The WTO's Agreement on Agriculture and the Right to Food in Developing Countries', *International Political Science Review*, vol. 34, no. 1, pp. 21–38.

Josling, T. (2015), 'Rethinking the Rules for Agricultural Subsidies', *The E-15 Initiative: Strengthening the Global Trade System*, International Centre for Trade and Sustainable Development (ICTSD), available at http://e15initiative.org/wp-content/uploads/2015/09/E15-Subsidies-Josling-Final.pdf, accessed 22 March 2021.

Panos, K. and M. George (2014), 'WTO Domestic Support Disciplines: Options for Alleviating Constraints to Stockholding in Developing Countries in the Follow-Up to Bali', FAO Commodity and Trade Policy Research Working Paper No. 45, available at http://www.fao.org/fileadmin/templates/est/meetings/stocks/Konandreas-Mermigkas_16Feb2014.pdf, accessed 22 March 2021.

Schmitz A, T.G. Schmitz and F. Rossi (2006), 'Agricultural Subsidies in Developed Countries: Impact on Global Welfare', *Review of Agricultural Economics*, vol. 28, no. 3, pp. 416–25.

Sharma, S.K. (2016), 'Domestic Support under Agreement on Agriculture', in S.K. Sharma, *WTO and Food Security: Implications for Developing Countries*, Singapore: Springer.

——— (2018), 'WTO and Policy Space for Agriculture and Food Security: Issues for China and India', *Agricultural Economics Research Review*, vol. 31, no. 2, pp. 207–19.

——— (2020), 'A Quantitative Analysis of Proposals on Domestic Support in WTO Agriculture Negotiations: Need for Reaffirming the Development Agenda', CWS Working Paper No. 200/63, Centre for WTO Studies (CWS), Delhi, available at https://wtocentre.iift.ac.in/workingpaper/Working%20Paper%2063.pdf, accessed 22 March 2021.

Sharma, S.K. and A. Das (2017), 'Food Sovereignty under WTO: An Unfulfilled Promise at Buenos Aires', *Economic and Political Weekly*, vol. 52, no. 52, pp. 16–20.

——— (2018), 'EU-Brazil Proposal on Farm Support: Strengthening Agricultural Reforms or Undermining Them?', *Agricultural Economics Research Review*, vol. 31, no. 1, pp. 75–86.

Sharma, S.K., A. Sawant, P. Vats, S. Naik and T. Lahiri (2020a), 'Disciplining Trade-Distorting Support to Cotton in the US: An Unfinished Agenda in WTO Negotiations', *Agriculture Economics Research Review*, vol. 2, July–December.

Sharma, S.K., T. Lahiri, S. Neogi and R. Akhter (2020b), 'Revisiting Domestic Support to Agriculture at the WTO: Ensuring a Level Playing Field', CWS Working Paper No. 200/56, Centre for WTO Studies, Delhi, available at https://wtocentre.iift.ac.in/workingpaper/WorkingPaper56.pdf, accessed 22 March 2021.

South Centre (2014), 'The WTO's Bali Ministerial and Food Security for Developing Countries: Need for Equity and Justice in the Rules on Agricultural Subsidies', *South Bulletin*, no. 74, available at https://www.southcentre.int/question/the-wtos-bali-ministerial-and-food-security-for-developing-countries-need-for-equity-and-justice-in-the-rules-on-agricultural-subsidies/, accessed 22 March 2021.

Tania, S. and J.K. Mapulanga-Hulston (2016), 'Examining the Synergy Between the Right to Food and Agricultural Trade Policies', *African Journal of International and Comparative Law*, vol. 24, no. 2, pp. 293–26.

Taylor, M. (2014), *The Political Ecology of Climate Change Adaptation: Livelihoods, Agrarian Change and the Conflicts of Development*, Oxon and New York: Routledge.

World Trade Organization (WTO) (2012), 'G-33 Proposal on Some Elements of TN/AG/W/4/Rev. 4 for Early Agreement to Address Food Security Issues', WTO Doc No. JOB/AG/22.

——— (2017a), 'Special Session on Effectively Constraining Trade Distorting Domestic Support Using Fixed Caps from New Zealand, Australia, Canada and Paraguay', WTO Doc No. JOB/AG/100.

——— (2017b), 'Special Session on Elimination of AMS to Reduce Distortions in Global Agricultural Trade From China and India', WTO Doc. No. JOB/AG/102.

——— (2018), 'Special Session on Elimination of AMS Beyond *De-Minimis* to Reduce Distortions in Global Agricultural Trade from China and India', WTO Doc No. JOB/AG/137.

IV

Costs, Profits and Incomes

7

Economic Liberalization and Fertilizer Policies in India

Prachi Bansal and Vikas Rawal

Introduction

The use of chemical fertilizers has been key to agricultural growth in India since the 1970s. The widespread adoption of chemical fertilizers along with other modern inputs became possible because of specific policies that were introduced in the wake of the green revolution. Fertilizer policies following the green revolution were designed to meet the dual objective of expanding domestic capacity for fertilizer production and making fertilizers available to farmers at affordable prices. During this period, state policy ensured an increase in the supply of raw materials required for manufacturing fertilizers. The public sector and cooperatives led the production of fertilizers, and both fertilizer prices and the distribution of fertilizers across states were regulated by the government. The system of controls and subsidies was designed to provide assured returns to fertilizer manufacturers as well as keep fertilizer prices low for farmers.

Significant changes were brought about in these policies after the 1990s. These policy changes have had profound implications for Indian agriculture. Decontrolling the prices of all non-urea fertilizers was the most significant change brought about during the post-liberalization period. This resulted in a surge in prices of fertilizers and a bias towards urea consumption. This chapter analyses how the decontrolling of fertilizers prices and distribution was brought about in different phases by the government. The chapter also shows the effect of decontrolling on the prices, consumption, production and imports of these fertilizers.

Continuing with its efforts to decontrol fertilizer prices, the Indian government introduced a shift in the subsidy regime with a scheme called the Nutrient Based Subsidy scheme in 2010. This scheme delinked the subsidy regime from the prices of chemical fertilizers and consequently made possible the complete decontrolling of non-urea fertilizer prices. This policy change resulted in a massive rise in the prices of non-urea fertilizers, which has had severe implications for the Indian peasantry. This chapter attempts to critically review these policy changes. The Indian state has given a differential treatment to the use of urea fertilizers, which is important to examine in order to understand the political economy of fertilizer sector reforms. The chapter also discusses the major urea policies that the Indian government has implemented since 1991.

The rest of the chapter is organized as follows. The second section reviews the major debates on fertilizer subsidy in India. The third section discusses different stages in which prices and distribution of fertilizers were decontrolled after 1991. These include the Concession Scheme, the Nutrient Based Subsidy Scheme and policies specifically related to urea. The recent implementation of the Direct Benefit Transfer Scheme is discussed in the fourth section. The fifth section briefly discusses three recent policy changes: the requirement that urea be coated with neem oil, the reduction in the size of urea bags and the imposition of GST. The main findings of the chapter is summarized in the sixth section.

Major Debates on Fertilizer Subsidies in India

Fertilizer subsidies were introduced in India in the early 1970s as the use of chemical fertilizers was considered indispensable for achieving agricultural growth and food self-sufficiency under the green revolution strategy. With the adoption of the Structural Adjustment Programme in 1991, the debate on fertilizer subsidies shifted to the fiscal burden of these subsidies. India's joining the WTO in 1995 and the enactment of the Fiscal Responsibility and Budget Management (FRBM) Act in 2003 added to the pressure for cutting agricultural subsidies.

Critics of India's fertilizer policies have faulted these on various grounds including the rising fiscal burden of subsidies, the lopsided pattern of nutrient use, the overuse of fertilizers leading to the excess nitrification of soil, the low productivity of fertilizers and low fertilizer use efficiency. A number of official policy documents as well as scholars have argued that fertilizer subsidies should be reduced or terminated (see, for example, Ashra and Chakravarty 2007; Bathla, Joshi and Kumar 2020; Mahendra Dev 2011; Gulati 1990; Gulati and Banerjee 2015; Gulati and Narayanan 2000; Planning Commission 2015; Pratap Rao Bhosale Committee (JPC) 1992; Shanta Kumar Committee 2015; Vaidyanathan 2000).

Gulati and Sharma (1995), Gulati and Narayanan (2000) and Vaidyanathan (2000) argued that subsidies resulted in inefficiencies in production as well as use of fertilizers and should be withdrawn in a phased manner. Sagar (1991) argued that a part of the reduction in fertilizer subsidies could be absorbed by improvements in efficiency of fertilizer production and use, and a part via increases in food prices combined with targeted food subsidies.

The Pratap Rao Bhosale Committee (JPC) (1992) argued that fertilizer subsidies should be reduced and farmers should instead be compensated through higher minimum support prices (MSPs).[1] More recently, the Twelfth Five-Year Plan document also argued that increasing MSP and crop-specific packages with additional price incentives may be sufficient to address the issue of loss of income on account of a rise in the prices of inputs (Planning Commission 2015). However, this argument has not found favour with most critics of fertilizer subsidies, as such a change would result in an increased expenditure on food subsidies (Meenakshi 1992; Parikh, Kumar and Darbha 2003). Acharya (2000) has discussed many problems with the proposal to reduce input subsidies and compensate farmers by raising support prices. First, since the government procures only a few crops, merely increasing the MSP will not benefit all farmers. Second, to the extent that such a move is effective, the policy change is likely to be highly inflationary, with food inflation having a cascading effect on inflation in prices of other goods as well. Third, with the highly unequal distribution of land and production, most rural households in India are net buyers of food. As a result, high food inflation not only hurts the urban poor but also a vast majority of rural households. Finally, substituting fertilizer subsidies with higher food subsidies may not even result in a decline in the fiscal burden unless the overall level of support is reduced in the process.

One of the strongest arguments against input subsidies has been that these have crowded out investment in agriculture (Mahendra Dev 2011; Parikh *et al.* 1995; Kumar, Sen and Kurien 2004; Planning Commission 2002). Jha (2007) attributes the poor performance of agriculture in the post-reform period to the prioritization of agricultural subsidies as a way to meet recurring expenditure over agricultural investment that would improve productive capacity in the long run. Parikh *et al.* (1995) used an applied general equilibrium model to argue that agricultural growth would rise if reductions in input subsidies were used to finance irrigation investments.

There are three problems with the argument that fertilizer subsidies should be replaced with investments in irrigation. First, fertilizer use and irrigation are complementary inputs for agricultural growth and not substitutes. Complementary investments are also required for improving nutrient management at the farm-level. More generally, investment in infrastructure and fixed capital has to be combined with the optimum deployment of different variable inputs to achieve higher productivity. Given this, policies to ensure that farmers get modern inputs at affordable prices and investments in irrigation development (and other kinds of investment) have to be treated as complementary rather than alternative strategies. Second, the level of public expenditure on agriculture in India is relatively low. In 2012–15, while agriculture (including crops, livestock and fisheries) accounted for about 12.6 per cent of gross value added in the country, the share of agriculture in total budgetary expenditure was only about 7.5 per cent. This points to the need for increasing the total public expenditure on agriculture. Third, the argument that higher input subsidies have prevented the state from investing more in agriculture stems from the idea that the fiscal deficit must not be allowed to rise because, under the standard neoclassical assumptions of full-employment and full-capacity utilization in the economy, a higher fiscal deficit can be inflationary. However, in a demand-constrained economy that is characterized by high unemployment and a high degree of unutilized capacity, increasing public expenditure in sectors such as agriculture is likely to be expansionary rather than being inflationary (Patnaik 2003; 2006).

While most of the quoted studies have merely asserted that fertilizer subsidies can be substituted by investment to achieve growth, Storm (1994) examined the macroeconomic impact of expenditure on subsidies and irrigation on growth. Using a dynamic nine-sector computable general equilibrium (CGE) model, he estimated marginal returns per rupee of public expenditure for three policy options: a rise in public agricultural investment, a rise in fertilizer subsidy and a rise in public foodgrain procurement. The model showed that, of the three policies, marginal returns from expenditure were highest for fertilizer subsidies in the short run. In the medium run, an additional rupee of public investment raised the GDP by Rs 5.3, an additional rupee spent on fertilizer subsidies raised the GDP by Rs 3.14 and an additional rupee spent on public procurement of foodgrain raised the GDP by Rs 3.58. His simulations showed that the highest growth in GDP is obtained when an increase in public investment in agriculture is combined with an increase in input subsidies.

Decontrolling the Fertilizer Industry

The post-liberalization period saw a distinct change in the direction of fertilizer policies, from uniform and controlled prices towards a regime of decontrolled fertilizer prices. Until 1991, fertilizer prices were controlled through the Retention Price Scheme (RPS) and the distribution of fertilizers was controlled under the Essential Commodities Act (ECA), 1955. The RPS was introduced in 1977 in the wake of a sharp increase in the cost of fertilizer production due to the oil crisis. Under the RPS, the value of fertilizers produced was estimated by adding a 12 per cent post-tax return on the net worth to manufacturing cost which, in turn, was estimated for all manufacturers depending on the technology used, levels of capacity utilization and norms for inputs required. The RPS initially covered urea, ammonium sulphate (AS) and calcium ammonium nitrate (CAN). In 1979, phosphatic fertilizers were also brought under the scheme and in 1985, ammonium chloride (ACL) was brought under the RPS (C.H. Hanumantha Rao Committee 1998; G.V.K. Rao Committee 1987). The RPS ensured that fertilizer manufacturers received an assured return by compensating them for the difference between the value of fertilizers produced and the subsidized price. Along with this, the system of price controls kept the prices of fertilizers low for farmers.

With the increase in the production and use of fertilizers, expenditure on fertilizer subsidies under the RPS increased from 0.22 per cent of agricultural GDP in 1976–77 to 2.64 per cent of agricultural GDP in 1986–87.

The initial changes made to the fertilizer policies were ad-hoc and some of these had to be reversed immediately. In July 1991, soon after the process of economic liberalization began, the government announced a 40 per cent increase in the prices of urea. However, this was partially rolled back (by 10 percentage points) in August 1991. At the same time, ACL, AS and CAN were removed from the RPS and their prices were decontrolled.

These changes, however, could not be sustained and the focus shifted to decontrolling the prices and distribution of fertilizers other than urea. This was done in two stages: through the Concession Scheme introduced in the early 1990s and then through the Nutrient Based Subsidy Scheme launched in 2010. Although several official committees have recommended ways of decontrolling urea prices, these could not be implemented.

The Concession Scheme

The decade 1980–91 was marked by stagnation in the prices of fertilizers. However, the subsidy burden was increasing and so were the input costs for manufacturing fertilizers. There was also an increase in the cost of imported fertilizers. The aftermath of this crisis and the government's immediate introduction of ad-hoc changes required a comprehensive review. Thus, the government constituted a joint parliamentary committee on fertilizer pricing (JPC) under the chairmanship of Pratap Rao Bhosale in December 1991. The committee submitted its report in August 1992 and recommended that the prices (along with movement and distribution) of fertilizers containing phosphate and potash be decontrolled, that the prices of urea be reduced by 10 per cent, and that nitrogenous fertilizers, which had been removed from the RPS, be brought back under the scheme.

The motive behind decontrolling phosphatic and potash fertilizers was that these were imported (or manufactured using imported raw materials), and thus required a considerable outlay of foreign exchange. In 1990–91, about half of diammonium phosphate (DAP) and almost all potash fertilizers were imported (Table 7.1). The committee also argued that, unlike urea, these fertilizers were mainly used for commercial crops and by rich farmers, and therefore need not be subsidized. The class of farmers who

Table 7.1 *Consumption and import of P and K fertilizers in 1990–91,* in '000 tonnes

Fertilizer	Quantity imported ('000 tonnes)	Quantity consumed ('000 tonnes)
Diammonium phosphate (DAP)	2,155	4,248
Muriate of potash (MoP)	2,120	1,630
Sulfate of potash (SoP)	59	32

Source: Based on data from *Fertilizer Statistics,* 2016–17, The Fertilizer Association of India, New Delhi.

used phosphatic and potash fertilizers could also be partially compensated, the Bhosale Committee argued, through higher MSPs for the high value crops that such farmers grow (Pratap Rao Bhosale Committee [JPC] 1992).

Decontrolling the prices of fertilizers containing phosphate and potash on the basis of the Bhosale Committee recommendations in August 1992 resulted in a surge in the prices of these fertilizers. In light of this, the government was forced to introduce a new system of price controls and concessions in October 1992 to partially mitigate the price rise. However, the level of prices was allowed to remain higher than it was under the RPS. The new system of controls and concessions worked in an ad-hoc manner between October 1992–93 and 1996–97. During this period, state governments fixed the maximum retail prices (MRPs) of different fertilizers in their states, and the central government provided a certain amount as concession per tonne of fertilizers to fertilizer manufacturers to cover losses incurred on account of these new state-level price controls. In 1996–97, the central government provided a concession of Rs 1,000 per tonne each for DAP and MoP, and Rs 435–999 per tonne for other complex NP and NPK (nitrogen, phosphorous, potash) fertilizers. Since the rates of concession were fixed in an ad-hoc and arbitrary manner until 1996–97, this scheme came to be known as the Ad-hoc Concession Scheme.

With the implementation of the ad-hoc Concession Scheme, the price of DAP increased from Rs 4,680 per tonne in 1991–92 to Rs 9,450 in the kharif season of 1995–96 and Rs 9,938 per tonne in the rabi season of 1995–96.[2] Similarly, the price of single super phosphate (SSP) rose from Rs 1,440 per tonne in August 1991 to Rs 2,954 per tonne in the rabi season of 1995–96. The price of MoP more than doubled, from Rs 1,700 in August 1991 to Rs 3,714–4,300 per tonne in the rabi season of 1995–96. Over the period of the ad-hoc Concession Scheme, urea emerged as the cheapest fertilizer of all.

This distortion in prices led to a steep fall in the consumption of P- and K-based fertilizers. Figure 7.2 shows the impact of decontrolling

Figure 7.1 *Consumption of urea, DAP, SSP and MoP, 1990–91 to 2016–17*, in '000 tonnes

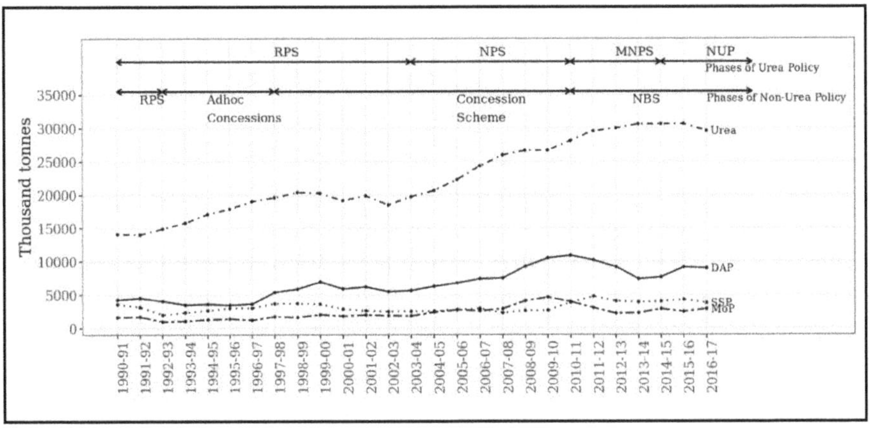

Source: Based on data from *Fertilizer Statistics*, 2016–17, The Fertilizer Association of India, New Delhi.

and the ad-hoc concessions on the consumption of DAP, SSP and MoP. Consumption of DAP declined by about a million tonnes between 1992 and 1995. Correspondingly, production of DAP also fell from 2,874 thousand tonnes in 1991–92 to 1,952 thousand tonnes in 1993–94. Total production of DAP and other NPK fertilizers fell from 6,368 thousand tonnes in 1991–92 to 4,859 thousand tonnes in 1993–94. Total production of SSP also declined from 3,650 thousand tonnes in 1990–91 to 2,257 thousand tonnes in 1993–94 (Appendix Table 1). Urea consumption, on the other hand, as shown in Figure 7.1, continued to rise during this period.

In 1996–97, the central government introduced a system of a uniform national prices for P and K fertilizers (except SSP) and a system for calculating the concessions to be given to fertilizer manufacturers. The method of estimating the rates of concession under the new scheme was developed by the Bureau of Industrial Costs and Prices. Under this scheme, the rates of concession were estimated quarterly and were based on an estimation of cost that covered not just the costs of raw materials and other inputs but also marketing costs and cost of raising capital. The concessions for complex NP and NPK fertilizers were determined in proportion to the different nutrients contained in these fertilizers using the concession for domestic DAP as the reference. The rates of concession were revised frequently to account for changes in input costs.

In 2000, the responsibility for implementing this scheme was transferred from the Department of Agriculture and Cooperation to the Department of Fertilizers. It is noteworthy that while most of the domestic production of DAP was based on imported phosphoric acid, a few plants were set up in this period with captive production of phosphoric acid. The Tariff Commission conducted a study in 2003 on the differences in manufacturing costs between plants having captive production of phosphoric acid and plants using imported phosphoric acid. On the basis of this study, the commission recommended that different rates of concession should be used for plants with captive production of phosphoric acid and plants using imported phosphoric acid (Planning Commission 2006). India's consumption of phosphoric acid in the year 2000–01 was 3.2 million tonnes out of which only about 1 million tonnes were produced domestically.

The international prices of P and K fertilizers, and of the inputs required for manufacturing these fertilizers, increased steeply in 2007–08 and 2008–09 (Figure 7.2). Since concessions during this period were directly linked to import parity prices, and this was a period in which oil prices and international prices of fertilizers shot up, the rates of concessions went up year after year. Table 7.2 shows that the average concession rate reached a peak of Rs 36,488 per tonne in 2008–09. In contrast, the price of DAP had to be controlled and remained at Rs 9,350 per tonne since 2001–02. This increase in rates of concession, necessitated by a sharp rise in international prices, meant a huge increase in the subsidy from about 3.5 per cent of agricultural GDP in 1992 to about 8.12 per cent in 2008–09 (Figure 7.3). According to the Department of Fertilizers (2014), about 94 per cent of the increase in subsidy outgo between 2005 and 2010 was on account of increase in international prices and only 6 per cent was due to a rise in consumption of fertilizers. As shown in Figure 7.3, the increase in subsidy bill was much steeper for P and K fertilizers, which had been shifted to the Concession Scheme, than for urea, which was still under the RPS.[3]

Figure 7.2 *International prices of urea and DAP, 1990–2019,* USD per metric tonne

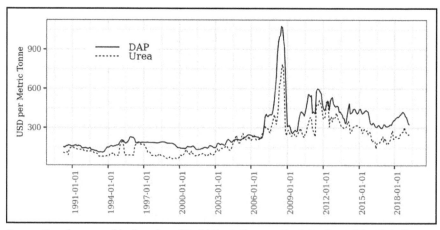

Source: Based on monthly data from World Bank Commodity Price Data (The Pink Sheet).

Table 7.2 *Average concession for domestically produced DAP, 2001–02 to 2009–10*, in Rs per tonne

Year	Average concession, in Rs/tonne
2001–02	3,510
2002–03	2,570
2003–04	3,254
2004–05	4,826
2005–06	5,759
2006–07	6,392
2007–08	8,489
2008–09	36,488
2009–10	10,532

Source: Based on data from *Fertilizer Statistics*, 2016–17, The Fertilizer Association of India, New Delhi.

The decontrolling of P and K fertilizers post-liberalization had a serious impact on the consumption of these fertilizers. The increase in prices was only partially contained due to the provision of concessions since 1997. Decontrolling fertilizer prices resulted in an increase in the retail prices of fertilizers other than urea, accentuation of nutrient imbalance and a slow-down in the use of non-urea fertilizers. While the cost to the farmer went up, paradoxically, the policy change did not result in any reduction in the fiscal burden of fertilizer subsidies.

Nutrient Based Subsidy Scheme

The increase in international prices in 2007–08 and 2008–09 was the primary reason for the increase in the fertilizer subsidy bill during this period, which was primarily absorbed through increasing concessions. This changed in 2010 with the introduction of the Nutrient Based Subsidy (NBS) Scheme, which took the process of decontrolling prices of fertilizers further. The NBS, which is in operation till date, covers 21 different kinds of fertilizers, the most important of which are DAP, MoP and SSP. Although urea is not covered under the NBS, other fertilizers containing nitrogen are covered under it.

The NBS Scheme introduced three main changes in the system of fertilizer subsidies. First, the subsidy given to manufacturers was delinked from international prices and the cost of production. Secondly, the subsidy was specified by the national government in terms of nutrient content – per unit of nitrogen (N), phosphorus (P), potash (K) and sulphur (S) – rather than for different fertilizer products. Thirdly, fertilizer manufacturers were given the freedom to set the retail prices of the fertilizers and the system of government regulation of prices of fertilizers (other than urea) was dismantled.

Along with these changes in the system of subsidies, the movement and distribution of 20 per cent of the production and imports of P and K fertilizers were back under the purview of the ECA.

Under the NBS regime, the government progressively reduced the rate of subsidy for P and K fertilizers (Figure 7.3 and Table 7.3). However, under the NBS regime, this subsidy is simply a top-up over and above decon-

Figure 7.3 *Expenditure on fertilizer subsidies as a proportion of agricultural GDP, 1991–92 to 2016–17*, in per cent

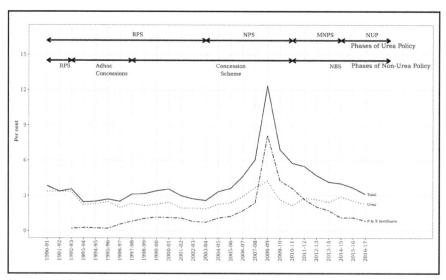

Note: Agricultural GDP is based on NAS series 2004–05 for the years 1990–91 to 2010–11 and NAS series 2011–12 for the years 2011–12 to 2016–17.
Source: Based on data from *Fertilizer Statistics*, 2016–17, The Fertilizer Association of India, New Delhi.

Table 7.3 *Subsidy for nitrogen, phosphorus and potash under Nutrient Based Subsidy Scheme, 2010–11 to 2017–18*, in Rs per kg of nutrient

Nutrient	2010–11	2011–12	2012–13	2013–14	2014–15	2015–16	2016–17	2017–18
Nitrogen	23.22	27.15	24.00	20.87	20.87	20.87	15.85	18.98
Phosphorous	25.62	32.33	21.80	18.67	18.67	18.67	13.24	11.99
Potash	23.98	26.75	24.00	18.83	15.50	15.50	15.47	12.39

Source: Based on data from *Fertilizer Statistics*, 2016–17, The Fertilizer Association of India, New Delhi.

trolled prices, and goes into the pockets of fertilizer companies (as they are not required to pass it on to farmers in the form of reduced prices).

It is not surprising that the introduction of such a scheme resulted in a surge in prices of fertilizers other than urea (Figure 7.4). The price of MoP increased from Rs 4,455 per tonne in 2009–10 to Rs 12,040 per tonne in 2011–12 (December), and has remained around that level since then. The price of DAP more than doubled from Rs 9,350 per tonne in 2009–10 to Rs 20,297 per tonne in 2011–12 (December) and to Rs 24,826 per tonne in 2018–19.

Figure 7.4 *Prices of fertilizers in terms of nutrients, 2004–05 to 2016–17*, in Rs per kg of nutrient

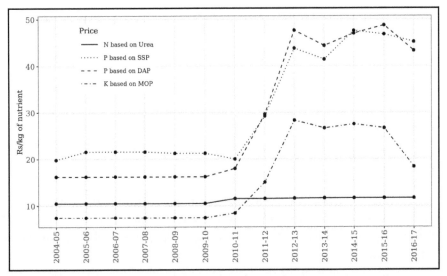

Note: Under NBS, retail prices are open and announced by the individual companies. The prices shown for 2010–11 to 2016–17 are indicative average prices.
Source: Based on data from *Fertilizer Statistics*, 2016–17, The Fertilizer Association of India, New Delhi.

Table 7.4 *Ratio of DAP, MoP and SSP prices to urea prices, 1991–2018*

Year	DAP to Urea	MoP to Urea	SSP to Urea
1991	1.50	0.50	0.57
2000	1.93	0.92	0.64
2003	1.93	0.92	0.69
2010	1.76	0.95	0.60
2018	4.53	2.44	1.40

Note: SSP price refers to the price of granular SSP.
Source: Based on data from *Fertilizer Statistics*, 2016–17, The Fertilizer Association of India, New Delhi and monthly bulletins from Department of Fertilizers, Government of India.

Figure 7.5 *Indian and international prices of DAP, 2010–2018*, in USD per metric tonne

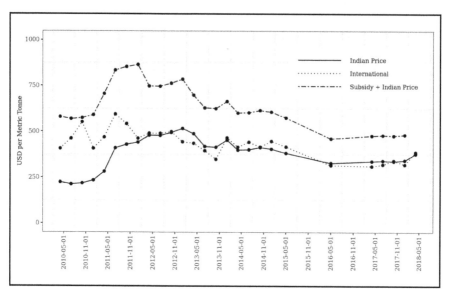

Source: Based on data from World Bank Commodity Price Data (The Pink Sheet) for international prices, monthly bulletins of Department of Fertilizers, Government of India for prices of Indian DAP, Fertilizer Association of India for data on subsidy and Federal Reserve Economic Data for exchange rate.

Figure 7.5 shows that after the implementation of the NBS scheme, Indian prices of DAP rose to the same level as international prices, and the movement of prices in India was closely aligned with the movement of international prices.

Implementation of the NBS scheme resulted in a sharp rise in the ratio of prices of non-urea to urea fertilizers. In 2018, DAP was 4.5 times more expensive than urea and MoP was 2.4 times more expensive than urea. SSP, which used to be cheaper than urea until 2010 and was the main phosphatic fertilizer used by poor farmers, was 1.4 times more expensive than urea in 2018 (Table 7.4).

Decontrolling the prices of fertilizers other than urea under the NBS regime accentuated the urea bias in Indian agriculture and resulted in a sharp decline in the consumption of DAP, SSP and MoP after 2010. Although DAP consumption started to rise slowly after 2014, the fall in MoP consumption was not arrested (See Figure 7.1). Imports of MoP fell from 6.3 million tonnes in 2010–11 to 2.4 million tonnes in 2012–13, and remained around that level since then (Appendix Table 1).

In conclusion, with the introduction of the NBS scheme, the state put in place a framework of fertilizer policies under which fertilizer manufacturers were allowed to sell fertilizers at profit-maximizing prices and were still given a substantial subsidy. The scheme provided no mechanism to ensure that the benefit of these subsidies was passed on by fertilizer manufacturers to farmers. The fluctuation in the prices of non-urea fertilizers on a very regular basis (almost monthly) implies that there is high instability in the market. Various decisions including stock maintenance by the seller or the farmer are influenced by this instability of prices.

Policies Related to Urea
The New Pricing Scheme: 2003 to 2014

Urea remained under the RPS until March 2003. In 2000, the Expenditure Reforms Commission (ERC) chaired by K.P. Geethakrishnan examined the issue of rationalizing fertilizer subsidies. The ERC recommended that movement and distribution of urea should be decontrolled with immediate effect, and that prices of urea should be decontrolled in a phased manner over a period of about five years. It was suggested that urea should be brought under the Concession Scheme with different rates of concession for urea plants using different kinds of feedstock, and the real prices of urea should be allowed to increase by about 7 per cent annually between 2001 and 2006. It was envisaged that the concessions would be reduced over time, to be covered by a gradual shift to natural gas-based plants, improvements in efficiency and a gradual rise in urea prices.

In consideration of these recommendations, the Department of Fertilizers appointed another committee under the chairmanship of A.V. Gokak to look into the possibility of introducing group-based concessions for urea. Based on the recommendations of this committee, in December 2002, a new scheme for urea units called the New Pricing Scheme (NPS) was implemented by the government. However, rather than changing the system of pricing and subsidies, the focus of the NPS was on decontrolling the distribution of urea and creating conditions for the technological modernization of the urea manufacturing industry.

The NPS was implemented in three phases.

Stage I was introduced on 1 April 2003 and lasted for one year. During this period, urea manufacturers were permitted to sell up to half of urea produced anywhere in the country, while movement and distribution of the remaining half continued to be regulated by the ECA.

A Working Group was constituted in December 2004, with Y.K. Alagh as Chair, to evaluate the performance of NPS. The Alagh Committee opposed the idea of decontrolling urea prices as envisaged by the ERC on the grounds that this would result in a huge increase in urea prices for farmers. The committee provided a roadmap of measures to shift urea manufacturing from naphtha-based to natural gas-based so that the cost of production could be brought down, which was argued to be a precondition for the eventual decontrolling of urea prices. In addition, the committee also recommended that the movement and distribution of urea be decontrolled completely.

Consequently, Stage II of the NPS, which ran from 1 April 2004 to 31 September 2006, focused on shifting urea production from naphtha to natural gas and increasing the efficiency of energy used per unit production of urea. The government invested in the domestic production and distribution of natural gas as well as in the creation of infrastructure for assured supply of natural gas through joint ventures with gas-rich countries such as Oman and Iran. The norms used for the calculation of subsidies were modified to provide incentives to energy-efficient and natural gas-based production and disincentivize production based on naphtha.

Stage III of the NPS ran from October 2006 to March 2010. The government notified a new investment policy in September 2008 for investments in urea manufacturing (for expansion of capacity in existing units as well as for the creation of new units). Under this policy, the government used an import parity price (with a floor of 250 USD/MT and a ceiling of 425 USD/MT) rather than the normative cost of production of urea to calculate the rate of subsidy for new urea plants or when additional capacity was created in existing plants. This incentive resulted in an increase in 2.3 million tonnes of capacity in existing plants. However, the policy failed to attract investments for new urea plants mainly because of shortage in availability of natural gas (Planning Commission 2011).

Policy changes under the NPS resulted in a sharp decline in the

Figure 7.6 *Consumption of naphtha (thousand tonnes) and offtake of domestically produced natural gas (million cubic metres) by fertilizer industry, 1990–91 to 2016–17*

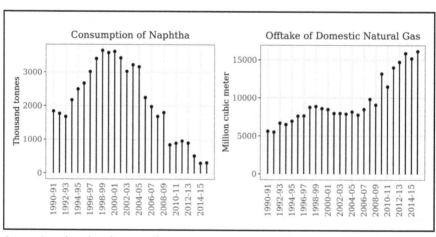

Source: Based on data from *Fertilizer Statistics*, 2016–17, The Fertilizer Association of India, New Delhi.

use of naphtha as feedstock in urea production. Figure 7.6 shows that the consumption of naphtha by the fertilizer industry fell from 3 million tonnes in 2002–03 to 0.8 million tonnes in 2009–10. During the same time, the offtake of domestically produced natural gas for fertilizer manufacturing increased from 7,955 million cubic meters in 2002–03 to 13,168 million cubic meters in 2009–10 (Figure 7.6). In order to meet the requirements of natural gas, the imports of liquified natural gas (LNG) were also encouraged. The Ministry of Petroleum and Natural Gas also expanded the gas pipeline network during these years.

The Modified NPS and the New Urea Investment Policy

Stage III of the NPS was extended up to September 2014 along with some modifications. The most important change introduced at this stage was the revision of norms for the estimation of costs other than that of raw material. These norms – termed as norms for 'fixed costs' although these also covered several components of variable costs – had remained unchanged since 2003.[4]

In 2012, a New Urea Investment Policy (NUIP) 2012 was announced in which additional incentives were provided in the form of compensation for the increase in gas prices.[5] NUIP also included a provision for assured buyback of urea for eight years starting from the date of production. However, this provision was withdrawn in 2014.[6]

New Urea Policy, 2015

In June 2015, the Government of India notified the New Urea Policy (NUP) for existing gas-based urea manufacturing units. The main components of the NUP were the introduction of a uniform gas price, that was a weighted average price of imported and domestic gas, and a further lowering of energy norms (Standing Committee on Chemicals and Fertilizers 2017).

The focus of urea policies since 2003 was to create conditions for shifting the domestic urea industry from naphtha-based production to the use of natural gas as the feedstock. While this has been achieved, the policies during this period failed to expand the domestic production of urea. At the same time, with sharply rising prices of fertilizers other than urea, the government was forced to keep the prices of urea low and compensate for increasing costs through higher subsidies (Figure 7.3). The prices of urea have remained fixed at Rs 5,360 per tonne since 2012. Contrary to the stated objectives of achieving self-sufficiency in the production of urea, the policies have resulted in a greater dependence on imports to meet the demand for urea (Appendix Table 1).

The focus of urea policies has been to create the conditions for an eventual decontrol of urea prices. This has not been possible so far because of the huge political implications it would have for the Indian state given that urea is the most widely used and the cheapest fertilizer available to the farmers. The government successfully shifted the domestic production of urea from naphtha-based to natural gas-based. However, no substantial increase in the domestic production of urea was achieved.

Direct Benefit Transfer Scheme for Fertilizer Subsidy

Various scholars have criticized fertilizer subsidies on the grounds that these disproportionately benefit rich farmers, farmers in the irrigated regions and farmers growing irrigated/commercial crops (Gulati 1990; Vaidyanathan 2000; Mahendra Dev 2011; Jha 2007; and Ashra and Chakravarty 2007). This has been used to argue for targeting of fertilizer subsidies to only poorer sections of the peasantry. Targeted fertilizer subsidies have also been advocated as a means of reducing the fiscal burden of fertilizer subsidies (Ministry of Finance 2016; Aadil and Rautela 2018). While a few scholars argued for targeting of fertilizer subsidies using coupons (Ashra and Chakravarty 2007), most recent contributions have argued for direct benefit transfers targeted to small and marginal farmers. Although proponents of direct benefit transfers to farmers have talked of a flat household-level transfer (as in the PM-KISAN scheme introduced in 2019), a per hectare transfer (Dalwai Committee 2018; Gulati and Banerjee 2015; Shanta Kumar Committee 2015 and as in the Rythu Bandhu Scheme in Telangana introduced in 2016) or transfers linked to the quantity of actual purchases of fertilizers (as sought to be implemented by the NITI Aayog), the relative merits of these have not been analysed.[7]

In October 2016, the government of India introduced a Direct Benefit Transfer (DBT) scheme for fertilizer subsidies on a pilot basis in seventeen districts. The NITI Aayog constituted a committee in September 2017 to prepare a roadmap for shifting to targeted cash transfers in lieu of fertilizer subsidies. In March 2018, the scheme was extended to the entire country.[8] In the first phase, point of sale (PoS) machines with Aadhaar-based biometric authentication were installed in fertilizer shops across the country and their use was made mandatory. Although the subsidy continued to be given to private companies, it was now computed on the basis of fertilizer sales recorded by the PoS machines rather than on the basis of the dispatch of fertilizers by fertilizer companies. During Phase I of the scheme, from October 2016 to July 2019, the fertilizer subsidy was paid to fertilizer companies. In this phase, by installing infrastructure to enable the biometric authentication of buyers and tying fertilizer subsidies to sales recorded through PoS machines, the government put in place the mechanism for targeted fertilizer subsidies.

There were no independent evaluations of the functioning of the DBT scheme during this phase. The only evaluation of the scheme, done by MicroSave, was commissioned by the NITI Aayog, which is spearheading the rollout of the DBT scheme (MicroSave 2018). The study showed that 81 per cent of sales were Aadhaar-authenticated.

Since no independent systematic evaluations of the DBT scheme were available, we travelled to Patiala (Punjab), Karnal (Haryana), Fatehabad (Haryana) and Bulandshahr (Uttar Pradesh) in August and September 2019, and interviewed about fifteen fertilizer dealers to inquire into the functioning of the DBT scheme. All the dealers we interviewed had PoS machines and reported using them. While the PoS machines required the Aadhaar numbers of the buyers to be recorded using fingerprint authentication, we found that no prospective buyer was turned away because they lacked an Aadhaar card. Since no subsidy was being transferred directly to customers and since there was no restriction on the amount of fertilizer that could be sold against a single Aadhaar number, it was common for dealers to record the sales of some customers against somebody else's Aadhaar information. Some dealers also reported problems like poor internet connectivity and the failure of biometric authentication by the PoS machines. Given that the subsidies were not being transferred directly to buyers, these problems were being dealt with by making entries in the PoS machines whenever internet connectivity was available and using the Aadhaar-authentication of any person available.

In July 2019, the Government of India announced launching of Phase II of the DBT scheme. In this phase, the government intended to shift to transferring the subsidy directly to the bank accounts of farmers, and to link fertilizer sales with land records and Soil Health Cards.[9] The PoS machines have been updated to provide area and crop-specific recommendations based on Soil Health Card data though these are not yet used to fix the subsidy entitlements of farmers. The shift in fertilizer subsidies from fertilizer companies to farmers necessarily requires the deregulation of fertilizer prices. The government has not yet announced whether the DBT will first be implemented for non-urea fertilizers only, or if there will be a phased deregulation of urea prices as well. No such roadmap has been made public by the government yet. The deregulation of urea prices would result in a dramatic rise in the prices of urea and the cost of cultivation. If implemented, this will add to already intense agrarian distress.

Targeting fertilizer subsidies using land records and Soil Health Cards would also be fraught with several problems. Given that land records in many states are not updated or computerized, that tenancy relations are informal, that the availability of formal sector credit is limited, and that rural markets are informal and interlocked, any system of targeting is likely to be fraught with errors and result in large-scale exclusion. Linking the transfer of subsidies to the mandatory use of Aadhaar-based authentication and PoS machines may result in large-scale exclusion in remote areas because of poor network connectivity and other technical constraints.

Other Recent Policy Changes

Over the last five years, three other changes have been introduced in the fertilizer policies. These are: making the neem oil coating of urea mandatory, the reduction in the size of the urea bags and a change in the taxation regime for fertilizers. In this section, we discuss the implications of these changes.

Neem Coating of Urea

The policy of introducing neem oil-coated urea started in June 2008, when the Fertilizer Control Order, 1985 was amended to allow fertilizer manufacturers to add micronutrients such as boron and zinc as well as neem oil to up to 20 per cent of their urea production. In September 2015, this policy was extended by making neem oil coating mandatory. It was argued that neem oil works as a nitrification inhibitor – that is, it would slow down the conversion of nitrogen into nitrates which are highly soluble and reduce the loss of nitrogen through leaching – and thus improve absorption of urea by plants, increase yields and cause a reduction in the use of urea. In addition, it was also argued that the coating of urea with neem oil would check the diversion of subsidized urea for non-agricultural uses.[10]

Based on a review of the literature, our assessment is that the scientific evidence on the impact of neem oil coating of urea on yields is very weak and limited. Almost all studies on the impact of neem oil coating of urea were conducted in experimental conditions and almost no evaluation existed of the impact in actual field conditions. A detailed review of the literature by Singh (2016) found that the impact of neem oil coating in most crops was small and diminished in soils with high pH levels. He found that the average increase in yield due to neem coating of urea was found to be 6.3 per cent in studies on paddy, 5.3 per cent in studies on wheat, 10.5 per cent in potato, 8.7 per cent in sugarcane, 4.3 per cent in cotton and 5.4 per cent in finger millet. The studies on maize found no increase at all. In about 30 per cent of the studies on paddy and wheat, neem oil coating was found to have no impact on yield.

Also, while neem oil coating was made mandatory for urea, it was not clear how the annual requirement of about 26,000 tonnes of neem oil (production of which, in turn, requires 2.6 lakh tonnes of neem seeds) was being met. There is some evidence suggesting that, in some cases, other oils and chemicals were used in place of neem oil.

Reduction in the Size of Urea Bag

In April 2018, Ministry of Chemicals and Fertilizers introduced a change in the size of urea bag, replacing the 50 kg bag with a 45 kg bag. It was argued that 'since farmers mostly assess the requirement of urea in terms of bags for agriculture purpose, it is estimated that the availability of urea in a 45 kg bag instead of a 50 kg bag may bring down consumption of urea by 10 per cent'.[11] It is not clear on what basis such a claim and policy decision were made. No reference was made to any pilot study, which might have been done to estimate the impact of such a change on urea consumption and to test if such an impact was likely to be sustained over time. While there was no evidence that shifting to smaller bags resulted in decline in urea consumption, the shift did seem to have resulted in higher cost of bagging and transportation. Fertilizer companies were demanding that they be compensated for this increased cost.

Imposition of GST on Fertilizers

The central government introduced a major change in the country's taxation system with the introduction of the Goods and Services Tax (GST) on 1 July 2017. GST, a centralized value-added tax, that replaced all central- and state-level VAT/sales taxes. The imposition of sales/VAT tax on fertilizers simply meant a reduction in government subsidy on fertilizers albeit in a round-about manner.

Before July 2019, the rates of VAT on fertilizers varied from zero tax to 5.5 per cent across the states. Under the new regime, a 5 per cent GST was imposed on all fertilizers resulting in an increase in taxation (or a net reduction in fertilizer subsidy) in many states.

Also, imported raw materials for manufacturing fertilizers carried a higher tax (ranging from 12 to 18 per cent). This resulted in manufacturers having to pay a higher tax on raw materials, and then claim a refund of excess payment towards input tax. Delays in input tax credit refunds added to problems of domestic manufacturers. High tax on raw materials particularly disadvantaged naphtha-based production of urea as naphtha was taxed at 18 per cent while natural gas was taxed at only 5 per cent. Under the earlier system of VAT, naphtha used for urea manufacturing was subject to only 4 per cent tax (Deshpande 2017).

Conclusions

The onset of economic reforms in 1991 shifted the focus of fertilizer policies away from playing a leading role in building the fertilizer industry and ensuring availability of fertilizers at affordable prices to farmers. Under neoliberalism, reducing the fiscal burden of fertilizer subsidy and foreign exchange burden of fertilizer-related imports became the overriding concerns of the state. Interestingly, the post-liberalization policies not only spectacularly failed in both these objectives, but they also resulted in a surge in prices of fertilizers other than urea, and vastly accentuated the urea bias in nutrient application in Indian agriculture. The analysis in this chapter shows that the decontrolling of prices of fertilizers other than urea through the NBS scheme resulted in a situation in which, while the state continued to incur a huge amount of expenditure on subsidies for these fertilizers, fertilizer companies were not required to pass on the benefits to farmers.

The shift to DBT for the disbursement of fertilizer subsidies was likely to have the most far-reaching effects on the Indian peasantry. With the pan-India rollout of the DBT scheme in 2018, the government put in place a framework for targeting fertilizer subsidies. Although mechanisms for targeting of subsidies were not yet enforced, the current policy had provisions for denying the benefit of fertilizer subsidies to farmers who did not have land registered in their own names or did not have registration under Aadhaar. The government was already preparing a roadmap for eliminating fertilizer subsidies and shifting to targeted cash transfers in lieu of fertilizer subsidies through PM-KISAN, a scheme for cash transfers to farmers introduced in March 2019. If implemented, the shift from fertilizer subsidies to targeted direct benefit transfers would be detrimental for farmers who can at least buy any amount of urea at subsidized and controlled prices presently.

We are thankful to Chirashree Dasgupta and Jesim Pais for their comments on the article. Usual disclaimer applies.

Notes

[1] The minimum support price is the floor price at which the government guarantees to procure crops from farmers.

[2] Kharif refers to the monsoon season (June–November in most parts of India) and rabi refers to the winter season (November–April in most parts of India). MRP of DAP and MoP are average MRPs of the MRP ranges that prevailed in the kharif and rabi seasons for the year 1995–96 across different states.

[3] A part of the rise in the subsidy bill may have been on account of a shift in fertilizer consumption towards urea because of an increase in the prices of fertilizers that had been moved to the Concession Scheme.

[4] Under the Modified NPS, the concessions to urea units included the minimum fixed cost of Rs 2,300 per tonne or actual fixed cost prevailing in 2012–13, along with an additional incentive of Rs 350 per tonne to existing urea units if their fixed cost is less than the minimum fixed cost of Rs 2,300 per tonne. Special compensation was announced for gas-based urea plants at Rs 150 per tonne for units that have completed thirty years of operation.

[5] The major addition this policy provided was that for each $1 increase in gas price beyond $6.50 per million Btu for new projects and $7.5 per million Btu for the revamp projects, compensation to the manufacturer increases by $20 per tonne for new urea units and $22 per tonne for revamped units.

[6] The Modified NPS also notified the shutting down of the three remaining naphtha-based units by 30 September 2014. However, these plants were re-opened in June 2015 and were allowed to operate using naphtha.

[7] See http://www.pmkisan.gov.in/ for details of the PM-KISAN Scheme and see http://rythubandhu.telangana.gov.in/ for details of the *Rythu Bandhu* Scheme.

[8] http://fert.nic.in/page/direct-benefit-transfer-dbt.

[9] The Soil Health Card scheme was launched by the Government of India in 2015.

Under the scheme, a large number of private testing facilities have been used to test soils, and farmers have been provided with Soil Health Cards bearing the results of soil tests for their land and recommendations on the appropriate dosage of fertilizers to be used. For more information, see https://soilhealth.dac.gov.in/Content/blue/soil/index.html.

[10] http://www.pib.nic.in/Pressreleaseshare.aspx?PRID=1559069, accessed 19 March 2021.

[11] Ministry of Chemicals and Fertilizers, Government of India, Rajya Sabha Unstarred Question No 2131, Savings with the usage of reduced quantity in urea bags, asked by C M Ramesh, Answered by Rao Inderjit Singh, Minister of State (Independent Charge) on 5 January 2018.

References

Aadil, A. and R. Rautela (2018), 'Enablers for Direct Benefit Transfers of Fertilizer Subsidy', MicroSave, available at http://www.microsave.net/wp-content/uploads/2018/10/IFN_148_Enablers_for_Direct_Benefit_Transfers_of_Fertiliser_subsidy-1.pdf.

Acharya, S.S. (2000), 'Subsidies in Indian Agriculture and Their Beneficiaries', *Agricultural Situation in India*, vol. 57, no. 5, August, pp. 251–60.

Ashra, S. and M. Chakravarty (2007), 'Input Subsidies to Agriculture: Case of Subsidies to Fertilizer Industry Across Countries', *Vision: The Journal of Business Perspective*, vol. 11, no. 3, pp. 35–58, available at https://journals.sagepub.com/doi/10.1177/097226290701100305.

Bathla, S., P.K. Joshi and A. Kumar (2020), *Agricultural Growth and Rural Poverty Reduction in India*, India Studies in Business and Economics, Singapore: Springer.

C.H. Hanumantha Rao Committee (1998), 'Fertilizer Pricing Policy: Report of the High-Powered Review Committee', Department of Fertilizers, Ministry of Chemicals and Fertilizers, New Delhi.

Dalwai Committee (2018), 'Structural Reforms and Governance Framework', Report of the Committee on Doubling Farmers' Income, vol. 13, Department of Agriculture, Cooperation and Farmers' Welfare, Ministry of Agriculture and Farmers' Welfare, Government of India, New Delhi, url: http://farmer.gov.in/imagedefault/DFI/DFI%20Volume%2013.pdf .

Department of Fertilizers (2014), 'Annual Report 2013–14', Department of Fertilizers, Ministry of Chemicals and Fertilizers, Government of India, available at http://fert.nic.in/sites/default/files/Annual_Report2013-14%20eng.pdf.

Deshpande, R.M. (2017), 'Impact of GST on Fertilizer Sector', *Indian Journal of Fertilizers*, 13 September, pp. 12–23.

Gulati, A. (1990), 'Fertilizer Subsidy: Is the Cultivator Net Subsidized', *Indian Journal of Agricultural Economics*, vol. 45, no. 1, pp. 1–9.

Gulati, A. and P. Banerjee (2015), 'Rationalizing Fertilizer Subsidy in India: Key Issues and Policy Options', Working Paper No. 307, August, Indian Council for Research on International Economic Relations, New Delhi, http://www.esocialsciences.org/Download/repecDownload.aspx?fname=A201671511465_53.pdfandfcategory=ArticlesandAId=11083andfref=repec.

Gulati, A. and S. Narayanan (2000), 'Demystifying Fertilizer and Power Subsidies in India', *Economic and Political Weekly*, vol. 35, no. 10, pp. 784–94.

Gulati, A. and A. Sharma (1995), 'Subsidy Syndrome in Indian Agriculture', *Economic and Political Weekly*, vol. 30, no. 39, pp. A93–A102.

Gupta, U. (2019), 'Direct Action Needed for Direct Benefits', *The Pioneer*, 6 May 2019, available at https://www.dailypioneer.com/2019/columnists/direct-action-needed-for-direct-benefits.html.

G.V.K. Rao Committee (1987), 'Report of the High-Powered Committee on Fertilizer Consumer Prices', Ministry of Agriculture, Government of India, Delhi.

Jha, R. (2007), 'Investment and Subsidies in Indian Agriculture', Australia South Asia
    Research Centre, Research School of Pacific and Asian Studies, Australian National
    University, Australia, available at https://ssrn.com/abstract=987147 or http://dx.doi.
    org/10.2139/ssrn.987147.

Kumar, S., T. Sen, and N.J. Kurien (2004), *Central Budgetary Subsidies in India*, National
    Institute of Public Finance and Policy, New Delhi, available at https://www.nipfp.
    org.in/media/medialibrary/2013/08/Subsidy-_Dec10-2004-FINAL.pdf.

Mahendra Dev, S. (2011), 'Macro and Farm Level Investment in India: Trends, Determinants
    and Policies, Food and Agriculture Organization of the United Nations', Rome,
    available at http://www.fao.org/fileadmin/templates/tci/pdf/India/Micro_and_farm_
    level_investment_in_India.pdf.

Meenakshi, J.V. (1992), 'Partial Decontrol of Fertilizer Prices', *Economic and Political Weekly*,
    vol. 27, no. 43–44, pp. 2347–48.

MicroSave (2018), 'DBT in Fertiizer: Independent Assessment Report', MicroSave, available
    at http://staging.microsave.net/searches/tag_by_resources/Direct%20benefit%20
    transfer

Ministry of Finance (2016), *Economic Survey of India: 2015–16*, Department of Economic
    Affairs, Ministry of Finance, New Delhi, available at https://www.indiabudget.gov.
    in/budget2016-2017/es2015-16/echapter-vol2.pdf

Parikh, K., A. Ganesh Kumar and G. Darbha (2003), 'Growth and Welfare Consequences of
    Rise in MSP', *Economic and Political Weekly*, vol. 38, no. 9, pp. 891–95.

Parikh, K., N.S.S. Narayana, M. Panda and A. Ganesh Kumar (1995), 'Strategies for Agricul-
    tural Liberalisation: Consequences for Growth, Welfare, and Distribution', *Economic
    and Political Weekly*, vol. 30, no. 39, pp. A90–A92.

Patnaik, P. (2003), 'The Humbug of Finance', in *The Retreat to Unfreedom: Essays on the
    Emerging World Order*, New Delhi: Tulika Books.

————— (2006), 'What is Wrong with Sound Finance', *Economic and Political Weekly*, vol.
    41, no. 43–44, pp. 4560–64.

Planning Commission (2002), *Tenth Five Year Plan: 2002–2007: Sectoral Policies and Program-
    mes*, vol. 2, Planning Commission, Government of India, New Delhi, available
    at https://niti.gov.in/planningcommission.gov.in/docs/plans/planrel/fiveyr/10th/
    volume2/10th_vol2.pdf.

————— (2006), 'Report of the Working Group on Fertilizer Industry for the Eleventh Five Year
    Plan', Department of Fertilizers, Ministry of Chemicals and Fertilizers, Government
    of India, available at https://niti.gov.in/planningcommission.gov.in/docs/aboutus/
    committee/wrkgrp11/wg11_fertliser.pdf.

————— (2011), 'Report of the Working Group on Fertilizer Industry for the Twelfth Five Year
    Plan', Department of Fertilizers, Ministry of Chemicals and Fertilizers, Government
    of India, New Delhi.

————— (2015), *Twelfth Five Year Plan (2012–17): Economic Sectors*, vol. 2, Planning
    Commission, Government of India, New Delhi, available at https://niti.gov.in/
    planningcommission.gov.in/docs/plans/planrel/fiveyr/12th/pdf/12fyp_vol2.pdf.

Pratap Rao Bhosale Committee (JPC) (1992), 'Fertilizer Pricing: Extracts from Report of the
    Joint Committee on Fertilizer Pricing', Government of India, New Delhi.

Roychoudhury, A. (2019), 'Govt Working to Directly Transfer Fertilizer Subsidy to Farmers',
    Business Standard, 19 April, available at https://www.business-standard.com/
    article/economy-policy/govt-working-to-directly-transfer-fertiliser-subsidy-to-
    farmers-119041900866_1.html.

Sagar, V. (1991), 'Fertilizer Pricing: Are Subsidies Essential?', *Economic and Political Weekly*,
    vol. 26, no. 50, pp. 2861–64.

Shanta Kumar Committee (2015), 'Report of the High-Level Committee on Reorienting
    the Role and Restructuring of Food Corporation of India', Government of India,
    New Delhi, available at http://fci.gov.in/app2/webroot/upload/News/Report%20

of%20the%20High%20Level%20Committee%20on%20Reorienting%20the%20 Role%20and%20Restructuring%20of%20FCI_English.pdf.

Singh, B. (2016), 'Agronomic Benefits of Neem Coated Urea: A Review', Paper presented at the Crossroads Asia Pacific Conference, International Fertilizer Association, Singapore, October 25–27, doi: 10.13140/RG.2.2.10647.98722.

Standing Committee on Chemicals and Fertilizers (2017), 'Implementation of New Urea Policy, 2015', Department of Fertilizers, Ministry of Chemicals and Fertilizers, Government of India, available at http://164.100.47.193/lsscommittee/Chemicals%20and%20 Fertilizers/16_Chemicals_And_Fertilizers_40.pdf.

Storm, S. (1994), 'The Macroeconomic Impact of Agricultural Policy: A CGE Analysis for India', *Journal of Policy Modeling*, vol. 16, no. 1, pp. 55–95.

The Fertilizer Association of India (2017), *Fertilizer Statistics: 2016–17*, The Fertilier Association of India, New Delhi.

Vaidyanathan, A. (2000), 'Agricultural Input Subsidies', *Agricultural Situation in India*, vol. 57, no. 5, August, pp. 261–65.

Appendix

Appendix Table 1 *Production and import of urea, DAP, MoP and SSP, 1990–91 to 2016–17*, in thousand tonnes

Year	Urea		DAP		MoP	SSP
	Production	Imports	Production	Imports	Imports	Production
1990–91	12,835.9	–	1,904.9	2,155	2,120	3,650.3
1991–92	12,831.3	391	2,873.6	2,077	2,040	2,984.8
1992–93	13,125.9	1,857	2,598.8	1,533	1,761	2,329.3
1993–94	13,150.2	2,840	1,951.5	1,569	1,428	2,257.2
1994–95	14,137.1	2,884	2,820.1	792	2,120	3,024.6
1995–96	15,805.6	3,782	2,645.3	1,475.5	2,356.2	3,201.9
1996–97	15,628.7	2,328	2,765.2	475	1,100.9	3,187.0
1997–98	18,594.5	2,389	3,665.6	1,536	2,380.4	3,832.5
1998–99	19,292.2	556	3,864.4	2,091.1	2,579.8	3,816.1
1999–00	19,807.7	533	3,860.8	3,268	2,946.1	3,532.7
2000–01	19,623.8	–	4,881.5	861	2,646	2,742.2
2001–02	19,003.1	220	5,091.2	932.7	2,810.2	2,504.6
2002–03	18,621.2	119	5,235.6	383.2	2,603.2	2,407.7
2003–04	19,038.3	143	4,708.7	734.1	2,579.3	2,543.4
2004–05	20,239.2	641	5,172.3	643.6	3,409.5	2,461.1
2005–06	20,085.1	2,056	4,554.3	2,437.7	4,577.5	2,795.2
2006–07	20,271.2	4,718	4,713.1	2,875.4	3,448.4	2,972.0
2007–08	19,838.8	6,928	4,211	2,723.6	4,420.8	2,246.3
2008–09	19,923.2	5,667	2,992.5	6,191.7	5,671.7	2,533.6
2009–10	21,120.7	5,210	4,246.1	5,888.9	5,286.5	3,093.0
2010–11	21,872.5	6,610	3,541.2	7,411	6,357	3,712.8
2011–12	21,992.3	7,834	3,951.3	6,905.2	3,984.6	4,324.0
2012–13	22,586.6	8,044	3,646.8	5,702.3	2,496.1	4,434.9
2013–14	22,718.7	7,088	3,628.2	3,261.1	3,180	4,211.5
2014–15	22,592.9	8,749	3,445.4	3,853	4,197	4,229.6
2015–16	24,461.3	8,474	3,787	6,008	3,243	4,329.6
2016–17	24,201.0	5,481	4,365	4,385	3,736	4,418.0

Source: Based on data from *Fertilizer Statistics*, 2016–17, The Fertilizer Association of India, New Delhi; and monthly bulletins from the Department of Fertilizers, Government of India.

8

Transformation of the Irrigation Economy in India

From Public to Private

Tapas Singh Modak

This chapter examines changes in the irrigation economy of India in the post-independence period by drawing upon secondary data and data from in-depth village surveys conducted by the Foundation for Agrarian Studies (FAS).[1] It argues that there was a shift from surface irrigation to groundwater irrigation over the years, and the growth of groundwater irrigation was associated with greater inequality in the ownership of irrigation equipment and in access to an assured source of irrigation. The evidence from village-level data shows that while intervention by the state protects the interests of small and poor cultivators, private control over water adversely affects access to irrigation, crop choice and profitability in agriculture.

The Development of Irrigation in India: A Brief Review

At the time of independence, agriculture in India faced a crisis of stagnation marked by low crop yield, low share of irrigated area, large areas of cultivated land lying fallow, deterioration in soil quality and seeds of poor quality (Nanavati and Anjaria 1965, cited in Ramakumar 2012). The expansion and improvement of irrigation facilities were thus seen as important instruments to overcome the crisis in agriculture and achieve self-sufficiency in foodgrain production. The green revolution of the 1960s established the importance of irrigation, among other inputs, to achieve higher productivity in agriculture (Vaidyanathan 1999). From the late 1970s onwards, there was an increase in the area under groundwater irrigation. At the same time, the policies by different state governments in India primarily focused on promoting groundwater use for irrigation through measures such as electricity supply at subsidized flat-rates or free of cost, subsidized institutional credit for construction of groundwater structures, and the expansion of the public tubewell programme in eastern India (Uttar

Pradesh, Bihar and West Bengal). Private investment in groundwater irrigation also registered a rapid increase since then over the years, with groundwater irrigation accounting for about 70 per cent of the total irrigated area in 2014 (NSSO 2015).

Therefore, broadly, irrigation development in India can be categorized into three phases. In the first phase after independence, the early 1950s witnessed significant investments in public surface irrigation schemes and an increase in the area irrigated under these schemes. Groundwater development did not receive much attention in this phase, as the major policy thrust was on canal irrigation. The second phase, beginning from the late 1970s, is marked by an increase in the area under groundwater irrigation (Vaidyanathan 1999). With the liberalization of the Indian economy in the 1990s, the share of area under public surface irrigation declined and there was a corresponding increase in the share of area under private groundwater irrigation. Private investments in groundwater irrigation increased rapidly, while public investment declined. This marks the third phase of irrigation development.

Trends in Public Investment in Irrigation

Over the decades, public policies and expenditure patterns relating to irrigation in India have undergone significant changes, and influenced irrigation systems across the country. In India, one important feature of agriculture has been the complementarity between public and private investments. It was argued by several scholars that public investment in India played an important role in inducing private investment, therefore significantly contributing to growth in agriculture (Rao 1993; Dhawan 1997; Shetty 1990). Thus, typically, public investment in irrigation or rural infrastructure (electrification) helped induce private financing in irrigation (Rawal 1999).

However, the relationship between public and private investments changed with the liberalization of the Indian economy. There was an overall stagnation in public investment in the agricultural sector. This section, specifically, reviews investment patterns with reference to India's irrigation systems in the post-independence period.

Table 8.1 shows the magnitude and composition of investment under different heads of the irrigation sector for various Five-Year Plans (henceforth FYP). It is evident from the Table 8.1 that the period under review saw significant changes in the irrigation sector. First, investment in major and medium irrigation schemes constituted the largest share of expenditure in the irrigation sector across the FYP, though a steep rise in prices and construction costs over time might account for this.

Secondly, considerable funding was given to minor irrigation works from the Third FYP (1960–61 to 1965–66), with groundwater receiving greater attention within the category of minor irrigation works. Public investment in minor irrigation works included direct investment by the government and institutional credit for private investment (mostly for groundwater irrigation). Institutional credit from the public sector rose sharply during the Third FYP (1960–61 to 1965–66) and Fourth FYP (1969–70 to 1973–74). More than 95 per cent of groundwater structures were established by farmers' own investment with the help of credit facilities from the Government of India and other financial institutions (Shah 1993; Vaidyanathan 1994, cited in Narayanamoorthy and Deshpande 2005). This shift in the expenditure pattern from major and medium irrigation to minor irrigation works, specifically for groundwater irrigation, and greater supply of institutional credit may have helped in the expansion of the area irrigated by groundwater in the country after the 1960s.

Thirdly, from the late 1990s, there was a noticeable decline in institutional credit for minor irrigation schemes. For example, between the Fourth FYP (1969–70 to 1973–74) and the Seventh FYP (1985–86 to 1989–90), public sector institutional credit as a proportion of the total investment in irrigation remained at around 15 per cent, and declined to 3 per cent during the Tenth FYP (2002–03 to 2006–07) to only 1 per cent during the Eleventh FYP (2007–08 to 2011–12). Even the share of institutional credit as proportion of total investment in minor irrigation ranged between 40 to 50 per cent till Eighth FYP, and declined to 7.5 per cent during Eleventh FYP.

In the period between the Fourth and the Seventh FYPs, the total investment in minor irrigation schemes ranged between 30 to 50 per cent; this declined to 18.5 per cent during the Eleventh FYP.

In sum, though significant attention was directed towards irrigation as a part of the development of agriculture in the early decades after independence, public expenditure to expand irrigation slackened since the Seventh FYP, particularly from the mid-1980s onwards. Farmers invested in groundwater irrigation separately from the state as a response to the stagnation in public investment in irrigation, particularly surface irrigation schemes (Ramakumar 2012). These shifts in the investment pattern may affect the trends in area irrigated by different sources over time, as shown below.

Shift in Sources of Irrigation: From Public Canals to Private Tubewells

Table 8.3 shows the trends in area irrigated by different sources between 1950–51 and 2015–16. The total net irrigated area in the country increased from 20.9 million hectares (mha) in 1950–52 to 67.3 mha in 2015–16. In the same period, the gross area irrigated increased over four

Table 8.1 *Magnitude and composition of investment in the irrigation sector for different Plan periods, 1951–56 to 2002–07*, at current prices in Rs crore

Five Year Plans (FYPs)	Period	Major and medium irrigation	Minor irrigation			Command Area Development	Total
			Government	Institutional credit	All		
First FYP	1950–51 to 1954–55	376 (85)	66 (15)	Neg. (–)	66 (15)	–	442 (100)
Second FYP	1955–56 to 1959–60	380 (70)	142 (26)	19 (4)	162 (30)	–	542 (100)
Third FYP	1960–61 to 1965–66	576 (57)	326 (32)	115 (11)	442 (43)	–	1,018 (100)
Annual Plans	1966–67 to 1968–69	430 (44)	321 (33)	235 (24)	556 (56)	–	986 (100)
Fourth FYP	1969–70 to 1973–74	1,242 (52)	506 (21)	661 (27)	1,167 (48)	–	2,410 (100)
Fifth FYP	1974–75 to 1978–79	2,516 (62)	628 (15)	799 (20)	1,426 (35)	148 (4)	4,090 (100)
Annual Plan	1979–80	2,079 (64)	496 (15)	481 (15)	977 (30)	215 (7)	3,271 (100)
Sixth FYP	1980–81 to 1984–85	7,369 (64)	1,979 (17)	1,438 (12)	3,417 (30)	743 (6)	11,529 (100)
Seventh FYP	1985–86 to 1989–90	11,107 (59)	3,132 (17)	3,061 (16)	6,193 (33)	1,448 (8)	18,748 (100)

Table 8.1 (*continued*)

Five Year Plans (FYPs)	Period	Major and medium irrigation	Minor irrigation			Command Area Development	Total
			Government	Institutional credit	All		
Annual Plan	1990–91	2,635 (60)	812 (18)	676 (15)	1,488 (34)	286 (6)	4,408 (100)
Annual Plan	1991–92	2,824 (60)	844 (18)	674 (14)	1,518 (32)	334 (7)	4,676 (100)
Eighth FYP	1992–93 to 1996–97	21,669 (64)	6,231 (18)	4,242 (12)	10,472 (31)	1,938 (6)	34,080 (100)
Ninth FYP	1997–98 to 2001–02	49,290 (78)	8,635 (14)	2,662 (4)	11,297 (18)	2,223 (4)	62,809 (100)
Tenth FYP	2002–03 to 2006–07	83,647 (81)	13,924 (13)	3,257 (3)	17,182 (17)	2,535 (2)	1,03,364 (100)
Eleventh FYP*	2007-08 to 2011-12	174,473 (79)	37,606 (17)	3,059 (1)	40,665 (18)	4,922 (2)	2,20,060 (100)

Notes: Figures in parentheses indicate row share. Major irrigation schemes are those with a Culturable Command Area (CCA) of more than 10,000 hectares; medium irrigation schemes have a CCA of more than 2,000 hectares and up to 10,000 hectares; and minor irrigation schemes have a CCA of less than 2,000 hectares. The Command Area Development (CAD) programme was initiated in 1974–75 to improve utilization of the irrigation potential, and optimize agricultural production and productivity, through an integrated and coordinated approach to efficient water management.
* The figures for 2007–08, 2008–09 and 2009–10 are the actual expenditure, and for 2010–11 and 2011–12 are the approved outlay.
Source: Water and Related Statistics, Central Water Commission 2013.

Table 8.2 *Plan-wise outlay on irrigation and flood control by the centre, states and union territories, 1960–61 to 2011–12, at current prices,* in Rs crore and per cent

Five-Year Plan (FYP)	Period	Actual plan outlay (in Rs crore)	Percentage of total plan outlay
Third FYP	1960–61 to 1965–66	664	7.8
Annual Plans	1966–67 to 1968–69	471	7.1
Fourth FYP	1969–70 to 1973–74	1,354	8.6
Fifth FYP	1974–75 to 1978–79	3,877	9.8
Annual Plan	1979–80	1,288	10.6
Sixth FYP	1980–81 to 1984–85	10,930	10
Seventh FYP	1985–86 to 1989–90	16,590	7.6
Annual Plan	1990–91	3,974	6.8
Annual Plan	1991–92	4,232	6.5
Eighth FYP	1992–93 to 1996–97	32,525	7.5
Ninth FYP	1997–98 to 2001–02	55,420	6.5
Tenth FYP	2002–03 to 2006–07	1,03,315	6.8
Eleventh FYP	2007–08 to 2011–12	2,10,326	5.8
Twelfth FYP	2012–13 to 2016–17	4,22,012	5.5

Source: 'Statistical Appendix, A 40–46', *Economic Survey, 2010–11*, Government of India (cited in Jha and Acharya 2011) and 'Statistical Appendix, A 46–47', *Economic Survey 2014–15*.

times, from 22.6 mha in 1950–51 to 96.6 mha in 2015–16. I discuss below the major changes in the development of different sources of irrigation during the period under review.

First, in the early FYP periods, substantial investment in major and medium irrigation schemes for the construction of dams, barrages and canal networks resulted in an expansion of canal-irrigated area. The net irrigated area under canals was 8.3 mha in 1950–51, which increased to 17.5 mha in 1990–91. In subsequent years, particularly after 1990, there was a sharp decline in the area irrigated by canals. Several studies have discussed the reasons for the shrinking of public irrigation systems. These include poor operation and maintenance, degraded infrastructure, low productivity and financial returns, inequity in the allocation of water, water logging and salinity in the command area (Dhawan 1997; Shah 2008; Namboodiri and Gandhi 2009; Mukherji 2016).

Secondly, groundwater emerged as a major source of irrigation in India after 1970. The area irrigated by groundwater was only 6 mha

Table 8.3 *Trends in net irrigated area, gross irrigated area, and cropping intensity in India, by source, 1950–51 to 2015–16,* in million hectares and per cent

| Year | Canal | Tanks | Wells | | Other sources | Total net irrigated area | Gross irrigated area | Cropping intensity (in per cent) |
			tube-wells	other wells				
1950–51	8.3	3.6	*	6	3	20.9	22.6	111.1
1955–56	9.4	4.4	*	6.7	2.2	22.8	25.6	114.1
1960–61	10.4	4.6	0.1	7.2	2.4	24.7	28	114.7
1965–66	11	4.3	1.3	7.4	2.5	26.3	30.9	114
1970–71	12.8	4.1	4.5	7.4	2.3	31.1	38.2	117.7
1975–76	13.8	4	6.8	7.6	2.4	34.6	43.4	120.9
1980–81	15.3	3.2	9.5	8.2	2.6	38.7	49.8	123.1
1985–86	16.2	2.8	11.9	8.5	2.5	41.9	54.3	126.7
1990–91	17.5	2.9	14.3	10.4	2.9	48	63.2	130
1995–96	17.1	3.1	17.9	11.8	3.5	53.4	71.4	131.8
2000–01	16	2.5	22.6	11.3	2.9	55.2	76.2	131.1
2005–06	16.7	2.1	26.0	10	6	60.8	84.3	136.5
2010–11	15.6	2	28.5	10.6	6.9	63.7	88.9	139.6
2013–14	16.3	1.8	31.1	11.3	7.5	68.1	95.8	142
2014–15	16.2	1.8	31.6	11.4	7.5	68.4	96.8	141.5
2015–16	15.2	1.7	32.2	11.0	7.3	67.3	96.6	141.2

Note: 1. * includes under 'other wells', as separate figures were not collected for these years. *Source*: Ministry of Agriculture and Farmers' Welfare, Government of India, available at https://www.indiastat.com/

in 1950–51, which increased to 12.9 mha in 1970–72 and 43.2 mha in 2015–16. Figure 8.1 shows that number of groundwater structures, namely dug wells, shallow tubewells, and deep tubewells, substantially increased between 1986–87 and 2000–01. For instance, the total number of groundwater structures was 12.2 million in 1986–97, which increased to 18.5 million in 2001. Between 2000–01 and 2013–14, however, there was a slowdown in the growth of number of groundwater structures, particularly dug wells, and shallow tubewells. But the number of deep tubewells increased significantly from 0.5 million in 2000–01 to 2.6 million in 2013–14. The reason could be the decline in groundwater levels in many parts of India (Mukherji 2016).

Thus, between 1950–51 and 2015–16, there was a shift in the share of area irrigated by different sources in total net area irrigated (see Figure 8.2). Surface water irrigation (canal and tank) accounted for 57 per cent

Figure 8.1 *Number of groundwater structures in India, 1986–87 to 2013–14*, in million

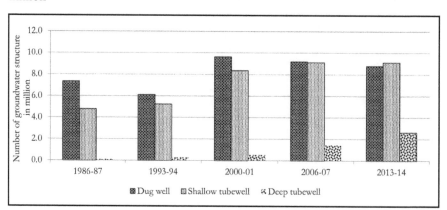

Source: Minor Irrigation Census, Government of India 2001, 2005, 2014, 2017.

Figure 8.2 *Growth of net irrigated area under different sources, 1950–51 to 2015–16*, in per cent

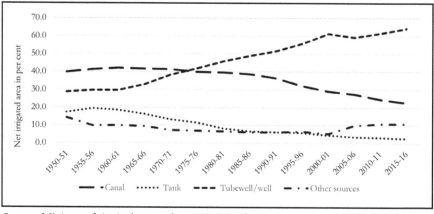

Source: Ministry of Agriculture and Farmers' Welfare, Government of India, available at https://www.indiastat.com/

of total net area irrigated in 1950–51, but declined to about 25 per cent in 2015–16. In the same period, the share of groundwater irrigation in the total net area irrigated increased rapidly, from 28.7 per cent in 1950 to 64.2 per cent in 2015–16. Tubewell irrigation, in particular, saw dramatic changes in this period; in 1950, there was a complete absence of tubewells; but by 2015–16, they constituted a share of 45.7 per cent in net area irrigated.

Thirdly, private investment in tubewell irrigation was a major factor that contributed to the expansion of groundwater irrigation. Table 8.4 shows that about 99 per cent of all groundwater structures in the country were under private ownership in 2013–14. More than 10 per cent of deep

Table 8.4 *Share of public and private structures by type of groundwater structure, in 1993, 2001, 2006 and 2013–14,* in per cent

Year	Dug well			Shallow tubewell			Deep tubewell		
	Public	Private	All	Public	Private	All	Public	Private	All
1993–94	1.5	98.5	100	0.6	99.4	100	11.5	88.5	100
2000–01	2.0	98.0	100	0.9	99.1	100	10.5	89.5	100
2006–07	3.9	96.1	100	1.7	98.3	100	4.1	95.9	100
2013–14	1.7	98.3	100	0.9	99.1	100	1.7	98.3	100

Source: *Minor Irrigation Census*, Government of India 2001, 2005, 2014, 2017.

tubewells in the country were under government ownership in 1993–94 and 2000–01, which declined to only 1.7 per cent in 2013–14. In general, the capital cost for constructing a deep tubewell is much higher compared to that for constructing a dug well or a shallow tubewell. Thus, public deep tubewells, particularly to support the small and marginal farmers under different programmes were installed by the government. However, as Table 8.4 shows, direct intervention by government even for deep tubewells declined over time.

Factors Affecting Access to Groundwater Irrigation

The expansion in groundwater irrigation and private control over groundwater has led to concerns of equity in the ownership of groundwater structures and access to irrigation. This section examines some of the factors that govern ownership of and access to groundwater for irrigation.

Ownership of Groundwater Irrigation

In India, the legalities surrounding groundwater ownership are complex, consisting of a range of statutory and constitutional provisions at the central and state levels (Garduno *et al.* 2011). Legislation governing groundwater in India does not treat it as common property or an open access resource. Access to groundwater, its regulation and control of its use are largely derived from British laws (Cullet 2014). The right to groundwater follows from the right to ownership of land, which in turn is derived from the Indian Easement Act, 1882. In other words, 'groundwater is attached, like a chattel to land property and . . . there is no limitation on how much groundwater a particular landowner may withdraw' (Singh 1991).

Following from this, the unequal distribution of land across households belonging to different socio-economic classes and castes inevitably leads to inequalities in access to groundwater for irrigation. About 85 per cent of farmers in India are marginal and small farmers (that is, those who own up to one hectare and between one and two hectares of operational land, respectively), while they cultivate only about 50 per cent of the operational agricultural land (NSSO 2015). Inequality in distribution of land and the lack of credit to invest in tubewells have reduced the direct ownership of groundwater irrigation structures among small and marginal farmers. Table 8.5 shows the percentage of farm households of different land-size categories that owned groundwater structures. In the large farmer category, 20.8 per cent owned dug wells, 22.7 per cent owned shallow tubewells, and 10.1 per cent owned deep tubewells. In contrast, only 2.4 per cent of all marginal farmers owned dug wells, 3.7 per cent owned shallow tubewells, and 0.5 per cent owned deep tubewells.

Evidence from micro-level studies also indicates that inequalities in the ownership of groundwater structures are closely related to inequality in land distribution (Shah 1993; Bhatia 1992; Janakarajan 1993; Dubash 2002; A. Sarkar 2011; Rawal 2002). Bhatia (1992) argued that inequalities in land and water ownership compound each other. As installation of tubewells required considerable capital investment, it becomes affordable

Table 8.5 *Distribution of landholdings and ownership of groundwater structures by size of landholding in India, 2013–14 and 2016–16,* in number, million hectares and per cent

Size of landholding category	Total number of holders in 2015–16 (in millions)	Total area of holding in 2015–16 (in million ha)	Average size of holding in 2015–16 (ha)	Share (%) of farmers who own groundwater structures in 2013–14		
				Dug well	Shallow tubewell	Deep tubewell
Marginal farmer	92.8	35.9	0.4	2.4	3.7	0.5
Small farmer	24.8	35.2	1.4	9.4	10.2	2.3
Semi-medium farmer	13.9	37.7	2.7	10.0	13.0	4.2
Medium farmer	5.9	33.8	5.8	9.4	11.3	6.3
Large farmer	1.0	16.9	17.4	20.8	22.7	10.1
All	138.3	159.6	1.2	4.9	6.2	1.5

Note: Large farmer households are those with over 10 hectares of operational land. Medium farmer households have operational land between 4 and 10 hectares. Semi-medium farmer households have operational land between 2 and 4 hectares. Small farmer households have operational land between 1 and 2 hectares. Marginal farmers have less than 1 hectare of operational land.
Source: Data on the number of holders and total holdings in 2015–16 are from the *All-India Report on Agriculture Census*, Government of India 2017. Data on the number of tubewells in 2013–14 are from the *Minor Irrigation Census*, Government of India 2017.

primarily for the large owners. Thus, better access to land in the village is closely associated with better groundwater irrigation (A. Sarkar 2011).

Prakash (2005), based on a study of Sangpura village (Mehsana district) in Gujarat, showed that the relationship between groundwater irrigation and social differentiation starts with the basic inequality in the ownership of land. The study argued that the development of private groundwater irrigation on existing unequal distribution of land ownership helped large farmers, who were already well-off and sociopolitically powerful in the village, to gain more surplus from agriculture. It also showed that caste structures are closely correlated with the class hierarchy and upper-caste households had control over means of production, in particular groundwater irrigation in the village (ibid).

Role of Groundwater Markets in Access to Irrigation

It has been argued that the problem of unequal ownership of groundwater structures can be addressed by the 'market'. Groundwater market is an arrangement where few better-off peasants in the village own pump sets and tubewells, and sell water for irrigation to other farmers at a price higher than the average groundwater withdrawal costs. The groundwater markets in the form of water exchange and distribution have been widely prevalent in many parts of India and other South Asian countries (Shah 1993; Shah and Raju 1987; Bhatia 1992; Dubash 2002; Prakash 2005; Janakarajan 1993; Pant 1994; A. Sarkar 2011; Wood 1999; Shah and Ballabh 1997; Kishore 2004; Rawal 2002; Fujita, Kundu and Jaim 2003; Mukherji 2004; Mukherji, Shah and Banerjee 2012).

Some studies propose that private water markets provide access to irrigation for large number of small and marginal farmers, and thus promote equity in access to groundwater irrigation (Shah 1991, 1993; Shah and Ballabh 1997; Mukherji 2007). Although most of these studies found that the private ownership of tubewells is associated with unequal distribution of tubewells and a new form of social inequality, it has been argued that water markets are highly beneficial to the small and marginal farmers as they provide irrigation access to resource-poor farmers who do not own tubewells. Shah (1993) advocated electricity pricing as a policy prescription to bring more competition in the water markets, as there is a strong and direct linkage between electricity pricing and groundwater use.[2] He argues that a high flat-rate tariff for electricity, instead of pro-rata tariffs, will create incentives for pumping and will encourage competition among water sellers. This is because under a flat-rate tariff, the marginal cost is almost zero, which encourages water sellers to sell more water and spur competition among them. This competition among water sellers is also a strong incentive for keeping the costs of extraction low. A groundwater market also leads to increase in pumping capacity, which enhances tubewell efficiency (Meinzen-Dick 1996). In other words, it has been argued that a competitive groundwater market is associated with better utilization of groundwater and can act as an incentive to check the costs of irrigation.

Other studies, however, show that water markets lead to exploitative relationships between tubewell owners and water buyers (Janakarajan 1993) and accentuate rural inequalities (Bhatia 1992; Wood 1999; Dubash 2002; Rawal 2002; Sarkar 2011; Modak 2017).Wood (1999), in his study on irrigation markets in north Bihar, found that unequal ownership of pump sets was associated with reverse tenancy. Small and marginal farmers who are unable to mobilize the investment for irrigation and other inputs for irrigated crops, were forced to lease out their land to the owners of pump sets. Vaidyanathan (1999) argued that purely private exploitation would lead to either monopolistic exploitation or highly skewed distribution of the benefits in favour of better-off farmers. Bhatia (1992), in her study in north Gujarat, found that the monopoly power of groundwater market harassed non-owners. The excessive control over the groundwater market by a few creates difficulties for poor sharecroppers as cultivation becomes more capital-intensive. The landlords preferred to lease out their land to owners of pump sets to guarantee cheap water services. As a result, landless and poor farmers gradually lost the limited cultivation opportunity through sharecropping. Janakarajan's study on Tamil Nadu (1993) also pointed out how the control over water was used as a means to reinforce social and economic power. He found a triadic relation where water sellers received loans for installation of tube wells from merchants on liberal norms, and in exchange, water sellers set a condition to water buyers that they had to sell their output to the same merchants from whom the water sellers received their loans.

Studies also showed that marginal and small farmers who purchased water from water markets paid much higher amounts as irrigation cost when compared to water sellers (Bhatia 1992; Prasad 2002; Sarkar 2011; Modak 2018). It led to a greater disparity in the net returns from cultivation on account of higher price paid for irrigation in the water market.

Rawal (2002) argued that the oligopolistic structure of the water market gave opportunities to the water sellers to extract substantial surplus through high charges on water. In the long-term, concentration of ownership of tubewells in the hands of big landowners further strengthens their social and economic position in the village through control over irrigation water. On the contrary, based on two case studies of non-market interventions in water sharing, he showed that that democratic institutions at village level (panchayats) or cooperative societies are more capable of equitable arrangements of water sharing for the small and marginal farmers.

Depletion of Groundwater and Its Impact on Ownership

It is a fact that the development of groundwater irrigation contributed significantly to agricultural development in the country in terms of expansion of irrigated area, increase in cropping intensity, and higher productivity and profitability. But a new set of problems also emerged along with this development – overexploitation of groundwater resources in many parts of the country. The estimation of Central Ground Water Board (CGWB) shows that in 2016 about 16 per cent of total number of assessment units of the country were classified as overexploited, about 4 per cent as critical, and about 10 per cent as semi-critical (GoI 2017). The situation was alarming and a matter of concern for Punjab, Haryana, Rajasthan, Tamil Nadu and Karnataka where the share of overexploited assessment units among total units in each state ranged from 30 to 60 per cent.

Typically, the decline of groundwater level is associated with an increase in the well density and a progressive increase in the depth of wells. This has important social and economic consequences. As the number of wells tapping an aquifer increase and become deeper, the volumes of water extracted also increase. After a point, the yield per well declines and the investment incurred per unit of water lifted increases. The operating costs per unit of water also increase as water has to be lifted from a greater depth (Vaidyanathan 1999). As lifting water from a greater depth requires new technology and substantial investment, falling groundwater levels have further excluded a large number of marginal and small farmers from ownership of and access to irrigation. This has implications for equity, especially in a situation in which farmers have little opportunity for additional income generation (Dhawan 1982, cited in A. Sarkar 2011) and cannot exit agriculture. Hence, the privately owned sources of groundwater irrigation continued to be the reason for inter and intra-generational inequity, even though it contributed significantly in the overall growth of Indian agriculture (Nagaraj and Chandrakanth 1997).

Many micro-level studies have shown the implications of a declining water table for equity in ownership and access to groundwater for irrigation (Bhatia 1992; Moench 1992; Nagaraj and Chandrakanth 1997; A. Sarkar 2011; Modak 2018). Inequality in the distribution of tubewells is most pronounced in groundwater-depleted states like Punjab, Gujarat, Tamil Nadu and Karnataka, as compared to states with an abundance of groundwater like West Bengal.

To conclude, official data and literature both confirm a shift in the irrigation economy of India from public canal irrigation in the two decades after independence to private investment-led groundwater irrigation from the mid-1980s onwards. This shift has implications for equity in access to irrigation.

Village Surveys: An Introduction

This article uses household-level data of seven villages, collected as a part of the Project on Agrarian Relations in India (PARI) of the Foundation for Agrarian Studies (FAS) through surveys conducted in different agro-ecological regions of India (Figure 8.3).[3] PARI uses a consistent methodology of farm accounting to provide empirical data on production systems at the level of cultivator households. Details of the location and year of survey of each village are listed in Table 8.6.

In-depth census surveys were conducted between 2006 and 2010 in the seven study villages included in this chapter. Harevli, a canal- and groundwater-irrigated village located in the sugarcane-growing district of

Table 8.6 *List of study villages with location, year of survey, agro-ecological zone and features of crop irrigation*

Village and district	State	Survey year	Agro-ecological zone	Features of irrigation and crops cultivated
Alabujanahalli (Mandya)	Karnataka	2009	Southern Dry Zone	Canal irrigation; sugarcane, paddy, finger millet, sericulture
Harevli (Bijnor)	Uttar Pradesh	2006	Bhabar and Tarai Zone	Canal and groundwater irrigation; wheat, sugarcane
Gharsondi (Gwalior)	Madhya Pradesh	2008	Gird Zone	Limited canal and groundwater irrigation; soybean, wheat, mustard
Amarsinghi (Malda)	West Bengal	2010 and 2015	New Alluvial Zone	Groundwater irrigation; aman (monsoon) paddy, boro (summer) paddy, jute
Panahar (Bankura)	West Bengal	2010 and 2015	Old Alluvial Zone	Groundwater irrigation; aman paddy, boro paddy, potato, sesame
Siresandra (Kolar)	Karnataka	2009	Eastern Dry Zone	Groundwater irrigation; finger millet, vegetables, sericulture
Rewasi (Sikar)	Rajasthan	2010	Transitional Plain Zone of Inland Drainage	Rainfed irrigation; pearl millet, wheat, mustard, fenugreek

Note: The listed agro-ecological zones are as per the National Agriculture Research Project (NARP) classification.

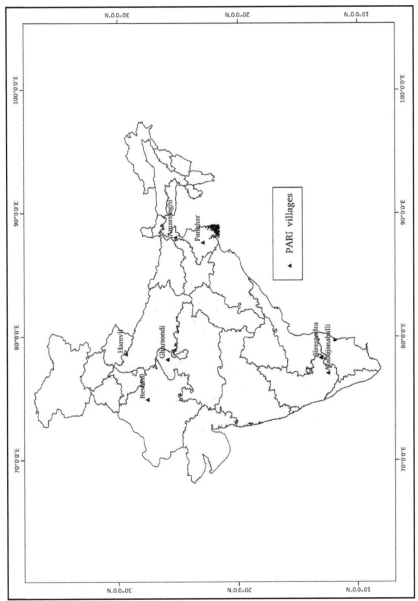

Figure 8.3 *Location of PARI study villages*

Bijnor in western Uttar Pradesh, was surveyed in 2006. In 2008, a census survey was conducted in Gharsondi, a village in Bhitarwar tehsil of Gwalior district in central Madhya Pradesh. In June 2009, two villages were surveyed in Karnataka state: Alabujanahalli, a canal-irrigated village in Mandya district, and Siresandra, a dry village in Kolar district. Rewasi, a dry village in the semi-arid region of Sikar district in Rajasthan, was surveyed in 2010. A census survey in 2010 and a sample survey in 2015 were conducted in Amarsinghi village (Malda district) and Panahar village (Bankura district), two groundwater-irrigated regions of West Bengal.

Socio-economic classification of households was undertaken for each village, based on the three classical criteria used to differentiate the peasantry: control over the means of production, relative use of family and hired labour, and the surplus that a household is able to generate within a working year. Based on these general criteria, households in the study villages were categorized broadly into the following five classes: landlords, capitalist farmers, peasants, manual workers, and households dependent on business, salaries or other sources of income. Within each village, the peasantry was further subdivided based on specific conditions of the village (Ramachandran 2011). Only households primarily dependent on crop cultivation and allied activities in the study villages were considered for this chapter.

The specific category of socio-economic classes was used in each village: Rich capitalist farmer, Peasant 1, Peasant 2, Peasant 3 and Peasant 4 in Alabujanahalli (Karnataka); Landlord, Peasant 1 (rich), Peasant 2 (upper middle), Peasant 3 (lower middle) and Peasant 4 (small) in Harveli (Uttar Pradesh); Landlord/Big capitalist farmer, Peasant 1/Rich capitalist farmer, Peasant 2 (upper middle), Peasant 3 (lower middle) and Peasant 4 (small) in Gharsondi (Madhya Pradesh); Peasant (upper) and peasant (lower) in Amarsinghi (West Bengal); Landlord/capitalist farmer, Peasant (upper) and peasant (lower) in Panahar (West Bengal); Landlord and rural rich, Peasant 1, Peasant 2, Peasant 3 and Peasant 4 in Rewasi (Rajasthan); and Peasant 1, Peasant 2, and Peasant 3 in Siresandra (Karnataka). Appendix Table 1 shows the distribution of cultivator households by socio-economic class and description of socio-economic classes in the study villages in details.

Nature of Ownership, Access to Irrigation and Agricultural Production

I have categorized the study villages under four distinct irrigation regimes on the basis of type of irrigation infrastructure (public investment in canals or groundwater irrigation versus private investment in groundwater irrigation) and area irrigated by different sources of irrigation.[4] The four categories are canal irrigation, groundwater irrigation, a combination of canal and groundwater irrigation, and dry villages with groundwater irrigation (Tables 8.7 and 8.8).[5]

Table 8.7 *Categorization of villages by source of irrigation and type of infrastructure*

Type of infrastructure	Canal	Canal plus groundwater	Groundwater	Dry villages with groundwater irrigation
Public	Alabujana-halli	Gharsondi and Harevli	Amarsinghi	Siresandra
Private	NA	Gharsondi and Harevli	Amarsinghi and Panahar	Rewasi and Siresandra

Source: PARI survey data.

Table 8.8 *Proportion of gross cropped irrigated area (GCA) by different sources, selected villages,* in per cent

Village	District	Canal/ river	Tubewell/ borewell	Multi-source	Pond/ tank	Unirri-gated	All
Alabujanahalli	Mandya	60.5	1.3	24.6	6.3	7.3	100
Harevli	Bijnor	8.4	47.3	37.1	0	7.2	100
Gharsondi	Gwalior	20.7	9.4	26.1	0	43.8	100
Amarsinghi	Malda	4.2	81.6	3.3	0.6	10.3	100
Panahar	Bankura	3.4	84.1	0.7	0.5	11.3	100
Rewasi	Sikar	0	63.1	0	0	36.9	100
Siresandra	Kolar	0.4	45.4	0	2	52.2	100

Source: PARI survey data.

In the following subsections, I examine how the type of irrigation infrastructure determines ownership and access to irrigation in the study villages, and their impact on agricultural production systems across socio-economic classes. While access to irrigation was not the sole factor determining household production decisions, it was nonetheless a vital component that influenced cropping pattern and the level of productivity in agriculture, along with agroclimatic characteristics, inputs, capital, technology and market conditions. In other words, cropping pattern choices were driven by access to resources, of which a critical resource is access to water or irrigation (Das and Swaminathan 2017).

Canal Irrigation

The public canal system was the predominant source of irrigation in Alabujanahalli village. The village is located in Maddur taluk (sub-district) of Mandya district, Karnataka state, and belongs to the Kaveri-irrigated region of south Karnataka. It receives irrigation water from a network of tanks that are fed by canals from the Krishnarajasagar dam on the Kaveri river. In 2009, two-thirds of the total crop land in the village was irrigated solely by the network of tanks, while the remaining one-third was irrigated by a combination of tanks and tubewells (Table 8.8).

All the rich capitalist farmer households and Peasant 1 households owned tubewells fitted with electric pumps that were used for supplementary irrigation. The average value of the irrigation equipment of a household was Rs 12 lakhs for rich capitalist farmer and Peasant 1 households. In contrast, only 27 per cent of Peasant 3 households and 9 per cent of Peasant 4 households owned irrigation equipment, mostly diesel and electric pumps, for drawing and supplying water from tank networks to crop fields. The average value of the irrigation equipment of a household was Rs 35,492 for a Peasant 3 household and Rs 14,763 for a Peasant 4 household.

It is interesting to note that inequality in ownership of irrigation equipment among farm households did not affect access to irrigation in the survey year. The public canal irrigation system ensured water for cultivation across cultivator classes. Over 90 per cent of the gross cropped area belonging to all socio-economic classes were irrigated (Table 8.9). In years of shortage or drought, inequality in ownership of irrigation equipment among cultivator households may have an adverse effect on access to irrigation.

Secure and low-cost irrigation meant that all farm households in Alabujanahalli cultivated water-intensive crops such as paddy and sugarcane. A large extent of the cultivated land (about 80 per cent of the gross cropped area [GCA]) of Peasant 2, Peasant 3 and Peasant 4 households was under sugarcane and paddy. Irrigation cost constituted only 1.5 per cent of total paid-out cost for all socio-economic classes in Alabujanahalli, a fact that can be attributed to the low cost of canal irrigation and the almost

Table 8.9 *Proportion of irrigated gross cropped area (GCA) as a share of total GCA by socio-economic class, Alabujanahalli, in 2008–09* in per cent

Socio-economic class	Irrigated GCA (in per cent)
Rich capitalist farmer	93
Peasant 1	96
Peasant 2	97
Peasant 3	90
Peasant 4	92
All	92

Source: PARI survey data, 2009.

Table 8.10 *Average cost of irrigation and irrigation cost as a proportion of total paid out-cost on operational holding by socio-economic class, Alabujanahalli, at 2015–16 prices*, in Rupees per hectare and per cent

Socio-economic class	Average irrigation cost (in Rs per hectare)	Irrigation cost as a percentage of total paid-out cost
Rich capitalist farmer	1,413	1.3
Peasant 1	1,708	1.4
Peasant 2	1,926	1.9
Peasant 3	1,704	1.5
Peasant 4	1,475	1.3

Source: PARI survey data, 2009.

equal average per hectare cost of irrigation across classes (Table 8.10).[6] Thus, in a public canal-irrigated village, despite the ownership of irrigation equipment being skewed towards rich capitalist farmer households, a public irrigation system ensured equitable supply of water for agriculture and reduced the cost of irrigation across farm households.

Combination of Canal and Groundwater Irrigation

Harevli (in Bijnor district, Uttar Pradesh) and Gharsondi (in Gwalior district, western Madhya Pradesh) were in the command area of canals. Harevli received water from a public canal that was part of the Eastern Ganga Canal project and Gharsondi was irrigated by a canal on the Harsi dam. Canal irrigation, however, provided insufficient water for cultivation in both villages in the year preceding the survey. Shortage of canal water created a demand for alternative sources of irrigation and private tubewells emerged in both study villages as an alternative, particularly for rabi (winter) cultivation.

There were three landlord households in Harveli and twelve landlord/big capitalist farmer households in Gharsondi. The peasant households of the two villages were further classified into four classes: rich peasants, upper middle, lower middle and small peasants (Ramachandran 2016). Inequality in ownership of irrigation equipment for private tubewell irrigation was very high across socio-economic classes in both villages. All the landlord/big capitalist and Peasant 1 (rich)/capitalist farmer households owned tubewells and electric pumps, whereas only 17 per cent of Peasant 4 households in Gharsondi and 18 per cent of Peasant 4 households in Harevli owned irrigation equipment. The difference in the average value of irrigation equipment owned by households across classes was large. Most submersible tubewells run by electric pumps were owned by the large landowning Tyagi (economically and socially dominant caste) households, while Peasant 3 and Peasant 4 households mainly owned diesel pumps. A similar pattern of unequal distribution of irrigation equipment across classes was observed in Gharsondi.

Inadequate supply of canal water on the one hand and inequality in the ownership of private irrigation equipment on the other, led to differentiation in access to irrigation across classes. Most of the land in both the villages belonged to landlords and rich capitalist farmers, and was irrigated by the public canal system as well as privately owned electric tubewells (Table 8.11). Tubewells fitted with electric pumps were used for rabi cultivation and as supplementary irrigation for kharif (summer) crops. On the other hand, Peasant 4 households had very little access to tubewell irrigation and were primarily dependent on canal irrigation, which was erratic. Crop land owned by Peasant 3 and Peasant 4 households was irrigated through tubewells operated by diesel pump sets or by water purchased from other tube well owners.

This disparity in access to irrigation had a visible impact on the cropping pattern. For example, in Harevli, the landlords, rich peasants and middle peasants cultivated sugarcane, which requires irrigation throughout the year, on about 60 per cent of their GCA as they had greater access to tubewell irrigation. In contrast, the Peasant 4 households in the village cultivated kharif paddy on 52 per cent of their GCA, using water for irrigation mainly from the public canal.

Table 8.11 *Share of gross irrigated area by source and socio-economic class, Harevli (2006) and Gharsondi (2008)*, in per cent

Socio-economic class	Harevli				Gharsondi			
	Canal	Tube-well & diesel pump	Tube-well & electric pump	Multiple sources	Canal	Tube-well & diesel pump	Tube-well & electric pump	Multiple sources
Landlord/big capitalist farmer	–	–	54	46	16	0	20	64
Peasant 1 (rich)/ capitalist farmer	5	15	37	43	19	0	26	55
Peasant 2 (upper middle)	6	48	13	32	35	0	14	51
Peasant 3 (lower middle)	18	22	17	42	75	0.2	11	14
Peasant 4 (small)	41	23	15	21	76	0.5	6	17

Source: PARI survey data.

There was an acute shortage of water supply from the canal system in Gharsondi in the survey year, primarily on account of a bad monsoon. The main kharif crop, soybean, was completely destroyed due to lack of irrigation and pest attack. Cultivation became primarily dependent on tubewell irrigation. As a result, landlords and rich capitalist farmers who owned tubewells and had an assured source of irrigation cultivated a much higher proportion of paddy on their GCAs (9 per cent) as compared to Peasant 4 households (only 0.8 per cent). In contrast, Peasant 3 and Peasant 4 households cultivated unirrigated crops such as black gram and sesame in the kharif season. In the rabi season, Peasant 3 and Peasant 4 households cultivated wheat intercropped with rapeseed, in order to reduce their losses.

Thus, outcomes were significantly different across socio-economic classes in adverse conditions, such as shortage of canal water. Landlord and rich capitalist households used their own tubewells for supplementary irrigation to avert losses. In contrast, lower middle (Peasant 3) and small peasant (Peasant 4) households had to depend on purchased water or shift their cropping pattern to unirrigated crops.

Groundwater Irrigation

Agricultural land in Panahar village (Bankura district) in West Bengal was primarily irrigated by groundwater. The village is located in the command area of the Kangsabati project but receives very little water for irrigation from it. Electricity for irrigation came to the village in the mid-1980s. About 85 per cent of the total irrigated area was under tubewell irrigation by 2010. Private tubewell irrigation was the predominant source of irrigation.

Expansion of electrified tubewells for irrigation in Panahar was undertaken primarily by the large landowners. Ownership of submersible tubewells was skewed in favour of large farmer households: all seven landlord households together owned eleven out of a total of sixteen electrified submersible tube wells in 2010. Despite the concentration in ownership of tube wells, all farm households had access to tubewell irrigation in all seasons. A majority of cultivators purchased water for irrigation from the water market and sale of water from tubewells predominated in the water market. About 96 per cent of gross irrigated area operated by lower peasant households was irrigated by purchased water (Table 8.12). Village-level data do not show a significant difference in the cropping pattern across socio-economic classes in Panahar village. Most farm households in Panahar cultivated water-intensive crops such as *boro* or summer paddy. Potato was cultivated in the rabi season. The private water market ensured a regular supply of water for cultivation.

Disparities came to the fore when we studied the cost of irrigation.

Table 8.12 *Proportion of gross cropped area (GCA) irrigated by purchased water, by socio-economic class, Amarsinghi and Panahar, 2009,* in per cent

Village	Landlord/big capitalist farmer	Peasant (upper)	Peasant (lower)
Amarsinghi	NA	74	90
Panahar	13	72	96

Source: PARI survey data, 2010.

Table 8.13 *Average cost of irrigation and irrigation cost as a percentage of total paid-out cost on operational holding, by socio-economic class, Amarsinghi and Panahar, at 2015–16 prices,* in Rupees per hectare and per cent

Socio-economic class	Amarsinghi		Panahar	
	Average cost of irrigation (in Rs)	Irrigation cost as a percentage of total paid-out cost	Average cost of irrigation (in Rs)	Irrigation cost as a percentage of total paid-out cost
Landlord/big capitalist farmer	NA	NA	7,355	6.5
Peasant (upper)	9,211	10.7	8,897	7.8
Peasant (lower)	12,480	16.7	10,684	13.4

Source: PARI survey data, 2010.

In general, the cost of irrigation is higher for villages that depend on ground-water irrigation as compared to canal-irrigated villages. In Panahar, all land-lord/big capitalist households used their own tubewells for cultivation. As a result, the average cost of irrigation was low, at Rs 7,355 per hectare of operated land at constant prices in 2015–16, and constituted only 6.5 per cent of total paid-out cost (Table 8.13). In contrast, most of the lower peasant households purchased water from the private water market, paying a much higher price for irrigation. The average cost of irrigation per hectare of operated land for them was Rs 10,684 per hectare of operated land at constant prices in 2015–16, and constituted 13.4 per cent of total paid-out cost.

    Amarsinghi village is situated in Ratua I block in Malda district, in the New Alluvial Plains of West Bengal. Electricity for irrigation came to the village in 2007. Shallow tube well owners gradually shifted to electric-powered submersible tubewells. There were no diesel-powered shallow tubewells in the village in 2015. A public deep tubewell was installed in the village in 2008 by the Irrigation and Waterways Department of the

Government of West Bengal, managed by an eighteen-member cooperative group. A majority of cultivators in the village bought water for irrigation. In 2010, 90 per cent of lower peasant households and 74 per cent of upper peasant households bought water (Table 8.12); 44 per cent of cultivator households purchased water from the cooperative-run tubewell and 63 per cent from private water sellers.

These two state interventions, electrification and the installation of a tubewell by the government, substantially reduced the costs of irrigation for the major irrigated crops. For example, the average irrigation cost per hectare in 2010 for the primary irrigated crop, *boro* rice, was Rs 14,030 for households that used private diesel-powered tubewells and Rs 9,869 for households that used private electric-powered tubewells. In the same year, households that had access to the cooperative deep tubewell had a much lower irrigation cost as compared to the prevalent rates in the private water market: Rs 4,653 per hectare for *boro* rice. Higher rates in the private water market increased the total paid-out cost and reduced profits. To cite an example, the profitability of *boro* paddy in Amarsinghi in 2010 was high for households that used the cooperative deep tubewell as compared to those that used private tubewells.

Dry Villages with Groundwater Irrigation

Cultivators in Rewasi village (Sikar district) in the Western Dry agro-climatic zone of Rajasthan mainly practiced rainfed agriculture in the survey year. There was no public source of irrigation and cultivation was entirely dependent on private tubewell irrigation. Eleven open wells were functional in Rewasi in 2010. Electric-powered submersible tubewells were fitted into the base of open wells to extract groundwater from greater depths.

On account of the scarcity of rainfall and limited availability of irrigation, ownership of and access to irrigation controlled the agricultural production system in Rewasi. Table 8.14 shows that only about 25 per cent of operational holdings belonging to Peasant 3 and Peasant 4 households was irrigated in the kharif season. In the survey year, in the kharif season, Peasant 3 and Peasant 4 households incurred losses from crop production as 70 per cent of their crops were completely destroyed due to limited access to irrigation. In the rabi season, 49 per cent and 59 per cent, respectively, of operational holdings belonging to Peasant 3 and Peasant 4 households were sown, and the rest of the land was left fallow due to lack of access to water. The average cost of irrigation for Peasant 3 and Peasant 4 households was high, as many such households received water on payment from other tube-well owners. The average irrigation cost per acre of operational holding incurred by Peasant 3 and Peasant 4 households was Rs 11,302 and Rs 12,706, respectively, at constant prices in 2015–16, while it was only Rs

Table 8.14 *Share of irrigated, unirrigated and fallow land in total operational holdings, by season, by socio-economic class, Rewasi, 2010*, in per cent

Socio-economic class	Kharif			Rabi		
	Irrigated	Unirrigated	Fallow	Irrigated	Unirrigated	Fallow
Landlords and rural rich	44	42	14	72	0	28
Peasant 1	49	30	21	76	0	24
Peasant 2	44	36	20	80	0	20
Peasant 3	24	65	11	49	0	51
Peasant 4	26	59	15	59	0	41

Source: PARI survey data, 2010.

5,486 for landlord/rich peasants, Rs 6,521 for Peasant 1 households and Rs 7,873 for Peasant 2 households.

Siresandra village is located in the water-scarce district of Kolar, in the Eastern Dry Region of Karnataka. Private tube wells were the primary source of irrigation in the village, although electricity for irrigation was free in the state. Siresandra was characterized by severe depletion of groundwater and falling water tables. Inequality in ownership and access to groundwater structures had further increased with groundwater depletion and was clearly evident.

Drip irrigation technology was used in vegetable cultivation to reduce the wastage of water (B. Sarkar 2017). However, the use of irrigation was limited to rich farm households (Peasant 1) in the village in 2009, all Peasant 1 households in Siresandra owned tubewells whereas only 53 per cent of Peasant 3 households owned tubewells, many of which were not operational and could not extract water from greater depths, particularly in the summer months. In addition, the use of groundwater for irrigation was restricted among Peasant 2 and Peasant 3 households in the survey year, as tubewell owners did not have surplus water to sell to other peasants. Table 8.15 shows the extent of total GCA that belonged to Peasant 2 and Peasant 3 households in the village, and was under cultivation in the kharif season. Cultivation in this season was primarily dependent on the monsoon rains. Only 13 per cent and 10 per cent of the GCA belonging to Peasant 2 and Peasant 3 households, respectively, were under rabi cultivation, but this proportion was 43 per cent for Peasant 1 households.

Evidence from this water-scarce village shows that water markets do not develop automatically. Although the data are from a single village, they raise questions about water markets providing access to irrigation for

Table 8.15 *Proportion of cultivated area in total gross cropped area (GCA), by season and socio-economic class, Siresandra, 2009,* in per cent

Class	Annual crops	Kharif crop	Rabi crop	Total
Peasant 1	32	26	43	100
Peasant 2	24	63	13	100
Peasant 3	14	76	10	100

Source: PARI survey data, 2009.

small and marginal farmers in different agro-climatic regions. Also, markets may not develop due to the limited natural availability of groundwater. In Siresandra, despite there being a demand for irrigation water, the available groundwater was not shared or distributed through a market mechanism but was utilized only by the owners of groundwater structures. This control over groundwater further resulted in a high level of social inequality.

Conclusions

Irrigation in India underwent major transformation after independence. The 1950s and 1960s were marked by significant investment in public irrigation schemes and an increase in the area irrigated under public surface irrigation. From the late 1970s, however, private investment in groundwater irrigation registered a rapid increase throughout the country. After the green revolution began, the policies adopted by different state governments focused on promoting groundwater use by means of electricity supply at subsidized rates or free of cost, subsidized institutional credit for tubewell installation, and expansion of public tubewell programmes. These policies contributed significantly to an increase in the area irrigated by groundwater throughout the country. Groundwater emerged as a major source of irrigation, accounting for 62.3 per cent of the total net irrigated area in 2013. Although the development of groundwater irrigation contributed significantly to Indian agriculture, the shift towards private groundwater irrigation was associated with greater inequality in ownership of irrigation source and equipment.

Groundwater ownership rights in India are tied to land ownership. As the distribution of land across households of different classes and castes is extremely unequal, there is an inherent inequality in the ownership of and access to groundwater. Scholarly studies have shown that inequality in land distribution and the lack of credit for investment in tubewells have reduced direct ownership of groundwater irrigation structures by small and marginal farmers. Private groundwater irrigation was accompanied by the emergence of an informal water market in many parts of the country. Specifically, in the absence of government interventions for public-owned irrigation, private groundwater markets became the primary source of irrigation in the countryside. Poor farm households that cannot invest in their own tubewells, primarily relied on water markets gain access to water for agriculture. Several scholars argue that groundwater markets lead to efficient use of groundwater and provide better access to irrigation for a large number of small and marginal farmers. At the same time, some studies argue that informal water markets, which are mostly controlled by rich farmers, are associated with an exploitative relationship between water sellers and buyers.

The results from village studies show that the shift in the irrigation economy towards private groundwater irrigation in India is associated with higher inequality in the ownership of groundwater structures and access to assured irrigation for all cultivator households. State intervention in irrigation can protect the interests of small and poor cultivators, whereas private control over water affects crop choices, increases risk and lowers profitability in agriculture. Inequality in access to irrigation is an important contributory factor to contemporary agrarian distress, especially among small and poor cultivators.

Notes

[1] A part of this chapter is taken from my article 'From Public to Private Irrigation: Implications for Equity in Access to Water' published in the *Review of Agrarian Studies*, vol. 8, no. 1, pp. 28–64.

[2] According to Shah *et al.* (2012), a shift to flat-rate tariff from metering for tubewell irrigation from late 1970s was a result of high and rising transaction cost in a meter-based electricity system. As the number of tubewells increased substantially in the 1970s and 1980s, state electricity boards (SEBs) found that the transaction costs were higher than the costs recovered from the agricultural sector, and also had logistical difficulties in regulating billings. The change from metered tariff to flat tariff has reduced the marginal cost of groundwater extraction to near zero level, which created a 'free power illusion' among famers. As a result, the number of tubewells and the demand for electricity connection for the operating tubewells increased substantially in the country.

[3] Twenty-five villages in eleven states have been surveyed under PARI. See http://fas. org.in/category/research/project-on-agrarian-relations-in-india-pari/ for details.

[4] It is worth noting that combined canal and groundwater irrigation is practised in many parts of the country. For example, fields may receive water from more than one source (a public canal as well as a private tubewell) in different seasons or even in a single season. The official statistics on irrigation in India do not give information on crop lands that are irrigated by more than one source (Rawal 2001). PARI data can fill this gap by providing information on crop lands that receive water from multiple sources.

[5] The main distinction between two categories, 'groundwater irrigation' and 'dry villages with groundwater irrigation', was that the former had high groundwater potential and the availability of groundwater was not a matter of concern throughout the year, while in the latter category the villages were mostly located in the dry regions, experienced a continuous depletion of groundwater resource and had limited availability of irrigation.

[6] Paid-out cost was calculated using the definition of Cost A2 by the Commission for Agricultural Costs and Prices (CACP).

References

Bhatia, B. (1992), 'Lush Fields and Parched Throats: Political Economy of Groundwater in Gujarat', *Economic and Political Weekly*, vol. 27, no. 51–52, 19 December.

Central Ground Water Board (CGWB) (2014), 'Dynamic Groundwater Resources in India (as on 31 March 2011)', Ministry of Water Resources, River Development, and Ganga Rejuvenation, Government of India, Faridabad.

Central Water Commission (CWC) (2013), 'Water and Related Statistics', Ministry of Water Resources, Government of India, New Delhi, available at http://cwc.gov.in/main/downloads/Water%20and%20Related%20Statistics-2013.pdf, accessed 9 May 2018.

Cullet, P. (2014), 'Groundwater Law in India: Towards a Framework Ensuring Equitable Access and Aquifer Protection', *Journal of Environmental Law*, pp. 55–81, available at http://jel.oxfordjoirnals.org/content/26/1/55, accessed 9 May 2018.

Das, A. and M. Swaminathan (2017), 'Cropping Pattern, Productivity, and Incomes from Crop Production', in M. Swaminathan and S. Baksi, eds, *How do Small Farmers Fare? Evidence from Village Studies in India*, New Delhi: Tulika Books.

Dhawan, B.D. (1997), 'Large-Scale Canal Irrigation: How Cost Effective?', *Economic and Political Weekly*, vol. 32, no. 26, 28 June.

———— (1982), *Development of Tubewell Irrigation in India*, New Delhi: Agricole Publishing Academy.

———— (1991), 'Developing Groundwater Resources: Merits and Demerits,' *Economic and Political Weekly*, vol. 26, no. 8, 23 February.

Dubash, N.K. (2002), *Tubewell Capitalism: Groundwater Development and Agrarian Change*, New Delhi: Oxford University Press.

Fujita, K., A. Kundu and W.M.H. Jaim (2003), 'Groundwater Market and Agricultural Development in West Bengal: Perspectives from a Village Study', *The Japanese Journal of Rural Economics*, vol. 5, pp. 51–65.

Garduno, H., S. Romani, B. Sengupta, A. Tuinhof and D. Richard (2011), 'Indian Groundwater Governance: Case Study', World Bank, available on-line at www.worldbank.org/water

Government of India (GoI) (2001), *2nd Census of Minor Irrigation Schemes 1993–94*, Minor Irrigation Division, Ministry of Water Resources, Government of India, New Delhi, available at http://micensus.gov.in/mi2census/default.htm, accessed 15 June 2018.

———— (2005), *3rd Census of Minor Irrigation Schemes 2000–01*, Minor Irrigation Division, Ministry of Water Resources, Government of India, New Delhi, available at http://micensus.gov.in/mi3census/index.htm, accessed 15 June 2018.

———— (2014), *4th Census of Minor Irrigation Schemes 2006–07*, Minor Irrigation Division, Ministry of Water Resources, Government of India, New Delhi, available at http://micensus.gov.in/MIProg.html, accessed 15 June 2018.

———— (2015), 'All-India Report on Agriculture Census, 2010–11', Department of Agriculture and Cooperation, Ministry of Agriculture and Farmers' Welfare, Government of India, New Delhi, available at http://agcensus.nic.in/document/ac1011/ac1011rep.html, accessed on 15 June 2018.

———— (2017), *5th Census of Minor Irrigation Schemes 2013–14*, Minor Irrigation Division, Ministry of Water Resources, Government of India, New Delhi, available at http://mowr.gov.in/report-5th-mi-census, accessed `15 June 2018.

Howes, S. and R. Murgai (2003), 'Karnataka: Incidence of Agricultural Subsidies', *Economic and Political Weekly*, vol. 38, no. 16, 19 April.

Janakarajan, S. (1993), 'Triadic Exchange Relations: An Illustration from South India', *IDS Bulletin*, vol. 24, no. 3, Institute of Development Studies, Brighton.

Jha, P. and N. Acharya (2011), 'Expenditure on the Rural Economy in India's Budgets since the 1950s: An Assessment', *Review of Agrarian Studies*, vol. 1, no. 2, available at http://www.ras.org.in/expenditure_on_the_rural_economy_in_indias_budgets_since_the_1950s, accessed 9 May 2018.

Kishore, A. (2004), 'Understanding Agrarian Impasse in Bihar', *Economic and Political Weekly*, vol. 39, no. 31, 31 July–6 August 2004, pp. 3484–91.

Meinzen-Dick, R. (1996), 'Groundwater Markets in Pakistan: Participation and Productivity', Research Report No 105, International Food Policy Research Institute, Washington D.C.

Modak, T.S. and A. Bakshi (2017), 'Changes in Groundwater Markets: A Case Study of Amarsinghi Village, 2005 to 2015', *Review of Agrarian Studies*, vol. 7, no. 2, available at http://ras.org.in/changes_in_groundwater_markets, accessed 9 May 2018.

Modak, T.S. (2018), 'From Public to Private Irrigation: Implications for Equity in Access to Water', *Review of Agrarian Studies*, vol. 8, no. 1, pp. 28–64.

Moench, M. (1992), 'Chasing the Water Table: Equity and Sustainability in Groundwater Management', *Economic and Political Weekly*, vol. 27, nos. 51–52.

Mukherji, A. (2004), 'Groundwater Markets in Ganga-Meghna-Brahmaputra Basin: Theory and Evidence', *Economic and Political Weekly*, vol. 30, no. 31, pp. 3514–20.

———— (2007), 'The Energy-Irrigation Nexus and Its Impact on Groundwater Markets in Eastern Indo-Gangetic Basin: Evidence from West Bengal, India', *Energy Policy*.

———— (2008), 'Spatio-Temporal Analysis of Markets for Groundwater Irrigation Services in India: 1976–77 to 1997–98', *Hydrogeology Journal*, vol. 16, no. 6, January.

———— (2016), 'Evolution of Irrigation Sector', *Economic and Political Weekly*, vol. 51, no. 52, 28 December.

Mukherji A, T. Shah and P. Banerjee (2012), 'Kick-Starting a Second Green Revolution in West Bengal', *Economic and Political Weekly*, vol. 47, no. 18.

Namboodiri, N.V. and V.P. Gandhi (2009), 'Institutional Analysis of the Performance of Surface Water Institutions in India', in L. Crase and V. Gandhi, eds, *Reforming Institutions in Water Resource Management: Policy and Performance for Sustainable Development*, London and New York: Earthscan.

Nagaraj, N. and M.G. Chandrakanth (1997), 'Intra and Inter-Generational Equity: Effects of Irrigation Well Failures', *Economic and Political Weekly*, vol. 32, no. 13, pp. A41–A44.

Nanavati, M.B. and J.J. Anjaria (1965), *The Indian Rural Problem*, Indian Society of Agricultural Economics, Bombay.

National Sample Survey Office (NSSO) (2015), 'Household Ownership and Operational Holdings in India', National Sample Survey 70th Round, Report No. 571, Ministry of Statistics and Programme Implementation, Government of India.

Narayanamoorthy, A. and R.S. Deshpande (2005), *Where Water Seeps!: Towards a New Phase in India's Irrigation Reforms*, New Delhi: Academic Foundation.

Pant, N. (1994), 'Performance of the World Bank Tubewells in India', in F. Kahnaert and G. Levine, eds, *Groundwater Irrigation and the Poor: Options for Development in the Gangetic Basin*, World Bank, Washington D.C.

Prakash, A. (2005), *The Dark Zone: Groundwater Irrigation, Politics and Social Power in North Gujarat*, Hyderabad: Orient Longman.

Prasad, G.S.G. (2002), 'Public Resource and Private Appropriation', *Economic and Political Weekly*, vol.57, no.1, pp. 28–29.

Planning Commission (2007), 'Groundwater Management and Ownership', Report of the Expert Group, Government of India, New Delhi.

Ramachandran, V.K. (2011), 'The State of Agrarian Relations in India Today', *The Marxist*, vol. 27, nos. 1–2, January–June.

———— (2015), 'Socio-Economic Classes in the Study Villages', presented at the Symposium on Results from Village Surveys, organized by the Foundation for Agrarian Studies, Durgapur, 11–13 September.

———— (2016), 'Socio-Economic Classes in Gharsondi Village', presented at the workshop on Results from Village Surveys in Madhya Pradesh, organized by the Foundation for Agrarian Studies, Bangalore, July 18–19.

———— (2017), 'Socio-Economic Classes in the Three Villages', in M. Swaminathan and A. Das, eds, *Socio-Economic Surveys of Three Villages in Karnataka: A Study of Agrarian Relations*, New Delhi: Tulika Books.

Ramakumar, R. (2012), 'Large-Scale Investments in Agriculture in India', *IDS Bulletin*, vol. 43, July.

Rao, P.S. (1993), 'Review of Selected Literature on Indicators of Irrigation Performance', International Irrigation Management Institute (IIMI), Colombo, Sri Lanka.

Rawal, V. (1999), 'Irrigation Development in West Bengal', PhD thesis, Indira Gandhi Institute of Development Research, Mumbai

———— (2001), 'Irrigation Statistics in West Bengal-1', *Economic and Political Weekly*, vol. 36, no. 27, 7 July.

———— (2002), 'Non-Market Interventions in Water-Sharing: Case Studies from West Bengal, India', *Journal of Agrarian Change*, vol. 2, no. 4, October.

Sarkar, A. (2011), 'Socio-Economic Implications for Depleting Groundwater Resources in Punjab: A Comparative Analysis of Different Irrigation Systems', *Economic and Political Weekly*, vol. 46, no. 7, 12 February.

Sarkar, B. (2017), 'Cropping Pattern, Yield and Crop Income: Findings from Three Villages Surveyed in Karnataka', in M. Swaminathan and A. Das, eds, *Socio-Economic Surveys of Three Villages in Karnataka: A Study of Agrarian Relations*, New Delhi: Tulika Books.

Shah, T. (1991), 'Water Markets and Irrigation Development in India', *Indian Journal of Agricultural Economics*, vol. 46, no. 3, pp. 335–48.

———— (1993), *Groundwater Markets and Irrigation Development: Political Economy and Practical Policy*, Bombay: Oxford University Press.

———— (2008), 'Groundwater Management and Ownership: Rejoinder', *Economic and Political Weekly*, vol. 43, no. 17.

———— (2009), *Taming the Anarchy: Groundwater Governance in South Asia: Resource for the Future*, Colombo and Washington D.C.: International Water Management Institute.

———— (2012), *India's Groundwater Irrigation Economy: The Challenge of Balancing Livelihoods and Environment*, Colombo and Washington D.C.: International Water Management Institute.

Shah, T. and V. Ballabh (1997), 'Water Markets in North Bihar: Six Village Studies in Muzaffarpur District', *Economic and Political Weekly*, vol. 37, no. 18.

Shah, T. and K.V. Raju (1987), 'Working of Groundwater Markets in Andhra Pradesh and Gujarat Results of Two Village Studies', *Economic and Political Weekly*, vol. 26, no. 3, pp. A23–A28.

Shah, T., M. Giordano and A. Mukherji (2012), 'Political Economy of the Energy–Groundwater Nexus in India: Exploring Issues and Assessing Policy Options', *Hydrogeology Journal*, vol. 20, no. 5, pp. 995–1006.

Shetty, S.L. (1990), 'Investment in Agriculture: A Brief Review of Recent Trends', *Economic and Political Weekly*, vol. 25, nos 7–8, 17 February.

Singh, C. (1991), *Water Rights and Principles of Water Resources Management*, Bombay: N.M. Tripathi Pvt. Ltd.

Swaminathan, M. and V. Rawal, eds (2015), *Socio-Economic Surveys of Two Villages in Rajasthan: A Study of Agrarian Relations*, New Delhi: Tulika Books.

Vaidyanathan, A. (1994), 'Performance of Indian Agriculture since Independence', in K. Basu, ed., *Agrarian Questions*, New Delhi: Oxford University Press.

———— (1999), *Water Resource Management: Institutional and Irrigation Development in India*, New York: Oxford University Press.

Wood, G.D. (1999), 'Private Provision after Public Neglect Bending Irrigation Markets in North Bihar', *Development and Change*, vol. 30, no. 4, pp. 775–94.

Appendix

Appendix Table 1 *Distribution of cultivator households in the study villages, by socio-economic class,* in number and per cent

Village	Socio-economic class	Number of households	Share of total cultivator households
Alabujanahalli	Rich capitalist farmer	2	1.4
	Peasant 1	9	6.5
	Peasant 2	39	28.3
	Peasant 3	30	21.7
	Peasant 4	58	42.0

Note: In Alabujanahalli, there was no traditional class of landlords. Two households with relatively large holdings that did not engage in any family labour, classified as 'rich capitalist farmer' households. Peasant households, whose earnings were primarily from cultivation, were classified as Peasant 1, Peasant 2, Peasant 3 and Peasant 4 on the basis of landholding (ownership and operational), income sources and asset-holding. The value of household assets for Peasant 1 household was above Rs 50 lakhs, for Peasant 2 households was from 20 lakhs to Rs 50 lakhs, for Peasant 3 households was from 10 lakhs to Rs 20 lakhs and for Peasant households was below 10 lakhs.

Harevli	Landlord	3	4.3
	Peasant 1 (rich)	10	14.5
	Peasant 2 (upper middle)	13	18.8
	Peasant 3 (lower middle)	15	21.7
	Peasant 4 (small)	28	40.6

Note: There were three landlord households in Harveli. These households had the largest extent of owned landholdings in the village. The peasant households were further classified into four classes on the basis of landholdings (owned and operational holdings), income sources and assets. These classes are Peasant 1 (rich), Peasants 2 (upper middle), Peasant 3 (lower middle) and Peasant 4 (small).

Appendix Table 1 *(continued)*

Village	Socio-economic class	Number of households	Share of total cultivator households
Gharsondi	Landlord/Big capitalist farmer	12	8.5
	Peasant 1/Rich capitalist farmer	6	4.2
	Peasant 2 (upper middle)	22	15.5
	Peasant 3 (lower middle)	44	31.0
	Peasant 4 (small)	58	40.8

Note: In Gharsondi, there were twelve landlord/big capitalist farmer households. Landlords or big capitalist farmers had highest landholdings and asset value in the village. Peasant households incurred primarily from agriculture and animal husbandry. These households are categorized on the basis of landholding of the villages (ownership and operational holding), income sources and asset holding. Peasant 1 (rich/capitalist farmer) households own substantial extent of land (average landholding is around 27.5 acres). The value of asset holding of Peasant 1 households was around Rs 56 lakhs to Rs 98 lakhs. Their share of earnings from agriculture and allied services was about 90 per cent of their total income. Peasant 2 (upper middle) households having asset valued ranges from Rs 24 lakhs to Rs 55 lakhs. The average landholding of this class was 12 acres. Peasant 3 (lower middle) households had an average landholding of 5 acre and assets valued ranges between 8.8 lakhs to 24 lakhs. The major sources of income were agriculture and allied services which constituted about 80 per cent of their total income. The average holding of Peasant 4 (small) households were 2.3 acre. The asset holding of this category ranges between 64,000 and 13 lakhs. The maximum asset holding of 13 lakhs was of only one household while the rest of the category lies between 64,000 and 10 lakhs. They also did manual labouring out apart from crop cultivation.

Amarsinghi	Peasant (upper)	18	33.3
	Peasant (lower)	36	66.7

Note: There were no landlord/capitalist farmer households. Peasant households were classified into 'upper' and 'lower' on the basis of a labour ratio criterion.

Panahar	Landlord/Big capitalist farmer	7	4.6
	Peasant (upper)	52	34.2
	Peasant (lower)	93	61.2

Note: There were seven landlord/capitalist farmer households in Panahar. Of these, three were Muslim households and were descendants of a Muslim jotedar family. The other four households were goala families that initially had small holdings but purchased land over time. No member of these seven families worked on the fields. Some employed full-time farm servants, but most relied on daily hired labour to cultivate their fields. All the other peasant households had less than 2 hectares of operational holdings. These households worked on all or some of the major manual operations on the land. These households were further classified into 'upper' and 'lower' peasant households on the basis of a labour ratio criterion.

Appendix Table 1 *(continued)*

Village	Socio-economic class	Number of households	Share of total cultivator households
Rewasi	Landlord and rural rich	8	5
	Peasant 1	14	8.8
	Peasant 2	26	16.3
	Peasant 3	59	36.9
	Peasant 4	53	33.1

Note: Eight households that were among the richest households in Rewasi were classified as 'landlords and rural rich'. These households wielded considerable social and political power in the village. Peasant households were further classified on the basis of asset ownership. Households having means of production valued at more than 20 lakhs per households were classified as 'Peasant I'; households having means of production valued between 10 lakhs and 20 lakhs per households were classified as 'Peasant 2'; households with means of production valued between 5 lakhs and 10 lakhs per household were classified as 'Peasant 3'; and the households having means of production valued less than 5 lakhs were classified as 'Peasant 4'.

Siresandra	Peasant 1	4	6.7
	Peasant 2	24	40.0
	Peasant 3	32	53.3

Note: There were no landlords or capitalist farmers in the village. Peasant households were classified into Peasant 1, Peasant 2, and Peasant 3 households on the basis of asset ownership and value. The value of household assets for Peasant 1 was above Rs 50 lakhs, for Peasant 2 was from 15 lakhs to Rs 50 lakhs and for Peasant 3 was below Rs 15 lakhs.
Source: PARI survey data.

9

Price Support and Access to MSPs in Indian Agriculture

Biplab Sarkar

Introduction

About 70 per cent of the Indian population was rural as per the Census of India 2011.[1] In most Indian villages, a majority of the households are associated with agricultural production and allied activities – as owners and operators of land, as hired workers, or as providers of inputs and other services. But agriculture and allied sectors contribute only 17 per cent to the total national income. In 2018–19, share in gross value added was only 9.4 per cent for crop production, 5.1 per cent for livestock production, 1.3 per cent for forestry, and 1.2 per cent for fishing and aquaculture. The overall growth of gross value added in agriculture at constant (2011–12) basic prices was only 2.4 per cent in 2018–19 and was negative for crop production. These figures reflect the poor development of the agricultural sector in general, and crop production in particular. It also manifests the low incomes of all those who work in the agricultural sector.

Perhaps the most tragic manifestation of the crisis of farming livelihoods and rural poverty in the last two decades has been the large-scale farmers' suicides. Official statistics indicate that more than 3 lakh farmers committed suicide between 1997 and 2018. The available studies show that the farmers who committed suicide were mostly small and medium farmers, and they attribute these suicides to loss of farm income, indebtedness and an absence of alternative livelihood opportunities. They have also argued that the decline of farm income was associated with rising costs of cultivation, crop losses and the price risks associated with agricultural markets (Reddy and Mishra 2009; Ramachandran 2011; Rawal and Swaminathan 2011; Mahendra Dev 2012; Gaurav and Mishra 2014; Merriott 2017).

Policies to ensure steady, sustainable and adequate incomes to farmers must thus be central to agricultural and rural development policy. Such policies have historically taken the form of interventions with respect to costs of inputs and prices of outputs. A historically preferred policy mechanism has been to regulate the market by means of administered output prices.

The declared objective of agricultural price policy in India, from the 1960s, was to ensure remunerative prices to producers to encourage higher investment and production as well as safeguard the interests of consumers by making cereal supplies available at reasonable prices. In each season, the Government of India announces minimum support prices (MSPs) for agricultural commodities; it also organizes purchase operations, wherever required, through public, cooperative and other designated agencies to ensure that prices do not fall below the MSP for each commodity. It decided on the MSP taking into account the crop-wise recommendations of the Commission for Agricultural Costs and Prices (CACP).

In this context, the present chapter attempts to examine two sets of questions related to agricultural price policy in India. First, we investigate how much of the cost of production was covered by the MSPs for agricultural produce. What percentage of total produce was procured by government agencies. Secondly, it examines the divergence between the farm harvest prices (FHPs) at which farmers sold their produce and the MSPs.[2] In the third section, the first set of questions is examined by choosing rice, wheat, cotton, sugarcane, jute and *arhar*. The question is further investigated in the fourth section using the results from a detailed village survey dataset.

MSP: The Official Methodology

The initial determinants of MSPs for agricultural commodities in India are the crop-wise surveys carried out by the Department of Economics and Statistics (DES), Ministry of Agriculture, Government of India. Since 1970–71, the DES has been conducting crop surveys under a scheme known as the 'Comprehensive Scheme for Studying Cost of Cultivation/Production of Principal Crops' (CCPC henceforth). The CCPC scheme involves collecting data on twenty-three crops (annual and seasonal) every year.[3] At present, these surveys are conducted in nineteen states of the Indian Union; in almost all cases, the actual surveys are conducted by local universities. On the receipt of field data from these universities, the DES generates the following cost of production estimates and provides it to the CACP. The three-tiered system of calculation of production costs for crops is given below. As the actual cost data are received by the DES with a lag of at least two to three years, the CACP uses projected costs of production for the most recent year relevant for the MSP.

A	A1= All actual expenses in cash and kind incurred in production by the cultivator
	A2= A1 + Rent paid for leased in land
	A2+FL = A1 + Rent paid for leased in land + Imputed value of family labour
B	B1= A1 + Interest on value of owned capital assets (excluding land)
	B2= B1 + Rental value of owned land and rent paid for leased-in land
C	C1= B1 + Imputed value of family labour
	C2= B2 + Imputed value of family labour
	C2*= C2 + Additional value of human labour based on use of higher wage in consideration with the statutory minimum wage rate
	C3= C2* + 10 per cent of C2*

In 2002, the Government of India appointed a High Level Committee on Long Term Grain Policy (HLC). The HLC recognized that the MSP policy 'was critical in India's achievement of food grains self-sufficiency' and suggested certain modifications to the then existing system. Among its recommendations, one was to set MSPs on the basis of C2 cost of production in the more efficient producing regions/states (HLC 2002). However, the HLC also suggested that at least A2+FL should be covered by the MSP in the other high-cost regions/states. In other words, the price policy should be based on producers in the 'efficient' or lower-cost regions.

In 2004, the Government of India appointed a National Commission on Farmers (NCF). In its landmark reports from 2004 to 2006, the NCF made a series of recommendations designed, *inter alia*, to strengthen India's food security and sovereignty, strengthen farming and related activities, ensure adequate and sustainable incomes to the rural population, and make farming and related activities an attractive and remunerative option for young men and women in rural India. The NCF argued that implementation of MSP had to be improved for crops other than paddy and wheat; it recommended that MSP should be at least 50 per cent more than the weighted C2 cost of production. In other words, the costs in all major producing regions would need to be considered in estimating C2, and MSP should give a fixed return over C2. This, it was argued, would make cultivation remunerative. These recommendations, which were radical in the Indian context and were accepted with enthusiasm by peasant organizations in the country, have not been accepted as policy by the central government.

Cost of Cultivation and MSP: Crop-Wise Analysis

In this section, we analyse three themes: (1) the number of states covered for estimating costs of production of individual crops; (2) the proportion of C2+50 per cent that is actually accounted for by MSP in each crop; (3) the quantity of total produce procured by government agencies. The crops covered here are rice, wheat, cotton, sugarcane, jute and *arhar*.

The MSP announced by the Government of India has stagnated in the recent years. Between 2014 and 2019, the MSP for almost all commodities grew by less than 5 per cent a year (see Appendix Table 1). While MSP for paddy was hiked annually by 32 per cent in 2008–09, 18 per cent in 2009–10 and 16 per cent in 2012–13, the increase was only 4–5 per cent for all the years after 2013–14. The annual growth rates of MSP between 2007–08 and 2012–13 were 19 per cent for *arhar*, 17 per cent for sugarcane, 16 per cent for groundnut and 16 per cent for *ragi*. Between 2013–14 and 2018–19, these growth rates declined to 6 per cent, 5 per cent, 3 per cent and 6 per cent for *arhar*, sugarcane, groundnut and ragi respectively.

In what follows, we examine the relationship between MSP and the costs of production for each crop separately. This section uses cost of production data from 2009–10 to 2017–18 collected by the Directorate of Economics and Statistics, Ministry of Agriculture and Farmers' Welfare.

Paddy

The CCPC surveys on paddy cultivation covers eighteen states – Andhra Pradesh, Assam, Bihar, Chhattisgarh, Gujarat, Haryana, Himachal Pradesh, Jharkhand, Kerala, Karnataka, Madhya Pradesh, Maharashtra, Odisha, Punjab, Tamil Nadu, Uttarakhand, Uttar Pradesh and West Bengal. No other crop is as extensively covered by the survey as paddy. The MSP for paddy announced by the central government is given in Table 9.1. Table 9.2 presents the percentage of C2+50 per cent covered by MSP.

At the national level, MSP as a share of C2+50 per cent declined from 76 per cent in 2009–10 to 69 per cent in 2017–18 (see Table 9.2). In West Bengal, the largest producer of rice in India, the MSP was 63 per cent of the C2+50 per cent. In Maharashtra, MSP was as low as 38 per cent of C2+50 per cent in 2015–16 and 2017–18. MSP was not above C2+50

Table 9.1 *Minimum support price for rice, 2009–10 to 2018–19 at current prices,* in rupees per quintal

Year	2009–10	2010–11	2011–12	2012–13	2013–14	2014–15	2015–16	2016–17	2017–18	2018–19
Paddy (F)/ Grade A	1,030	1,030	1,110	1,280	1,345	1,400	1,450	1,510	1,590	1,770
Paddy Common	1,000	1,000	1,080	1,250	1,310	1,360	1,410	1,470	1,550	1,750

Source: Directorate of Economics and Statistics, Ministry of Agriculture and Farmers' Welfare.

Table 9.2 *C2+50% for rice (at current prices, rupees per quintal) and percentage of C2+50% (in brackets) covered by all-India MSP, 2009–10 to 2017–18*

State/Year	C2+50% and MSP as proportion of C2+50% (in brackets)								
	2009–10	2010–11	2011–12	2012–13	2013–14	2014–15	2015–16	2016–17	2017–18
Andhra Pradesh	1,399	1,375	1,465	1,703	1,864	1,923	1,982	1,896	2,261
	(72)	(73)	(74)	(73)	(70)	(71)	(71)	(78)	(69)
Assam	1,237	1,237	1,500	1,529	1,786	2,142	2,099	2,363	2,143
	(81)	(81)	(72)	(82)	(73)	(63)	(67)	(62)	(72)
Bihar	1,338	1,385	1,292	1,622	1,712	1,582	1,907	1,736	1,905
	(75)	(72)	(84)	(77)	(77)	(86)	(74)	(85)	(81)
Chhattisgarh	1,251	1,247	1,396	1,443	1,746	1,845	2,062	1,939	1,909
	(80)	(80)	(77)	(87)	(75)	(74)	(68)	(76)	(81)
Gujarat	1,142	1,018	1,709	1,949	1,816	1,644	1,646	1,660	1,674
	(88)	(98)	(63)	(64)	(72)	(83)	(86)	(89)	(93)
Haryana	1,725	1,957	1,876	1,872	2,084	2,297	2,315	2,374	2,172
	(60)	(53)	(59)	(68)	(65)	(61)	(63)	(64)	(73)
Himachal Pradesh	1,209	1,017	993	1,467	1,780	1,650	2,225	2,304	2,065
	(83)	(98)	(109)	(85)	(74)	(82)	(63)	(64)	(75)
Jharkhand	1,851	1,957	1,990	2,206	1,912	1,625	2,024	1,803	1,972
	(54)	(51)	(54)	(57)	(69)	(84)	(70)	(82)	(79)
Karnataka	1,209	1,341	1,449	1,932	1,786	1,794	2,009	1,900	3,194
	(83)	(75)	(75)	(65)	(73)	(76)	(70)	(77)	(49)
Kerala	1,322	1,555	1,681	1,936	2,020	2,219	2,505	2,558	3,598
	(76)	(64)	(64)	(65)	(65)	(61)	(56)	(57)	(43)
Madhya Pradesh	1,408	1,418	1,441	1,562	1,701	2,124	2,565	1,806	2,360
	(71)	(71)	(75)	(80)	(77)	(64)	(55)	(81)	(66)
Maharashtra	2,112	2,281	1,751	2,031	2,263	3,356	3,703	3,299	4,099
	(47)	(44)	(62)	(62)	(58)	(41)	(38)	(45)	(38)
Odisha	1,190	1,433	1,832	1,722	2,099	2,108	2,175	2,140	2,091
	(84)	(70)	(59)	(73)	(62)	(65)	(65)	(69)	(74)
Punjab	1,160	1,255	1,356	1,417	1,565	1,638	1,592	1,638	1,624
	(89)	(82)	(82)	(90)	(86)	(85)	(91)	(92)	(98)
Tamil Nadu	1,346	1,420	1,668	1,883	1,887	2,097	2,153	2,285	2,507
	(74)	(70)	(65)	(66)	(69)	(65)	(65)	(64)	(62)
Uttar Pradesh	1,219	1,210	1,437	1,527	1,538	2,220	2,312	2,214	2,344
	(82)	(83)	(75)	(82)	(85)	(61)	(61)	(66)	(66)
Uttarakhand	1,228	1,224	1,584	1,859	1,690	1,345	1,403	1,520	2,542
	(81)	(82)	(68)	(67)	(78)	(101)	(100)	(97)	(61)
West Bengal	1,298	1,534	1,629	1,854	2,050	2,117	2,135	2,246	2,448
	(77)	(65)	(66)	(67)	(64)	(64)	(66)	(65)	(63)
India	1,317	1,402	1,538	1,686	1,823	2,011	2,109	2,057	2,233
	(76)	(71)	(70)	(74)	(72)	(68)	(67)	(71)	(69)

Note: MSP for Punjab and Haryana is for Grade-A paddy.
Source: Directorate of Economics and Statistics, Ministry of Agriculture and Farmers' Welfare.

Table 9.3 *Procurement of paddy, major states, India, 2017–18*

State	Total production ('000 Tonnes)	Procurement ('000 tonnes)	Procurement as % of production	Marketed Surplus Ratio (MSR)
Andhra Pradesh	8,166	4,000	49	92
Chhattisgarh	4,931	3,255	66	NA
Haryana	4,523	3,992	88	99
Madhya Pradesh	4,124	1,096	27	93
Odisha	6,551	3,287	50	77
Punjab	13,382	11,833	88	99
Tamil Nadu	6,639	1,011	15	92
Telangana	6,262	3,618	58	NA
Uttar Pradesh	13,274	2,875	22	78
West Bengal	14,967	1,673	11	69

Note: MSR is the actual sale in the market divided by the total production in the state.
Source: Agricultural Statistics at a Glance 2019, Directorate of Economics and Statistics, Ministry of Agriculture and Farmers' Welfare.

per cent in any state in the time period under consideration except on two occasions: Himachal Pradesh in 2011–12 (109 per cent) and Uttarakhand in 2014–15 (101 per cent). Even if we take just C2 costs as the benchmark, eight out of eighteen states had MSP lower than their average C2 costs in 2017–18. C2 was only 57 per cent of MSP in Maharashtra in 2017–18.

The procurement pattern of paddy shows wide variations (see Table 9.3). In 2017–18, the total amount of rice procured was 34 per cent of the total production in India (38184 thousand tonnes out of 112758 thousand tonnes). Only five States – Punjab, Haryana, Chhattisgarh, Telangana, Odisha – had at least 50 per cent of the total produce procured by government agencies[5] (Table 9.3). The procurement of paddy was lowest in West Bengal, Tamil Nadu and Uttar Pradesh. While the largest producer of paddy, West Bengal, had only 11 per cent of total production procured by government agencies in 2017–18, other advanced rice growing states like Punjab and Haryana had 88 per cent of total production procured by government agencies.

The marketed surplus ratio (proportion of total output that is sold or disposed of) for all states in Table 9.3 was higher than 65 per cent. Since these states also had a large number of farmers with holding size less than 1 hectare, the low level of procurement affected these farmers the most.

Wheat

The CCPC surveys on wheat covered fourteen states – Bihar, Chhattisgarh, Gujarat, Haryana, Himachal Pradesh, Jharkhand, Karnataka,

Table 9.4 *Minimum support price for wheat, 2009–10 to 2018–19 at current prices*, in rupees per quintal

Year	2009–10	2010–11	2011–12	2012–13	2013–14	2014–15	2015–16	2016–17	2017–18	2018–19
All-India MSP	1,100	1,120	1,285	1,350	1,400	1,450	1,525	1,625	1,735	1,840

Source: Directorate of Economics and Statistics, Ministry of Agriculture and Farmers' Welfare.

Table 9.5 *C2+50% for wheat (at current prices, rupees per quintal) and percentage of C2+50% (in brackets) covered by all-India MSP, 2009–10 to 207–18*

State/Year	2009–10	2010–11	2011–12	2012–13	2013–14	2014–15	2015–16	2016–17	2017–18
Bihar	1,186 (93)	1,147 (98)	1,202 (107)	1,294 (104)	1,363 (103)	1,846 (79)	1,954 (78)	1,703 (95)	1,912 (91)
Chhattisgarh	2,280 (48)	1,513 (74)	1,806 (71)	2,157 (63)	2,732 (51)	1,859 (78)	1,881 (81)	1,811 (90)	3,172 (55)
Gujarat	1,176 (94)	1,063 (105)	1,325 (97)	1,878 (72)	1,671 (84)	1,861 (78)	1,859 (82)	1,788 (91)	2,037 (85)
Haryana	1,249 (88)	1,160 (97)	1,276 (101)	1,561 (86)	1,567 (89)	2,626 (55)	2,887 (53)	2,757 (59)	2,012 (86)
Himachal Pradesh	1,789 (61)	1,584 (71)	1,828 (70)	2,151 (63)	2,218 (63)	2,601 (56)	2,137 (71)	1,978 (82)	2,659 (65)
Jharkhand	2,320 (47)	2,444 (46)	1,276 (101)	1,465 (92)	1,541 (91)	3,531 (41)	5,793 (26)	5,566 (29)	2,687 (65)
Madhya Pradesh	1,213 (91)	1,251 (90)	1,278 (101)	1,438 (94)	1,612 (87)	1,691 (86)	1,834 (83)	1,527 (106)	1,665 (104)
Maharashtra	2,023 (54)	1,885 (59)	1,948 (66)	2,408 (56)	2,522 (56)	2,989 (49)	3,072 (50)	3,133 (52)	3,472 (50)
Punjab	1,225 (90)	1,308 (86)	1,333 (96)	1,458 (93)	1,446 (97)	1,623 (89)	1,625 (94)	1,654 (98)	1,754 (99)
Rajasthan	1,064 (103)	1,000 (112)	1,239 (104)	1,370 (99)	1,496 (94)	1,734 (84)	1,778 (86)	1,758 (92)	2,046 (85)
Uttar Pradesh	1,249 (88)	1,206 (93)	1,396 (92)	1,564 (86)	1,581 (89)	2,254 (64)	2,135 (71)	1,891 (86)	2,196 (79)
Uttarakhand	1,334 (82)	1,212 (92)	1,564 (82)	1,445 (93)	1,413 (99)	1,916 (76)	1,805 (85)	1,639 (99)	2,148 (81)
West Bengal	1,854 (59)	1,816 (62)	1,989 (65)	2,059 (66)	2,107 (66)	2,379 (61)	2,924 (52)	2,780 (58)	2,312 (75)
India	1,248 (88)	1,245 (90)	1,359 (95)	1,534 (88)	1,591 (88)	2,033 (71)	2,052 (74)	1,908 (85)	2,003 (87)

Source: Directorate of Economics and Statistics, Ministry of Agriculture and Farmers' Welfare.

Table 9.6 *Procurement of wheat, 2017–18*

State	Total production ('000 Tonnes)	Procurement ('000 tonnes)	Procurement as % of production	Marketed surplus ratio (MSR)
Gujarat	3,069	7	0	97
Haryana	10,765	7,432	69	81
Madhya Pradesh	15,911	6,725	42	74
Punjab	17,830	11,706	66	89
Rajasthan	9,369	1,245	13	78
Uttar Pradesh	31,879	3,699	12	55

Source: Agricultural Statistics at a Glance 2019, Directorate of Economics and Statistics, Ministry of Agriculture and Farmers' Welfare.

Maharashtra, Madhya Pradesh, Punjab, Rajasthan, Uttarakhand, Uttar Pradesh and West Bengal – in 2017–18. In 2017–18, only 87 per cent of C2+50 per cent was covered by the MSP at the national level. MSP as a share of the national C2+50 per cent was highest (95 per cent) in 2011–12 and lowest (71 per cent) in 2014–15 (see Tables 9.4 and 9.5). In 2017–18, none of the states had MSP higher than the average C2+50 per cent.

Between 2009–10 and 2017–18, the MSP exceeded C2+50 per cent in different states for some years: Bihar from 2011–12 to 2013–14, Gujarat in 2010–11, Haryana in 2011–12, Jharkhand in 2011–12, Madhya Pradesh in 2011–12, 2016–17 and 2017–18, and Rajasthan from 2009–10 to 2011–12 (see Table 9.5). The largest amount of procurement by government agencies happened in Punjab and Haryana, where 66 per cent to 69 per cent of the total production was procured in 2017–18 (see Table 9.6). The procurement was very low in Uttar Pradesh, which was the largest producer of wheat. Here, the amount of wheat procured constituted only about 12 per cent of the total production in 2017–18. The marketed surplus ratio in Uttar Pradesh was only 55 per cent. A low procurement implies that a large number of farmers depended on market prices, which in most cases, were less than the MSP.

Cotton

The CCPC surveys on cotton cultivation covered ten states – Andhra Pradesh, Gujarat, Haryana, Karnataka, Madhya Pradesh, Maharashtra, Odisha, Punjab, Rajasthan and Tamil Nadu. The MSP as a proportion of C2+50 per cent declined from 84 per cent in 2009–10 to 63 per cent in 2017–18 (see Table 9.8). In 2017–18, the range for MSP as a share of C2+50 per cent was between 43 per cent and 72 per cent. The highest

Table 9.7 *Minimum support price for cotton, 2009–10 to 2018–19 at current prices*, in rupees per quintal

Year	2009–10	2010–11	2011–12	2012–13	2013–14	2014–15	2015–16	2016–17	2017–18	2018–19
Medium Staple	2,500	2,500	2,800	3,600	3,700	3,750	3,800	3,860	4,020	5,150
Long Staple	3,000	3,000	3,300	3,900	4,000	4,050	4,100	4,160	4,320	5,450

Source: Directorate of Economics and Statistics, Ministry of Agriculture and Farmers' Welfare.

Table 9.8 *C2+50% for cotton (at current prices, rupees per quintal) and percentage of C2+50% (in brackets) covered by all-India MSP, 2009–10 to 2017–18*

State/Year	C2+50% and MSP as proportion of C2+50% (in brackets)								
	2009–10	2010–11	2011–12	2012–13	2013–14	2014–15	2015–16	2016–17	2017–18
Andhra Pradesh	3,610 (83)	4,958 (61)	5,336 (62)	6,133 (64)	6,379 (63)	6,993 (58)	7,601 (54)	6,817 (61)	8,326 (52)
Gujarat	3,338 (90)	3,622 (83)	4,901 (67)	6,520 (60)	5,017 (80)	5,489 (74)	5,760 (71)	5,901 (71)	5,994 (72)
Haryana	3,620 (83)	4,201 (71)	4,844 (68)	5,694 (68)	6,274 (64)	8,360 (48)	10,581 (39)	6,881 (60)	7,121 (61)
Karnataka	3,581 (70)	4,326 (58)	4,456 (63)	5,363 (67)	5,521 (67)	6,127 (61)	7,343 (52)	6,201 (62)	6,679 (60)
Madhya Pradesh	2,971 (84)	3,474 (72)	3,689 (76)	3,963 (91)	4,679 (79)	8,347 (45)	8,378 (45)	7,924 (49)	6,116 (66)
Maharashtra	4,007 (75)	5,405 (56)	5,978 (55)	6,180 (63)	6,055 (66)	6,948 (58)	6,905 (59)	6,532 (64)	8,321 (52)
Odisha	3,390 (74)	3,856 (65)	5,067 (55)	6,099 (59)	6,142 (60)	9,522 (39)	7,436 (51)	6,431 (60)	6,514 (62)
Punjab	3,531 (85)	4,421 (68)	5,639 (59)	5,617 (69)	6,110 (65)	5,836 (69)	11,205 (37)	5,982 (70)	6,123 (71)
Rajasthan	2,794 (107)	2,937 (102)	3,620 (91)	4,045 (96)	5,895 (68)	5,733 (71)	6,106 (67)	6,855 (61)	5,983 (72)
Tamil Nadu	3,863 (78)	4,280 (70)	6,329 (52)	6,741 (58)	8,000 (50)	5,655 (72)	5,919 (69)	10,062 (41)	10,129 (43)
India	3,557 (84)	4,390 (68)	5,118 (64)	5,936 (66)	5,764 (69)	6,466 (63)	6,896 (59)	6,511 (64)	6,887 (63)

Note: States which are included in the medium staple category are Karnataka, Madhya Pradesh and Odisha. The rest of the states are reported in long staple cotton MSP.
Source: Directorate of Economics and Statistics, Ministry of Agriculture and Farmers' Welfare.

C2+50 per cent was in Tamil Nadu and the lowest C2+50 per cent was in Gujarat and Rajasthan in 2017–18. From 2009–10 to 2017–18, MSP was more than C2+50 per cent in only one state for just two years, Rajasthan in 2009–10 and 2010–11.

Sugarcane

The CCPC surveys on sugarcane cultivation covered nine states – Andhra Pradesh, Bihar, Haryana, Karnataka, Maharashtra, Punjab, Tamil Nadu, Uttar Pradesh and Uttarakhand. In the case of sugarcane, the central government announces what is called the 'fair and remunerative price' (FRP) to be paid by sugar mills to sugarcane farmers. In 2017–18, the MSP as a share of C2+50 per cent was 88 per cent in Maharashtra and 71 per

Table 9.9 *Fair and remunerative price (FRP) for sugarcane, 2009–10 to 2018–19 at current prices*, in rupees per quintal

Year	2009–10	2010–11	2011–12	2012–13	2013–14	2014–15	2015–16	2016–17	2017–18	2018–19
All-India FRP	130	139	145	170	210	220	230	230	255	275

Source: Directorate of Economics and Statistics, Ministry of Agriculture and Farmers' Welfare.

Table 9.10 *C2+50% for sugarcane (at current prices, rupees per quintal) and percentage of C2+50% (in brackets) covered by all-India FRP, 2009–10 to 2017–18*

State/Year	C2+50% and MSP as proportion of C2+50% (in brackets)								
	2009–10	2010–11	2011–12	2012–13	2013–14	2014–15	2015–16	2016–17	2017–18
Andhra Pradesh	195	225	275	241	222	328	321	354	360
	(67)	(62)	(53)	(71)	(95)	(67)	(72)	(65)	(71)
Haryana	200	202	245	272	297	NA	NA	NA	210
	(65)	(69)	(59)	(63)	(71)				(121)
Karnataka	134	140	184	194	196	215	207	215	194
	(97)	(100)	(79)	(88)	(107)	(102)	(111)	(107)	(131)
Maharashtra	182	187	208	227	229	274	284	275	290
	(71)	(74)	(70)	(75)	(92)	(80)	(81)	(84)	(88)
Tamil Nadu	150	166	193	224	242	257	255	283	363
	(87)	(84)	(75)	(76)	(87)	(86)	(90)	(81)	(70)
Uttar Pradesh	158	186	212	237	248	260	264	258	299
	(82)	(75)	(68)	(72)	(85)	(85)	(87)	(89)	(85)
Uttarakhand	160	192	219	191	240	223	284	298	290
	(81)	(73)	(66)	(89)	(87)	(99)	(81)	(77)	(88)

Source: Directorate of Economics and Statistics, Ministry of Agriculture and Farmers' Welfare.

cent in Andhra Pradesh. An analysis of state-wise C2+50 per cent figures shows that the MSP exceeded C2+50 per cent in two states for a few years: Haryana in 2017–18, and Karnataka from 2013–14 to 2017–18 (see Tables 9.9 and 9.10). C2+50 per cent was lowest in Karnataka and highest in Andhra Pradesh for most of the years.

Jute

The CCPC surveys on jute cultivation covered three states – Assam, Odisha and West Bengal. MSP for jute was less than 70 per cent of C2+50 per cent in the time period under consideration in all the three states except for two occasions: West Bengal in 2012–13 and 2017–18 (see Tables 9.11 and 9.12). In 2016–17, the MSP covered only 52 per cent of the cost of production in Odisha, the lowest among the three states.

Arhar

The CCPC surveys on *arhar* cultivation covered ten states – Andhra Pradesh, Bihar, Chhattisgarh, Gujarat, Karnataka, Madhya Pradesh, Maharashtra, Odisha, Tamil Nadu and Uttar Pradesh in 2017–18. However, cost of cultivation data was not available regularly for Bihar, Chhattisgarh

Table 9.11 *Minimum support price for jute, 2009–10 to 2018–19 at current prices,* rupees per quintal

Year	2009–10	2010–11	2011–12	2012–13	2013–14	2014–15	2015–16	2016–17	2017–18	2018–19
All-India MSP	1,375	1,575	1,675	2,200	2,300	2,400	2,700	3,200	3,500	3,700

Source: Directorate of Economics and Statistics, Ministry of Agriculture and Farmers' Welfare.

Table 9.12 *C2+50% for jute (at current prices, rupees per quintal) and percentage of C2+50% (in brackets) covered by all-India MSP, 2009–10 to 2017–18*

State/Year	C2+50% and MSP as proportion of C2+50% (in brackets)								
	2009–10	2010–11	2011–12	2012–13	2013–14	2014–15	2015–16	2016–17	2017–18
Assam	2,306 (60)	4,010 (39)	3,017 (56)	3,879 (57)	3,928 (59)	3,941 (61)	5,423 (50)	6,037 (53)	5,363 (65)
Odisha	2,232 (62)	3,285 (48)	3,428 (49)	3,796 (58)	3,774 (61)	5,244 (46)	6,407 (42)	6,145 (52)	NA
West Bengal	2,167 (63)	2,848 (55)	2,960 (57)	3,135 (70)	3,430 (67)	3,983 (60)	4,445 (61)	4,690 (68)	4,841 (72)

Source: Directorate of Economics and Statistics, Ministry of Agriculture and Farmers' Welfare.

and Tamil Nadu in the time period under consideration. Therefore, we have considered the remaining seven states for the analysis. These seven states together accounted for 84 per cent of the total area cultivated under *arhar* and 83 per cent of the total production of *arhar* in India.

The national MSP for *arhar* declined from 72 per cent of C2+50 per cent in 2010–11 to 59 per cent of C2+50 per cent in 2014–15 (see Tables 9.13 and 9.14). Across the states, the MSP was about 43 per cent to 73 per cent of the C2+50 per cent for *arhar* in 2014–15. However, in 2017–18, the

Table 9.13 *Minimum support price for arhar, 2009–10 to 2018–19 at current prices*, in rupees per quintal

Year	2009– 10	2010– 11	2011– 12	2012– 13	2013– 14	2014– 15	2015– 16	2016– 17	2017– 18	2018– 19
All-India MSP	2,300	3,500	3,700	3,850	4,300	4,350	4,625	5,050	5,450	5,675

Note: In 2010–11 and 2011–12, Rs 500 was additionally given as bonus during the harvesting period. This is included in the values given in the table.
Source: Directorate of Economics and Statistics, Ministry of Agriculture and Farmers' Welfare.

Table 9.14 *C2+50% for arhar (at current prices, rupees per quintal) and percentage of C2+50% (in brackets) by the MSP, 2009–10 to 2017–18*

State/Year	C2+50% and MSP as proportion of C2+50% (in brackets)								
	2009– 10	2010– 11	2011– 12	2012– 13	2013– 14	2014– 15	2015– 16	2016– 17	2017– 18
Andhra Pradesh	4,725 (49)	6,539 (54)	4,777 (77)	6,725 (57)	7,052 (61)	9,573 (45)	13,408 (34)	9,364 (54)	9,809 (56)
Gujarat	5,191 (44)	3,050 (115)	4,644 (80)	5,620 (69)	5,834 (74)	6,826 (64)	6,656 (69)	5,214 (97)	6,629 (82)
Karnataka	3,969 (58)	4,539 (77)	3,964 (93)	4,652 (83)	4,587 (94)	5,945 (73)	7,717 (60)	5,609 (90)	6,124 (89)
Madhya Pradesh	3,476 (66)	4,398 (80)	3,640 (102)	4,178 (92)	4,245 (101)	6,853 (63)	10,781 (43)	4,816 (105)	6,473 (84)
Maharashtra	3,654 (63)	5,486 (64)	4,708 (79)	4,653 (83)	4,473 (96)	8,573 (51)	8,976 (52)	6,249 (81)	6,821 (80)
Odisha	4,437 (52)	4,847 (72)	6,044 (61)	6,472 (59)	6,328 (68)	10,209 (43)	10,085 (46)	9,707 (52)	6,662 (82)
Uttar Pradesh	6,255 (37)	4,267 (82)	4,418 (84)	6,157 (63)	7,077 (61)	6,277 (69)	8,087 (57)	6,487 (78)	6,392 (85)
India	Na	4,881 (72)	4,455 (83)	5,110 (75)	5,083 (85)	7,432 (59)	Na	Na	Na

Source: Directorate of Economics and Statistics, Ministry of Agriculture and Farmers' Welfare.

MSP was more than 80 per cent of the C2+50 per cent for *arhar* almost in all states with one exception: Andhra Pradesh (56 per cent).

Procurement of *arhar* was organized under the Price Stabilization Fund (PSF) scheme of the Government of India. The procurement operations were carried out by National Agricultural Cooperative Marketing Federation of India Ltd. (NAFED). The highest amount of *arhar* procured from 2010–11 to 2014–15 was in 2013–14, when a paltry 2 per cent of the marketed surplus was procured across the country. NAFED procured 19,989 tonnes of *arhar* in 2015–16. However, the situation of arhar procurement changed significantly after 2015. The total procurement of *arhar* in 2016–17 was 1,95,993 tonnes, almost 10 times higher than the previous year. It was 8,73,758 tonnes in 2017–18 and 2,91,000 tonnes in 2018–19.

Farm Harvest Price and MSP: Crop-Wise Analysis

This section uses detailed data from the data archive of the Foundation for Agrarian Studies (FAS), Bengaluru, collected as part of its Project on Agrarian Relations in India (PARI), to show the divergence between MSP and FHP of paddy and wheat in fifteen villages of eight states in India.

We selected the villages based on two criteria: first, gross cropped area devoted to paddy and wheat; second, share of market arrivals to total production in the village. Only those villages were selected in which paddy and wheat were sown as mono-crops in at least 10 per cent of the cropped area and where at least 10 per cent of the total production was marketed. Wheat was also cultivated as an intercrop in some villages, but these villages were not considered in our analysis, as the official data (with which we shall compare our results) did not give any estimates of costs for intercrops.

Paddy

We estimated the weighted average of farm harvest prices of paddy for the twelve villages and calculated the deviation from MSP for the respective year. Table 9.15 shows that the average FHPs in seven out of twelve villages were lower than the official MSPs for the relevant year. In other words, MSP did not act as a floor price for paddy in all the villages surveyed under PARI. The difference between FHP and MSP was negative in the villages that belonged to the major paddy producing states. It was not a one-year drop. If we look at the official FHP statistics for these states, weighted average FHPs were lower than the official MSP in most of the cases.

On the other hand, in Hakamwala (Punjab), the average FHP of paddy was almost 1.5 times higher than the MSP. A basmati variety of paddy was cultivated in Hakamwala. Basmati is a high value paddy variety with a good domestic and export market.

We also compared MSP for paddy with the actual FHP for each

Table 9.15 *Minimum support price (MSP) and farm harvest price (FHP) for 100 kg of paddy, selected villages*, in rupees

Survey village	State	Year	For 100 kg of paddy		FHP – MSP
			MSP	FHP	
Ananthavaram	Andhra Pradesh	2005–06	570	618	48
Bukkacherla	Andhra Pradesh	2005–06	570	564	–6
Kothapalle	Andhra Pradesh	2005–06	570	548	–22
Harevli	Uttar Pradesh	2005–06	570	610	40
Alabujanahalli	Karnataka	2008–09	900	884	–16
Panahar	West Bengal	2009–10	1,000	891	–109
Amarsinghi	West Bengal	2009–10	1,000	910	–90
Kalmandasguri	West Bengal	2009–10	1,000	830	–170
Tehang	Punjab	2009–10	1,000	1,035	35
Hakamwala	Punjab	2009–10	1,000	1,535	535
Katkuian	Bihar	2011–12	1,080	1,125	45
Nayanagar	Bihar	2011–12	1,080	928	–152

Source: Survey data.

cultivator surveyed. In Ananthavaram (Andhra Pradesh), the unit price obtained was below the MSP for 36 per cent of cultivators. The corresponding proportion was 40 per cent in Bukkacherla (dry zone in Rayalaseema, Andhra Pradesh), 81 per cent in Kothapalle (north Telengana, Andhra Pradesh) and 30 per cent in Harevli (western Uttar Pradesh).

In Alabujanahalli (Karnataka), surveyed in 2008–09, for 75 per cent cultivators in the pre-kharif season and 50 per cent of the cultivators in the kharif and rabi seasons, the MSP did not act as a floor price. The situation was worse in the villages surveyed in West Bengal and Bihar, where procurement seemed non-operational. On the other hand, cultivators in villages of Punjab received paddy prices either equal to or higher than the MSP. Paddy was cultivated as a commercial crop in these villages and farmers marketed almost 95 per cent of their production under very strong government procurement system.

Wheat

The weighted average of FHP for wheat was estimated for twelve villages and the deviation from the MSP for each respective year was calculated. Here, the picture was different from that of paddy. The average FHP of wheat in all the villages was higher than the announced MSP (see Table

Table **9.16** *Minimum support price (MSP) and farm harvest price (FHP) for 100 kg of wheat,* in rupees

Survey village	State	Year	For 100 kg of wheat		FHP – MSP
			MSP	FHP	
Harevli	Uttar Pradesh	2005–06	700	809	109
25F Gulabewala	Rajasthan	2006–07	850	861	11
Gharsondi	Madhya Pradesh	2007–08	1,000	1,119	119
Rewasi	Rajasthan	2009–10	1,100	1,319	219
Tehang	Punjab	2010–11	1,170	1,239	69
Hakamwala	Punjab	2010–11	1,170	1,256	86
Nayanagar	Bihar	2011–12	1,285	1,290	5

Source: Survey data.

9.16). The MSP did act as the floor price in these villages. This suggests that with an active MSP and procurement policy, the MSP can work as the floor price.

When we compared MSP for wheat with the actual FHP for each cultivator, we could see the variation in actual output prices across households. Except in Nayanagar village in Bihar, almost all cultivators received wheat price either equal to or higher than the MSP. Nayanagar was surveyed in 2011–12 and here the unit price obtained was below the MSP for 56 per cent of the wheat cultivators.

Conclusions

This chapter was based on an examination of primary and secondary sources of data on the pricing policy for agricultural produce in India. The main secondary data source used was the CCPC. The main primary sources of data were the census-type household surveys conducted by FAS in different agro-ecological regions of India. The following are the main findings.

CCPC data show that, first, the MSPs announced by the government to ensure remunerative prices did not compensate for the actual cost of production incurred per unit of output for rice, wheat, cotton, sugarcane, jute and *arhar* in a majority of states. The MSPs also did not come anywhere near the levels proposed by the NCF. Secondly, the low level of procurement ensured that the poor and middle-level farmers did not benefit from the MSP in most parts of the country, and large sections of them were forced to make distress sales to private traders.

FAS survey data showed that in seven out of 12 villages, the average FHP of paddy was lower than the corresponding MSPs. At the same time, for all wheat growing survey villages, the average FHP of wheat was higher than the corresponding MSPs. This shows that, on the one hand, MSP does work as a floor price for wheat, and on the other hand, that it was not implemented effectively for paddy in all parts of the country.

Notes

[1] According to 2011 population census, of the 1.21 billion Indians, 0.83 billion lived in rural areas while 0.37 billion lived in urban areas (Census of India 2011).

[2] FHP is defined as the average of output prices at which cultivators sold their produce to traders at the village site or nearby market during a specified marketing period after the beginning of the harvest season.

[3] The twenty-three crops include seven cereals (paddy, wheat, maize, sorghum or jowar, pearl millet or bajra, barley and ragi), five pulses (gram, *tur* or arhar, *moong*, *urad* and lentil or *masur*), seven oilseeds (groundnut, rapeseed/mustard, soybean, sesamum, sunflower, safflower, niger seed) and five commercial crops (copra or dried coconut, cotton, jute, sugarcane and tobacco).

[4] Cost A1 includes value of seed (both home-produced and purchased), value of manures (homegrown and purchased), value of fertilizers, insecticides and pesticides, irrigation charges, hired human labour, hired and owned bullock labour, owned and hired machine charges, marketing expenses, land revenue and other taxes, interest on working capital, depreciation of implements and farm buildings.

[5] This includes the approved amount procured by states under the decentralized procurement schemes.

References

Census of India (2011), *Population Finder 2011*, Office of the Registrar General and Census Commissioner, Ministry of Home Affairs, Government of India, available at https://censusindia.gov.in/census.website/data/population-finder

Gaurav, S. and S. Mishra (2014), 'Farm Size and Returns to Cultivation in India: Revisiting an Old Debate', *Oxford Development Studies*, vol. 43, no. 2, pp. 165–93.

HLC (2002), 'Report of the High-Level Committee on Long-Term Grain Policy', Department of Food and Public Distribution, Ministry of Consumer Affairs, Food and Public Distribution, Government of India.

Mahendra Dev, S. (2012), 'Small Farmers in India: Challenges and Opportunities', Working Paper No. 14, Indira Gandhi Institute of Development Research, Mumbai, June.

Merriott, D. (2017), 'Factors Associated with the Farmer Suicide Crisis in India', *Journal of Epidemiology and Global Health*, vol. 6, pp. 217–27.

Ramachandran, V.K. (2011), 'The State of Agrarian Relations in India Today', *The Marxist*, vol. 27, nos 1–2.

Rawal, V. and M. Swaminathan (2011), 'Returns from Crop Cultivation and Scale of Production', Paper presented in a workshop on Policy Options and Investment Priorities for Accelerating Agricultural Productivity and Development in India, organized by Indira Gandhi Institute of Development Research and Institute for Human Development, 10–11 November, India International Centre, New Delhi.

Reddy, D.N. and S. Mishra (2009), *Agrarian Crisis in India*, New Delhi: Oxford University Press.

Appendix

Appendix Table 1 MSP *(at current prices) fixed by the central government, 2007–08 to 2018–19*

Commodity	MSP fixed by the central government (rupees per quintal)											
	2007–08	2008–09	2009–10	2010–11	2011–12	2012–13	2013–14	2014–15	2015–16	2016–17	2017–18	2018–19
Paddy Common	745	900	1,000	1,000	1,080	1,250	1,310	1,360	1,410	1,470	1,550	1,750
Paddy (F)/Grade 'A'	775	930	1,030	1,030	1,110	1,280	1,345	1,400	1,450	1,510	1,590	1,770
Jowar-Hybrid	600	840	840	880	980	1,500	1,500	1,530	1,570	1,625	1,700	2,430
Jowar-Maldandi	620	860	860	900	1,000	1,520	–	1,550	1,590	1,650	1,725	2,450
Bajra	600	840	840	880	980	1,175	1,250	1,250	1,275	1,330	1,425	1,950
Ragi	600	915	915	965	1,050	1,500	1,500	1,550	1,650	1,725	1,900	2,897
Maize	620	840	840	880	980	1,175	1,310	1,310	1,325	1,365	1,425	1,700
Tur (Arhar)	1,550	2,000	2,300	3,000	3,200	3,850	4,300	4,350	4,625	5,050	5,450	5,675
Moong	1,700	2,520	2,760	3,170	3,500	4,400	4,500	4,600	4,850	5,225	5,575	6,975
Urad	1,700	2,520	2,520	2,900	3,300	4,300	4,300	4,350	4,625	5,000	5,400	5,600
Groundnut	1,550	2,100	2,100	2,300	2,700	3,700	4,000	4,000	4,030	4,220	4,450	4,890
Sunflower seed	1,510	2,215	2,215	2,350	2,800	3,700	3,700	3,750	3,800	3,950	4,100	5,388
Soybean black	910	1,350	1,350	1,400	1,650	2,200	2,500	2,500	–	–	–	–
Soybean yellow	1,050	1,390	1,390	1,440	1,690	–	2,560	2,560	2,600	2,775	3,050	3,399
Sesamum	1,580	2,750	2,850	2,900	3,400	4,200	4,500	4,600	4,700	5,000	5,300	6,249
Niger seed	1,240	2,405	2,405	2,450	2,900	3,500	3,500	3,600	3,650	3,825	4,050	5,877

Appendix Table 1 *(continued)*

Commodity	MSP fixed by the Central Government (Rs/Qtl)											
	2007–08	2008–09	2009–10	2010–11	2011–12	2012–13	2013–14	2014–15	2015–16	2016–17	2017–18	2018–19
Medium staple cotton	1,800	2,500	2,500	2,500	2,800	3,600	3,700	3,750	3,800	3,860	4,020	5,150
Long staple cotton	2,030	3,000	3,000	3,000	3,300	3,900	4,000	4,050	4,100	4,160	4,320	5,450
Wheat	1,000	1,080	1,100	1,170	1,285	1,350	1,400	1,450	1,525	1,625	1,735	1,840
Barley	650	680	750	780	980	980	1,100	1,150	1,225	1,325	1,410	1,440
Gram	1,600	1,730	1,760	2,100	2,800	3,000	3,100	3,175	3,425	4,000	4,400	4,620
Lentil (Masur)	1,700	1,870	1,870	2,250	2,800	2,900	2,950	3,075	3,325	3,950	4,250	4,475
Rapeseed/ mustard	1,800	1,830	1,830	1,850	2,500	3,000	3,050	3,100	3,350	3,700	4,000	4,200
Safflower	1,650	1,650	1,680	1,800	2,500	2,800	3,000	3,050	3,300	3,700	4,100	4,945
Jute (TD5)	1,055	1,250	1,375	1,575	1,675	2,200	2,300	2,400	2,700	3,200	3,500	3,700
Sugarcane	81.18	81.18	129.84	139.12	145.0	170.0	210.0	220.0	230.0	230.0	255.0	275.0
Copra (milling)	3,660	4,450	4,450	4,525	5,100	5,250	5,250	5,550	5,950	6,500	7,500	9,521
Copra (ball)	3,910	4,700	4,700	4,775	5,350	5,500	5,500	5,830	6,240	6,785	7,750	9,920

Note: MSPs include bonuses awarded by the government.
Source: CACP.

Appendix Table 2 Year-on-year growth rates and annual growth rates of MSP

Commodity	Year-on-year growth rate (%)											Annual growth rate – log (%)	
	2008–09	2009–10	2010–11	2011–12	2012–13	2013–14	2014–15	2015–16	2016–17	2017–18	2018–19	2007–08 to 2012–13	2013–14 to 2018–19
Paddy Common	32	18	0	8	16	5	4	4	4	5	13	12	6
Paddy (F)/Grade 'A'	30	17	0	8	15	5	4	4	4	5	11	12	5
Jowar-Hybrid	40	0	5	11	53	0	2	3	4	5	43	16	8
Jowar-Maldandi	39	0	5	11	52	–	0	3	4	5	42	15	10
Bajra	40	0	5	11	20	6	0	2	4	7	37	12	8
Ragi	53	0	5	9	43	0	3	6	5	10	52	16	12
Maize	35	0	5	11	20	11	0	1	3	4	19	11	5
Tur (Arhar)	29	15	30	7	20	12	1	6	9	8	4	19	6
Moong	48	10	15	10	26	2	2	5	8	7	25	18	8
Urad	48	0	15	14	30	0	1	6	8	8	4	17	6
Groundnut	35	0	10	17	37	8	0	1	5	5	10	16	4
Sunflower seed	47	0	6	19	32	0	1	1	4	4	31	16	6
Soybean black	48	0	4	18	33	14	0	–	–	–	–	–	–
Soybean yellow	32	0	4	17	–	–	0	2	7	10	11	10	6
Sesamum	74	4	2	17	24	7	2	2	6	6	18	17	6
Niger seed	94	0	2	18	21	0	3	1	5	6	45	18	9

Appendix Table 2 (*continued*)

Commodity	Year-on-year growth rate (%)											Annual growth rate – log (%)	
	2008–09	2009–10	2010–11	2011–12	2012–13	2013–14	2014–15	2015–16	2016–17	2017–18	2018–19	2007–08 to 2012–13	2013–14 to 2018–19
Medium staple cotton	39	0	0	12	29	3	1	1	2	4	28	11	6
Long staple cotton	48	0	0	10	18	3	1	1	1	4	26	11	5
Wheat	8	2	2	15	5	4	4	5	7	7	6	6	6
Barley	5	10	4	26	0	12	5	7	8	6	2	10	6
Gram	8	2	19	33	7	3	2	8	17	10	5	15	9
Lentil (*masur*)	10	0	20	24	4	2	4	8	19	8	5	12	10
Rapeseed/ mustard	2	0	1	35	20	2	2	8	10	8	5	11	7
Safflower	0	2	7	39	12	7	2	8	12	11	21	12	11
Jute (TD5)	10	15	6	31	5	4	13	19	9	6	–	14	12
Sugarcane	60	7	4	17	24	5	5	0	11	8	–	17	6
Copra (milling)	22	0	2	13	3	0	6	7	9	15	27	7	12
Copra (ball)	20	0	2	12	3	0	6	7	9	14	28	6	12

Note: MSPs include bonuses awarded by the government.
Source: CACP.

10

Costs of Cultivation and Profitability in Indian Agriculture

A Plot-level Analysis

Ashish Kamra

Introduction

Most studies on Indian agriculture trace the roots of the ongoing agrarian crisis to the declining profitability on cultivation (Bhatia 2006; Rao and Mahendra Dev 2010; Mishra 2008; Srivastava, Chand and Singh 2017; Ramakumar 2010). This declining profitability is attributed to the neoliberal policies of the Indian state, which has resulted in reduced state support for the farmers who constitute an overwhelmingly large section of India's workforce (Bhalla and Singh 2009; Bhatia 2006; Mishra 2008). It is in this context that this chapter outlines how cost of cultivation and profitability in Indian agriculture have evolved in the presence of neoliberal policies.

Profitability in agriculture, like in any other enterprise, is a function of cost of inputs on the one hand and revenue generated through sales of produce on the other. Revenue in turn is a function of selling price of the agricultural produce and yield. One reason for low profitability in Indian agriculture is the high cost of inputs including fertilizers, seeds, irrigation and credit (Raghavan 2008; Srivastava, Chand and Singh 2017). On the revenue side, low and stagnant market prices for outputs keep profit margins low (Bhatia 2006; Narayanamoorthy 2013). The reasons for low prices are manifold, including but not limited to low procurement prices, absence of procurement infrastructure and the low density of Agricultural Produce Marketing Committee (APMC) markets or *mandis* (Chatterjee and Kapur 2016; Narayanamoorthy and Suresh 2013).

Low returns of farm cultivation are extensively documented for India. Most of this literature uses data from Situation Assessment Surveys (SAS) of the National Sample Survey Office (NSSO) or from the 'Comprehensive Scheme for Studying Cost of Cultivation/Production of Principal Crops' (CCPC) of the Directorate of Economics and Statistics (DES), Ministry of Agriculture.

Literature based on the data from SAS have argued that consumption expenditure for landless, small and marginal farmers exceed their farm profits signalling that farm returns remain extremely low for a large proportion of farmers (see chapter 11 by Aparajita Bakshi, this volume). These studies make it clear that a differential farm profitability exists in Indian farm sector. It should be noted that these assessment surveys cannot be used to construct a time series or a trend in profits because the successive survey rounds differ in their reach, sampling design, definitions and cost accounting (B. Sarkar 2017).[1] In other words, all these studies are limited to cross-sectional analysis of profits and incomes.

The literature that uses data from the CCPC analyses input costs, incomes, yields and profits across different time periods. Some of this literature focuses on particular crops (Bhatia 2006; Raghavan 2008; Narayanamoorthy 2013; Tripathi 2017; Singh *et al.* 2019; Sharma 2016). Some others focus on state-specific analysis (Kumari, Singh and Ahmad 2020; Singh *et al.* 2017; Kumar, Sunandini and Suhasini 2020; Ahmad 2018). Sen and Bhatia (2004) is the most comprehensive study on cost, incomes and profits in Indian agriculture, which covers all the major crops across all the major states. The authors used plot-level CCPC data for their study. But the reference period for this study ended at 1999–2000. To the author's knowledge, no such comprehensive study has been attempted after that period.

Sen and Bhatia (2004) argue that there was overwhelming evidence that the cost of inputs in farming was on an increase ever since neoliberal policies were introduced. It was also argued that agricultural productivity, which increased after the green revolution, continued to increase in the early 1990s but signs of stagnating yields were visible by the late 1990s. At the same time, the coupling of domestic agriculture prices with the international commodity prices led to a situation where the domestic prices also stagnated or declined. This coupling was also accompanied by a lacklustre state price support mechanism in the form of minimum support prices (MSP), which not only increased at a slow rate but also continued to exclude the majority of farmers from its ambit. It was this misguided 'getting the prices right' policy that led to a decline in profitability for farmers across states and crops. The farmers got hit by a double whammy of 'right prices' where input prices rose and farm harvest prices (FHP) fell. This decline in profitability was differential in nature; the decline was steeper for small and marginal farmers than for large farmers.[2]

Methodology
This chapter uses plot-level data generated under the CCPC scheme.[3] These data are collected annually for twenty-nine crops across twenty states and encompasses 8,100 operational holdings. Under the scheme, data is

collected on various inputs used in farming. It is implemented by various universities across states. Once the data is collected from the field, it takes around two to three years to complete data processing for the data to be useful in any analysis.[4] The latest available plot-level data are for 2016–17.

This chapter analyses data for thirteen crops for a period of seventeen years from 2000–01 to 2016–17. These crops include the cereal crops of paddy, wheat, maize and *bajra*; pulses, which include *arhar*, gram, *moong* and urad; soybean, the oilseed; cotton, the fibre crop; and onion and potato. For every crop, selected important growing states were identified for an overview of input costs, value of output and profitability. The inflation-adjusted real values of these variables were estimated using GDP deflators at 2011–12 prices.

Profitability in agriculture can be defined in multiple ways depending upon (1) the definition of input costs used; and (2) the concept of selling price used to define the revenue generated. Literature on input costs uses different concepts of cost as defined under the CCPC scheme. Broadly speaking, the cost concepts under the scheme are differentiated on the basis of whether only the actual paid-out costs are included or the imputed costs are also considered as part of the total cost. Thus, three major types of costs emerge. Cost A2 is the actual cost that farmers pay out for purchasing various inputs including seeds, fertilizers, pesticides, hired labour and machinery. Cost A2+FL includes the A2 cost along with imputed costs of family labour. Cost C2 is the most comprehensive cost concept as, apart from A2 cost and the imputed costs of family labour, it also includes imputed rent of owned land and imputed interest on owned capital. Everything else remaining equal, using cost A2 would give 'net income' while using cost C2 would give 'farm business income'.

On the revenue side, the literature either uses Gross Value of Output (GVO) as defined under the CCPC scheme or the MSP as the selling price to estimate gross revenue. In few cases, international prices or *mandi* prices are also used to calculate selling prices.[5]

In this chapter, I use the cost concept of A2+FL *minus* the depreciation. This is defined as the 'operational cost' (in Rs/hectare) in the plot-level summary data published by DES. Operational cost includes the value of hired and owned labour (human, animal and machine), value of seeds (purchased or home grown), value of pesticides and insecticides, value of manure (purchased or owned), irrigation charges, interest paid (or imputed) on working capital and other miscellaneous expenses. I do not use the conventional definition of A2+FL as the main cost concept because depreciation cannot be estimated at the state-level using plot-level data. Further information from DES would be required to compute the same, which is not publicly available. Using the 'operational cost' concept does not alter the overall conclusions of this chapter. For calculating the selling price, I use the GVO concept outlined under the CCPC scheme to arrive at estimates of 'operational profits'.

In this chapter, I have also attempted an analysis of operational profits across farm sizes. To my knowledge, only Sen and Bhatia (2004) have attempted such an analysis before. For their study, they had access to the entire dataset generated under the CCPC scheme. But for this chapter, I only had access to the plot-level data, which was compiled using the larger and more granular datasets. While arriving at the farm size-level estimates, I used the same methodology as mentioned in CSO (2008). I included plot-level data for that particular farm size and assumed everything else to be the same under the sampling design. Methodologically, this means that farm size estimates assume that all the farms existing in the country belong to that particular farm size category.

It must be noted that I am attempting an operational holding-level analysis and not a household-level analysis although I use the phrase 'small and marginal farmers' to denote farmers operating less than 2 hectares of land. It may be the case that a large farmer had fragmented land and operates less than 2 hectares of land for a particular crop. For this chapter, such a farmer have been put under the category of small and marginal farmer. These two assumptions however do not impact the general conclusions made in this chapter.

Before going ahead with the analysis, it is important to acknowledge some of the problems associated with data generated under the CCPC scheme (see Kamra and Ramakumar 2019). Two expert committees constituted by the government in 1979–80 (S.R. Sen Committee) and 1990 (Hanumantha Rao Committee) raised a number of issues related to the methodology of the scheme. As a result of the recommendations of these committees, the scheme shifted from a single-crop approach to a crop-complex approach in order to improve its estimates. However, the sampling framework continued to have major shortcomings (Surjit 2008; Nawn 2013). For example, the scheme does not operate in all the states and covers only twenty-five crops leaving out some important vegetables, fruits and plantation crops from its ambit. Thus, any all-India estimate of costs would be biased but it would still be indicative of what was happening on ground. At the same time, the scheme does not take into consideration changing cropping patterns in many states (Surjit 2008). The scheme also fails to adequately accommodate various institutional arrangements, such as tenancy, in its sample.

Methods used to calculate imputed costs, such as the rental value of owned land, and interest rates charged for fixed capital and working capital under the scheme are also debated. Sen and Bhatia (2004) pointed out that the rental value of owned land is calculated on the basis of the share of rent in the gross value of output, even though the two review committees had recommended more comprehensive methods to compute this variable. Similarly, the interest cost on owned fixed capital was estimated at 10 per cent per annum and the interest cost on working capital was estimated at 12.5 per cent for half the period of a crop. Through different sources like All India Debt and Investment Survey (AIDIS) and other studies, we know that interest rates charged to farmers are much higher than what is assumed under the scheme. The two committees recommended that the two interest rates be calculated by taking the weighted average of the actual interest rates canvassed from sample cultivators but this is yet to be implemented. The exclusion of transport costs also contributes to underestimating the costs of cultivation.

There are also problems with respect to the collection, processing and analysis of data, and of the quality of data. Surjit (2008) and Nawn (2013) point out problems related to the classification of farms into different size classes for sampling purposes, problems associated with the FARMAP software, which result in substantial inaccuracies in the estimation of gross cropped area and net sown area, and problems arising from incorrect coding. The implementation of the scheme by the universities is also reported to be unsatisfactory, according to the Ministry of Statistics and Programme Implementation.

Despite these issues, data from the CCPC scheme provides a general idea about how costs, revenue and profitability have varied in Indian agriculture across different states and different crops. As such, these issues do not change the interpretation of data in this chapter.

The rest of the chapter is divided into five sections. The following section which is the third section of the chapter studies the trends in costs of different inputs. Costs of seeds, fertilizers, pesticides, labour, machines and irrigation are discussed in detail. The fourth section examines the movement of MSP and revenue realized by the farmers and its relationship with international prices. The impact of input costs and revenues realized on the real profitability across different crops and different states is analysed in the fifth section. The sixth section assesses the differential nature of this profitability with respect to farm size. The seventh section summarizes and concludes the chapter.

Cost of Inputs

Between 2000–01 and 2016–17, the real operational cost (in Rs/hectare) increased across all the crops and states except for wheat in Punjab and Gujarat and potato in Bihar. Change in operational cost during this period shows a clear pattern (see Table 10.1). The increase was lowest for the agriculturally developed states of north India. In these states, the compound annual growth rate (CAGR) for real operational costs did not rise

Table 10.1 *Compound annual growth rate (CAGR) of real operational cost between 2000–01 and 2016–17, selected crops and states, India,* in per cent per annum

States	Paddy	Wheat	Maize	Bajra	Arhar	Gram	Moong	Urad	Soybean	Cotton	Onion	Potato
Haryana	1.7	1.2		1.9						2.6		
Himachal Pradesh			3.8									
Punjab	1.2	-0.1								1.7		
Uttar Pradesh	2.8	1.7	2.7	3.2				2.4				0.8
Andhra Pradesh	0.7		4.6				1.4	3.4		3		
Karnataka			1.7		2.2					4.9	5.9	
Kerala	1.1											
Tamil Nadu	0.5							4.4				
Assam	3.9											
Bihar	2.3	0.6	1.7									-0.4
Odisha	3.8						2.5					
West Bengal	3.3											1.1
Gujarat		-0.1		3.7	3.7					5.9		
Maharashtra				5.9	10.1	4.8*	5.4	4.8	3.9*	5	2.1	
Rajasthan		1.9	2.1	4.3		3.4	2.6			5.8		
Madhya Pradesh	3.5	3	7		6.1	4.2		4.8	3.7	11.9		

Note: * Data are for 2003–04 to 2016–17.
Source: Compiled by author using CCPC scheme data.

beyond 2.5 per cent between 2000–01 and 2016–17. On the other hand, the western and central states saw the highest increase in operational costs. Maharashtra saw the largest increase in operational costs generally hovering around a CAGR of 5 per cent. The southern and eastern states saw a moderate and fluctuating increase in the real operational cost across different crops. Amongst different crops, cotton saw the highest increase in real operational cost, growing even at a CAGR as high as 12 per cent in Madhya Pradesh. Wheat registered the slowest increase in real operational cost. These differences across CAGR were a result of differential intensity of input use and differential increases in costs of individual inputs across crops and states.

The increase in real operational cost for different crops cannot be said to be consistent. In the case of the four cereal crops except *bajra*, the real operational cost remained stagnant for most states till 2008–11 and shot up dramatically after that. We see a similar trend in case of pulses, soybean and onion. Only in case of cotton do we see a consistent increase in real operational cost even during the early 2000s. In the case of potato, we see a decline/stagnation in real operational cost between 2000–01 and 2016–17.

Cost of Seeds

Under the CCPC scheme, cost of seeds includes the cost of purchased as well as farm produced seeds. Although a majority of farmers depend upon farm produced seeds in India, their dependence on purchased seeds is increasing. As a result of the liberalization of seed policy, state actors in seed production were replaced by private and multinational seed producers (see the introductory chapter to this volume by Ramakumar). From 1984 to 1995, around 50–60 per cent of the purchased seed requirement was met by the private sector; in 2010, about 80 per cent of turnover in seed business came from private companies (Manjunath, Rao and Dastagiri 2013). This resulted in an increase in the cost price of seeds for farmers. Seeds (produced by private players) are costlier and their prices are often reported spuriously. Due to this, the actual cost of cultivation on account of purchased seeds could be higher than what the CCPC scheme reports (Raghavan 2008).

Real cost of seeds changed differently for different states and crops between 2000–01 and 2016–17. Like the overall real cost, the highest increase in seed costs was in cotton followed by maize. The seed cost increase in cotton was different for different states and increased at a CAGR of 3 to 10 per cent (see Table 10.2). The increase in seed costs for cotton coincided with the emergence of Bt Cotton hybrid seeds in India. The use of private Bt Cotton hybrid seeds no doubt increased the yield of cotton, but it was also accompanied by an increase in the operational costs. This increase came not only in the form of direct increase in the seed prices (coupled with

Table 10.2 *Compound annual growth rate (CAGR) of real input cost of seeds between 2000–01 and 2016–17, selected crops and states, India,* in per cent per annum

States	Paddy	Wheat	Maize	Bajra	Arhar	Gram	Moong	Urad	Soybean	Cotton	Onion	Potato
Haryana	1.8	0.9		0.6						9.6		
Himachal Pradesh			4.1									
Punjab	1.8	1.8								8.0		
Uttar Pradesh	3.3	2.7	10.2	3.4				5.4				0.9
Andhra Pradesh	-0.1		6.4				2.4	5.6		0.7		
Karnataka			2.9		2.8					3.8	9.3	
Kerala	1.7											
Tamil Nadu	1.0							3.3				
Assam	-0.9											
Bihar	0.2	1.1	3.7									0.7
Odisha	-1.2						-0.3					
West Bengal	1.9											1.2
Gujarat		1.7		4.9	5.8	5*				3.1		
Maharashtra				2.6	6.4		2.8	4.2	2.9*	3.4	3.8	
Rajasthan		1.2	6.6	4.5		6.9	0.9			8.3		
Madhya Pradesh	0.9	1.7				6.1			3.2	3.6		

Note: * Data are for 2003–04 to 2016–17.
Source: Compiled by author using CCPC scheme data.

a seed replacement rate of about 100 per cent), but also through increased usage of other inputs like fertilizers that are usually applied in Bt hybrids (see Ramakumar, Raut and Kamble 2017).

Compared to cotton, maize and pulses, the rate of increase in seed costs was less for paddy and wheat, the two most prominent foodgrains in India. Interestingly, in paddy and wheat, at least 50 per cent of the seed production and distribution of seeds continues with the public sector.

Cost of Fertilizers

Fertilizer is an important component of the operational cost for major crops in India. The fertilizer policy in India saw major shifts towards deregulation, especially after 2010 (see chapter by Bansal and Rawal in this volume). This policy shift had a direct impact on the cost of fertilizers for farmers. If we consider paddy and wheat, the trend in the overall real cost of fertilizers per hectare is mixed. While the costs declined or increased marginally in states like Punjab and Haryana, they rose in other states like West Bengal and Madhya Pradesh between 2000–01 and 2016–17. At the same time, the real costs of fertilizers rose considerably in crops like cotton and pulses in many states (see Table 10.3).

The mixed trend in growth of real fertilizer costs was because of three different reasons. First, paddy and wheat farmers continued to rely heavily on nitrogen-based fertilizers (N). CCPC data suggest that, on an average, nitrogen-based fertilizers constituted 60 to 65 per cent of all the fertilizers applied by paddy and wheat farmers between 2000–01 and 2016–17. On the other hand, only 50 to 55 per cent of fertilizers applied were nitrogen-based among cotton farmers; the rest were either phosphatic or potassic fertilizers. Due to the skewed subsidy reform policy in India, nitrogen-based fertilizers were available cheaper than phosphatic and potassic fertilizers. The Nutrient Based Subsidy (NBS) policy of 2010 deregulated the selling prices of phosphatic and potassic fertilizers. This increased their prices drastically. As a result, crops like cotton, which relied more on phosphatic and potassic fertilizers, saw a higher increase in their real fertilizer costs as compared to paddy and wheat. Secondly, the rate of overall fertilizer use also differed across crops and states. The total quantity of fertilizers used per hectare in cotton was clearly higher than those used in paddy and wheat after the introduction of Bt Cotton seeds (for a field study, see Ramakumar, Raut and Kamble 2017). According to the CCPC data, the total quantity of fertilizers applied in cotton doubled from 89 kg/ha in 2000–02 to 178 kg/ha in 2014–17. But in the case of paddy and wheat, the fertilizer consumption increased only moderately from 125–32 kg/ha in 2000–02 to 140–45 kg/ha in 2014–17. Such differences in fertilizer use also led the mixed results across crops with regard to real costs of fertilizers.

Table 10.3 *Compound annual growth rate (CAGR) of real input cost of fertilizers between 2000–01 and 2016–17, selected crops and states, India,* in per cent per annum

States	Paddy	Wheat	Maize	Bajra	Arhar	Gram	Moong	Urad	Soybean	Cotton	Onion	Potato
Haryana	-1.2	-1.8		4.2						4.1		
Himachal Pradesh		-1.7	-1.1									
Punjab	-2.2	-1.7								3.3		
Uttar Pradesh	2.3	0.3	2.0	-0.1				22.9				1.4
Andhra Pradesh	1.4		3.4				-4.3	-0.8		2.6		
Karnataka			-0.7		-1.3					4.2	2.4	
Kerala	2.0											
Tamil Nadu	-0.9							8.8				
Assam	4.4											
Bihar	2.3	-0.5	-1.8									-1.9
Odisha	0.6						-8.1					
West Bengal	3.4											0.0
Gujarat		-0.9		1.7	0.6					6.1		
Maharashtra				0.5	10.2	4.5*	5.0	1.0	-0.2*	2.9	5.3	
Rajasthan		0.4	2.2	6.4		8.7	13.8			-0.6		
Madhya Pradesh	4.3	1.3				2.0			2.4	7.9		

Note: * Data are for 2003–04 to 2016–17.
Source: Compiled by author using CCPC scheme data.

Even before the introduction of NBS, fertilizer prices had been rising. Raghavan (2008) pointed out that the increase in the rate of growth of fertilizer prices in the 1980s was around 4.5 per cent per annum in wheat, which rose in the 1990s to 6.2 per cent per annum. In the 1990s, the 'retention price scheme' was substituted with a 'new fertilizer policy' as part of the liberalization policies. The new policy escalated the prices of fertilizers, making cultivation unaffordable for small and marginal farmers (Raghavan 2008). Data show that the situation only worsened in the 2000s and 2010s (see Ramakumar's introductory chapter and chapter by Bansal and Rawal in this volume).

Cost of Insecticides/Pesticides

The real cost per hectare of pesticides/insecticides/weedicides saw one of the largest increases between 2000–01 and 2016–17 (Table 10.4). Except for cotton and wheat in the northern states, the real cost of insecticides as well as its share in the total operational cost increased drastically in most of the crops across states (see also Ramakumar's introductory chapter to this volume). Madhya Pradesh and Gujarat saw the highest increase in real cost of insecticides across crops, and the per annum increase in real cost was as high as 25 per cent in certain cases. Data show that the increase in insecticide consumption started as early as the 1970s. The all-states average expense per hectare (not adjusted for inflation) on insecticides for wheat, which was less than one rupee in the 1970s and just over Rs 25 in the 1980s, shot up by 365 per cent in the 1990s and by as much as 1,115 per cent in the early 2000s (Raghavan 2008).

As in the case of fertilizers, the type and quantity of insecticides or weedicides used by farmers differed across crops and states. These differences had a bearing on the differential growth rates reported in Table 10.4.

Cost of Human and Machine Labour

Labour cost was the largest component of all the items of operational cost for most crops. Except for paddy, the contribution of human labour costs in total operational cost increased for most crops in most states (Table 10.5). Within human labour, casual labour costs saw the largest increase whereas attached labour costs declined in most states and crops. This shift of human labour from family labour and attached labour to hired wage labour was, of course, indicative of a broader development of the capitalist mode of production. The most important reason for higher labour costs was the rising wage rates for agricultural labourers.

At the same time, the fall in human labour costs in many states and crops indicated a sharp shift towards substitution of human labour with machine labour. Machine costs increased sharply between 2000–01

Table 10.4 *Compound annual growth rate (CAGR) of real input cost of insecticides between 2000–01 and 2016–17, selected crops and states, India,* in per cent per annum

States	Paddy	Wheat	Maize	Bajra	Arhar	Gram	Moong	Urad	Soybean	Cotton	Onion	Potato
Haryana	1.5	-2.1								-2.5		
Himachal Pradesh			4.3									
Punjab	2.7	-1.7								-3.6		
Uttar Pradesh	6.0	7.1						10.0				4.7
Andhra Pradesh	1.9		7.8				12.2	4.9		-3.2		
Karnataka			15.9		-1.6					2.5		
Kerala	9.5											
Tamil Nadu	3.5							6.3				
Assam	5.9											
Bihar		70.0										8.5
Odisha	3.6											
West Bengal	7.0											2.0
Gujarat		18.1		25.4	20.4					7.1		
Maharashtra					37.6	14.3*	21.8	19.4	19.8*	3.2	6.4	
Rajasthan		11.4				-14.6	2.6			-4.0		
Madhya Pradesh	17.2	16.1				20.6			13.2	25.0		

Note: * Data are for 2003–04 to 2016–17.
Source: Compiled by author using CCPC scheme data.

Table 10.5 *Compound annual growth rate (CAGR) of contribution of real human labour cost to total operational cost between 2000–01 and 2016–17, selected crops and states, India, in per cent per annum*

States	Paddy	Wheat	Maize	Bajra	Arhar	Gram	Moong	Urad	Soybean	Cotton	Onion	Potato
Haryana	-5.7	-0.7		3.6						1.0		
Himachal Pradesh			3.4									
Punjab	1.1	-1.5								3.5		
Uttar Pradesh	-10.9	-8.0		-6.9								
Andhra Pradesh	-5.9		-3.5				-5.0	1.0		2.5		
Karnataka					-7.4							
Kerala	-100.0											
Tamil Nadu	-8.2							6.4				
Assam	-13.1											
Bihar	1.2	-4.3	29.5									
Odisha	-10.7						-13.8					
West Bengal	-28.0											-11.0
Gujarat		-16.4		-6.7						-16.8		
Maharashtra				4.3	11.3	6.7*	11.3	2.1	16.0*	9.7		
Rajasthan		0.9		-4.1		21.1				-6.3		
Madhya Pradesh	0.9	7.0				-0.2			-0.4			

Note: * Data are for 2003–04 to 2016–17.
Source: Compiled by author using CCPC scheme data.

Table 10.6 *Compound annual growth rate (CAGR) of contribution of real machine cost to total operational cost between 2000–01 and 2016–17, selected crops and states, India,* in per cent per annum

States	Paddy	Wheat	Maize	Bajra	Arhar	Gram	Moong	Urad	Soybean	Cotton	Onion	Potato
Haryana	0.9	1.2		3.3						2.4		
Himachal Pradesh		1.8	9.5									
Punjab	-1.0									-2.3		
Uttar Pradesh	0.8	0.4	1.7	-0.1				4.1				1.9
Andhra Pradesh	5.2		4.8				18.1	-2.2		4.8		
Karnataka			2.4		6.7					7.1	9.6	
Kerala	4.8											
Tamil Nadu	3.8							-0.8				
Assam	9.5											
Bihar	2.6	0.1	4.7									8.9
Odisha	10.8						33.0					
West Bengal	6.5											0.4
Gujarat		5.0		-0.2	1.8					-1.2		
Maharashtra				4.0	8.6	6.0*	12.6	12.2	3.1*	4.0	6.6	
Rajasthan		0.0	10.7	-1.3		-3.2	0.0			2.1		
Madhya Pradesh	16.7	3.2				0.8			3.3	11.0		

Note: * Data are for 2003–04 to 2016–17.
Source: Compiled by author using CCPC scheme data.

and 2016–17 across crops and states (Table 10.6). But the pace of this shift differed across crops and states, as data in Tables 10.5 and 10.6 show. In paddy, the shift away from human labour towards machine labour was clear; the contribution of machine labour to operational cost increased in major paddy growing states (Table 10.6) whereas the contribution of total labour cost decreased (Table 10.5). Even in other crops, the increase in the contribution of real cost of machinery to total cost remained higher than that of real cost of labour. Other studies have shown that the purchase of tractors and tillers increased significantly after 2000 in rural India (A. Sarkar 2013).

Hired machinery continued to form a major component of total machinery cost. Th rise in hiring costs was accompanied by increases in petrol/diesel prices and electricity tariffs, which together led to a substantial rise in the total real machinery costs per hectare.

From the analysis of costs, we now move to the analysis of revenues, or the gross value of output (GVO).

Value of Output, Yield and Prices

The value of output as reported in the CCPC reflects the actual prices realized by the farmers (Rao and Mahendra Dev 2010). Sen and Bhatia (2004) compared the data on yields across CCPC data and other published data at the state level and found that the differences were within the limits of statistical tolerance. In other words, the CCPC data gave a close-to-accurate estimate of yields and value of output. Since the value of output showed variations on a year-on-year basis due of the high variability in yields, the data presented in this section are averaged over three-year periods (see Figures 10.1 to 10.12).[6]

Except for pulses and to some extent *bajra*, the real value of output stagnated or even declined for most crops in most states after 2008–11. In some cases, the stagnation began during 2011–14. Within pulses, the real value of output grew consistently in all states for *arhar*, gram and *urad* whereas signs of stagnation showed up for *moong* from 2008–11. The stagnation in value output per unit hectare was driven by two factors: yield per hectare and output prices. The interplay of these two factors defined the trends in real value of output.

In cereals, there was a decline or stagnation in real value of output for wheat after 2011 in major states except Bihar; in Bihar, there was a major improvement in wheat yields between 2008–09 and 2016–17. This overall stagnation in real value of output was a direct result of a decline in real MSPs for wheat (which was mostly procured by the states at the MSP) after 2008–11.[7] The decline of real value of output in wheat actually began in 1999–2000 (Bhatia 2006). The same was the case for *bajra*, though at a slower rate. For maize and paddy, there was an increase in yields and a

Figure 10.1 *Real value of output, yield and MSP for paddy, selected states, India, 2000–02 to 2014–17, in Rs/ha and Rs/q*

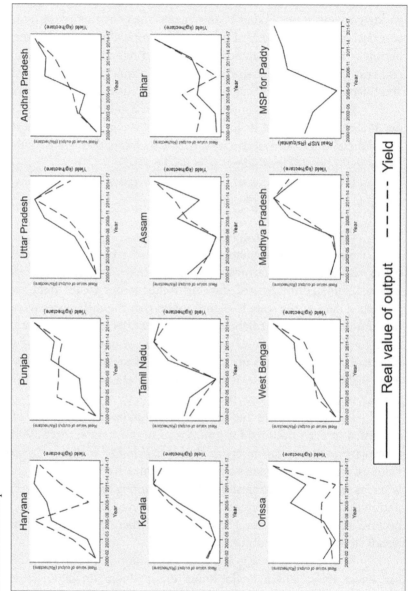

Figure 10.2 *Real value of output, yield and MSP for wheat, selected states, India, 2000–02 to 2014–17,* in Rs/ha and Rs/q

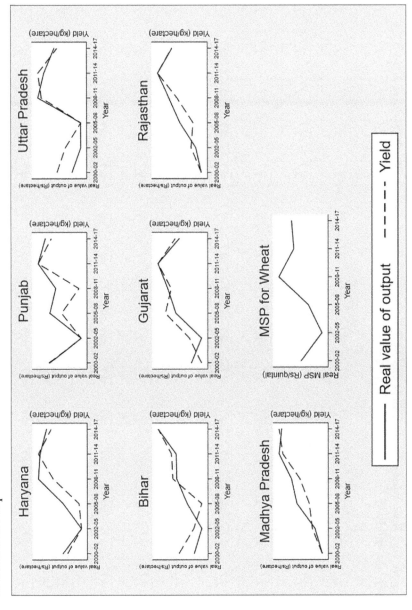

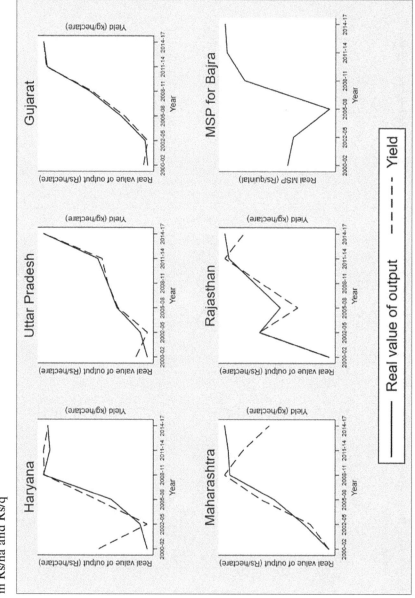

Figure 10.3 *Real value of output, yield and MSP for bajra, selected states, India, 2000–02 to 2014–17,* in Rs/ha and Rs/q

Figure 10.4 *Real value of output, yield and MSP for maize, selected states, India, 2000–02 to 2014–17,* in Rs/ha and Rs/q

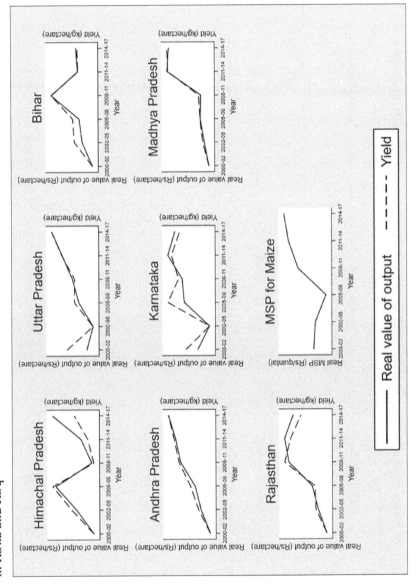

Figure 10.5 *Real value of output, yield and MSP for arhar, selected states, India, 2000–02 to 2014–17, in Rs/ha and Rs/q*

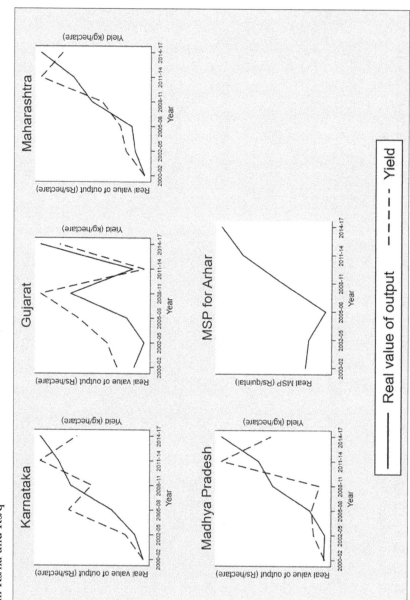

Figure 10.6 *Real value of output, yield and MSP for gram, selected states, India, 2000–02 to 2014–17, in Rs/ha and Rs/q*

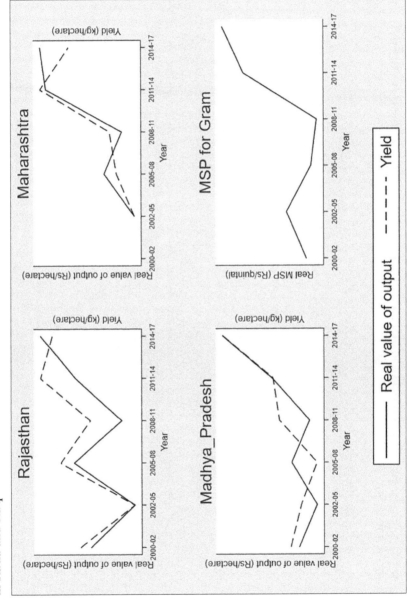

Figure 10.7 *Real value of output, yield and MSP for urad, selected states, India, 2000–02 to 2014–17, in Rs/ha and Rs/q*

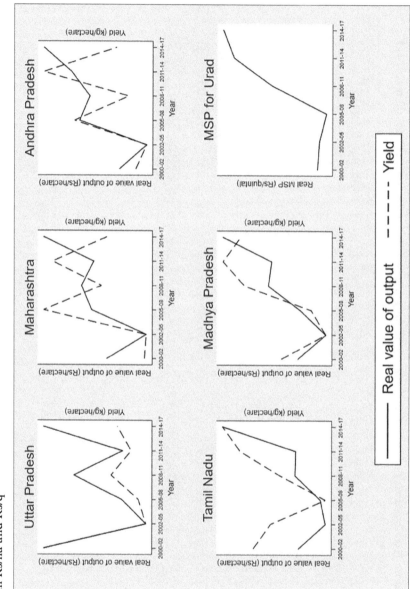

Figure 10.8 *Real value of output, yield and MSP for moong, selected states, India, 2000–02 to 2014–17, in Rs/ha and Rs/q*

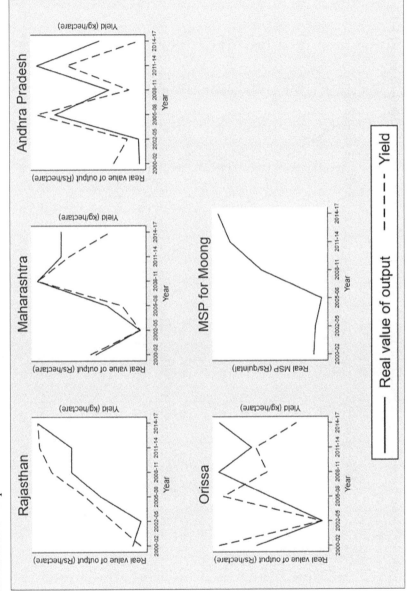

Figure 10.9 *Real value of output, yield and MSP for soybean, selected states, India, 2000–02 to 2014–17, in Rs/ha and Rs/q*

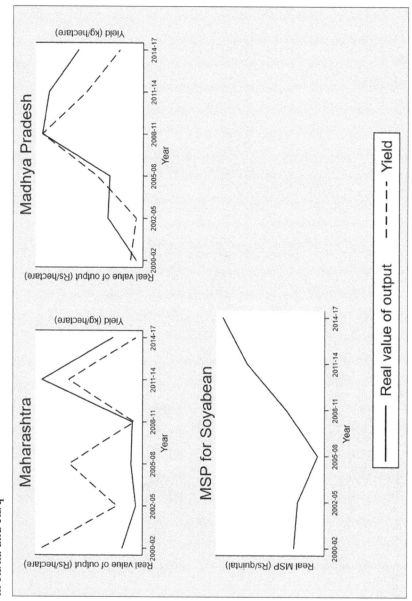

Figure 10.10 *Real value of output, yield and MSP for cotton, selected states, India, 2000–02 to 2014–17, in Rs/ha and Rs/q*

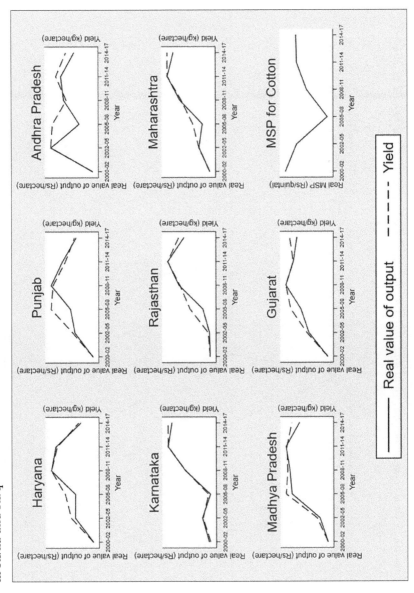

Figure 10.11 *Real value of output, yield and MSP for onion, selected states, India, 2000–02 to 2014–17,* in Rs/ha and Rs/q

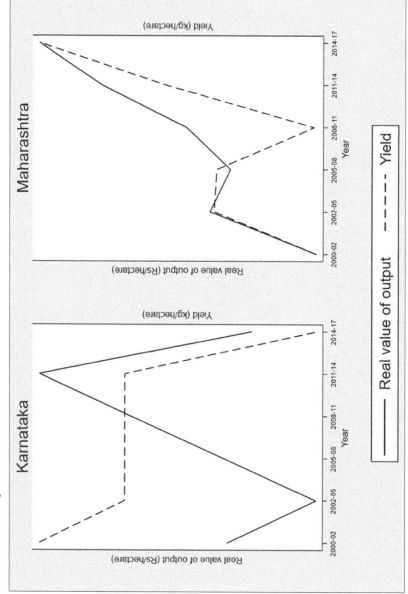

Figure 10.12 *Real value of output, yield and MSP for potato, selected states, India, 2000–02 to 2014–17, in Rs/ha and Rs/q*

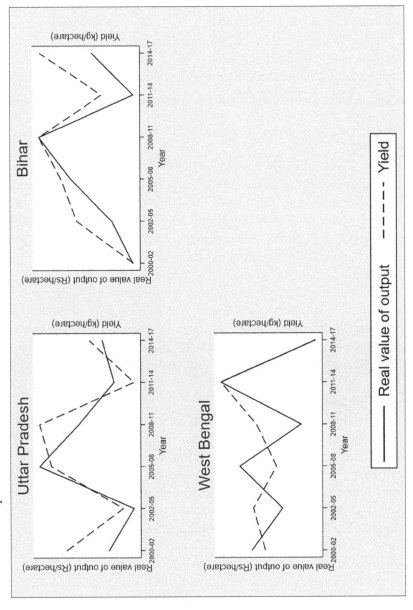

moderate rise in real MSPs, as a result of which the real value of output for these two crops grew at a consistent pace.

In pulses, there was a consistent and high rate of increase in real MSPs after 2008. As a result, although the yield fluctuated on a year-on-year basis, there was an increase in total value of output per hectare for *arhar*, gram and *urad*. Due to the fluctuating yields of *moong*, even a sharp increase in MSP could not ensure an increase in the value of output of *moong* after 2008, especially in major producing states like Maharashtra, Andhra Pradesh and Odisha.

In the case of soybean, there was a stagnation/decline in yields, which resulted in a decline of real value of output per hectare, especially after 2011.

Cotton farmers were affected both by a stagnation in yields as well as stagnation/decline in real MSP. This was despite the major cotton-growing states shifting to Bt Cotton seeds. The real MSP for cotton had been decreasing since 1999–2000 (Bhatia 2006). In fact, the real MSP of cotton for the period 2014–17 was lower than what it was during 2000–02. As a result, the real value of output per hectare of cotton decreased after 2011 in almost all the major cotton-growing states.

For vegetable crops, there were fluctuations in the real value of output. This was possibly because of the absence of an MSP framework for onion and potato, leaving them at the mercy of volatile open market prices. Between 2000–01 and 2016–17, the real value of output per hectare declined for onion in Karnataka and for potato in West Bengal.

Profitability Rates

There was an overarching trend of declining real profitability across crops and states between agriculture year 2000–01 and 2016–17 (see Figures 10.13 to 10.24). Very few states saw increasing profitability in cereal production. Punjab was the only state for which real profitability per hectare increased in paddy. Andhra Pradesh's and Kerala's real profitability in paddy production stagnated after 2008–11. In Haryana, the real profitability of paddy stagnated after 2005–08. Steep declines in real profitability in paddy production were also witnessed in Uttar Pradesh, Madhya Pradesh, Assam, Odisha and West Bengal; in these states, the real profitability per hectare for paddy was higher in 2000–02 than in 2014–17. For some of these states, particularly Haryana, Madhya Pradesh and Odisha, the signs of stagnation in profitability were visible during the late 1990s itself (see Sen and Bhatia 2004). But the decline was particularly stark between 2013–14 and 2016–17.

In wheat, the decline in real profitability was milder compared to paddy. But the real profitability per hectare in wheat production declined in

Figure 10.13 *Real profitability for paddy per hectare, selected states, India, 2000–02 to 2014–17*, in Rs/ha

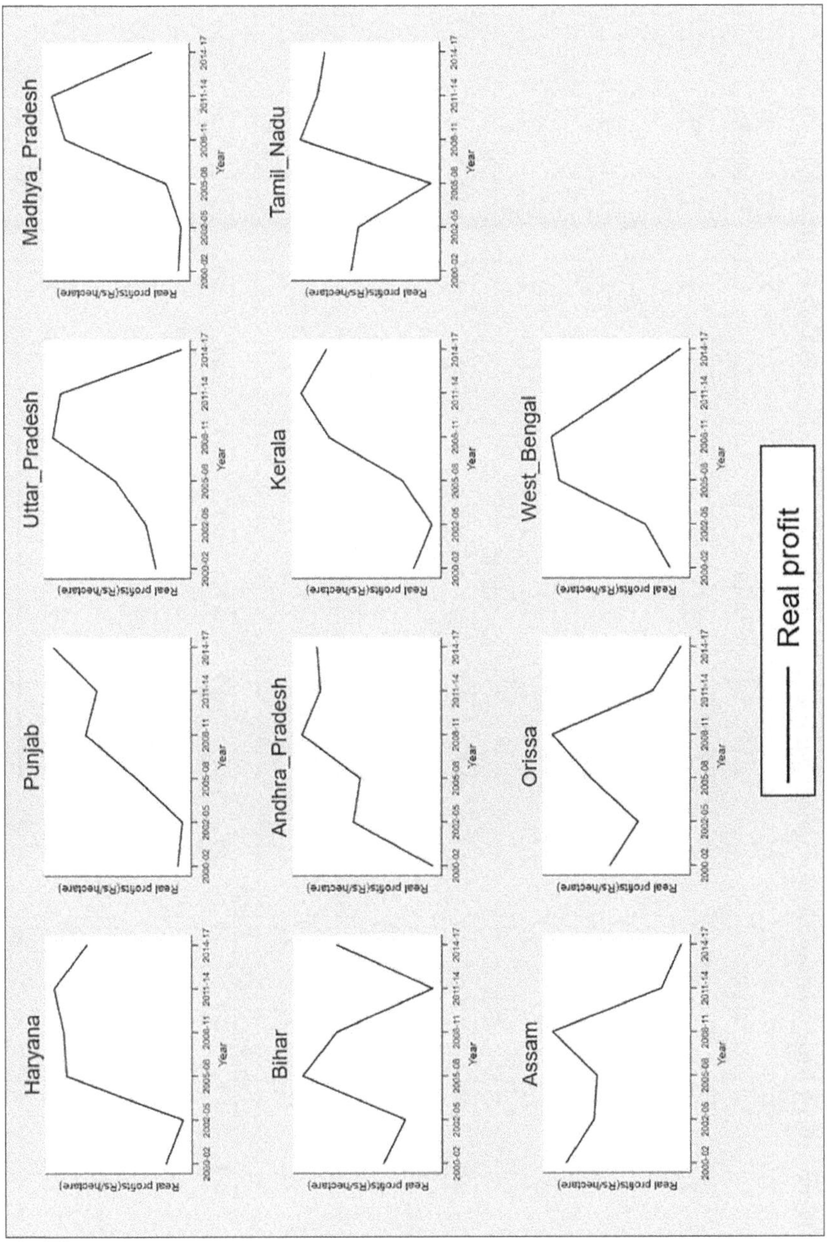

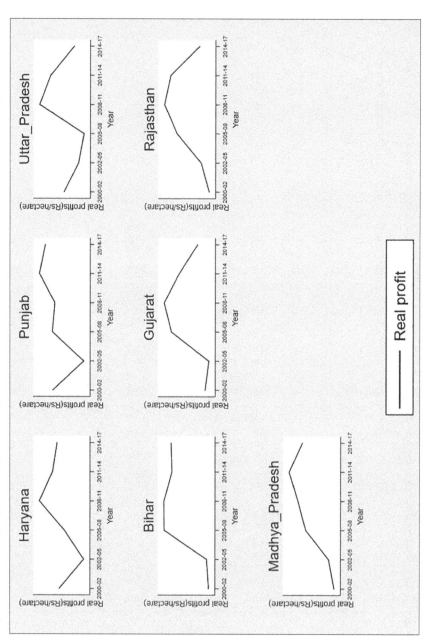

Figure 10.14 *Real profitability for wheat per hectare, selected states, India, 2000–02 to 2014–17*, in Rs/ha

Figure 10.15 *Real profitability for bajra per hectare, selected states, India, 2000–02 to 2014–17*, in Rs/ha

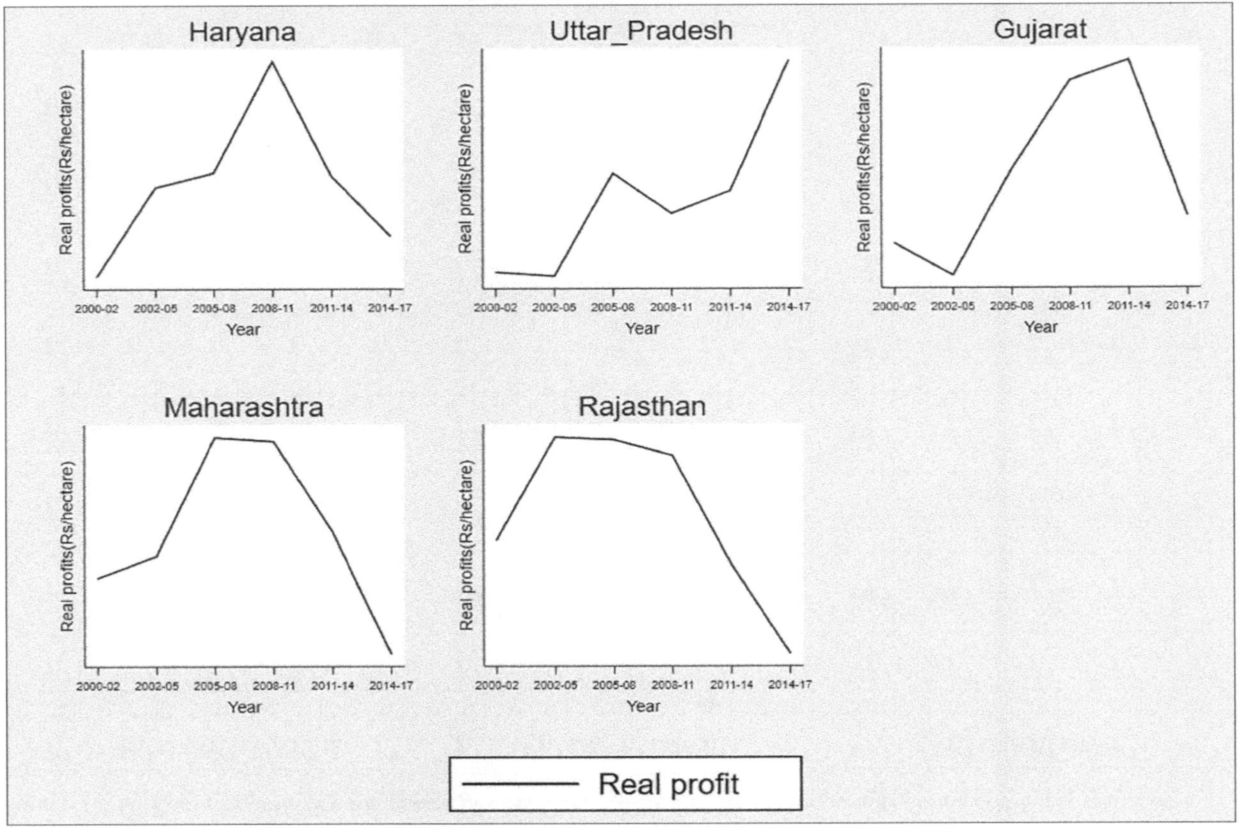

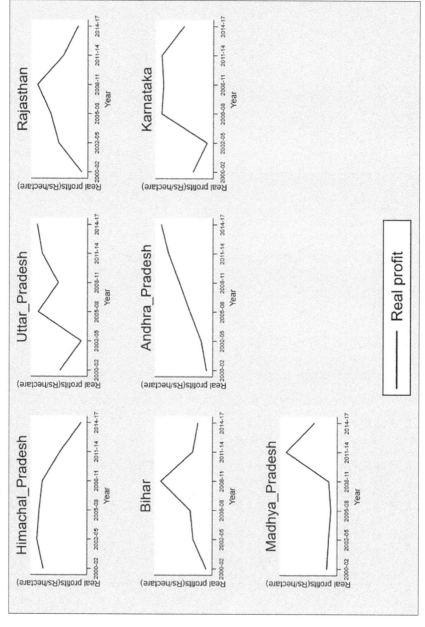

Figure 10.16 *Real profitability for maize per hectare, selected states, India, 2000–02 to 2014–17,* in Rs/ha

Figure 10.17 *Real profitability for arhar per hectare, selected states, India, 2000–02 to 2014–17, in Rs/ha*

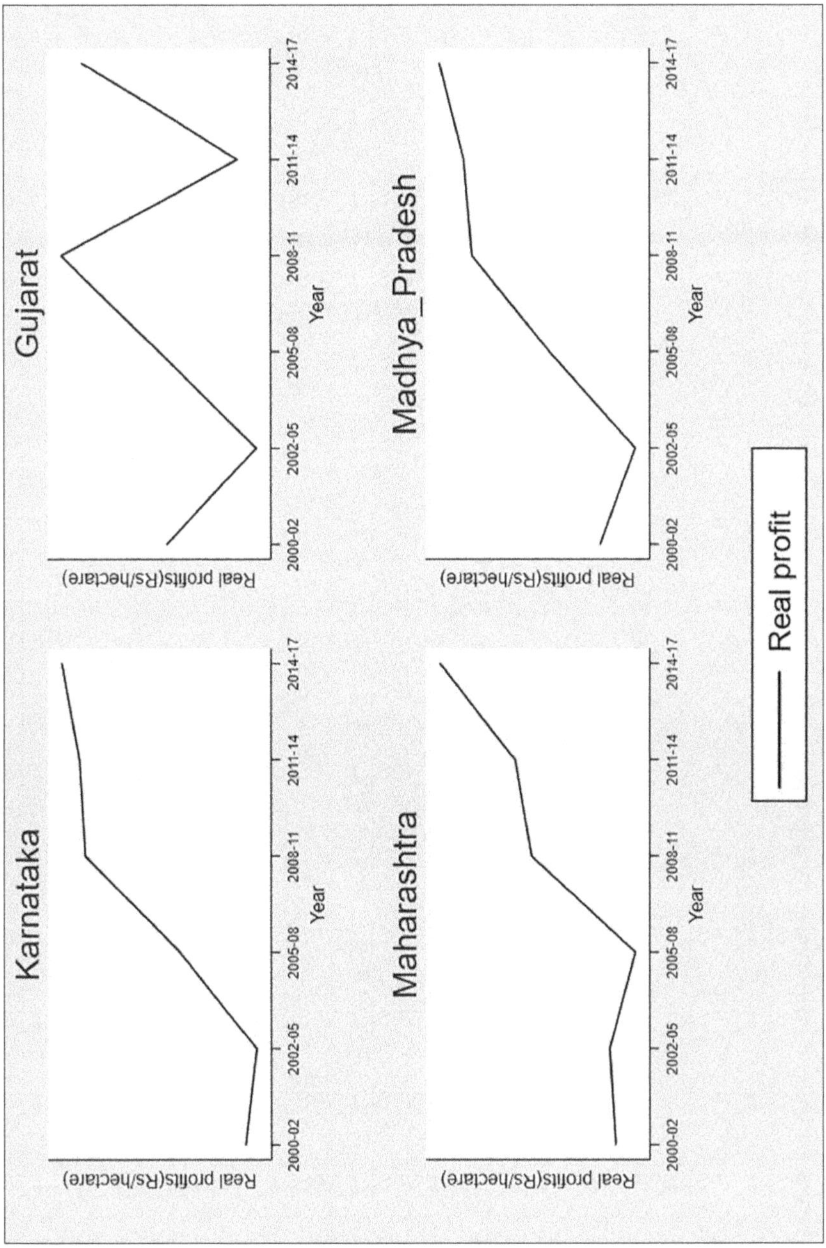

Figure 10.18 *Real profitability for gram per hectare, selected states, India, 2000–02 to 2014–17, in Rs/ha*

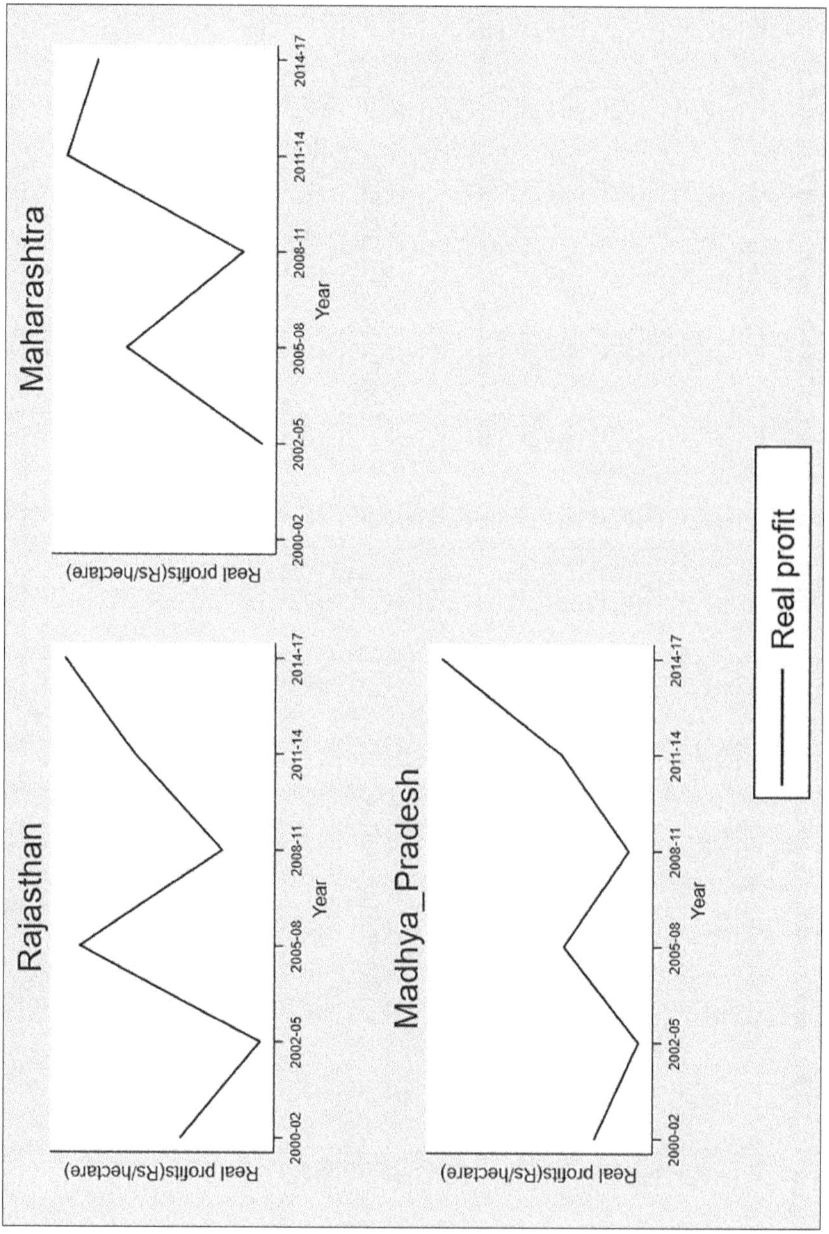

Figure 10.19 *Real profitability for moong per hectare, selected states, India, 2000–02 to 2014–17*, in Rs/ha

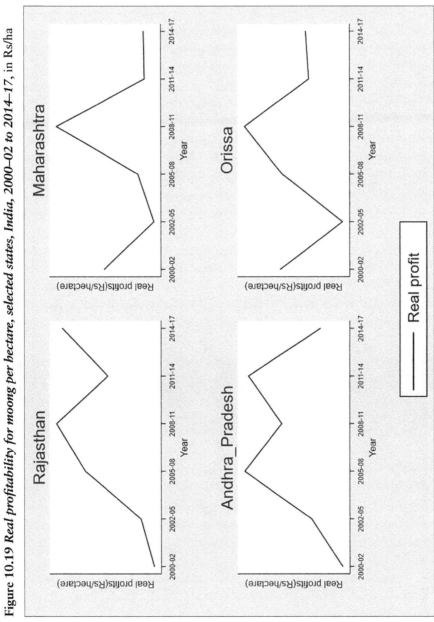

Figure 10.20 *Real profitability for urad per hectare, selected states, India, 2000–02 to 2014–17*, in Rs/ha

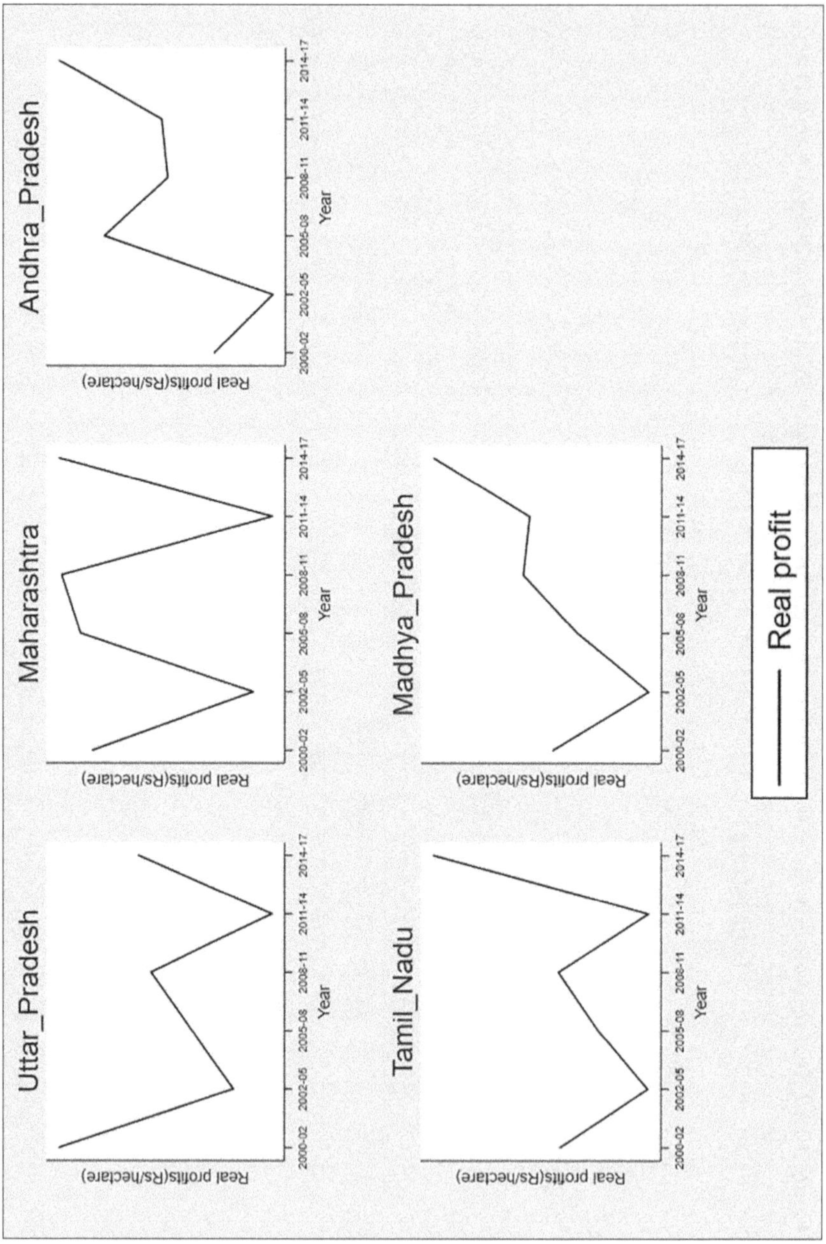

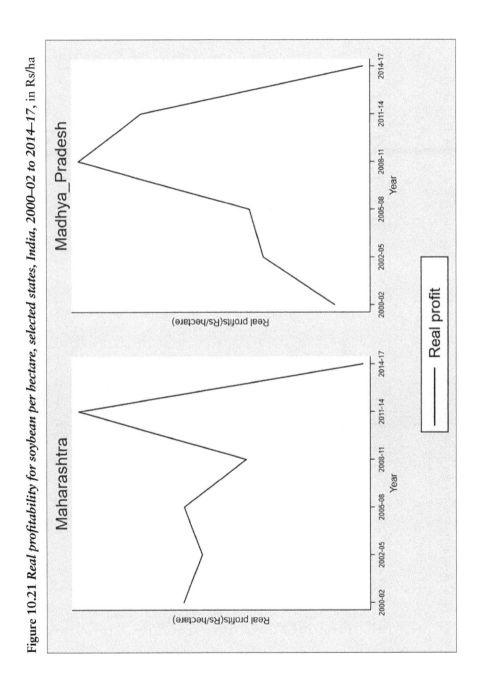

Figure 10.21 Real profitability for soybean per hectare, selected states, India, 2000–02 to 2014–17, in Rs/ha

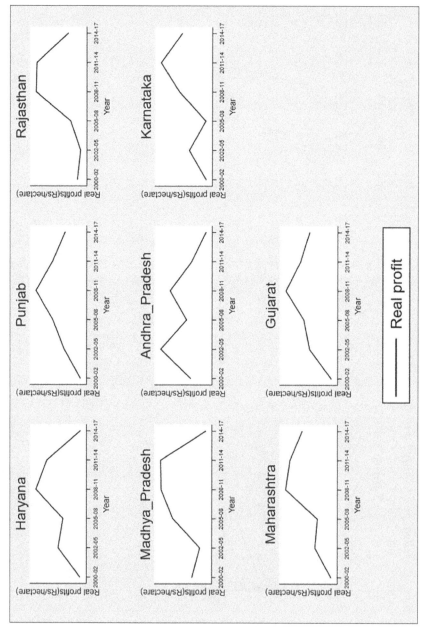

Figure 10.22 *Real profitability for cotton per hectare, selected states, India, 2000–02 to 2014–17,* in Rs/ha

Figure 10.23 *Real profitability for onion per hectare, selected states, India, 2000–02 to 2014–17,* in Rs/ha

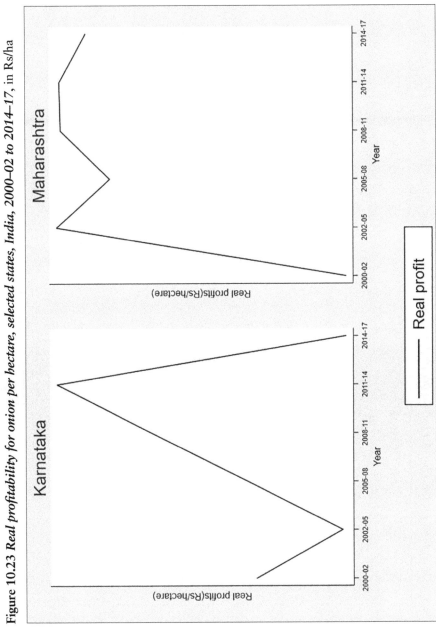

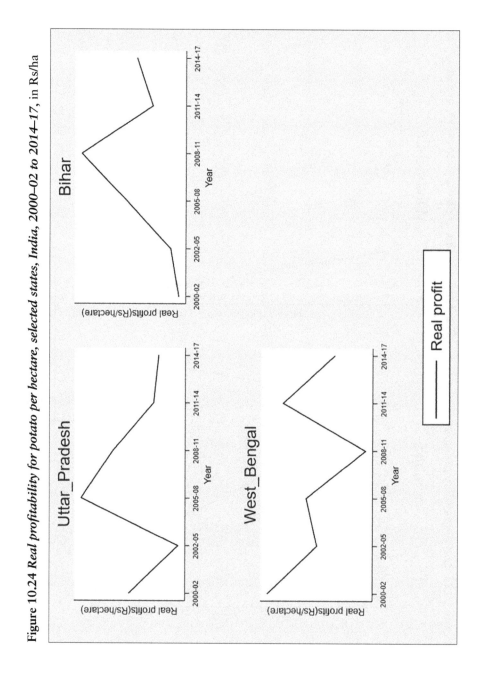

Figure 10.24 *Real profitability for potato per hectare, selected states, India, 2000–02 to 2014–17*, in Rs/ha

all the major wheat-producing states after 2014. In Uttar Pradesh, Gujarat and Rajasthan, the real profitability between 2014 and 2017 fell to levels recorded in the early 2000s. Same was the case for *bajra*, where except in Uttar Pradesh the real profitability during 2014–17 was similar (or even lower) than the levels recorded during 2000–2005.

Despite high variability in yields, real profitability increased consistently for *arhar*, gram and *urad* between 2000–01 and 2016–17 as a direct result of increases in MSP. But *moong* production saw a decline in real profitability with its profitability in 2014–17 recording the levels recorded for the early 2000s.

In both Maharashtra and Madhya Pradesh, which are the major soybean-producing states in India, the real profitability per hectare during 2014–17 was actually lower than what was recorded during 2000–02 despite an increase in yields and real MSP.

In cotton, the stagnating real value of output had a direct impact on its real profitability. The decline in real profitability in cotton started during 2008–11 but it was particularly sharp during 2014–17. Except for Maharashtra, the real profitability levels in cotton in 2014–17 reached close to or below the levels recorded in the early 2000s.

Profitability Rates Across Farm Sizes

Trends in profitability rates for crops discussed in the previous section were state-level averages. In reality, profitability rates vary across farm sizes due to the differential nature of costs faced, technology use and market access. This section compares real profitability of crops in different states across farm sizes. For this purpose, farmers were categorized into two groups: (1) small and marginal farmers operating a plot size less than 2 hectares; and (2) large farmers operating a plot size greater than 2 hectares.[8]

In cereals, large farms were more profitable than small farms. The difference in real profitability between small and marginal farmers and large farmers was rather stark in paddy production (Figure 10.25). The case with wheat was similar, but the corresponding difference was narrower than was the case in paddy (Figure 10.26). For example, the difference in real profitability between the two sets of farmers in paddy was, on an average, Rs 4,000 per hectare in 2000–02 and Rs 6,500 per hectare in 2014–17. In wheat, the corresponding figures were Rs 2,800 in 2000–02 and Rs 4,200 in 2014–17. Thus, the profitability for larger farms in paddy and wheat were consistently higher than the profitability for smaller farms and the difference increased with time. Similar conclusions can be drawn for *bajra* as well (Figure 10.27). At the same time, in maize, the differences in real profitability between small farms and large farms were insignificant (Figure 10.28).

Like in the case of cereals, in pulses too, levels of profitability were

Figure 10.25 *Real profitability across farm size for paddy, selected states, 2000–02 to 2014–17*, in Rs/ha

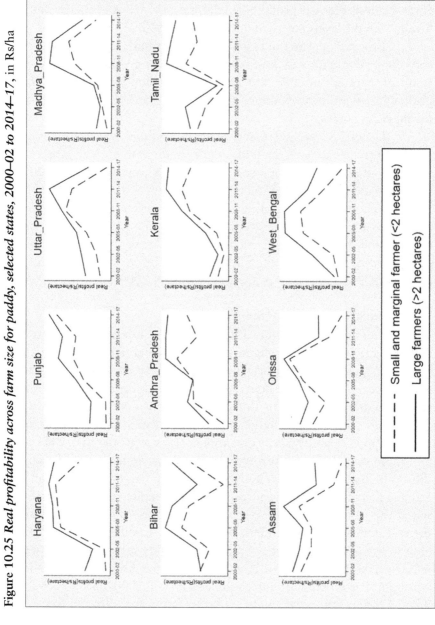

Figure 10.26 Real profitability across farm size for wheat, selected states, 2000–02 to 2014–17, in Rs/ha

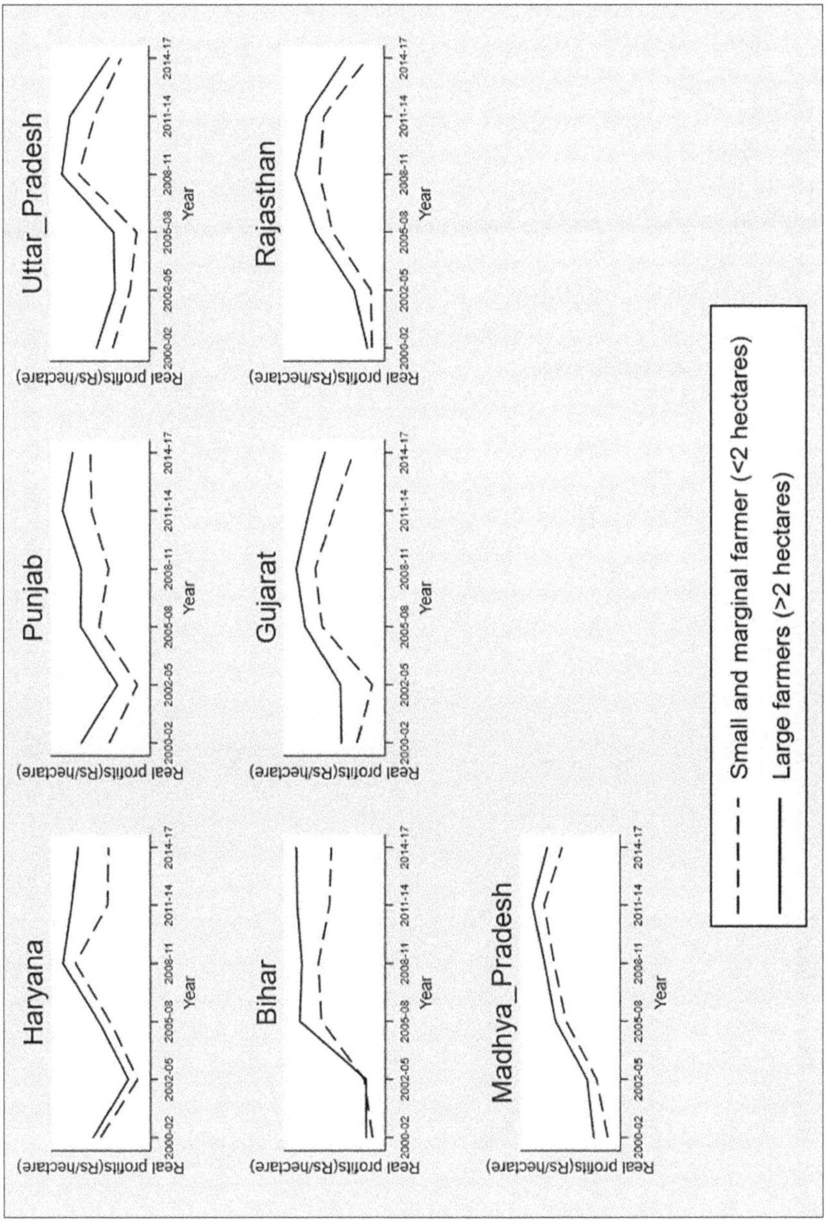

Figure 10.27 *Real profitability across farm size for bajra, selected states, 2000–02 to 2014–17*, in Rs/ha

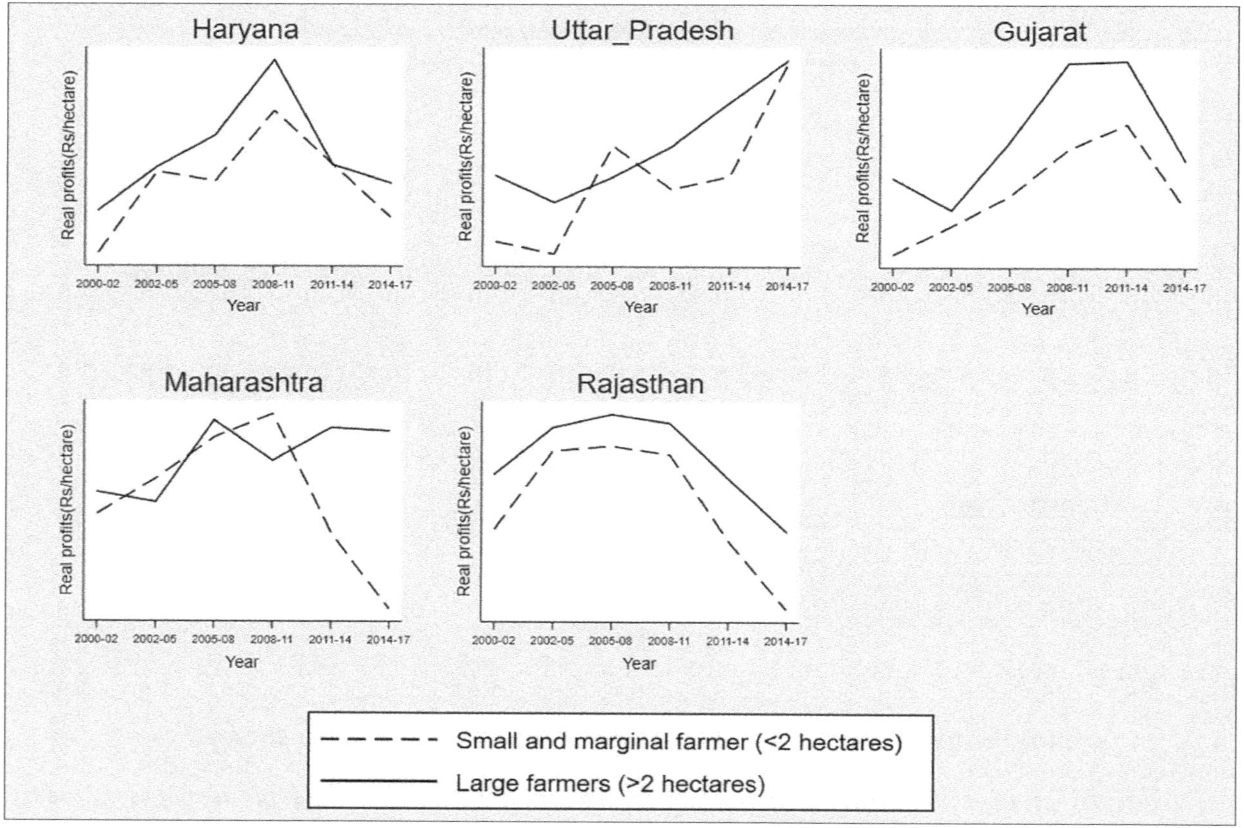

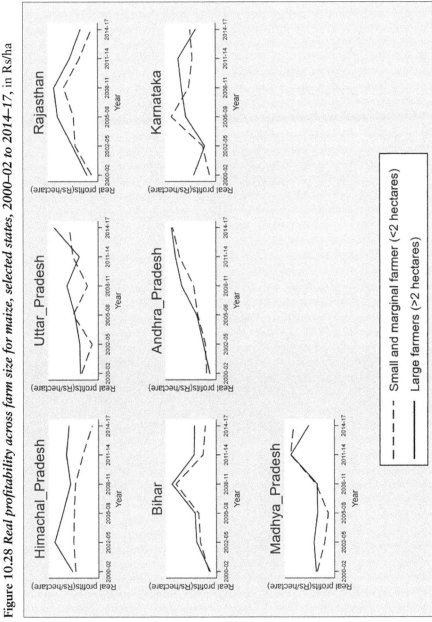

Figure 10.28 *Real profitability across farm size for maize, selected states, 2000–02 to 2014–17*, in Rs/ha

Figure 10.29 *Real profitability across farm size for arhar, selected states, 2000–02 to 2014–17, in Rs/ha*

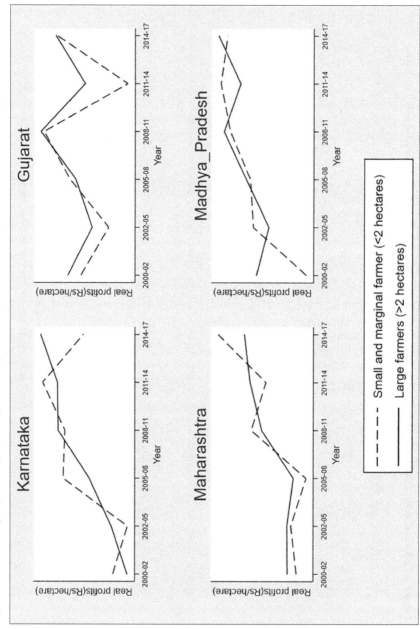

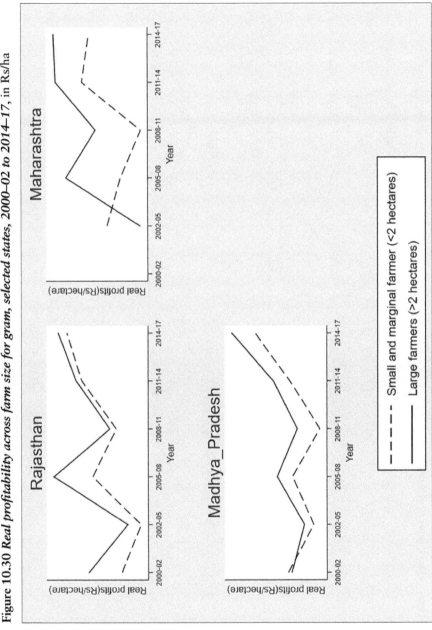

Figure 10.30 *Real profitability across farm size for gram, selected states, 2000–02 to 2014–17,* in Rs/ha

Figure 10.31 *Real profitability across farm size for moong, selected states, 2000–02 to 2014–17*, in Rs/ha

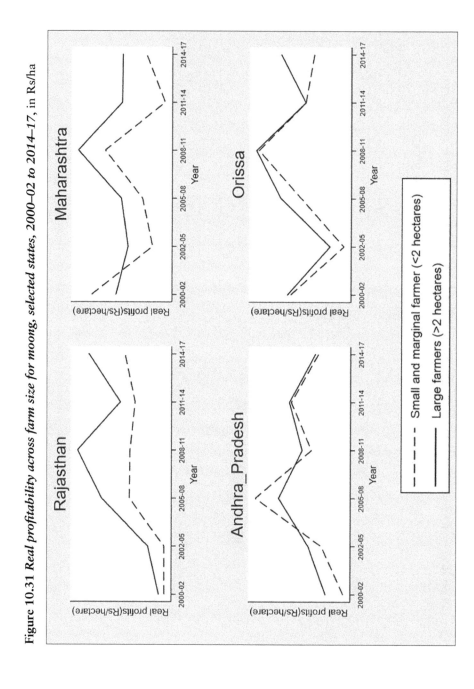

Figure 10.32 *Real profitability across farm size for urad, selected states, 2000–02 to 2014–17*, in Rs/ha

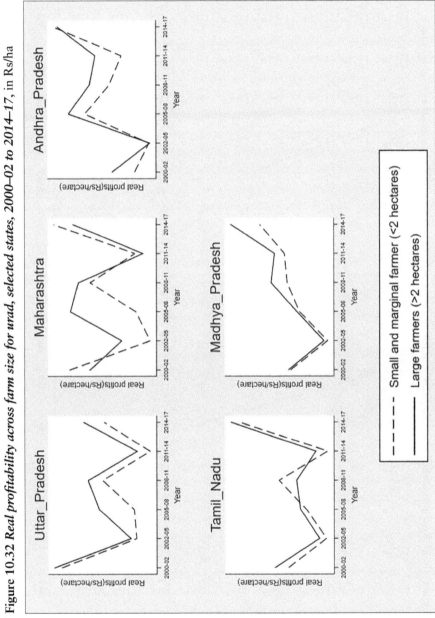

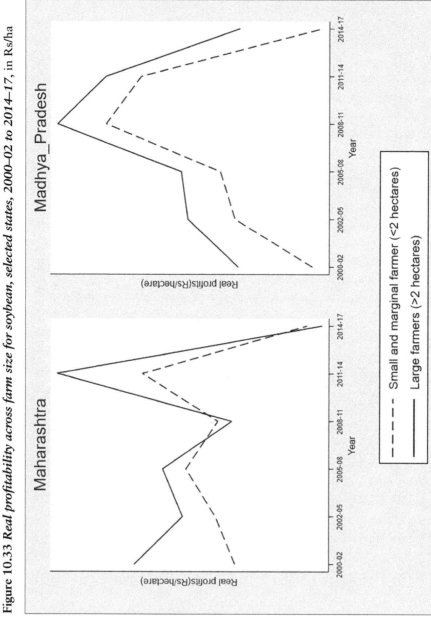

Figure 10.33 *Real profitability across farm size for soybean, selected states, 2000–02 to 2014–17*, in Rs/ha

Figure 10.34 *Real profitability across farm size for cotton, selected states, 2000–02 to 2014–17,* in Rs/ha

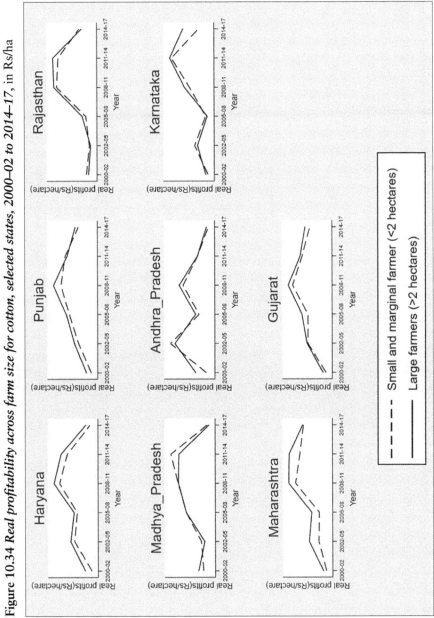

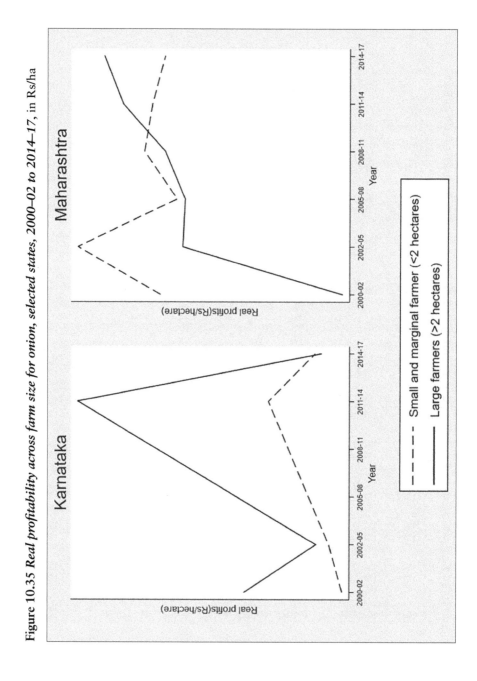

Figure 10.35 *Real profitability across farm size for onion, selected states, 2000–02 to 2014–17*, in Rs/ha

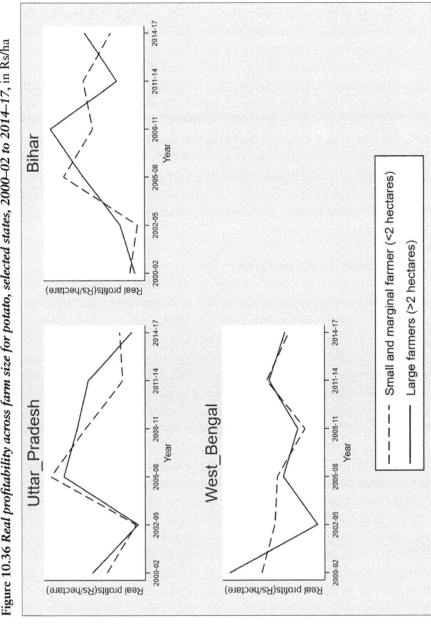

Figure 10.36 Real profitability across farm size for potato, selected states, 2000–02 to 2014–17, in Rs/ha

higher for large farms than small farms (see Figures 10.29 to 10.32). In soybean, we see contrasting cases (Figure 10.33). In Madhya Pradesh, the real profitability for small farms as well as large farms changed at a similar pace. But in Maharashtra, the trend actually reversed; real profitability for large farms in 2000–02 was higher than that of small and marginal farmers while it was the opposite case in 2014–17.

In cotton also, the real profitability of large farms was usually higher than of small farms (Figure 10.34). But the difference decreased with time in the major cotton-producing states except Gujarat and Karnataka. Combined with the fact that real profitability in cotton had actually decreased with time for everyone, it may be concluded that profitability levels decreased for large farms at a faster rate when compared with small farms.

The real profitability in onion fluctuated too much across farm sizes to decipher any clear pattern (Figure 10.35). In potato, the real profitability for small farmers declined at a slower pace when compared with large farmers (Figure 10.36).

Summary and Conclusions

Data from the CCPC scheme clearly establishes the fact that the real costs of cultivation per hectare increased at an alarming pace in Indian agriculture between 2000–01 and 2016–17. Studies show that the real cost of cultivation per hectare was on a rise since the mid-1990s itself. This increase in cost was differentiated geographically; costs per hectare increased at a much higher pace in states like Maharashtra and Madhya Pradesh compared to states like Haryana and Punjab. The increase in input costs was a direct result of the policies of liberalization. Privatization of the seed sector and consequent withdrawal of state support in the seed sector led to a substantial increase in seed costs. Similarly, deregulation of non-urea fertilizers led to not just an overuse of urea but also a drastic increase in cost incurred on potassic and phosphatic fertilizers. The increase in fertilizer cost was usually also accompanied by an increase in cost of pesticides/insecticides/weedicides.

If the costs of cultivation increased on the one hand, the real value of output either stagnated or declined on the other hand, especially after 2010–11. This stagnation was a direct result of the stagnation in yields of major crops as well as a saturation of output prices. The price stagnation was, in part, an outcome of the government's reluctance to increase MSPs as in the past and improve and expand the procurement system. In some cases, the real MSP actually declined between 2000–01 and 2016–17. Any attempt to privatize the output market would, in all likelihood, further depress prices in the future.

The 'double whammy' of prices – increase in input prices and decrease/stagnation in output prices – led to a situation where per hectare profitability for various crops stagnated or declined after the early 2010s. Profitability levels for many crops in many states in the mid-2010s had fallen to levels recorded in the early 2000s. The government's 'getting prices right' policy appears to have shifted the terms of trade against farmers as they purchased their inputs at a higher cost and sold their output at relatively stagnant or lower prices. Finally, the decrease in profitability is not differentiated across land size classes. Smaller farms had lesser profitability per hectare than larger farms, and they also faced a more rapid fall in profitability than larger farms.

Notes

[1] So far, two Situation Assessment Surveys have been conducted. The first one was conducted in 2002–03. The latest survey was conducted in 2012–13.

[2] Small and marginal farmers are defined here as farmers operating less than 2 hectares plot for a particular crop.

[3] The data are available publicly. Plot-level data were processed to state-level summary data using the methodology described in the manual on cost of cultivation studies released by the CACP, available at http://mospi.nic.in/sites/default/files/publication_reports/manual_cost_cultivation_surveys_23july08_0.pdf, accessed 21 January 2021.

[4] The data entry and processing make use of a DOS-based computer package called FARMAP provided by the Food and Agricultural Organization (FAO). The Directorate of Economics and Statistics is in the process of deploying FARMAP 2.0 to speed up the data collection and processing of this data but it is not clear when it would be implemented.

[5] GVO is calculated using the farm gate prices in the CCPC scheme.

[6] The years are combined based on the fact that CACP freezes the blocks for a period of three years for the survey and then select the blocks again. Since the data for 1999 is not available, the first time reference is a two-year period, i.e. 2000–02. Rest of the three-year periods coincide with CACP three-year window period.

[7] The value of MSPs considered in this paper do not include the bonus added by individual states.

[8] In reality, farms operating greater than 2 hectares plot cannot be categorized as 'large'. This was done only for theoretical purposes.

References

Ahmad, N., D.K. Sinha, K.M. Singh and R.R. Mishra (2018), 'Revisiting Policies for Enhancing Minimum Support Price (MSP): Evidences from Cost of Cultivation Data of Bihar (India)', *International Journal of Pure and Applied Bioscience*, vol. 6, no. 2, pp. 277–86.

Bhalla, G.S. and G. Singh (2009), 'Economic Liberalisation and Indian Agriculture: A State-Wise Analysis', *Economic and Political Weekly*, vol. 44, no. 52, pp. 34–44.

Bhatia, M.S. (2006), 'Sustainability and Trends in Profitability of Indian Agriculture', *Agricultural Economics Research Review*, vol. 19, pp. 89–100.

Chatterjee, S. and D. Kapur (2016), 'Understanding Price Variation in Agricultural Commodities in India: MSP, Government Procurement, and Agriculture Markets', *India Policy Forum*, July, pp. 12–13.

Central Statistical Organisation (CSO) (2008), *Manual on Cost of Cultivation Surveys*, available at http://mospi.nic.in/sites/default/files/publication_reports/manual_cost_cultivation_surveys_23july08.pdf, accessed 21 January 2021.

Kamra, A. and R. Ramakumar (2019), 'Underestimation of Farm Costs: A Note on the Methodology of the CACP', *Review of Agrarian Studies*, vol. 9, no. 1, pp. 112–26.

Kumar, P.S., G.P. Sunandini and K. Suhasini (2020), 'Trend in Cost of Cultivation of Sorghum in Andhra Pradesh and Telangana States of India', *Economic Affairs*, vol. 65, no. 4, pp. 505–09.

Kumari, P., K.M. Singh and N. Ahmad (2020), 'Yield Gap and its Determinants in Pulse Crops of Bihar: Facts from Plot-Level Data of Cost of Cultivation Scheme', *Multilogic in Science*, vol. 9, no. 32, pp. 455–58.

Manjunatha, B.L., D.U.M. Rao and M.B. Dastagiri (2013), 'Trends in Seed Production, Growth Drivers and Present Market Status of Indian Seed Industry: An Analytical Study', *Indian Journal of Agricultural Sciences*, vol. 83, no. 3, pp. 315–20.

Mishra, S. (2008), 'Risks, Farmers' Suicides and Agrarian Crisis in India: Is There a Way Out?', *Indian Journal of Agricultural Economics*, vol. 63, no. 1, pp. 38–54.

Narayanamoorthy, A. (2013), 'Profitability in Crops Cultivation in India: Some Evidence from Cost of Cultivation Survey Data', *Indian Journal of Agricultural Economics*, vol. 68, no. 1, pp. 104–21.

Narayanamoorthy, A. and R. Suresh (2013), 'An Uncovered Truth in Fixation of MSP for Crops in India', *Review of Development and Change*, vol. 18, no. 1, pp. 53–62.

Nawn, N. (2013), 'Using Cost of Cultivation Survey Data: Changing Challenges for Researchers', *Economic and Political Weekly*, vol. 48, nos 26–27, pp. 139–47.

Raghavan, M. (2008), 'Changing Pattern of Input Use and Cost of Cultivation', *Economic and Political Weekly*, vol. 43, no. 26, pp. 123–29.

Ramakumar, R. (2010), 'Continuity and Change: Notes on Agriculture in "New India"', in Anthony D'Costa, eds, *A New India? Critical Perspectives in the Long Twentieth Century*, London: Anthem Press.

Ramakumar, R., K. Raut and T. Kamble (2017), 'Moving Out of Cotton: Notes from a Longitudinal Survey in Two Vidarbha Villages', *Review of Agrarian Studies*, vol. 7, no. 1, pp. 107–32.

Rao, N.C. and S. Mahendra Dev (2010), 'Agricultural Price Policy, Farm Profitability and Food Security', *Economic and Political Weekly*, vol. 45, nos 26–27, pp. 174–82.

Sarkar, A. (2013), 'Tractor Production and Sales in India, 1989–2009', *Review of Agrarian Studies*, vol. 3, no. 1, pp. 55–72.

Sarkar, B. (2017), 'The Situation Assessment Surveys: An Evaluation', *Review of Agrarian Studies*, vol. 7, no. 2, pp. 111–22.

Sen, A. and M.S. Bhatia (2004), *Cost of Cultivation and Farm Income in India*, New Delhi: Academic Foundation.

Singh, J., T. Dutta, J. Singh and N. Singh (2019), 'Farm Size and Technical Efficiency Relationship in Major Cotton-Producing States: Empirical Evidence from the Cost of Cultivation Survey Data', *Restaurant Business*, vol. 118, no. 11, pp. 1314–29.

Singh, J., S.K. Srivastava, A.P. Kaur, R. Jain, K. Immaneulraj and P. Kaur (2017), 'Farm-Size Efficiency Relationship in Punjab Agriculture: Evidences from Cost of Cultivation Survey', *Indian Journal of Economics and Development*, vol. 13, no. 2, pp. 357–62.

Sharma, P. (2016), 'Costs, Returns and Profitability of Soybean Cultivation in India: Trends and Prospects', *Economic Affairs*, vol. 61, no. 3, pp. 413–25.

Srivastava, S.K., R. Chand and J. Singh (2017), 'Changing Crop Production Cost in India: Input Prices, Substitution and Technological Effects', *Agricultural Economics Research Review*, vol. 30, Conference issue, pp. 171–82.

Surjit, V. (2008), 'Farm Business Incomes in India: A Study of Two Rice Growing Villages of Thanjavur Region of Tamil Nadu', PhD thesis, University of Calcutta, Kolkata.

Tripathi, A.K. (2017), 'Price and Profitability Analysis of Major Pulses in India', *Asian Journal of Agriculture and Development*, vol. 14, no. 2, pp. 83–102.

11

Inadequacy of Agricultural Incomes in India

Aparajita Bakshi

Introduction

One of the defining features of economic transformation and structural change in India is the increasing complexity of incomes and income sources within rural geographies and within rural households. While agricultural production is largely confined to rural locations, production and economic activities in rural areas are no longer confined to agriculture. As a matter of fact, national accounts estimates show that less than 50 per cent of rural net domestic product (NDP) in the country is sourced from agriculture. This also implies decreasing reliance of rural households on agriculture for livelihoods, and diversification of household incomes to non-agricultural sources.

In this chapter, we are concerned with the levels of agricultural incomes that accrue to rural households. We ask the question, are agricultural incomes adequate for sustaining livelihoods of households that depend on it? Though the title of the chapter suggests a presumption and a giveaway, it is through detailed empirical analysis that we conclude that agricultural incomes are inadequate for very large sections of the rural population. We also explore how farm size, and the caste and class of rural households present differential outcomes on the question of adequate agricultural incomes. We use data from the Situation Assessment Survey of Agricultural Households (SAS) conducted by the National Sample Survey Office (NSSO) in 2011–12 and data from sixteen village surveys conducted by the Foundation for Agrarian Studies (FAS) over the period of 2006 to 2010 for our analysis.

In a 2017 working paper, the NITI Aayog discussed some interesting findings (Chand, Srivastava and Singh 2017). Using data from the Central Statistics Office (CSO) on rural and urban NDP, the paper showed that the sectoral share of agriculture in the rural NDP decreased from 72.4 per cent in 1970–71 to 39.2 per cent in 2011–12. Thus, less than 40 per cent of rural incomes originated in agriculture in 2011–12. NSS data on employment shows that the employment share of agriculture also declined (from 85.5 per cent to 64.1 per cent), but not as much as the decline in the share of output.

Differing rates of reduction of output and employment point to one of the core problems of Indian agriculture in general: that of low productivity (measured as low output per worker). According to the NITI Ayog study, the productivity of a rural non-farm worker was 2.76 times that of a farm worker. The disparity between productivity or per worker income of farm and non-farm workers within rural areas had increased continuously between 1970–71 and 2004–05, after which it showed a decline. The rural–urban difference in per worker incomes was also sharp; the productivity of urban workers was close to three times that of their rural counterparts throughout the three-decade period. Thus, farm workers earned much less than non-farm workers in rural areas, and rural workers earned much less than urban workers. The differences in productivity between rural farm and non-farm workers, and rural workers and urban workers are indicative of the low levels of agricultural incomes in India. They also indicate a more serious malaise: the continued dependence of workers on agricultural incomes in spite of wide disparities in income between agriculture and other sectors.

The Levels of Agricultural Incomes

The Situation Assessment Survey (SAS) of Agricultural Households (NSS 70th round, 2013) was conducted as a repeat survey of Situation Assessment Survey of Farmer Households (NSS 59th round, 2003). The SAS of 2003 was conducted in a period of agricultural deceleration and amidst widespread concern over an agricultural crisis in the country. SAS 2013, in contrast, was conducted in a period of agricultural revival (Ramakumar 2014; Deokar and Shetty 2014). The revival of agricultural growth was attributed to policy changes since 2004 by Deokar and Shetty (2014). Some of the important policy changes after 2004 were the improvement of agricultural terms of trade and increase in minimum support prices (Deokar and Shetty 2014; Mahendra Dev and Rao 2010), increase in budgetary allocations to various departments related to agriculture and animal husbandry, launch of a number of projects with specific focus on increasing agricultural production (such as the National Horticulture Mission) and the reform of extension services (Deokar and Shetty 2014, Planning Commission 2005).

Further, the two surveys are not strictly comparable due to the change in the scope of the survey. SAS 2003 surveyed 'farmer' households, defined as households with at least one member as farmer who operated some land and engaged in some agricultural activities in the broad sense. SAS 2013 broadened the scope to include all 'agricultural' households, defined as those 'receiving some value of produce more than Rs 3,000 from agricultural activities and having at least one member self-employed in agriculture either in the principal status or in subsidiary status during last 365 days'. Chandrasekhar and Mehrotra (2016) estimated comparable incomes of agricultural households from SAS 2003 and 2013. They concluded that between 2003 and 2013, the average monthly incomes of agricultural households increased by a factor of 1.34 in constant prices.

In the agricultural year 2012–13, agricultural households comprised 57.8 per cent of rural households in India. Even though the survey targeted agricultural households, crop production and animal farming were the principal sources of income (the source yielding maximum income) for only 67 per cent agricultural households. Among the remaining agricultural households, the principal source of income was wages and salaries for 22 per cent, non-agricultural enterprises for 4.7 per cent and other sources for the rest.

A large majority of agricultural households were marginal and small farmers. Table 11.1 shows the distribution of agricultural households by size class of land possessed. Land possessed refers to all land owned, leased in or otherwise occupied by households and excludes land leased out. In 2012–13, 69.6 per cent of agricultural households were marginal farmer households possessing up to 1 hectare (ha) of land, and 17.1 per cent were small farmers possessing between 1 ha and 2 ha. The proportion of large farmers possessing more than 10 hectares was only 0.4 per cent.

The NSS SAS estimated only four major sources of income for agricultural households: crop production, animal farming, non-farm busi-

Table 11.1 *Distribution of agricultural households by size class of land possessed, 2012–13*

Size class of land possessed	Estimated no. of households	Per cent
Landless	57,265	0.1
up to 1 ha	6,27,81,241	69.6
1 – 2 ha	1,54,37,225	17.1
2 – 4 ha	82,76,129	9.2
4 – 10 ha	33,08,731	3.7
>10 ha	3,43,271	0.4
All	9,02,03,863	100.0

Source: Author's calculation from NSS SAS 2013 unit-level data.

ness, and wages and salaries. Other sources of income, such as transfers, remittances and financial incomes, were excluded though we can assume that these sources would constitute a small proportion of incomes of agricultural households. The average income of agricultural households was Rs 6,426 per month. Cultivation constituted 47.9 per cent of household incomes, livestock 11.9 per cent, wages and salaries 32.2 per cent and non-farm business 8 per cent.

In order to address the question of adequacy of agricultural incomes, first, we need to define agricultural incomes, and second, we need to set some benchmark for 'adequate income'. All incomes that accrue to agricultural households are not agricultural incomes, as agricultural households receive incomes from multiple non-agricultural sources. Ideally, agricultural incomes should consist of incomes from crop production, animal husbandry and wages earned from agricultural employment. The SAS data does not allow us to segregate incomes from agricultural and non-agricultural wages as 'wages and salaries' constitute a single category. Thus, we do not get an estimate of 'agricultural incomes'. We can only get estimates of incomes from crop production and animal husbandry, and in this part of the analysis, we refer to incomes from these two sources as 'agricultural incomes'.

One measure of 'adequate incomes' could be incomes sufficient to meet household consumption expenditures. This can be easily estimated from SAS data as the survey collected data on consumption expenditures. Figure 11.1 compares the average consumption expenditures of households in each income decile to average incomes, incomes from crop production and agricultural incomes. The figure throws light on the scale of the problem in rural India. For the bottom six deciles of the income distribution (comprising 60 per cent of agricultural households), average annual incomes fell short of average consumption expenditures. If we consider incomes from crop production or incomes from crop production and animal husbandry (agricultural income), then only the top two income deciles received incomes adequate to cover household consumption expenditures. Hence, about 80 per cent of the agricultural households in rural India did not receive adequate incomes from crop production and animal husbandry, according to NSS SAS estimates.

One may disagree with the 'income sufficient to meet consumption' definition of adequate incomes that I have used and argue that if consumption expenditures are high due to the extravagance of rural agricultural households, the benchmark we have used would overestimate the proportion of households receiving inadequate incomes and magnify the problem. One conservative estimate of income inadequacy that we can use is the official poverty line. The last of the official poverty lines estimated in India was the Tendulkar poverty line of 2009–10. We have used the 2009–10

Figure 11.1 *Average consumption, income, crop income and agricultural income per agricultural household per year, by annual income deciles, rural India, 2013*

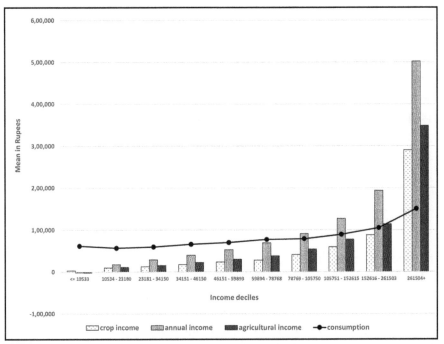

Source: Author's calculation from NSS SAS 2013 unit-level data.

Tendulkar poverty line for rural India of Rs 672.8 per month per capita and estimated the proportion of agricultural households with incomes below this benchmark. According to our estimates, annual incomes of 42.7 per cent of the agricultural households was below the Tendulkar poverty line. Further, agricultural incomes of 67 per cent households and crop incomes of 74.5 per cent households were below the poverty line. Thus, whether we use a poverty line measure or an actual consumption measure, our inference that a majority of the households do not receive adequate incomes from agriculture holds true.

Small Farm Size and Inadequacy of Agricultural Incomes

SAS 2013 data show that marginal farmer households owning less than one hectare of land have a net income deficit, as their annual consumption expenditure was higher than their income. It is important to emphasize here that this category comprises 70 per cent agricultural households in India.

The problem faced by marginal and small farmer households in India is of persistent income deprivation. This is clearly shown in Figure 11.2 and Table 11.3. Figure 11.2 plots the mean annual income, consumption, agricultural incomes and crop incomes by land deciles. The horizon-

Table 11.2 *Average annual income and consumption expenditure of agricultural households, by size class of land possessed, 2013*

Size class of land possessed	Estimated number of households	Annual income		Annual consumption expenditure	
		Mean	Median	Mean	Median
Landless	57,265	79,019	70,195	49,470	44,500
up to 1 ha	6,27,81,241	56,760	36,680	68,450	59,450
1 – 2 ha	1,54,37,225	89,848	64,100	77,622	67,400
2 – 4 ha	82,76,129	1,33,162	88,180	93,684	78,400
4 – 10 ha	33,08,731	2,40,278	1,40,800	1,21,513	96,740
>10 ha	3,43,271	5,75,918	3,01,620	1,73,701	1,23,500
All	9,02,03,863	78,153	44,958	74,670	63,200

Source: Author's calculation from NSS SAS 2013 unit-level data.

tal line indicates the Tendulkar poverty line for rural India of 2009–10 (Rs 672.8 per capita per month for average household size of 5.11, that is, Rs 41,256). Average consumption of each land decile stood above the poverty line in 2012–13. Average annual incomes were lower than consumption for 70 per cent of the households possessing less than 1.01 ha of land. Even these lower levels of incomes surpass the poverty line for all land deciles. However, the picture was remarkably different if we considered incomes from crop production and livestock.

If agricultural households relied solely on income from crop production and livestock, only households in the top land decile possessing more than 2.227 ha of land would be able to make adequate incomes to meet their consumption expenditures. Further, only those households in the top three land deciles possessing more than 1.01 ha would be able to earn adequate incomes to meet poverty-line consumption. Bhalla (2008) had shown using NSS SAS data for 2003 that in fourteen out of eighteen major states, the income of farmer households owning up to 2 hectares of land was insufficient to meet their consumption needs.

The shortfall of annual incomes over consumption would evidently be met through depletion of household assets and savings or borrowings. This would lead to diversion of formal sector production credit to consumption and dependence on informal sources of credit. The results are all of a piece with trends on rural credit in India, which show heavy reliance on informal sources of credit, particularly professional moneylenders, on the part of landless and marginal farmer households. According to the SAS reports, 63.7 per cent of outstanding loans of landless agricultural households, 32.4 per cent of the loans of households possessing less than 0.4 ha

Figure 11.2 *Average consumption, income, crop income and agricultural income per agricultural household per year, by land possessed deciles, rural India, 2013*

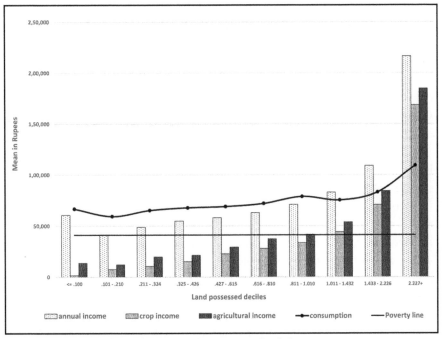

Source: Author's calculation from NSS SAS 2013 unit-level data.

Table 11.3 *Proportion of households receiving incomes from source below the Tendulkar poverty line, by size class of land possessed, 2013*, in per cent

Size class of land possessed	Total income	Agricultural income	Crop income
Landless	19.5	52.9	100.0
up to 1 ha	50.1	78.8	86.9
1 – 2 ha	31.0	47.8	54.9
2 – 4 ha	20.7	32.8	38.3
4 – 10 ha	16.3	22.8	25.3
>10 ha	10.2	14.4	24.9
All	42.7	67.0	74.5

Source: Author's calculation from NSS SAS 2013 unit-level data.

and 27.4 per cent of the loans of households possessing less than 1 ha were borrowed from professional moneylenders.

The problem of income inadequacy was most common among marginal farmers possessing less than a hectare of land. Half of the marginal farmer households received total incomes less than the poverty line, while

78.8 per cent of them did not earn agricultural incomes to meet the poverty line (Table 11.3). It must be also noted that 22.8 per cent of the medium farmer households and 14.4 per cent of the large farmer households also did not receive adequate incomes from agriculture to meet the poverty line. This shows how widespread the problem of income inadequacy is in Indian agriculture. The problem of inadequate agricultural incomes was also experienced by all social groups in the country. Our estimates show that agricultural incomes of 68 per cent of ST, 79.8 per cent of SC, 65.9 per cent OBC and 59.9 per cent of other agricultural households were below the Tendulkar poverty line (Table 11.4).

As a result of such widespread income deficit, agricultural households were increasingly looking for alternate sources of income – a phenomenon often referred to as income diversification in the livelihoods literature. In a country like India, coping with the income shortfall in agriculture is manifested in two ways. First, agricultural households engage in other income-generating activities to mitigate the income shortfall in agriculture. Thus, a significant portion of the income portfolio of agricultural households are sourced from other activities. The reliance on crop production decreases as land size decreases. While households with medium and large holdings derived 70 per cent or higher share of household income from crop production, households with marginal holdings received only 29.6 per cent and small farmers received only 56.6 per cent of annual incomes from crop production (Table 11.5). Wage employment played a significant role in mitigating income risks. Agricultural households with marginal and small holdings relied significantly on wage incomes. As a matter of fact, the contribution of wages to total incomes (46.7 per cent) was much higher than of crop production for households with marginal holdings. In contrast, only 2.7 per cent of household incomes of large agricultural households was sourced from wages and salaries.

The second aspect of the income crisis is that, most of the income

Table 11.4 *Proportion of households receiving agricultural incomes below the Tendulkar poverty line, by social group, 2013*, in per cent

Social group	Agricultural incomes
Scheduled Tribe (ST)	68.0
Scheduled Caste (SC)	79.8
Other Backward Class (OBC)	65.9
Others	59.9
All	67.0

Source: Author's calculation from NSS SAS 2013 unit-level data.

Table 11.5 *Income portfolio of households, by size class of land possessed*, in per cent

Size class of land possessed	Share in annual income					Average number of sources per household	Inverse HHI
	Crop production	Animal farming	Non-farm business	Wages and salaries	Annual income		
Landless	0.00	36.86	1.79	61.35	100.0	1.92	1.95
up to 1 ha	29.56	14.02	9.72	46.71	100.0	2.27	2.99
1 – 2 ha	56.61	12.12	8.02	23.25	100.0	2.25	2.53
2 – 4 ha	69.38	10.75	4.90	14.97	100.0	2.24	1.93
4 – 10 ha	78.02	7.41	4.36	10.22	100.0	2.17	1.60
>10 ha	87.58	5.94	3.76	2.73	100.0	2.23	1.29
All	48.18	12.18	7.85	31.79	100.0	2.26	2.82

Source: Author's calculation from NSS SAS 2013 unit-level data.

and employment options available for poor households in rural India are precarious in nature, leading poor households to depend on multiple low-income activities to meet household consumption needs. This is captured by the inverse Herfindahl-Hirschman Index (HHI) in Table 11.5. The inverse HHI measures the concentration of income from individual sources among different types of households. The HHI is the sum of the squares of income shares from each source of income. The inverse HHI is the reciprocal of the HHI. If the maximum number of income sources is n, then the index lies between 1 and n, where higher index values signify more diversified income portfolios. In our case, the highest value the index can take is 4. The value of inverse HHI was above 2 for agricultural households with marginal (2.99) and small holdings (2.53) showing that their income portfolios were significantly diversified and there was lower concentration or specialization of income from single sources.

Some Insights from Village Studies

The magnitude and nature of distress in agricultural incomes come out quite clearly in the village studies conducted by the Foundation for Agrarian Studies, Bengaluru, that have been collecting detailed data on incomes from villages surveyed in different parts of India since 2006 as part of the Project on Agrarian Relations in India (PARI). The method of data collection and estimation of household incomes in these surveys are fairly elaborate and are designed to yield good estimates of household incomes in a country such as India where thin and imperfect markets, complexity

Table 11.6 *Location and agro-ecology of survey villages, 2005 to 2010*

Village[2]	Block	District	State	Agro-ecological type
Ananthavaram (2006)	Kollur	Guntur	Andhra Pradesh	canal-irrigated paddy cultivation
Bukkacherla (2006)	Raptadu	Anantapur	Andhra Pradesh	dry and drought-prone, groundnut
Kothapalle (2006)	Thimmapur	Karimnagar	Andhra Pradesh	groundwater-irrigated, multi-crop system
Harevli (2006)	Najibabad	Bijnor	Uttar Pradesh	100% canal-irrigated with supplementary groundwater, wheat–sugarcane
Mahatwar (2006)	Rasra	Ballia	Uttar Pradesh	groundwater-irrigated, wheat–paddy rotation
Warwat Khanderao (2007)	Sangrampur	Buldhana	Maha-rashtra	rainfed-cotton region
Nimshirgaon (2007)	Shirol	Kolhapur	Maha-rashtra	irrigated sugarcane and multi-crop system
25F Gulabewala (2007)	Karanpur	Sri Ganganagar	Rajasthan	canal and groundwater irrigation with cotton, wheat and mustard cultivation
Gharsondi (2008)	Bhitarwar	Gwalior	Madhya Pradesh	canal and groundwater irrigation, soybean, wheat, pulses, oilseeds and fodder cultivation
Alabujanahalli (2009)	Maddur	Mandya	Karnataka	canal irrigation, sugarcane, paddy and *ragi* cultivation. sericulture
Siresandra (2009)	Kolar	Kolar	Karnataka	tubewell drip irrigation; *ragi* and vegetables grown; sericulture
Zhapur (2009)	Gulbarga	Gulbarga	Karnataka	unirrigated; cereals and oilseeds mixed cropping; stone quarrying
Rewasi (2010)	Sikar	Sikar	Rajasthan	tubewell and sprinkler irrigation; pearl millet in kharif and wheat, mustard, fenugreek, onion in rabi; high remittance incomes

Table 11.6 *(continued)*

Village	Block	District	State	Agro-ecological type
Panahar (2010)	Kotulpur	Bankura	West Bengal	tubewell irrigation; paddy in kharif, paddy and oilseeds in summer, potato in winter
Amarsinghi (2010)	Ratua I	Maldah	West Bengal	tubewell irrigation, river lift irrigation in small area; jute in pre-kharif, paddy in kharif, paddy, lentils and oilseeds in summer, and potato in winter; vegetables grown all year
Kalmandasguri (2010)	Coch Behar II	Koch Bihar	West Bengal	unirrigated, small area irrigated by tube wells; jute and kharif paddy are the main crops; potato grown in irrigated area; fishing in ponds

of land and labour contracts, seasonality and uncertainty of agricultural production and all forms of agricultural and non-agricultural employment lead to multiple problems in valuation and quantification of income flows. The detailed questionnaire and income calculation methodology used by the foundation are available in public domain.[1] In this chapter, I use the FAS-PARI data from sixteen villages surveyed between 2006 and 2010 to analyse how widespread the problem of low agricultural incomes was. The location and characteristics of the villages where the surveys were conducted are in Table 11.6. Each of the villages represented different agro-ecological typologies within the states, thus capturing the diversity of production conditions and production relations in the country.

Levels of Household and Agricultural Incomes

Household incomes in the villages ranged from Rs 7,458 per capita per annum in Mahatwar in eastern Uttar Pradesh to Rs 41,627 in 25F Gulabewala in the Ganga canal region in Rajasthan (valued in 2010–11 prices). The variation in mean incomes across villages was associated with production conditions in agriculture, as well as village specific factors that determined access to non-agricultural sources of income. The villages in eastern Uttar Pradesh and West Bengal, where landholding sizes were among the lowest, also had low levels of income. Incomes in unirrigated villages such as Bukkacherla, Warwat Khanderao, Zhapur were lower than incomes in their corresponding irrigated villages namely Ananthavaram, Nimshirgaon and Alabujanahalli respectively, which were located in the same respective states, namely Andhra Pradesh, Maharashtra and Karnataka. At the same time, the desert village of Rewasi in the Shekhawati region in Rajasthan had higher incomes than other unirrigated villages due to the existence of migration and high remittance flows into the village. Siresandra, another unirrigated village in Karnataka had the second highest mean income among the villages due to large-scale sericulture farming carried out by households.

To put these income estimates in some perspective, we may compare them with various benchmarks and calculate an approximate head count measure of poverty. Since the FAS-PARI surveys calculate income flows and do not collect information on consumption, it would be analytically incorrect to compare these estimates with a consumption-based poverty line, such as the Tendulkar poverty line. Hence, I have used a statutory minimum wage-based poverty line to calculate the poverty levels in the villages. The Labour Bureau in India periodically announces statutory minimum wages in scheduled occupations based on many considerations, including calorie requirements for the intensity of physical labour in the occupation and cost of living. The statutory minimum wage is the wage to support a household comprising three adult units. I have calculated a poverty benchmark that is equivalent to 300 days of employment at state-specific minimum wages in agriculture. Thus, a household receiving below this amount is considered as poor in our definition. We have not adjusted for household size.

The proportion of poor households in the villages ranged from as high as 72 per cent in Panahar in West Bengal to a low of 17.7 per cent in Siresandra in Karnataka (Table 11.7). The incidence of poverty was the result of absolute levels of incomes (circumscribed by production conditions and opportunities for work) and/or the income inequality in the villages (which most often was related to inequality in ownership of land and other means of production). For example, the richest village, 25F Gulabewala also had high levels of poverty due to huge inequalities in ownership of land and other assets. On the other hand, levels of poverty in Amarsinghi and Kalmandasguri were largely on account of low absolute incomes, as inequalities were quite low in these villages. High levels of poverty in Bukkacherla resulted from low incomes and high inequality in land ownership.

So far, our discussion was on total household incomes. Agricultural incomes constituted a fraction of total household incomes in the villages, whichever way we choose to define agricultural incomes. Incomes from crop production, including fruits and vegetables, did not surpass 50 per cent of total household incomes in all but two of the villages (Table 11.8). If incomes from allied activities such as animal husbandry, fishing and sericul-

Table 11.7 *Mean per capita household income, at constant (2010–11) prices and percentage of poor households, study villages,* in rupees

Village[2]	Per capita annual income	Income per person per day	Percentage of poor households
Mahatwar, UP	7,458	20	47.4
Amarsinghi, WB	11,310	31	69.3
Panahar, WB	12,947	35	72.2
Kalmandasguri, WB	13,084	36	52.4
Kothapalle, AP	13,697	38	48.1
Bukkacherla, AP	13,889	38	51.7
Warwat Khanderao, MH	15,967	44	28.8
Zhapur, KA	16,117	44	40.4
Harevli, UP	18,754	51	35.8
Nimshirgaon, MH	20,517	56	19.0
Gharsondi, MP	22,879	63	38.4
Alabujanahalli, KA	23,665	65	28.8
Ananthavaram, AP	24,040	66	42.6
Rewasi, RJ	25,128	69	21.0
Siresandra, KA	29,298	80	17.7
25F Gulabewala, RJ	41,627	114	39.7

Note: Villages in the table are arranged in ascending order by column 2.

ture were included, the share of agricultural incomes ranged from 21.4 per cent of household incomes in Panahar to 73.2 per cent in Harevli. Adding agricultural wages and rental incomes from agricultural land increased the share further. However, even after including the allied activities, agricultural wages and rental incomes from land within the definition of agricultural incomes, in only eight of the sixteen villages was the share of such incomes higher than 50 per cent. In that sense, the FAS-PARI village data show that only about half of the villages were 'agricultural' in the sense that the major portion of village incomes and livelihoods originated in agriculture and allied activities. The importance of agriculture as a major source of income is certainly on decline. That is not to say that agriculture and hence agricultural policies are of no significance to the Indian economy. The significance of agriculture lies in the fact that a very large section of rural households depends on agriculture, even when agricultural incomes and employment per household and as a share of total are shrinking.

Let us now turn to the question of adequacy of agricultural incomes. Here, I have made estimates using the statutory minimum wage

Table 11.8 *Share of agricultural incomes in total household incomes, FAS-PARI villages,* in per cent

Village	Crops, orchards, plantations	Crops, orchards, plantations, allied activities	Crops, orchards, plantations, allied activities, agricultural wages, rents
Kothapalle, AP	9.0	28.3	36.9
Mahatwar, UP	11.5	22.6	24.1
Rewasi, RJ	15.2	32.7	34.9
Panahar, WB	15.6	21.4	36.1
Kalmandasguri, WB	17.6	29.6	40.9
Bukkacherla, AP	21.8	46.5	56.5
Ananthavaram, AP	24.5	57.6	67.8
Siresandra, KA	24.7	65.5	72.5
Zhapur, KA	24.9	36.6	47.2
Amarsinghi, WB	25.5	33.8	47.4
Nimshirgaon, MH	27.3	40.0	46.6
Alabujanahalli, KA	34.3	49.2	60.3
Gharsondi, MP	40.2	50.9	54.4
Warwat Khanderao, MH	42.1	50.0	60.0
25F Gulabewala, RJ	54.4	63.8	69.7
Harevli, UP	57.3	73.2	80.5

Note: Villages in the table are arranged in ascending order by column 2.

in India for 300 days as an accepted standard of adequate annual incomes for a household. Table 11.9 shows that if households depended on agricultural production alone, more than 70 per cent of the households in all the study villages did not meet the poverty line cut-off. Even after including all forms of agricultural and allied sector incomes, more than 50 per cent of the households did not meet the poverty cut-off in any of the villages, with the sole exception of Siresandra. The magnitude of the problem was thus large and widespread, as indicated by both primary and secondary data.

The Differentiated Nature of the Problem

A unique feature of the FAS-PARI database is that an attempt was made to classify households in rural 'classes', the word 'class' as understood and discussed in the literature on agrarian relations and peasant class differentiation. Rural classes were identified in the PARI villages based on the following criteria:[3]

Table 11.9 *Proportion of households that did not receive poverty line incomes from source*, in per cent

Village	Agricultural production	Agriculture and allied production	Agriculture, allied and wages
Warwat Khanderao, MH	72.40	65.60	56.40
Harevli, UP	72.50	63.30	56.00
25F Gulabewala, RJ	73.00	68.60	61.30
Nimshirgaon, MH	75.30	68.80	60.50
Alabujanahalli, KA	78.20	66.30	50.60
Gharsondi, MP	79.10	67.70	63.10
Siresandra, KA	82.30	53.20	40.50
Rewasi, RJ	84.00	65.80	63.00
Bukkacherla, AP	86.30	79.50	72.30
Ananthavaram, AP	90.40	72.90	69.30
Zhapur, KA	94.50	85.30	80.70
Mahatwar, UP	94.90	93.60	93.60
Panahar, WB	96.00	95.60	94.80
Amarsinghi, WB	97.60	97.60	97.60
Kothapalle, AP	97.80	84.90	84.10
Kalmandasguri, WB	98.60	97.30	95.20

Note: Villages in the table are arranged in ascending order by column 2.

(1) Ownership of the means of production and other assets;
(2) The labour ratio, defined as the ratio between the sum of labouring out of members of the household in agricultural and non-agricultural work and the number of days of labour hired in by the household;
(3) Rent exploitation, or rent received or paid by the household;
(4) Net income of the household, gross value of output from agriculture and investment in agriculture per hectare;
(5) The sources of income of the household.

The PARI villages were varied in terms of the levels of development of productive forces and nature of agrarian relations. Hence, there were subtle differences in the classes identified in each of these villages based on the above-mentioned criteria. In this analysis, we have used broad aggregation of classes in the villages. The broad classes used are:[4]

- *Landlord/big capitalist farmer/capitalist landlord*: these households owned the largest and best land within the village, invested in modern agricultural machinery and technology, and the landlords among them came from families that historically owned land in the villages. They did not participate in the main agricultural operations, for which they hired labour.

- *Small farmers and other farmers*: The defining feature of farmer or peasant households was that they participated in the major agricultural operations on land and derived a significant part of their incomes from cultivation. Small farmers operated less than 2 hectares of irrigated land (where 1 hectare of irrigated land was considered equivalent to 2 hectares of unirrigated land) and other farmers operated holding larger than 2 irrigated hectares.

- *Manual workers*: These households derived the major part of their incomes from wage employment in agriculture and non-agriculture, even though they may also have operated small holdings of land. The labour they spent in manual wage employment far outweighed their labour deployment in cultivation or other occupations.

- *Non-farmers*: These households were primarily employed in different kinds of non-agricultural activities, such as salaried employment, business and trade, rents from non-agricultural assets, elderly population depending on pensions and remittances.

Table 11.10 shows the proportion of households of different socio-economic classes who received incomes less than 300 days of minimum wages in agriculture. In most of the villages, there were no landlord or capitalist farmer households in this category. In the few villages such as Bukkacherla, Gharsondhi, Mahatwar, Panahar and Zhapur, where we found landlord capitalist farmer household making less than minimum wage income, it was a result of some income shocks during the survey year. In Gharsondhi, Bukkacherla and Mahatwar, the survey was conducted during a drought year while in Panahar, the potato prices crashed in the year of the survey. The largest proportion of households that did not receive adequate agricultural incomes were among the small farmer households, though in some villages the proportion of 'other farmer' households affected by low agricultural incomes was also high. A very large section of small farmers, more than 50 per cent in most cases, received agricultural incomes less than poverty line incomes. If we excluded agricultural wages, the percentage rose further.

Thus, the income problem in agriculture was not an undifferentiated phenomenon. There was a class of landlords and capitalist farmers, who by virtue of their better access to land and capital, did make adequate incomes within agriculture, and also took advantage of various non-agricultural income opportunities that opened up with the deeper penetration of markets and development of capitalism in the economy. We have shown

Table 11.10 *Proportion of households that did not receive poverty line incomes from agriculture, by socio-economic classes,* in per cent

Village	Landlord/big capitalist farmer/capitalist landlord	Other farmer	Small farmer	Manual worker	Non-farmer	Total
Siresandra, KA	0.0	0.0	25.0	92.3	100	40.5
Alabujanahalli, KA	0.0	4.3	43.4	64.4	81.3	50.6
Harevli, UP	0.0	4.8	53.3	89.3	91.7	56.0
Warwat Khanderao, MH	0.0	15.4	30.2	82.9	84.6	56.4
Nimshirgaon, MH	0.0	37.3	25.2	80.5	83.2	60.5
25F Gulabewala, RJ	0.0	0	0	87.7	78.1	61.3
Rewasi, RJ	0.0	7.9	74.8	81	87.5	63
Gharsondi, MP	8.3	27.1	76.1	81.4	74.5	63.1
Ananthavaram, AP	0.0	0.0	56.2	89.6	80.1	69.3
Bukkacherla, AP	60.0	43.8	69.2	80.6	90.8	71.9
Zhapur, KA	25.0	40.0	84.6	88.2	88.9	80.7
Kothapalle, AP	0.0	100.0	58.2	95.2	93.8	83.8
Mahatwar, UP	25.0	100.0	91.3	100	97.7	93.6
Panahar, WB	42.9	100.0	94.4	98.4	100.0	94.8
Kalmandasguri, WB	–	–	89.7	100.0	100.0	95.2
Amarsinghi, WB	–	–	94.4	100.0	100.0	97.6
Total	13	18.2	58.0	86.9	88.5	70.9

Notes: – = not applicable; There were no landlord or other farmer households in Amarsinghi and Kalmandasguri in West Bengal; The villages in the table are arranged in ascending order by column 7.

in an earlier publication the deep fissures that have emerged within the agrarian economy, one of extreme inequality where landlords and large farmers received incomes five to ten times higher than incomes of small farmers (Bakshi and Modak 2017). This study had noted that '. . . in spite of variations [across villages] . . . the fact remains that landlord and large farmer households received much higher incomes than small farmers. In fact, the classes of landlords and large farmers were quite distinct from the rest of the peasantry in terms of incomes received' (Bakshi and Modak 2017: p. 137, parenthesis added).

When we discuss India's agrarian crisis in the economic discourse, we often ignore this specific class character of the crisis. It is not a crisis for all, but a crisis for certain sections of the peasantry comprising small farmers and manual workers. The fact that more than 50 per cent of the small farmers and 80 per cent of the manual worker households did not receive adequate agricultural incomes, even after accounting for agricultural wage incomes, indicates a crisis at two levels for these sections – the crisis of low productivity in small farms and the crisis of employment within agriculture. The smallness of farms and overall disenfranchisement of small farmers through market forces that have limited the access of small farmers to credit, subsidized inputs and agricultural technology, have rendered small-scale farming unprofitable. On the other hand, larger farms did not create adequate wage employment opportunities for small farmers and manual workers due to the growth of mechanization, and even when they did in some cases (as in the case of increased labour absorption in Bt Cotton or labour-intensive vegetable production), wages were kept depressed to maintain profits.

The kind of differentiation we observe across socio-economic classes was not entirely present across the caste and religious stratifications of the peasantry. This was because of the fact that small farmers and manual workers were among the most caste-heterogeneous classes. While it was true that more than two-third of the Scheduled Caste (SC) households received low agricultural incomes (as SCs are over-represented in the classes of small peasantry and manual workers), it was also true that a significant proportion of households belonging to other castes and religious groups (59 per cent on the average) also did not receive agricultural incomes equivalent to 300 days of minimum wage. In only a few villages where there were extreme caste-based inequalities in ownership structures, did we find significantly fewer non-Dalit households who had low agricultural incomes. The cases in point are 25F Gulabewala in Rajasthan where Jat Sikh households owned all land and Mazhabi Sikh (SC) households did not, and Harevli in western Uttar Pradesh where Tyagi (Brahmin) households were the major landowners.

At this point, I would also like to emphasize that while the picture of caste-based inequalities in agricultural incomes was relatively blurred due to the overwhelming problem of small-scale farming by a large majority of farmers across caste and religious groups, this in no way meant that caste-based income inequalities were less pronounced in rural India. These inequalities persisted, and are even intensified under capitalist growth conditions. The inequalities in property structures now find new manifestations in rising income inequalities, through unequal access to remunerative sources of non-agricultural and urban employment. As the share of agriculture in total household incomes declined, non-agricultural incomes, particularly incomes from remunerative and steady sources, such as salaries and businesses, have become the major driver of rural income inequalities (Bakshi 2015).

The inadequacy of agricultural incomes poses a serious challenge for subsistence and survival for a large section of rural households, a chal-

Table 11.11 *Proportion of households that do not receive poverty line incomes from agriculture, by caste and religious groups,* in per cent

Village	All other caste and religious group	Muslim	Scheduled caste (SC)	Scheduled tribe (ST)	All house-holds
Siresandra, KA	20.0	–	75.9	–	40.5
Alabujanahalli, KA	47.6	–	70.6	0	50.6
Harevli, UP	35.7	69.2	80.0	–	56.0
Warwat Khanderao, MH	45.9	75.5	88.0	–	56.4
Nimshirgaon, MH	52.4	34.8	80.6	–	60.5
25F Gulabewala, RJ	21.0	–	87.8	–	61.3
Rewasi, RJ	59.9	–	71.4	81.0	63.0
Gharsondi, MP	56.8	84.6	70.4	84.8	63.1
Ananthavaram, AP	59.2	100.0	75.3	89.7	69.4
Bukkacherla, AP	67.2	50.0	94.6	–	72.2
Zhapur, KA	68.8	100.0	91.3	85.7	80.7
Kothapalle, AP	83.3	100.0	83.7	100.0	83.8
Mahatwar, UP	85.5	–	98.9	–	93.6
Panahar, WB	90.2	66.7	98.5	100.0	94.8
Kalmandasguri, WB	96.3	100.0	91.8	80.0	95.2
Amarsinghi, WB	97.1	–	98.2	100.0	97.6
All villages	59.0	76.2	87.4	86.5	70.9

Notes: – = not applicable. There were no households in the social group in the village. The villages in the table are arranged in ascending order by column 6.

lenge they seek to meet through increased participation in non-agricultural employment. The travesty of the situation, however, lies not in mass exit from agriculture but in the very absence of such mass exit and the continued dependence on agriculture at very low levels of incomes. The expansion of the non-agricultural sector and the transfer of labour from agriculture to non-agriculture is a common phenomenon in the process of economic expansion and development. Such a process is even welcome, when accompanied by rising productivities in both agriculture and non-agriculture, leading to higher incomes in both sectors.

In India, however, that is not the case. The lingering of a large section of the peasantry in agriculture and related activities, in spite of low levels of agricultural incomes, is an indication of failure of growth in both agriculture and non-agriculture. The failure of agriculture lies in the low productivity of the sector, veritably tied to the diseconomies of scale in small

Table 11.12 *Inverse HHI of income diversification, by socio-economic classes*

Village	Landlord/big capitalist farmer/capitalist landlord	Other farmer	Small farmer	Manual worker	Non-farmer	All house-holds
Bukkacherla, AP	1.17	1.24	1.05	1.81	1.25	1.3
Zhapur, KA	1.38	1.28	1.44	1.36	1.55	1.4
Ananthavaram, AP	1.27	1.15	1.51	1.48	1.38	1.44
Kothapalle, AP	1.13	1	1.32	1.79	1.27	1.51
25F Gulabewala, RJ	1.27	1.15	2.7	1.62	1.61	1.51
Harevli, UP	1.26	1.21	1.67	1.69	1.54	1.56
Gharsondi, MP	1.23	1.36	1.48	1.78	1.73	1.57
Nimshirgaon, MH	1.44	1.85	1.55	1.51	1.75	1.6
Siresandra, KA		1.28	1.58	1.83	1.53	1.6
Warwat Khanderao, MH	1.64	1.37	1.58	1.76	1.52	1.61
Mahatwar, UP	1.96	1.99	1.88	1.56	1.46	1.69
Alabujanahalli, KA		1.49	1.47	1.99	1.95	1.69
Rewasi, RJ	1.85	1.71	1.62	1.97	1.58	1.71
Panahar, WB	1.57	0.23	1.91	1.75	1.2	1.76
Amarsinghi, WB	–	–	1.76	2.15	1.57	1.88
Kalmandasguri, WB	–	–	2.16	2.39	1.73	2.18
All villages	1.38	1.41	1.58	1.7	1.51	1.59

Note: The villages in the table are arranged in ascending order by column 7. There are three exceptions – the three dry villages of Bukkacherla, Mahatwar and Rewasi – where landlords and other farmers had more diverse portfolios due to the limitations of agriculture.

holder agriculture and the absence of state support. The failure of non-agriculture lies in the inability of this sector to absorb the surplus labour and provide adequate incomes and employment, which forces households to stay on in agriculture in the absence of any remunerative alternative. The result is not just chronic income deprivation, as we have observed in our analysis, but also uncertainty and poor conditions of employment. Households and workers have to rely on multiple sources of income within a year to make ends meet, and the income portfolio is so diversified that there is no specialization in any single source. Table 11.12 shows that the inverse HHI that measures income diversification shows highest diversification among small farmers and manual worker households. In our earlier work, we have argued and given evidence from the same village data that the reason why small farmer households do not exit farming in spite of its heavy reliance on non-agricultural incomes is the low wages and days of employment available in non-agricultural sector (Bakshi and Modak 2017).

Conclusions

In this chapter, I made three points on agricultural incomes based on empirical evidence from SAS 2013 and detailed villages surveys in sixteen villages conducted by the Foundation for Agrarian Studies (FAS) between 2006 and 2010.

First, incomes derived from agriculture and related activities, which included crop production, horticulture, allied activities and agricultural wages, were low for a large majority of households depending on such incomes. The incomes derived from such sources were inadequate to meet any poverty standard, be it the consumption-based poverty line or an income-based poverty line. In addition, the NSS-SAS data showed that there was a sizeable section of agricultural households who actually dissaved, that is, their incomes did not fulfil their consumption needs.

Secondly, this inadequacy of incomes was not a problem that equally affected all sections of the peasantry. There were also deep income inequalities within the peasantry, and a section of landlords and capitalist farmers had distinctly higher agricultural incomes than small peasants. The agricultural income crisis was most acutely a problem confronting the small peasantry. The roots of the problem lay in the crisis of small-scale farming in the context of declining state support and increasing exclusion from markets that do not favour the asset-poor.

Thirdly, it would be myopic to understand the problem within the bounds of agriculture, as there was a larger issue at stake: the issue of transition to non-agricultural incomes and livelihoods. Instead of exiting agriculture to find remunerative employment outside the sector, small farmers stay on in agriculture in spite of low incomes. This was due to the poor show of the non-agricultural sector that was not able to absorb the surplus labour from agriculture, and provide adequate incomes and employment to the rural population. Without resolving this larger problem of creating skill-appropriate employment that would enable farmers to exit farming, the problem of agricultural incomes cannot be resolved.

The union government's approach to doubling farmers' income seeks to overcome the problem of scale faced by the small farmers by measures like land-pooling by encouraging tenancy and contract farming, formation of farmer producer companies, and increased role of private sector in agricultural marketing (GoI 2018). Each of these measures eventually allows for concentration of land and production in the hands of larger farmers and private capital, with the intention of accelerating small and marginal farmers' exit from agriculture. If gainful employment is not created outside agriculture, such policy direction can only lead to further immiserisation of the small farmers.

Notes

[1] See Survey Method Toolbox at the FAS website, http://fas.org.in/survey-method-toolbox/, accessed 9 December 2020.

[2] Acronyms of states in which the villages are located are used in Tables 11.7 to 11.10. AP: Andhra Pradesh, UP: Uttar Pradesh, MH: Maharashtra, RJ: Rajasthan, MP: Madhya Pradesh, KA: Karnataka, WB: West Bengal.

[3] See Ramachandran (2011), for a discussion of the methodology used for identifying classes and characteristics of each of the classes.

[4] For further details on this classification, see Sivamurugan and Swaminathan (2017).

References

Bakshi, A. (2015), 'Nature of Income Diversification in Village India with Special Focus on Dalit Households', Project report for Indian Council for Social Science Research, New Delhi.

Bakshi, A. and T.S. Modak (2017), 'Incomes of Small Farmer Households', in M. Swaminathan and S. Baksi, eds, *How do Small Farmers Fare?: Evidence from Village Studies in India*, New Delhi: Tulika Books, pp. 126–70.

Bhalla, G.S. (2008), *Condition of the Indian Peasantry*, Delhi: National Book Trust.

Chand, R., S.K. Srivastava and J. Singh (2017), 'Changing Structure of Rural Economy of India: Implications for Employment and Growth', Discussion paper, NITI Aayog, New Delhi.

Chandrasekhar, S. and N. Mehrotra (2016), 'Doubling Farmers' Income by 2022: What Would It Take?', *Economic and Political Weekly*, vol. 51, no. 18, pp. 10–13.

Deokar, B.K. and S.L. Shetty (2014), 'Growth in Indian Agriculture: Responding to Policy Initiatives since 2004–05', *Economic and Political Weekly*, vol. 49, nos 26–27, pp. 101–04.

Government of India (GoI) (2018), *Report of the Committee on Doubling Farmers' Income*, vol. 14, Department of Agriculture, Cooperation and Farmers' Welfare, Ministry of Agriculture and Farmers' Welfare.

Mahendra Dev, S. and C.N. Rao (2010), 'Agricultural Price Policy, Farm Profitability and Food Security', *Economic and Political Weekly*, vol. 45, nos 26–27, pp. 174–82.

Planning Commission (2005), 'Mid-Term Appraisal of Tenth Five Year Plan (2002–2007)', Government of India, available at https://niti.gov.in/planningcommission.gov.in/docs/plans/mta/midterm/cont_eng1.htm, accessed 24 June 2022.

Ramachandran, V.K. (2011), 'The State of Agrarian Relations in India Today', *The Marxist*, vol. 27, nos 1–2, January–June, pp. 51–89.

Ramakumar, R. (2014), 'Economic Reforms and Agricultural Policy in India', Paper presented in Foundation for Agrarian Studies Tenth Anniversary Conference, Kochi, India, 9–12 January 2014.

Sivamurugan, T. and M. Swaminathan (2017), 'PARI Villages: An Introduction', in M. Swaminathan and S. Baksi, eds, *How do Small Farmers Fare?: Evidence from Village Studies in India*, New Delhi: Tulika Books, pp. 25–61.

V

Credit and Insurance

12

Trends in Agricultural Credit in India

An Account of Change and Continuity

Pallavi Chavan and R. Ramakumar

This chapter analyses the trends in agricultural credit in India with special reference to the period between 2011 and 2018. In earlier papers published in 2007 and 2014, we had discussed the slowdown in agricultural credit growth in the 1990s, followed by a striking revival in the 2000s (see Ramakumar and Chavan 2007, 2014). This revival, however, was marked by a disquieting pattern of distribution of agricultural credit. In this paper, we extend our analysis till 2018 and discuss the more recent features of agricultural credit growth in India. We underline features of both change and continuity in the distribution of agricultural credit.

Introduction

Agriculture has been an integral part of banking policy in India since the nationalization of banks in 1969. Prior to that, commercial banks had a peripheral role in providing banking services to rural areas. Agricultural credit was essentially the domain of credit cooperatives. However, as the demand for agricultural credit increased manifold with the onset of the green revolution, which could not be met by cooperatives exclusively, commercial banks were roped into agricultural credit provision in a major way. What began was the policy of 'social and development banking' aimed at enhancing the access of under-served economic sectors, including agriculture, to bank credit (Wiggins and Rajendran 1987). The adoption of social and development banking catapulted banks as the most important source of rural and agricultural credit, making agricultural credit in India almost synonymous with bank credit to agriculture (Misra, Chavan and Verma 2016).

The three major instruments of the policy of social and development banking were branch licensing policy, priority sector lending policy and interest rate policy. While the outcomes of each of these policies has had a bearing on agricultural credit given by banks, it is the priority sector lending policy that has influenced bank credit to agriculture the most. Agriculture enjoys a separate sub-target of 18 per cent within the total priority sector lending target of 40 per cent of (adjusted net) bank credit.

In our earlier papers in 2007 and 2014 cited earlier, we discussed trends in the growth of bank credit to agriculture and allied activities (referred to as 'agricultural credit') in the 1990s and 2000s – the phase of financial liberalization – in comparison with the 1970s and 1980s – the phase of social and development banking. We analysed these trends against the backdrop of the changes in the definition of agriculture within the priority sector lending policy. We also discussed changes in the rural bank branch network that resulted from changes in the branch licensing policy in the 1990s and 2000s and found that these changes in the number of rural branches were associated with changes in agricultural credit.

In this chapter, we extend the analysis till 2018 using data from the annual 'Basic Statistical Returns of Scheduled Commercial Banks in India' (BSR), published by the Reserve Bank of India (RBI). Our effort is to relate the trends in agricultural credit to the changes in banking policy in general, and priority sector lending policy in particular, in the decade of 2010s.[1]

The chapter is divided into five sections. The second section contains a brief review of the trends in the 1990s and 2000s drawing primarily from our earlier papers. This review provides a background to the discussion on the more recent trends. The third section contains an analysis of some of the changes in priority sector lending policy in agriculture in the 2010s. The fourth section discusses the recent trends in the growth and distribution of agricultural credit. The fifth section is a concluding section.

A Brief Review of Agricultural Credit in the 1990s and 2000s

In this section, we provide a summary of the major arguments discussed in our two past papers on agricultural credit in the 1990s and 2000s (see Ramakumar and Chavan 2007, 2014).

1. There was a perceptible slowdown in agricultural credit growth in the 1990s as compared to the earlier decades. Agricultural credit growth in the 1990s slowed down despite reasonable high growth in overall bank credit (see also Ramachandran and Swaminathan, eds 2005; Shetty 2006).

2. The growth in agricultural credit recovered significantly to double digits in the 2000s. The Comprehensive Credit Policy of 2004 – the policy of doubling of agricultural credit in three years – had a role to play in this revival.

3. The slowdown in the 1990s and the revival in the 2000s of agricultural credit growth was experienced in all the regions of India.

However, when credit growth slowed down in the 1990s, the under-banked North-Eastern and eastern regions bore a disproportionate brunt of the slowdown. When credit growth revived in the 2000s, the relatively well-banked southern region benefitted dispropor-tionately from the revival.

4. There was a close relationship between the slowdown and revival of agricultural credit growth and the fall and rise in the number of rural bank branches. The number of rural bank branches fell between 1995 and 2005, but this fall was more than compensated for by a rise in the number of rural bank branches after 2005. The fall in the number of rural bank branches in the 1990s was related to the withdrawal of the branch licensing policy; and the rise in the number of rural bank branches in the 2000s resulted mainly from a fresh thrust on opening rural bank branches under the policy of financial inclusion (see Ramakumar 2018).

5. Though agricultural credit revived in the 2000s, there were a num-ber of disquieting features with regard to its growth and distribu-tion. As a result, much of the additional credit flow in agriculture bypassed the small and marginal farmers of India. Five of these disquieting features are worth noting.

    (i) To begin with, agricultural credit given in the 2000s was increasingly *indirect* credit and not *direct* credit. Indirect credit is credit given to institutions and organizations that support agricultural production, while direct credit is credit given directly to farmers/producers in allied activities. The rise in indirect credit was striking in the northern and eastern regions of India. The RBI itself had pointed to the perils of favouring indirect credit over direct credit as being detrimental to food security and financial inclusion of farmers (RBI 2004).

    (ii) Secondly, a large proportion of the credit provided in the 2000s, including as *direct* credit, was in the form of large-sized loans whose recipients could not have been farmers. For example, the share of loans exceeding the credit limit of Rs 10 crore and Rs 25 crore in agricultural credit increased. One reason was the provision of more of large-sized indirect credit. However, even within direct credit, such a shift was discernible; there was a sharp fall in the share of small borrowal accounts with a credit limit of up to Rs 2 lakh.

    (iii) Thirdly, the share of agricultural credit, including *direct* credit, given by urban and metropolitan branches increased. This phenomenon was more prominent in Maharashtra (owing to Greater Mumbai district) and West Bengal (owing to Kolkata district). Both Greater Mumbai and Kolkata districts are entirely metropolitan and have little agricultural activity.

(iv) Fourthly, the largest share of agricultural credit in a year was disbursed in the month of March – the last month of the financial year – during which there is limited agricultural activity.

(v) Finally, agricultural credit was increasingly diverted away from long-term agricultural credit in favour of short-term agricultural credit. Although short-term credit is important for seasonal agricultural operations, long-term credit is also important as it supports capital formation in agriculture.

Most of these changes in agricultural credit were correlated with a series of changes in the definition of agriculture under the priority sector lending policy. The important definitional changes in agriculture in the 1990s and 2000s were:

(1) *Inclusion of indirect agricultural credit under priority sector*: Indirect agricultural credit was newly included under priority sector credit in 1993. Of course, there was a cap of 4.5 per cent on the share of indirect credit within the 18 per cent target for agriculture. However, the remaining part of indirect credit was eligible for inclusion under the total priority sector target of 40 per cent.

(2) *Addition of new forms of financing commercial, export-oriented, and capital-intensive agriculture*: In the 1990s and 2000s, a new and wide range of activities were included under agricultural credit. These activities included the credit given to food and agro-based processing units, agri-clinics and agri-business centres; cold storage units and warehouses in rural and non-rural centres; and traditional and non-traditional plantations irrespective of the landholding size of the borrower.

(3) *Rise in the credit limit for many existing forms of indirect credit*: A steep rise was effected in the credit limits for various forms of indirect agricultural credit, often defying the argument of inflation.

(4) *Inclusion of credit to corporate farmers under agricultural credit*: A portion of agricultural credit given to corporates, partnership firms and institutions engaged in direct agricultural production and production in allied activities, such as beekeeping, piggery, poultry, fisheries and dairy, (in short, credit to corporate farmers) was made eligible for inclusion under direct agricultural credit, while the rest of it was accounted for under indirect agricultural credit.

It is important to distinguish between credit to corporate farmers and corporate agricultural credit. The latter included credit given to corporates for various indirect agricultural activities, such as construction of warehouses or cold storages.

Concerns on the distribution of agricultural credit, like the ones discussed earlier, were noted by several official sources (GoI 2010, 2015).[2] For instance, the Task Force on Credit-related Issues of Farmers noted that more agricultural credit was flowing to institutions than farmers (GoI 2010). It also highlighted that large loans through urban and metropolitan branches were being 'booked as agricultural lending', and that there was widespread window-dressing by banks to meet targets for agricultural credit.

Changes in Agricultural Credit Policy, 2011 to 2018

In the 2010s, several changes in the priority sector lending policy in general, and those concerning agriculture in particular, were introduced as in the earlier decades. In this section, we focus only on the changes that may have had a direct bearing on what constitutes agricultural credit. In fact, some of these changes were specifically aimed at addressing the concerns related to the distribution of agricultural credit, which were discussed in the foregoing section. These changes were:

(1) *Reorganization of agricultural credit*: Instead of the conventional distinction between direct and indirect credit, agricultural credit was divided in 2016 into three new categories: farm credit, agricultural infrastructure and ancillary activities. The category of farm credit corresponded to the earlier category of direct agricultural credit. Indirect credit was largely bifurcated into credit for agricultural infrastructure (such as storage and warehouse construction) and ancillary activities (such as on-lending by commercial banks to other financial institutions). A fallout of this change was that the 4.5 per cent cap on indirect agricultural credit within the 18 per cent target for agriculture stood redundant; no new caps were introduced for the three newly introduced categories.

Yet, even after the trifurcation of agricultural credit in 2016, the RBI continued to publish data based on the two-way direct–indirect classification. As such, it appears that the new category of farm credit is reported as direct credit in the BSR.

(2) *Limiting the role of credit to corporate farmers*: The classification of credit to corporate farmers underwent three changes after 2007. First, from 2007 onwards, one-third of the credit to corporate farmers above Rs 1 crore in aggregate per borrower (in addition to all the credit of less than Rs 1 crore) was treated as direct credit. The rest (two-thirds of the credit to corporate farmers above Rs 1 crore in aggregate per borrower) was included under indirect agricultural credit. Secondly, from 2012 onwards, credit to corporate farmers up to Rs 2 crore in aggregate per borrower was included under direct credit; credit above Rs 2 crore was included under

indirect credit. Thirdly, from 2016 onwards, only the credit to corporate farmers of up to Rs 2 crore was included under the priority sectors; credit exceeding Rs 2 crore was no longer eligible for inclusion under priority sectors. Credit to corporate farmers of up to Rs 2 crore was included under farm credit (or direct credit).

Furthermore, to give priority to credit to farmers over corporate farmers, a new lending cap was introduced. Banks had to ensure that their credit to farmers (excluding credit to corporate farmers) did not fall below the past systemic average share of such credit. This past systemic average share was announced annually by the RBI. The idea behind this new cap was to ensure that, given the lack of a cap on indirect credit, credit to farmers received priority over credit to corporate farmers.

(3) *Introducing a new sub-target for small and marginal farmers*: From 2016, a new sub-target was introduced for small and marginal farmers.[3] Consequently, agricultural credit under priority sectors had two formal targets: 18 per cent for agriculture as a whole; and 8 per cent for small and marginal farmers (to be raised to 10 per cent by 2023–24). In addition, as discussed before, an informal target was to be announced by the RBI every year for credit to farmers (excluding corporate farmers). Theoretically, then, the difference (i.e. of 10 per cent) between the targets for total agricultural credit and credit to small and marginal farmers became the *maximum* share of credit to medium and large farmers, corporate farmers and all other types of indirect credit.[4]

(4) *Quarterly monitoring of targets*: In any policy involving financial or economic targets, a bunching is observed towards the end of the monitoring period. In order to reduce the 'March bunching' in the achievement of priority sector targets, the monitoring of these targets was made both quarterly *and* annually from 2016. The yearly shortfall in target achievement was based on an average of the positions for all the four quarters and not on the end-year position.

(5) *Enhancing the participation in priority sector lending*: To enhance the flow of credit to various priority sectors, new banking institutions were brought into its foray. Foreign banks, which originally followed a lower target and a differential composition of priority sectors, were brought on par with domestic banks. From 2018, all priority sector targets, including that of agriculture and small and marginal farmers, were made applicable to all foreign banks with twenty or more branches in a phased manner. Similarly, priority sector lending targets were made applicable to small finance banks (SFBs).[5]

(6) *Trading of priority sector lending portfolio*: In 2016, priority sec-

tor lending certificates (PSLCs) were introduced.[6] The PSLCs were introduced to enable the under-achieving banks to meet their lending targets by purchasing from the over-achieving banks the right to under-shoot these targets. It also aimed to incentivize the over-achieving banks to specialize in lending to specific types of priority sectors depending on their comparative advantage (RBI 2015, 2016).

The inter-bank trading of these certificates did not involve any transfer of the underlying credit risk.[7] On each reporting date, the achievement for a bank was worked out as the sum of own-out-standing priority sector credit and the net nominal value of PSLCs issued and purchased.

The PSLCs were purely meant for meeting priority sector targets during a given year and were valid only up to March.[8] The nominal value of the portfolio traded was deducted from the seller and added to the portfolio of the buyer towards the achievement of the priority sector lending target. However, their trading premiums (fees paid by the buyer to the seller) were entirely market-driven depending on the extent of demand and supply for a given type of certificate. Four PSLCs were designed towards meeting four types of priority sector lending targets: overall priority sector credit, agricultural credit, credit to small and marginal farmers, and credit to micro-enterprises.[9]

7. *Achievement of priority sector targets weighted by region*: In order to address the regional disparities in priority sector credit, a higher weight (of 125 per cent) was assigned to the incremental credit flow in districts identified as having lower allocation of priority sector credit and a lower weight (of 90 per cent) was assigned to the incremental credit flow in districts identified as having higher allocation of priority sector credit.[10] Banks' achievement of targets will be decided based on the weighted volume of priority sector credit from 2022 onwards.

While a few of these policy changes are yet to come into play, most others have been implemented. Did these changes in the 2010s address the disquieting features in the distribution of agricultural credit? In the next section, we attempt to examine this question.

Features of Growth in Agricultural Credit, 2011–18
Moderation in Agricultural Credit Growth
First, if agricultural credit grew rapidly between 2001 and 2011, there was a moderation in its growth between 2011 and 2018. The annual growth of real agricultural credit was 9.6 per cent between 2011 and 2018 as compared to 17.8 per cent between 2001 and 2011 (Table 12.1).

Secondly, within agricultural credit, while there was a slowdown of growth in direct and indirect agricultural credit, it was certainly more pronounced for indirect credit. Indirect credit posted a negative growth rate between 2011 and 2018. This too was in contrast to the period between 2001 and 2011, when the major driver of the revival in agricultural credit growth was indirect credit.

Thirdly, due to the high growth in agricultural credit between 2001 and 2011, there was a spurt in the ratio of agricultural credit to agricultural GDP (gross domestic product). However, between 2011 and 2018, while the ratio continued to inch up, its rate of increase was slower than between 2001 and 2011 (see Figure 12.1).

Fourthly, the moderation in agricultural credit growth in the 2010s was experienced across all geographical regions (Table 12.2). However, it was most pronounced in the southern region and most modest in the north-eastern region. Between 2011 and 2018, the annual growth in agricultural credit in the North-Eastern region was 16 per cent as compared to only about 6 per cent in the southern region. Historically, the southern region has been a well-banked region and the North East has been an under-banked region (Misra, Chavan and Verma 2016).

Fifthly, an important factor associated with the increase in the growth of agricultural credit in the under-banked regions was the growth

Table 12.1 *Rate of growth of credit to agriculture, total bank credit and agricultural GDP, at constant prices, India, 1972 to 2018*, in per cent per annum

Period	Annual growth rates of				
	Credit to agriculture	Direct agricultural credit	Indirect agricultural credit	Total bank credit	Agricultural GDP
1972–81	16.1	11.3	16.4	8.4	2.3
1981–91	6.8	8.7	0.1	8.0	3.5
1991–2001	2.6	2.4	4.0	7.3	2.8
2001–11	17.8	17.6	19.2	15.7	3.3
(1) 2001–04	18.7	13.2	41.4	13.7	2.1
(2) 2004–07	26.7	27.7	24.1	23.5	4.6
(3) 2007–11	11.0	13.7	1.7	12.2	3.8
2011–18	9.6	11.2	–0.7	6.7	2.8*

Note: * Based on 2011–12 NAS (National Account Statistics) series. The decade of 2001–11 is divided into three sub-periods to highlight the growth trends between 2004 and 2007 – the period of implementation of the Comprehensive Credit Policy.
Source: 'Basic Statistical Returns of Scheduled Commercial Banks in India', RBI, various issues; 'National Accounts Statistics', Central Statistics Office (CSO), various issues.

Figure 12.1 *Agricultural credit to agricultural GDP ratio, India, 1971–72 to 2017–18*, in per cent

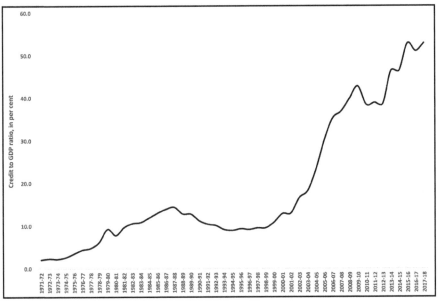

Source: 'Basic Statistical Returns of Scheduled Commercial Banks in India,' RBI, various issues; and 'National Accounts Statistics', Central Statistics Office (CSO), various issues.

in the number of rural bank branches. After 2005, there was a significant expansion in rural bank branches across India (Ramakumar and Chavan, 2011). However, the spurt was particularly striking after 2011 with an annual mandate for banks to open at least 25 per cent of their new branches in unbanked rural centres. As Table 12.3 shows, rural branches contributed 39 per cent to the increase in the number of branches between 2011 and 2016; the corresponding share between 2006 and 2011 was only 13 per cent. Further, this share was significantly higher in the relatively underbanked regions, which helped narrow the regional gap in rural branch network to a noticeable extent.

Decline in the Share of Indirect Agricultural Credit

As Table 12.1 shows, the moderation in growth rate of total agricultural credit after 2011 was primarily due to the negative growth rate of indirect agricultural credit. Consequently, the share of indirect credit in total agricultural credit fell to single digits in the 2010s as against its steep rise in the 2000s (Table 12.4).[11] What prompted this fall in the share of indirect credit, and could it be interpreted as an increased allocation of credit to farmers?

Unfortunately, we do not have a break-up of indirect agricultural

Table 12.2 *Rate of growth of deflated agricultural credit by state, 1991–2017*, in per cent per annum

Region/State	1991–2001	2001–11	2011–17
Northern region	3.8	18.3	7.8
Haryana	−0.2	18.3	9.1
Himachal Pradesh	−1.8	22.1	10.8
Jammu and Kashmir	−3.3	16.3	19.6
Punjab	2.1	15.8	12.0
Rajasthan	5.7	16.7	11.5
NCT of Delhi	16.2	22.8	−4.2
North-Eastern region	−5.9	18.5	16.0
Arunachal Pradesh	−0.3	11.3	6.3
Assam	−6.9	19.1	17.5
Manipur	0.1	20.8	4.5
Meghalaya	−7.6	15.9	18.7
Nagaland	−9.6	15.3	16.9
Tripura	−0.2	16.1	−
Eastern region	−1.2	13.7	8.6
Bihar	−4.1	12.3	9.9
Odisha	0.1	17.9	4.8
West Bengal	1.4	20.7	−
Central region	0.7	12.2	9.3
Madhya Pradesh	1.7	11.4	1.9
Uttar Pradesh	0.01	12.8	10.7
Western region	3.4	16.4	11.9
Goa	−7.3	14.9	2.9
Gujarat	2.9	16.6	12.1
Maharashtra	3.9	16.4	11.9
Southern region	2.0	18.5	6.3
Andhra Pradesh	1.8	18.4	0.5
Karnataka	3.7	14.6	10.2
Kerala	2.8	19.3	8.1
Tamil Nadu	0.3	21.7	8.3
India	2.4	17.8	9.6

Note: Growth rates are worked out after deflating the credit figures using the state domestic product figures. Figures for Andhra Pradesh, Madhya Pradesh, Bihar and Uttar Pradesh include those for Telangana, Chhattisgarh, Jharkhand and Uttarakhand, respectively, maintaining comparability.
– : Cannot be estimated due to non-availability of state domestic product figures for 2017.
Source: 'Basic Statistical Returns of Scheduled Commercial Banks in India,' RBI, various issues and 'Handbook of Statistics on Indian Economy', various issues.

Table 12.3 *Contribution of various types of branches to the change in the total number of branches, by region/state, 2006–16,* in per cent

Region/State	Contribution to the change in total number of branches during 2006–11					Contribution to the change in total number of branches during 2011–16				
	Rural	Semi-urban	Urban	Metro	Total	Rural	Semi-urban	Urban	Metro	Total
Northern region	14	31	26	28	*100*	*44*	*26*	*16*	*15*	*100*
Haryana	18	33	43	6	100	45	23	26	5	100
Himachal Pradesh	41	48	11	0	100	76	21	3	0	100
Jammu & Kashmir	18	41	41	0	100	52	25	23	0	100
Punjab	18	46	21	14	100	53	29	11	7	100
Rajasthan	12	37	33	17	100	43	35	15	8	100
NCT of Delhi	1	0	0	98	100	5	4	0	91	100
North-Eastern Region	10	45	45	0	*100*	*36*	*40*	*23*	*0*	*100*
Arunachal Pradesh	0	100	0	0	100	37	63	0	0	100
Assam	7	46	47	0	100	37	38	26	0	100
Manipur	−20	20	100	0	100	46	37	16	0	100
Meghalaya	9	38	53	0	100	28	36	37	0	100
Mizoram	−15	15	100	0	100	16	39	45	0	100
Nagaland	14	86	0	0	100	20	80	0	0	100
Tripura	35	25	40	0	100	48	35	17	0	100
Eastern Region	17	37	36	11	*100*	*42*	*30*	*19*	*9*	*100*
Bihar	12	42	32	14	100	45	33	13	9	100
Jharkhand	14	44	41	0	100	50	34	16	0	100
Odisha	19	46	35	0	100	47	33	21	0	100
Sikkim	58	42	0	0	100	80	20	0	0	100
West Bengal	18	22	37	23	100	38	25	24	14	100
Central Region	15	33	34	18	*100*	*45*	*28*	*17*	*10*	*100*
Chhattisgarh	12	37	51	0	100	41	33	25	0	100
Madhya Pradesh	1	40	36	23	100	31	37	15	16	100
Uttar Pradesh	19	28	32	21	100	51	23	15	11	100
Uttarakhand	22	46	32	0	100	46	32	21	0	100
Western Region	11	28	19	41	*100*	*36*	*29*	*12*	*23*	*100*
Goa	31	69	0	0	100	48	52	0	0	100
Gujarat	16	30	16	37	100	43	27	9	21	100
Maharashtra	7	23	23	47	100	30	28	15	27	100
Southern Region	10	38	30	22	*100*	*31*	*38*	*14*	*17*	*100*
Andhra Pradesh	15	26	38	21	100	35	31	9	24	100

Table 12.3 *(continued)*

Region/State	Contribution to the change in total number of branches during 2006–11					Contribution to the change in total number of branches during 2011–16				
	Rural	Semi-urban	Urban	Metro	Total	Rural	Semi-urban	Urban	Metro	Total
Karnataka	8	24	25	44	100	40	26	17	18	100
Kerala	0	66	33	0	100	0	77	23	0	100
Tamil Nadu	10	47	24	19	100	35	38	12	16	100
India	*13*	*34*	*30*	*24*	*100*	*39*	*31*	*16*	*14*	*100*

Note: The selection of the periods used in the table is based on the definitions of various types of branches in the BSR. After 2006, BSR classification of branches was based on Census of India 2001 and later on the 2011 census from 2017 onwards. The choice of 2011 as the dividing year was because in this year, the RBI introduced the mandate for banks to open at least 25 per cent of their branches in unbanked rural centres. Data for Telangana are included in the figures of Andhra Pradesh to maintain comparability.

Source: 'Basic Statistical Returns of Scheduled Commercial Banks in India', RBI, various issues.

credit to identify which of its components were responsible for the fall in its share. However, one factor associated with the fall could have been the change in the classifications of credit to corporate farmers (see the detailed explanation in the third section of the chapter – Changes in Agricultural Credit Policy – on the three changes in this category).

The inclusion of credit to corporate farmers partly as direct agricultural credit (all loans up to Rs 1 crore and one-third of the loans above Rs 1 crore) and partly as indirect agricultural credit (two-thirds of the loans above Rs 1 crore) from 2007 distinctly changed the relative shares of these two categories. The share of direct agricultural credit began to rise thereafter. From 2012, when all such loans of up to Rs 2 crore were included under direct credit, the share of direct credit increased further. Finally, from 2016, credit to corporate farmers of only up to Rs 2 crore was included under direct credit, and the remainder was no longer included under indirect credit or under the priority sector as a whole. This change in guidelines precipitated a continued rise in the share of direct credit and the fall in the share of indirect credit. In other words, a fall in the share of indirect credit need not be interpreted as an increased allocation of credit to farmers. Farmers continued to face stiff competition from the corporates for agricultural credit.

Concentration of Agricultural Credit in Large Loan Sizes

Like between 2001 and 2011, there was a concentration of agricultural credit in large loan sizes between 2011 and 2018 also. As noted

Table 12.4 *Shares of direct and indirect agricultural credit to total agricultural credit, India, 1985 to 2018,* in per cent

Year	Share in total agricultural credit (%)		
	Direct credit	Indirect credit	Total
1985	83.2	16.8	100.0
1990	86.8	13.2	100.0
2000	84.5	15.5	100.0
2005	76.1	23.9	100.0
2006	72.1	27.9	100.0
2007	74.5	25.5	100.0
2008	77.5	22.5	100.0
2009	77.1	22.9	100.0
2010	76.1	23.9	100.0
2011	82.0	18.0	100.0
2012	83.4	16.6	100.0
2013	86.0	14.0	100.0
2014	84.3	15.7	100.0
2015	87.7	12.3	100.0
2016	89.8	10.2	100.0
2017	91.4	8.6	100.0
2018	91.0	9.0	100.0

Source: 'Basic Statistical Returns of Scheduled Commercial Banks in India', RBI, various issues.

in Ramakumar and Chavan (2007, 2014), the shift of agricultural credit towards large-sized loans between 2001 and 2011 was primarily associated with the growth in indirect agricultural credit of various types. However, indirect agricultural credit posted a negative growth rate between 2011 and 2018. As a result, there was a fall in the share of large-sized agricultural loans too, such as in loans with a credit limit of Rs 10 crore and above. Between 2011 and 2018, the share of loans with a credit limit of Rs 10 crore and above in total agricultural credit fell from 19.5 per cent to about 9 per cent (Table 12.5).

At the same time, this decline did not alter the fact that agricultural credit continued to display a concentration in large loan sizes. In 2018, about 24 per cent of total agricultural credit consisted of loans with a credit limit of over Rs 10 lakh, and 60.5 per cent of total agricultural credit consisted of loans with a credit limit of over Rs 2 lakh.

Similar was the case with direct agricultural credit (Table 12.6). At

Table 12.5 *Distribution of amount outstanding under total agricultural credit by scheduled commercial banks, by credit limit size classes of loans, 1990 to 2018, in per cent*

Credit limit size class of loans (Rs)	Share of amount outstanding in total amount outstanding (%)					
	1990	2000	2005	2011	2015	2018
Up to 2 lakh	82.6	67.6	51.9	41.4	42.6	39.5
2 lakh to 10 lakh	4.3	11.7	17.9	24.6	34.0	36.4
10 lakh to 10 crore	11.8	13.3	14.4	14.6	14.5	15.5
10 lakh to 1 crore	7.6	6.6	6.4	7.4	9.4	10.7
1 crore to 10 crore	4.2	6.7	8.0	7.2	5.1	4.8
10 crore and above	1.3	7.4	15.9	19.5	8.9	8.7
10 crore to 25 crore	1.3	1.7	3.3	3.0	1.5	1.4
Above 25 crore		5.7	12.6	16.5	7.4	7.3
Total credit	100.0	100.0	100.0	100.0	100.0	100.0

Source: 'Basic Statistical Returns of Scheduled Commercial Banks in India', RBI, various issues.

one end, only 40 per cent of direct agricultural credit in 2018 consisted of loans with a credit limit of less than Rs 2 lakh. It is highly unlikely that a small or marginal farmer in India would borrow more than Rs 2 lakh a year for agricultural activities.[12] At the other end, about 22 per cent of direct agricultural credit consisted of loans with a credit limit of more than Rs 10 lakh. Even after capping the credit to corporate farmers at Rs 2 crore, loans exceeding Rs 10 crore, and even Rs 25 crore, still found a place as part of direct agricultural credit. In between these two ends of the spectrum, there was a rise also in the share of loans with credit limits between Rs 2 lakh and Rs 10 lakh. A major reason for this increase could have been the interest subvention offered on direct credit up to Rs 3 lakh.[13]

In the foregoing discussion, following the definition in RBI (2019), we considered Rs 2 lakh as the maximum potential loan size for small and marginal farmers. Admittedly, any analysis using credit limits (unadjusted for inflation) as a benchmark may be problematic, as a farmer may need higher amount of credit due to the rise in input costs. However, it is not possible to adjust for inflation while comparing loan sizes reported in the BSR.

An alternative may be to analyse the share of actual credit given by banks to small and marginal farmers with landholdings up to 2 hectares. The share of small and marginal farmers in total and direct agricultural credits showed an unmistakable decline over the 1990s which stagnated in the 2000s. However, over the 2010s, there was a rising, although somewhat

Table 12.6 *Distribution of amount outstanding under direct agricultural credit by scheduled commercial banks, by credit limit size classes of loans, 1990 to 2018,* in per cent

Credit limit size class of loans (Rs)	Share of amount outstanding in total amount outstanding (%)					
	1990	2000	2005	2011	2015	2018
Up to 2 lakh	92.0	78.5	66.7	48.0	46.3	40.0
2 lakh to 10 lakh	3.6	12.8	21.4	28.3	37.3	37.3
10 lakh to 10 crore	3.8	7.0	8.6	12.8	12.2	16.8
10 lakh to 1 crore	2.6	3.9	4.5	7.1	9.1	13.6
1 crore to 10 crore	1.2	3.1	4.1	5.7	3.1	3.2
10 crore and above	0.3	1.6	3.4	10.9	4.2	5.2
10 crore to 25 crore	0.3	0.4	1.4	2.4	0.9	0.9
Above 25 crore		1.2	2.0	8.5	3.3	4.3
Total direct credit	100.0	100.0	100.0	100.0	100.0	100.0

Source: 'Basic Statistical Returns of Scheduled Commercial Banks in India', RBI, various issues.

chequered, trend in their share (Figure 12.2). Yet, even in 2018, only 45 per cent and 58 per cent of the total and direct agricultural credits, respectively, was reported as credit to small and marginal farmers. If we compare these shares with the share of loans having a credit limit of up to Rs 2 lakh (in tables 12.5 and 12.6), it emerges that small and marginal farmers still continue to be closely represented by the loan size of Rs 2 lakh.

Further, while the increase in the share of small and marginal farmers in agricultural credit was a positive development, we would add a few qualifications too. First, although the banking system as a whole was able to meet the sub-target for small and marginal farmers, there was under-achievement at the level of individual banks. This was important because priority sector achievements are measured at the bank level and not at the systemic level. In 2019, public sector banks as a group reported an average overachievement of (+)0.8 percentage points on the sub-target of 8 per cent for small and marginal farmers. However, private sector banks as a group reported an average shortfall of about (–)1.1 percentage points (Table 12.7). Although bank-level achievements of the sub-target are not known, under-achievers are bound to be in the group if the average achievement is lower than the target or very close to the target for a given bank group. The underachievement persisted even after the introduction of PSLCs in 2016.[14]

Secondly, even in 2015, only 49 per cent of the small and marginal farmers in the country were covered by direct agricultural credit (Table 12.8).

Figure 12.2 *Share of small and marginal farmers in total and direct agricultural credit, 1994–2018*, in per cent

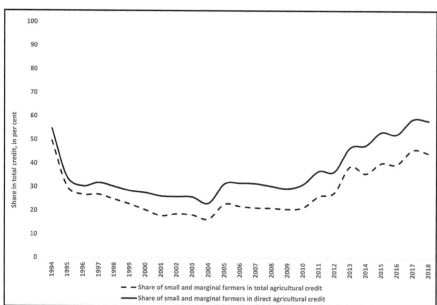

Note: Data from 2017 onwards also include credit given by small finance banks.
Source: Calculated taking data from Database on Indian Economy (DBIE), RBI; RBI (2019); 'Statistical Tables Relating to Banks in India', RBI various issues.

For this, we considered the number of direct agricultural loan accounts with a credit limit of up to Rs 2 lakh from the BSR and compared it with the number of small and marginal landholdings as reported in the Agricultural Census, 2015–16. The national coverage of 49 per cent may be misleading, as there were marked variations across states. Chhattisgarh, Jammu and Kashmir, West Bengal and Bihar covered less than 25 per cent of their small and marginal farmers through bank credit. Among the major states, only Punjab and Tamil Nadu reported more than 100 per cent coverage of small and marginal farmers.[15] In other words, the coverage of small and marginal farmers with bank credit remained poor in large parts of the country.

Concentration of Agricultural Credit in Urban/Metropolitan Centres

As between 2001 and 2011, significant proportion of agricultural credit was provided from urban and metropolitan bank branches between 2011 and 2018 also. Even in 2018, about 25 per cent of the total agricultural credit and about 23 per cent of direct agricultural credit was outstanding in urban and metropolitan branches (Table 12.9).

If we compare the figures presented in Tables 12.5, 12.6 and 12.9,

Table **12.7** *Achievement of priority sector targets, by bank groups, 2017–19*, in percentage points

Bank group	Agricultural target	Target for small and marginal farmers	Target for individual farmers (excluding corporates/corporate farmers)
2017			
Public sector banks	0.3	0.7	0.8
	(48)	–	–
Private sector banks	–1.5	–2.5	–1.2
	(32)	–	–
Foreign banks*	–8.4	–	–
	(100)	–	–
2018			
Public sector banks	0.0	0.9	1.1
	(24)	–	–
Private sector banks	–1.8	–2.0	–0.9
	(38)	–	–
Foreign banks*	–1.3	–2.8	–5.1
	(67)	–	–
2019			
Public sector banks	0.1	0.8	0.6
	(45)	–	–
Private sector banks	–1.7	–1.1	–0.9
	(32)	–	–
Foreign banks*	2.1	1.0	–1.4
	(0)	–	–

Notes: – signifies underachievement, + signifies overachievement from target, * relates to foreign banks with twenty branches or more. Figures in brackets indicate percentage of banks failing to meet the target in each group. Figures on bank-level achievements are only available for the agricultural target.
Source: 'Report on Trend and Progress of Banking in India', various issues; 'Statistical Tables relating to Banks in India', various issues.

the whole of large-sized direct agricultural credit could be attributed to credit provided from urban and metropolitan bank branches. In other words, there was a division of direct agricultural credit into two parts: one, small-sized loans taken by the peasantry (approximately 40 per cent); and two, large-sized loans taken by corporate farmers (approximately 60 per cent).

At the regional level, the dominance of urban and metropolitan branches was visible in the western, southern and eastern regions, as already noted in Ramakumar and Chavan (2014). Within these regions, the

Table 12.8 *Coverage of small and marginal farmers by direct agricultural credit, by state, 2015*, in per cent

State	Small and marginal farmers covered by direct agricultural credit (per cent)	Amount of direct agricultural credit per hectare (Rs thousand)
Nagaland	311	25
Punjab	243	110
Tamil Nadu	119	236
Andhra Pradesh	83	102
Telangana	60	56
Karnataka	58	52
Uttar Pradesh	56	128
Kerala	55	680
Haryana	54	80
Mizoram	52	32
Goa	49	125
Jharkhand	47	40
Gujarat	47	26
Meghalaya	47	26
Rajasthan	46	44
Madhya Pradesh	43	37
Arunachal Pradesh	43	14
Assam	41	34
Odisha	39	39
Tripura	35	45
Manipur	34	20
Maharashtra	33	24
Uttarakhand	31	51
Himachal Pradesh	25	41
Bihar	23	95
West Bengal	21	30
Jammu and Kashmir	15	42
Chhattisgarh	12	11
India	49	64

Note: Direct loan accounts for small and marginal farmers are taken as small borrowal accounts (credit limit of up to Rs 2 lakh), following the suggested definition in RBI (2019). States arranged in a descending order of their coverage of small and marginal farmers.
Source: 'Basic Statistical Returns of Scheduled Commercial Banks in India', RBI; Agricultural Census of India, 2015–16.

Table 12.9 *Share of agricultural credit outstanding, by population groups, by direct and indirect credit, India, 1995 to 2018,* in per cent

Year	Share of agricultural credit outstanding from branches in (%)				
	Rural	Semi-urban	Urban	Metropolitan	Total
Total agricultural credit					
1995	51.7	29.3	9.5	9.5	100.0
2005	43.0	26.4	11.7	19.0	100.0
2006	37.1	25.3	13.8	23.8	100.0
2011	37.9	29.0	18.4	14.7	100.0
2016	41.7	34.3	15.1	8.8	100.0
2018	39.2	36.0	15.2	9.7	100.0
Direct credit					
1995	56.5	31.2	8.2	4.0	100.0
2005	52.9	31.4	10.0	5.7	100.0
2006	48.0	32.0	12.6	7.5	100.0
2011	43.2	31.2	16.5	9.1	100.0
2016	44.5	35.8	14.0	5.6	100.0
2018	41.5	35.8	14.8	7.9	100.0
Indirect credit					
1995	23.9	18.5	16.8	40.8	100.0
2005	11.4	10.2	17.2	61.2	100.0
2006	9.1	7.8	17.0	66.0	100.0
2011	13.6	19.0	27.1	40.2	100.0
2016	16.3	22.0	24.6	37.2	100.0
2018	7.1	38.7	19.9	34.3	100.0

Note: As regards periodization in this table from 2006 onwards, see notes under Table 12.3. Branches for the years prior 2006 shown in the table were classified using the Census of India of 1991.
Source: 'Basic Statistical Returns of Scheduled Commercial Banks in India', RBI, various issues.

three states responsible for pulling up the shares of urban and metropolitan branches in total agricultural credit were Maharashtra, Tamil Nadu and West Bengal (see tables 12.10 and 12.11). In 2018, about 39 per cent of the total agricultural credit and 35 per cent of direct agricultural credit in West Bengal was outstanding in urban and metropolitan branches. The corresponding shares were, respectively, 32 per cent and 27 per cent in Maharashtra and 25.5 per cent and 24 per cent in Tamil Nadu. Telangana was a new addi-

Table 12.10 *Share of bank branches located in urban and metropolitan centres in outstanding direct credit to agriculture, by regions, India, 1991 to 2018*, in per cent

Year	Share of urban/metropolitan branches in outstanding direct credit, by regions (%)					
	Northern	North-Eastern	Eastern	Central	Western	Southern
1991	11.4	14.1	10.4	9.2	12.9	12.2
1994	11.7	11.3	8.0	8.7	12.7	11.8
1995	13.1	8.8	8.9	8.4	11.8	12.6
2005	12.8	13.4	18.4	9.4	29.7	15.7
2006	19.7	16.0	18.6	11.8	37.1	19.0
2011	25.8	12.5	30.3	17.0	34.5	25.9
2016	19.1	13.3	20.5	13.0	26.8	21.9
2018	21.7	15.2	22.0	20.1	25.4	24.6

Note: On the periodization in this table, see notes in tables 12.3 and 12.9.
Source: 'Basic Statistical Returns of Scheduled Commercial Banks in India', RBI, various issues.

tion to this category of states in 2018; its percentages were 36 per cent and 34.8 per cent, respectively. In 2018, the largely metropolitan district of Kolkata accounted for about 19 per cent of all direct agricultural credit in West Bengal. Similarly, the metropolitan district of Hyderabad accounted for about 24 per cent of all direct agricultural credit in Telangana (Table 12.11).

Concentration of Agricultural Credit in the March Quarter
The intra-year concentration of agricultural credit in the March quarter also continued in the 2010s as in the 2000s. Even though priority sector target monitoring was made quarterly and annual, the largest quarter-to-quarter intra-year rise in the net amount outstanding of agricultural credit continued to be in the March quarter (Figure 12.3).[16]

The June quarter marks the beginning of the agricultural season in India when farmers renew their agricultural credit lines with banks. Yet, as Figure 12.3 shows, the June quarter showed a negative or near-zero net outstanding change in total agricultural credit in most years. Net outstanding credit increased gradually through the September and December quarters and increased significantly in the March quarter.

In India, a large part of agricultural credit is short-term and administered through Kisan Credit Cards (KCCs). A KCC limit is fixed by the bank for a five-year period including a short-term limit for working capital and a long-term limit for term loans towards capital investment.[17] Any

Table 12.11 *Share of bank branches located in urban and metropolitan centres in credit to agriculture, West Bengal, Maharashtra, Tamil Nadu and Telangana, 2011 and 2018*, in per cent

State/Item	Year	Share of agricultural credit outstanding in branches (%)				
		Rural	Semi-urban	Urban	Metropolitan	Total
West Bengal						
Agricultural credit	2011	31.3	13.1	11.8	43.7	100.0
	2018	42.8	18.3	18.0	20.9 (20.5)	100.0
Direct credit	2011	35.1	14.1	10.4	40.5	100.0
	2018	46.7	18.2	15.5	19.6 (19.3)	100.0
Indirect credit	2011	22.0	10.4	15.5	52.0	100.0
	2018	21.2	18.7	32.0	28.2 (27.3)	100.0
Maharashtra						
Agricultural credit	2011	30.9	21.7	11.6	35.8	100.0
	2018	28.5	39.2	13.6	18.7 (9.7)	100.0
Direct credit	2011	34.3	25.0	11.2	29.4	100.0
	2018	31.2	41.6	14.1	13.1 (5.1)	100.0
Indirect credit	2011	21.0	12.1	12.9	54.0	100.0
	2018	8.2	20.4	9.8	61.6 (45.9)	100.0
Tamil Nadu						
Agricultural credit	2011	32.7	33.9	16.8	16.6	100.0
	2018	32.9	41.5	16.9	8.6 (4.3)	100.0
Direct credit	2011	35.3	38.7	18.6	7.4	100.0
	2018	32.8	43.2	17.4	6.6 (2.4)	100.0
Indirect credit	2011	23.0	15.8	10.2	51.0	100.0
	2018	34.3	21.5	11.0	33.2 (27.9)	100.0
Telangana						
Agricultural credit	2018	40.2	23.7	7.7	28.4 (25.6)	100.0
Direct credit	2018	41.6	23.6	7.9	26.9 (24.3)	100.0
Indirect credit	2018	32.1	24.2	6.7	37.0 (32.8)	100.0

Note: Figures in brackets under West Bengal, Maharashtra, Tamil Nadu and Telangana relate to the shares of Kolkata, Greater Mumbai, Chennai and Hyderabad in the total, direct and indirect agricultural credit of the respective states. These are districts with almost all metropolitan centres/branches. In 2018, all branches in Greater Mumbai and Kolkata, and 99 per cent of the branches in Chennai and Hyderabad were metropolitan. Telangana was formed in 2014, and hence, data for 2011 for the state are not reported here.
Source: 'Basic Statistical Returns of Scheduled Commercial Banks in India', RBI, various issues.

Figure 12.3 *Net outstanding of total agricultural credit, by quarters, September 2007–March 2020,* in Rs crore

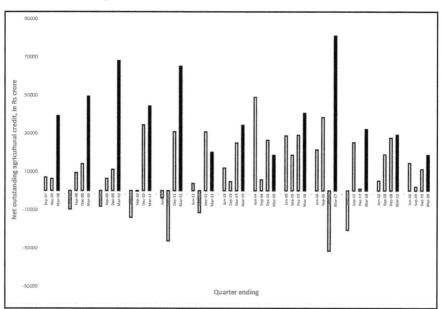

Note: Bar for the March quarter is shaded black.
Source: Sectoral Deployment of Bank Credit, DBIE, RBI.

withdrawal during the year against the short-term limit is payable including the interest payment within a year's time. Even if we assume that a large part of the repayment of the short-term credit happened in the June quarter, leading to a negative net outstanding in this quarter, the high positive net outstanding during the March quarter would still be perplexing. The sanction of new credit on such a large scale is unlikely to happen during a quarter that witnesses little or no agricultural activity.

Earlier, one of the factors identified for the concentration of agricultural credit in March was the rise in indirect agricultural credit (GoI 2010). However, indirect agricultural credit fell in absolute terms between 2011 and 2018. Nevertheless, the concentration of agricultural credit in the March quarter has continued.

Shift Away from Long-term Agricultural Credit

Between 2011 and 2018, there was a decline in the share of long-term direct agricultural credit in total agricultural credit (Figure 12.4). This too was a continuation of the trends between 2001 and 2011. Long-term agricultural credit includes credit given to cultivators or producers for minor irrigation, reclamation and land development, purchase of tractors and agricultural machinery, plantations, crop loans converted into term

Figure 12.4 *Share of short-term credit and long-term credit in direct agricultural credit, commercial banks, India, 1973–74 to 2015–16,* in per cent

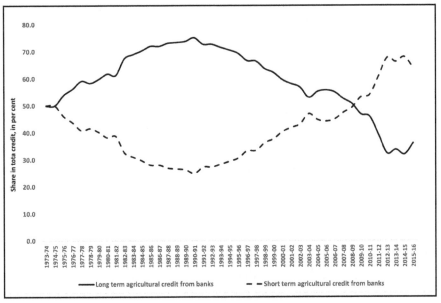

Note: The series terminate in 2015–16 due to non-availability of more recent data.
Source: 'Handbook of Statistics on Indian Economy', RBI, various issues.

loans, and all loans given to allied activities like dairy, fishing, poultry and beekeeping.

Historically, there has been a strong correlation between long-term credit flow and capital formation in agriculture (see Chavan 2013). Thus, long-term credit flow is critical in increasing agricultural growth.

The proliferation of KCCs may be one reason for the sharp rise in the share of short-term credit in total credit. Banks may classify the entire KCC loan as a short-term loan without accounting for the long-term loan component separately. This, surely, leads to an underestimation of long-term credit. However, this qualification should not be overstated. First, the decline in the share of long-term credit had set in from the beginning of the 1990s itself, much before the introduction of KCCs in 1998.[18] Secondly, a major concern with KCCs has been the wide gap between the number of cards issued and number of cards actually used by farmers. In particular, commercial banks have had a very low percentage of KCCs in use.[19] Hence, there may not be an obvious link between the declining share of long-term credit and the use of KCCs.

Concluding Observations

In this chapter, we analysed the pattern of agricultural credit growth and distribution between 2011 and 2018 and brought out the features of change and continuity as compared to the 1990s and 2000s. The important feature of change was of the moderation in agricultural credit growth between 2011 and 2018 as compared to its high growth in the 2000s. This moderation between 2011 and 2018 stemmed primarily from a negative rate of growth in indirect agricultural credit. This change was important because it was indirect agricultural credit that was the basis for the sharp increase in the growth of total agricultural credit in the 2000s. Regardless of this change, there were several continuities in the distribution of agricultural credit.

First, the share of relatively large-sized agricultural loans remained unacceptably high. In 2018, loans with credit limits exceeding Rs 10 lakh constituted about 25 per cent of total agricultural credit; and loans with credit limit exceeding Rs 25 crore constituted about 7 per cent. Even within direct agricultural credit, the problem of dominance of large-sized loans remained stark. In 2018, only 40 per cent of the direct agricultural credit had a credit limit of up to Rs 2 lakh.

Secondly, a large proportion of total agricultural credit, and even direct agricultural credit, continued to be provided through urban and metropolitan branches. In 2018, these branches accounted for about 25 per cent of total agricultural credit and 23 per cent of direct agricultural credit, respectively.

Thirdly, within a year, the March quarter, which entailed limited agricultural activity, continued to have the highest concentration of (net) agricultural credit. The 'March-bunching' continued even though monitoring of priority sector targets was made both quarterly and annual since 2016.

Finally, there was a continued decline in the share of long-term agricultural credit in total agricultural credit in the 2010s.

In our earlier papers, we had highlighted how the concentration of agricultural credit in large loan sizes by urban and metropolitan branches and at end-March every year had a close association with the increasing growth and share of indirect agricultural credit in the 2000s. Between 2011 and 2018, indirect agricultural credit growth, however, had turned negative and yet, the pattern of distribution of agricultural credit persisted.

Was the decline in indirect agricultural credit credible then? The answer is no. Among the various definitional changes that happened in the 2000s and 2010s, a major change related to agricultural credit to corporate farmers. This was credit given to corporates, partnership firms and institutions engaged in direct agricultural production. It was included under priority sector credit for the first time in 2007 and was bifurcated between direct and indirect agricultural credit. The subsequent definitional changes ensured a progressive shift of corporate farmer credit from indirect agricultural credit to direct agricultural credit. Finally, in 2016, corporate farmer credit with a credit limit of only up to Rs 2 crore was included under direct agricultural credit. Corporate farmer credit exceeding Rs 2 crore was no longer included as part of indirect agricultural credit. The fall in the growth and share of indirect agricultural credit was a likely fallout of these changes. The share of indirect agricultural credit started to fall from 2007 onwards, while its growth slowed down significantly between 2007 and 2011, and eventually turned negative between 2011 and 2018.

Although banks were disincentivized from giving credit above Rs 2 crore to corporate farmers as such credit no longer carried the priority sector tag, the limit of Rs 2 crore was itself much higher than the credit normally sought by a farmer, particularly a small and marginal farmer. The introduction of a sub-target of 8 per cent for small and marginal farmers in 2016 was a positive change aimed at increasing the allocation of credit to these sections. However, such a sub-target may have limited import so long as corporate farmers find a place under direct agricultural credit. Under a liberalized set up, banks find greater commercial sense in giving a few large-sized loans to corporates/institutions from urban or metropolitan branches than giving many small-sized loans to farmers from rural branches. Hence, it may not be a surprise if the sub-target for small and marginal farmers eventually turns into a ceiling rather than a floor.

Notes

[1] A detailed account of the changes in banking policy in the 1990s and 2000s can be found in Ramakumar and Chavan (2007, 2014).

[2] Also see Reddy (2001), who noted that 'the definition of priority sector lending has been broadened significantly in recent years, thus overestimating credit flows to actual agricultural operations'.

[3] Small and marginal farmers included, among others, farmers, landless agricultural labourers, tenant farmers, oral lessees and sharecroppers with landholding of up to 2 hectares and loans to self-help groups (SHGs) or joint liability groups (JLGs) of small and marginal farmers.

[4] Of course, the target of 8 per cent could be breached in practice by banks.

[5] The overall priority sector target for SFBs was fixed at 75 per cent as compared to 40 per cent for all other banks with the target for agriculture being 18 per cent for all.

[6] Apart from PSLCs, outright purchases of priority sector lending portfolio, investments in securitized priority sector assets, deposits in Rural Infrastructure Development Fund (RIDF) and other funds listed in priority sector lending guidelines of the RBI were the other avenues available to banks in meeting the target shortfall.

[7] In this regard, they differed from inter-bank participation certificates, which involved a transfer of credit risk to the purchasing bank, as indicated in the priority sector guidelines of the RBI.

[8] In this regard, they differ from outright purchases and securitized investments in priority sector lending, which remain on the books of banks till the repayment of the underlying loans or reselling of the portfolio.

[9] See RBI (2016).

[10] The list of districts would be prepared on the basis of per capita priority sector credit to be periodically reviewed by the RBI.

[11] Although the segregation of agricultural credit between direct and indirect credit is

no longer valid after the change in the priority sector lending policy in 2016, these heads continue to be reported in the BSR, as shown in Table 12.4.

[12] In fact, RBI (2019) has recommended that small and marginal farmers should be defined not on the basis of their landholding but the amount of credit they take. Accordingly, it has specified Rs 2 lakh as the limit for identifying agricultural credit to small and marginal farmers.

[13] The interest subvention scheme for direct agricultural credit was introduced in 2006–07. For details, see https://www.nabard.org/content.aspx?id=602

[14] One way to ascertain the effectiveness of PSLCs is to see how far they aided in mitigating the extent of shortfall in achieving priority sector targets. The other way is to see how far they have aided the growth in priority sector lending; see the third section of the chapter – Changes in Agricultural Credit Policy – for the various objectives behind the introduction of PSLCs. A comparison of the growth in trading volume and the growth in credit underlines a possible disconnect (Appendix Table 1). The growth in trading volume of all PSLCs, possibly aided by a low base, has been staggeringly high. However, the growth in underlying priority sector credit (also called as the 'organic lending' [excluding PSLCs trading] [RBI 2020]) does not suggest any striking change from its past trend after the introduction of PSLCs.

[15] A possible interpretation of this could be that small and marginal farmers in these states held more than one loan account with the banking system. Nagaland too shows above 100 per cent coverage of small and marginal farmers. However, this was on account of a very small number of landholdings reported for the state, possibly reflecting an underestimation.

[16] Ideally, an assessment of quarterly credit should be made using flow of credit disbursed during each quarter. However, in the absence of data on disbursements, the change in outstanding has been considered here. As outstanding reflects both principal and interest outstanding, large-scale repayments should lead to a reduction in net outstanding. Similarly, large-scale sanction of new loans should lead to an increase in net outstanding.

[17] See RBI 'Master Circular – Kisan Credit Card (KCC) Scheme', 3 July 2017, available at https://www.rbi.org.in/Scripts/BS_ViewMasCirculardetails.aspx?id=11034, accessed 25 June 2022.

[18] KCCs were introduced in 1998. Furthermore, investment credit needs were covered under KCC only in 2004. See RBI 'Master Circular – Kisan Credit Card (KCC) Scheme', 3 July 2017.

[19] As per a study by National Bank for Agriculture and Rural Development (NABARD), commercial banks (including regional rural banks [RRBs]) accounted for around 47 per cent of the cumulative KCCs issued by 2014–15. However, only about 35 per cent of these cards were 'live' or active (Mani 2016). By contrast, about 77 per cent of the KCCs issued by credit cooperatives were live.

References

Chavan, P. (2013), 'Credit and Capital Formation in Agriculture: A Growing Disconnect', *Social Scientist*, vol. 41, no. 9, September–November, pp. 59–67.

Government of India (GoI) (2010), 'Report of the Task Force on Credit-Related Issues of Farmers', Chairperson: U.C. Sarangi, Submitted to the Ministry of Agriculture, Government of India, New Delhi.

———— (2015), *Economic Survey: 2014–15*, Ministry of Finance, Government of India, New Delhi.

Mani, G. (2016), 'Study on Implementation of KCC Scheme', Working Paper No. 64, National Bank for Agriculture and Rural Development (NABARD), Mumbai.

Misra, R., P. Chavan and R. Verma (2016), 'Agricultural Credit in India in the 2000s: Growth, Distribution and Linkages with Productivity', *Margin*, vol. 10, no. 2, pp. 169–97.

Ramachandran, V.K. and M. Swaminathan, eds (2005), *Financial Liberalisation and Rural Credit in India*, New Delhi: Tulika Books.

Ramakumar, R. (2018), 'Financial Inclusion in India: A Review', in *Rural India Perspective 2017*, National Bank for Agriculture and Rural Development (NABARD), New Delhi: Oxford University Press.

Ramakumar, R. and P. Chavan (2007), 'Revival of Agricultural Credit in the 2000s: An Explanation', *Economic and Political Weekly*, vol. 42, no. 52, pp. 57–64.

——— (2011), 'Changes in the Number of Rural Bank Branches in India, 1991 to 2008', *Review of Agrarian Studies*, vol. 1, no. 1, pp. 141–48.

——— (2014), 'Bank Credit to Agriculture in India in the 2000s: Dissecting the Revival', *Review of Agrarian Studies*, vol. 4, no. 1, pp. 50–79.

Reddy, Y.V. (2001), 'Indian Agriculture and Reform: Concerns, Issues and Agenda', *RBI Bulletin*, May.

Reserve Bank of India (RBI) (2004), 'Report of the Advisory Committee on Flow of Credit to Agriculture and Related Activities from the Banking System', Chairperson: V.S. Vyas, Reserve Bank of India, Mumbai.

——— (2015), 'Report of the Internal Working Group to Revisit the Existing Priority Sector Lending Guidelines', Reserve Bank of India, Mumbai.

——— (2016), 'Priority Sector Lending Certificates', 7 April, Reserve Bank of India, Mumbai.

——— (2019), 'Report of the Internal Working Group to Review Agricultural Credit', Chairperson: M.K. Jain, Reserve Bank of India, Mumbai.

——— (2020), 'Report on the Trend and Progress of Banking in India: 2019–20', Reserve Bank of India, Mumbai.

Shetty, S.L. (2006), 'Policy Responses to the Failure of Formal Banking Institutions to Expand Credit Delivery for Agriculture and Non-farm Informal Sectors: The Ground Reality and Tasks Ahead', Revised version of the seminar paper, Monthly Seminar Series on India's Financial Sector, Indian Council for Research on International Economic Relations (ICRIER), New Delhi, 14 November.

Wiggins, S. and S. Rajendran (1987), 'Rural Banking in Southern Tamil Nadu: Performance and Management', Final Research Report No. 3, The University of Reading, United Kingdom.

Appendix

Appendix Table 1 *Trading volume growth and premiums of PSLCs, and growth in priority sector credit, All banks, 2013–20*

Category	Growth (per cent per annum)							Weighted average premium (per cent)			
	2013–14	2014–15	2015–16	2016–17	2017–18	2018–19	2019–20	2016–17	2017–18	2018–19	2018–19
Trading volume of all PSLCs	–	–	–	–	269.9	77.8	42.9	–	–	–	–
Overall priority sector credit	28.4	9.3	16.0	2.4	6.8	15.3	9.2	0.7	0.59	0.31	0.35
Agricultural credit	41.1	11.2	16.5	3.3	5.5	9.9	8.6	1.87	1.29	0.79	1.17
Credit to small and marginal farmers	–	–	–	–	12.2	11.3	17.2	1.72	1.54	1.15	1.58

Note: As PSLCs and sub-target for small and marginal farmers were introduced in 2016, data for past years are not available for related heads. Growth in credit is reported in current prices to make it comparable with the growth trading volume.
Source: 'Report on Trend and Progress of Banking in India', various issues.
– Not available/not applicable.

13

Agricultural Insurance in India

History, Issues and Recent Performance

Awanish Kumar

Why is agricultural insurance necessary? What are the persistent challenges with agricultural insurance schemes in India? Has the Pradhan Mantri Fasal Bima Yojana (PMFBY) launched in 2016 been able to address and overcome those issues? In this chapter, I will try to answer some of these questions. The first section introduces the concept and operationalization of crop insurance. The second section provides a historical background to the debates regarding crop insurance and identifies some of the longstanding issues related to the conceptualization and implementation of erstwhile crop insurance schemes in India. The third section analyses the available data about the functioning of the PMFBY on the parameters identified in the previous section. The final section concludes the paper highlighting some important issues about PMFBY and suggests some possible policy remedies.

Introduction

One of the most important developmental problems of India is that a majority of the rural Indian workforce still finds an occupation in agriculture, while the contribution of agriculture to the Gross Domestic Product (GDP) has reduced drastically. Agriculture in India has remained a low productivity, low-income economic activity. Within the agricultural sector, about 85 per cent of farmers can be classified as small and marginal farmers (NSSO 2014). In the absence of irrigation and dwindling public support, a large section of these farmers predominantly relies upon monsoon rains for cultivation as about two-thirds of the total cultivated area has no access to assured irrigation (Singh 2010). According to the *Accidental Deaths and Suicides in India* report 2015, the number of farmers who committed suicide rose from 5,650 in 2014 to 8,007 in 2015 signifying a jump of about 42 per cent. The same report says that the most important reasons for farmers' suicides are indebtedness and crop failures (Bhushan and Kumar 2017).

On an average, 1.2 crore hectares of crop area in India is affected annually by natural calamities leading to loss of production and reduced yields (Singh 2010). The small and marginal farmers are highly vulnerable to risks associated with natural and man-made events (Skees 2000, Raju and Chand 2008). Such risks can be categorized as climatic risks, market risks, resource risks and production risks. The incidence and severity of risks to farmers vary with institutional frameworks, policy environments and climactic factors (Hazell, Pomareda and Valdes, eds 1986). Nevertheless, about 50 per cent of the variation in crop yields in India can be explained by variations in rainfall (Singh 2010).

Agriculture is a risky economic activity, and Indian agriculture is riskier because of its heavy dependence on monsoon rains (ibid.). The farmers attempt to tide over the risks by changing cropping patterns, changing the sowing period, increasing the intensity of family labour use, working in the non-farm sector, entering into sharecropping and fixed rent tenancy contracts and distress sale of assets. The government is expected to provide risk sharing/risk pooling arrangements, which typically translate into various schemes related to irrigation and extension services, subsidies on inputs, compensation against yield losses, minimum support prices (MSP), employment guarantee schemes and reduced interest rates on credit (Walker, Singh and Asokan 1986).

In this overall framework of risk mitigation, agricultural insurance is a comprehensive mechanism of providing cover for all possible risks in crop operations i.e., a part of an overall risk management strategy with a multi-peril coverage. This is especially true for a country like India where farming losses have enormous consequences for rural society (Raju and Chand 2008). Crop insurance is a component of agricultural insurance and an important mechanism against natural risks, which protects farmers against uncertainty of crop production and help minimize income instability (Ahsan, Ali and Kurian 1982). Crop insurance policies benefit the farmers in two ways: they can either increase mean income levels or reduce income variability. The former falls into the category of transfer benefits while the latter are referred to as risk benefits (Walker, Singh and Asokan 1986).

Crop insurance has also been an integral part of agricultural policy in many countries. In the case of the United States, crop insurance schemes are subsidized by the government, but administered by private companies. According to the European Commission, there are different types of crop insurance policies, such as single risk insurance (e.g. hailstorms), combined insurance and yield insurance. However, the implementation of crop insurance schemes varies according to the member nations of the European Union. In several member states, insurance is subsidized by the government but administered by private companies (European Commission 2006).

Prabhu (1988) lists some of the important lessons from the international experiences of crop insurance. First, crop insurance is a public policy towards managing income variability though it must be clearly understood that crop insurance schemes only cover yield risks and income variability resulting from such risks. Price volatility and resultant income variability cannot be tackled through crop insurance and must be managed through other appropriate policies. Secondly, multi-peril crop insurance programmes are almost always offered by the public sector and are heavily subsidized. Thirdly, premiums for crop insurance schemes must reflect the varying degrees of risks associated with certain crops and locations. Benefits from crop insurance schemes might get affected if a uniform premium is applied to a diverse region, such as in the case of India with its agro-ecological and socio-economic diversity. Fourthly, crop credit insurance might not be related to loan recovery as is often believed (see Dandekar 1976; Hazell, Pomareda and Valdes, eds 1986). Since institutional credit is limited in its availability to farmers, crop credit insurance schemes might also lead to worsening of income distribution in rural areas. Finally, there is a strong case for recognizing the 'political hazard' in crop insurance programmes since the rural power structures are controlled by elites that has influence over public policies in developing countries like India.

In India, crop insurance plays an important role in sustaining household incomes in times of drought, a frequent calamity in India. As the then Planning Commission, in its approach paper to the Eleventh Five-Year Plan, noted that 'all farmers do not have the ability to bear downside risks and this is evident from the spate of farmer suicides when new seeds fail to deliver expected output, or expenditure on bore wells proves infructuous, or when market prices collapse unexpectedly' (GoI 2006, p. 30).

The approach paper noted that more than two-thirds of the total crop acreage was vulnerable to drought in varying degrees. In such scenarios, crop insurance played an important role in terms of credit flow from formal institutions and crop insurance, as collateral, protects farmers from turning into defaulters. Therefore, crop insurance is often recommended for all loanee/indebted farmers as it increases the chances of repayment of loans (Dandekar 1976; Hazell, Pomareda and Valdes, eds 1986).

Crop Insurance in India: A Brief History

The early debates on crop insurance began immediately after India attained independence. These debates are pertinent even now for the range of questions raised by economists and policy-makers. Rajendra Prasad assured the members of the central legislature in 1947 that the government would examine the feasibility of a crop insurance programme in the country. The government introduced two pilot schemes in 1948 but the state governments did not respond positively. The first crop insurance bill was passed in 1965 and a model scheme was launched, but due to the requirement of financial contributions by state governments, no state came forward to implement the programme. After a lull, renewed discussions began during the third plan and finally in July 1970, an expert committee on crop insurance, chaired by Dharam Narain, was appointed. The committee, however, concluded that it was not advisable to introduce any crop insurance programme in the country (Dandekar 1976).

In these discussions, a major point of debate was on the relative plausibility of the *individual* approach versus *homogenous* or *pooled area* approach (Dandekar 1976, 1985; Agarwal 1979; Raju and Chand 2008). The *individual* approach towards crop insurance recognizes the individual plot as the unit of insurance. This approach, obviously, is suitable for a small-plot agricultural system as we have in India. However, this approach may require extensive investment – like a weather station in every village – and background work by the local bureaucracy – like by the department of land revenue. Some also deem it impractical. Some others suggest a larger area, such as the village or panchayat, to be considered as the unit of insurance and losses to be measured using a threshold-yield level. The latter approach is called *homogenous* or *pooled area* approach. Indian agriculture is marked by localized disasters, which affect yields of farmers differently in the same large region. A larger unit of insurance will be inadequate in this regard. In contrast, a smaller unit of insurance allows for the diversity and disproportionate burden of natural disasters to be reflected in the calculation of threshold yields, which become the basis for claim payments.

The first insurance scheme in India was initiated in 1972, based on the 'individual approach' and was implemented in Gujarat. Since then, new schemes were launched every five years with certain modifications in the scheme guidelines in terms of area, crops and premiums. The Pilot Crop Insurance Scheme (PCIS) was operational during 1979–84, and this scheme changed the approach to an area-based approach as was recommended by V.M. Dandekar.

Several shortcomings were noted in this period including the following: crop insurance was linked to crop loans and hence owing to poor access to institutional credit, insurance coverage remained low; the unit of insurance was very large; there was lack of awareness among the farmers about the crop insurance scheme; and major commercial crops like cotton and sugarcane were excluded from the crop insurance scheme (Raju and Chand 2008; Singh 2010; also see Dandekar 1985).

In 1985, another scheme named the Comprehensive Crop Insurance Scheme (CCIS) was initiated and was under operation till the kharif season of 1999. The CCIS was also linked to crop loans. However, unlike earlier schemes, a few crucial reforms were introduced. The CCIS was compulsory for all loanee farmers. It covered a larger area and was adopted in fifteen states and two union territories. Premium rates were made uniform across all farmers and regions. Nevertheless, the major shortcomings of the CCIS remained the same as in the earlier schemes. The coverage continued to be confined to loanee farmers and certain crops with low premiums (Seeta Prabhu and Ramachandran 1986; Raju and Chand 2008). Indemnity payments were heavily skewed towards Gujarat and to a certain degree Maharashtra and Andhra Pradesh. Even in relatively better performing states like Maharashtra, the coverage of the scheme was poor (Patil and Borude 1993).

The National Agricultural Insurance Scheme (NAIS) was introduced from the rabi season of 1999–2000. A new agency called the Agricultural Insurance Company of India Limited (AIC) replaced the General Insurance Company. The AIC was incorporated in December 2002 and took over the implementation of NAIS. A major shift in this scheme was that it was available to both loanee and non-loanee farmers and it covered all foodgrains and oilseeds. Another innovative aspect was that the scheme operated based on both the area approach for natural calamities with larger impact and the individual approach for localized events like hailstorms, cyclones and floods (Raju and Chand 2008; Singh 2010).

Salient Issues with Crop Insurance Schemes

The NAIS was evaluated as having better impact and coverage than the earlier programmes though the overall coverage remained low. But a persistent feature has been extremely high claims to premium ratio with very skewed uptake across regions with Gujarat emerging as one of the top beneficiaries (Vyas and Singh 2006; Gangopadhyay 2004; Sinha 2004). Low coverage has coexisted with inadequacy of the cover, in terms of the sum insured over the years as part of different crop insurance schemes (Damodaran 2016). Data available from the Situation Assessment Survey (SAS) of the NSSO in 2013 provide further evidence of the enormity of exclusion from the NAIS. Both in the July–December 2018 season and the January–June 2019 season, the share of agricultural households who insured their crops ranged from 8.3 per cent in paddy and 6.8 per cent in wheat to 25.4 per cent in cotton and 27.5 per cent in soybean (NSSO 2020). The major reasons why farmers were not insuring at a mass scale were 'not aware' or 'not aware about availability of facility' (see Table 13.1).

Another issue that was discussed and debated concerned the relative efficacy of yield-based crop insurance versus weather-based insurance. This debate was also linked to the role of the private sector in agricultural insurance since it was the private sector that was heavily involved in the formula-

Table 13.1 *Distribution of major reasons for not insuring crops and selected crops, 2018–19,* in per cent

Crop	Reason for not insuring their crops being					Share of households insuring this crop
	Not aware about insurance	Not aware about availability of facility	Not inter-ested	No need	Insurance facility not available	
Paddy	44.2	15.6	21.1	3.4	3.8	8.3
Wheat	39.8	13.9	24.2	5.7	3.7	6.8
Arhar (*tur*)	36.4	15.8	18.3	8.7	5.1	16.6
Sugarcane	43.6	16.8	22.3	4.9	5.4	4.3
Soybean	44.2	11.1	17.4	3.5	2.1	27.5
Cotton	34.4	11.9	26.3	3.8	2.2	25.4

Note: Only five most important reasons are listed. Numbers may add up to more than 100 as farmers stated more than one reason.
Source: NSSO (2020).

tion and implementation of the weather-based crop insurance programmes (Sinha 2004). The Weather Based Crop Insurance Scheme (WBCIS) was piloted in a few states such as Andhra Pradesh, Bihar, Chattisgarh, Gujarat, Haryana, Karnataka, Madhya Pradesh, Maharashtra, Punjab, Rajasthan and Uttar Pradesh during the kharif season of the year 2003. The WBCIS was based on indicators that could be objectively assessed, such as rainfall and other weather-related variables. Here, the indemnity was measured on the realization of a weather index i.e., rainfall, temperature, humidity and wind speed, which were in turn highly correlated with the extent of losses. Table 13.2 shows the various comparative issues associated with yield-based crop insurance (such as NAIS) and weather-based insurance (such as WBCIS).

A few scholars advocated a weather-based insurance model for India (see Reddy 2004; Mishra 1995). However, a study based on field data by Gine, Townsend and Vickery (2008) highlighted that the insurance take up even in weather-based schemes was poor and was affected by various factors, such as household wealth, participation in village networks and familiarity with insurance vendors. Other scholars like Nair (2010a; 2010b) were more cautious. They suggested infrastructural changes including more weather stations and concluded that yield-based and weather-based insurance schemes, at least in Indian conditions, may actually work together as complements and not as substitutes. Gangopadhyay (2004) argued for an NGO-led insurance programme, which would have low transaction costs as compared to private sector companies.

Table 13.2 *A comparison of the relative efficacy of yield-based and weather-based insurance schemes*

Parameters	Yield-based crop insurance (NAIS)	Weather-based crop insurance (WBCIS)
Scope of insurance cover	covers yield shortfall	covers anticipated shortfall in yield due to adverse weather parameters; however, weather parameters appear to account for majority of crop losses.
Scope of perils covered	all natural and non-preventable perils	rainfall, minimum and maximum temperature, soil moisture, relative humidity, sunlight, day length etc.
Target group	all farmers growing insured crops	farmers and others
Crops	all crops for which past yield data is available	all crops for which correlation is established between yield and weather parameters
Scheme approach	homogeneous-area approach (taluk/block/*mandal*)	homogeneous-area approach (jurisdiction of rain gauge)
Scope for intro-duction of insurance	can be introduced for all crops with yield data	can be introduced for crops with good sensitivity to weather parameters; but technical challenges remain.
Premium rates	high	relatively lower and flexible
Sum insured	loan amount/150 per cent of the value of production	flexible; can range from input cost to value of production
Control on adverse selection/moral hazard	relatively less control	almost complete control
Time taken for settlement of claims	may range from 6 to 9 months from occurrence of loss	within two weeks from close of indemnity period
Administrative set-up	relatively large	relatively small
Transaction cost	high	moderate and affordable
Transparency	not transparent	transparent

Source: Reproduced from Raju and Chand (2008) and Singh (2010) with minor modifications.

A group-led approach in place of a homogenous-area approach was also suggested as more practical than an individual-based approach (Ghosh and Yadav 2008). Notwithstanding a lot of counterevidence, all crop insurance schemes were based on the homogeneous-area approach where several problems are encountered, such as the problem of moral hazard, adverse selection and non-availability of valid data to measure indemnity.

A report from the Comptroller and Auditor General (CAG), covering the period between the kharif season of 2011 and the rabi season of 2015–16, arrived at the following conclusions (see CAG 2017):

(1) About two-thirds of the farmers surveyed by the CAG were not even aware of the crop insurance schemes;

(2) There was no database of farmers kept by either the centre/state governments or the AIC for the purpose of payment of premiums or settling claims. Thus, without knowing the number of farmers being insured, Rs 10,617 crore was paid as premium subsidy and Rs 21,989 crore was paid as liability claims to the AIC and private insurance companies.

(3) Major discrepancies were noticed between the data on area sown and area insured;

(4) Coverage of farmers, as a whole, and small and marginal farmers, in particular, was very poor, and their coverage under the scheme was not more than 13 per cent;

(5) Sharecroppers and tenant farmers were largely excluded from the purview of the scheme;

(6) No data was available with the governments on the number of Scheduled Castes (SC) or Scheduled Tribes (ST) farmers covered under the programme;

(7) Only one state – Odisha – had notified the village as the lowest possible unit of defined area. All other states continued to use the block as the lowest possible unit of defined area.

(8) In many places, several malpractices were noted. The deductions of premium were done without the knowledge of the farmers, sometimes even in the case of non-notified crops.

(9) There were also major delays in processing the claims and paying the farmers. Most shockingly, the CAG report also noted that for the kharif season of 2016, insurance companies collected premium amounting to Rs 9,041.25 crore while paying out only Rs 570.1 crore of the total claims (made at Rs 2,324.01 crore). In other words, more than 75 per cent of total claims were lying unpaid by many of the private insurance companies while their profits kept on rising.

In sum, crop insurance schemes in India were not popular among farmers mainly due to the following issues in conceptualization and implementation: higher premium, low awareness and limited coverage, complexity of loss assessments and delay in settling insurance claims. An important issue was also the role and extent of involvement of private companies in crop insurance programmes. Overall, as a cumulative impact of these issues, out of the gross cropped area of 19.53 crore hectares in the country, only 4.28 crore hectares, or 22 per cent of the total area, was covered under crop insurance in 2014 (Damodaran 2016).

In the next section, I will try to analyse the performance of PMFBY based on the parameters identified above to see if the scheme has been able to overcome some of these longstanding challenges.

Has PMFBY Overcome the Persistent Challenges in Crop Insurance?

The Pradhan Mantri Fasal Bima Yojana (PMFBY) was launched in January 2016 as an extension of the NAIS with certain key changes adopted such as lower premiums, wider coverage and faster settlement of claims. The PMFBY replaced the earlier MNAIS while the WBCIS continues to operate concurrently. The state governments have the power to decide whether they want WBCIS or PMFBY or both.

In PMFBY, the premiums were reduced to 2 per cent of the sum insured for all kharif crops, 1.5 per cent of the sum insured for all rabi crops and 5 per cent of the sum insured for commercial or horticultural crops. The artificial cap on the sum insured was removed to incentivize farmers to join the scheme. According to the PMFBY's operational guidelines, all risks were covered under the scheme including yield losses due to non-preventable risks, prevented sowing, post-harvest losses and localized calamities. The latter two categories were not considered in the previous schemes. The field assessments of actual crop damages and faster settlements of claims were to be accomplished using modern technology, such as GPS, smart phones and remote sensing. All pronounced provisions taken together, the new promise of low premiums and no artificial capping of the sum insured along with faster claim settlements could turn the PMFBY, as Damodaran (2016) noted, into a 'game-changer for Indian agriculture'.

Formulation and Conceptualization

Let us first look at some of the continuities between the earlier crop insurance programmes and PMFBY at the level of policy formulation and conceptualization.

(1) *Focused on yield risk alone*: The first and foremost issue about any crop insurance policy is to understand that it only attempts at managing yield risks and income variability resulting from such risks. In the post-liberalization period, price volatility and resultant income variability was a major cause of farmers' suicides and agrarian dis-

tress. However, the government, despite the demands made by several organizations, ignored the issue for a comprehensive crop and income insurance scheme. So, like earlier crop insurance schemes, the PMFBY merely serves to cover the risks associated with yield loss and nothing else. There is no multi-peril strategy to cover other risks like market risks. In this way, PMFBY does not assure any support against income variability.

(2) *Insurance as a neoliberal intervention*: The other issue is regarding the philosophy of government intervention based on insurance and not on public investment on agriculture, such as investment in public irrigation. The major shift towards crop insurance, as opposed to risk-reducing public investments, as the flagship policy of the government also signifies a neoliberal stance of public policy in general, and agricultural policy in particular.

(3) *Compulsory/universal scheme with caveats*: The longstanding issues related to low awareness and limited coverage continues to plague the scheme. The PMFBY continues the tradition of mandatory coverage of loanee farmers while only theoretically covering non-loanee farmers. The small and marginal farmers, particularly belonging to Dalit and Adivasi categories, are excluded since they are excluded from crop loans and cannot afford the premium to join the PMFBY. The PMFBY also continues to work with the artificial distinction between the loanee and non-loanee farmers. While registration under PMFBY is compulsory for loanee farmers, it is not so for the non-loanee farmers. So, even if everyone is eligible theoretically, the scheme is not universal in its spirit and implementation. This becomes obvious when we look at the numbers with respect to the coverage of the scheme. Additionally, the loanee farmers face a lot of issues because of malpractices prevalent in the sector. For instance, a lot of media reports indicated that the premium amount is often deducted from the bank account of loanee farmers without their consent and sometimes even knowledge. The income security of the loanee farmers was further compromised with non-payments of the previous year's claims even as advance premium payments were deducted from the next year's loans. In the most recent amendments in the year 2020, the scheme has been made completely voluntary for all farmers.

(4) *Area approach continues*: The scheme continues the much debated and criticized area approach to implementation. A section of scholars has praised the area-based approach for its prevention of moral hazard problems (see Rai 2019). However, as pointed out earlier, the persistence of the area-based approach was the primary reason

why farmers shied away from crop insurance schemes in the past. Despite its pronouncements about using technology (such as use of drones for crop-cutting exercises), the PMFBY has not brought down the unit of insurance to the farm level.

(5) *State governments juggle with the scheme*: The scheme, though is named after the Prime Minister and gives a sense that it is a fully centrally sponsored scheme, demands 50 per cent of the financial contributions from the states. In the case of Bihar, for example, the state government had to annually pay Rs 600 crore as premium subsidy, which was one-fourth of the state's total agricultural budget of Rs 2,718 crore in 2016. Further, the tall promises made by the scheme in its operational guidelines eventually passed through the notifications made by the states. For instance, the states notify the crops during every season and also decide upon the sum insured, indemnity levels and coverage. A farmer cultivating any crop other than the one notified stands ineligible for the scheme. The experience shows that many state governments delayed notifying the scheme, excluded many important crops and often failed to provide the threshold yield for every unit of insurance (Bhushan and Kumar 2017).

(6) *Unit of loss measurement*: The unit of measurement for loss calculation continues to be block/tehsil level as the crop-cutting experiments are done at the block or tehsil level. As discussed above, the homogenous area-based approach ignores the specificities of individual farms and farmers. This was an old demand of peasant organizations, but the government invested nothing to institute structures and capacities to collect data at the village and farm levels. The artificial uniformity imposed, and the resulting underestimation of losses, was one reason why farmers were not inclined towards joining insurance schemes.

(7) *Complexity of loss assessments*: The PMFBY proposes to calculate threshold yield for a given area for the purpose of settling claims by looking at weighted averages of yield over the last seven years excluding up to two calamity years. This was against the interests of most farmers in the semi-arid and dry regions. While notifying the sum insured and reimbursing losses, according to the Swaminathan Commission report 2006, there is no attempt to calculate the costs.

Implementation

Let us now move on to the performance of PMFBY on some of the major indicators that I have identified as longstanding problems in erstwhile crop insurance programmes in the country. This is to see if PMFBY has been able to overcome the obstacles of the previous schemes as advertised.

(1) *Coverage*: Before the launch of PMFBY in 2015–16, a total of 4.86 crore farmers were part of the previous schemes on an annual basis (Banerjee and Anand 2019). In 2016–17, the number of farmers' applications covered by PMFBY increased to 5.83 crore. In 2017–18, however, with the unfolding of the numerous problems with the scheme, this number got reduced by about 50 lakh and the total number of farmers' applications stood at 5.33 crore only.

More recent trends are shown in Table 13.3. First, the number of farmers' applications picked up after 2017–18 and stood at 6.13 crore in 2020–21. However, while the number of farmers' applications for kharif crops rose, the number of farmers' applications for rabi crops fell from about 2.27 crore applications in 2018–19 to 2.02 crore applications in 2020–21. Secondly, regardless of the number of farmers' applications, the number of farmers insured fell from about 3.64 crores in 2018–19 to 2.67 crores in 2020–21. This applied to both the kharif and rabi seasons. Thirdly, the coverage of loanee farmers increased while the coverage of non-loanee farmers remained largely stagnant. Fourthly, while the number of farmers' applications under PMFBY rose, the number of farmers' applications under the Revised Weather Based Crop Insurance Scheme (RWBCIS) fell to just about 7,00,000 applications in 2020–21.

We see similar trends in terms of area insured under PMFBY. In 2018–19, the total area insured was about 5.7 crore hectares. By 2020–21, the total area insured fell to about 4.9 crore hectares. Overall, over the five years of its implementation, there was a fatigue experienced by farmers under PMFBY.

(2) *Claims versus compensation to farmers under PMFBY*: While the number of farmers insured was falling, the farmers' share of total premium under PMFBY was showing an upward trend between 2016–17 and 2018–19 (see Table 13.4).

The premium amount paid by the farmers insured under PMFBY rose from Rs 4,042 crores in 2016–17 to Rs 4,189 crores in 2017–18 and Rs 4,853 crores in 2018–19. In terms of the gross premium paid to the insurance companies, despite a fall in the number of farmers insured, the gross premium paid increased from Rs 21,573 crores in 2016–17 to Rs 29,357 crores in 2018–19. Interestingly, the reported claims and paid claims remained almost identical over the last few years.

This exact tally between reported and paid claims under PMFBY appear suspicious when we look at the difference between the gross premium paid to insurance companies and the estimated claims along with the number of rejections of claims in the last few years

Table 13.3 *Coverage of PMFBY plus RWBCIS, India, 2018 to 2020,* in number and '000 ha

Season	States/UTs that notified PMFBY	Loanee farmers' applications (crores)	Non-loanee farmers' applications (crores)	PMFBY applications (crores)	RWBCIS applications (crores)	Total farmers' applications (crores)	Number of farmers insured (crores)	Area insured ('000 ha)
Kharif 2018	22	2.04	1.15	3.07	0.13	3.20	2.17	29,258
Rabi 2018–19	21	1.34	0.94	2.20	0.07	2.27	1.47	27,815
2018–19, total	–	3.38	2.09	5.27	0.20	5.47	3.64	57,073
Kharif 2019	20	2.38	1.68	3.83	0.23	4.06	2.00	31,446
Rabi 2019–20	19	1.31	0.53	1.77	0.07	1.84	0.97	23,797
2019–20, total	–	3.69	2.21	5.60	0.30	5.90	2.97	55,243
Kharif 2020	19	2.69	1.43	4.08	0.03	4.11	1.68	27,209
Rabi 2020–21	18	1.24	0.78	1.98	0.04	2.02	0.99	22,646
2020–21, total	–	3.93	2.21	6.06	0.07	6.13	2.67	49,855

Source: Administrative Dashboard, available at https://pmfby.gov.in/adminStatistics/dashboard, accessed 14 April 2021.

Table 13.4 *Premiums paid versus reported and paid claims, PMFBY, India, 2016–17 to 2019–20*, in crores and Rs crores

Financial year	Farmers' applications insured (crores)	Sum insured (Rs crore)	Farmers' share in premium (Rs crore)	Gross premium (Rs crore)	Reported claims (Rs crore)	Paid claims (Rs crore)	Farmers' applications benefited (crores)
2016–17	5.83	2,03,120	4,042	21,573	16,773	16,759	1.6
2017–18	5.33	2,02,267	4,189	24,652	22,118	22,114	1.7
2018–19	5.77	2,30,061	4,853	29,357	28,941	28,004	2.2
Kharif 2019	4.22	1,42,969	3,018	23,542	20,975	20,090	1.9

Source: Lok Sabha Unstarred Question No. 1564, answered on 11 February 2020, available at http://164.100.47.194/Loksabha/Questions/Qtextsearch.aspx, accessed 27 June 2022.

Table 13.5 *Premium paid, estimated and denied claims, PMFBY, India, 2016–17 to 2019–20*, in Rs crore

Financial Year	Gross premium (Rs crore)	Estimated claims (Rs crore)	Gross premium – estimated claims (Rs crore)	Number of individual claims rejected/denied by insurance companies
2016–17	21,875	16,774	5,101	NA
2017–18	25,350	21,926	3,424	92,869
2018–19	29,106	23,176	5,930	2,04,742
2019–20	NA	NA	NA	9,28,870

Source: Lok Sabha Unstarred Question No. 1564, answered on 11 February 2020; and Lok Sabha Unstarred Question No. 483 answered on 5 February 2021, available at http://164.100.47.194/Loksabha/Questions/Qtextsearch.aspx, accessed 27 June 2022.

(see Table 13.5). Tables 13.4 and 13.5 are based on two different answers to questions in the Parliament in 2020 and 2021 respectively, but they show different figures.

The difference between gross premium paid and estimated claims can be understood as a proxy for profits accrued to private insurance companies. This number stood at Rs 5,930 crore in 2018–19. In the same period, the number of individual claims denied by insurance companies kept rising and it was more than 9 lakh in 2019–20.

Given this feature, it would not be incorrect to say that while the PMFBY failed to overcome some of the longstanding issues in crop insurance schemes, it made a unique contribution in terms of opening the doors of crop insurance business to private companies. The empanelled private companies included major firms including ICICI-Lombard General Insurance Company Ltd., HDFC-ERGO General Insurance Company Ltd., IFFCO-Tokio General Insurance Company Ltd., Cholamandalam MS General Insurance Company Ltd., Bajaj Allianz General Insurance Company Ltd., Reliance General Insurance Company Ltd., Future General India Insurance Company Ltd., Tata-AIG General Insurance Company Ltd., SBI General Insurance Company Ltd. and Universal Sompo General Insurance Company Ltd. These insurance companies were given a cluster of districts for operation under competitive bidding. The private insurance companies charged high actuarial premium rates, and more so in backward states like Bihar.

(3) *Delay in payments of claims*: The most important issue in PMFBY was regarding the delay in payment of claims. A correlate of the impunity through which the insurance companies were operating under PMFBY is shown in Table 13.6. The pending claims of farmers increased from Rs 1,114 crore in 2016–17 to Rs 4,588 crore in 2017–18 and Rs 6,814 crore in kharif 2018. The last column of Table 13.6 shows that the share of pending claims in total estimated claims was about 7 per cent in 2016–17, which increased to about 28 per cent in 2017–18. Till 19 March 2019, about 75 per cent of all claims made during kharif 2018 were pending with the insurance companies.

Table 13.6 *Delay in payments of claims, PMFBY, India, 2016–17 to 2019–20,* in Rs crore and per cent

Season	Estimated claims (in Rs crore)	Approved claims (in Rs crore)	Claims pending (in Rs crore)	Claims pending as % of estimated claims
Kharif 2016	10,505	10,422	221	2.10
Rabi 2016–17	5,990	5,502	923	15.41
2016–17, total	*16,495*	*15,924*	*1,144*	*6.94*
Kharif 2017	16,239	13,706	4,439	27.34
Rabi 2017–18	210	62	149	70.95
2017–18, total	*16,448*	*13,768*	*4,588*	*27.89*
Kharif 2018 (till 19 March 2019)	8,996	3,583	6,814	75.74

Source: RTI information from Ministry of Agriculture.

Table 13.7 *Number of farmers benefited, PMFBY, India, 2016–17 to 2018–19*, in number and per cent

Financial year	Number of farmers applications insured	Farmers benefitted with respect to paid claims	% of farmers benefitted
2016–17	5.83	1.49	25.6
2017–18	5.28	1.75	33.1
2018–19	5.68	1.65	29.0

Source: Lok Sabha Unstarred Question No. 1564, answered on 11 February 2020.

Table 13.8 *State-wise number of farmers insured, PMFBY, India, 2016–17 to 2018–19*, in lakhs and lakh ha

State	FY 2016–17		FY 2017–18		FY 2018–19	
	No. of farmers applications insured (lakh)	Area insured (lakh ha)	No. of farmers' applications insured (lakh)	Area insured (lakh ha)	No. of farmers' applications insured (lakh)	Area insured (lakh ha)
Andhra Pradesh	17.8	15.6	18.3	21.5	24.5	22.3
Assam	0.6	0.4	0.6	0.4	0.7	0.5
Bihar	27.1	24.8	23.0	21.3	NA	NA
Chhattisgarh	15.5	24.1	14.7	22.2	15.7	22.7
Gujarat	19.8	30.2	17.6	26.6	21.7	26.1
Haryana	13.4	20.8	13.5	19.3	14.4	20.5
Karnataka	29.5	26.1	20.9	18.1	19.2	22.2
Kerala	0.8	0.3	0.6	0.5	0.6	0.4
Madhya Pradesh	74.6	126.1	69.5	121.2	73.4	129.5
Maharashtra	120.1	73.0	102.1	59.0	147.3	88.2
Odisha	18.2	13.2	18.9	13.5	20.8	14.6
Rajasthan	91.9	103.8	88.1	98.5	69.3	74.3
Tamil Nadu	15.0	12.3	14.6	11.7	20.5	11.1
Uttar Pradesh	72.9	65.1	54.2	47.1	61.3	51.3
West Bengal	41.3	19.9	40.6	16.8	51.8	18.0
All India	583.7	570.8	528.0	515.0	568.1	519.3

Source: Lok Sabha Unstarred Question No 1564, answered on 11 February 2020, available in http://164.100.47.194/Loksabha/Questions/Qtextsearch.aspx, accessed 27 June 2022.

(4) *Farmers benefitted under PMFBY*: The number of farmers insured under PMFBY saw a decline over the three years of its implementation. The same was true for farmers who benefitted under the scheme with respect to approved claims. In 2016–17, the share of farmers who benefitted was about 26 per cent of the total farmers applications insured. In 2017–18, it increased to about 33 per cent while in 2018–19, the share declined to about 29 per cent (see Table 13.7).

A related issue that received a lot of media coverage was the actual quantum of claims paid to the farmers under the PMFBY. In 2018, for instance, some 2,000 farmers in the Beed district of Maharashtra received less than five rupees as compensation for claims made in lakhs of rupees (Banerjee and Anand 2019). Recently, farmers also took many insurance companies to court regarding the meagre amounts of claims paid to them (Kulkarni 2019).

(5) *Regional disparity in the coverage of PMFBY*: Crop insurance in India was always skewed towards some states like Maharashtra and Gujarat that accounted for a huge share of insured farmers. A number of new states such as Madhya Pradesh, Rajasthan and Uttar Pradesh have performed well in terms of coverage under PMFBY (see Table 13.8).

At the same time, a curious aspect of the PMFBY was also the withdrawal of certain states from the scheme. In kharif 2020, only nineteen states participated in and notified PMFBY, and by rabi 2020, the number fell to eighteen states. A prominent example was Bihar that started its own scheme that provided a fixed payment to farmers to mitigate crop losses (Das 2018). Another important reason for many other states withdrawing from the scheme was because of amendments in the operational guidelines that drastically reduced the share of the central government in premium payments and substantially increased the fiscal burden on state

Table 13.9 *Share of states/UTs in gross premium paid, PMFBY, India, 2018 to 2020*, in Rs crore and per cent

Variable	FY 2018	FY 2019	FY 2020
State/UTs premium (in Rs crore)	10,750	12,334	13,729
GoI premium (in Rs crore)	10,383	11,373	12,312
Gross premium (in Rs crore)	25,355	27,527	29,883
State/UTs premium as a share of gross premium (%)	42.4	44.8	45.9

Source: Administrative Dashboard, available at https://pmfby.gov.in/adminStatistics/dashboard, accessed 14 April 2021.

governments (see Table 13.9). The share of the gross premium paid by states and union territories rose between 2018 and 2020. This also led to the failure of many states to pay their share in premium subsidy in time, resulting in delays in claim payments.

Conclusions

The paper tried to highlight some longstanding issues with the design and implementation of crop insurance schemes in India over the years. Some of these issues were higher premiums, low awareness, limited coverage, complexity of loss assessments and delays in settling insurance claims. An additional issue was regarding the role of private insurance companies in crop insurance schemes. I tried to show that despite the claims made by the government on PMFBY, the scheme continued to be plagued with several design and conceptualization issues. Further, a closer look at the data available for PMFBY showed that the scheme was struggling to overcome the shortcomings identified for the previous insurance schemes like NAIS. A universal and comprehensive scheme with a special focus on the vulnerable sections is the need of the hour.

References

Agarwal, A.K. (1979), 'Crop Insurance: Need for a New Approach', *Economic and Political Weekly*, vol. 14, no. 39, pp. A125–A127.

Ahsan, S.M., A.A.G. Ali and N. John Kurian (1982), 'Toward a Theory of Agricultural Insurance', *American Journal of Agricultural Economics*, vol. 64, no. 3, pp. 520–29.

Banerjee, A. and I. Anand (2019), 'The Modi Regime and Worsening Agrarian Crisis', in R. Azad, S. Chakraborty, S. Ramani and D. Sinha, eds, *A Quantum Leap in the Wrong Direction?* Hyderabad: Orient Blackswan.

Bhushan, C. and V. Kumar (2017), *Pradhan Mantri Fasal Bima Yojana: An Assessment*, New Delhi: Centre for Science and Environment.

Comptroller and Auditor General of India (CAG) (2017), 'Report of the Comptroller and Auditor General of India on Performance Audit of Agriculture Crop Insurance Schemes', Ministry of Agriculture and Farmers' Welfare, New Delhi.

Damodaran, H. (2016), 'Some Assurance: How New Crop Insurance Scheme can be a Game-Changer', *The Indian Express*, 21 January.

Dandekar, V.M. (1976), 'Crop Insurance in India', *Economic and Political Weekly*, vol. 11, no. 26, pp. A61–A80.

———— (1985), 'Crop Insurance in India – A Review, 1976–77 to 1984–85', *Economic and Political Weekly*, vol. 20, nos 25–26, pp. A46–A59.

Das, A.S.T. (2018), 'Bihar Dumps Centre's Insurance Scheme for Farmers, Launches its Own Scheme to Tackle Crop Loss', *The New Indian Express*, 6 June 2018, https://www.newindianexpress.com/nation/2018/jun/06/bihar-dumps-centres-insurance-scheme-for-farmers-launches-its-own-scheme-to-tackle-crop-loss-1824619.html, accessed 14 April 2021.

European Commission (2006), 'Agricultural Insurance Schemes', Institute for the Protection and Security of the Citizen: Agriculture and Fisheries Unit, available at https://ec.europa.eu/agriculture/sites/agriculture/files/external-studies/2006/insurance/summary_en.pdf.

Gangopadhyay, S. (2004), 'An Alternative to Crop Insurance', *Economic and Political Weekly*, vol. 39, no. 44, pp. 4763–64.

Ghosh, N. and S.S. Yadav (2008), 'Problems and Prospects of Crop Insurance: Reviewing Agricultural Risk and NAIS in India', New Delhi: Institute of Economic Growth.

Gine, X., R. Townsend and J. Vickery (2008), 'Patterns of Rainfall Insurance Participation in Rural India', *The World Bank Economic Review*, vol. 22, no. 3, pp. 539–66.

Government of India (GoI) (2006), 'Towards Faster and More Inclusive Growth: An Approach to the 11th Five Year Plan', New Delhi: Planning Commission, November.

Hazell, P., C. Pomareda and A. Valdes, eds (1986), 'Crop Insurance for Agricultural Development: Issues and Experience', *International Food Policy Research Institute*, Baltimore: The Johns Hopkins University Press.

Kulkarni, P. (2019), 'Why Farmers Across India are Complaining of Being Cheated by Prime Minister's Crop Insurance Scheme, *Scroll.in*, 27 February, available at https://scroll.in/article/914641/why-farmers-across-india-are-complaining-of-being-cheated-by-prime-ministers-crop-insurance-scheme, accessed 13 June 2019.

Mishra, P.K. (1995), 'Is Rainfall Insurance a New Idea? Pioneering Work Revisited', *Economic and Political Weekly*, vol. 30, no. 25, pp. A84–A88.

Nair, R. (2010a), 'Crop Insurance in India: Changes and Challenges', *Economic and Political Weekly*, vol. 45, no. 6, pp. 19–22.

———— (2010b), 'Weather-Based Crop Insurance in India: Towards a Sustainable Crop Insurance Regime?', *Economic and Political Weekly*, vol. 45, no. 34, pp. 73–81.

National Sample Survey Office (NSSO) (2020), *Situation Assessment of Agricultural Households and Land and Livestock Holdings of Households in Rural India, 2019*, New Delhi: Central Statistical Organisation.

Patil, M.M. and S.G. Borude (1993), 'Comprehensive Crop Insurance Scheme in Raigad District', *Economic and Political Weekly*, vol. 28, nos 12–13, pp. A25–A28.

Prabhu, K.S. (1988), 'Crop Insurance: The International Experience', Review Article, *Economic and Political Weekly*, vol. 23, no. 17, pp. 833–36.

Prabhu, K.S. and S. Ramachandran (1986), 'Crop-Credit Insurance: Some Disturbing Features', *Economic and Political Weekly*, vol. 21, no. 42, pp. 1866–69.

Rai, R. (2019), 'Pradhan Mantri Fasal Bima Yojana: An Assessment of India's Crop Insurance Scheme', ORF Issue Brief No. 296, May 2019, Mumbai: Observer Research Foundation.

Raju, S.S. and R. Chand (2008), 'Agricultural Insurance in India: Problems and Prospects', NCAP Working Paper No. 8, New Delhi: National Centre for Agricultural Economics and Policy Research (Indian Council of Agricultural Research).

Reddy, A.A. (2004), 'Agricultural Insurance in India: A Perspective', Paper presented at the Sixth Global Conference of Actuaries, 18–19 February, New Delhi.

Singh, G. (2010), 'Crop Insurance in India', Working Paper No. 2010-06-01, June, Ahmedabad: Indian Institute of Management.

Sinha, S. (2004). 'Agriculture Insurance in India: Scope for Participation of Private Insurers', *Economic and Political Weekly*, vol. 39, no. 25, pp. 2605–12.

Skees, J.R. (2000), 'A Role for Capital Markets in Natural Disasters: A Piece of the Food Security Puzzle', *Food Policy*, vol. 25, pp. 365–78.

Vyas, V.S. and S. Singh (2006), 'Crop Insurance in India: Scope for Improvement', *Economic and Political Weekly*, vol. 41, nos 43–44, pp. 4585–94.

Walker, T.S., R.P. Singh and M. Asokan (1986), 'Risk Benefits, Crop Insurance, and Dryland Agriculture', *Economic and Political Weekly*, vol. 21, nos 25–26, pp. A81–A88.

VI

Agricultural Marketing
and Food Security

14

Regulatory Aspects of Agricultural Market Reforms in India with Special Reference to Contract Farming

A Critical Assessment

Sukhpal Singh

Introduction

Agricultural market reform is a long pending and vexed policy issue. These reforms were always considered to be a state subject as per the Indian Constitution. As such, the first attempt at the reforms in agricultural marketing was made by the union government with the design of a model Agricultural Produce Market Committee (APMC) Act in 2003, which provided for new market channels for farmers and buyers alike, i.e. direct purchase, private wholesale markets and contract farming (hereafter CF). These new channels were made legal under the model APMC Act for the first time (S. Singh 2018).

Agricultural market reforms are much needed and long overdue in the light of the changing global and local markets in agriculture. The emergence of new stakeholders, i.e. wholesale cash and carry players, food retail supermarkets (domestic and foreign), online retailers/aggregators, processors, exporters and farmer producer companies in agricultural produce markets has led to new demands on the existing market structures (APMCs), which most of them are unable to meet. The APMCs were not organized and managed keeping in view the new players to meet the new and changing demands for quality produce and consistent supply. This has been due to poor policy attention paid to wholesale agricultural produce markets over the years, especially in fresh produce (wet) wholesale markets (S. Singh 2018). The major objectives of market reforms were: to achieve better efficiency in terms of lower transaction cost, better price discovery, spatial and temporal integration across markets, and an improvement in the producer's share in consumer rupee.

After the introduction of the model Agricultural Produce and Livestock Markets (APLM) Act, 2017 (MoAFW 2017), the Ministry of

Agriculture and Farmers' Welfare (MoAFW) decided to separate CF from the APMC domain citing a conflict of interest. It was argued that the APMCs were discouraging CF because the contract-farmed produce did not have to pass through APMC *mandi*, and trader and the commission agent business would be adversely affected. Therefore, a separate model Agricultural Produce and Livestock Contract Farming and Services (Promotion and Facilitation) Act, 2018 (hereafter APLCFSA, 2018) was floated by the MoAFW, which was broadly on the lines of the Punjab Contract Farming Act, 2013. Ironically, the APMCs had a larger conflict of interest with the private wholesale markets as they were direct competitors. Yet, the provision of APMCs giving permission to the private wholesale markets was retained in the APLM, 2017. The APLCFSA, 2018 also mentioned that a benefit of keeping CF and services out of the purview of the APMC was that buyers would not need to pay the market fee and commission charges. This, it was argued, would result in a saving of 5–10 per cent in their transaction costs (S. Singh 2018).

With the passage of the three Farm Acts at the central level in September 2020 (but repealed in November 2021 after protests from farmers), particularly the The Farmers (Empowerment and Protection) Agreement on Price Assurance and Farm Services Act, 2020 (hereafter FAPAFS, 2020), we had a union contract farming legislation along with a union legislation to bypass the APMC *mandi*s. These Farm Acts were expected to change the way agricultural markets are regulated across the country in multiple ways. For example, in states like Bihar that had completely deregulated the *mandi* system by repealing its APMC Act in 2006, agricultural markets would have to be brought back to regulation.

This chapter examines the major aspects of the two CF Acts – the model APLCFSA, 2018 and the FAPAFS, 2020. It also suggests mechanisms to ensure that CF remains effective in efficiently discovering prices and lowering costs of marketing for farmers. The next and second section examines the CF mechanism itself for its inclusiveness, impact and effectiveness. The third section discusses the major aspects of, and lacunae in, the model APLCFSA, 2018. The FAPAFS, 2020 is discussed in the fourth section. The final section concludes the article with some suggestions for improving the contract farming regulation and leveraging CF as a mechanism for inclusive and sustainable agricultural development.

Contract Farming (CF): Theory, Practice and Regulation

CF is defined as a system for the production and supply of agricultural and horticultural produce by farmers/primary producers under advance contracts. The essence of such arrangements is a commitment to provide an agricultural commodity of a type (quality/variety), at a specified time, price, place and quantity to a known buyer. CF basically involves five things: a pre-determined price, quality, quantity or acreage, place of delivery and time of delivery (S. Singh 2002a). It is generally undertaken when there is market failure due to perishability of the produce, quality of the produce and the technicalities of producing a new/different product (Bijman 2008). Farmers prefer contract farming not only due to better prices and output market certainty but also due to input market certainty and access to technology (Maskure and Henson 2005; Abebe *et al.* 2013). They participate in CF, or avoid it, due to many other factors too including the nature of crop, government policy, resource use or nature of company (Gedgaew, Simaraks and Terry-Rambo 2017).

In fact, for a contracting entity, CF can be described as a halfway house between independent farm production and corporate/captive farming. It is a step towards complete vertical integration or disintegration depending on the context. Due to the efficiency (co-ordination and quality control in a vertical system) and equity (smallholder inclusion) benefits of this hybrid system, CF has been promoted aggressively in the developing world by various agencies (Glover 1987).

CF is known by different variants: the centralized model, which is a company–farmer arrangement; the outgrower scheme, which is run as a government/public sector/joint venture; the nucleus-outgrower scheme involving both captive farming and CF by the contracting agency; the multipartite arrangement involving many types of agencies; the intermediary model where intermediaries are involved between the company and the farmer; and satellite farming that refers to any of the above models (Eaton and Shepherd 2001; GoI 2003; Bijman 2008). In fact, CF varies depending on the nature and type of contracting agency, technology, crop/produce, and the local and national contexts (Swain 2011).

CF is also seen to remove market imperfections in different markets (produce, capital/credit, land, labour, information and insurance markets), facilitate better co-ordination of local production activities (often involving initial investments in processing and extension) and help in reducing transaction costs (Grosh 1994; Key and Runsten 1999; IFPRI, 2005; Bijman 2008). In terms of institutional economics, the logic for CF could come from the creation of positive externalities like employment and market development or infrastructure (Key and Runsten 1999).

CF has also been attempted/used in many situations as a policy step by the state to bring about crop diversification and improve farm incomes and employment (Benziger 1996; S. Singh 2002a). The increasing cost of cultivation was the reason for the emergence of CF in Japan and Spain in the 1950s (Asano-Tamanoi 1988) and in the Indian Punjab in the early 1990s (S. Singh 2002a).

Some scholars recommend CF as the only way to make small-scale farming competitive as the services provided by contracting agencies cannot be provided by any other agencies (Eaton and Shepherd 2001). CF is also an alternative to corporate farming, which may be costly, risky, difficult to manage and not a viable option as is the case in India due to the ceilings on landholdings and land leasing restrictions (S. Singh 2006). Further, in India, the growth of food supermarkets and emerging quality issues in international trade like sanitary and phyto-sanitary measures, organic trade, fair trade and ethical trade, are also argued to be fertile grounds for the promotion of CF. Even the new Intellectual Property Rights (IPR) regime, which encourages protection and exploitation of proprietary genetics, is likely to accelerate the practice of CF (Wold, Hueth and Ligon 2001).

There is a widespread practice of CF across crops, states and agencies (public, private and multinational) in India covering twenty-five crops and livestock products with more than 100 CF projects or schemes, mostly by private domestic and multinational corporations for domestic processing or for export. Some of them also have bank linkages for the provision of credit to farmers (Swain 2016). There are different models practiced by different players, which range from bipartite- to multipartite- and intermediary-based. Given the diversity of rural and agricultural landscape in India, a single contracting agency like Frito-Lay practices five different models in different states for the same commodity i.e., potato chips. Most crops covered under CF are those with some market failure either in terms of farmer involvement or market signals. Most of these are high value crops that require new and higher investments. Therefore, they need risk coverage – both production risk and market risk, but particularly the latter (S. Singh 2011).

That the practice of CF is also problematic is borne out by many studies. It is known that many CF agreements are generally one-sided and against the farmer's interest (S. Singh 2000, 2002a, 2004; Nagaraj et al. 2008; Ruml and Qaim 2020). Studies also show that there are limitations in treating CF as a pro-poor agricultural development strategy (Ragasa, Lambrecht and Skufoalor 2018). Therefore, there has been general as well as product- or crop-specific regulations in different countries like the general farming contract law in Spain, and the crop-specific law in Kenya (Pultrone 2012). For some time now, Food and Agriculture Organization (FAO) has been seized by this problem and has been designing and propagating responsible contracts and contract practices (FAO 2012; FAO and IISD 2018). There have also been attempts at designing more practical and workable contracts (Bogetoft and Olesen 2002), as design has been found to be important in contract performance (Abebe et al. 2013). In the remaining part of this section, we review some of these issues.

Exclusion in CF

Smallholder exclusion is a global problem in CF in developing countries (Ton *et al.* 2018). There is no doubt that CF generally benefits farmers when compared with the existing channels of marketing (S. Singh 2002a; Kumar 2006; Narayanan 2013; Kharumnuid *et al.* 2017; Kaur and Singla 2018). But it is also true that contracting agencies prefer larger farmers to reduce their transaction costs (S. Singh 2002a, 2004; G. Singh and Asokan 2005; Kumar 2006; Asokan and G. Singh 2006; S. Singh 2007). Of course, there are a few exceptions in some regions and some crops like gherkins (S. Singh 2012; Sen and Raju 2006; Sharma 2016a, 2016b, Sharma and S.P. Singh 2015). In some other cases, small farmers select themselves out when large farmers are part of the CF programme (Narayanan 2013a; Ze-ying *et al.* 2018). But even in crops like gherkins, Swain (2011) has shown that the landholdings of contract growers were much larger (7.4 acres) and better irrigated compared with those of non-contract growers (4.9 acres). This bias in favour of large/medium farmers is perpetuating the practice of reverse tenancy in regions like Punjab where large farmers lease in land from marginal and small farmers and undertake CF (S. Singh 2002a, 2009a).

In Gujarat, among the sample farmers, only one contract grower with McCain had operational land holdings of less than 5 acres (S. Singh 2008a). The average landholding of contract farmers was 19 acres while the corresponding figure in farm gate sales and AMPC sales channels was only 5 and 9 acres, respectively. Similarly, contract growers for Frito-Lay (Pepsi) in Punjab had average operational holdings of 63 acres, with only 22 acres of owned land and the rest leased in. None of the sample contract growers with Frito-Lay had less than 10 acres of land, in spite of the fact that the average size of holdings in Punjab was 9 acres and 70 per cent of the holdings were of size below 10 acres (S. Singh 2008b). Another study of CF in Punjab showed that the average size of the operational holdings of contract growers was more than 1.5 times that of non-contract growers. It found no small or marginal farmer practising CF (Kumar 2006). Another study noted that 'the majority of the acreage registered in the project [CF by Punjab Agro Foodgrains Corporation (PAFC)] is held by larger farmers, who tended to receive greater benefits . . .' (Witsoe 2006, p. 16).

In fact, one of the parastatal agencies in Punjab – Punjab State Co-operative Marketing Federation (Markfed) – placed advertisements in local newspapers a few years ago publicizing its basmati paddy CF programme where it asked potential contract growers to contact its district managers if they were willing to grow in at least three acres. The questions which arise from this kind of offers are: How many small or marginal farmers can spare 3 acres for basmati paddy? How many can spare it for CF? How many would like to spare it for CF with Markfed?

A recent study of CF in chicory and sugar beet in Punjab found that the companies excluded marginal and small farmers. In one case, only 6 per cent of contract farmers were small despite the fact that 28–32 per cent of the farmers in the operating area were marginal or small. Operated landholdings of contract farmers in both cases were double of their non-contract counterparts. Farm size had a significant and positive impact on CF participation, and so had the possession of farm machinery. In terms of the income effect, only two coefficients – size of operational holding and contract participation – turned out to be significant, further reaffirming the fact that larger farmers benefitted more from CF participation (Kaur and Singla 2018).

In India, most CF projects are in the states of Punjab, Haryana, Gujarat, Maharashtra, Karnataka and Tamil Nadu, which are agriculturally more developed states. Does it mean that farmers from other states would not benefit from commercialization and vertical co-ordination of agriculture? Most states outside this set of states are areas with the highest concentration of small and marginal farmers. This essentially means that contracting companies do not encourage participation of small and marginal farmers who need help in risk-taking capability and innovation (Glover 1987).

Breach of Contracts

Defaults by farmers and firms is another global phenomenon in CF (Pultrone 2012) which has been reported in India too (S. Singh 2002a; Haque 2003; S. Singh 2004; Kumar *et al.* 2013). CF in gherkin and iceberg lettuce was relatively smooth as there was no, or a very thin, local market. There was also flexibility in contracts due to the short duration of the crops (G. Singh and Asokan 2005; Khairnar and Yeleti 2005). But even in gherkins there was a partial breach of contracts as the firms did not procure contracted produce as per contract in the case of 63 per cent of contract farmers in Andhra Pradesh (Swain 2011).

Studies in Punjab and Andhra Pradesh show that contract growers faced many problems like reduced purchase citing poor market, non-purchase of produce, delayed deliveries at the factory, delayed payments, low prices, poor quality of inputs supplied and pest attacks on the contracted crop leading to crop failure or rise in cost of production (S. Singh 2002a; Swain 2011). In the case of broiler chickens in Tamil Nadu, the firms manipulated provisions of the contracts – they picked up birds before due date or sometimes delayed the pick-up depending on the market demand leading to losses for contract growers; payments were also delayed up to 60 days. But growers were locked into these contracts due to the firm-specific fixed investments made (G. Singh and Asokan 2005). In fact, broiler CF cannot really be representative of CF in agriculture as it is more of a case of 'putting out work' or 'wage labour contracting'; the contracting agency provides all the inputs ranging from day-old chicks to feed and vaccination, and the contract grower only provides labour for feeding the birds and supervision where land requirement is not a big factor.

Even state-sponsored programmes of CF did not deliver in Punjab. In general, across crops and regions, the CF programmes could not achieve the stated area goals. The farmers also did not plant the entire contracted area with the contract crops, and the difference between the contracted and actual area cultivated was as high as 50 per cent in the case of winter maize in Ludhiana and 20 per cent in that of hyola in Ludhiana and Patiala. The private seed company provided the seeds and no other extension service. None of the companies procured the produce and they advised the farmers to sell in open market either because open market prices were higher than the contract price or because the quality was not as desired. Due to this experience, a large majority (60 per cent) of the farmers were not willing to enter into CF arrangements again (Dhaliwal, Kaur and Singh 2003). There were also instances of corruption and malpractice in the PAFC-run CF programme due to conflicts of interest among implementing agencies and lack of monitoring (Ramachandran and Dogra 2006; S. Singh 2006). Since most CF agencies did not provide crop insurance, production risk was not covered in most cases.

World Bank reports also showed the deficiencies in the CF programme of the state government in Punjab. These reports noted a set of necessities for CF to be successful: care should be exercised in the selection of crops; there should be quick and effective contract enforcement and dispute resolution; fiscal risks to the government should be limited; the number of parties in the contract should be minimum; and farmers' organizations should be developed towards transaction costs, while increasing information flow and improving farmers' negotiation position (World Bank 2003, 2004).

CF and Natural Resource Sustainability

CF leads to a transfer of responsibility for many production decisions from the individual farmer to the contracting company (Opondo 2000). However, it is not clear if the responsibility for environment impacts too is shifted (Eaton 1998). There is hardly any rigorous evidence on the environmental impacts of CF as most studies focus on the impact on small producer livelihoods (Minten, Randrianarison and Swinner 2006).

CF influences the direction of ecological change in two ways. One, the contracting agency lays down the production schedule for the farmers. By determining the crop to be grown and the husbandry practices to be followed, the contracting agency influences the impact CF will have on the environment. Two, it is the task of the government to lead conservation measures, i.e. advisory, financial and material measures. The farmer's access to these measures is, to a large extent, determined by the government policy.

Thus, the contracting agency and the government have a larger role to play in environmental/ecological change than the farmer, since they occupy a 'privileged' position in the realm of decision-making (Opondo 2000).

The environmental implications of CF include monocultures, which lead to depletion of soil quality, and overuse of chemical fertilizers and pesticides (ibid.). The contracting firms tend to aggravate environmental crisis as most of the contracts are short-term (one or two crop cycles) and the firms tend to move on to new growers and lands after exhausting the natural potential of the local resources, particularly land and water, or when productivity declines due to other reasons (Raynolds 2000). The overexploitation of groundwater, salination of soils, decline in soil fertility and pollution are examples of environmental degradation due to CF (Rickson and Burch 1996). The firms do not pay heed as the costs of such effects are externalized. CF might also lead to increasing investments in developing countries, which have low environmental standards; as a result, the natural resource base might be irreversibly depleted or damaged (Minten, Randrianarison and Swinner 2006).

There is also evidence that CF can contribute to environmental sustainability. In some African cases, CF programmes that evolved from corporate farming inherited all the ecological concerns of the previous management and continued to meet ecological responsibilities (Eaton 1998). Similarly, as an exception, in Tasmania in Australia, there were companies contracting growers for pyrethrum – a natural pesticide – and poppies for opium that integrated soil conservation into its structures and programmes. Even the crop – pyrethrum – was planted by the contracting company. These companies also insisted on crop rotation and weeding (Rickson and Burch 1996). Another study in Madagascar (Minten, Randrianarison and Swinner 2006) found that CF had important positive environmental effects, resulting from spill-over effects on land use and land intensification and the reduction of pressure on valuable forest land. In the export-oriented vegetable supply chain managed by a local company, strict standards were practiced by the company to conserve land. Pesticide application was either monitored by the company or in several cases applied by the representatives of the company to ensure correct dosage and timing. Compost application was also supervised, and the farmers were taught how to make compost. Compost use for contract crops had spill-over effects for many years. For instance, the growers were not using compost earlier, but some farmers reported that even if CF ended, they would continue using compost. In India too, there are many contracting agencies that work with organic growers for production and export of produce like cotton, basmati rice and other certified organic products (S. Singh 2009b).

In India, the irrigation intensity of the major contract crops, i.e. tomato, potato and chillies, was more than that of wheat in Punjab during the late 1990s under Pepsi Foods (a PepsiCo subsidiary). For example, potato required 8–12 rounds of irrigation as against only 5–6 rounds for wheat. Pesticides and fertilizers were also used at much higher levels than those used in the traditional crops. Potato cultivation required 108 kg of NPK (nitrogenous [N], phosphatic [P] and potassic [K]) fertilizers per acre as against 78 kg for wheat and 60 kg each of P and K fertilizers. Tomato crop required 60–90 kg of N, 60–100 kg of P, and 60–120 kg of K per acre depending on the quality of soil. Similarly, the chips potato crop required 4–5 pesticide sprays and the seed potato crop required 6–7 pesticide sprays (S. Singh 2002a). This was so despite the statement in PepsiCo's website that it follows a policy of 'application of environmentally sound agricultural practices' (Aragon-Correa and Rubio-Lopez 2007). Tomato crop under CF required as many as 14 pesticide sprays, which was even higher than that in cotton (S. Singh 2002a). In most of these cases, the farmer's awareness of the negative effects of pesticides was also poor (Gandhi and Patel 1997).

During the last decade, in Punjab, CF was promoted by the State government to encourage diversification of cropping pattern away from wheat and paddy to less water consuming crops. It was found that the number of hours of water consumption for paddy was 265.71 hours per acre compared with only 183.86 hours per acre for contract-grown basmati paddy. Similarly, CF-promoted maize had water use of only 18.35 hours per acre. In other words, crops grown under CF arrangement were water-saving. Overall, contract growers' weighted water consumption per acre was 120.49 hours compared with 129.58 hours for non-contract growers. What is notable here is that water consumption decreased not because of any new agricultural practices promoted by the contracting agencies but just because of greater area devoted to the new crops of basmati paddy and maize. In fact, contract farmers were practicing more intensive agriculture than the non-contract farmers and were devoting significantly higher number of water hours to basmati and maize than that by non-contract farmers across all crops. Thus, increased commercialisation of the various crops under CF propelled these contract farmers to use inputs more intensively. Further, the crop combination of potato and sunflower promoted under CF was more water-intensive, though more remunerative than wheat (M.P. Singh 2007). In gherkin and paddy seed CF also, the irrigation intensity of the contract crops was found to be higher as compared with that of non-contract crops (Swain 2011).

McCain Foods, a subsidiary of the Canadian multinational company McCain, practices CF with growers in Gujarat. It had made micro-irrigation compulsory for contract growers given the low groundwater table. Banaskantha district, where the company undertook CF of potato, had the seventh highest level of exploitation of ground water in Gujarat. Though this clause was not mentioned in the contract, all contract farmers had sprinkler systems. This and other forms of input supplies led to lower farmer defaults and reflected higher involvement of the firm with the growers (S. Singh 2008a). Earlier, Pepsi in Punjab had advised farmers to apply insecticides just after the white-borer larvae had broken out of their eggs and not when they matured. This way, a lesser amount of insecticides was used more effectively. Also, the company promoted the use of locally relevant traditional techniques like the use of a local grass called 'sarkanda' for the protection of plants from winter, and black ash for covering the soil to prevent crust formation and give warmth to the seeds (S. Singh 2001).

In sum, environmental concerns are increasingly being intermediated by the nature of market demand. In Kenya, most of the environmental management efforts were influenced by consumer preferences in the industrialized countries. This led to drastic reduction in the misuse of pesticides (Opondo 2000). But markets may not always signal the importance of ecological concerns due to various market imperfections, externalities and poor monitoring. For example, in Kenya, soil erosion was not attended to by the contracting agencies as that was not reflected in the product quality and was a negative externality in the contract (ibid.). Therefore, it is important to proactively provide mechanisms to ensure environmental compliance and concerns. It is not that CF *per se* leads to environmental degradation. But it can contribute to it.

The APLCFS Act, 2018: Rationale and Limitations

The model legislation of 2018 had given the operational efficiency of small farms (calling them 'handkerchief size') as the reason for promoting CF. It was not clear how the scale of farm operations can change due to CF; scales can be achieved under CF only through group contracts. But there was no mention of group contracts in the model Act. Group contracts were already in practice in Gujarat in crops like potato. Group contracts were also the deliberate choice of Thailand to leverage CF for agricultural development (S. Singh 2018). But it was not included in the APLCFS, 2018.

APLCFS Act, 2018 also bid farewell to regulation as an objective; the Act's title itself mentioned only promotion and facilitation. The Act also had provisions for the producer leasing out agricultural land to the sponsor-lessee for CF. But this was inconsistent to the prevailing laws in many states that disallowed tenancy (MoAFW 2018). This clause was also included in the Act at a time when a separate model land-leasing Act was being proposed by the Niti Aayog. In essence, the law allowed sponsors full access to farm land, and not just through contracts with farmers (S. Singh 2018).

The biggest anti-thesis of CF in the Act was the provision that a board would ensure the purchase of the entire pre-agreed produce of the grower by the contracting agency. This provision was against the very logic of quality promotion and standards in the market. Though protection of producer interest could be argued as the reason, it could also be problematic to implement this provision. When a contract specifies quality standards beforehand, why should a buyer buy lower quality produce? In practice, contracting agencies do buy a part of the lower quality produce as part of the agreement to give a market outlet for the farmers. But this is also always a source of conflict, as the prices offered for this lower quality produce (sometimes on flimsy grounds) are very low or nominal.

The APLCFS Act, 2018 also linked contract prices to the market prices, which was against the spirit of CF. Why should an agency undertake CF if it had to go for market prices which may not be efficiently discovered? The reason for undertaking CF is that the desired quality and cost are not available to the agency in the open market. In fact, Haryana had in 2005 linked the contract price to the MSP for the concerned crop in its amended APMC Act. At that time, this was argued to be undesirable, as contract prices cannot be tied to any other price mandatorily (S. Singh 2018).

The (now repealed) Union CF Act, 2020

The clauses of FAPAFS Act, 2020 led to widespread confusion between CF and corporate farming. Many provisions of the Act such as the definition of the production agreement, gave rise to this concern (MoAFW, 2020; S. Singh 2020a). The 'production agreement' was defined in FAPAFS Act, 2020 as: 'where the sponsor agrees to provide farm services, either fully or partially and to bear the risk of output, but agrees to make payment to the farmer for the services rendered by such farmer'. It was unclear how this could be contract farming where a farmer is paid for the services rendered, and not for the produce. It was also unclear how the sponsor could bear the risk of output when it was produced by the farmer. The sponsor could at best reduce the farmer's market risk as it agrees to buy in advance at a pre-agreed price (S. Singh 2020b).

Secondly, CF was also confused with the direct purchase by corporates from farmers. A trade and commerce agreement, stated as one of the types of CF agreements in the Act, was not a contract arrangement. Direct purchase was legal along with CF for many years. Many large corporates, especially fresh produce-selling supermarket players in India, were using this channel of direct purchase to buy a part of their requirement of fresh vegetables and fruits. For this, they used collection centres in the growing rural areas but without signing any contract with the farmers. The use of the term 'farming agreement' in the Act's title was itself unusual as it led to confusion with other arrangements like sharecropping or land leasing (S. Singh 2020a). CF is essentially about contract; farming is only a part of it.

The FAPAFS Act, 2020 also defined 'farming produce' very narrowly and excluded many important crops that were already being culti-vated under CF in India. Examples were medicinal plants, stevia, castor oilseed, mint/mentha and so on. It also included farmer producer organiza-tions (FPOs) under the definition of a 'farmer', which was undesirable as these FPOs themselves undertook CF in many parts of India and were never involved in production. FPOs cannot typically be called farmers.

The Act also introduced a new entity called 'farm service provider' or an 'aggregator'. It was defined as a person (who could also be an FPO) and acted as an intermediary between a farmer (or a group of farmers) and the sponsor and could be a party to the contract with a clearly specified role. This provision was completely unnecessary as service provision could be a part of the CF arrangement itself. Perhaps what was being referred to was the agro-input and other professional service agencies that undertake CF for other buyers, and not for their own needs. This was the practice in India across many crops and states where agro-input companies have organized CF projects for processors and exporters under the amended APMC Acts in the states. There was no need to separate out this set of players as they also undertook CF activities like any other players.

Further, some of these entities could also end up as intermediar-ies in CF between farmers and companies as shown by the experience of Thailand and Indian Punjab. In Punjab, there were brokers, intermediar-ies and even franchisees and sub-franchisees that led to a very long and complex chain of intermediaries in CF. It defeated the very purpose of CF as a direct link between farmers and agribusiness entities. In fact, many of these intermediaries pocketed even state subsidies in the name of providing extension services to contract growers (S. Singh 2002a).

The FAPAFS Act, 2020 specifically mentioned that in the case of seed CF, the sponsor would make payment of not less than two-thirds of the agreed amount at the time of delivery and the remaining after due certifica-tion but not later than thirty days of delivery. In seed CF, it is well known that, many times, standing crops are asked to be ploughed down by the sponsor if quality seed is not expected to be produced from a given plot of land. The compensation for this loss is a big issue for farmers, which was was not addressed at all in the Act.

But the FAPAFS Act, 2020 specifically mentioned that quality, grade and standards for pesticide residue, food safety, good farming practices, and labour and social development standards may be adopted in the contract. It even went to the extent of specifying third-party assayers to monitor and to ensure impartiality and fairness (S. Singh 2020c). It was unfortunate that social and labour aspects were only suggested and not made manda-tory given the fact that child labour and labour exploitation in wages and work conditions are widely prevalent in CF in India (S. Singh 2008c, 2017;

Banday *et al.* 2018; D'Çruz *et al.* 2021). This issue has also been adversely affecting India's export prospects in the global markets in fair trade and ethical products (S. Singh 2020c). There are also serious violations of various labour-related laws like the Child Labour Act, 1986 and Minimum Wages Act, 1948, as well as practices like gender-based wage disparity and unfair wages. The FAPAFS Act, 2020 addressed these issues only by mentioning various market-based standards, and not in terms of laws of the land.

Also, very basic aspects of CF like acreage, quantity, and time of delivery were not specified in the Act. These specifications are essential parts of any contract, and clear regulations should have been introduced in the law that claimed to be regulatory. They were very clearly stated in the 2003 model APMC Act besides additional optional provisions (S. Singh 2020c). In fact, the APMC Act also included a model CF agreement. After having kept dispute resolution outside the purview of civil courts, the FAPAFS Act, 2020 surprisingly stated that all farming agreements must meet the ordinary requirements of contract law to be valid. If these contracts were not to be dealt with by civil courts, why this condition? The FAPAFS, 2020 also left out many sophisticated aspects of modern CF practices like contract cancellation clauses and damages therein, and 'tournaments' in CF where farmers are made to compete with each other and paid as per relative performance. Such tournaments are banned in CF in many countries.

The FAPAFS Act, 2020 linked bonus and premium over and above the guaranteed price with the *mandi* price or the electronic market price. This is typically against the spirit of CF. The contracted price, like many other basic aspects of contract, should be left to the parties to negotiate and cannot be tied to any other channel. If one is citing the problems of price discovery in APMC *mandis* as the reason for introducing a new law on CF, why should the contract price be mandated to follow the *mandi* price? (S. Singh 2020c).

As per FAPAFS, 2020, permanent structures or modifications to land/premises of the farmers were allowed if the sponsor agreed to remove them at his/her cost after the end/expiry of agreement (failing which the farmer would own them). However, who would bear the cost of removing them if the farmer did not need these structures was not specified in the Act.

The Act clearly stated that the contracting agency could not lay any claim on the farmer's land and could not even lease it out. But provisions in the dispute resolution section allowed recovery of dues from the farmers by way of arrears of land revenue. This strange clause raised fears about whether farmer land or assets were actually protected from such recovery by companies.

In sum, the terms 'empowerment' and 'protection' to farmers mentioned in the title of the Act were given a miss in the clauses. The FAPAFS Act, 2020 was more about facilitation and promotion of CF rather than regulation of CF. That the Act went all the way to facilitate CF was clear from the mention that stock limits under the Essential Commodities Act (ECA) would not apply to the contracted farm produce. Why was this provision of another Act be specifically mentioned in this Act which had nothing to do with CF directly or indirectly? (S. Singh 2020c).

Conclusions: Issues and Mechanisms

The discussion on the experience with the APLCFS Act, 2018 and the FAPAFS Act, 2020 shows that these Acts were meant to open up the agricultural markets without adequate safeguards for farmers. The various lacunae in these Acts showed that they were prepared in a hurry without adequate discussion and debate (S. Singh 2018). They would not have served the purpose of making CF efficient and inclusive (S. Singh 2016). This was unfortunate, as CF could be an efficient vehicle to bring new crops, technologies and markets to farmers.

What are the pre-conditions for a successful interlocking across agribusiness firms and small producers? There should be increased competition for procurement instead of monopsony, a stable and guaranteed market for the farmers, an effective payment mechanism, market information for farmers to effectively bargain with companies and large volumes of transactions through groups of farmers to lower transaction costs and foster cooperation (Kirsten and Sartorius 2002; Bijman 2008). Many CF agreements fail because of lack of trust emerging from the behaviours of contracting companies and lack of transparency (Ruml and Qaim 2020). Hence, building of relationships of trust with farmers is essential for company reputation. There should be mutual respect, fair and transparent negotiation processes, realistic assessment of benefits, long-term commitment, equitable sharing of risk and sound business plans (Mayers and Vermeulen 2002). Innovative pricing mechanisms like bonus at the end of the processing cycle, shares in company equity, dividends, fixed price for producers and quality-based pricing that rewards performance can all help in improving contract performance.

The organization of the growers into collectives can make them benefit from CF. India's encouragement to FPOs is a right step in this direction (S. Singh and T. Singh 2014). Governments must also encourage more equitable contracts by facilitating group contracts, providing information, designing model contracts and monitoring, supervising or regulating contracts as was the case with oil palm grower contracts in the Philippines. This was also the case with sugarcane and cotton contracts in Zambia (Schupbach 2014). In this section, we try to focus on what may be needed to ensure that small farmers are included in CF.

Smallholder Inclusion

Case studies show that in many cases where smallholders were included in viable and sustainable value chains rather than engage with open markets, farmers were better off. There are many crops in India like gherkin, baby corn, chillies and vegetables where smallholders can also be part of the value chains (see S. Singh 2012). For becoming inclusive, business models in agribusiness need to appreciate adaptation to smallholder context, understand and leverage the smallholder linkage benefits in both procurement and marketing, and focus on procurement, quality and upgrading issues in the supply chain.

The crops suitable for smallholder participation should be chosen carefully; for instance, it is better that crops are of short duration. Voluminous crops like potato are not fit for smallholders as they can be produced on large scale and are amenable to mechanized cultivation. On the other hand, labour-intensive crops like gherkins or tomatoes are not amenable to mechanical handling and require constant and regular crop care – these are more suitable for CF with smallholders. Many of these crops are also those which would not be grown without a contract, such as organic cotton or gherkins, as they have no open markets.

Private sector investments can also help in inclusion as shown by Plenty Foods in Sri Lanka. Here, the company was committed to working with small farmers as part of its business model, which involved direct CF. Over years, with Oxfam intervention, there was a shift from individual contracts to group contracts that lowered transaction costs. The company also set up crop-based steering committees in the villages with farmer organizations to transfer technology, know-how and farming techniques. The committees selected a lead farmer to liaise with different service providers including Plenty Foods. Plenty Foods had a four-party CF agreement with the Department of Agriculture (DoA), financial service providers and producer organizations. The DoA provided the required extension services. This led to the formation of thirty-two groups of 500 farmers, with 70 per cent of the crop management committees led by women (Jayadevan 2011). This was similar to the national-level four-sector cooperation plan attempted in Thailand as part of its national plans for CF in the 1980s and the 1990s (S. Singh 2005).

In India, if CF is to be the way for farmer's participation in high value product chains, then it is important to make a place for smallholders. One way to do that is to encourage and promote group CF. The state should make it attractive for agencies to work with groups rather than individuals, which will lower transaction costs for all. All incentives given for CF should be for those working with smallholders or their groups as in Thailand (S. Singh 2005). But the state should not directly involve itself in CF projects (Lambrecht and Ragasa 2018; S. Singh 2002b).

The CF agencies should proactively involve NGOs in their CF operations and even organise farmer cooperatives or groups for more sustainable CF programmes (Mayers and Vermeulen 2002). In contract arrangements with small producers in West African countries, the cotton companies started transferring some of the operational or functional responsibilities like distribution of inputs, equipment orders and credit repayment management to the village associations in the 1970s. They provided these associations with management skills. The companies relied on traditional village authority structures for organizing the associations but limited the associations to one per village to simplify company purchase, delivery and marketing. This arrangement accounted for a significant part of each cotton company's success (Bingen, Serrano and Howard 2003).

The state and development agencies can also make it attractive for agencies to work with smallholders by extending low interest credit, and free training and extension support to such growers. For example, in Thailand, the state's bank (Bank for Agriculture and Agricultural Co-operatives or BAAC) provided such loans and the Department of Agricultural Extension (DoAE) provided extension support to contract growers and their groups (S. Singh, 2005). There are many cases of such support by state agencies in Malaysia and South Africa to facilitate the inclusion of specific types of smallholders into CF arrangements (Bijman 2008; Morrison, Murray and Ngidang 2006). Specific tax and other incentives like market fee waiver could also be offered to those proactively involving smallholders or their groups/agencies in their operations.

Producers' organizations and NGOs also need to monitor and negotiate more equitable contracts. The government should play an enabling role by ensuring legal provisions and institutional mechanisms, like helping farmer cooperatives producer companies and producer groups, to facilitate smooth functioning of the CF linkage and avoid its ill-effects. FPOs in India have a potential to deal with contracting agencies on behalf of smallholders (S. Singh and T. Singh 2014).

Beyond Inclusion
Legal protection to contract growers as a group must be considered to protect their interest. There are cases of legal protection given to subcontracting industries in Japan in their relations with large firms. These laws specify the duties (to have a written and clear terms contract with the subcontractor) and forbidden acts for the large parent firm. The latter includes refusal to receive delivery of commissioned goods, delaying the payment beyond an agreed period, discounting of payment, returning of commissioned goods without a good reason, forced price reduction, compulsory purchase by subcontractors of parental firm's products, and forcing subcontractors to pay in advance for materials supplied by the parent firm (Sako 1992). In the farm-

ing sector, there is the Model Producer Protection Act, 2000 of Iowa state in the USA, which requires contracts to be in plain language and disclose material risks. It provides a three-day cancellation period for the producer to review and discuss production contracts with their advisors. It also provides for producers to be the first priority for payments due under a contract in case of company bankruptcy. Besides, it protects producers against undue cancellation of contracts by companies and prohibits 'tournaments'.

Contracts must be transparent and require frequent and independent scrutiny so that they remain competitive with open market transactions. Wide publicity of contract terms can help stimulate competition.

Vigorous bargaining cooperatives or other agricultural producer organizations are needed to negotiate equitable contracts (Goldsmith 1985; Key and Runsten 1999). Such organizations have been able to secure the standardization of contracts and their scrutiny by a government agency in the USA (Wilson 1986). Bargaining groups have negotiated input purchase and output sale collectively (Welsh 1990). In Japan too, farmers have managed their relationships with companies well through cooperatives (Asano-Tamanoi 1988). The groups or farmers' organizations like cooperatives not only lower transaction costs of firms but also lower input costs for farmers and give them better bargaining power as in the case of the potato growers' co-operative in north Thailand (see Ornberg 2003).

In India, above the two Acts discussed in this chapter, the state should incentivize a move towards CF from direct purchase so that farmer's market risk is reduced considerably. Similarly, there is a need to incentivise smallholder inclusion in CF as evidence shows that they are excluded in most cases (S. Singh 2012). To encourage CF, there is a need to link lower cost credit with CF (S. Singh 2005). To top it all, there should be policy bias towards group contracts (as in Thailand) so that information asymmetry between firms and growers is reduced, transaction cost of dealing with small growers falls and there is better bargaining power with growers.

More importantly, there is a need to promote FPCs to organize and encourage market-oriented and business-like cooperatives (S. Singh and T. Singh 2014). China has progressed well on involvement of FPCs contracting with buyers in various crops with written and informal contracts (Jia and Huang 2011).

There is also a need to incorporate ecological concerns into CF programmes and policies. This can be done by way of effective land-use planning based on soil depth, soil quality, land slope and water availability. It is also important to understand the nature of previous land uses and make it mandatory to follow crop rotation, if necessary.

Finally, it is important to underline that irrespective of the expansion of CF and direct purchase, India's large mass of marginal and small farmers need public wholesale markets. These markets need to be reformed and expanded, as they are the last resort for a large majority of farmers. Reforms should take the form of free licensing for better competition, e-payment of market fee, ensuring open auction, better infrastructural facilities, representation of FPCs in APMC managements and even denotification of commission agents or *arthiyas* (as Madhya Pradesh did in 1985). The reform of APMC markets is important as they should remain to serve as competitors to CF and direct purchase channels.

References

Abebe, G.K., J. Bijman, R. Kemp, O. Omta and A. Tswgaye (2013), 'Contract Farming Configuration: Smallholders' Preference for Contract Design Attribute', *Food Policy*, vol. 40, pp. 14–24.

Aragon-Correa, J.A. and E.A. Rubio-Lopez (2007), 'Proactive Corporate Environmental Strategies: Myths and Misunderstandings', *Long Range Planning*, vol. 40, pp. 357–81.

Asano-Tamanoi, M. (1988), 'Farmers, Industries, and the State: The Culture of Contract Farming in Spain and Japan', *Comparative Studies in Society and History*, vol. 30, no. 3, pp. 432–52.

Asokan, S.R. and G. Singh (2006), *Contract Farming of Medicinal Herbs and Organic Crops in India*, CMA Monograph No. 224, Ahmedabad: Centre for Management in Agriculture, Indian Institute of Management (IIM).

Banday, M.U.L., S. Chakraborty, P. D'Cruz and E. Noronha (2018), 'Abuse Faced by Child Labourers: Novel Territory in Workplace Bullying', in D'Cruz, E. Noronha, A. Mendonca and N. Mishr, eds, *Indian Perspectives on Workplace Bullying: A Decade of Insights*, Singapore: Springer Nature, pp. 173–204.

Benziger, V. (1996), 'Small Fields, Big Money: Two Successful Programs in Helping Small Farmers Make the Transition to High Value-Added Crops', *World Development*, vol. 24, no. 11, pp. 1681–93.

Bijman, J. (2008), 'Contract Farming in Developing Countries', Working Paper, Development Co-operation, Ministry of Foreign Affairs and Wageningen University, The Netherlands.

Bingen, J., A. Serrano and J. Howard (2003), 'Linking Farmers to Markets: Different Approaches to Human Capital Development', *Food Policy*, vol. 28, pp. 405–19.

Bogetoft, P. and H.B. Olesen (2002), 'Ten Rules of Thumb in Contract Design: Lessons from Danish Agriculture', *European Review of Agricultural Economics*, vol. 29, no. 2, pp. 185–204.

D'Cruz, P., E. Noronoha, M.U.L. Banday and S. Chakraborty (2021), 'Place Matters: (Dis) embeddedness and Child Labourers' Experiences of Depersonalised Bullying in Indian Cottonseed Global Production Network's', *Journal of Business Ethics*, 4 January 2021, doi: https://doi.org/10.1007/s10551-020-04676-1.

Dhaliwal, H.S., M. Kaur and J. Singh (2003), 'Evaluation of Contract Farming Scheme in the Punjab State', Department of Economics, Punjab Agricultural University, Ludhiana.

Eaton, C. (1998), 'Contract Farming: Structure and Management in Developing Countries', in D. Burch, G. Lawrence, R.E. Rickson and J. Goss, eds, *Australian Food and Farming in a Globalised Economy: Recent Developments and Future Prospects*, Monash Publications in Geography No. 50, Melbourne, Australia: Monash University, pp. 127–44.

Eaton, C. and A.W. Shepherd (2001), *Contract Farming: Partnerships for Growth*, Rome: FAO.

Food and Agriculture Organization (FAO) (2012), *Guiding Principles for Responsible Contract Farming Operations*, Rome: FAO.

FAO and International Institute for Sustainable Development (IISD) (2018*), Model Agreement for Responsible Contract Farming*, with commentary, Rome: FAO.

Gandhi, V.P. and N.T. Patel (1997), 'Pesticides and the Environment: Comparative Study of Farmer Awareness and Behaviour in Andhra Pradesh, Punjab and Gujarat', *Indian Journal of Agricultural Economics*, vol. 52, no. 3.

Gedgaew, C., S. Simaraks and A. Terry-Rambo (2017), 'Trends in Hybrid Tomato Seed Production Under Contract Farming in Northeast Thailand', *Southeast Asian Studies*, vol. 6, no. 2, pp. 339–55.

Glover, D. (1987), 'Increasing the Benefits to Smallholders from Contract Farming: Problems for Farmers' Organisations and Policy Makers', *World Development*, vol. 15, no. 4, pp. 441–48.

Goldsmith, A. (1985), 'The Private Sector and Rural Development: Can Agribusiness Help the Small Farmer?', *World Development*, vol. 13, nos 11–12, pp. 1125–38.

Government of India (GoI) (2003), *Contract Farming Agreement and its Model Specifications*, Ministry of Agriculture, Department of Agriculture and Co-operation, Krishi Bhawan, New Delhi, 17 September.

Grosh, B. (1994), 'Contract Farming in Africa: An Application of the New Institutional Economics', *Journal of African Economies*, vol. 3, no. 2, October, 231–61.

Haque, T. (2003), 'Land Reforms and Agricultural Development: Retrospect and Prospect', in S. Pal, Mruthyunjaya, P.K. Joshi and R. Saxena, eds, *Institutional Change in Indian Agriculture*, New Delhi: National Centre for Agricultural Economics and Policy Research (NCAP), pp. 267–84.

IFPRI (2005), 'High Value Agriculture and Vertical Coordination in India: Will the Smallholders Participate?', A Draft Research Report, Washington: IFPRI.

Jayadevan, G. (2011), 'Growing Partnerships: Private Sector Working with Farmers in Sri Lanka', in D. Wilson, K. Wilson and C. Harvey, eds, (2011), *Small Farmers, Big Change: Scaling Up Impact in Smallholder Agriculture*, Warwickshire and Oxford: Practical Action Publishing and Oxfam, pp. 81–94.

Jia, X. and J. Huang (2011), 'Contractual Arrangements Between Farmer Co-operatives and Buyers in China', *Food Policy*, vol. 36, pp. 656–66.

Key, N. and D. Runsten (1999), 'Contract Farming, Smallholders, and Rural Development in Latin America: The Organisation of Agroprocessing Firms and Scale of Outgrower Production', *World Development*, vol. 27, no. 2, pp. 381–401.

Khairnar, S. and V. Yeleti (2005): 'Contract Farming in India: Impact and Implications', in R. Chand, ed., *India's Agricultural Challenges: Reflections on Policy, Technology and Other Issues*, CENTAD, New Delhi, pp. 105–28.

Kaur, P. and N. Singla (2018), 'Can Contract Farming Double Farmers' Income?', *Economic and Political Weekly*, vol. 53, no. 51, pp. 68–73.

Kirsten, J. and K. Sartorius (2002), 'Linking Agribusiness and Small-Scale Farmers in Developing Countries: Is There a New Role for Contract Farming?', *Development Southern Africa*, vol. 19, no. 4, pp. 503–29.

Kharumnuid, P., S. Sarkar, P. Singh, S. Priya, B.S. Tomar and D.K. Singh (2017), 'An Assessment of Contract Farming System for Potato Seed Production in Punjab: A Case Study', *Indian Journal of Horticulture*, vol. 74, no. 3, pp. 453–57.

Kumar, P. (2006), 'Contract Farming Through Agribusiness Firms and State Corporation: A Case Study in Punjab,' *Economic and Political Weekly*, vol. 41, no. 52, pp. 5367–75.

Kumar, S., Subhash Chandra, D.R. Singh and K.R. Chaudhary (2013), 'Contractual Arrangements and Enforcement in India: The Case of Organic Basmati Paddy Farming', *Indian Journal of Agricultural Economics*, vol. 68, no. 3, pp. 449–56.

Lambrecht, I. and C. Ragasa (2018), 'Do Development Projects Crowd-Out Private Sector Activities? Evidence from Contract Farming Participation in Northern Ghana', *Food Policy*, vol. 74, pp. 9–22.

Maskure, O. and S. Henson (2005), 'Why do Small-Scale Producers Choose to Produce Under Contract? Lessons from Non-Traditional Vegetable Exports from Zimbabwe', *World Development*, vol. 33, no. 10, October, pp. 1721–33.

Mayers, J. and S. Vermeulen (2002), *Company–Community Forestry Partnerships: From Raw Deals to Mutual Gains?*, London: International Institute for Environment and Development (IIED).

Minten, B., L. Randrianarison and J.F.M. Swinner (2006), 'Global Supply Chains, Poverty and the Environment: Evidence from Madagascar', in J.F.M. Swinnen, ed., *Global Supply Chains, Standards and the Poor*, Oxon, United Kingdom: CAB International, pp. 147–58.

Ministry of Agriculture and Farmers' Welfare (MoAFW) (2017), *Model Act (The---State/ UT Agricultural Produce and Livestock Marketing (Promotion & Facilitation) Act, 2017*, April, MoAFW, Department of Agriculture, Cooperation and Farmers' Welfare, Government of India.

——— (2018), *Model Act (The State/UT Agricultural Produce and Livestock Contract Farming and Services (Promotion and Facilitation) Act, 2018*, February, MoAFW, Department of Agriculture, Cooperation and Farmers' Welfare, Government of India.

——— (2020), The Farmers (Empowerment and Protection) Agreement on Price Assurance and Farm Services Bill, No. 11 of 2020, Ministry of Agriculture and Farmer Welfare (MoAFW), Government of India.

Morrison, P.S., W.E. Murray and D. Ngidang (2006), 'Promoting Indigenous Entrepreneurship Through Small-Scale Contract Farming: The Poultry Sector in Sarawak, Malaysia', *Singapore Journal of Tropical Geography*, vol. 27, no. 2, pp. 191–206.

Nagaraj, N., M.G. Chandrakanth, P.G. Chengappa, H.S. Roopa and P.M. Chandakavate (2008), 'Contract Farming and its Implications for Input Supply, Linkages between Markets and Farmers in Karnataka', AERR, Conference no. 21, pp. 307–16.

Narayanan, S. (2013), 'Profits from Participation in High Value Agriculture: Evidence of Heterogeneous Benefits in Contract Farming Schemes in Southern India', *Food Policy*, vol. 44, pp. 142–57.

Opondo, M. (2000), 'The Socio-Economic and Ecological Impacts of the Agro-industrial Food Chain on the Rural Economy in Kenya', *Ambio*, vol. 29, no. 1, pp. 35–41.

Ornberg, L. (2003), 'Farmers' Choice: Contract Farming, Agricultural Change and Modernisation in Northern Thailand', Paper presented at the Third International Convention of Asia Scholars (ICAS3), Singapore, August 19–22.

Pritchard, B. and J. Connell (2011), 'Contract Farming and the Remaking of Agrarian Landscapes: Insights from South India's Chilly Belt', *Singapore Journal of Tropical Geography*, vol. 32, no. 3, pp. 236–52.

Pultrone, C. (2012), 'An Overview of Contract Farming: Legal Issues and Challenges', *Uniform Law Review*, vol. 17, nos 1–2, pp. 263–89.

Ragasa, C., I. Lambrecht and D. Skufoalor (2018), 'Limitations of Contract Farming as a Pro-Poor Strategy: The Case of Maize Outgrower Scheme in Upper West Ghana', *World Development*, vol. 102, pp. 30–56.

Rickson, R.E. and D. Burch (1996), 'Globalised Agriculture and Agri-Food Restructuring in Southeast Asia: The Thai experience', in D. Burch, R.E. Rickson and G. Lawrence, eds, *Globalisation and Agri-Food Restructuring: Perspectives from the Australasia Region*, Brookfield (USA), Avebury, pp. 323–44.

Ramachandran, R. and C.S. Dogra (2006), 'Punjab- Caught in A Contract', *Outlook*, 23 January, pp. 24–26.

Ruml, A. and M. Qaim (2020), 'Smallholder Farmers' Dissatisfaction with Contract Schemes in spite of Economic Benefits: Issues of Mistrust and Lack of Transparency', *The Journal of Development Studies*, vol. 57, no. 7, pp. 1106–19, doi: https://doi.org./ 10.1080/00220388.2020.1850699

Sako, M. (1992), *Prices, Quality and Trust: Inter-Firm Relations in Britain and Japan*, Cambridge: Cambridge University Press.

Schupbach, J.M. (2014), 'Foreign Direct Investment in Agriculture: The Impact of Outgrower

Scheme Large-Scale Farm Employment on Economic Wellbeing in Zambia', PhD Thesis, University of Zurich.

Sen, S. and S. Raju (2006), 'Globalization and Expanding Markets for Cut-Flowers: Who Benefits?', *Economic and Political Weekly*, vol. 41, no. 26, pp. 2725–31.

Sharma, N. (2016a), 'Determining Growers' Participation in Contract Farming in Punjab', *Economic and Political Weekly*, vol. 51, no. 2, pp. 58–65.

———— (2016b), 'Does Contract Farming Improve Farmers' Income and Efficiency? A Case Study from Punjab', *Economic and Political Weekly*, vol. 51, no. 40, pp. 63–69.

Sharma, N. and S.P. Singh (2015), 'Exploring Contract Relationships in Punjab: A Case Study of Potato and Basmati Paddy', *Journal of Land and Rural Studies*, vol. 3, no. 2, pp. 165–86.

Singh, G. and S.R. Asokan (2005), *Contract Farming in India- Text and Cases*, New Delhi: Oxford and IBH Publishing Co. Pvt. Ltd.

Singh, M.P. (2007), 'Contract Farming and Emerging Agrarian Structure: The Case of Punjab', PhD Thesis, Centre for the Study of Regional Development, Jawaharlal Nehru University, New Delhi.

Singh, S. (2000), 'Theory and Practice of Contract Farming: A Review', *Journal of Social and Economic Development*, vol. 2, no. 2, July–December.

———— (2002a), 'Contracting Out Solutions: Political Economy of Contract Farming in the Indian Punjab', *World Development*, vol. 30, no. 9, pp. 1621–38.

———— (2002b), 'Contract Farming: Let Firms, Farmers Deal Directly', *The Tribune*, 23 December, p.13.

———— (2004), 'Crisis and Diversification in Punjab Agriculture: Role of State and Agribusiness', *Economic and Political Weekly*, vol. 39, no. 52, pp. 5583–89.

———— (2005), 'Role of the State in Contract Farming in Thailand: Experience and Lessons', *ASEAN Economic Bulletin*, vol. 22, no. 2, pp. 217–28.

———— (2006), 'Organic Cotton Supply Chains and Small Producers: Governance, Participation and Strategies', *Economic and Political Weekly*, no. 41, no. 42, *Review of Agriculture*, pp. 5359–66.

———— (2007), 'Contract Farming for Agricultural Development in Gujarat: Evidence and Issues', in R.H. Dholakia, ed., *Frontiers of Agricultural Development in Gujarat*, Ahmedabad: Indian Institute of Management (IIM).

———— (2008a), 'Understanding Practice of Contract Farming in India: A small Producer Perspective', in A. Gulati, P.K. Joshi and M. Landes, eds, *Contract Farming in India: A Resource Book*, ICAR, IFPRI and USDA, available at www.icar.org.in.

———— (2008b), 'Marketing Channels and their Implications for Smallholder Farmers in India', in E.B. McCullough, P.L. Pingali and K.G. Stamoulis, eds, *The Transformation of Agri-food Systems: Globalization, Supply Chains, and Smallholder Farmers*, Oxon and New York: Earthscan Press, pp. 279–310.

———— (2008c), 'Gender and Child Labour in Cottonseed Production in India: A Case Study of Gujarat', *Indian Journal of Labour Economics*, vol. 51, no. 3, pp. 445–58.

———— (2009a), 'Supply Chains for High Value Crops: A Case Study of Mint in Punjab', *Indian Journal of Agricultural Marketing*, vol. 23, no. 1, pp. 93–102.

———— (2009b), *Organic Produce Supply Chains in India: Organisation and Governance*, New Delhi: Allied Publishers.

———— (2011), 'Contract Farming for Sustainable Agricultural Development in India: A Smallholder Perspective', Indira Gandhi Institute of Development Research, Proceedings of workshop on Policy Options and Investment Priorities for Accelerating Agricultural Productivity and Development in India, held at India International Centre, New Delhi, 10–11 November.

———— (2012), *Modern Food Value Chains in India: Emerging Potential for the Poor*, New Delhi: Samskriti.

———— (2015), 'Reforming Markets, Lessons from Bihar', *The Tribune*, Chandigarh, 6 February, p. 9.

————— (2016), 'Smallholder Organisation through Farmer (Producer) Companies for Modern Markets: Experiences of Sri Lanka and India', in J. Bijman, R. Muradian and J. Schuurman, eds, *Cooperatives, Economic Democratization and Rural Development*, Cheltelham, UK and Massachusetts, USA: Edward Elgar, pp. 75–100.

————— (2017), '"White Gold" for Whom? A Study of Institutional Aspects of Work and Wages in Cotton GPNs in India', in E. Noronha and P. D'Çruz, eds, *Critical Perspectives on Work and Employment in Globalizing India*, edited by Ernesto Noronha and Premila D'Çruz, 15–36, Singapore: Springer.

————— (2018), 'Reforming Agricultural Markets in India: A Tale of Two Model Acts', *Economic and Political Weekly*, vol. 53, no. 51.

Singh, S. (2020a): 'Two Acts and a Half', *Outlook*, 5 October.

————— (2020b), 'Farmers' Freedom at Stake', *Frontline*, 23 October, pp. 27–31.

————— (2020c), 'Separating Grain from the Chaff', *The Pioneer*, 5 February, p. 7.

Singh, S. and T. Singh (2014), *Producer Companies in India: Organisation and Performance*, New Delhi: Allied Publishers.

Swain, B.B. (2011), 'Contract farming in Andhra Pradesh: A Case of Rice Seed and Gherkin Cultivation', *Economic and Political Weekly*, vol. 46, no. 42, pp. 60–68.

————— (2016), 'Contract Farming in Indian Agriculture: 'Can Agribusiness Help the Small Farmers?', *Indian Journal of Agricultural Economics*, vol. 71, no. 3, pp. 285–97.

Ton, G., W. Vellema, S. Desiere, S. Weituschat and M. D'Haese (2018), 'Contract Farming for improving Smallholder Incomes: What Can we Learn from Effectiveness Studies', *World Development*, vol. 104, pp. 46–64.

Welsh, R. (1990), 'Vertical Co-ordination, Producer Response, and the Locus of Control over Agricultural Production Decisions', *Rural Sociology*, vol. 62, no. 4, pp. 491–507, Winter.

Wilson, J. (1986), 'The Political Economy of Contract Farming', *Review of Radical Political Economics*, vol. 18, no. 4, pp. 47–70.

Witsoe, J. (2006), 'India: Second Green Revolution? The Sociological Implications of Corporate-led Agricultural Growth', D Kapur, ed., *India in Transition: Economic and Politics of Change*, Centre for the Advanced Study of India, Philadelphia, Fall.

Wolf, S., B. Hueth and E. Ligon (2001), 'Policing Mechanisms in Agricultural Contracts', *Rural Sociology*, vol. 66, no. 3, pp. 359–81.

World Bank (2003), *India: Revitalising Punjab's Agriculture*, Rural Development Unit, South Asia Region, Washington: World Bank.

————— (2004), *Resuming Punjab's Prosperity: The Opportunities and Challenges Ahead*, Washington and New Delhi: World Bank.

Ze-ying, H., X. Ying, Z. Di, W. Chen and W. Ji-min (2018), 'One Size Fits All? Contract Farming Among Broiler Producers in China', *Journal of Integrative Agriculture*, vol. 17, no. 2, pp. 473–82.

15

Reform of Agricultural Markets in India

A Critical Analysis

Sudha Narayanan

Background

Why is agricultural marketing so crucial for the farmer? Agriculture and allied sectors accounted for only 17.7 per cent of the GDP of India in 2020.[1] Yet, as much as 54.6 per cent of India's workforce, as per the Census of 2011, relied on this sector for employment and incomes.[2,3] Although agricultural households earned incomes from several sources, a significant share was still earned from agriculture and allied activities. As per the Situation Assessment Survey of Agricultural Households (SAS) in 2018–19, agricultural households earned 37.2 per cent of their income from crop cultivation, 15.5 per cent of their income from animal husbandry and 39.8 per cent of their income from wages.

Agricultural household incomes have, however, remained low relative to household expenses as well as their debts. As per the SAS, 2013 income measures up to only 78.67 per cent of outstanding debt and for most households operating less than 2 hectares of land, they barely cover household expenses. This finding on farm incomes is broadly echoed in other earlier estimates (Chand, Prasanna and Singh 2011; Chand, Saxena and Rana 2015). Chand, Prasanna and Singh (2011) found that the income earned by 62 per cent of farmers in India who own less than 0.80 hectare of cultivable land was lower than the poverty line during 2007–09. A later estimate suggests that farmers with landholding below 0.63 hectare do not earn enough income from agriculture to be counted among the non-poor. In other words, about 53 per cent of farm households in India would be living in poverty if they did not have earnings from non-farm sources (Chand, Saxena and Rana 2015). Aparajita Bakshi (see Chapter 11, this volume) notes further that the outcomes for smaller land class sizes and disadvantaged communities are worse. She cites evidence from detailed village surveys that reinforce these observations.

This situation prevailed despite significant changes in the agricultural sector that were expected to increase farmer incomes – with new opportunities emerging, new market players in the sector, increased prospects of participating high-value commodity supply chains and increased world commodity prices (Birthal, Joshi and Gulati 2005). For a brief period in the 2000s, food price inflation and higher world prices implied that prices of agricultural produce were higher relative to non-agricultural produce. For example, the period 2004–05 to 2010–11, the terms of trade improved in favour of agriculture, increasing from 87.82 in 2004–05 to 104.1 in 2010–11 (Ramakumar 2019).[4] Chand, Saxena and Rana (2015) found that income of farmer per rupee cost, including hired labour, in fact, showed a surge after 1999–2000. But the terms of trade stagnated thereafter from 2010–11 (see Mahendra Dev and Rao 2010; Dholakia and Sapre 2013; Ramakumar 2019). The growth in farmers' income that began around 2004–05 could not be sustained after 2011–12, when growth in farm income plummeted to 1 per cent per annum. This may be an important reason for the sudden rise in agrarian distress in the recent years. Overall, there is ample evidence that the decade of 2010–20 has been an especially challenging one for farmers (ibid.).

While there are many potential pathways to achieving increases in farmer incomes – for example, by investing in yield-increasing technologies, enhancing input use efficiency and changing the cropping pattern, there exists substantial scope to improve incomes via securing stable and better price realization of the farmer and for increasing his/her share in what the consumer eventually pays. The constitution of the Doubling Farmers' Incomes Committee (Government O.M. No. 15–3/2016-FW dated 13 April 2016) with a focus on 'monetization of farmers' produce' and the Expert Committee on the Integration of Spot and Commodity Markets (GoI 2018) indicated a renewed focus on the functioning of agricultural spot markets that in turn could help achieve these goals.

The structure, regulation and performance of agricultural markets have a strong bearing on farmer incomes. Can farmers sell their produce to buyers of their choice? Do they have a say in the prices that they can get? Are these prices stable, remunerative and just? These are the goals that underpin our discussion of agricultural markets in India. This chapter does not attempt to answer all these questions but lays out a broad discussion of the nature of agricultural marketing in India with a view to providing a foundation and context for further discussion, research and exploration.

In this chapter, we focus on *primary markets* – these are markets where bilateral trade for agricultural commodities occurs according to some rights and obligations between the seller and buyer, where the seller is typically a farmer. In this type of market, there may or may not be intermediaries. Even where intermediaries exist, their role is restricted to facilitating these bilateral transactions. Market participants in this segment include farmers, buyers, commission agents, aggregators and processors. Further, it is important in the context of marketing and market reform to study the entire market ecosystem rather than an exclusive focus on the transaction or the place of transaction. A transaction process flow in the primary market would therefore include transport, warehousing and storage, assaying, *mandi*-based or direct marketing and financing. We do not focus on *secondary or tertiary markets,*[5] where the first buyers who procure produce from farmers sell them further to others downstream along the supply chain, such as retailers, exporters and consumers, important though they are. Nor do we discuss futures markets for agricultural commodities that are linked to commodity markets. Too often, discussions on agricultural markets in India focus exclusively on field crops. This chapter retains such focus but also briefly discusses the marketing systems for plantation and livestock sectors.

The chapter begins by describing the regulatory framework for markets, for field crops and then for plantation crops, poultry, fish and livestock. The section that follows offers a review of literature on the consequences for farmers. The final section brings in the discussion on the range of marketing reforms that have unfolded until the recent Farm Laws, that were passed in September 2020. The tumultuous events of 2020 in the form of the three new farm legislations in agricultural marketing and the consequent protests and the temporary suspension of these laws presents serious challenges and promises to influence the future course of agricultural marketing in India. In this chapter, we restrict ourselves to presenting the current status without necessarily proposing a way forward, in the interests of ensuring that the contents of the chapter remain relevant, notwithstanding the course of events.

Spot Markets in Indian Agriculture: History and Context
Field Crops

The architecture of spot markets for agricultural commodities has thus far involved two levels of market interventions with respect to agricultural commodities. First, interventions by the central government, and second, interventions by the state governments. These interventions maybe legislative interventions in the form of laws or policy interventions by government orders. The federal structure adopted by the Constitution of India in 1950 divided the power to legislate on various subjects between the center and the state under three lists: List I (Union List), List II (State List) and List III (Concurrent List).[6] Since agriculture is an item in List II, state legislatures are empowered to legislate matters in this regard. Specifically, 'agriculture', 'trade and commerce within the state' and 'markets and fairs' (Entries 14, 26 and 28 respectively in List II, Seventh Schedule) are all state subjects as per the Indian Constitution. Agricultural spot markets like *mandi*s and auction platforms are governed by the respective state Agricultural Produce Marketing Committee (APMC) legislations. At the same time, the centre has an overarching responsibility via Article 301 to ensure that there is free inter-state trade within the country – of ensuring 'freedom of trade, commerce and intercourse'.

At the state level, Agricultural Produce Marketing Regulations (APMR) laws, often called APMC Acts for the committee that it empowers, govern the functioning of spot markets. The APMC Act provides a regulatory framework for trading within the state of certain 'notified' commodities, typically field crops, and typically mandates that purchases of certain agricultural commodities be through government-regulated markets (*mandi*s) with the payment of designated commissions and marketing fees. These *mandi*s are physical market places where buyers and sellers meet and commodities are auctioned or tendered. As Patnaik (2011) points out, there is considerable diversity across states in the APMC laws and the ways in which these operate. As of July 2020, most states had made deep reform of these laws, allowing private players to transact outside the *mandi* and to establish private market yards (Table 15.1). In most cases, though, trade in the market areas would still attract a *mandi* fee that would accrue to the APMC that has oversight of the market area.

In general, the government-organized market places are of two broad types – one, those that come directly under the APMC in the form of market yards and sub-market yards; and two, the rural primary markets (RPM) that are governed by panchayats, local government and the APMCs. GoI (2017a) reported that there were about 2,284 regulated markets, 2,339 principal market yards and 4,276 sub-market yards in India. The country also had about 22,932 rural periodic markets (as on March 2017) accessed by farmers. These markets operated at intervals of a week or more, though in a few cases they functioned daily. One periodic market catered to an average area of 146 sq km or a radius of 7 km and were typically owned and managed by different agencies, namely, individuals, panchayats, municipalities, including State Agricultural Marketing Boards (SAMBs)/APMCs. Since 2002, state governments have also been operating farmers' markets to enable the direct sale by farmers to consumers. Examples of these are the Rythu Bazaar (Andhra Pradesh and Telangana), Raitar Santhe (Karnataka), Apni Mandi (Haryana and Punjab), Shetkari Bazaar (Maharashtra), Uzhavar Santhaigal (Tamil Nadu) and Krishak Bazaar (Odisha). About 488 such markets existed in India in 2017.

The variation in state legislations is perhaps a core feature of Indian agricultural spot markets. This is apart from the fact that, historically, different marketing forms have evolved together as the dominant mode of transaction for different commodities typically driven by commodity char-

Figure 15.1 *Marketing channels used by farmers for select kharif crops, 2012*

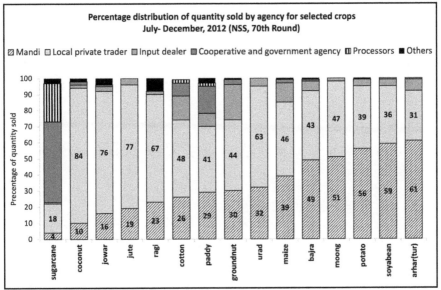

Source: Computed based on unit-level data.

acteristics and end use. For example, sugarcane, cotton and oilseeds tend to be supplied to processors as opposed to horticultural crops, which are more likely to involve traders. SAS 2012–13, the only nationally representative dataset available for marketing channels of farmers, suggests that the *mandi* and local private traders dominated the landscape of market actors (Figure 15.1). Direct sales to processors or to governments were fairly limited, except for a few crops. Even processors who contract often end up transacting with farmers through intermediaries or agents. This is evident from more recent studies on agricultural markets (Chatterjee *et al.* 2020). In the reform process, *mandis* remained the focus, and a number of committees have suggested reforms that are broadly consistent (Appendix Table 1). However, it is also apparent that there is enormous diversity in the marketing channels used in reality. As such, a single-minded or exclusive focus on *mandis* would be inadequate to improve prices received by the farmers (Mookherjee 2016). Any reform would need to address other transactional forms, such as contract farming and direct marketing.

At the centre or federal level of the government, the key factors that shape spot markets are threefold: provisions in the Essential Commodities Act, 1955 (ECA), the operation of the procurement system – wherein the government undertakes purchases at pre-established minimum support prices (MSPs) – and trade policies that change periodically in response to market conditions and demands from interest groups.

Table 15.1 *Status of agricultural marketing reform across states, as of July 2020*

State/union territory	Limiting regulation within APMC yard	Separation of powers between Director (Mktg.) and MD, Mandi Board	Single unified trading licence	Single point levy of market fee	Private wholesale market	Direct marketing (outside *mandi*)	Declaring warehouse, silos/cold storages, as deemed market	E-trading	De-regulation of marketing of fruits and vegetables
Andhra Pradesh	No	No	Yes	Yes	Yes	Yes	Yes	Yes	Yes
Arunachal Pradesh	Yes	Yes	Yes	Yes	Yes	Yes	Yes	Yes	Yes
Assam	Yes	Yes	Yes	Yes	Yes	Yes	Yes	Yes	Yes
Bihar					No APMC Act				
Chhattisgarh	No	Yes	Yes	Yes	Yes	Yes	No	Yes	Yes
Goa	Yes	Yes	Yes	Yes	Yes	Yes	Yes	Yes	Yes
Gujarat	Yes	Yes	Yes	Yes	Yes	Yes	Yes	Yes	Yes
Haryana	No	Yes	Yes	Yes	Yes	Yes	Yes	Yes	No
Himachal Pradesh	Yes	Yes	Yes	Yes	Yes	Yes	Yes	Yes	Yes
Jharkhand	No	No	Yes	Yes	Yes	Yes	Yes	No	Yes
Karnataka	Yes	Yes	Yes	Yes	Yes	Yes	Yes	Yes	Yes
Kerala					No APMC Act				
Madhya Pradesh	No	Yes	Yes	Yes	Yes	Yes	No	Yes	Yes
Maharashtra	No	Yes	Yes	Yes	Yes	Yes	No	Yes	Yes
Manipur					No APMC Act				
Meghalaya	Yes	Yes	Yes	Yes	Yes	Yes	Yes	Yes	Yes

State							
Mizoram	No	No	Yes	Yes	No	Yes	No
Nagaland	Yes	No	Yes	Yes	Yes	Yes	Yes
Odisha	Yes	Yes	Yes	Yes	Yes	Yes	Yes
Punjab	No	No	Yes	Yes	No	Yes	No
Rajasthan	No	Yes	Yes	Yes	No	Yes	Yes
Sikkim	No	No	Yes	Yes	No	Yes	No
Tamil Nadu	No	Yes	Yes	Yes	Yes	Yes	No
Telangana	No	No	Yes	Yes	Yes	Yes	No
Tripura	Yes	Yes	Yes	Yes	Yes	Yes	Yes
Uttar Pradesh	No	Yes	Yes	Yes	Yes	Yes	Yes
Uttarakhand	Yes	Yes	Yes	Yes	Yes	Yes	Yes
West Bengal	No	No	Yes	Yes	No	Yes	Yes
Delhi	No	No	No	No	No	No	Yes
Chandigarh	No	No	Yes	Yes	No	Yes	No
Puducherry	No	No	Yes	Yes	Yes	Yes	Yes
Jammu & Kashmir	No APMC Act						
Ladakh							
Andaman and Nicobar Islands							
Dadra and Nagar Haveli							
Daman and Diu							
Lakshadweep							

Source: Directorate of Marketing and Inspection (DMI), Government of India, available at https://dmi.gov.in/Documents/Reform_Status.pdf.

The ECA imposes restrictions on storage and movement of certain 'essential' commodities by private parties, mainly to protect consumers. The MSPs are announced for twenty-three commodities at the beginning of the season, which the government in principle will use to procure the produce should market prices fall below them. It is therefore a price support to prevent prices from falling below a certain threshold, although in practice, procurement is often independent of price movements and overwhelmingly focussed on rice and wheat. Procurement of other crops such as pulses, oilseeds and cotton remain limited. With respect to ECA and MSP, although these are driven by the centre, the states also have a role. In the case of ECA, states are free to set stocking limits based on the centre's notification. In the case of MSP and procurement, states participate in a decentralized procurement (DCP) scheme and provide, in some cases, bonuses over MSPs on commodities that are procured. States are also free to undertake and design procurement operations of their own, without central support, to ensure remunerative prices. Thus, both the ECA and the procurement operations, while driven largely by the centre, also provide a substantial role for the states. Trade policy, in contrast, is determined exclusively by the central government and, in an increasingly integrated world, exerts a strong influence on spot markets for cash crops that are linked to world markets.

The governance architecture of the larger market ecosystem – including warehousing and storage, transport, assaying and finance – also tends to be layered with roles distributed both across different authorities nationally and across administrative levels, i.e. centre and states.

The *warehousing market* is regulated by various regulations and guidelines imposed by the Central Warehousing Corporation (CWC), State Warehousing Corporation (SWC) and the Warehousing Development and Regulatory Authority (WDRA). *Transport controls* derived from the ECA and taxes on cross-border trade, until recently, posed barriers for inter-state movement of goods. For *assaying* too, thus far, India had multiple sets of grades and standards, with various authorities that set quality standards for different segments of the agricultural markets (examples include AGMARK and FSSAI). *Assaying,* in general, has historically been mandatory only for goods stored in warehouses and traded in exchanges. In the spot markets, neither is assaying mandatory nor is there a transparent system of assessing the quality of produce. Transactions in the spot market in *mandi*s or private markets are governed by heterogenous and non-transparent standards that are largely enforced by buyers.

Plantation Crops, Livestock, Poultry and Fishery
The description so far of the APMC Acts governs 'notified' commodities and these are typically restricted to field crops. The marketing regu-

lation for some of the fastest growing subsectors of the economy – livestock, poultry and fishery – or key foreign exchange earners, such as tea and spices – has historically followed a very different trajectory in India. Many of the institutions and regulations for the marketing of plantation crops have colonial origins and are managed typically by commodity boards, some of which were established at the cusp of Indian independence; these find force via dedicated Acts of the Parliament (Appendix Table 2). While some commodity boards (for example, the Coconut Development Board and the Coir Board) are more focused on research and development or export promotion, those such as the Spices Board and Tea Board India actively regulate auctions of commodities. A majority of domestic marketing of spices and tea is organized around auctions in commodity exchanges, with detailed protocols for grading and operations of the auction. Indeed, the tea sector has seen attempts at building a pan-India tea auction via an integrated electronic platform. For rubber, coconut and coffee, the boards have a more limited role in providing support without an explicit involvement in organizing marketplaces.

As for poultry, livestock and fisheries, there are large differences across these subsectors. Only 22 per cent of India's milk market is organized. But the legacy of Operation Flood has resulted in a well-organized system of milk routes and farmgate collection of milk from small milk producers for further retailing and processing. This sector has seen the emergence of a large number of private players, many of whom build contractual relationships with farmers for milk procurement. In poultry too, the emergence of contract farming is noteworthy, where broiler firms place day-old chicks with farmers, and provide feed and vaccines with a promise to buyback grown hens at pre-established rates (Ramaswami, Birthal and Joshi 2009). The layer industry, where chickens are raised for their eggs, is often organized along similar lines although backyard poultry still dominates. Each of these sectors is increasingly seeing private sector players invest in digital technologies to improve traceability and food safety standards along the supply chain.

In most of the meat sector, of which buffalo meat is the most important, domestic marketing is largely informally organized. The export sector, in contrast, is more well organized to ensure traceability and food safety, where packers typically integrate vertically to ensure closer oversight and control over the health of the animals and rearing practices.

The fish sector too tends to be segmented – with a large informal marine and inland aquaculture sector that has traditional supply chains, with an export-oriented segment, notably for shrimp, that has stronger vertical linkages along the supply chain to meet global food standards. In each of these sectors, state governments do play a role, often via cooperative federations of farmers or through providing regulatory frameworks (for example, for fish auctions) to protect the interests of the farmers.

In contrast to research on markets for field crops, there is relatively less research on the functioning of either of these commodity exchanges or livestock supply chains and their implications for farmers. Since several plantation crops are important export commodities for India, many studies focus on this aspect; these studies note that since the reform of these boards after the 1990s, domestic markets have been increasingly well integrated with global markets leading to greater volatility of prices faced by farmers. In a few commodities such as tea, India appears to have market power globally. Dairy is an exception, where a number of studies show mixed evidence of positive impacts on farmers.

How Has the Agricultural Marketing System Served Farmers?

Against the context provided in the previous section, this section highlights the consequences of the current marketing structure for farmers and summarizes the challenges and issues faced by farmers (Harriss 1980; Kapur and Krishnamurthy 2014).

Market Access and Monopsony

There is perhaps an inherent trade-off between ensuring that farmers have markets as close to the point of production as possible, and also ensuring that these markets are large enough to prevent collusion, to ensure transparent price discovery and to enable regulation. Establishing a large network of markets with a wide spread runs the risk of creating thin markets, with just a few buyers per market. As per the 'State of Indian Agriculture: 2015–16' (GoI 2016), the density of regulated markets in different parts of the country varied widely – from 119 sq km in Punjab to 11,215 sq km in Meghalaya. The national average area served by a regulated market was 449 sq km. The National Commission for Farmers (2004) had recommended that a regulated market should be available to farmers within a radius of 5 km (corresponding to a market area of about 80 sq km). The density per unit of output or per farmers too suggests large variations across states (GoI 2017a).

Consequently, in the current scenario, we have on the one hand, areas (and crops) for which *mandis* and rural markets are easily accessible and used but remain thin, in ways that foster monopsonies that undermine farmer interests. Studies document non-transparent price discovery processes, often through collusive trader behaviour (Banerji and Meenakshi 2004, 2008) or hoarding as in the case of onions (Madaan *et al.* 2019). In other areas, *mandis* are too far away and the transactions costs to farmers, especially smallholders, to sell in *mandis* are high enough that private traders remain a more attractive marketing alternative (Figure 15.1; Negi *et al.* 2018; Shilpi and Umali-Deininger 2008).

It is well recognized by now that though the APMC Act was designed to protect farmers' interests, it perversely rendered farmers dependent on middlemen – who were financiers, information brokers and traders, all rolled into one. This dependency often turned exploitative; farmers received but a fraction of the price paid by the final consumer, with middlemen cornering a large part of the rest (World Bank 2008; Acharya 2004; Gulati 2012). For instance, for potatoes in West Bengal, farmers received 25–50 per cent of the wholesale prices (Mitra *et al.* 2013). The supply chain for commodities also tends to be very long, with each commodity passing through as many as five to six agents before reaching the end user. Consequently, agricultural marketing in the country is characterized by high transaction costs, which results in a wide disconnect between the prices received by producers and the prices paid by consumers (GoI 2013). A 2012 study (S. Singh 2012a) in Gujarat estimated that farmers obtained 37 per cent and 48 per cent of the retail price of fruits and vegetables, indicating scope for improving the farmer's share of the retail price. A recent study by the Reserve Bank of India (RBI) in 2018–19 noted that the farmer's share in consumer's rupee ranged between 32 per cent and 68 per cent for horticulture and 40–89 per cent for foodgrains and oilseeds (RBI 2019). Interestingly, in farmer's markets like the Uzhavar Sandhai in Tamil Nadu and Rythu Bazaar in Andhra Pradesh, farmers obtained 15–40 per cent more than the prevailing *mandi*/wholesale prices and consumers paid 15–30 per cent less than retail prices (GoI 2017a).

Fragmented Markets

Since states exert influence and control over the procurement, storage and movement of commodities, the absence of uniformity in policies across states has led to fragmented markets. Interstate barriers to movement of commodities can originate from statutory orders (say, under the ECA), variations in taxes and other fees, and physical restrictions on movements (GoI 2013). In fact, recent research on agricultural markets in India conclude that they are inefficient (Mattoo, Mishra and Narain 2007; Umali-Deininger and Deininger 2001), and are characterized by a high level of wastage (Mattoo, Mishra and Narain 2007) and an absence of spatial market integration (GoI 2017b; Acharya *et al.* 2012). Chatterjee (2018) suggests that barriers to interstate trade in agricultural commodities might result in price increases for the farmer to the extent of 11 per cent.

Other issues that have been highlighted are the variation in taxes, non-transparent levies and various charges on the sale of farm produce that could be as high as 14.5 per cent in Punjab and as low as 3 per cent in Gujarat and 3.6 per cent in Rajasthan (GoI 2013). These charges manifest themselves in the form of high transaction costs, and a wide disconnect between the prices received by producers, the prices paid by consumers and prices across states (ibid.). APMCs are authorized to collect market fee ranging between 0.50 and 2.0 per cent of the sale value of the produce. In addition, commission charges vary from 1 to 2.5 per cent in foodgrains and 4 to 8 per cent in fruits and vegetables. Further, other charges, such as purchase tax, weighment charges and *hamali* (payment of wages to the carriers of food items) charges are also required to be paid. In some states, this works out to total charges of about 15 per cent.

Poor price dissemination mechanisms also mean that farmers are unable to negotiate a better price for their produce although existing interventions on price information dissemination have been ambivalent at best (Fafchamps and Minten 2012; Mitra *et al.* 2013; Goyal 2010; Jensen 2007).

Price for Quality

Assaying in spot markets is not mandatory and is done almost entirely in a subjective manner by the trader or commission agent. Farmers typically do not grade or sort in the farm itself and if at all they do, it is done after the sales. The limited extent to which produce is assayed or graded represents a missed opportunity for farmers to capture a premium associated with selling better quality produce, which can be achieved with modest expenses on grading and sorting. In general, not only is there need to upgrade infrastructure to grade, sort and assay, but also to bring down the costs of assaying and increase the awareness among farmers regarding the benefits of assaying.

The Problem of Aggregation

An important aspect of low prices accruing to farmers is the small scale of agriculture. In general, farmers tend to be price takers. Given the small quantities of sale per farmer, they typically lack the bargaining power and face high transaction costs of marketing per unit of commodity. Aggregation of produce for sale has often been prescribed as a way for farmers to command better prices and has been the driving premise for collective marketing arrangements. The agricultural marketing cooperatives movement has a long history in India and there are fine examples of successful aggregation models in marketing (for example, areca nut marketing cooperatives in Karnataka discussed in Gopikuttan and Naik 2021). Recent forms of other collective institutions, including farmer producer organizations (FPO), are steps towards addressing this issue (S. Singh 2012b; S. Singh and T. Singh 2014). The literature on this is somewhat limited in the context of the benefits in terms of better prices. In general, even as there are several examples of success in cooperative marketing, FPOs in India currently face formidable operational challenges (Neti, Govil and Rao 2019; S. Singh and T. Singh 2014).

Storage Issues and Credit

Another key constraint in monetizing farm produce is the inability of farmers to store for a better price (Kumar and Das 2020). It is typical to see prices plunge as market arrivals surge during the harvest season and pick up as the season tapers off. Most farmers have limited financial strength or staying power to postpone their sales and wait for better prices – leading to distress sales. Often, farmers are forced to sell immediately to dissolve their debts. Interlinked credit–output transactions continue to be pervasive, despite some studies noting that these are absent in some contexts (Chatterjee *et al.* 2020; Minten, Vandeplas and Swinnen 2012). Despite the spread of formal financing for farmers, farmers in many regions continue to rely on commission agents for loans (both production and consumption credit) and often sell their output to their creditors to extinguish their debts (Aggarwal *et al.* 2017). Nationally representative surveys suggest that for those who do this, output price is discounted to account for implicit interest rates (Narayanan and Dhanapal 2021).

Evidence of farmers' inability to save has been documented in several contexts. In a study of warehouses, NIPFP (2015) found that a bulk of the users of warehouses were traders. Smaller outputs and long distances from warehouses have deprived small farmers of access to modern storage facilities, particularly for perishable items (IDFC 2013). The government's focus has been on encouraging farmers to use warehouses to expand their access post-harvest credit. Lending against agricultural commodities stored in warehouses is generally considered safe, as the commodity is a good collateral. However, presently, the main users of warehouses and the main beneficiaries of pledge financing are traders who use pledge financing to hedge and manage liquidity constraints (NIPFP 2015). In general, pledge loans and warehouse receipt financing are yet to gain traction as financing instruments for farmers (GoI 2018).

A study on cold storages for potato in Bihar is more encouraging and reported that the number of cold storages at the state level in Bihar increased between 2000 and 2009 from 195 to 320, an increase of 64 per cent (Minten *et al.* 2014). In the case of cold storages, Minten *et al.* (2014) found that 91 per cent of the users of cold storages were farmers, including smallholders. Because of better storage conditions of their seeds, farmers benefited directly from the existence of these cold storages and an extra market channel. Even those who did not directly participate could benefit because prices were smoothened. Due to the availability of an extra marketing channel (the storage option), it can be expected that prices would increase, on an average, during the harvest. For those smaller farmers who sell relatively more directly after the harvest, there could be benefits from these higher prices.

Minten *et al.* (2014) also pointed out that more competition in the cold storage sector was desirable so as to drive down the cost of storage. While the subsidies given out by the government helped to stimulate the setting up of cold storages, it was insufficient, as yet, to lower storage costs and create a more competitive environment for cold storages. The storage costs of cold storages were still very high on account of high overheads like investments in generators due to poor power supply. Cold storages required a constant supply of electricity. Poor electricity supply in areas forced operators to maintain back-up generators. These were costly and increased the cost of warehousing. Inadequate competition was also cited as another reason for high storage costs, especially in cold storages. Cold storage capacity increased by 43 per cent between 2009 and 2017, but varied widely across states (GoI 2018). Such findings augur well in terms of clearing a critical supply bottleneck.

Post-Harvest Losses

There is considerable scope to reduce post-harvest losses. The total post-harvest losses of agriculture commodities were earlier estimated at about Rs 44,000 crore at 2009 wholesale prices. These losses were deemed to be on account of poor storage and transport at points of exchange. Investments in reducing these losses would help farmers monetize a larger share of their marketed surplus.

A high-level expert committee on cold storage constituted by Department of Agriculture and Co-operation (NCCD 2015) estimated that 25 per cent to 30 per cent of fruit and vegetables, and 8 per cent to 10 per cent of food grains were wasted annually due to lack of post-harvest technology and non-existence of integrated transport, storage and marketing facilities. A Ministry of Agriculture study estimated in 2014 (Tripathy 2017) that about 7 per cent of the food grains and 30 per cent of fruit and vegetables were lost due to inadequate handling facilities. Approximately 10 per cent of valuable spices were also lost due to lack of proper post-harvest infrastructural facilities. Patnaik (2011) reported that a recent study conducted by ICAR (2010), which showed that post-harvest losses of various commodities in the range of 3.9–6.0 per cent for cereals, 4.3–6.1 per cent for pulses, 5.8–18.0 per cent for fruits and 6.8–12.4 per cent for vegetables.

Price Support and Procurement

Government intervention in markets takes many forms: price support for different groups of commodities under the MSP/procurement policy, the market intervention system (MIS) for the procurement of perishable agricultural and horticultural commodities and the price support scheme (PSS) for three categories of crops, i.e. oilseeds, cotton and pulses. These are meant to provide a price floor for the farmers.

The MSP, which is supposed to function as a price floor, often lies below the reigning marketplace and has proven to be a somewhat blunt instrument. Even as a price floor, it barely covers the cost of production in many states. Recent policy announcements on pegging MSP to cost of cultivation have only underscored the fact that the MSP did not necessarily assure the farmer a remunerative price.

In recent years, the MSP and government procurement, especially of paddy and wheat, have been discussed and critiqued widely (GoI 2015; Chand 2003). Among other things, the following claims were often voiced: very few farmers directly benefit from MSP (6 per cent only), only large farmers benefit from MSP, and only farmers of Punjab and Haryana (and to some extent western Uttar Pradesh) benefit from MSP. These arguments have often formed the basis for a call to reform the system.

More recent research suggests that these claims are not entirely correct (Gupta, Khera and Narayanan 2021). Not only has the source of procurement diversified to new geographies outside Punjab, Haryana and western Uttar Pradesh, they were also increasingly inclusive of small and marginal farmers. Despite a large farmer bias nationally in terms of procurement, this has not crowded out small farmer participation and majority of the beneficiaries are marginal and small farmers on both the extensive (participation) and the intensive (quantity sold to procurement agencies) margins. They also offer perhaps the only credible insurance to farmers (Chatterjee *et al.* 2020). There are several concerns with government price support as it is implemented today. These concerns include focus on only rice and wheat, the fiscal costs of procurement and storage without a clear plan for distribution, and their welfare and distributional implications for the farmers. Some states such as Madhya Pradesh and Haryana experimented briefly with price deficiency payments (the Bhavantar Bhugtan Yojana and Bhavantar Bharpayee Yojana, respectively) that paid out the shortfall of the traded price from the MSP or an established guarantee price to farmers. These have, however, since been abandoned. This is an area that demands deeper understanding and discussion before embarking on any reform.

Uncertainty in Policy

At a macro level, there are significant sources of price volatility that lead to price risks faced by farmers. These include changes in trade policy, as in rice and cotton, and in the regulations under ECA. Another source of uncertainty is the frequent bans on futures markets that transmit volatility to spot markets (see Table 15.2). While there is not much research so far on the key impacts of these policies on the prices farmers obtain, the uncertainties can thwart efficiency-enhancing investments in marketing and enhance the need for sophisticated understanding of price movements and market functioning.

Table 15.2 *Some recent examples of bans on futures trading until 2020*

Commodity	Trading suspension period
Tur, urad	23 January 2007
Jute	15 December 2005 – 15 July 2006
Rice	27 February 2007
Wheat	27 February 2007 – 21 May 2009
Chana	7 May 2008 – 4 December 2008; 27 July 2016 – 14 July 2017
Potato	7 May 2008 – 4 December 2008; 18 June 2014
Rubber, sugar	26 May 2008 – 14/15 May 2009; Rubber: 7 May – 4 December 2008 on MCX (Multi Commodity Exchange)
Soy oil	7 May 2008 – 4 December 2008
Castor seed	27 January 2016 – 5 January 2017
Guar seed, guar gum	27 March 2012 – 14 May 2013

Source: GoI (2018).

Current Policy Efforts: A Review and Assessment

The previous section highlighted some of the persistent and stubborn problems in agricultural marketing that continue to limit the ability of farmers to get better and fairer prices. There is evidence of several initiatives by different states and some encouraging examples. These learnings have by and large provided a useful basis for further reform of the agricultural marketing system. At the same time, deep reform has been hard to achieve. This section reviews recent efforts to improve the marketing ecosystem for agricultural commodities until the three Farm Acts were introduced with dramatic suddenness, first as ordinances in June 2020, and then as Acts of the Parliament in September 2020 (they were, of course, repealed in November 2021).

Mandi Reforms: NALM and e-Nam

There was early recognition that the essential structure of the APMC markets would need to change. Recommended changes typically included a separation of regulatory powers from operational responsibility that would resolve any conflicts of interests; a move towards unified licensing so that one licence would suffice to trade in any *mandi* within the state; freeing up of constraints to allow new forms of engagement in the market area outside the *mandi*, and so on (Appendix Table 1).

Early efforts at reframing the architecture of agricultural spot markets came with the model APMC Act, 2003. The model Act sought to remove some of the limitations of the old APMC Act by opening up the markets to the private sector and cooperatives and by allowing direct farm sales and contract farming. The Act also envisaged use of technological infrastructure for marketing and online trading of agricultural produce. The objective was to bring transparency and efficiency, and provide freedom to farmers to sell their produce to the agent of their choice – whether a contract-sponsor, a public *mandi* or a private market. The extent of adoption of the model Act by states remained discouraging for over a decade, despite potential benefits (Purohit 2016; Purohit, Imai and Sen 2017; Chand 2016). While several states adopted key areas of reforms, in reality, most of the states diluted the model Act provisions and only partly implemented them (Chand 2016; Patnaik 2011). Bihar, on the other hand, went so far as to abolish the APMC Act entirely in 2006, which spawned makeshift marketplaces across the state devoid of any infrastructure (S. Singh 2015).

Since then, however, several states have attempted more substantive and earnest reform. Table 15.1 illustrates the state of reform in different states; in contrast to the situation earlier, despite implementation problems, several states appear to have moved forward on these reforms. At the same time, even where some features have purportedly been implemented, it is unclear whether these changes have taken place in practice. For example, as Patnaik (2011) observes, the model Act of 2003 stipulated prohibition of commission agents in any transaction of agricultural produce of the farmers. The states of Madhya Pradesh, Chhattisgarh, Mizoram, Nagaland and Sikkim adopted this specific provision but it is doubtful if this had been implemented faithfully. In 2014, the union government called for the denotification of horticultural crops, implying that fruits and vegetables should no longer come under the regulatory ambit of the APMC Acts. While many states denotified fruits and vegetables, some states continued to regulate a few key commodities like apple in Himachal Pradesh. Likewise, the denotification of horticultural crops did not fully do away with *mandi* fees and charges (Table 15.1).

More recent initiatives included the e-NAM (e-National Agriculture Market), which represented a renewed attempt to redress persistent issues. Discussions on a national unified market may be dated back to the mid-term appraisal of the Eleventh Five-Year Plan (GoI 2011, p. 84), which expressed a need to bring down the barriers in agricultural markets across states. In the Twelfth Five-Year Plan, a task group explicitly articulated the need to have a National Agricultural Market (NAM). The announcement in the Union Budget, 2016–17 of the establishment of such a platform therefore marked the culmination of years of discussion and represented a significant first step towards implementation (GoI 2016). Despite the progress with e-NAM rollout, the state legislative frameworks seem to have continued to hinder the development of a unified framework or 'rules of the game'. In reality, the complex relationship shared by commission agents in *mandi*s and farmers who sell to them – where credit and output sale were linked – was hard to dislodge. Infrastructural constraints for assaying and a basic mistrust by traders and farmers of scientific quality assessments were other challenges to the uptake of e-trading (Aggarwal, Jain and Narayanan 2017).

The possibility of e-NAM's success within the APMC framework was predicated on coordinated reform of all state APMC Acts. Without this, the state with the most restrictive APMC Act would determine the extent to which an electronic platform can be truly national. A crucial element is that there might be conflicts between the legal and regulatory frameworks of the states versus the framework proposed by the centre. It was at this juncture that a model legislation titled National Agricultural Produce and Livestock Marketing (Promotion and Facilitation) Act, 2017 (NALM) was proposed by the centre as the latest effort in spot market reform. Together with the Model Contract Farming Act, 2018, this Act aimed to set a new institutional framework for spot market transactions in India (S. Singh 2019).

Contract Farming and Other Direct Marketing Channels

A key challenge in the agricultural marketing ecosystem in India has been the variable success of private players to participate on a large scale. Barring a few exceptions, these problems were especially true of contract farming arrangements and direct purchases by retailers and processors from farmers through private *mandi*s. The 2003 model Act (APMC Act) had outlined a framework for contract farming operations that would safeguard the interests of both the firms and farmers equitably. It also paved the way for private market yards and direct buying and selling, among other things. This was later complemented by the creation of agri-export zones (AEZs) across the country, where firms involved in agri-processing for exports would benefit from tax-breaks and specific infrastructural facilities. Contract farming in high-value crops also became part of a larger strategy for diversification, weaning farmers away from the rice–wheat system that so dominated Indian agriculture.

Both contract farming and direct selling to supermarkets appear to hold considerable benefits to participating farmers (Nutalapthi *et al.* 2020; Suganthi 2013). However, only a few farmers tend to be included in these supply chains. Likewise, contract farming has only succeeded in niche commodities for exports or in specific sectors like poultry, but has largely failed to gain traction where domestic spot markets offered competition (Singh and Asokan 2005). The small scale of holdings implied that firms had to negotiate with a large number of farmers, increasing the transaction costs and monitoring costs.

Commodity exchanges in India too faced severe challenges

(Sahadevan 2002a, 2002b). The emergence of a large number of agri-tech start-ups and e-platforms hold uncertain outcomes for farmers. Institutional innovations like cooperatives and farmer producer companies (FPCs) appear to be one way to address the constraints of small scale of farm operations but here too, success has been variable at best (Neti, Govil and Rao 2019; S. Singh and T. Singh 2014). The model Contract Farming Acts of 2018–19 aimed to provide a framework that would not deter and instead encourage contract farming that would balance the interests of firms and farmers alike (see chapter 14 by Sukhpal Singh in this volume for a detailed and critical discussion).

Transport, Storage, Warehousing, Assaying

There has been substantial progress in reducing inter-state barriers as well. With the enforcement of the GST and removal of checkpoints at the state boundaries, the transport of produce is much less burdensome than earlier. This is an important step towards the idea of a nationally integrated market. Despite the easing of physical and tax barriers, as long as statutory regulations, like those under the ECA were in force in the states, these barriers could be used to restrict inter-state trade. As the inter-state ministerial committee noted, since 1993, the central government had decided to treat the entire country as a single food zone, but states were imposing orders to restrict movements. While each state is empowered to take decisions to moderate prices, the unpredictability and uncertainty of policy announcements could often pose barriers for internal trade.

The Three Farm Laws

The previous section outlined the progress in marketing reforms until 2020. In June 2020, three farm bills were introduced as ordinances and were later promulgated as Acts in September 2020. Although it is the case that marketing reforms have been discussed for long (Appendix Table 1), the three ordinances or Acts themselves hardly saw any discussion at all. These three Acts marked a clear departure from the somewhat consistent trajectory of reform thus far.

The first of the three Acts, the Farmers' Produce Trade and Commerce (Promotion and Facilitation) Act, 2020, wrested control away from states by limiting the APMC's oversight and jurisdiction to the APMC 'market yard', terming all areas outside the market yard as 'trade area' and freeing trade completely in the trade area, and providing a 'facilitative framework for electronic trading'.[7] The second Act, the Essential Commodities (Amendment) Act, 2020 amended the Essential Commodities Act of 1955 that allowed the centre and the states to impose stocking limits on private traders to prevent hoarding and market manipulation.[8] The new amended

Act removed some of these restrictions, which could be deployed only in 'exceptional circumstances'. This easing was welcomed especially by large businesses who had found those restrictions constraining. The third Act, the Farmers (Empowerment and Protection) Agreement on Price Assurance and Farm Services Act, 2020 allowed 'sponsors' to engage with farmers via written contracts and frees downstream players in the supply chain from state APMC regulations by permitting them to operate outside the purview of any State Act or of the Essential Commodities Act of 1955.[9]

Since their promulgation, several critiques of these Acts appeared in the popular press. A key issue was the constitutional validity of these Acts and the manner in which it was passed and later suspended by the Supreme Court of India (Ramakumar 2020). Beyond that is the question of whether the trajectory of existing reform by the states was so wanting in terms of content or pace as to warrant an approach by the centre that undermines the states' role in agricultural marketing. As has been explained so far in the chapter, states have taken the lead in implementing these reforms, often with laudable innovations, with the centre providing the broad direction. Indeed, in recent years, several states have allowed private agribusinesses to establish private market yards or collection centres, to undertake contract farming and to buy directly from farmers (Table 15.1). Private sector players operated within the ambit of the state-level APMCs, under the same regulatory umbrella in which APMC market yards served as the backbone that brought buyers and sellers together to trade in one place. The new reforms under the Farm Acts now create a different structure, outside the regulatory purview of APMCs, and therefore of state governments, fully under central government control.

There were also concerns regarding the contents of the Acts themselves, that seemed to depart from the logic of the path of reform thus far. For, although purporting to serve the interests of farmers, all the three Acts focused not directly on farmer's welfare but on improving the 'ease of doing business' for supply chain actors, especially non-traditional private players, such as agri-tech companies and retailers. Till then, however, virtually no rules existed for this new space: transactions were not needed to be recorded or documented, and nothing ensured competition or the absence of collusion (Narayanan 2020). The devices farmers had for dispute resolution too were weak at best. In essence, therefore, though the Acts professed to free trade for farmers, they really removed constraints on buyers and shifted control over trade from the states, as originally envisioned in the Constitution, towards the centre. The centre could now fully regulate and control agriculture in ways that fostered consolidation of select businesses that found favour with the government in power.[10]

The three Farm Acts were repealed on 24 November 2021. This

most recent misadventure with agricultural marketing reforms offers a moment of self-reflection for policy-making in Indian agriculture. Just as the Acts were never going to solve the Indian farmer's marketing problems, the repeal of these three Acts is not going to reverse the growth of private players in agricultural marketing. The union government has the capacity to make landmark changes, but the ability to enact true reforms rests in the hands of the state governments. The state governments are best placed to assimilate and respond to the diversity of institutional and socio-economic contexts and agroclimatic regions and incorporate local concerns for robust and sustainable solutions. States need to go back to the basics and to the suggestions that many expert committees have proposed for agricultural market reform – especially delinking the regulatory and operational roles of the APMCs. The union government, for its part, should turn its attention in the short term to offer a stable and predictable policy environment vis-à-vis imports and exports, the functioning of national commodity exchanges and futures markets, and the provision of inclusive platforms for discussions on public procurement, price support, safeguards against the consolidation of corporate interests, data policies and state-level market reforms.

Notes

[1] Officially, agriculture includes crops, livestock and allied sectors include forestry and fishery. The data presented here are for agriculture and allied activities. For this paper, we focus only on farming activities including crops, livestock and fishery.

[2] The figures are for the share of agriculture and allied sector in total employment as per the Census of India, 2011 (GoI 2016, p. 35). The National Sample Survey estimates that in 2011–12, 48.9 per cent of total workforce was employed in agriculture.

[3] Data are for the year 2014–15 at 2011–12 constant prices (GoI 2016).

[4] Terms of trade measure how much the agriculture sector prices change relative to those of the non-agricultural sector. The terms of trade index with a value less than 100 suggests that agricultural is at a relative disadvantage in the very broad sense that the prices that farmers earn for their produce is less than what they would spend on non-agricultural commodities.

[5] Secondary and tertiary markets include those that are organized via commodity exchange such as NeML (National e-Markets Limited) as well as other kinds of transactions that involve the commodity's changing hands from one link in the supply chain all the way to the end-user.

[6] Article 246, Constitution of India.

[7] http://egazette.nic.in/WriteReadData/2020/222039.pdf.

[8] http://egazette.nic.in/WriteReadData/2020/222038.pdf.

[9] http://egazette.nic.in/WriteReadData/2020/222040.pdf.

[10] https://economictimes.indiatimes.com/blogs/et-commentary/drama-at-the-farm-gate.

References

Acharya, S.S. (2004), 'Agricultural Marketing in India', *Millennium Study of Indian Farmers*, vol. 17, New Delhi: Academic Foundation.

Acharya, S.S., R. Chand, P.S. Birthal, S. Kumar and D.S. Negi (2012), 'Market Integration and Price Transmission in India: A Case of Rice and Wheat with Special Reference to the World Food Crisis of 2007/08', Rome: Food and Agriculture Organization.

Aggarwal N, S. Jain and S. Narayanan (2017), 'The Long Road to Transformation of Agricultural Markets in India: Lessons from Karnataka', *Economic and Political Weekly*, vol. 52, no. 41, pp. 47–55.

Banerji, A. and J.V. Meenakshi (2008), 'Millers, Commission Agents and Collusion in Grain Markets: Evidence from Basmati Auctions in North India', *The BE Journal of Economic Analysis and Policy*, vol. 8, no. 1, pp. 1–26, https://doi.org/10.2202/1935-1682.1786

Banerji, A. and J.V. Meenakshi (2004), 'Buyer Collusion and Efficiency of Government Intervention in Wheat Markets in Northern India: An Asymmetric Structural Auctions Analysis', *American Journal of Agricultural Economics*, vol. 86, no. 1, pp. 236–53.

Birthal, P.S., P.K. Joshi and A. Gulati (2005), 'Vertical Coordination in High-Value Commodities Implications for Smallholders', MTID Discussion Paper 85, Washington D.C.: International Food Policy Research Institute.

Chand, R., P. Prasanna and A. Singh (2011), 'Farm Size and Productivity: Understanding the Strengths of Smallholders and Improving their Livelihoods', *Economic and Political Weekly*, vol. 46, nos 26–27, pp. 5–11.

Chand, R., R. Saxena and S. Rana (2015), 'Estimates and Analysis of Farm Income in India, 1983–84 to 2011–12', *Economic and Political Weekly*, vol. 50, no. 22, pp. 139–45.

Chand, R. (2003), 'Government Intervention in Foodgrain Markets in the New Context', National Institute of Agricultural Economics and Policy Research (NIAP) Policy Paper No. 19, National Centre for Agricultural Economics and Policy Research, New Delhi.

Chand, R. (2016), 'e-Platform for National Agricultural Market', *Economic and Political Weekly*, vol. 51, no. 28, pp. 15–18.

Chatterjee, S., M. Krishnamurthy, D. Kapur and M. Bouton (2020), 'A Study of the Agricultural Markets of Bihar, Odisha and Punjab', Final Report. Philadelphia: Center for the Advanced Study of India, University of Pennsylvania.

Chatterjee, S. (2018), 'Market Power and Spatial Competition in Rural India', Working Paper, Princeton, NJ: Princeton University.

Dholakia, R.H. and A. Sapre (2013), 'Inter-sectoral Terms of Trade and Aggregate Supply Response in Gujarat and Indian Agriculture', Working Paper, No. 2013-07-02, Indian Institute of Management (IIM), Ahmedabad.

Fafchamps, M. and B. Minten (2012), 'Impact of SMS-Based Agricultural Information on Indian Farmers', *The World Bank Economic Review*, vol. 26, no. 3, pp. 383–414.

Government of India (GoI) (2011), 'Mid-Term Appraisal for Eleventh Five Year Plan 2007–2012', Planning commission, Government of India, available at https://niti.gov.in/planningcommission.gov.in/docs/plans/mta/11th_mta/MTA.html.

———— (2013), 'Final Report of Committee of State Ministers In-charge of Agricultural Marketing Reforms', Ministry of Agriculture, Department of Agriculture and Co-operation, available at http://dmi.gov.in/Documents/stminprreform.pdf, accessed on 15 November 2017.

———— (2015), 'Report of the High-Level Committee on Reorienting the Role and Restructuring of the Food Corporation of India', January 2015.

———— (2017a), 'Post-Production Interventions: Agricultural Marketing', Report of the Committee on Doubling Farmers' Income, Department of Agriculture, Cooperation and Farmers' Welfare, vol. 4, Ministry of Agriculture and Farmers' Welfare, Government of India.

———— (2017b), *Economic Survey 2016-17*, Department of Economic Affairs, Government of India.

———— (2018), 'Expert Committee Report on the Integration of Spot and Derivatives Markets', Department of Economic Affairs, Government of India.

Gopikuttan, G.S. and G. Naik (2020), 'Deregulation of Agricultural Markets in India', Working Paper No. 631, Indian Institute of Management, Bangalore.

Government of Karnataka (2013), 'Report of Agricultural Marketing Reforms Committee', Co-operation Department, Government of Karnataka, available at http://krishimaratavahini.kar.nic.in/HTML/Downloads/English per cent20Recommendations per cent20of per cent20committe.pdf

Goyal, A. (2010), 'Information, Direct Access to Farmers, and Rural Market Performance in Central India', *American Economic Journal: Applied Economics*, vol. 2, no. 3, pp. 22–45.

Gulati, A. (2012), 'Reforming Agriculture in India 2011: A Symposium on the Year That Was', *Seminar*, vol. 629. https://www.india-seminar.com/semframe2.html

Gupta, P., R. Khera and S. Narayanan (2021), 'Minimum Support Prices in India: Distilling the Facts', https://doi.org/10.31235/osf.io/ufw9k

Harriss, B. (1980), 'Regulated Foodgrains Markets: A Critique', *Social Scientist*, vol. 8, no. 8, pp. 22-31.

IDFC with CESS, IRMA and IGIDR (2013), *India Rural Development Report, 2012–2013*', Noida: Orient Blackswan Private Limited.

Jensen, R. (2007), 'The Digital Provide: Information (technology), Market Performance, and Welfare in the South Indian Fisheries Sector', *The Quarterly Journal of Economics*, vol. 122, no. 3, pp. 879–24.

Kapur, D. and M. Krishnamurthy (2014), 'Understanding Mandis: Market Towns and the Dynamics of India's Rural and Urban Transformations', CASI Working Paper No 14-02, Center for the Advanced Study of India, Pennsylvania: University of Pennsylvania.

Kumar, A.G. and V.K. Das (2020), 'Do Storage and Structural Factors Determine Agricultural Commercialization in India', Working Paper No. 2020-004, Indira Gandhi Institute for Development Research, Mumbai.

Madaan, L., A. Sharma, P. Khandelwal, S. Goel, P. Singla and A. Seth (2019), 'Price Forecasting and Anomaly Detection for Agricultural Commodities in India', available at https://www.cse.iitd.ac.in/~aseth/commodity-prices.pdf

Mahendra Dev, S. and N.C. Rao (2010), 'Agricultural Price Policy, Farm Profitability and Food Security', *Economic and Political Weekly*, vol. 45, nos 26–27, pp. 174–82.

Mattoo, A., D. Mishra and A. Narain (2007), *From Competition at Home to Competing Abroad: A Case Study of India's Horticulture*, New Delhi: Oxford University Press.

Minten, B., T. Reardon, K. Singh and R. Sutradhar (2014), 'The New and Changing Roles of Cold Storages in the Potato Supply Chain in Bihar', *Economic and Political Weekly*, vol. 49, no. 52, pp. 98–108.

Minten, B., A. Vandeplas and J. Swinnen (2012), 'Regulations, Brokers and Interlinkages: The Institutional Organization of Wholesale Markets in India', *Journal of Development Studies*, vol. 48, no. 7, pp. 864–86.

Mitra, S., D. Mookherjee, M. Torero and S. Visaria (2013), 'Asymmetric Information and Middleman Margins: An Experiment with West Bengal Potato Farmers', The Bureau for Research and Economic Analysis of Development (BREAD) Working Paper No. 401.

Mookherjee, D. (2016), 'Agriculture: A Revolution Waiting to Happen Beyond the Mandis', *Business Today*, available at http://www.businesstoday.in/magazine/cover-story/agriculture-a-revolution-waiting-to-happen-beyond-the-mandis/story/227502.html, accessed 15 November 2017.

Narayanan, S. (2020), 'The Three Farm Bills: Is this the Marketing Reform India Needs?', *The India Forum*, 2 October 2020.

Narayanan, S. and S. Dhanapal (2021), 'Interlinked Credit-Output Transactions in India: Testing an Old Model with New Data', Mimeo.

National Centre for Cold-Chain Development (NCCD) (2015), 'All India Cold-chain Infra-structure Capacity Assessment of Status and Gap', New Delhi: National Centre for Cold-Chain Development, Autonomous Body of Ministry of Agriculture and Farmers' Welfare.

Negi, D.S., P.S. Birthal, D. Roy and M.T. Khan (2018), 'Farmers' Choice of Market Channels and Producer Prices in India: Role of Transportation and Communication Net-works', *Food Policy*, vol. 81, pp. 106–21.

Neti, A., R. Govil and M.R. Rao (2019), 'Farmer Producer Companies in India: Demystifying the Numbers', *Review of Agrarian Studies*, vol. 9, no. 2, pp. 92–113, available at http://ras.org.in/fc5e6f86c86e8548e3eb17f4ec8fbc9f.

National Institute of Public Finance and Policy (NIPFP) (2015), 'Report on Warehousing in India Study Commissioned by the Warehousing Development and Regulatory Authority', available at http://wdra.nic.in/Report.pdf, accessed 15 November 2017.

Nuthalapati, C.S.R., R. Sutradhar, T. Reardon and M. Qaim (2020), 'Supermarket Procure-ment and Farmgate Prices in India', *World Development*, vol. 134, https://doi.org/10.1016/j.worlddev.2020.105034.

Patnaik, G. (2011), 'Status of Agriculture Reforms, workshop on 'Policy Options and Invest-ment Priorities for Accelerating Agricultural Productivity and Development in India' organized by Indira Gandhi Institute of Development Research (IGIDR) and Institute of Human Development (IHD), 10–11 November, New Delhi.

Purohit, P., K.S. Imai and K. Sen (2017), 'Do Agricultural Marketing Laws Matter for Rural Growth? Evidence from the Indian States', Discussion Paper No. 2017–17, Research Institute of Economics and Business (RIEB), Kobe, Japan: Kobe University.

Purohit, P. (2016), 'Measurement of Regulations of the Agricultural Produce Markets', *Economic and Political Weekly*, vol. 51, no. 28, pp. 36–45.

Ramakumar, R. (2019), 'Crumbs for Farmers', *Frontline*, vol. 36, no. 4, 16 February–1 March.

———— (2020), 'Farm Acts – Unwanted Consumer Adventurism', *The Hindu*, 6 October, https://www.thehindu.com/opinion/lead/farm-acts-unwanted-constitutional-adventurism/article32776232.ece.

Ramaswami, B., P.S. Birthal and P.K. Joshi (2019), 'Grower Heterogeneity and the Gains from Contract Farming', *Indian Growth and Development Review*, vol. 2, no. 1, pp. 56–74, https://doi.org/10.1108/17538250910953462

Reserve Bank of India (RBI) (2019), 'Supply Chain Dynamics and Food Inflation in India', *RBI Bulletin*, October 2019, Reserve Bank of India, Mumbai.

Sahadevan, K.G. (2002a), 'Price Discovery, Return and Market Conditions: Evidence from Commodity Futures Markets', *The ICFAI Journal of Applied Finance*, vol. 8, no. 5, pp. 25–39.

———— (2002b), 'Sagging Agricultural Commodity Exchanges: Growth Constraints and Revival Policy Options', *Economic and Political Weekly*, vol. 37, no. 30, pp. 3153–60.

Shilpi, F. and D. Umali Deininger (2008), 'Market Facilities and Agricultural Marketing: Evi-dence from Tamil Nadu, India', *Agricultural Economics*, vol. 39, no. 3, pp. 281–94.

Singh, G. and S.R. Asokan (2005), *Contract Farming in India: Text and Cases*, New Delhi: Oxford and IBH Publishing Co. Pvt. Ltd.

Singh, S. (2012a), 'Marketing Channels and their Implications for Smallholder Farmers in India', in Ellen B. McCullough, P. Pingali and K. Stamoulis, eds, *The Transformation of Agri-Food Systems: Globalization, Supply Chains and Smallholder Farmers*, London: Routledge.

Singh, S. (2012b), 'New Markets for Smallholders in India: Exclusion, Policy and Mechan-isms', *Economic and Political Weekly*, vol. 47, no. 52, pp. 95–105.

———— (2015), 'Reforming Markets, Lessons from Bihar', *The Tribune*, available at http://www.tribuneindia.com/news/comment/reforming-markets-lessons-from-bihar/37892.html., accessed on 15 November 2017.

————— (2019), 'Reforming Agricultural Markets in India, A Tale of Two Model Acts', *Economic and Political Weekly*, vol. 53, no. 51, pp. 15–18.

Singh, S. and T. Singh (2014), *Producer Companies in India: Organization and Performance*, New Delhi: Allied Publishers Pvt. Limited.

Suganthi, D. (2013), 'Behaviour of Premium Paid by Supermarket and Trade-off Facing Farmers, *Indian Journal of Agricultural Economics*, vol. 68, no. 3, pp. 422–30

Tripathy, S.N. (2017), 'Minimizing Post-Harvest Loss is Catalyst to Agricultural Development in Andhra Pradesh', in *Agricultural Situation in India*, Ministry of Agriculture and Farmer's Welfare, Government of India, New Delhi.

Umali Deininger, D.L. and K.W. Deininger (2001), 'Towards Greater Food Security for India's Poor: Balancing Government Intervention and Private Competition', *Agricultural Economics*, vol. 25, nos 2–3, pp. 321–35.

World Bank (2008), 'India: Taking Agriculture to the Market', Washington D.C.: World Bank. https://openknowledge.worldbank.org/handle/10986/7919, License: CC BY 3.0 IGO.

Appendix

Appendix Table 1 *Select committees on agri-commodities markets*

Sl No	Name of Committee	Year	Objectives
1.	Expert Committee on Strengthening and Developing of Agricultural Marketing (Guru Committee)	2001	• to develop output marketing; • to strengthen agricultural marketing; • to promote agricultural commodity marketing via organized regulated markets.
2.	Inter-Ministerial Task Force on Agricultural Marketing Reforms	2002	• to identify priority areas to work out a road map for strengthening the agricultural marketing system in the country.
3.	The Expert Committee to study the impact of Futures Trading on Agricultural Commodity Prices (Abhijit Sen Committee)	2008	• to study the impact of futures trading on the wholesale and retail prices of agricultural commodities; • to suggest ways to minimize such impact; • to make recommendations to increase farmers participations in futures trading.
4.	Committee of State Ministers in-charge of Agricultural Marketing to Promote Reforms	2013	• to facilitate development of efficient and competitive markets, rationalization of market fee, promotion of grading, standardization, packaging and quality certification, and dissemination of market information and market intelligence.
5.	Committee to suggest steps for fulfilling the objectives of Price Discovery and Risk management of Commodity derivatives market (Kolamkar Committee)	2014	• to examine whether commodity futures markets are delivering price discovery and hedging.
6.	Committee on the Integration of Spot and Derivative Markets (Ramesh Chand Committee)	2016	• to examine spot and derivative markets for both agricultural and non-agricultural commodities for better integration
6.	Standing Committee on Agriculture (2018–2019), 16th Lok Sabha Ministry of Agriculture and Farmers' Welfare (Department of Agricultural, Cooperation and Farmers Welfare), "Agriculture Marketing and Role of Weekly GraminHaats"	2019	• to examine agricultural marketing ecosystem with a focus on rural markets.

Appendix Table 2 *Select commodity boards*

Tobacco Board	• statutory body established on 1 January, 1976 under Section (4) of the Tobacco Board Act, 1975.
Coffee Board	• statutory organization constituted under Section (4) of the Coffee Act, 1942
Tea Board	• statutory body established on 1 April, 1954 as per Section (4) of the Tea Act, 1953
Rubber Board	• statutory organization constituted under Section (4) of the Rubber Act, 1947
Coconut Development Board; Coir Board	• Coconut Development Board: established on 12 January 1981. • Coir Board: A statutory body established by the Government of India under a legislation enacted by the Parliament namely Coir Industry Act, 1953 (45 of 1953)
Spices Board	• Statutory body established on 26 February, 1987 under Section (3) of the Spices Board Act, 1986.
Others	• National Medicinal Plants Board (NMPB); Government of India set up on 24 November 2000. • National Oilseeds and Vegetable Oils Development (NOVOD) Board is a statutory body established under an Act of Parliament [NOVOD Board Act, 1983].

16

Food Security Policy and Reforms in the Public Distribution System

Anmol Somanchi

Despite prolonged periods of steady economic growth over the last two decades of the twenty-first century, the status of food security in India remains precarious. Adequately nutritious diets remain unaffordable for a significant share of the rural poor (Raghunathan, Heady and Herforth 2020). As per the 2020 Global Hunger Index, India ranks 97 out of 107 countries globally, worse than all its neighbours including Bangladesh, Myanmar, Nepal, Pakistan, and Sri Lanka. Estimates from the National Family Health Survey 2019–20 (NFHS-5) show that child nutrition indicators declined between 2015–16 and 2019–20 in large states and alarming 'pauses and reversals' in infant mortality declines were observed since 2016 (Drèze *et al*. 2020). The Covid-19 pandemic is likely to have further worsened the situation.

It is in such a context that the Public Distribution System (PDS) stands as an important source of basic food security and social protection. On the back of an expansive network of fair price shops (or ration shops) established across the country over the years, the PDS currently provides subsidized foodgrains (primarily rice and wheat) to nearly 900 million people under centre- and state-funded programmes (Khera and Somanchi 2020).

Evolution of the Public Distribution System

The PDS found its root in the system of food rationing established by the British during the Second World War. While the system was dismantled after the war, it had to be reintroduced at the time of independence in the face of severe inflationary pressures (Bhatia 1985). In the early years after independence, until the early 1960s, the PDS was largely an urban phenomenon, relied heavily on food imports, and was used primarily to maintain food price stability. The reach of the PDS expanded considerably between 1960 and 1990 on the back of various reforms to national food policy (see Figure 16.1). The first of these was the reintroduction of control on grain trade in 1957. This was accompanied by opening of new ration shops and a growth in the quantity of grains distributed.

The next fillip came with the setting up of the Foodgrains Prices Committee in 1964, which further strengthened the position of the PDS. The government committed itself to announce a minimum support price (MSP) to promote agriculture and the stocks procured were to be utilized towards meeting the needs of the PDS. If grain availability from such procurement fell short of PDS demand, the government had to resort to imports and others measures, such as monopoly procurement and levy on farmers, millers, traders (George 1984; Nawani 1994). This converted the PDS from a price stability instrument to a welfare programme aimed at supporting consumers. Over the next three decades, as Figure 16.1 shows, the reach of the PDS steadily grew. This expansion, in large part, was due to the active involvement of state governments in food policy and the increased need for foodgrains for the implementation of various special programmes targeted at specific regions or the rural poor (Mooji 1998). In 1992, the 'revamped' PDS was launched with the aim of covering 1,750 blocks in hilly, remote,

Figure 16.1 *Expansion of PDS between 1950 and 1996*

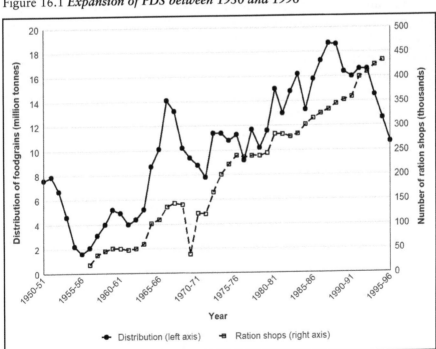

Source: Mooji (1998).

and inaccessible regions. While the PDS largely benefited urban households in the early years, this bias towards urban households largely disappeared by the 1990s in most states except West Bengal (Dev and Suryanarayana 1991).

All through this period, the PDS was a universal scheme without any specific target population. Every citizen was eligible for a ration and could purchase grains from the PDS. However, despite three decades of general expansion, the PDS 'failed in providing cheap food and food security on a mass scale to households that [were] undernourished or vulnerable to under-nourishment' (Swaminathan 2000). Data from National Sample Surveys (NSS) suggest that its coverage was quite patchy. In 1993–94, only 27 per cent of rural and 29 per cent of urban households purchased grains from the PDS. Some observers attributed this to the steady increase in issue prices since the mid-1980s (George 1996) while others blame poor administration, corruption and lack of political will (Swaminathan 2000). At the same time, the PDS came under severe criticism for large-scale leakages and lack of progressiveness in the benefits (Jha 1992). This prompted some to argue for dismantling the PDS system while others argued for it to be replaced by direct income transfers (Parikh 1994). Following the structural adjustment policies in 1991, 'targeting' started to gain popularity as a means of reducing food subsidies.

Placing PDS reforms in a historical context, Mooji (1998) argued that the direction of food policy in subsequent years would be determined by the interplay of economic forces: structural adjustment policies would force the central government to curtail their food subsidy bill while increased political competition at the state-level would make the PDS an important political issue.

Universal PDS to Targeted PDS

With the aim of increasing the subsidy to worse-off households and enhancing its role towards food security, the PDS was converted into a targeted scheme in June 1997. The population was divided into two categories – 'below poverty line' (BPL) and 'above poverty line' (APL). BPL households could buy grains from the PDS (initially 10 kg per month and later 35 kg per month) at 50 per cent of the economic cost of procurement. Till 2000–01, APL households could purchase grains at 75 per cent of economic cost, after which they stopped receiving any subsidy and had to purchase grains at the full economic cost. In 2000, the Antyodaya (Antyodaya Anna Yojana [AAY]) category was added covering 1 crore, later increased to 2 crore, 'poorest of the poor' households. AAY households were entitled to initially 25 kg per month, later revised to 35 kg per month, of grains irrespective of family size at the rate of Rs 3 per kg for rice and Rs 2 per kg for wheat (Department of Food and Public Distribution 2016).

Poor Coverage and Targeting

While the aim of this reform was to enhance the access for poor households, a large body of subsequent work showed that the targeted PDS (TPDS) failed to do exactly that. When the TPDS was launched in 1997, the first challenge for the government was to 'estimate' the number of eligible people under the BPL category. It was decided that coverage of BPL households would be based on state-wise head-count ratios of poverty drawn from the NSS surveys of consumption expenditure in 1993–94.[1] However, there were already complaints that the NSS poverty estimates, especially for rural areas, were underestimates (Swaminathan 2000). As the central government's allocation to each state was based on the low share of poverty in each state, various states had to introduce 'caps' on the number of BPL households.

The problem of 'estimation' was followed by the problem of 'identification'. Households belonging to the BPL category had to be identified but subject to the maximum levels already set by the head-count ratios. States were responsible for identifying eligible households under the BPL category and Antyodaya schemes. Initially, most states relied on the results of a survey organized in 1992–93 to identify the beneficiaries of the Integrated Rural Development Programme (IRDP) (Swaminathan and Misra 2001). Later, a BPL Survey was organized in 2002 to identify eligible households. Here, the government scored households based on thirteen different parameters covering asset ownership, occupation, land ownership, etc. But not only were the BPL surveys a very costly exercise, they also resulted in large-scale errors of inclusion and exclusion. In 2004–05, nearly half of households in the lowest monthly per capita expenditure (MPCE) quintile did not have a BPL/AAY ration card (Drèze and Khera 2010; Himanshu and Sen 2011). A majority of Scheduled Caste (SC), Scheduled Tribe (ST), and Other Backward Class (OBC) households were excluded from the PDS (Rahman 2014; Swaminathan 2008). In total, only 34 per cent of households had a BPL or an AAY card. On the other hand, between 20 per cent and 25 per cent of households in the two highest consumption quintiles possessed a BPL or an AAY ration card.

Numerous state-specific studies from Maharashtra, Andhra Pradesh and Rajasthan also documented the large-scale inclusion and exclusion errors in the TPDS (Swaminathan and Misra 2001; Dutta and Ramaswami 2001; Khera 2008). While some of these errors could perhaps have been reduced with better survey designs, the very idea of targeting welfare entitlements based on poverty lines continued to be fraught with unresolved issues (Deaton and Drèze 2014). The worst affected states by the switch to a targeted system were Kerala and Tamil Nadu, which historically had relatively high PDS coverage and purchases prior to 1997–98 (Swaminathan 2008). In most states, the shift to the TPDS resulted in a decline in per-capita PDS purchases between 1999–2000 and 2004–05 (Khera 2011a).

Initially, states were directed to disburse PDS grains at a price no more than 50 paise above central issue prices (CIP). This directive was later scrapped, and states were given flexibility in setting PDS issue prices. Moreover, the CIPs were also revised upwards. From under Rs 400/quintal for common rice in 1997, the CIP was increased to Rs 600/quintal in 2000 and remained so till 2013 (Bhattacharya *et al.* 2017). This meant that in some places, the difference between the PDS issue price and market prices of cereals was negligible. It is worth noting that the shift to the TPDS resulted in a significant decline in access in urban areas and increased the utilization of the PDS among the poorest two quintiles (it declined among the others) but any potential progressive effects were largely eroded by the significant exclusion errors (Himanshu and Sen 2013a).

Large-scale Leakages

Along with a decline in coverage and access, leakages from the system in the form of diverted grains increased during the early 2000s. At the national level, the share of PDS grain not reaching the beneficiaries increased from just over 24 per cent in 1999–2000 to 39 per cent in 2001–02 and further to 54 per cent in 2004–05 (Khera 2011a). This was quite likely a result of numerous factors including reduced coverage of the PDS, decline in the consumer base of fair price shops, low levels of utilization, and the shift of PDS away from the places where it worked well (Himanshu and Sen 2013a; Isaac and Ramakumar 2010).

There were two important dimensions to the leakage problem worth noting. First, leakages of wheat were significantly larger than rice. Indeed, evidence suggested that the PDS worked much better in rice-consuming states (Khera 2011a). Per capita wheat purchases remained low and leakages increased during this period. Second, leakages were significantly higher for the APL allocation than the BPL allocation. Drèze and Khera (2015) found that the leakages from the APL quota were more than twice as high as the leakages from the BPL quota in 2011–12. They argued that this was because APL allocations fluctuated arbitrarily, and APL households often did not know what they were entitled to as a result. This is supported by Overbeck (2016) who found that the APL quota of states was an important predictor for the overall level of leakages between 2004 and 2011.

Steady Revival

While the PDS seemed to be in the dumps in the early years of the TPDS, there was a significant improvement in coverage, utilization and leakages between 2004–05 and 2011–12. At the national level, the share of households with a BPL or AAY card increased from 30 per cent to 44 per cent, coverage significantly improved among SC, ST, OBC households, and many households in the bottom three declines moved from APL to BPL entitlements (Rahman 2014). Consequently, the share of population accessing grains from the PDS also rose from 25 per cent in 2004–05 to 43 per cent in 2009–10 to 50 per cent in 2011–12 (Himanshu and Sen 2013a). By 2011–12, 67 per cent and 55 per cent of the households in the poorest two quintiles were purchasing grains from the PDS and rice purchases from the PDS accounted for 46 per cent of the total household rice purchases (Rahman 2014).

The improvement in coverage and utilization was matched by a decline in leakages during the same period. At the national level, leakages fell from 54 per cent in 2004–05 to 42 per cent in 2011–12. Estimates based on the India Human Development Survey, a more detailed and careful survey, for the same period (2011–12), pegged leakages at an even lower level of 32 per cent. While this decline might still appear moderate (as it indeed was), it nonetheless showed an improvement in the functioning of PDS. The state-level trends are also worth emphasizing (Khera 2011a, 2011b; Himanshu and Sen 2011a). The erstwhile poorly performing states of Bihar, Chhattisgarh and Odisha saw significant improvements and states like Andhra Pradesh, Himachal Pradesh, Kerala and Tamil Nadu, where the PDS was already functioning relatively well, were able to consolidate their position further.

These improvements were largely the outcome of various bold initiatives by many state governments. For instance, Tamil Nadu and Himachal Pradesh moved towards universalization of their PDS, Chhattisgarh did away with private PDS dealers and implemented a stronger monitoring system, and various other states supplemented the central subsidy to reduce issues prices and/or expand coverage.[2] As with many other welfare programmes, Kerala was always one of the best performers on all indicators of PDS functionality (coverage, access and leakage). As noted earlier, the shift from a universal to targeted approach severely hurt the PDS in Kerala. Crucially, the coverage caps fixed by the centre excluded many vulnerable households. To remedy these issues, starting 2009–10, Kerala decided to automatically include all Dalit, Adivasi and fisherperson households as well as all destitute persons. Subsequently, in 2010–11, all agricultural labourer households and traditional industrial worker households were made automatically eligible to subsidized grains irrespective of their APL/BPL status. As a result of these policy changes, aimed explicitly at moving away from consumption-based targeting to a 'class approach', the number of BPL households increased from 20 lakhs to 35 lakhs, covering 42 per cent of households in the state (see Isaac and Ramakumar [2010] for an account).

Another important factor contributing to the PDS revival was the significant increase in global food prices, which in turn led to a rise in domestic food prices. On the demand side, the value of the subsidy from the PDS increased making it a more meaningful entitlement for households. On the supply side, the increase in market prices made it more profitable for PDS dealers to divert grains into the open market. Empirical evidence suggests that the demand-side effect was stronger than that of the supply side; exogenous increases in the value of PDS subsidy resulting from the variations in local prices (along with differences in the PDS issue prices across states and over time) led to increases in PDS purchases in most states (Kaul 2018; Chakrabarti, Kishore and Roy 2017).

The National Food Security Act

In 2013, the Indian Parliament passed the National Food Security Act (NFSA), which brought major reforms to the national food security policy and the PDS. These included converting the PDS from a welfare scheme into a legal entitlement, restructuring the process of grain procurements and distribution, expanding the coverage of the PDS, reducing issue prices and discarding the APL–BPL method of targeting households. The NFSA also made maternity entitlements of Rs 6,000 for pregnant women, supplementary nutrition to mothers and children under the Integrated Child Development Services (ICDS) and mid-day meals, a legal right.

The NFSA expanded the coverage of the PDS to reach 75 per cent of the rural population and 50 per cent of the urban population. Before the NFSA, coverage of BPL/AAY cards was just about 50 per cent of the total population; with the exception of a few states, the NFSA led to significant expansion in PDS coverage. While NFSA continued with a targeted approach and did not universalize the PDS, it did do away with the APL–BPL style of targeting. Households were now categorized into 'Priority' households (PHH) and 'Antyodaya' households (AAY), and the APL category was disbanded. Entitlements of 5 kg per person per month were fixed for PHH, while Antyodaya households were to be provided 35 kg per household per month irrespective of family size. The selection of households into the PHH and AAY categories was left to the state governments. Various states adopted a simple 'inclusion–exclusion' approach to identify eligible households, often using the 2011 Socio-Economic Caste Census (SECC) data or other data they had recently collected. Further, CIPs were reduced considerably (nearly halved) and fixed at 3/2/1 per kg for rice/wheat/millets, respectively.

The NFSA came into effect in September 2013 but its roll-out at the state level happened with a significant lag as state governments struggled to prepare new beneficiary lists, computerize their ration cards and streamline various other processes of distribution. The delay in the release of the

SECC data also contributed to this. Despite the provision for food security allowance in the case of failures to provide benefits, no such allowances were paid to compensate for the delay. The earliest states to implement the NFSA were Delhi, Haryana, Himachal Pradesh, Punjab and Rajasthan between September and December 2013, while Kerala and Tamil Nadu implemented the NFSA only in November 2016 (Department of Food and Public Distribution, 2020).

Status of PDS Coverage and State-wise Variations

Table 16.1 presents estimates of state-wise coverage of the PDS before and after the introduction of the NFSA. At the national level, 44 per cent of the population had a BPL or AAY card in 2011–12. If we drop Andhra Pradesh, which had a PDS coverage of 89 per cent, the national coverage was even lower. The NFSA 2013 aimed to increase the coverage to 67 per cent of the total population. For all the states, except Andhra Pradesh and Karnataka, this entailed a significant expansion. In some states, which included poor large states, food surplus states, and few North-Eastern states (i.e. Haryana, Gujarat, Jharkhand, Karnataka, Manipur, Nagaland, Punjab, Rajasthan and Uttar Pradesh), the coverage increased by a magnitude of 2–3 times. Multiple surveys conducted after the roll-out of NFSA found that coverage across states was largely compliant with the NFSA coverage targets. However, by 2020, there was an under-coverage of over 100 million people as the central government continued to rely on the outdated 2011 census estimates of population.[3] At the national level, the PDS covered only 59 per cent of the population as against the 67 per cent mandated by the NFSA. This problem was seen across all states but was particularly amplified in large states with relatively higher population growth (i.e. Bihar, Gujarat, Jharkhand and Uttar Pradesh).

As was the case before the NFSA, various states continued to develop their own schemes and run an 'expanded PDS' even after the NFSA was launched. This resulted in at least three significant state-wise variations (Khera and Somanchi 2020). First, some states continued with an 'expanded' PDS providing subsidized grains to a larger population than covered by the NFSA. These included all the southern states and also, interestingly, poorer states like Chhattisgarh, Odisha and West Bengal (see columns 5 and 6 in Table 16.1). In these states, besides NFSA cards, two additional types of ration were in circulation: ration cards with 'NFSA-Equivalent Entitlements or More' (NEEM) and rations cards with 'Lesser Entitlements Against NFSA' (LEAN).[4] NEEM cardholders received grains as per the NFSA norms (similar entitlements and prices) while for LEAN cardholders, entitlements were lower and prices were higher than those for the NFSA/NEEM cardholders. Second, while expanding coverage, several

Table 16.1 *State-wise coverage of the public distribution system*

States	Population with BPL or AAY card in 2011–12 (%)	Population coverage mandated by NFSA 2013 (%)	Population with NFSA ration cards in 2020 (%)	Population with NEEM (state) ration cards in 2020 (%)	Population with LEAN (state) ration cards in 2020 (%)
India	44	67	59	7	4
Andaman and Nicobar Islands	10	17	15	0	77
Andhra Pradesh	89	54	50	28	0
Arunachal Pradesh	37	63	55	0	6
Assam	47	81	70	0	0
Bihar	52	84	70	0	0
Chandigarh	0	47	25	0	–
Chhattisgarh	60	79	67	7	13
Dadra and Nagar Haveli	38	69	52	0	0
Delhi	6	43	39	0	0
Goa	13	36	35	0	51
Gujarat	33	63	49	0	0
Haryana	22	50	42	0	0
Himachal Pradesh	29	54	38	0	61
Jammu and Kashmir	26	59	52	0	33
Jharkhand	36	80	68	0	0
Karnataka	69	66	64	0	11
Kerala	31	46	44	29	28
Lakshadweep	28	34	32	0	0
Madhya Pradesh	42	75	64	0	0
Maharashtra	35	62	56	3	0
Manipur	35	88	81	0	–
Meghalaya	56	72	62	0	–
Mizoram	57	65	57	0	–
Nagaland	32	75	58	0	–
Odisha	53	78	72	2	0
Puducherry	43	51	48	0	–
Punjab	30	51	45	0	0

Table 16.1 *(continued)*

States	Population with BPL or AAY card in 2011–12 (%)	Population coverage mandated by NFSA 2013 (%)	Population with NFSA ration cards in 2020 (%)	Population with NEEM (state) ration cards in 2020 (%)	Population with LEAN (state) ration cards in 2020 (%)
Rajasthan	25	65	62	0	0
Sikkim	58	67	55	0	18
Tamil Nadu	41	51	47	38	0
Telangana	NA	54	49	23	0
Tripura	38	68	62	0	32
Uttar Pradesh	28	76	63	0	0
Uttarakhand	33	61	56	0	42
West Bengal	38	66	61	19	14

Notes: NEEM – NFSA Equivalent Entitlements or More; LEAN – Lower Entitlements as against NFSA (see Khera and Somanchi [2020] for further details); – implies no publicly available information was found; NA – not applicable.
Sources: Estimates by Jean Drèze, Reetika Khera and Meghana Mungikar (see IndiaSpend [2020]); Khera and Somanchi (2020) and Rahman (2014).

states lowered the issue prices of PDS even beyond the NFSA mandate. Rice was distributed free of cost in Tamil Nadu while it was sold at less than the NFSA price of Rs 3 in Chhattisgarh, Jharkhand and Odisha. Third, some states expanded the PDS basket to include salt, *dal* and edible oil also.

Overall, in 2020, the PDS coverage reached the 66 per cent mandate set by the NFSA only if we account for the NEEM cards also. While a small portion of NEEM coverage was paid for by the centre via the concept of 'tide-over grains', a significant share of it was paid out of state budgets.

Functionality of PDS post-NFSA

Unfortunately, no nationally representative consumption survey is available since the roll-out of the NFSA to conclusively evaluate its performance. This data gap has had to be filled by independent smaller scale surveys. The most comprehensive study so far is Drèze *et al.* (2019) which presents results from a census survey of 36 villages in six poor states covering 3,800 households conducted in May 2016. The survey presented positive evidence on various aspects of the PDS relevant to the roll-out of the NFSA.

First, about 80 per cent of sample households had a BPL/AAY ration card, a significant increase from 58 per cent pre-NFSA as reported by the same households.[5] Second, the proportion of fake, duplicate, ghost (identity fraud) ration cards were found to be low with the exception of Bihar. Third, both inclusion and exclusion errors were found to be less than 10 per cent, which was a massive improvement over the situation under the earlier APL–BPL classification.

Lastly, the purchase entitlement ratio (PER), defined as the actual household purchases from the PDS in a month as a ratio of their legal entitlement – a good indicator of cumulative leakages in the system – was high in all the sample states. In four of the six sample states (Chhattisgarh, Madhya Pradesh, Odisha and West Bengal), households were receiving more than 90 per cent of their entitlements, and even in the two 'laggard' states (Bihar and Jharkhand), the PERs were 84 per cent. Despite certain unresolved issues like limited grievance redressal and below-par standards of transparency and accountability, the authors concluded that the PDS had indeed come a long way from the days of rampant corruption and mistargeting. These findings were more or less consistent with the findings from other state-specific surveys covering Andhra Pradesh, Bihar, Chhattisgarh, Jharkhand, Odisha and West Bengal.[6]

The Case of Jharkhand

The improvement in the PDS with the passage of the NFSA can be demonstrated using the case of Jharkhand. Throughout the period between 2000 and 2008, leakages from the PDS were as high as 80–85 per cent. In 2004–05, only 26 per cent of households in the state had a BPL or AAY ration card and grain purchases from the PDS were negligible: 0.15 kg and 0.11 kg per month respectively for rice and wheat. By 2011–12, however, things had reversed. Coverage of BPL/AAY cards increased to 36 per cent, share of households purchasing grains from the PDS rose by nearly 6 times (5.5 per cent to 30 per cent), and leakages were effectively halved (44 per cent).[7] Jharkhand implemented the NFSA in October 2015, which resulted in a significant expansion of coverage, especially in rural areas. Further, evidence from multiple small surveys with comparable methodologies conducted in recent years suggested that leakages were falling year-on-year (see Figure 16.2). In early 2017, for instance, households that purchased grains from the PDS received over 90 per cent of their entitlements (Drèze et al. 2017) and overall leakages – defined as the share of grains allocated to the state that did not reach beneficiaries – stood at 20 per cent (Muralidharan, Niehaus and Sukhtankar 2020). That similar results were found in another sample survey of Particularly Vulnerable Tribal Groups (PVTGs) suggests that the PDS had indeed improved its functioning in the state. Further, access to PDS was strongly negatively correlated with the occurrence of hunger among the PVTG sample during the three months preceding the

Figure 16.2 *Trends of PDS leakages in Jharkhand*

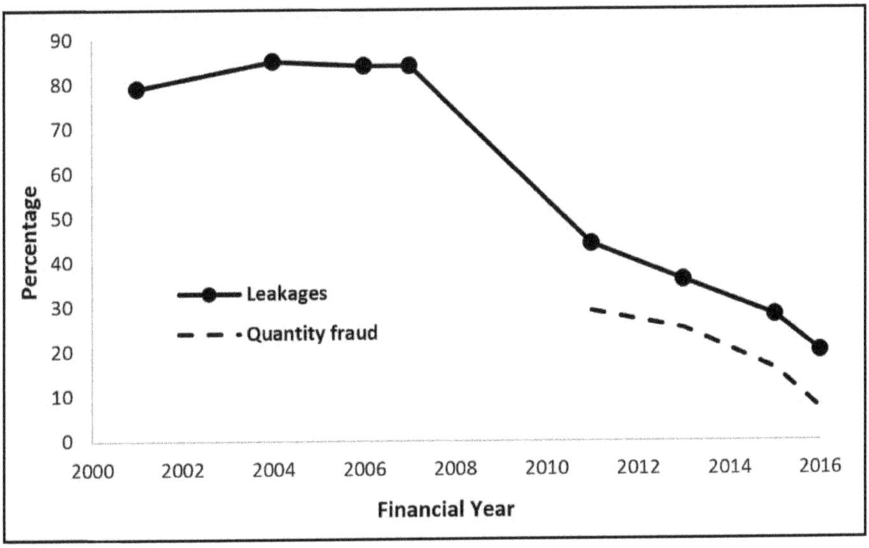

Notes: The figure presents two separate measures of corruption in the PDS in Jharkhand presented in various sources. The solid line presents 'leakages', defined as the share of grains allocated to the state which did not reach beneficiaries. This is calculated by matching off-take data (from the Monthly Foodgrain Bulletin or State Food Department data) with data on household PDS purchases (from NSS Consumption and Expenditure surveys or primary survey by researchers at Abdul Latif Jameel Poverty Action Lab). These estimates are from large sample surveys and are largely representative of the state. The dashed line presents 'quantity fraud' defined as the share of monthly entitlements that households did not receive. These are based on small sample survey and are not representative of the entire state. The year 2000–01 is defined as FY2000 and so on.
Source: Drèze and Khera (2015), Khera (2011a) and Muralidharan, Niehaus and Sukhtankar (2020) for leakage estimates (solid line); Drèze, Khera and PEEP Team (2013), Drèze et al. (2017), Drèze et al. (2019) and Khera (2011b) for quantity fraud estimates (dashed line).

survey. It was both remarkable and surprising that even in a corruption-ridden state like Jharkhand, vulnerable beneficiaries like PVTGs also largely received a bulk of their monthly entitlements (Somanchi 2020).

Recent Evidence on Effectiveness of PDS

At one level, the PDS can be looked up on as an income transfer programme. The value of this income transfer equals the quantity purchased from the PDS multiplied by the difference between PDS issue prices and open market prices.[8] Following this approach, Drèze and Khera (2013) found that even in the pre-NFSA form, the PDS had an important effect on poverty reduction. In 2009–10, for instance, the poverty gap would have been higher by 18 to 22 per cent at the national level in the absence of the PDS; the gains were larger – 40 to 80 per cent – in states like Tamil Nadu and Chhattisgarh with a well-functioning PDS. If the imputed value of mid-day meals was also included, the national poverty gap reduction was even higher at 40 per cent (Himanshu and Sen 2013a). These national-level impacts were despite the fact that the effect on poverty reductions were smaller in states like Bihar, Jharkhand, Uttar Pradesh and West Bengal where the PDS performed poorly.

On the issue of the effects of PDS on nutritional outcomes, the evidence has been mixed. Some of the earlier studies, which focused on the PDS during the 1990s and early 2000s, found little or no impact of food subsidies on nutritional indicators.[9] In contrast to these, a set of more recent studies found that the PDS (even in its pre-NFSA form) did indeed have modest to moderate positive effects on nutrition. Studying the expansion of the PDS in Chhattisgarh in early 2000s, Krishnamurthy, Pathania and Tandon (2017) reported that households increased their consumption of protein and other nutrients relative to the bordering districts from neighbouring states. Similarly, Rahman (2016) reported a moderate improvement in household nutrient intake and diet quality resulting from the universalization of the PDS in the eight districts of the Kalahandi-Balangir-Koraput (KBK) region in Odisha. Interestingly, Kaul (2018) found that increases in the value of PDS subsidy resulted in small but significant increases in caloric intakes for *all* food groups, not just cereals. The only evidence on the specific impact of the roll-out of NFSA on nutritional outcomes was reported in Shrinivas *et al.* (2018). Exploiting variations in entitlements and issue prices across states resulting from the expansion of the PDS after the roll-out of the NFSA, the authors found that the PDS increased dietary diversity, crowded-in consumption of non-staple food and increased calorie intake.

How does one reconcile these different sets of results? It is hard to be sure but the null effects of PDS on nutritional outcomes found in the earlier studies could be a result of the lower levels of PDS access prior to 2004–05, the retention of only wheat-consuming states (where leakages were high) in the sample (as in Kochar 2005), and difficulties in accurately identifying the type of ration card that households possessed during the entire period of analysis (as in Kaushal and Muchomba 2015).

In addition to the income-transfer and nutritional outcomes, emerging evidence suggests that the PDS could be benefitting households through other pathways as well. Shrinivas, Baylis and Crost (2018) found that expansion of PDS subsidy after NFSA reduced labour supply and increased wages, which in turn reduced income inequality by redistributing incomes from richer to poorer households. These welfare-enhancing effects were strongest during the periods of economic shock (proxied by rainfall). This suggested that improvements in labour market outcomes could be an additional benefit from in-kind transfers. Further, anecdotal evidence from the field suggests that the effects of the PDS on caste dynamics, either direct or indirect (via labour-market effects), may be another aspect worth investigating.[10]

It must, however, be noted that some of these studies may not have high external validity given their use of small samples and/or focus on only a group of states. More substantive evidence is required to validate these findings. Moreover, a national evaluation of the PDS after roll-out of the NFSA using nationally representative data remains to be done. If the PDS has indeed consolidated its position further (as the early evidence suggests), its effects on outcomes, particularly poverty and nutrition indicators, could be even stronger than those found in the pre-NFSA studies.

Cash Versus In-Kind Transfers

In the recent years, an issue that has often dominated debates surrounding the PDS was whether the expansive and costly system of delivering foodgrains should be replaced by a system of cash transfers wherein the value of the PDS subsidy is deposited into the bank accounts of beneficiaries. This has been prompted in large part due to the high levels of leakages that have plagued the PDS over the years. Even in 2011–12, just over 40 per cent of the PDS grains did not reach households. Theoretically, cash transfers are perceived to be more efficient given lower transaction costs, reduced scope for leakages, and greater freedom for households to choose how to spend the money. Further, the state's heavy involvement in the national grain markets that the PDS necessitates has been frowned upon (though it must be noted that total procurement far exceeds the requirements of the PDS). Based on these arguments, there have been calls for replacing the PDS with cash transfers.[11]

The arguments in favour of cash transfer may hold some conceptual merit but the performance of recent cash transfer experiments make clear that a hasty transition towards cash transfers could be highly disruptive. In the context of a fractured rural banking network, limited digital infrastructure and low levels of technological literacy (see Ramakumar 2018), a move to cash transfers can be exclusionary if households struggle to keep up with the technological requirements or find it difficult to access the banking system. While the coverage of bank accounts has significantly increased in the recent years, data on the national PDS portal as of December 2020 suggested that only 17 per cent of ration cards were linked with a bank account and 32 per cent of ration cards were linked with a mobile number.[12] In the centrally governed union territories of Puducherry, Chandigarh, and Dadra and Nagar Haveli, the government replaced the PDS with cash transfers in September 2015. A full year into the programme, roughly 20 per cent of the beneficiaries did not receive their benefits and close to two-thirds preferred the PDS over cash transfers (Muralidharan, Niehaus and Sukhtankar

2017). Only when beneficiaries got an option to choose between cash transfers and grains did the levels of exclusion fall slightly and the proportion in favour of Direct Benefit Transfer (DBT) increased marginally.

Similarly, in 2018, the Jharkhand government piloted the 'DBT for rations' scheme in the Nagri block of the state. A study of the pilot by the Right to Food Campaign, Jharkhand found that on an average, households received only two of the four instalments due to them since the start of pilot (Sen 2018). Further, on an average, households said that the whole process of withdrawing money and purchasing their monthly entitlement of grains took 12 hours on an average. These findings were confirmed by other sources as well (Giri *et al.* 2019). The opposition to this reform was so strong (large demonstrations were held), that the government was forced to roll it back (Mukesh 2018). It is important to account for such 'transition costs' associated with dismantling an expansive network of PDS shops that reaches most corners of the country. In fact, even in steady state, the 'length of the last mile' is often quite long, as demonstrated by the case of the payment systems in Mahatma Gandhi National Rural Employment Guarantee Scheme (MGNREGS) (Narayanan, Dhorajiwala and Kambhatla 2020).

Contrary to the key theoretical claim underpinning the case for cash transfers, they are not immune to leakages and fraud. Low awareness levels of the financial system, limited digital literacy, and loopholes in the sophisticated payment and authentication systems resulted in large-scale frauds being reported in cash transfer programmes. These issues arose despite a hurried and high-handed exercise of linking bank accounts with Aadhaar (Dhorajiwala, Drèze and Wagner 2018). Fraudsters found ingenuous ways of getting around the technological systems including the misuse of the one-time password (OTP) system, reconstruction of fingerprints on rubber and collusion between concerned officials and bank staff. Such scams were especially prevalent among scholarship schemes but also with other transfers.[13] The experience of the largest cash transfer initiative in the recent years – the Covid-19 relief transferred to over 240 million Jan Dhan bank accounts held by women – also faced similar issues. Estimates based on numerous surveys conducted during the lockdown suggested that nearly a third of women/households eligible for transfers did not receive it (Somanchi 2021).

There have been suggestions that instead of imposing cash transfers on beneficiaries, it may be more prudent to provide them an option between in-cash transfer and in-kind grains (Muralidharan, Niehaus and Sukhtankar 2018; Agarwal and Krishna 2018). In this context, it is important to understand beneficiary preferences. Using a novel dataset collected from over 1,200 households across nine states in 2011, Khera (2014) presented several interesting patterns regarding beneficiary preferences across in-kind and in-cash transfers. Most important of these was that in states where the PDS worked well (measured in terms of leakages), a large proportion of beneficiaries preferred PDS grains over cash transfers. Even for all the survey states combined, close to two-thirds of the households preferred the PDS. A major explanation that households gave was that they felt more food secure with PDS grains as opposed to cash transfers. Another factor was the poor development of rural markets – for an average rural household, the nearest PDS outlet was located about 1 to 2 km closer than the closest grain market. Further, the penetration of bank branches in rural areas is low, in sharp contrast to the near universal presence of PDS outlets in villages (Narayan 2015).

Another set of interesting results come from a relatively more recent field study where researchers elicited individual preferences for cash transfers as trade-offs with other forms of public investment (Khemani, Habyarimana and Nooruddin 2019). Based on responses from 3,800 respondents in rural Bihar, the authors noted that 86 per cent of them preferred direct investment in public health and nutrition over cash transfers. While the authors did not present the PDS as a trade-off, the results suggested that beneficiary preferences between in-cash and in-kind transfers were more complex than usually presumed in the literature. This is also demonstrated by the results of a micro-pilot by the Maharashtra government in two PDS shops in Mumbai, wherein beneficiaries could choose to receive cash transfers in lieu of PDS grains, only 24 per cent of the beneficiaries opted for the cash transfer even though they were allowed to change their preference every month (Gadgil 2018).

Finally, as Narayanan (2011) highlighted based on the international experience, in-kind transfers were found to be successful for a whole class of food and health interventions while cash transfers were found to be more suitable for interventions like old-age pensions and widow pensions or as supplementary child income. In line with this, Gadenne *et al.* (2017) found evidence that in-kind transfers via the PDS could be shielding households from price shocks and acting as a form of insurance since the value of PDS entitlements was not eroded by inflation. They documented considerable price risk across the country, especially for landless households, in response to which they found households cutting back on calorie intakes. Between 2003 and 2012, they found that various state-level expansions of the PDS (both in terms of coverage and price reductions) were positively correlated with a weakening of the relationship between price and calorie intake. Further, there were reasons to believe that a cash transfer equal in value to grain subsidy may not have the same effects; in Tamil Nadu, households used the income transfer from PDS to purchase not only other food items from the open market but also rice which was already provided under the PDS (Rahman 2015; Pingali, Mittra and Rahman 2017). As per one estimate, a pure cash transfer required to maintain the same levels of calorie intake would cost several times more than the food subsidy bill under the present system (Himanshu and Sen 2013b).

Aadhaar and the PDS: Pain Without Gain[14]

After 2015–16, Aadhaar-based biometric authentication (ABBA) was made mandatory to access PDS grains in various states, ostensibly to plus leakages and enhance efficiency. The claim was that integrating Aadhaar with the PDS would help in easy identification of 'millions' of ghosts, fake and duplicate beneficiaries, eliminate middlemen, and reduce corruption in the system. Further, Aadhaar would enable inclusion of persons who were previously excluded for lack of a document. Aadhaar was thus proclaimed to be a 'game-changer' for India's welfare system and the PDS made its prime target.[15]

The evidence so far suggests that Aadhaar has had limited effects on leakages. It is not difficult to explain why. Identity verification, the issue that Aadhaar aims to solve, is not the root cause of leakages in the PDS. There are primarily four types of fraud in the PDS – identity fraud, quantity fraud, eligibility fraud and quality fraud (Khera 2017). Aadhaar's role was largely limited to plugging identity fraud by clearing the PDS lists of duplicates and ghosts. It had no role to play in preventing dealers from underselling, overcharging or quality fraud. We do not know the share of each of these frauds in the total leakages; yet, the impression established quite widely by successive governments and Unique Identification Authority of India (UIDAI) was that a lion's share of the fraud comes from duplicates, ghosts and fakes that have crept into the PDS lists over the years. In this way, the citizen was portrayed as the prime corrupt actor and Aadhaar was portrayed as a magic bullet (Somanchi 2019). As Ramakumar (2011c) noted when the project was still in its infancy, 'such an inversion of the problems in the PDS and an exaggerated focus on leakages and fake ration cards [was] a necessary self-justification for the government and the UIDAI.'

While reliable data on the number of fake cards has been hard to come by, data from various states suggest they make up a tiny share of total ration cards. Mohanty (2017) reported that only 4 per cent of all ration cards that were deleted in Odisha were on account of being fake or duplicates; this accounted for less than 1 per cent of the total ration cards in the state. Similarly, Muralidharan, Niehaus and Sukhtankar (2020) reported that by 2017 the share of fakes/ghosts in the total ration cards in Jharkhand was at most 3 per cent. Drèze et al. (2019) also reported smaller share of fakes on the PDS lists in other states. Surveys and ground reports have suggested that the cleaning up of PDS lists that accompanied the roll-out of the NFSA was responsible for a significant reduction in identity fraud.

The widely circulated figure by the government that 2.33 crore 'fake' ration cards were deleted due to Aadhaar was simply misleading, as a majority of these deletions happened even before Aadhaar was introduced and were for various reasons like death, migration, ineligibility and marriage, in which Aadhaar had no role to play (Khera 2017; Ramakumar 2011c).

An important source of corruption in the PDS that has, however, persisted is that of quantity fraud – dealers taking cuts from beneficiaries' entitlements every month. Aadhaar, as expected, was toothless in tackling this form of corruption since it did nothing to alter the power balance between beneficiaries and PDS dealers, which was the source of the corruption in this case. Two independent studies, including a randomized controlled trial (RCT), found that the mandatory ABBA in the PDS had no effects on quantity fraud and leakages in Jharkhand (Drèze *et al.* 2017; Muralidharan, Niehaus and Sukhtankar 2020). It is possible that the detailed transaction records that ABBA generated could help save some money by allowing the government to track the quantities of grains that did not get sold and adjust for those in subsequent allocations. Muralidharan, Niehaus and Sukhtankar (2020) found that such 'reconciliation' of records did indeed lead to savings in Jharkhand. However, these savings came at the cost of significant reduction in benefits received by beneficiaries and the 'reconciliation' reform had to be called-off after three months in the light of large-scale opposition from both dealers and beneficiaries (Drèze *et al.* 2020)

On the other hand, there was mounting evidence from various sources to suggest that the mandatory imposition of Aadhaar was leading to exclusion of genuine beneficiaries. This was because the ABBA system rested on a set of 'fragile technologies', all of which needed to simultaneously work for successful authentication (Drèze 2016). Breakdown at various points in the authentication system led to temporary or permanent exclusions. To begin with, households that failed to link their Aadhaar number to their PDS card (known as Aadhaar 'seeding') get excluded. For instance, it appears that 90 per cent of ration cards that were deleted when Aadhaar was mandated in Jharkhand belonged to genuine households (Muralidharan, Niehaus and Sukhtankar 2020). Further, manual errors, mismatch in details like name and age between Aadhaar and the administrative databases can all lead to exclusions and delays.

Even after successful Aadhaar seeding, genuine households were excluded due to failures with fingerprint authentication. A survey of nearly 900 households in Jharkhand found that 43 per cent of households that failed to purchase PDS grains in May 2017 reported Aadhaar-related factors as the reason (Drèze *et al.* 2017). The issues included lack of internet connectivity, repeated authentication failures and absence of any override mechanisms. The excluded families often were single-member families, elderly couples and manual labourers. These findings were largely corroborated by an RCT conducted around the same time, which found that ABBA increased exclusion, particularly among households that failed to seed their Aadhaar numbers (Muralidharan, Niehaus and Sukhtankar 2020). Again, the excluded households were found to be poorer, less educated and less likely to be upper caste. In addition to exclusions, both studies found an increase in transaction costs for beneficiaries as they had to make repeated trips when authentication failed or wait for long hours in the queue when internet connectivity was down.

Evidence from other states besides Jharkhand also suggest significant exclusion. Roughly 2.5 million people were excluded in the states of Rajasthan and Andhra Pradesh due to Aadhaar-related reasons (Abraham *et al.* 2018). Even official data from the UIDAI suggests that authentication failures stood at 12 per cent for government services in the recent years (Sachdev 2018). Not surprisingly, a significant share of beneficiaries surveyed across three states seemed to prefer the old system over the Aadhaar-based system – 65 per cent in Jharkhand, 45 per cent in Andhra Pradesh and 35 per cent in Rajasthan (Abraham *et al.* 2018; Drèze *et al.* 2017).

To those following the Aadhaar project closely from its early days, the exclusion observed on the ground and borne out by credible survey estimates, were worrying but not all that surprising. As early as 2012, based on an analysis of UIDAI's own proof-of-concept studies, which highlighted possibility of large-scale authentication failure, Ramakumar (2012) noted: 'it would be an irony that a project that is marketed in the name of "including the poor" would end up excluding them massively from whatever meagre provisions they obtain from the state today.'

Conclusions

From a system of wartime rationing, and subsequently as an instrument of price stability after independence, the PDS has gradually evolved into being the central pillar of welfare policy in India today. This was most clearly demonstrated during the Covid-19 lockdown when free rations from the PDS emerged as welfare benefits with the highest coverage.[16] Until very recently, however, this was not the case. While the PDS saw significant expansion between 1960 and 1990, its coverage had remained patchy. The shift from a universal to a targeted PDS in 1997, aimed at targeting benefits to worse-off households and reducing leakages, had the opposite effect as access to the PDS reduced and leakages increased in almost all the states. Multiple state government-led initiatives in the early 2000s, coupled with a rise in global food prices, saw a revival of the PDS from around 2004–05. By 2011–12, leakages had reduced and access to PDS had expanded. The

NFSA, passed in 2013, made subsidized foodgrains from the PDS a legal entitlement for 67 per cent of the population. Numerous small-scale surveys in the wake of NFSA roll-out by the states suggested that PDS coverage had expanded, distribution was largely regular and households were receiving a bulk of their legal entitlements.

Despite the considerable progress in the recent years, some key issues persist. Most important of these was that by 2020 the coverage of the PDS under NFSA was not in compliance with the target mandates of the NFSA; the government had fixed PDS coverage based on the outdated 2011 population figures. Particularly considering the recent health and economic crisis related to the Covid-19 pandemic, the government must urgently expand PDS coverage to account for population growth. The other major concern was the inclusion of only rice and wheat in the PDS basket. Given that nutritious diets remained largely unaffordable for a large section of the population (Raghunathan, Heady and Herforth 2019), there was a strong case for the inclusion of pulses and millets in the PDS. It is certainly implementable as demonstrated during the lockdown when the PDS delivered 1 kg of pulses per family free of cost as an emergency measure. Finally, much more needs to be done to put in place a strong and responsive grievance redressal mechanism. Both awareness of entitlements and rights and accountability mechanisms are important as reinforcing features to preserve the integrity of the system (Drèze 2004).

Instead of resolving these issues, however, the government has obsessively focused on technological reforms aimed solely at curtailing fiscal costs forgetting that the prime objective of the PDS and the NFSA are to eliminate hunger and food insecurity. Moreover, far from the days of rampant corruption and targeting errors, the PDS has gained much needed integrity and works well in many parts of the country. This has been the result of many years of efforts by various state governments (nudged in part by the centre) culminating in the NFSA. Not capitalizing on the positive momentum to further strengthen the PDS – by increasing coverage, enhancing entitlements and expanding the commodity basket – would be a lost opportunity to make important progress towards achieving food security.

The author would like to thank R. Ramakumar for motivating him to write this chapter and for his guidance, and Vikas Rawal and other participants at the seminar on 'Indian Agriculture: Policy Shifts and Emerging Challenges' held at Tata Institute of Social Sciences Mumbai, for thoughtful discussions. He is particularly indebted to S.V.R. Murthy for his detailed comments.

Notes

[1] This was based on the methodology of the 'Expert Group on Estimation of Proportion and Number of Poor' chaired by D.T. Lakdawala (DFPD 2016).

[2] See Khera (2011a) and Rahman (2014) for a discussion on state-specific initiatives.

[3] Estimates by Jean Dreze, Reetika Khera and Meghana Mungikar; see IndiaSpend (2020).

[4] See Khera and Somanchi (2020) for further details.

[5] There are potential recall concerns since households were asked to report if they had a ration card five years before the survey (pre-NFSA). But the ration card is such an important document that most households were certain whether they possessed one or not before NFSA. Moreover, in most sample states, the roll-out of the NFSA was accompanied by distribution of new ration cards, which was used as an additional benchmark to aid in recall.

[6] See Chatterjee (2014), Bhattacharya and Puri (2015), Drèze, Khera and Pudussery (2015), Khanduja et al. (2019), and NCAER (2015).

[7] The estimates cited in this paragraph for coverage of BPL/AAY cards and share of households purchasing PDS grains are sourced from Rahman (2014), and estimates of per capita PDS grain purchases and leakages are sourced from Khera (2011a).

[8] This is valid only if PDS purchases are inframarginal, i.e., they do not account for the entire grain purchases of the households, as is mostly the case with PDS purchases.

[9] See Balasubramanian (2015), Kaushal and Muchomba (2015), Kochar (2005) and Tarozzi (2005).

[10] During a field survey in rural Madhya Pradesh in 2016, our survey team met multiple upper-caste landlords who were unhappy with the NFSA because Dalit agricultural labourers had started demanding higher wages and had reduced labour supply after they started receiving the grains.

[11] Banerjee (2016), George and Subramanian (2015), Jha and Ramaswami (2010), Kapur, Mukhopadhyay and Subramanian (2008), Kotwal, Murugkar and Ramaswami (2011, 2012), Parikh (1994), Saini and Gulati (2017) and Chaudhuri and Somanathan (2011).

[12] See National Food Security Portal, available at: https://nfsa.gov.in/public/nfsadashboard/PublicRCDashboard.aspx, accessed 30 December 2020.

[13] See Angad (2020), Bisht (2020), Karmarkar (2020), Rajasekaran (2020), Sircar and Sachdev (2020), Somanchi (2018) and Virmani (2019).

[14] This title is borrowed from our previous work (Drèze et al. 2017). See Khera (2017), Khera (2018) and Somanchi (2019) for a broader discussion on Aadhaar in welfare from which this section draws.

[15] On the broader set of myths and illusions that the projects initial marketing hinged on, see Ramakumar (2011a, 2011b).

[16] See Totapally et al. (2020).

References

Abraham, R., E.S. Bennett, R. Bhusal, S. Dubey, Q. Li, A. Pattanayak and N.B. Shah (2018), 'State of Aadhaar Report 2017–18', New Delhi: IDinsight.

Agarwal, T. and A. Krishna (2018), 'Food Subsidy: PDS, Cash, or Both?', *Ideas for India*, 31 October.

Angad, A. (2020), 'Direct Benefit Transfer is Direct Siphoning of School Scholarship', *Indian Express*, 2 November.

Balasubramanian, S. (2015), 'Is the PDS Already a Cash Transfer? Rethinking India's Food Subsidy Policies', *Journal of Development Studies*, vol. 51, no. 6, pp. 642–59.

Banerjee, A. (2016), 'Universal Basic Income: The Best Way to Welfare', *Ideas for India*, 16 September.

Bhattacharya, S. and R. Puri (2015), 'Preliminary Results from the Bihar Time-Motion Study', World Bank Draft Paper.

Bhattacharya, S., V.L. Falcao and R. Puri (2017), 'The Public Distribution System in India: Policy Evolution and Programme Delivery Trends', in H. Alderman, U. Gentilini and R. Yemtsov, eds, *The 1.5 Billion Question: Food, Vouchers, or Cash Transfers*, Washington D.C.: World Bank.

Bhatia, B.M. (1985), *Food Security in South Asia*, New Delhi: Oxford and IBH Publishing Co.Pvt. Ltd.

Bisht, G. (2020), '1,100 Students Got Scholarship Fraudulently: CBI Probe into Rs 250-cr Scam in Himachal', *Hindustan Times*, 18 July.

Chakrabarti, S., A. Kishore and D. Roy (2016), 'Arbitrage and Corruption in Food Subsidy Programmes: Evidence from India's Public Distribution System', Selected paper prepared for presentation at the Agricultural & Applied Economics Association's Annual Meeting, Boston, MA, 31 July–2 August 2016.

Chatterjee, M. (2014), 'An Improved PDS in a 'Reviving' State: Food Security in Koraput, Odisha', *Economic and Political Weekly*, vol. 49, no. 45, pp. 49–59.

Chaudhuri, A.R. and E. Somanathan (2011), 'Impact of Biometric Identification-Based Transfers', *Economic and Political Weekly*, vol. 46, no. 21, pp. 77–80.

Deaton, A.S. and J. Drèze (2014), 'Squaring the Poverty Circle', *The Hindu*, 25 July.

Department of Food and Public Distribution (2016), *Annual Report 2015-16*, New Dehi: Government of India

Dhorajiwala, S., J. Drèze and N. Wagner (2018), 'A Birdge to Nowhere', *The Hindu*, 27 March.

Drèze, J. (2004), 'Democracy and the Right to Food', *Economic and Political Weekly*, vol. 39, no. 17, pp. 1723–31.

———— (2016), 'Dark Clouds over the PDS', *The Hindu*, 10 September

Drèze, J., A. Gupta, S.A. Parashar and K. Sharma (2020), 'Pauses and Reversals of Infant Mortality Decline in India in 2017 and 2018', *SSRN*, available at https://ssrn.com/abstract=3727001

Drèze, J. and R. Khera (2010), 'The BPL Census and a Possible Alternative', *Economic and Political Weekly*, vol. 45, no. 9, pp. 54–63.

———— (2013), 'Rural Poverty and the Public Distribution System', *Economic and Political Weekly*, vol. 48, nos 45–46, pp. 55–60.

———— (2015), 'Understanding Leakages in the Public Distribution System', *Economic and Political Weekly*, vol. 45, no. 7, pp. 39–42.

Drèze, J., P. Gupta, R. Khera and I. Pimenta (2019), 'Casting the Net: India's Public Distribution System after the Food Security Act', *Economic and Political Weekly*, vol. 54, no. 6, pp. 36–47.

Drèze, J., N. Khalid, R. Khera and A. Somanchi (2017), 'Aadhaar and Food Security in Jharkhand: Pain without Gain', *Economic and Political Weekly*, vol. 52, no. 50, pp. 50-60.

Drèze, J., R. Khera and J. Pudussery (2015), 'Food Security: Bihar on the Move', *Economic and Political Weekly*, vol. 50, no. 34, no. pp. 44–52.

Drèze, J., R. Khera and the PEEP Team (2013), 'A PEEP into Another India', *Outlook*, 24 March.

Dutta, B. and B. Ramaswami (2011), 'Targeting and Efficiency in the Public Distribution System Case of Andhra Pradesh and Maharashtra', *Economic and Political Weekly*, vol. 36, no. 18, pp. 1524–32.

Gadenne, L., S. Norris, M. Singhal and S. Sukhtankar (2017), 'Price Risk and Poverty', *Ideas for India*, 15 May.

Gadgil, M. (2018), 'Direct Benefit Transfer Pilot Receives Luke Warm Response', *Mumbai Mirror,* 14 December.

George, P.S. (1984), 'Some Aspects of Public Distribution of Foodgrains in India', *Economic and Political Weekly*, vol. 19, no. 12, pp. A106–A110.

———— (1996), 'Public Distribution System, Food Subsidy, and Production Incentives', *Economic and Political Weekly*, vol. 31, no. 39, pp. A140–A144.

George, S. and A. Subramanian (2015), 'Transforming the Fight Against Poverty in India', *New York Times,* 22 July.

Giri, A., R. Rautela, V.P. Sharma and S. Sampath (2019), *Experimenting with Cash Transfers in Food Subsidies: Lessons from the Nagri Pilot,* MicroSave Consulting, August.

Himanshu and A. Sen (2011), 'Why Not a Universal Food Security Legislation?', *Economic and Political Weekly,* vol. 46, no. 12, pp. 38–47.

——— (2013a), 'In-Kind Food Transfers – I: Impact on Poverty', *Economic and Political Weekly,* vol. 48, nos 45–46, pp. 46–54.

——— (2013b), 'In-Kind Food Transfers - II: Impact on Nutrition and Implications for Food Security and Its Costs', *Economic and Political Weekly,* vol. 48, no. 47, pp. 60–73.

IndiaSpend (2020), 'More than 100mn Excluded from PDS as Govt Uses Outdated Census 2011 Data', *IndiaSpend,* 16 April.

Issac, T.M.T. and R. Ramakumar (2010), 'Expanding Welfare Entitlements in the Neo-Liberal Era: The Case of Food Security in Kerala', *Indian Journal of Human Development,* vol. 4, no. 1, pp. 99–119.

Jha, S. (1992), 'Consumer Subsidies in India: Is Targeting Effective?', *Development and Change,* vol. 23, no. 4, pp. 101–28.

Jha, S. and B. Ramaswami (2010), 'How Can Food Subsides Work Better? Answers for India and Phillippines', ADB Economics Working Paper Series No. 221, *SSRN.*

Kapur, D., P. Mukhopadhyay and A. Subramanian (2008), 'The Case for Direct Cash Transfers to the Poor', *Economic and Political Weekly,* vol. 43, no. 15, pp. 37–41.

Karmarkar, S. (2020), 'Minority Students' Scholarship "Scam" Surfaces in Assam, Five Teachers Among 21 Arrested', *National Herald,* 9 November.

Kaul, T. (2018), 'Household Responses to Food Subsidies: Evidence from India', *Economic Development and Cultural Change,* vol. 67, no. 1, pp. 95–129.

Kaushal, N. and F. Muchomba (2015), 'How Consumer Price Subsidies Affect Nutrition', *World Development,* 74, pp. 25–42.

Khanduja, P., M. Thapliyal, V. Ravi and N. Parakh (2019), *A Study to Assess the Nutrtional Gaps in PDS Households,* Microsave Consulting, July 2019.

Khemani, S., J. Habyarimana and I. Nooruddin (2019), 'What Do Poor People Think About Direct Cash Transfers?', *Brookings Blog (Future Development),* 8 April.

Khera, R. (2008), 'Access to the Targeted Public Distribution System: A Case Study in Rajasthan', *Economic and Politcal Weekly,* vol. 43, no. 44, pp. 51–56.

——— (2010), 'Not All That Unique', *Hindustan Times,* 3 August.

——— (2011a), 'Trends in Diversion of Grain from the Public Distribution System', *Economic and Political Weekly,* vol. 46, no. 21, pp. 106–14.

——— (2011b), 'Revival of the Public Distribution System: Evidence and Explanations', *Economic and Political Weekly,* vol. 46, nos 44–45, pp. 36–50.

——— (2017), 'Impact of Aadhaar on Welfare Programmes', *Economic and Political Weekly,* vol. 52, no. 50, pp. 61–70.

——— (2018), 'Introduction', in R. Khera, ed. *Dissent on Aadhaar,* Noida: Orient Blackswan.

Khera, R. and A. Somanchi (2020), 'A Review of Coverage of the Public Distribution System', *Ideas for India,* 19 August.

Kochar, A. (2005), 'Can Targeted Food Programs Improve Nutrition? An Empirical Analysis of India's Public Distribution System', *Economic Development and Cultural Change,* vol. 54, no. 1, pp. 203–35.

Kotwal, A., M. Murugkar and B. Ramaswami (2011), 'PDS Forever?', *Economic and Political Weekly,* vol. 46, no. 21, pp. 72–76.

Kotwal, A., M. Murugkar and B. Ramaswami (2012), 'Political Economy of Food Subsidy in India', *The Copenhagen Journal of Asian Studies,* vol. 30, no. 2, pp. 100–21.

Krishnamurthy, P., V. Pathania and S. Tandon (2017), 'Food Price Subsidies and Nutrition: Evidence from State Reforms to India's Public Distribution System', *Economic Development and Cultural Change,* vol. 66, no. 1, pp. 55–90.

Mahendra Dev, S. and M.H. Suryanarayana (1991), 'Is PDS Urban Biased and Pro Rich?', *Economic and Poltical Weekly*, vol. 26, no. 41, pp. 2357–59 and 2361–66.

Mohanty, M. (2017), 'Aadhaar Seeding Responsible for only 4% of the Cancelled Ration Cards in Odisha', *Economic Times*, 14 November.

Mooji, J. (1998), 'Food Policy and Politics: The Political Economy of the Public Distribution System in India', *Journal of Peasant Studies*, vol. 25, no. 2, pp. 77–101.

Mukesh, A.S.R.P. (2018), 'State Stops DBT in Nagri', *The Telegraph*, 9 August.

Muralidharan, K., P. Niehaus and S. Sukhtankar (2017), 'Direct Benefit Transfers in Food: Results from One Year of Process Monitoring in Union Territories', University of California, San Diego.

——— (2018), 'We Need a Choice-Based Approach in the Public Distribution System', *Hindustan Times*, 3 October.

——— (2020), 'Identity Verification Standards in Welfare Programs: Experimental Evidence from India', NBER Working Paper no. 26744.

Narayanan, S. (2011), 'A Case for Reframing the Cash Transfer Debate in India', *Economic and Political Weekly*, vol. 46, no. 21, pp. 41–48.

Narayanan, R., S. Dhorajiwala and S. Kambhatla (2020), *Length of the Last Mile: Delays and Hurdles in NREGA Wage Payments*, Bangalore: Azim Premji University and LibTech India.

Narayan, S. (2015), 'Ten Facts That Set the Record Straight on Cash Transfers', *The Wire*, 15 August.

Nawani, NP. (1994), 'Indian Experience on Household Food and Nutrition Security', Regional Expert Consultation FAO-UN Bangkok.

National Council for Applied Economics Research (NCAER) (2015), *Evaluation Study of Targeted Public Distribution System in Selected States*, New Delhi: NCAER .

Overbeck, D. (2016), 'Leakage and Corruption in India's Public Distribution System', Paper presented at the 12th Annual Conference on Economic Growth and Development at the Indian Statistical Institute, Delhi, 19–21 December.

Parikh, K. (1994), 'Who Gets How Much from PDS: How Effectively Does It Reach the Poor?', *Sarvekshana*, vol. 17, no. 3, pp. 1–34.

Pingali, P., B. Mittra and A. Rahman (2018), 'The Bumpy Road from Food to Nutrition Security - Slow Evolution of India's Food Policy', *Global Food Security*, vol. 15, pp. 77–84.

Puri, R. (2017), 'India's National Food Security Act (NFSA): Early Experiences', *LANSA Working Paper Series* , vol. 14.

Raghunathan, K., D. Heady and A. Herforth (2020), 'Affordability of Nutritious Diets in Rural India', *Food Policy*, vol. 99.

Rahman, A. (2014), 'Revival of Rural Public Distribution System: Expansion and Outreach', *Economic and Political Weekly*, vol. 49, no. 20, pp. 62–68.

——— (2015), 'Do Publicly Provided Subsidized Foodgrains Crowd-out the Open Market Demand?', Spandan Working Paper Series No. WP/06/2015.

——— (2016), 'Universal Food Security Programme and Nutritional Intake: Evidence from the Hunger Prone KBK Districts in Odisha', *Food Policy*, vol. 63, pp. 73–86.

Rajasekaran, I. (2020), 'PM-KISAN Scam: Defrauding Farmers', *Frontline*, 9 October.

Ramakumar, R. (2011a), 'Aadhaar: On a Platform of Myths', *The Hindu*, 17 July.

——— (2011b), 'Identity Concerns', *Frontline*, 2 December.

——— (2011c), 'PDS in Peril', *Frontline*, 02 December.

——— (2012), 'A Tale of Errors', *Frontline*, 13 July.

——— (2018), 'Financial Inclusion in India: A Review', in D. Roy, G. Nair and G. Mani, eds, *Rural India Perspective 2017*, New Delhi: Oxford University Press India.

Sachdev, V. (2018), 'Aadhaar Authentication for Govt Services Fails 12% of Time: UIDAI', *The Quint*, 27 March.

Saini, S. and A. Gulati (2017), 'Price Distortions in Indian Agriculture', World Bank Group – ICRIER Working Paper.

Sen, J. (2018), 'Why People Are Protesting Against Jharkhand's Experiment With Direct Benefit Transfers', *The Wire*, 1 March, available at https://thewire.in/rights/jharkhand-nagri-ration-pds-direct-benefit-transfer, accessed 6 July 2022.

Shrinivas, A., K. Baylis and B. Crost (2018), 'Labor Market Effects of Social Transfer Programs :Evidence from India's Public Distribution System', Job market paper, University of Illinois Urbana-Champaign.

Shrinivas, A., K. Baylis, B. Crost and P. Pingali (2018), 'Do Staple Food Subsidies Improve Nutrition?: Evidence from India's Public Distribution System', Working Paper.

Sircar, S. and V. Sachdev (2020), '"Riteish Deshmukh", Hanuman and Pak Spy Get PM KISAN Cash Payments', *The Quint*, 10 December.

Somanchi, A. (2018), 'Aadhaar Fraud is Not Only Real but Worth More Closely Examining', *The Wire*, 3 May, available at https://thewire.in/economy/aadhaar-fraud-uidai, accessed 6 July 2022.

———— (2019), 'Aadhaa(r) Adhura Welfare', in R. Azad, S. Chakraborty, S. Ramani and D. Sinha, eds, *A Quantum Leap in the Wrong Direction?*, Noida: Orient Blackswan.

———— (2020), 'Food and Social Security at the Margins: The Parhaiyas of Jharkhand', *SSRN*.

———— (2021), 'Cash Transfers 'At-Scale' in India: Evidence from the Covid-19 Relief Transfers to Jan Dhan Accounts', Unpublished draft.

Totapally S., P. Rao, P. Sonderegger *et al.* (2020), *The Efficacy of Government Entitlements in Helping BPL Families Navigate Financial Impacts of Covid-19*, Dalberg.

Swaminathan, M. (2000), *Weakening Welfare: The Public Distribution of Food in India*, New Delhi: LeftWord Books.

———— (2008), 'Programmes to Protect the Hungry: Lessons from India', DESA Working Paper, October.

Swaminathan, M. and N. Mishra (2001), 'Errors of Targeting', *Economic and Political Weekly*, vol. 36, no. 26, pp. 2447–54.

Tarozzi, A. (2005), 'The Indian Public Distribution System as Provider of Food Security: Evidence from Child Nutrition in Andhra Pradesh', *European Economic Review*, vol. 49, no. 5, pp. 1305–30.

Virmani, A. (2019), 'Senior Social Welfare Department Official, 11 Others Arrested for Involvement in Multi-Crore SC/ST "Scholarship" Scam in Uttarakhand', *First Post*, 2 June, available at https://www.firstpost.com/india/senior-social-welfare-department-official-11-others-arrested-for-involvement-in-multi-crore-scst-scholarship-scam-in-uttarakhand-6743691.html, accessed 6 July 2022.

Contributors

Aparajita Bakshi is an associate professor at the School of Economics, R.V. University, Bengaluru. She holds a PhD in economics from the University of Calcutta through the Indian Statistical Institute, Kolkata. Her areas of research include development economics, rural transformation, livelihoods, poverty and inequality, and local governance and statistical systems in India.

Prachi Bansal is a senior research fellow at the Centre for Informal Sector and Labour Studies, Jawaharlal Nehru University (JNU), New Delhi. Her doctoral dissertation is on labour absorption in Indian agriculture. Her areas of research are agrarian studies, labour economics, food security and development economics.

Vaishali Bansal is a PhD student working on food security in India at the Centre for Economic Studies and Planning, Jawaharlal Nehru University (JNU), New Delhi. She has been part of several field-based studies on issues related to agrarian relations, food security, household incomes, livelihoods and industrial transformation. She also actively writes on issues of hunger and food security in popular media.

Pallavi Chavan is an economist with research experience in development economics, rural banking, financial regulation and agricultural economics. She holds a PhD in economics from the University of Calcutta through the Indian Statistical Institute, Kolkata.

Ashish Kamra is a research manager at Precision Development (PxD). He holds an MA in development studies from the Tata Institute of Social

Sciences, Mumbai. His areas of research interest include agricultural costs and prices, and big data analytics.

Awanish Kumar is British Academy Newton International Fellow at the University of Edinburgh, United Kingdom. He holds a PhD in development studies from the Tata Institute of Social Sciences, Mumbai. He is also the book reviews editor at the *Economic and Political Weekly*, Mumbai. His areas of research interest are agrarian studies, social policy and social movements.

Sridhar Kundu is a Senior Research Analyst (Economist) at the Bharti Institute of Public Policy, Indian School of Business, Mohali. He holds a PhD in economics from the Centre for the Study of Regional Development, Jawaharlal Nehru University (JNU), New Delhi. His areas of research interest are fiscal policies, poverty, inequality and energy economics.

Teesta Lahiri was a research fellow (legal) at the Centre for WTO Studies (CWS), New Delhi under the Ministry of Commerce and Industry, Government of India. She has an LLM in constitutional law from the National Law University, Odisha. Her areas of research interest are trade policy and free trade agreements.

Tapas Singh Modak is an associate fellow at the Foundation for Agrarian Studies (FAS), Bengaluru. He holds a PhD in social sciences from the Tata Institute of Social Sciences, Mumbai. His areas of research interest are agricultural economics, irrigation economics, water policy and village studies.

Sudha Narayanan is a research fellow at the South Asia Regional Office, International Food Policy Research Institute (IFPRI), New Delhi. She holds a PhD in economics from Cornell University. Her areas of research interest are agricultural economics, agricultural markets, contract farming, food and nutrition policy, and human development.

Suvayan Neogi was a research fellow at the Centre for WTO Studies (CWS), New Delhi under the Ministry of Commerce and Industry, Government of India. He is pursuing a PhD in economics from Symbiosis International (Deemed University), Pune. His areas of research interest include agricultural economics, international economics, WTO studies and food security.

R. Ramakumar is a professor at the School of Development Studies, Tata Institute of Social Sciences (TISS), Mumbai. He is also a non-ministerial expert member at the Kerala State Planning Board. He holds a PhD in quantitative economics from the Indian Statistical Institute, Kolkata. Earlier, he served as the Dean of the School of Development Studies and the National Bank for Agriculture and Rural Development (NABARD) Chair Professor at TISS, Mumbai. His areas of research interest are agrarian studies, agricultural economics and public finance.

Vikas Rawal is a professor at the Centre for Economic Studies and Planning, Jawaharlal Nehru University (JNU), New Delhi. He obtained his PhD in development studies from the Indira Gandhi Institute of Development Research (IGIDR), Mumbai. His research is mainly focused on agrarian conditions, food security, inequality and employment.

Geetanjoy Sahu is an associate professor at the Centre for Science, Technology and Society, School of Habitat Studies, Tata Institute of Social Sciences (TISS), Mumbai. He holds a PhD in political science from the Institute for Social and Economic Change (ISEC), Bengaluru. His areas of research interest are environmental jurisprudence, environmental regulation and policy, land and forest rights, the political economy of public policy implementation, and environmental movements.

Biplab Sarkar is an associate professor at the Department of Management Studies, PES University, Bengaluru. He holds a PhD in economics from the University of North Bengal through the Indian Statistical Institute, Kolkata. His areas of research interest include agricultural prices and profitability, rural development, and public policy.

Sachin Kumar Sharma is an associate professor at the Centre for WTO Studies (CWS), New Delhi, under the Ministry of Commerce and Industry, Government of India. He holds a PhD in economics from Jawaharlal Nehru University (JNU), New Delhi. His areas of research interest include trade policy, free trade agreements, subsidies, food security, CGE modelling and human development.

S.L. Shetty is the founding Director of the Economic and Political Weekly Research Foundation (EPWRF), Mumbai. He holds a PhD in Economics from the University of Mumbai. Earlier, he was the executive director, Department of Economic Analysis and Policy (DEAP), Reserve Bank of India. His areas of research interest include macroeconomic policy, monetary and fiscal policies, and development issues in the financial sector.

Gurpreet Singh is a senior policy analyst at the Centre for Budget and Governance Accountability (CBGA), New Delhi. He holds a PhD in economics from the Centre for Economic Studies and Planning, Jawaharlal Nehru University (JNU), New Delhi. His areas of research interest include agricultural financing, labour and political economy of development.

Sukhpal Singh is a professor and former chairperson at the Centre for Management in Agriculture, Indian Institute of Management (IIM), Ahmedabad. He holds a PhD in economics from the Institute for Social and Economic Change (ISEC), Bengaluru. He is the founding co-editor of *Millennial Asia: An International Journal of Asian Studies*. His areas of research interest are agricultural economics and policy, agricultural markets, value chains, contract farming, and farmer producer companies.

Anmol Somanchi is a graduate student in economics at the Ecole d'économie de Paris, Paris School of Economics, Paris. He holds an MA in Development Studies from the Tata Institute of Social Sciences (TISS), Mumbai. His areas of research interest are development economics, political economy, food and social security, and programme evaluation.

Madhura Swaminathan is a professor at the Economic Analysis Unit, Indian Statistical Institute (ISI), Bangalore. She holds a PhD in economics from the University of Oxford. She is also the Chairperson of the M.S. Swaminathan Research Foundation (MSSRF), Chennai, and a member of the Council of Advisors at the World Food Prize Foundation. Her areas of research are agriculture and food security, agrarian studies, poverty and inequality.

Milton Keynes UK
Ingram Content Group UK Ltd.
UKHW010829291123
433443UK00008B/131/J